Guide to Health Claims Examining

Insurance Career Development Center

INSURANCE CAREER DEVELOPMENT CENTER

Mosby Lifeline

St. Louis Baltimore Boston Carlsbad Chicago Naples New York Philadelphia Portland
London Madrid Mexico City Singapore Sydney Tokyo Toronto Wiesbaden

Mosby Lifeline

Dedicated to Publishing Excellence

Publisher: David T. Culverwell
Editor-in-Chief: Richard A. Weimer
Editor: Eric Duchinsky
Senior Developmental Editor: Cecilia F. Reilly
Developmental Editor: Nancy Peterson
Assistant Editors: Christine Ambrose; Carla Goldberg
Book Design and Production: Reuter & Associates
Manufacturing Supervisor: Betty Richmond
Cover Design: Avenue K, St. Louis
Illustrations: Julie Larick

Fourth edition

Printed in the United States of America

Composition by:
Reuter & Associates

Printing/Binding by:
Plus Communications, Inc.

Mosby–Year Book, Inc.
11830 Westline Industrial Drive
St. Louis, Missouri 63146

International Standard Book Number 0815148135

94 95 96 97 98 / 9 8 7 6 5 4 3 2 1

Disclaimer

This text is a guide for learning the medical billing and health claims examining fields. Decisions should not be based solely on information within this guide. Decisions impacting the practice of medical billing and health claims examining must be based on individual circumstances including legal/ethical considerations, local conditions and payor policies.

The information contained in this text is based on experience and research. However, in the complex, rapidly changing medical environment, this information may not always prove correct. Data used are widely variable and can change at any time. Readers should follow current coding regulations outlined by official coding organizations.

CPT is a listing of descriptive terms and five-digit numeric identifying codes and modifiers for reporting medical services performed by physicians. This presentation includes only CPT descriptive terms, numeric identifying codes and modifiers for reporting medical services and procedures that were selected by Mosby Lifeline for inclusion in this Publication.

The most current CPT is available from the American Medical Association.

No fee schedules, basic unit values, relative value guides, conversion factors or scales or components thereof are included in CPT.

Mosby Lifeline has selected certain CPT codes and service/procedure descriptions and assigned them to various specialty groups. The listing of a CPT service or procedure description and its code number in this Publication does not restrict its use to a particular specialty group. Any procedure or service in this Publication may be used to designate the services rendered by any qualified physician.

The American Medical Association assumes no responsibility for the consequences attributable to or related to any use or interpretation of any information or views contained in or not contained in this Publication.

The publisher and author do not accept responsibility for any adverse outcome from undetected errors, opinion and analysis contained in this text that may prove inaccurate or incorrect, or the reader's misunderstanding of an extremely complex topic. All names used in this book are completely fictitious. Any resemblance to persons or companies, current or no longer existing, is purely coincidental.

Acknowledgements

Many people have contributed to the development and success of *Guide to Health Claims Examining.* We extend our thanks and deep appreciation to the many students and classroom instructors who have provided us with helpful suggestions for this edition of the text.

We would like to express our thanks to the following individuals who believed in the program in its initial stages and helped us work through the glitches associated with any new product:

Jolene Buck, Ameritech College, Van Nuys, CA
Anna B. Little, Ladera Career Paths, Los Angeles, CA
Hollis Anglin and Colleen Wheatley, Dawn Training Institute, New Castle, DE
Tami Freedman, College America, San Francisco, CA
Bob Malone and Gloria Stender, Grand Rapids Educational Centers, Grand Rapids, MI
Ruby Herold, Heritage College of Health Careers, Denver, CO
Donna Montfoort, BSN, Carolyn Dykes, C.P.C. and Patti Overman, C.P.C., John Alden Life Insurance Company, Phoenix, AZ
Jennifer L. Spalding, R.N., MPA, Annis Collins, R.N., MS and Femi Daramola, United Health Plan, Inglewood, CA
Lowell P. Theard, PH.D, MD, and Katherine Rogers, MHA, Culver Healthcare Associates, Culver City, CA

We would like to thank those Insurance Career Development Center consultants who helped with this text, Mayra I. Caraballo and especially Caitlind L. Alexander for her loyalty and commitment, which was instrumental in bringing this edition to successful completion.

Thanks to the CPA firm of Miller, Kaplan, Arase and Company. To Mannon Kaplan, C.P.A., thank you for believing in and supporting ICDC, for all of your knowledge and wisdom. A special thank you to George Nadel Rivin, C.P.A,. and Joseph C. Cahn, C.P.A., for their valued consultation. For having the faith and commitment to see it through, we truly appreciate you and your partners, Jeffrey S. Slomiak, C.P.A., Edwin Kanemaru, C.P.A., Kenneth R. Holmer, C.P.A., Douglas S. Waite, C.P.A., James E. Veale, C.P.A., Charles Schnaid, C.P.A., and Donald G. Garrett, C.P.A..

We also wish to express our thanks to the expert staff at Mosby Lifeline who gave freely of their support. An extra special thank you to Editor Eric Duchinsky for realizing the need to publish such a text and for having the courage to undertake this project. Thanks to Editor-in-Chief Richard A. Weimer, Senior Developmental Editor Cecilia F. Reilly, Developmental Editor Nancy Peterson, and Assistant Editors Christine Ambrose and Carla Goldberg.

And finally, to Thomas, Sean and Sydney Adams, thank you for allowing me to spend the time and energy required to concentrate on this project. To Floree Brown, thank you for all of your love and support. I would like to dedicate this book to the memory of my father, Nathaniël Brown Sr.

Sharon E. Brown, President
Insurance Career Development Center, Inc.

Preface

Health claims examining and medical billing are two of the fastest-growing employment opportunities in the United States today. Insurance companies, medical offices, hospitals and other health care providers are in great need of trained personnel to create and process medical billing claims.

With the aid of this textbook, you can learn the skills necessary to become a successful health claims biller or examiner. The material has been designed to be comprehensive, yet user-friendly. The text follows a logical learning format by beginning with a broad base of information and then, step by step, following the course of a health claim from billing to examining.

This text is intended to be used with Insurance Career Development Center's *Guide to Medical Billing* and the Health Claims Examiner/Medical Biller Curriculum Program, which is divided into eight modules consisting of 100 hours each. A pad of Payment Worksheets accompanies the text. Their use in processing claims is explained in Chapter 8.

Special Features

Some special features of the text enhance understanding and retention of the material covered:

Each chapter begins with **learning objectives** to focus the student on the most pertinent topics covered in that chapter. The straightforward, **easy-to-understand writing style** presents information clearly and concisely. **Questions for Review** at the end of each chapter reinforce key concepts. Answering questions without looking back into the chapter will help students determine if they have grasped the principles within the chapter or if there is a need for further study. They also serve to prepare students for exams. Answers are contained in the instructor materials for this course. **Exercises** provided with most chapters give students the opportunity to put their knowledge into practice. These hands-on, real-life exercises will ensure competence in medical billing and claims examining.

The most important ingredient to success in this course is the desire to learn, without which the learning process is ineffective. The desire to learn can lead you to a rewarding career in the medical billing or health claims examining fields.

Contents

1. Introduction to Insurance 1
   - A. The Rising Cost of Health Care 2
   - B. Employee Benefits 2
   - C. Types of Insurance 3
   - D. Functional Areas in an Insurance Company 4
   - E. The Department of Insurance 5
   - F. Summary 6
   - G. Assignments 6
   - H. Questions for Review 7

2. Contracts 9
   - A. Contract Validity 10
   - B. Group Contracts 10
   - C. Summary 11
   - D. Assignments 11
   - E. Questions for Review 12
   - F. Exercises 2-1 to 2-5 13

3. Eligibility 19
   - A. Employee Eligibility 20
   - B. Dependent Eligibility 21
   - C. Employee Effective Date of Coverage 22
   - D. Dependent Effective Date of Coverage 23
   - E. Open Enrollment 23
   - F. Termination of Coverage 23
   - G. Continuation of Coverage 24
   - H. Disclaimers 29
   - I. Summary 30
   - J. Assignments 30
   - K. Questions for Review 31
   - L. Exercises 3-1 to 3-5 32

4. Benefit Structures 37
   - A. Benefit Definitions 38
   - B. Basic Benefits 40
   - C. Common Basic Benefits 41
   - D. Basic Major Medical Benefits 43
   - E. Comprehensive Major Medical Benefits 44
   - F. Summary 44
   - G. Assignments 44
   - H. Questions for Review 45

5. General Plan Provisions 47
   - A. Acts of Third Parties 48
   - B. Subrogation 49
   - C. Preexisting Conditions 51
   - D. Possible Preexisting Conditions 57
   - E. Mandates 59
   - F. Summary 60
   - G. Assignments 60
   - H. Questions for Review 61
   - I. Exercise 5-1 62

6. Cost-Containment Programs 63
   - A. Preadmission Testing 64
   - B. Precertification of Inpatient Admissions 64
   - C. Utilization Review 64
   - D. Second Surgical Opinion Consultations 65
   - E. Managed Care 66
   - F. Managed Competition 67
   - G. Medical Case Management 67
   - H. Summary 68
   - I. Assignments 68
   - J. Questions for Review 69
   - K. Appendix 6-1: Potential Medical Case Management Claims 70

7. Usual, Customary, and Reasonable Fees 73
   - A. UCR Definitions 74
   - B. Resource-Based Relative Value Study 75
   - C. Calculating UCR 75
   - D. Fee Schedules 77
   - E. Summary 77
   - F. Assignments 77
   - G. Questions for Review 78
   - H. Exercises 7-1 to 7-5 79

8. Claims Administration 85
   - A. Maintenance of Claim Files 86
   - B. Claim File Documentation 87
   - C. Claim Investigation 89
   - D. Referrals 89
   - E. Pended Claims 89
   - F. Claims Examiner's Responsibilities 93
   - G. Claim Processing 95
   - H. Good Claims Practice 96
   - I. Payment Worksheet 97
   - J. Processing the Claim 99

K. Computing Stop Loss 102
L. Quick Reference Formulas....104
M. Processing Drug Claims....105
N. Handling Prescription Claims 105
O. Red Book and Blue Book....106
P. Summary....107
Q. Assignments 107
R. Questions for Review....108

9. Fraud 109
A. Forms of Fraud 110
B. Fraud Indicators 111
C. Investigation 113
D. Checkpoint for Spotting Provider Fraud and Insurance Abuse....114
E. Summary....115
F. Assignments 115
G. Questions for Review....115

10. Physician's Services 117
A. Custodial Care (99321 - 99333) 118
B. Emergency Department Services (99281 - 99288) 118
C. Consultations (99241 - 99263)....119
D. Second Surgical Opinion Consultations (99271 - 99275)....119
E. Immunizations (90700 - 90749) 119
F. Nervous/Mental Care and Treatment (90801 - 90899) 120
G. Biofeedback (90900 - 90915) 120
H. Dialysis (90918 - 90999)....120
I. Ophthalmology (92002 - 92499) 121
J. Speech Therapy (92507 - 92508) 121
K. Cardiovascular (92950 - 93981) 121
L. Physical Medicine (97010 - 98929)....121
M. Maintenance Therapy 122
N. Summary....122
O. Assignments 122
P. Questions for Review....123

11. X-Ray and Laboratory Services 125
A. X-ray and Laboratory Services 126
B. Component Charges 127
C. Summary....127
D. Assignments 127
E. Questions for Review....128
F. Appendix 11-1: Common Laboratory Tests 129
G. Appendix 11-2: Laboratory Profile Index....138

12. Surgery....147
A. Surgical Procedures 148
B. General Guidelines 149
C. Cosmetic Surgery 154
D. Obesity Surgery....161
E. Co-Surgeons 162
F. Assistant Surgeons....162
G. Summary....163
H. Assignments 163
I. Questions for Review....164
J. Appendix 12-1: Assistant Surgeon Procedures 167

13. Anesthesia 169
A. General Anesthesia 170
B. Regional Anesthesia....170
C. Intravenous Sedation....170
D. Acupuncture 171
E. Handling Procedures....171
F. Calculating Anesthesia....172
G. Modifiers....172
H. Qualifying Circumstances 173
I. Miscellaneous 173
J. Summary....173
K. Assignments 173
L. Questions for Review....174

14. Hospital Services 175
A. UB-92 Billing Form 176
B. Inpatient Hospital Claims 176
C. Room and Board 177
D. Outpatient Hospital Claims....178
E. Miscellaneous Facilities 178
F. Summary....181
G. Assignments 181
H. Questions for Review....182

15. Coordination of Benefits....185
A. Definitions 186
B. Order of Benefit Determination Rules 187
C. Right to Receive and Release Information....188

D. Facility of Payment 188
E. Right of Recovery....188
F. Miscellaneous Guidelines 189
G. Health Maintenance Organizations 189
H. Preferred Provider Organizations 189
I. Civilian Health and Medical Programs of the Uniformed Services 190
J. Recognizing the Presence of Dual Coverage 190
K. COB Worksheet 191
L. Summary....193
M. Assignments 193
N. Questions for Review....193
O. Exercise 15-1....193

16. Medicare 195
A. TEFRA/DEFRA 196
B. Medicare Eligibility 196
C. Providers of Service 197
D. The Two Parts of Medicare 197
E. Approved or Reasonable Charges....199
F. Medicare Assignments of Benefits 199
G. Nonduplication of Medicare 201
H. Maintenance of Benefits 203
I. Coordination with Medicare 204
J. Medicare Supplement 205
K. Estimating Medicare Coverage....205
L. Diagnosis-Related Group Billing 206
M. Summary....207
N. Assignments 207
O. Questions for Review....207

17. Medicaid 209
A. Health Insurance Payment Demand 210
B. Handling Procedures....213
C. Summary....213
D. Assignments 213
E. Questions for Review....214

18. Podiatric Surgery 215
A. General Guidelines 216
B. Surgical Coding....216
C. Conditions of the Foot and Treatment Procedures....217
D. Assistant Surgeon 222
E. Referrals 222
F. Summary....223
G. Assignments 223
H. Questions for Review....224

19. Ambulance Expenses 225
A. Guidelines for Coverage....226
B. Air Ambulance 226
C. Paramedics 227
D. Mobile Intensive Care Unit 227
E. Van Transportation Unit 227
F. Summary....227
G. Assignments 227
H. Questions for Review....228

20. Durable Medical Equipment....229
A. DME Billing Procedures....230
B. Prosthetic Devices 232
C. Medical/Surgical Supplies 232
D. Summary....232
E. Assignments 232
F. Questions for Review....233
G. Appendix 20-1: Durable Medical Equipment and Coverage Guidelines....234

21. Adjustments....251
A. Statistical Adjustment 252
B. Supplemental Adjustment....252
C. Full Credit Adjustment 252
D. Partial Credit Adjustment 253
E. Summary....253
F. Assignments 254
G. Questions for Review....254

22. Dental Terminology 255
A. Common Dental Terms and Procedures 256
B. Summary....280
C. Assignments 280
D. Questions for Review....281
E. Exercises 22-1 to 22-5....283

23. Anatomy and Physiology of the Mouth....289
A. The Oral Cavity....290
B. The Jaw....292
C. Diseases of the Mouth....292
D. The Teeth 293

E. Growth and Development of Teeth 298
F. Diseases of the Teeth.................................298
G. Summary..299
H. Assignments 299
I. Questions for Review.................................300
J. Exercises 23-1 to 23-5...............................301

24. Dental Services and Coding 307
A. Dental Professionals 308
B. Dental Treatment 308
C. Dental Coding..308
D. Diagnostic 309
E. Preventive 311
F. Restorative..312
G. Endodontics 316
H. Periodontics 318
I. Prosthodontics 320
J. Oral Surgery 326
K. Orthodontic Services................................328
L. Adjunctive General Services.......................329
M. Summary..330
N. Assignments 330
O. Questions for Review.................................331
P. Appendix 24-1: Dental Code List 333

25. Temporomandibular Joint Dysfunction 349
A. Coverage for TMJ......................................350
B. Appliances 351
C. Services and Supplies 352
D. Summary..353
E. Assignments 353
F. Questions for Review.................................354

26. Dental Claim Form 355
A. The ADA Dental Claim Form 356
B. Patient Information Sheet 359
C. Summary..362
D. Assignments 362
E. Questions for Review.................................363

27. Dental Benefit Structures 365
A. Types of Dental Plans 366
B. Understanding Dental Contracts 367
C. General Guidelines 369
D. Cost Containment.....................................373
E. Major Medical Coverage for Dental Procedures 376
F. Temporary Restorations.............................378
G. X-rays 379
H. Anesthesia..379
I. Sedative Fillings..380
J. Cosmetic Services 380
K. Unspecified and By Report Procedures 380
L. Summary..381
M. Assignments 381
N. Questions for Review.................................381

28. Processing Dental Claims 383
A. The Claim Form 384
B. Eligibility..384
C. Other Insurance 384
D. Provider Authority.....................................384
E. Coverage of Services 384
F. Evaluating the Services 385
G. Processing the Claim 385
H. Completing the Claim Payment Worksheet 385
I. Dental Form Letters 388
J. Handling Fraudulent Dental Claims 388
K. Summary..389
L. Assignments 389
M. Questions for Review.................................390
N. Exercises 28-1 to 28-3...............................391
O. Appendix 28-1: Dental Prevailing Conversion Factors 394

29. Dental Claims 395
A. Dental Claims Beginning Financials............396
B. Claims 29-1 to 29-15 397

1

Introduction to Insurance

In this chapter you will learn:

- The role of insurance companies in the US economy.
- To recognize the different departments in an insurance company and discuss their functions.
- To identify the responsibilities of the Department of Insurance.

Because of the rising costs of health care and replacement of personal property, it is virtually impossible for each person to have the necessary funds available to cover his or her expenses in a disaster, whether it is a large-scale disaster or a personal one. For this reason, insurance has become a necessary part of life in American society.

Essentially, insurance is an agreement whereby insurance carriers collect fees or "premiums" from individuals or companies on a regular basis. In return, they agree to pay for specific benefits. These benefits can be the payment of health-care expenses, the replacement or repair of personal property, or the payment for expenses of others who may have been injured by you or your property.

Insurance companies operate on the principle that most of those who pay premiums will not need services, or that the services they will need will cost less than the premiums paid. As you can see, it becomes very important for an insurance company to place restrictions on the amount and type of benefits that will be paid. These restrictions can include eligibility requirements, deductibles, maximum benefits, exclusions to a policy, and many other "policy guidelines." The health claims examiner is responsible for ensuring that each claim or request for payment is within the guidelines set by the company or the policy.

The Rising Cost of Health Care

The inflation that has affected so many areas of the American economy has probably most severely impacted the cost of health care. Between 1960 and 1983, the cost of health care in the United States rose from $26.9 billion to $355.4 billion per year. Currently, health care in the United States costs more than $1 trillion per year. This astronomical figure has prompted the federal government to introduce major changes in the health-care system in an effort to control costs and help insure a higher percentage of Americans.

There are a number of reasons for the enormous increase in the cost of health care. The eight most significant factors are:

1. More people are seeking health care now compared with 20 years ago.
2. Medical treatments are more extensive and sophisticated than ever before. In addition, the equipment required for many treatments is extremely expensive. For instance, the cost of one MRI unit is about $500,000.
3. The cost of training health-care professionals, such as physicians, nurses, and laboratory technicians, is much greater than ever before.
4. The price that health-care professionals pay for malpractice insurance has increased dramatically because of the increase in lawsuits.
5. When a significant part of a person's medical expenses is paid for by a health plan, neither the patient nor the health-care provider has much incentive to control costs or limit the utilization of services.
6. There is little competition among health-care providers. Consequently, the marketplace does not place restraints on costs.
7. As people live longer, they require more health care, thus prolonging the need for care and increasing its cost.
8. Fraud by both providers and members is increasing.

For these reasons and many others, the cost of health care has been rising steadily and quickly for the past few decades. Unless major steps are taken to curb this increase, many Americans will find themselves unable to afford health care, and many companies will no longer be able to afford to insure their employees.

Employee Benefits

Although auto, home, and most other personal property insurance is purchased by an individual, health-care insurance is often supplied (partly or fully) by a person's employer. The supplying of health-care insurance comes under the heading of an employee benefit.

Health-care benefits are an extremely important part

of almost everyone's economic security. These benefits were once considered to be a fringe benefit by employers. Today, many employees consider the benefits to be a major consideration when seeking a job.

Benefits account for almost 40% of an employee's total compensation. In actuality, there are many definitions of employee benefits. In the broadest view, employee benefits are virtually any form of compensation other than direct wages paid or given to an employee. Other benefits include paid vacations, sick leave, pension plans, tuition reimbursement or payment plans, yearly bonuses, and many other "perks" that employers offer to attract the best employees.

Types of Insurance

There are various types of insurance coverage. The following list includes some of the most common:

- Accidental Death and Dismemberment Insurance pays a benefit to the beneficiary in the event of the insured person's death by accidental means. It also pays a benefit to the insured when an accident causes the loss of a limb.
- Dental Insurance covers preventive and therapeutic services of the teeth and gums.
- Disability Insurance covers an employee's salary, or a percentage of it, while the employee is on a disability leave. There is short-term disability insurance, up to 12 weeks, and long-term.
- Health Insurance covers medical and hospital services. Such policies are sold as individual policies or group policies.
- Life Insurance is coverage on a person's life. In the event of the insured person's death, a benefit is paid to the named beneficiary.
- Medicaid is a federal program established under Title XIX of the Social Security Act of 1965. Its purpose is to provide the needy with access to medical care.
- Medicare is the Federal Health Insurance Benefit Plan for the Aged and Disabled under Title XVIII of Public Law 89-97 of the Social Security Act. This program is for people 65 years of age and older and certain individuals who are totally disabled.
- Property and Casualty Insurance covers material items, paying for repair or replacement of the item.
- Workers' Compensation is a medical and disability reimbursement program that provides 100% coverage for job-related injury, illness, or conditions arising out of and in the course of employment.

Numerous other types of coverages also may be purchased from insurance companies. It is possible to be insured against almost any loss if you're willing to pay the premiums.

In addition, the term "insurance" is often incorrectly used to refer to all types of health coverage. In reality, insurance is only one type of health coverage. As part of this course, you will be expected to learn the correct terminology for referring to the various benefit plans. A listing of the most common plans follows.

Individual vs Group Insurance

Insurance coverage is categorized as being either individual or group. Individual insurance coverage covers one person or item. Premiums are usually higher because of the higher risks associated with insuring individuals on a case-by-case basis. With individual insurance, there is nowhere to spread risks, and the chance that losses may exceed the premiums collected is greater than in group insurance.

Group insurance covers one or more persons or items. A group consists of any number of people who have a common purpose other than obtaining insurance coverage. Under this definition, members of unions, trade associations, and other organizations are able to purchase insurance as a group rather than as individuals.

Conventional Insurance

In a conventional insurance arrangement, an employer or individual purchases an insurance plan and agrees to pay premiums to the insurance company. In return, the insurance company agrees to pay specific benefits.

The premium cost is based on the "experience" of the plan, which includes the actuarial statistics, inflation, and administrative expenses of the company.

In the past few years, the rise in health-care costs has affected the increase in premiums. As a result, it has become almost prohibitively expensive for small employers and individuals to purchase coverage. For many larger employers, benefits have been decreased, the portion paid by the employee has been increased, or the plan has become self-funded.

Self-Funded Plans

In a self-funded plan, the total and ultimate responsibility for providing all plan benefit payments rests solely with the employer. Because of this economic risk, it is not uncommon for portions of the benefits to be self-funded, whereas other portions are insured. For instance, the medical benefits may be self-funded, whereas the dental benefits may be insured. In self-funding, there are no insurance premiums because there is no associated insurance company. In addition, the plan is not governed by the Department of Insurance. The risk of loss is assumed by the employer. This potential risk may be decreased by the employer purchasing reinsurance or stop-loss insurance. Such insurance would reimburse the employer when losses exceed a specific amount agreed on by the employer and the reinsurance carrier.

In this book, the term "plan benefits" is used to refer to coverages—medical and/or dental—with no distinction made as to whether those benefits are insured or self-funded. Such a distinction is irrelevant for our purposes, because handling and processing of claims within both arrangements are nearly identical.

Third Party Administrators

A Third Party Administrator or TPA is a plan administration firm that deals solely with administering the eligibility and claim payment services for self-funded plans (along with various other administrative services). The administrator provides all the equipment and personnel required to meet the client's needs. In turn, the client supplies the funds or monies needed for payment of the administrator's services and for amounts paid out for claims payments. In contrast, the insurance company handles all its own plan administration along with providing all the equipment and personnel required.

In response to the increase in the number of self-funded plans, many insurance companies now offer what are known as Administrative Services Only (ASO) contracts. These contracts work basically the same as a TPA insofar as all of the funding is provided by the client, and the expertise, equipment, and personnel are provided by the insurance company (also referred to as the insurer). As with all areas of the benefit industry, a multitude of variations are possible on both of these concepts.

Functional Areas in an Insurance Company

Within each insurance company, there are a number of departments with varying responsibilities. Depending on the size of the company, a department may consist of a number of people or only one person. In fact, one person may perform the functions of several departments. However, each department is represented in each company, including the Human Resources, Marketing, Actuarial, New Business, Premium Services, Underwriting, Accounting, Claims, and Legal Departments.

The *Human Resources Department*, also called the Personnel Department, is responsible for matters relating to the company's employees. The Human Resources Department formulates company policy with respect to hiring, training, compensation, and ensuring company compliance with federal, state, and local employment laws and regulations. It also administers employment benefit plans, such as group insurance, tuition refund plans, and employee pensions.

The *Marketing Department* is responsible for getting insurance products to the company's customers. "Products" within the insurance industry refers to various benefit plans. This department normally conducts market research, works with other departments in the company to develop new products and revise current ones to meet the changing needs of the company's customers, prepares advertising campaigns, designs promotional materials, and establishes and maintains distribution systems for its products. Marketing is also in charge of selling the products.

The *Actuarial Department* is responsible for seeing that the company's operations are conducted on a mathematically sound basis. In conjunction with other departments, it designs and revises the company's products. The Actuarial Department is also chiefly responsible for establishing premium rates based on research performed to predict the profitability of its products. Research includes the use of a number of various studies such as morbidity rates, life expectancy studies, cost of services studies, and others. These studies can help companies to determine the cost of premiums according to how long a person is expected to live, the types of services the average person will need as they grow older, and the cost of these services.

The *New Business Department* does just what its name states: it processes new business acquired by the company. This department's primary responsibilities are to determine and verify that all information and forms submitted by the sales agents are complete and accurate. The New Business Department also schedules physical examinations for policies that require evidence of insurability.

All policies issued require premium payments to be made to keep the policy in force. The *Premium Services Department* handles and processes all premium payments received at the home office. This department handles the billing of premium notices and overdue statements to policyholders.

The *Underwriting Department* is responsible for making sure that the premium rates are accurate and that claim payments do not exceed the amounts assumed when the premium rates were calculated. The Underwriting Department makes determinations as to the insurability of applicants, both individuals and employer groups, based on their present experience and medical status.

The *Accounting Department* maintains the records to show if the company is being run in a profitable manner. This department is responsible for maintaining the company's general accounting records, preparing financial statements, controlling receipts and disbursements, overseeing the budgeting process, administering the payroll program, and working with the Legal Department to ensure that the firm is complying with government regulations and tax laws.

The primary responsibility of the *Claims Department* is the processing of claims in a correct and timely manner. The claims examiner reviews the claims submitted by members or providers of service for the correct application of the plan benefits. This area also includes a support staff of clerical and customer service personnel and often includes nurses and physicians for the administration of cost-containment programs.

The *Legal Department* makes sure that the company's operations comply with federal, state, and local laws and with the Department of Insurance regulations. It studies current and proposed legislation to determine the effects on the future operations and advises the Claims Department when claim disputes are received. This department also works with the Accounting Department in determining tax liabilities and represents the company in litigations.

The Department of Insurance

The entire insurance industry is overseen by a larger body called the Department of Insurance. The Department of Insurance for each state holds the primary legal authority over the operations of all insurance companies within that state. Therefore, it has influence over insured benefit plans but does not have legal authority over self-funded plans. The many responsibilities of the Department of Insurance are:

- Issues certificates and licenses authorizing insurance companies and insured products to operate or be sold in the state.
- Licenses agents to sell insurance and revokes licenses when warranted.
- Reviews the annual statements of insurance companies for verification of solvency.

- Ensures that policy forms include the required provisions and are printed in the proper format.
- Performs on-site inspections of insurance companies.
- Maintains an office for receiving and acting on consumer complaints.
- Ensures that insurance companies observe the rules affecting policy reserve maintenance and investment activities.

Summary

There are several types of insurance companies, and each provides benefits in exchange for premium payments from its members. Insurance companies are overseen by the Department of Insurance, which holds the primary legal authority over the operations of insurance companies within that state.

We will be concentrating on the functions of the Claims Department. As a Health Claims Examiner, you need to understand the principles that underlie the Claims Department's primary objective, which is to deliver timely, competent, fair, and friendly claim service. When conscientiously and consistently applied, these principles enable a company to build and maintain a respectable image with its customers and the general public. The maintenance of strong customer good will and the creation of a favorable public position are vital to the progress of a company as well as to each individual employee.

Assignments

Complete the Questions for Review.

Questions for Review

Directions: Answer the following questions without looking back into the material just covered. Write your answers in the space provided.

1. What is insurance? an ~~agreement~~ contract whereby insurance carriers collect fees from individuals on a regular basis in return they agree to pay for specific benefits always a contract

2. What are the two types of insurance plans and how do they differ? individual - covers 1 person or items, premiums higher Group insurance - covers more people - a group consists of any number of people who have a common purpose other then obtaining insurance coverage

conventional and self-funded

3. What does TPA stand for and what do these companies do? Third Party administrator Is an administration firm that deals solely with administering the eligibility + claim payment services for self-funded plans.

4. What are employee benefits? any form of compensation other then direct wages paid or given to an employee

5. Give five reasons for the rising cost of health care.

   a. More people are seeking health care now compared to 20 years ago.

   b. Cost of training health-care professionals is much higher

   c. Price health-care professionals pay for mal-practice insurance has increased dramatically

   d. Little competition among health-care providers no restraints on costs

e. fraud by both providers + members is on the increase

6. List five responsibilities of the Department of Insurance.

a. Issues certificates + licenses authorizing insurance companies + insured products to operate or be sold in the state

b. License agents to sell insurance + revokes licenses when warranted

c. Reviews annual statements of insurance companies for verification of solvency

d. Ensures that policy forms include the required provisions + are printed in the proper format

e. Performs on site inspections of insurance companies

7. What studies does the Actuarial Department of an insurance company use to help determine premiums? uses studies such as morbidity rates, life expectancy studies, cost of service studies and others

8. What work does the Underwriting Department of an insurance company do? makes sure premium rates are accurate, + claim payments do not exceed the amounts assumed when premium rates were calculated. Makes determinations as to insureability of applicants

9. What are the primary responsibilities of the Claims Department? is the processing of claims in a correct and timely manner

10. What other types of professionals will the Claims Department use as support staff and why? Support staff of clerical + customer service personnel sometimes nurses + Drs. for the administration of cost-containment programs

legal services - contract language

If you were unable to answer any of the questions, refer back to the section and complete the answers.

2

Contracts

In this chapter you will learn:

- To differentiate between basic comprehensive and major medical benefits.
- To determine order of benefits.
- The three usual roles for basic benefits.

A contract is a legal and binding written document that exists between two or more parties. Written contracts are in every aspect of society. Essentially, any agreement between two or more persons that is enforceable by law is considered a contract. Written contracts have several advantages over nonwritten (oral) contracts: the existence of a written contract cannot be denied, and the terms of a written contract can be enforced more easily in the event of death or incapacity (ie, insanity, coma) of one of the parties of the contract.

In health insurance, the contract is used to determine eligibility requirements and covered services and to determine how those covered services are to be paid. The contract also indicates services that are excluded and services that have limitations. Therefore, the Health Claims Examiner must learn to read and interpret the contract in order to pay the proper benefits.

Contract Validity

For a contract to be valid, the persons signing the contract must agree on the terms. For the parties to agree, there must be some form of offer and acceptance. To *offer* means to propose or undertake to do or give something in exchange for a return promise from the person to whom the act or gift is being offered. An offer must be communicated in one form or another before it can be accepted. However, acceptance need not always be communicated to create a contract.

For example, banks often send out a letter to their patrons informing them of a change in interest rates or other terms regarding their accounts. These letters often state that if the bank is not contacted within a specified period of time, it will be assumed that the patron has agreed to and accepted the new terms or rates.

For a contract to be valid and enforceable, the following principles must be met:

- The contract must be based on a mutual agreement by the parties to do or not to do a specific thing or things.
- The contract must be made by parties who are able and competent to enter into the contract and to enforce the terms of the contract. In some states, this may mean that minors may not enter into certain types of contracts.
- The contract must include consideration to pay money, deliver services, or promise to do or refrain from doing some lawful act that has not yet occurred (ie, a contract cannot be made to enforce an event that has already occurred).
- The purpose of the contract must be lawful. Contracts for unlawful acts are unenforceable.
- If the contract falls into a class of contracts required by law to be in a special form, the format of the contract must meet those laws or requirements.

Group Contracts

Every health benefit plan, whether it is insured or not, is required by law to have a written document describing the plan benefits. This written legal document is used both by the plan members and by the administrator in determining how claims are to be paid. If any settlement disputes develop, the document is entered as evidence of what is and is not covered, what allowances are provided toward specific services, what books are used for reference in calculating benefits, and what the appeal procedures are.

Insured plans call this written document a contract. Noninsured plans usually refer to the written document as a summary plan description. For our purposes, we will refer to the following documents generically as contracts without implying whether or not a plan is insured.

The group contract is an instrument through which an insurance company can meet the financial security needs of a group of persons. In essence, it is an agreement between the insurance company and the policyholder to insure the lives and health of the members of a defined group of persons and to pay the insurance benefits to the insured person or their beneficiaries. The specific terms and conditions of the contract are determined by negotiation between the insurance company and the policyholder. With the exception of benefit provisions, they are largely determined by standard provisions, generally accepted throughout the industry.

The group contract must consist of the following three parts:

1. The group master policy
2. The application of the group policyholder
3. The individual applications, if any, of the person insured.

The parties to a group contract are the insurance company and, in most cases, an employer. However, the policyholder may be a union or the trustee of a fund established by employers, unions, or both.

For a group contract to become valid, a written application must be made. For it to remain valid, premiums must be continued to be paid.

A basic principle of the law of contracts is consideration. Consideration can be a very broad term. For our purposes, *consideration* will be defined as anything that is given, done, promised, forbidden, or suffered by one party as an inducement for the agreement.

The most common form of consideration is the payment of money in exchange for a promise. For insurance, consideration is the premium paid by the group policyholder. The individual insured may contribute toward these premiums or provide the entire amount. In most cases, however, the premium is paid by the policyholder to the insurer, even though the individual insured may contribute part or all of the monies.

Summary

The term "contract," in a general context, is an agreement among two or more persons that is enforceable by law. For a contract to be valid, the parties must agree on its terms. There must also be some form of offer and acceptance. As soon as an offer has been properly communicated and accepted, a binding contract is formed. A group contract is the instrument through which an insurance company can meet the financial security needs of a group of persons.

The three contracts found on page 93 of the Student Exercise Manual will be used throughout the course to calculate benefits on sample claims and to add clarification to examples used to demonstrate the application of plan provisions.

These sample contracts are based on actual plans and should be used as examples of what is possible within the industry, because there is no such thing as a definitive plan. As you will discover, there are a multitude of possible contract provisions. Therefore, use these samples as learning tools only.

Assignments

Study the contracts beginning on page 93 of the Student Exercise Manual.
Complete the Questions for Review.
Complete the Contracts Exercises 2-1 to 2-5.

Questions for Review

Directions: Answer the following questions without looking back into the material just covered. Write your answers in the space provided.

1. Every health benefit plan, whether it is insured or not, is required by law to have a written document describing the plan benefits. (True or False) True
2. Define Offer. Propose or undertake to do or give something in exchange for a return promise from the person to whom the act or gift is being offered
3. Insured plans call this written document a contract
4. For a contract to be valid and enforceable, what five principles must be met?
   a. must be based on mutual agreement by the parties to do or not to do a specific thing or things
   b. Made by parties who are able + competent to enter into contract + to enforce the terms of the contract
   c. Contract must include consideration to pay $, deliver services, or promise to do or refrain from doing some lawful act that has not yet occurred
   d. purpose of contract must be lawful
   e. if contract falls into class of contracts required by law to be in a special form, the format of the contract must meet those laws + requirements
5. The group contract must consist of what three parts?
   a. Group Master Policy
   b. application of Group Policy holder
   c. individual application if any, of the person insured

If you were unable to answer any of the questions, refer back to the section and complete the answers.

Exercise 2-1

Directions: Read through the ABC Corporation contract (→ coverage cards) and list the amounts for the following provisions in the space provided. Do not concern yourself with the definitions of terms or how to calculate the amounts, since these subjects will be covered in another chapter.

1. What is the individual deductible amount? $100, three month carry-over provision
2. What is the dependent eligibility age limit? from birth to age 19, or to 25 if full time student or handicapped prior to 19/25.
3. What is the family calendar year deductible? family maximum deductible $200 aggregate
4. What is the individual coinsurance limit? $500 OOP per individual
5. What is the coinsurance percentage? 90% except 100% of hospital room + board expenses for 365 days per lifetime
6. What is the lifetime maximum amount? $300,000.00 per person
7. What is the Mental/Nervous lifetime outpatient amount? $10,000.00 per person (includes substance abuse + alcholism)
8. What is the Mental/Nervous lifetime inpatient amount? No inpatient maximum
9. How many hours must the employee work to be eligible? minimum of 30 hrs per week
10. Does the contract include dental coverage? yes
11. What is the family coinsurance limit? $1,000 OOP per family
12. Is the family coinsurance aggregate or nonaggregate? non aggregate
13. Is there a carryover provision on the individual deductible? yes
14. How many months must the employee work before coverage becomes effective? the first of month following 30 consecutive days of continuous employ.
15. What is the amount of the basic accident benefit? 100% of first $500 for services incurred within 90 days of date of accident Not subject to deductible

Exercise 2-2

Directions: Read through the Ninja Enterprises contract and list the amounts for the following provisions in the space provided.

1. What is the individual deductible amount? $150, 3 month carry over provision
2. What is the dependent eligibility age limit? birth to age 19 or to age 23 if full time student or handicapped prior to 19/23 unmarried natural children legally adopted + foster children included
3. What is the family calendar year deductible? Family Max. deductible $300 non-aggregate
4. What is the individual coinsurance limit? 1,250 OOP per individual
5. What is the coinsurance percentage? 80% network; 70% Non-network
6. What is the lifetime maximum amount? 1,000,000.00 per person
7. What is the Mental/Nervous lifetime outpatient amount? $15,000 per person combined in and out patient 30 days per lifetime
8. What is the Mental/Nervous lifetime inpatient amount? $15,000 per person combined inpatient + outpatient or 30 days per lifetime
9. How many hours must the employee work to be eligible? minimum of 20 hrs
10. Does the contract include dental coverage? No Covered through Simon Dental
11. What is the family coinsurance limit? 2,500 OOP for family
12. Is the family coinsurance aggregate or nonaggregate? non aggregate
13. Is there a carryover provision on the individual deductible? yes - 3 month carry-over
14. How many months must the employee work before coverage becomes effective? first of month following 2 consecutive months of employment
15. What is the amount of the basic accident benefit? 100% of 1st $300 for services incurred within 90 days of accident subject to $20 co pay. after $300 subject to calendar yr. deductible

Exercise 2-3

Directions: Read through the XYZ Corporation contract and list the amounts for the following provisions in the space provided.

1. What is the individual deductible amount? $125 - 3 month carry over provision
2. What is the dependent eligibility age limit? birth to age 19 or 23 if F.T. student or handicapped prior to 19/23, unmarried natural children, adopted or foster
3. What is the family calendar year deductible? $250 total - 2 family members must satisfy their individual calendar yr. deductible
4. What is the individual coinsurance limit? $400 OOP per individual
5. What is the coinsurance percentage? Standard coinsurance 80%
6. What is the lifetime maximum amount? $1,000,000.00 per person
7. What is the Mental/Nervous lifetime outpatient amount? 1,000,000.00 total inpatient & out patient
8. What is the Mental/Nervous lifetime inpatient amount? 500 calendar yr. maximum per person
9. How many hours must the employee work to be eligible? minimum of 30 hrs. per wk.
10. Does the contract include dental coverage? yes
11. What is the family coinsurance limit? $800 OOP per family - aggregate
12. Is the family coinsurance aggregate or nonaggregate? aggregate
13. Is there a carryover provision on the individual deductible? yes - 3 month carry-over provision
14. How many months must the employee work before coverage becomes effective? If written application is made prior to eligibility date, coverage becomes effective the 1st month following 3 months employment
15. What is the amount of the basic accident benefit? 100% of 1st $300. for services incurred within 90 days of accident

Exercise 2-4

Directions: Read through the following list of exclusions and place an E in the space provided if the service is excluded under the contract. Place an N/E in the space provided if the service is not excluded under the contract.

	ABC	NINJA	XYZ
1. Sex-altering treatments or surgeries or related studies.	E	E	E
2. Work-related injuries or illnesses.	E	E	E
3. Charges or services in excess of UCR.	E	E	E
4. Charge made for failure to keep an appointment.	E	E	E
5. Routine or preventative or experimental services.	E	E	E
6. Mental/Nervous expenses above $15,000.	NE	NE	NE
7. Orthopedic shoes (medically necessary) following foot surgery.	NE	NE	NE
8. Radial keratotomy.	E	E	E
9. Cosmetic surgery for breast following mastectomy.	NE	NE	NE
10. Services for which there is no charge in the absence of insurance.	E	E	E
11. Surgical correction of cleft palate.	NE	NE	NE
12. Custodial care.	E	E	E
13. Reversal of voluntary sterilization.	E	E	E
14. Contraceptive materials or devices.	E	E	E
15. Expenses resulting from self-inflicted injuries.	E	E	E
16. Elective abortions.	E	E	E
17. Expenses for weight reduction for someone 90 lb. overweight. (at least 100)	E	E	E
18. Charges for services not medically necessary.	E	E	E
19. Vitamins, food supplements, and/or protein supplements.	E	E	E
20. Experimental transplants.	E	E	E

Exercise 2-5

Directions: Read through the dental contracts and list the amounts for the following dental provisions in the spaces provided.

	ABC	NINJA	XYZ
1. What is the individual deductible amount?	$100	N/A	50
2. What is the dependent eligibility age limit?	19/25	N/A	19/23
3. What is the family calendar year deductible?	200	N/A	150
4. What is the calendar year maximum?	1500	N/A	1,000
5. What is the coinsurance percentage?	90%	N/A	80%
6. How many hours must the employee work to be eligible?	30 hrs	N/A	30 hrs
7. Are orthodontics covered?	yes	N/A	no
8. Is oral surgery covered?	no	N/A	yes
9. Are fluoride treatments covered for a 20-year-old?	yes	N/A	no
10. Does the missing and unreplaced rule apply?	yes	N/A	yes

3

Eligibility

In this chapter you will learn:

- To define eligibility and termination of coverage and explain their purposes.
- Basic eligibility guidelines.
- To determine the patient's eligibility status.
- To identify and explain COBRA.

Eligibility is defined as the quality or qualities that make someone eligible. Eligible is defined as fit to be chosen or legally or morally qualified. Therefore, as far as insurance is concerned, eligibility means those qualities or requirements that a person must meet to be covered by the plan. Do not confuse "eligible" with "effective." In insurance, these are two very different concepts. A person can be eligible for coverage without the coverage ever becoming effective. (The concept of coverage becoming effective will be covered later in this chapter.)

The definition of an eligible person varies from plan to plan. However, most plans have separate definitions for eligible employees or subscribers compared with eligible dependents. The requirements for the insured can include such things as number of hours worked for the policyholder and a minimum of months that the employee has been employed by the policyholder. The requirements for the dependents of the insured can include such things as being a lawful spouse or dependent child of the insured, being under a certain age limit, or attending school full-time.

It is important for the Health Claims Examiner to understand the concept of eligibility and the eligibility requirements under each contract in order to process claims correctly.

Employee Eligibility

Most contracts define participants (eg, employees, subscribers, members, insureds) according to the minimum number of hours that the employee or subscriber must work per specified period of time, which is usually per week. Generally, part-time employees—and full-time employees working fewer than 30 hours per week—are not considered eligible for coverage.

Other contracts define the subscriber in terms of membership in an organization, such as the CPA Society or real estate societies. A minimum number of hours worked may also apply in these circumstances.

Partners and proprietors are also considered participants as long as they engage in the conduct of business on a full-time basis or a minimum number of hours per week.

For example, refer to the XYZ Contract. As indicated therein, the employee must:

- Routinely work a minimum of 30 hours per week.
- Be considered a full-time employee. (Even though the contract does not specifically indicate this, it is an industry standard.) Therefore, unless the booklet or contract says otherwise, this is to be assumed.
- Work 3 consecutive months to be eligible. Coverage may become effective the first of the month following the completion of 3 months of work (application must still be made).

For example, suppose an employee is hired on 3/2/91 and works 40 hours per week. Since 6/2 is past the first of the month, coverage may become effective the first of the month following the completion of the 3-month waiting period, or 7/1/91.

Under many union contracts, eligibility depends on the number of hours the member worked during the previous year or the previous month. With unions, a member may work for multiple employers during a month or week. As long as the employer is a member of the union and the employee is a member of the union, hours are accumulated toward the satisfaction of the hourly requirement.

For instance, a common type of wording for union contracts is:

> If you are a bargaining unit employee, you will become eligible for benefits on the first day of the second month following any three consecutive months during which you worked for one or more contributing employers a minimum total of 300 hours. Once eligibility has been established, you and your dependents will be covered for a minimum of three consecutive months.

For example, if you worked:

January	110 hr	Your coverage will begin May 1.
February	0 hr	
March	190 hr	
Total	300 hr	

In this example, the requirements are:

- 300 hours in any consecutive 3-month period.
- Eligibility begins on the first day of the second month following the 3 consecutive months.
- Coverage will be for a minimum of 3 consecutive months.

It is not unusual for a plan to have different eligibility provisions for different classifications of employees. For instance, separate provisions may be given for employees classified as Active Officers, Board Members, Management Employees, or Retired Employees. Special provisions may also be applicable to employees who are laid off or on leave. Therefore, it is very important to check the plan provisions to determine whether there are a variety of classifications and, if so, to know how to verify the specific classifications of the claimants whose claims you are handling.

Dependent Eligibility

The first step in determining whether a dependent is eligible is to verify whether the dependent fits the definition of an eligible dependent. Defining a dependent is much more complex than defining an employee because of the complex family and social dynamics in our society. A plan must try as much as possible to define all the dependents that can exist and to place those definitions into either covered or noncovered categories.

In general, "dependent" means:

- The employee's legal spouse (either through marriage or through common-law status if recognized by the state in which they are residing. The employee and spouse cannot be divorced or legally separated, even if there is a court decree stating that the employee is responsible for providing medical coverage.)
- Dependent, unmarried children within the age limitations specified by the plan. The term "dependent" means that the child must rely on the employee for daily maintenance and care. The term "children" always includes one's natural children and may include:
  - Adopted children for whom the final court order has been issued or for whom it is specified by the adoption agreement during any state-mandated waiting period that the adoptive parents provide for all medical care.
  - Stepchildren residing with the employee.
  - Grandchildren residing with the employee, who depend on the employee for more than 50% of their support.
  - Foster children whose foster child agreement specifies that the state is not responsible for their health care and that the foster parents are responsible. (Usually, the state maintains responsibility for foster children's health care.)
  - Any other children related to the employee by blood or marriage, provided that they are living in a regular parent-child relationship and dependent on the employee for support and maintenance. In the case of grandchildren, a regular parent-child relationship does not exist if either of the child's parents also reside with the employee.

Plans will further specify that to be eligible, children must be under a certain age, usually 18 or 19 years. Unmarried children of a specified age limitation, usually 23 through 25 years of age, who attend a licensed or accredited school on a full-time basis, are also eligible. For coverage to continue during vacation periods, the child must be scheduled and registered to enter school on the next enrollment date.

In conjunction with this requirement, plans must define what is considered a "licensed" or "accredited" school. Many plans cover only colleges or universities. Other plans allow vocational schools and rehabilitation schools. The plan must specify what is considered to be full-time. Most schools define what constitutes a full-time student, and most plans accept the school-specific definition. However, this must be verified by reading the contract provisions.

Many states have enacted legislation concerning coverage for dependent children from birth. Although specific wording and intent are determined by individual state legislation, the laws generally provide that newborn children can be afforded the same eligibility for accident and health coverage as any other dependent and are covered from birth for treatment of a disease or injury. Preexisting limitations (covered later in this course) by definition cannot be applied to newborn children. This automatic coverage is for an initial 31-day period from date of birth. For such coverage to continue past the 31-day period, the employee must:

- Complete any required enrollment form.
- Elect to make any required contributions, effective from the date of birth.

The law does not usually create an obligation for plans to pay for well-baby or custodial care. A few states require insured plans to have well-child care provisions. Refer to the mandates listed in Chapter 5.

Many plans also specify that a person who is eligible as an employee cannot be enrolled as a dependent on the same plan. And, if both husband and wife are covered under the same plan as employees, one or the other, not both, may elect to cover their dependents. This prevents a particular child from being covered as a dependent under both parents.

Employee Effective Date of Coverage

For an eligible employee's coverage or dependent's coverage to become effective, the person is usually required to complete the necessary enrollment papers prior to the date of eligibility.

The rules defining the effective date of coverage vary, depending on whether the plan is considered a contributory or noncontributory plan.

In a contributory plan, the employees contribute to the cost of the coverage, usually through payroll deductions. In a noncontributory plan, the employer bears the complete cost of the coverage and the employee does not contribute.

In a contributory plan:

- The employee must complete the enrollment card listing himself or herself and the dependents he or she wants to be covered; usually, all eligible dependents must be listed.
- Such application must be received by the employer or by the plan administrator on or before the eligibility date of coverage for coverage to become effective on that date.
- The employee must also authorize the applicable payroll deductions.

If the enrollment card is not received on or before the eligibility date of coverage, but is received within 1 month (or 30 or 31 days) after the date of eligibility, the employee is considered to be a "late applicant" and coverage will begin either on the date of application or the first or fifteenth of the month following the date of application. (The plan provisions must specify which of the time limitations are to be applied.)

If the enrollment application is not submitted on or before or within 1 month (or 30 or 31 days) after the date of eligibility, the employee will be required to submit proof of good health, also known as *evidence of insurability* or a health questionnaire, as stipulated in the policy for himself and all eligible dependents seeking coverage. The questionnaire will be submitted to the medical consultants of the insurer or plan administrator for review. If the participant appears to be a good "risk," that is, he or she does not appear to have any active illnesses or conditions, coverage may be approved. If the participant appears to be a poor risk because of active illnesses, coverage will not be approved and the employee and dependents will not be able to obtain coverage under the plan at that time. (Some plans provide for open enrollment periods, which will be discussed later.) Dependents cannot be covered unless the employee is covered. Therefore, if the dependents are healthy but the employee is not and the employee's eligibility is denied, even though the dependents may be a good risk, they will not be covered under the plan.

In a noncontributory plan in which the employer pays the full cost, a request for coverage is not necessary except for record purposes and beneficiary designations. Coverage for employees and, in some instances, their dependents begins automatically on the employee's eligibility date, regardless of when the enrollment application is completed and submitted. If the insurer or administrator is not informed of an employee's eligibility on the appropriate date and a claim or an enrollment card is subsequently submitted, the insurer/administrator will automatically add the member and bill the employer for all back premiums due. After the back premiums are paid, the claim(s) will be paid. Evidence of insurability is not required in these cases and there are not considered to be any "late applicants" on the plan.

Be aware that a plan can be noncontributory for the employee and contributory for dependents. Therefore, a combination of the aforementioned rules may apply.

Whether the group is contributory or noncontributory, the usual effective date of coverage is deferred if on the effective date the employee is absent from work because of illness or injury. Most plans stipulate that for coverage to go into effect, the employee must have completed either a full day of active work on that date or a full day of active work on the last regularly scheduled work day and is able to work on the date of eligibility. If the employee does not meet these requirements, the coverage will become effective on the date he or she returns to active work.

Active work and actively at work usually means performing the regular duties for a full work day for the employer.

Dependent Effective Date of Coverage

The rules regarding the effective date of dependents are similar to the rules for employees, since the rules depend on whether the plan is contributory or noncontributory.

In the case of an employee, the plan usually makes a stipulation regarding being actively at work. A similar provision is also made for dependents. However, since a dependent often doesn't work, policies usually state that if a dependent is in the hospital, the coverage for that dependent becomes effective on the day after the date of discharge, or the date on which the dependent is able to perform all the duties he or she usually performs. In other words, if the dependent is of school age, coverage might begin when the child returns to school. An exception would be that of a newborn child, who is usually born in a hospital. In such a case, coverage begins immediately.

In a contributory plan, dependents are handled in the same way as with employees regarding late enrollment. However, many contributory plans require that for dependent coverage, all eligible dependents must be enrolled in the plan. This requirement is aimed at preventing adverse selection, in which an employee selectively chooses to put sick dependents on one plan and healthy dependents on another.

Open Enrollment

Open enrollment is a process that allows late applicants to enroll in a plan without having to complete evidence of insurability. This enrollment process usually occurs on the anniversary date of the coverage. The plans that provide this option are those in which an employer has multiple plan options. For instance, larger employers are required by law to offer their employees an HMO option. Also, these employers often offer a regular indemnity plan (deductible, coinsurance), an HMO, a low-indemnity plan (eg, higher deductibles, lower coinsurance payable by the plan), and perhaps a high-indemnity plan (lower deductible, higher coinsurance payable by the plan). By having an open enrollment period, employees may switch from one plan to another without penalties or a gap in coverage and without having to complete a health statement.

Termination of Coverage

The provisions for terminating an individual's coverage vary according to the type of group and how the employer wants the plan administered. In a union or association group, for instance, coverage terminates when the employer terminates the group's membership in the union or association. The most common termination provisions are those based on conditions pertaining to employment. Coverage is usually terminated under one of these conditions:

- The group policy terminates.
- The policy is amended to terminate the eligibility of the class of employees to which the individual belongs.
- The employee transfers out of a class covered by the policy.
- Active employment ceases.
- The employee ceases to pay the required contributions for the coverage.

When coverage ceases, regardless of the reason, some form of continuation of coverage may be available.

Continuation of Coverage

Many plans allow benefits to extend beyond the normal date or terms of eligibility. These extensions can be of several types, depending on the reason for the continuation (disability, COBRA). We will discuss the main situations in which benefits are extended beyond normal eligibility and the requirements for continuing such coverage.

Extension of Benefits

Most plans contain an extended benefits provision for totally disabled members. This type of provision requires that:

- The person was eligible and covered under the plan when his or her coverage terminated.
- As of the termination date, the person was totally disabled due to an injury or illness.
- Only covered expenses (as defined by the plan provisions) incurred for the illness or injury causing the disability will be considered eligible for benefit consideration.
- Coverage will last only for the length of time as specified in the policy.

The latter requirements indicate that first there must be documented proof that the person was totally disabled with an injury or illness when he or she terminated. Second, only eligible expenses incurred for the injury or illness causing the disability are considered for benefits after the termination date.

Refer to the three contracts. As indicated, ABC and XYZ Contracts both have a standard extension of benefits provision. Coverage will continue for 12 months from the date of termination under the plan or until the person is no longer totally disabled, whichever interval is less. Ninja Enterprises does not have an extension of benefits provision.

Therefore, in determining whether an extension of benefits provision is applicable, the following steps must be followed:

1. Was the member eligible and effective under the plan when coverage terminated? If no, the investigation would end, since the member could not continue coverage if he or she was not eligible and effective on the plan when coverage terminated. If yes, then:
2. Was the member totally disabled at the time the coverage terminated? If no, extension of benefits would not apply. If yes, then:
3. A letter from the attending physician must be obtained stating the condition or conditions causing the disability, the date the member became totally disabled, and the anticipated end of the total disability.
4. Also, if the employee is claiming disability, try to find out if he or she is employed anywhere. Sometimes, members apply for this type of extension because premiums are not required (continuation is provided for the maximum 12 months free of charge to the employee but only for the person totally disabled) and the member wants coverage between jobs.

Conversion Policies

Most states have legislatively mandated that insurance policies contain a continuation of coverage provision known as conversion. Conversion permits employees and dependents to continue their insurance protection on an individual basis when their coverage under a group plan ceases because:

- The employee's employment in the class of

employees insured under the group policy terminates.

- The policy is amended to terminate coverage for the class to which the employee belongs.
- The employee terminates employment with the employer.
- A dependent child reaches the plan limiting age.
- The employee and spouse are divorced or legally separated so that the spouse is no longer considered eligible under the provisions of the plan.

Evidence of insurability is not required, but the person must apply in writing and pay the required premiums within a specified time period of the date of termination of coverage under the group plan (usually 31 days). Those who voluntarily discontinue their insurance coverage while still employed are not eligible to convert, nor is the conversion privilege available when the employer's complete policy is terminated.

As a rule, conversion policies are extremely expensive. It is not uncommon for a quarterly conversion policy premium to be $5000 to $10,000. The reason for this high premium is that usually only those employees who are disabled and extremely ill convert their policy. Because of the high experience on the conversion policy, the resulting premiums are also very high.

Unfortunately, if an individual is so ill that he or she must cease working, it is extremely difficult to afford the high premiums. Nevertheless, it is an available option.

COBRA

On April 7, 1986, President Reagan signed into law HR3128, the Consolidated Omnibus Budget Reconciliation Act of 1985 (COBRA), also referred to hereafter as *continuation of coverage*. Within this act, there was a very significant provision, Title X, which has had profound effects on employee welfare benefit plans.

Previous to COBRA, employers were generally not required by statute to provide continuation of group insurance coverage for individuals who ceased to be eligible for such coverage. The objective of Congress through Title X was to require employers to permit employees and their dependents to purchase transitional health care coverage at favorable group rates until replacement coverage could be obtained. The intended result was to reduce the number of people without health care coverage.

Title X is composed of the following amendments:

Section 10001	Amendments to the Internal Revenue Code (IRC)
Section 10002	Amendments to the Employee Retirement Income Security Act (ERISA)
Section 10003	Amendments to the Public Health Service Act (PHSA)

The effect of these amendments is to require virtually every type of group health plan, insured or self-funded, to provide the option of self-payment for continuation of coverage. The scope of this new statute is said to be the broadest since the enactment of ERISA. And, since penalties for nonconformance will be administered by the IRS, noncompliance will be costly.

Cobra applicability

COBRA applies to all private employers who regularly employ 20 or more employees (including both full-time and part-time) on a typical working day. It applies to single employer health plans, multiple employer trust plans, collectively bargained plans, insured plans, and self-funded plans.

Under the amendment to the Public Health Service Act (Section 10003), certain state and local governmental employers of 20 or more employees are required to offer continuation of coverage even though these employers are exempt from both taxes and ERISA. The applicability of COBRA to state and local governmental employers is based on the receipt of funds under PHSA. If the state or local governmental employer received funds under PHSA, compliance is required.

In summation, all employee group health benefit plans are required to comply in offering continuation of coverage, with the exception of the following:

- Any group health plan for any calendar year if the employer normally maintained fewer than 20 employees on a typical business day during the preceding calendar year.

- Certain church plans.
- Group health plans maintained by state or local governmental employers who do not receive funds under PHSA.
- Group health plans maintained for employees by the government of the District of Columbia or any territory or possession of the United States.

Governmental and nongovernmental group health plans that are not collectively bargained were subject to the COBRA requirements as of the first of the plan year, beginning subsequent to June 30, 1986. The plan year, not the employer's fiscal year nor the insurance policy period, controls the compliance date.

For collectively bargained plans, the COBRA effective date is/was the first of the plan year beginning after the later of the following dates:

- December 31, 1986.
- The expiration date of the last agreement relating to the plan.

Section 10001 of Title X specifically states that any amendment made to a collective bargaining agreement relating to the plan, which amends the plan solely to conform to any requirement added by this law will not be treated as a termination of the agreement. The original expiration date of the agreement will still govern the COBRA effective date if later than December 31, 1986.

Most health plans became subject to COBRA by December 31, 1986.

Qualified beneficiaries

The option of self-payment continuation of coverage must be offered by the affected employers to certain individuals referred to as qualified beneficiaries. A *qualified beneficiary* is defined as anyone who, on the day before a Qualifying Event, is covered under the health coverage plan as an employee, a dependent spouse or a dependent child.

Qualifying event

The term *qualifying event* refers to one of the following events, which results in the loss of eligibility under the employer sponsored health plan:

- Voluntary or involuntary termination of employment, with the exception of termination for gross misconduct.
- Reduction in work hours.
- Eligibility of the employee only for Medicare.
- Death of the employee.
- Divorce or legal separation.
- Disqualification of a dependent child as an eligible dependent.

Employers are required to offer the self-pay continuation of coverage option to the following:

- Terminated or laid-off employees (except those terminated for gross misconduct); employees for whom a reduction in work hours would result in the loss of coverage; retired employees who are not eligible for Medicare.
- The surviving spouse and dependent children of a deceased employee.
- Divorced spouses and their dependent children.
- Spouses and dependent children of employees who are eligible for Medicare.
- Dependent children who cease to meet the plan definition of a "dependent child."

There are no length of service requirements connected to COBRA. As long as the employee was covered under the employer-sponsored health plan prior to the qualifying event, he or she has the right to elect continuation. This right also applies to the employee's spouse and dependent children, provided they were covered under the plan the day before the event.

The covered employee or spouse (when spouse is the elector) may act as the agent for the entire family. It is not necessary for each family member to make an individual election.

There is a great deal of ambiguity as to what constitutes "gross misconduct." Until formal regulations are issued or until the courts define it, the individual employer will have to decide what "gross misconduct" means.

Duration of coverage

COBRA requires that affected employers permit employees and covered dependents, at the time their coverage would cease because of a qualifying event, to elect continuation of their insurance coverage for up to

18, 29, or 36 months, depending on the circumstances.

For employees and their dependents, a maximum of 18 months is allowed after one of the following events:

- Voluntary or involuntary termination of employment other than for gross misconduct.
- Reduction of work hours below the plan eligibility requirements.

For employees or dependents who are permanently disabled at the time of their event, coverage may be continued for up to 29 months rather than 18 months. The plan may use the Social Security standard of permanent disability as a qualifying condition of the extended coverage. This provision became effective for plan years beginning on or after December 19, 1989.

For covered dependents only, a maximum of 36 months of continued coverage is allowed after one of the following events:

- Death of the employee.
- Divorce or legal separation from the employee.
- The employee becomes eligible for Medicare.
- A child ceases to be an eligible dependent as defined by the plan provisions.

If a second qualifying event occurs during the time of the continuation of coverage for dependents, the maximum time allowed can be increased from 18 to 36 months if a qualifying event occurs as indicated above. Also, it may be possible to extend coverage from 18 to 29 months if an employee becomes totally disabled while covered. However, coverage cannot be extended beyond 29 months for employees.

Notification of eligibility

One of the most important aspects of the COBRA Act is the requirement that eligible members be informed of their eligibility for COBRA. Many employers have interpreted this to mean that when an employee terminates coverage, usually in the form of employment termination, he or she will be informed of COBRA rights. However, this procedure addresses only a portion of those actually eligible for continuation of coverage.

Few personnel departments of large employers can maintain adequate monitoring of the mobility of all employees, much less of dependents. Yet, this segment of the eligible member base may represent a significant portion of continuation eligibility.

Figure 3-1 is an example of a document that may be used to enroll the applicant for continuation of coverage. In addition, the employer must provide notification of the availability of COBRA to all employees and their dependents. By early distribution of reference materials, liability for failure to notify affected employees/dependents can be avoided, and the responsibility for timely application would be shifted entirely to the affected employee if (1) dependents become overage, (2) if a divorce or separation occurs, or (3) if the employee abandons or terminates employment without advance notification. The applicant has 60 days from the date that such coverage is terminated due to a qualifying event in which to submit the application for continuation to the administrator or insurance company or 60 days from the date notice of the right to elect COBRA continuation is sent to the employee. Therefore, if the employer/plan fails to send out notification of the election right for 2 years after the actual event date, the employee would have to be given 60 days from the 2-year date in which to elect coverage. Mistakes like this can prove to be very costly to a plan.

Premium payments

After COBRA has been elected, 45 days is allowed in which to pay the initial premium including all retroactive premiums due since the termination of coverage as a regular employee. If the initial premium and all back premiums are not paid within this time, coverage will remain terminated and COBRA coverage will not become effective.

Normally, a monthly COBRA statement is provided to the employee, which reflects the premium due date for each month and the amount of the monthly premium based on the coverage elected by the applicant. However, the law permits a 30-day grace period from the premium due date. This allows the applicant 30 additional days in which to pay the required premium amount. If the premium is not mailed within the 30-day grace period, coverage will automatically lapse

ABC Company
333 Whata Way
Hollywood, CA 91731

CONTINUATION OF COVERAGE REQUEST

If you were eligible under your employer's group health insurance plan, you may be eligible to continue your coverage. In order to apply, this form must be completed and returned to the Administrator's office indicated above within 60 days of the date your eligibility under the group plan terminates. Within 14 days of our receipt of this request, you will be sent a copy of your Election Rights under the Consolidated Omnibus Reconciliation Act of 1985 (COBRA), Public Act 99-272, Title X.

EMPLOYEE NAME - LAST	FIRST	FACILITY	SOC. SEC.

COMPLETE HOME ADDRESS	CITY	STATE	ZIP

Qualifying Event: Check off the event and give the event date.

- ❑ Reduction in work hours. Effective: ______
- ❑ Employment Termination (Except due to "gross misconduct"). Last Work Day: ______
- ❑ Dependent Child Attained Maximum Age Defined by Plan. ______
- ❑ Legal Separation and/or Divorce. Date: ______
- ❑ Death of Covered Employee. Date: ______

CONTINUATION OF COVERAGE REQUESTED FOR: (Coverage(s) cannot be added. May be dropped only.)

❑ Employee Only	❑ Employee & Dependent(s)	❑ Dependent(s) Only
❑ Medical Only	❑ Medical Only	❑ Medical Only
❑ Dental + VSP Only	❑ Dental + VSP Only	❑ Dental + VSP Only
❑ Medical + Dental + VSP	❑ Medical + Dental + VSP	❑ Medical + Dent. + VSP

ALL DEPENDENTS MUST BE LISTED BELOW. LIST THE SOCIAL SECURITY NUMBER OF THE EMPLOYEE'S SPOUSE AND OVERAGE DEPENDENT CHILDREN.

NAME	SOC. SEC. #	BIRTHDATE	RELATIONSHIP

______
Signature of Applicant / Date Signed

Figure 3-1: Continuation of Coverage Request.

back to the last premium paid date.

The amount of the premium can be up to 102% of the premium costs for employees. The 2% is to cover administrative costs. For employees who are eligible for the 29-month extension, the premium can be up to 150% of the employee premium cost for months 19 through 29 (effective for plan years beginning December 19, 1989).

Normally, claims are not paid until the member has paid the premium for the month in which the services were incurred or until the grace period has lapsed. Consequently, if the member consistently pays at the end of the grace period, claim payments may be consistently delayed. (Again, the incurred date of services will be compared with the paid through date. If the premium for the month in which services were incurred has not been paid, processing will be delayed until the end of the grace period.)

Bounced checks or any type of nonpaid check may result in lapse of coverage if the check is returned from the bank after the premium due date and a replacement check was not received prior to the end of the grace period. The mailing date of premiums should be strictly monitored with no exceptions. The date of receipt is not important. Judgment of whether or not a payment was received timely is based on the postmark on the envelope. By law, if the payment was mailed within the specified time, it must be accepted as being paid timely.

It is very important that all applicants/members be treated equitably regarding the premium receipt policy, since deviations may set precedents and extend plan liabilities above acceptable limits.

Termination of coverage

An individual may terminate the continuation of coverage prior to the completion of the 18-, 29- or 36-month period. However, if coverage is terminated prior to completion of the maximum period, the employer is not required to offer a second election of extension. In other words, once continuation is discontinued, coverage will not be reinstated or restarted.

If any of the following events occurs before the end of the 18-, 29- or 36-month continuation periods, coverage will cease at the end of the month following the date of the occurrence:

- Termination of all of the employer's sponsored group health plans.
- Failure to pay required premium contributions within 30 days of premium due date.
- Becoming covered under another group sponsored health plan unless the replacement plan exempts coverage for a preexisting condition affecting the member. Under this circumstance, the member may continue COBRA with the COBRA plan covering only those expenses incurred as a result of the preexisting condition. The replacement plan would cover all other expenses. This change is effective for qualifying events occurring after December 31, 1989.
- Becoming entitled to Medicare coverage.

Since legislation regarding this provision is constantly being amended by Congress, it is important to stay abreast of changes.

Disclaimers

One of the best ways to protect yourself from possible legal action is to use disclaimers. Disclaimers use words such as "It appears that," or "This may be...." These words allow a general answer to the question without making any type of promise. If the biller or examiner makes a statement that is later found to be in error, it can cause numerous problems both in customer satisfaction and in possible legal issues.

All medical billers and claims examiners should practice using disclaimers in their conversations. When confirming a subscriber's eligibility and benefits, disclaimers should always be included. The following are disclaimers that may possibly be used in your verbal and written responses:

Eligibility—"We show that ___________ is currently effective on group ___________ . To receive benefits, he or she must be eligible at the time services are rendered."

Benefit—"These are the benefits now in effect for

this contract. To receive benefits, your membership must be in good standing on the dates services are rendered."

Remember that your main purpose when using disclaimers is to clarify an issue or answer a customer's question without making a promise that the company may be held to later.

Summary

Eligibility is probably the greatest factor to be considered when processing a claim. Thus, eligibility is the first thing that should be checked when a claim is received for payment. If the patient is not eligible, no further action need be taken on the claim.

Assignments

Complete the Questions for Review.

Complete the Eligibility and Disclaimer Exercises 3-1 to 3-5.

Questions for Review

Directions: Answer the following questions without looking back into the material just covered. Write your answers in the space provided.

1. Eligibility refers to the requirements that must be fulfilled for a person to be eligible for coverage.
2. Most contracts define employees in terms of according to number of hrs worked to get benefits
3. List the 5 conditions under which coverage is terminated.
   a. group policy terminates
   b. Policy is amended to terminate the eligibility of the class of employees to which individual belongs
   c. employee transfers out of a class covered by the policy
   d. active employment ceases
   e. Employee ceases to pay the required contributions for coverage
4. Conversion policies permits employees and dependents to continue their insurance protection on an individual basis when their coverage under a group plan ceases.
5. To whom does the COBRA act apply? employers who employ 20 or more employees. applies to single employer health plans, multiple employer trust plans, collectively bargained plans insured plans & self-funded plans
6. What is a qualified beneficiary? anyone who, on the day before the qualifying event is covered under the health coverage plan as an employee, dependent spouse or dependent child
7. What is a qualifying event? an event which results in the loss of eligibility under the employer sponsored health plan
8. What is the maximum time in which a dependent can continue COBRA? 18, 29 or (36) months depending on the circumstances
9. What is the maximum time in which an employee can continue COBRA? Not beyond 29 months for employees
10. How long does a member have to apply for COBRA after termination? 60 days

If you were unable to answer any of the questions, refer back to the section and then complete the answers.

Exercise 3-1

Directions: Indicate whether the person listed would be considered an eligible dependent (ED) or a noneligible dependent (NED) under the provisions of the plan. Assume that the first person is covered under the plan, and the second person is applying as his or her dependent.

1. Natalie's legally married spouse. ED
2. Nathaniel's dependent child age 4. ED
3. Bryant's cousin Terrell. NED
4. Tabari's divorced ex-spouse. NED
5. Tiron's son, aged 45, fully functional. NED
6. Renee's dependent child, aged 19, who is a full-time student. ED
7. Renita's brother Kenneth. NED
8. Ann's dog Pepper. NED
9. Elizabeth's adopted daughter. ED
10. Denise's mother-in-law. NED

Exercise 3-2

Directions: Place a "yes" or "no" next to each of the following to show whether coverage would be terminated under the circumstances given. Assume that each person listed is the member on the plan. Do not be concerned about whether the person is entitled to continuation of coverage.

1. Nancy goes from full-time to 20 hours per week. yes depends on plan
2. Alonzo is terminated by the company. yes
3. Kerri's company terminates the policy. yes
4. Sydney becomes self-employed but works on a contract basis for the same company. yes
5. Sean stops paying the premium for his insurance. yes
6. Thomas goes on vacation for 2 weeks. NO
7. Floree forgets to enroll during his company's open enrollment period. yes
8. Mia is transferred out of a class covered by the policy. yes
9. Mayra goes on maternity leave. NO
10. Carol gets married. NO

Exercise 3-3

Directions: Place a "yes" or "no" next to each of the following people to show which would be eligible for coverage under the Ninja contract:

1. Mother, Kanika, works 35 hours per week for Ninja. ____________
2. Father, Kenneth, is self-employed. He is Kanika's second husband. ____________
3. Ryan, 20-year-old son of Kanika and her first husband, Ryan, is currently unemployed and is not a full-time student. ____________
4. Ravyn, 20-year-old daughter (Ryan's twin) is going to the local university full-time. ____________
5. Jordan, 16-year-old daughter is a high school drop-out. ____________
6. Sheila is a 13-year-old foster child who lives with the family. ____________
7. Sharon is a 10-year-old legally adopted child. ____________
8. Paris is the 3-year-old daughter of Ravyn. ____________
9. Kytrena is Kanika's mother. She has Alzheimer's disease and is listed as a dependent on Kanika's income tax form. ____________
10. Caitlind is Kanika's mentally retarded sister. Kanika is not her legal guardian. ____________

Exercise 3-4

Directions: Reword the statements below to include the use of a disclaimer in the sentence.

1. Yes, your plan does include that coverage. It appears that your plan does include that coverage.

2. Yes, you are a member of that plan. It appears that you are a member of that plan

3. Yes, that is a covered service and we will be paying for it. It appears that it is a covered service and we'll let you know about payment

4. Your check will arrive in 5 days. We process claims as soon as possible.

5. Your deductible and stoploss have been met so you won't have to put out any more money on this bill. It appears your deductible & OOP has been met. We'll check on the remainder of your bill

6. You've worked for over 90 days so your company's insurance should cover the services. It appears you have worked for 90 days. We'll check your insurance coverage so medically nec. bills will be pd

7. Don't worry, your insurance will cover the bill. We'll check your policy to see if your insurance will cover it.

8. All hospitalization expenses are covered under your plan. It appears that hospitalization are covered under your plan.

9. We pay 80% of the billed amount. It appears we'll pay 80% of medically ness. of the billed amount after deductible

10. All preventive care is covered under your contract. It appears preventive care is covered under your contract.

Exercise 3-5

Directions: Reword the statements below to include the use of a disclaimer in the sentence.

1. Your insurance will cover the cost of these services. It appears your insurance will cover the medically ness services

2. Your policy includes coverage for those services, so we will pay a portion of the cost. It appears your policy includes those serves, so we may pay a portion of the cost

3. We process all claims upon receipt, so you should have your payment within 10 working days. We make all possible efforts to process claims upon receipt.

4. Yes, your child is an eligible dependent. It appears that your child is an eligible dependent as long as they meet age contract

5. If your claim reaches us by the 15th, it should be paid by the end of the month. If we have all information it should be pd by end of month

4

Benefit Structures

In this chapter you will learn:

- To interpret contract provisions.
- To identify the type of treatment as indicated by service provided.

Every health care plan is required by law to have a written description of the benefits available to the members of that plan. This plan document must indicate, in detail, and in layman's terms, the provisions of the coverage.

Three major types of coverage are currently available.

1. Basic only
2. Basic-Major Medical
3. Comprehensive Major Medical

Within these types there may be numerous variations.

Since the benefit payments calculated under each type of coverage can be identical, don't let the names confuse you. It's the concept that is important. Be sure that you understand the types of benefit payments prior to processing any claims, because accurate benefit payment calculation is essential to a good Health Claims Examiner. Inaccurate payments can cost an insurance carrier thousands of dollars.

Benefit Definitions

Following are some common terms that are used when dealing with benefits.

Accumulation Period—Period of time (normally January 1 through December 31) in which to satisfy the deductible, accumulate COB credit reserves, reach maximums, and so on.

Actively-at-Work Requirement—The provision of a group plan that requires that an otherwise eligible employee must be actively at work on the day he or she is scheduled to become covered. If the employee is not actively at work on the date that coverage should become effective, coverage will be delayed until the date of return to active work. For an eligible dependent, if the dependent is hospital-confined on the date coverage was to become effective, the coverage will not become effective until after release from the hospital.

Automatic Annual Reinstatement (AAR)—A contractually specified amount of money (credit) that may be added to the balance of available lifetime benefits. Usually, this applies to Major Medical benefits and is important only when a member has a catastrophic illness or injury and is calculated only when lifetime benefits have been exhausted.

Example: $1000 yearly reinstatement (AAR). Plan in effect since 1992.

Monies Payable by Plan	Lifetime Maximum
1992	
	$ 300,000
$150,000	-150,000
	$150,000
1993	
$175,000	$ 150,000 Remaining
	+ 1,000 1992 AAR
	+ 1,000 1993 AAR
	$ 152,000 Remaining and Payable
	-175,000
	$ 23,000 Unpaid/Over Max.

The maximum amount that can be reinstated in 1 year is either the amount specified in the plan or the amount paid out in that year, whichever is less. For example, if $800 had been paid out in 1992, only $800 could be reinstated. Usually, reinstatement is allowed for every year that the member is covered up to either the $1000 contract limit or the amount paid out, whichever is less. In essence, any amount not used will not be carried over to succeeding years.

Coinsurance—The arrangement by which both the member and the plan share, in a specific ratio of the covered losses under a policy. For example, the plan may reimburse the provider or member for 80% of covered expenses, and the member will be responsible for the remaining 20% of expenses.

Common Accident Provision—Only one deductible, under Major Medical, will be taken for all members of a family involved in the same accident. After the one deductible, remaining deductibles will be waived on all other members for expenses incurred for that accident only.

CoPay—The amount that the member/insured must pay "out-of-pocket" (OOP). This would normally be the 20% not paid by the coinsurance. The plan copay amount may or may not include the Major Medical deductible. The policy will state the specifics. This is also known as the out-of-pocket expense.

Covered Expense—Those expenses that are allowable under the plan. Services specifically excluded by the plan or in excess of UCR (usual customary and reasonable fees) are not considered to be covered expenses.

Example: Surgery is $500. The plan's UCR amount is $350. The covered expense would be $350. Therefore, any applicable deductible would be taken from the $350 allowance, and any remaining amount would be paid at the Major Medical coinsurance percentage. The difference between the submitted amount of $500 and the covered/allowable amount of $350 ($150) would be the member's responsibility.

Deductible—The amount of covered expenses that must be paid by the insured/member before benefits become payable by the insurer/plan under the Major Medical portion of the contract. Usually, this is a calendar year deductible (taken once each calendar year), but not always. The deductible is always taken out of the first eligible expense submitted each year.

- Individual Deductible—The amount of covered expense that must be paid by the individual family member before benefits become payable by the plan.
- Aggregate Deductible—All Major Medical deductibles applied for all family members are added together in order to attain the family limit.

Example: The family limit is $300 Aggregate. The individual limit is $100. No more than $100 may be applied per person.

Member	Amount Applied to Deductible
John	$ 100.00
Pat	50.00
Molly	25.00
Sally	80.00
Steve	45.00
	$ 300.00 **
Paul	0.00

**Family Limit has been met. Therefore, no more deductible will be taken on anyone in the family for the remainder of the calendar year.

- Nonaggregate Deductible—A specified number of individual deductibles must be satisfied before the family limit is met.

Example: The family limit is $300, Nonaggregate. The individual deductible is $100. Therefore, three family members must satisfy their deductible before the family limit is considered met.

Member	Amount Applied to Deductible
John	$ 100.00
Pat	50.00
Molly	25.00
Sally	80.00
Steve	45.00
	$ 300.00 **
Paul	65.00

**Although $300 has been applied to the deductible, the family limit has not been satisfied because only one individual deductible has been satisfied. Therefore, as claims are submitted on the members (except for John), monies will be applied toward the deductibles until two more individual deductibles have been satisfied. This type of deductible requirement is more cost-effective for the plan and more costly for the member.

Exclusions—Conditions or types of services that the policy does not cover.

Extended Benefits—The continued entitlement of a member, under certain circumstances, to receive benefits after the coverage has terminated. A doctor's certification of total disability is required before benefits can be extended. Usually, such coverage will continue only for expenses incurred from the condition that caused the disability and for a maximum of 12 months following the date of disability or the date that the member is no longer totally disabled, whichever is less.

Loss Date—The loss date is always the date of the accident. Regardless of the date of service, the loss date remains the same.

Maximum(s)—The maximum amount payable by the plan. The maximum may be a calendar year or a lifetime maximum. In addition, it may apply only toward expenses paid under Basic or only toward expenses paid under Major Medical or a combination of all payments, Basic and Major Medical. The policy must specify the type.

Out-of-Pocket Expense (OOP)—Expenses for which the insured is held responsible and must pay "out-of-pocket," such as the deductible and coinsurance. Also known as copay.

OOP Max—A yearly limit on the OOP that the insured is responsible for paying. When this limit or maximum is reached, the plan pays subsequent covered expenses at 100% (or other specified percentage) instead of the usual percentage for the remainder of the calendar year.

Per Period of Disability—Basic benefit waiting periods and deductibles; may be based on a per illness basis or a waiting period basis. With a per illness waiting period, for each new illness or injury a new benefit amount may be applicable or a new waiting period may apply. If there is a time period basis for renewal of the benefit, the patient must go for a specified time period without treatment of the specific illness or any illness. This most often applies to medical treatment while hospitalized or office visit benefits.

Preexisting Exclusion—When specified by the plan, a condition that is treated within a specified time period prior to the effective date of coverage. All charges related to the condition would not be covered at all for a stated period of time, or payment for the condition would be limited to a stated dollar amount.

Three-Month Carryover Provision (C/O)—Eligible charges incurred in the last quarter of the calendar year (October, November, December) and applied toward the member's deductible. These charges will apply toward satisfaction of the deductible for that member for the subsequent calendar year also. However, if the plan year is different from the calendar year, the last 3 months of the plan year will constitute the carryover deductible period. These monies may or may not be applied toward the family limit.

> *Example:* The deductible for John is $100.00 per year. The first claim payment submitted was for services in June 1993. Payment of $35.00 was applied toward the deductible. The second claim is for services dated November, 1993. The deductible paid on this claim is $65.00, thus satisfying the deductible for 1993. However, since $65.00 was satisfied during the last 3 months of 1993, $65.00 of the 1994 deductible will also be considered satisfied.

Basic Benefits

A Basic benefit provides a specified allowance for a certain type of service. Usually, the allowance is 100% of either UCR (as defined by the plan) or some other amount based on the relative value study (RVS) and conversion factors. (Calculating UCR and using conversion factors are explained in more detail in Chapter 7.)

A Basic benefit usually has a stated calendar year dollar maximum or number of visits or treatments or a combination of both.

For example, refer to the XYZ contract under "Surgical" benefits. As indicated, this Basic benefit pays 100% of the allowable using an $8.50 conversion factor. A maximum of $1600 is payable under the Basic benefits only per surgery or operative session. Any money charged in excess of either the $1600 or the allowable amount up to the UCR amount would be covered under Major Medical subject to any limitations specified by that provision. Basic benefits are always paid first. It is possible for a single expense to be covered under multiple Basic benefits. In this case, the first Basic benefit would be computed, then any excess would be allowed under any other applicable Basic benefit, and finally any remaining amount would be considered under Major Medical.

Following are some guidelines for calculating Basic benefits:

- Basic benefits are always paid first before applicable Major Medical benefits are calculated.
- Basic benefits are usually paid at 100% of the stated amount. Any other applicable percentage must be specifically stated in the policy.
- Basic benefits usually have a dollar or number limit.

Under a Basic only plan, any amount not paid by the Basic benefit would not be covered at all. The excess charges would be the patient's responsibility.

Common Basic Benefits

There are several different types of Basic benefits. The most common are listed below.

Accident Benefits

An accidental injury is a sudden and unforeseen event, definite as to time and place. This includes trauma happening involuntarily or as a result of a voluntary act entailing unforeseen consequences. The following is terminology related to accidental injuries:

- Aggravated physiologic weakness—Injury caused when an individual has a physical weakness that is aggravated by some voluntary activity. Overexertion or unusual physical exertion is also considered an accident if there is a specific time and circumstance involved. Do not consider routine bodily movements to be an injury if there is a history of a related illness, such as arthritis and chronic strain of the affected area. Strains or sprains resulting from an unknown cause would not be considered an accident.
- Aggressor acts while intoxicated—The aggressor is not usually considered responsible for his or her actions. Therefore, resulting injuries would be covered under this provision.
- Aggressor claims—When an investigation does not clearly show who the agressor was, the determination is usually is made in the claimant's favor. As a rule, a person who is the aggressor or who is injured in the commission of a crime is not usually covered under an accident benefit.
- Family altercations—If an employee injures a member of his or her family without provocation, the injuries would be considered accidental. Cases of this sort need to be investigated to ascertain the facts.
- Internal reaction with external trauma—Injury incurred as the result of an internal condition (eg, by falling after fainting) is considered accidental. There must be an external impact involved in the injury.
- Reactions to external stimulus—Unforeseen consequences of voluntary acts, such as insect bites, allergic reactions to poison ivy or other foliage, food poisoning, and animal bites. Reactions to drug therapy or "legal" or illegal drugs (in persons over the age of 16) are not considered accidents. Sunburn for anyone age 16 or older is also not considered an accident.

Benefits under this provision usually pay the first charges submitted up to a specified limit at 100% for all expenses incurred within a specified time period of the date of the accident. Amounts over the dollar limit or after the time limit are covered under other plan provisions.

Note: Any complication involved in treatment of what was originally deemed an "accident" would continue to be part of that accident. This includes reactions to drugs given as a result of the accident.

Nonaccidental Injuries

Injuries received as a result of any of the following are usually not considered accidental. These include:

- Injuries resulting from willful or reckless actions, which are known to result in serious bodily injury, including extremes such as playing Russian roulette, parachute jumping, high-speed auto racing on city streets, and injuries sustained in the commission of a crime.
- Intentionally self-inflicted injuries, such as those sustained during an attempted suicide.
- Injury sustained as a result of a family quarrel, unless the injured party takes legal action and receives a favorable court decision and it is the injured party who is the insured.
- Sunburn for any person over the age of 16. However, severe sunburn resulting from being stranded (eg, in a desert) is covered as an accident in a person of any age.
- Any trauma resulting from the normal risks a person takes when undergoing surgical or medical treatment for an illness. Included in this category would be similar circumstances to the following: the unintentional severing of a ureter during a hysterectomy, leaving a clamp or surgical instrument in the operative field, allergic reactions to prescribed medications.

- Injuries sustained in a fight or brawl, if it is determined that the member was the aggressor.
- A "bad trip" as the result of voluntary injection or ingestion of illegal drugs in anyone over 16 years of age. In a person under age 16, the first such experience may be considered "accidental."
- Any injury, with the exception of anything as obvious as a fracture, burn, or laceration, in which the patient cannot recall how it happened, except in a small child who cannot be expected to remember.

Attempted Suicide

Most plans will not cover attempted suicides as an accident. Some plans specifically exclude expenses incurred as a result of an attempted suicide or self-inflicted injury. Thus, the policy should be checked to determine whether such an exclusion is applicable.

Diagnostic X-Ray and Laboratory (DXL)

Benefits for x-rays and labs can be handled in a variety of ways. In the past, it was not uncommon to have what was called a "scheduled benefit." This type of benefit specified that a set dollar amount was allowed for each test. Today, most basic plans provide an alternative type of benefit called an "unscheduled" basic benefit, which limits payment only under the basic benefit to a specified dollar amount per calendar year based on UCR or based on a conversion factor and RVS units. Once the calendar year maximum has been paid, subsequent expenses would be paid under the Major Medical benefit. If a basic DXL benefit is provided by the plan, inpatient charges are usually excluded. That is, inpatient expenses would be covered only under Major Medical. However, outpatient hospital claims would allow a basic benefit for DXL charges. Therefore, it is important to read the benefit plan prior to determining benefits.

Hospital Benefits

With this basic benefit, there may be a per admission deductible that does not usually carry over to the major medical plan. This benefit usually applies not only to hospital expenses, but to outpatient surgery expenses and charges incurred as a result of an accident within a specified time period (generally 24 hours).

Another facet of this type of benefit is that a dollar limit is allowed per day for room and board and a separate allowance limit for ancillary expenses. As with other basic benefits, the provisions of this type of benefit vary widely from plan to plan.

Medical While Hospitalized (MWH)

Inpatient hospital care is often known as medical while hospitalized. The patient is admitted into a facility, and the physician visits him or her in the hospital.

Many types of MWH benefits are available. One of the more common types is called a **cumulative benefit.** To calculate benefits under this provision, the number of days hospitalized is multiplied by the benefit amount.

For example: A man was hospitalized from 3/1 through 3/14. His contract allows $21.00 for the first day and $7.00 per day thereafter.

Here, the day of admission and the day of discharge are counted to determine the maximum allowance. Then, $7.00 is multiplied by 13 days, which equals $91.00 plus $21.00 for the first day = $112.00. This is the maximum amount that can be paid out for this admission, regardless of how many doctors see the patient on a single day, or the actual number of visits during the 14-day period. Some provisions allow multiple doctors to receive the benefit, but most plans limit the benefit to one maximum, which may be split up and paid to multiple providers as long as it does not exceed the maximum as calculated above. For an example of this benefit type, see the XYZ Corporation contract.

A second type of benefit has multiple names, which may include the terms **nondisabling** or **per visit benefit.** In this type of benefit, there is a waiting period, a daily maximum, and a calendar year maximum. For instance, the provision may read: $10.00 per day payable after 7 days and $200.00 per calendar year.

Using the same hospitalization as above, this benefit is substantially different from the prior example. The day of admission and the day of discharge are counted to determine the maximum allowance. The 7-day waiting period is subtracted from the 14 days, and the remaining number of days (7) is multiplied by the daily benefit for the benefit amount of $70.00. Usually, this provision allows for the circumstance in which a patient is discharged and then readmitted within a specified period of time, and another 7-day waiting period is not required. The plan provisions must be checked for this and any other exceptions.

If surgery is performed during the hospitalization, there are many ways to apply an inpatient visit provision, depending on the wording of the benefit and how the services are provided. The following is a summary of some of the more common circumstances. These rules apply to visits performed by the operating surgeon.

- If surgery is performed, there should be no charge for a visit on the same day as a surgery, excluding diagnostic procedures such as proctosigmoidoscopy and other procedures with no follow-up days.
- If the surgery has follow-up days listed but the surgery is not performed on the day of admission:
  —Visits billed before the date of surgery are allowed. Calculate as indicated in the examples above, counting the date of admission and every day up to but not including the day of surgery.
  —Visits billed on the day of surgery are combined with the surgery charge. There should be no separate charge on the day of surgery. Allow up to the plan maximum for the surgery.
  —Visits billed on the days following surgery within the follow-up days listed are to be combined with the surgery charge. Visits billed after the follow-up days can be paid separately.
  —If surgery is performed on the first day of admission, all visits, billed separately from the surgery, occurring within the follow-up days should be combined with the surgery charge. The regular surgery benefit will be calculated in accordance with the plan provisions.

Office Visits

Like the MWH benefit, office visit benefits are usually based on a specified dollar limit per visit after a specified number of visits have been applied to the waiting period. The waiting period is often on a per illness basis. That is, a specified number of visits are not paid for under basic benefits for each illness. After the specified number of visits has been accumulated, basic benefits begin. The waiting period may be based on the illness, or it may be cumulative for all conditions based on a period of disability.

Surgery, Assistant Surgery, and Anesthesia

For surgery, assistant surgery, and anesthesia, determination of the basic benefit is based on the RVS and plan designated conversion factors. The assistant surgeon's allowance is almost always 20% of the surgeon's basic allowance. Consequently, the conversion factors are the same for the surgeon and the assistant surgeon. The anesthesia benefit may have the same or a different conversion factor. To get the basic benefit for all of these provisions, the conversion factor is multiplied by the RVS unit factor. Usually, there is a maximum amount allowed per operative session and often also for a calendar year. After the maximums are reached, these services would be covered only under Major Medical unless excluded under that contract's provisions.

Order of Basic Benefit Payments

To best use the funds available for basic benefits, these benefits should be applied in the following order:

1. Hospital benefits.
2. Surgery, assistant surgery, and anesthesia benefits.
3. Physician's visits (in- or outpatient).
4. DXL benefits.
5. Supplemental accident benefits.

Basic Major Medical Benefits

On a Basic only plan, amounts not paid by the basic benefits would not be payable at all. With a Basic-Major Medical plan, expenses not paid by the Basic portion of the contract may be payable under the Major Medical portion. Different limitations or restrictions may apply to Basic benefits than to Major Medical benefits. Generally, the following guidelines apply:

- Pay all applicable Basic benefits.
- Refer to the policy or plan document to see whether the excess amounts not paid under Basic plan would be eligible under Major Medical. The document should specifically exclude services not eligible under Major Medical.
- Apply all Major Medical limitations, deductibles, UCR maximums, and other limitations.
- Add the Basic allowance to the Major Medical allowance to determine the total claim payment.

Usually, the Major Medical portion has a specified dollar deductible amount that must be satisfied yearly before any payments are made. In addition, expenses under Major Medical are not usually paid at 100%, at least not initially. Normally, payments are calculated at 80%, 70%, and so on (this can be any percentage).

With a Basic-Major Medical plan, all Basic benefits will have two limitations (assuming the services are covered under both the Basic provisions and the Major Medical provisions):

1. The Basic benefit limitation.
2. The Major Medical UCR or plan limitation.

Comprehensive Major Medical Benefits

The comprehensive Major Medical plan does not have Basic benefits per se. However, there may be supplemental or built-in benefits that act the same as a Basic benefit. In other words, some charges may be covered at 100%, the same as in a Basic plan. All of the definitions previously covered also apply to this type of plan.

All services would be subject to the Major Medical deductible (unless it is waived for certain types of services) and would then be paid at the designated coinsurance rate. Limitations are usually based on a lifetime maximum or calendar year maximum.

Stop Loss

Many Major Medical contracts have a provision that provides for a greater reimbursement percentage (usually 100%) after payment of a certain dollar amount for a calendar year period. This provision limits the amount of money that the member/patient will be responsible for on allowable charges. Such a provision applies only toward "allowable" charges. Expenses not allowed under the plan such as UCR excess amounts and noncovered expenses would not be applied toward the stop loss. The patient would remain entirely responsible for payment.

An example of such contract wording would be "80% of the first $5000, 100% thereafter."

Summary

The three major types of coverage currently available are:

1. Basic only
2. Basic-Major Medical
3. Comprehensive Major Medical

It is important to understand the terminology associated with contracts and how benefit payments are calculated under each type of coverage. Quick and accurate benefit payments are what make a health claims examiner a valuable employee.

Assignments

Complete Questions for Review.

Questions for Review

Directions: Answer the following questions without looking back into the material just covered. Write your answers in the space provided.

1. Name the three major types of coverage which are currently available.
   a. Basic only
   b. Basic/Major Medical
   c. Comprehensive Major Medical
2. Co-insurance is the arrangement by which both the member and the plan share in a specific ratio of the covered losses under a policy.
3. Covered expenses are the amount of those expenses that are allowable under the plan.
4. What is an individual deductible? amount of covered expense that must be pd by member before the plan will pay
5. A Basic benefit provides a specified allowance for a certain type of service.
6. State the three usual rules for basic benefits.
   a. Basic benefits are always pd 1st. befor Major Med. is calculated
   b. usually pd at 100% of stated amount
   c. usually have a dollar or number limit
7. Expenses not paid by the basic portion of the contract may be payable under the Major Medical portion. (True or False) True
8. Define accumulation period. Period of time, usually 1-1 to 12-31 in which to satisfy a deductible
9. Define automatic annual reinstatement. a contractually specified amount of $ that may be added to the balance of available lifetime benefits
10. Explain the 3-month carryover provision. Eligible charges during last 3 months of year may be carried over as deductible for the next year.

If you were unable to answer any of the questions, refer back to the section and complete the answers.

5

General Plan Provisions

In this chapter you will learn:

- The purpose and identification of possible third party liability and preexisting claims.
- To thoroughly investigate possible third party liability and preexisting claims.

Acts of Third Parties and Subrogation are provisions that are included in many benefit plans to allow for recovery of money paid on claims incurred as a result of a third party's act or acts for which that party is financially responsible.

For example: A claimant is injured while on the premises of a grocery store. The losses are submitted to the benefit plan for payment. Subsequently, the claimant seeks recovery from the store. When recovery is successful, the claimant is required to reimburse the benefit plan for its losses.

Subrogation and Acts of Third Parties (ATP) (also known as Third Party Liability [TPL]) are similar but different. Many older plans had Subrogation, whereas many new plans have TPL.

State laws affect general plan provisions. Although a plan may contain one of these provisions, it may not always be allowed to function if prohibited by specific state statute or statutes.

A demand by the plan for reimbursement cannot be made until the insured has been compensated for the loss by the third party. Filing a lien against such compensation protects the plan by making it mandatory that the plan be reimbursed prior to the claimant's receiving such compensation. Although the loss claimed by the claimant may include medical expenses, property damage, loss of earnings, pain, suffering, and even future medical expenses, the plan is permitted to recover only the amount actually paid out as a result of the injury. A sample of a payment demand is shown in Figure 5-1. When any payments are received, they should be noted on a Right of Reimbursement Claims Ledger Sheet. A sample copy of such a ledger sheet is shown in Figure 5-2.

When a claim is received for expenses incurred as a result of an injury, determine how, when, and where the injury occurred. If this information is not indicated on the submitted forms, write to the member and request details. Samples of a letter and a questionnaire are shown in Figures 5-3 and 5-4.

If the injury occurred as the result of another party's acts and the plan has a TPL or subrogation provision, a letter informing the claimant regarding the appropriate provision should be sent along with an agreement. A sample copy of such a letter is shown in Figure 5-5. The claimant must sign an agreement indicating that if monies are received from another source to cover these expenses, he or she is legally obligated to reimburse the plan. A sample copy of an agreement is shown in Figure 5-6. This signed agreement is then kept on file with occasional follow-ups to track recovery; some payors file a lien against monies that the claimant might be entitled to. If the plan does not have either of these types of provisions, reimbursement from a third source cannot be sought.

As a rule, these provisions cannot be used to recover against the member's own auto liability carrier, homeowner's insurance carrier, or other carriers.

Acts of Third Parties

Under TPL, the plan advances money to the injured person with the understanding that, if the claimant is successful in obtaining reimbursement monies from a third party, the plan will be reimbursed for its losses. The plan's interests lie with the claimant, not with the third party.

An example of a third party provision is:

A special provision applies when you or your dependent covered under the plan is injured through the act or omission of another person. When this happens, the plan will advance the benefits under the policy only under the condition that you or your dependents agree in writing to the following:

1. To repay the plan in full any sums advanced to cover such claims paid by the plan from the judgment or settlement you or a dependent receives.
2. To provide the plan with a lien to repay the plan to the extent of benefits advanced by the plan. The lien may be filed with the person whose act caused the injuries, his or her agent, or the court or attorney of the person covered under the plan.

Thus, when such a claim is received, a repayment agreement must be sent to the claimant. This agreement requires the member to provide the information necessary to investigate the claim and subsequently, if appropriate, to file a lien with the member's attorney for reimbursement against any settlement procured by

ANY INSURANCE CARRIER, INC.
0123 Any Drive, Anywhere, USA 12345 • (800) 555-1234

Date:

Re: Policyholder: ________________
Control: ________________
Employee: ________________
Dependent: ________________

Dear

This is to advise you that benefits totaling ________________________ have been paid to date to ____ as a result of the accident on ____________________.

Under the terms of __________________________ group health coverage, the insurance carrier is entitled to claim reimbursement from any third party liability coverage applicable to the same incident. Therefore, subrogation rights are claimed. Please advise as soon as possible when we might expect payment.

Sincerely,

Figure 5-1: Sample of a Payment Demand Letter.

the member. Usually, payment of losses is not made until the claimant has signed the repayment agreement and returned it to the administrator.

Administration of this provision tends to be long-term and time-intensive. Therefore, many plans have retained special agencies responsible for tracking and recovering TPL monies. In exchange, the agency is paid from the proceeds that they recover.

Subrogation

Under Subrogation, the plan has an obligation to pay a benefit under the contract, but has a subrogated right for a portion of the recovery that the claimant may obtain from a third party. The plan has a direct interest with the third party.

An example of a subrogation provision is:

When benefits are paid to or for you or a dependent under the terms of the plan, the plan shall be subrogate, unless otherwise prohibited by law, to your right of recovery or the rights of recovery of a dependent against any person who might acknowledge to be liable or might be found legally liable by a court of competent jurisdiction for the injury that necessitated the hospitalization or the medical or surgical treatment for which the benefits were paid.

Such subrogation rights shall extend only to the recovery by the plan of the benefits it has paid for such

ANY INSURANCE CARRIER, INC.
0123 Any Drive, Anywhere, USA 12345 • (800) 555-1234

FOR RIGHT OF REIMBURSEMENT CLAIMS

Claimant: ______________________ Policyholder: ______________________

Date of Accident: ______________________ Control No: ______________________

Amount of Payment	Payee	Date Paid	Total Amount Paid to Date

Figure 5-2: **Right of Reimbursement Claims Ledger Sheet.**

ANY INSURANCE CARRIER, INC.
0123 Any Drive, Anywhere, USA 12345 • (800) 555-1234

Re:

Dear

The claim that you recently submitted for accidental bodily injuries expenses is under review. Circumstances of the accident indicate that a third party may be liable for the payment of your hospital/medical bills.

Accordingly, the policy in force between

____

and ____________________________________ contains a Third Party Liability exclusion, which provides that no medical or dental benefits are payable for injuries or illness caused by a third party if payment for such expenses has been or will be received from the third party or insurer. A copy of the entire provision is attached.

To assist us in evaluating the claim, please complete the enclosed questionnaire detailing particulars regarding the accident and parties involved. Any additional information would be greatly appreciated.

Additionally, if a third party is liable for your expenses, we have enclosed a Third Party Liability Reimbursement Agreement, to be signed, witnessed, and returned to us before benefits can be released.

If you have any questions regarding this matter, please do not hesitate to contact me.

Sincerely,

Figure 5-3: Sample of a letter requesting further information on a possible TPL claim.

treatment, and the plan shall pay fees and costs associated with such recovery.

When a claim is received for expenses incurred as a result of any injury involving another party, a subrogation letter along with a subrogation statement should be sent to the claimant.

The subrogation statement requires the member to provide information necessary to investigate the claim. The form also requires the member to agree to allow the plan to file a lien against any settlement made by the other party.

Although, technically, these two provisions are not the same, from the examiner's standpoint, the differences are moot. Don't be concerned with what the differences are at this point. Be concerned with the concepts behind them, what the objective is, and how to obtain that objective.

Preexisting Conditions

A preexisting condition is a condition that the patient was treated for within a specified time period prior to the member becoming effective under the plan. This provision must be read carefully because there are many variations. For example, it may apply to dependents only; time limits may be different for members versus dependents; or, the provision may be waived for all individuals who are covered on the effective date of the plan.

Whether the expense or expenses incurred are excluded completely or limited to a specific dollar benefit, most clauses provide that benefits will become payable after the member has been covered under the plan for a specific period of time and has not received any treatment for the preexisting condition.

ANY INSURANCE CARRIER, INC.
0123 Any Drive, Anywhere, USA 12345 • (800) 555-1234

1. Name and address of responsible third party.

City State Zip Code

2. Name and address of responsible third party insurance company and policy number.

Policy No.

City State Zip Code

3. If an accident, what were the circumstances?

4. If Any Insurance Carrier is to pay medical benefits under the terms of the contract, when is settlement expected or how often may we expect status reports?

5. Is legal counsel involved? If yes, please give name and address.

City State Zip Code

Figure 5-4: Sample of questionnaire requesting further information on a possible TPL claim.

ANY INSURANCE CARRIER, INC.
0123 Any Drive, Anywhere, USA 12345 • (800) 555-1234

Third Party Liability Exclusion Rider Effective ________________________
Attached to and made part of Group Insurance Policy No. ______________
Issued by ____

to ____

No benefits will be paid under this policy to or on behalf of an insured individual who has:

1. medical or dental charges or
2. loss of earnings

if the insured individual has received payment, in whole or in part, from a third party, or its insurer, for past or future medical or dental charges or loss of earnings as the result of negligence or intentional act of a third party.

If an insured party makes a claim to Any Insurance Carrier for medical, dental, or loss of earnings benefits under this policy prior to receiving payment from a third party, or its insurer, the insured individual (or legal representative of a minor or incompetent) must agree in writing to repay Any Insurance Carrier from any amount of money received by the insured individual from the third party, or its insurer. The repayment will be to the extent of the benefits paid by Any Insurance Carrier. However, the reasonable pro rata expenses, such as lawyer's fees and court costs, incurred in affecting the third party payment may be deducted from the repayment to Any Insurance Carrier.

The repayment agreement will be binding upon the insured individual (or legal representative of a minor or incompetent) whether:

1. the payment received from the third party, or its insurer, is the result of:
   a. a legal judgment, or
   b. an arbitration award, or
   c. a compromise settlement, or
   d. any other arrangement, or
2. the third party, or its insurer, has admitted liability for the payment, or
3. the medical or dental charges or loss of earnings are itemized in the third party payment.

Figure 5-5: Sample of a letter informing the claimant of TPL or subrogation provision.

ANY INSURANCE CARRIER, INC.
0123 Any Drive, Anywhere, USA 12345 • (800) 555-1234

Third Party Liability Reimbursement Agreement

I, ____, an insured individual (or his or her legal representative) under group insurance policy number ________________________ issued by Any Insurance Carrier to ______________________________, the policyholder, pursuant to the terms of the group insurance policy, do hereby agree to reimburse Any Insurance Carrier for any medical or dental expenses or loss of earnings benefits which are paid by Any Insurance Carrier or will be paid by it, which expenses or benefits arise out of the accident or sickness commencing _____________________, 19_________, if payment is received from a third party, or its insurer.

I understand that this agreement to reimburse shall be binding on me regardless of whether:

1) the payment received from the third party, or its insurer, is the result of a legal judgment, arbitration award, compromise settlement or otherwise; or,

2) such third party, or its insurer, has admitted liability in connection with such payment; or,

3) such medical or dental expenses actually incurred or loss of earnings realized are itemized in such third party payment.

I further understand that the reasonable pro rata costs, including attorney fees, actually incurred by me in effecting the third party payment for such medical or dental expenses or loss of earnings may be deducted from any such reimbursement.

____

(Witness) (Insured Individual or his or her Legal Representative)

Figure 5-6: Third Party Liability Reimbursement Agreement.

Handling Procedures

Improperly handled claims for preexisting conditions are a frequent source of complaints and lawsuits. An examiner has an obligation to:

- Investigate thoroughly, at the earliest appropriate time, preferably on the very first claim receipt. If the expenses result from an injury incurred after the effective date of the plan or are clearly not chronic, such as a cold or flu, an inquiry should not be made. Always consider the specific plan provisions.
- Notify the member and the provider, if appropriate, of the delay, in writing.
- Bring the investigation to a conclusion as rapidly as possible with either a decision to pay or a fully documented denial.

To qualify for payment on the basis of having satisfied the treatment free provision and the total limitation (no payment of preexisting conditions for 12 months), it must be determined that the patient did not receive any treatment for the preexisting condition from a doctor, hospital, clinic, or other medical practitioner. Advice from a practitioner without treatment may be considered "treatment" in the case of a preexisting condition. To determine whether a given condition is preexisting, the following procedures should be followed:

1. Identify all potentially preexisting conditions by noting the diagnosis and the length of time between the effective date of the plan and the first treatment documented on the claim form or in the claim file. Special attention should be paid to claims for chronic conditions or for major surgery with little or no preliminary diagnostic work or medical treatment.
2. Initiate the investigation as soon as appropriate by writing to the attending physician and all other consulting or referring physicians whose names can be determined. Write to the following sources as well:
   - All hospitals involved to request a copy of hospital records including the admitting history and physical, discharge summary, consultation, and operative reports.
   - Pharmacies to obtain drug names, dates filled, names and phone numbers of prescribing physicians.
   - Attending physicians to request copies of treatment histories that should detail the onset of the condition, referring physicians, and so on.
   - Claimants to request the names, addresses, and phone numbers of all doctors seen and all medications taken during the appropriate time period stipulated in the plan.

   Many insurance carriers have a standard form letter for requesting information regarding a preexisting condition. A copy of such a form letter is included as Figure 5-7.
3. Act immediately on leads or additional information supplied in response to the initial requests for information.
4. Bear in mind that the burden of proof lies with the plan to prove that a condition is preexisting. No matter how certain you may be that a condition is preexisting, a claim cannot be denied as such unless there is adequate documentation in the claim file.
5. If answers to the inquiries are not received, follow the administrator's guidelines for denying the claim. Do not deny the claim as preexisting. Instead, deny pending receipt of previously requested information.
6. Determining whether a condition is a chronic illness or a new illness is essential in deciding whether the preexisting exclusion would apply. For example, infectious conditions such as upper respiratory infection, otitis media, bronchitis, and urinary tract infection may occur again and again with resolution between episodes. If a period elapses between treatments, a new episode (and therefore, a new illness) may exist, in which the preexisting exclusion would not apply.
7. Related conditions and complications of existing conditions may pose problems in determining whether an illness is preexisting. Certain diseases are progressive, and a different diagnosis may be assigned to the successive stages of the disease. *The Merck Manual* may be helpful in researching

ANY INSURANCE CARRIER, INC.
0123 Any Drive, Anywhere, USA 12345 • (800) 555-1234

Re:

Control: ____________________
Insured: ____________________

Dear

We are presently processing a claim for the above patient. In order to give it full consideration, we need additional information. Please answer the questions outlined below. A pre-addressed envelope is provided for your convenience and a reasonable fee will be allowed for this service if you will include your bill with your reply. Your cooperation will be appreciated and will help expedite the matter for your patient. (Authorization to release information is attached.)

Sincerely yours,

Claims Representative

Condition(s) described on claim form as: ____
____

(1) Did you prescribe medication for, or treat the above condition or related symptoms from ____________ through ____________? ❑ Yes ❑ No If so, specify below:

Condition	Date Treated

(2)

Drug	Date Prescribed	Drug	Date Prescribed

(3) Was the patient referred to you by another physician? ❑ Yes ❑ No If so, please provide name and address of referring doctor. ____

Dated ______________________ Signed ______________________

Figure 5-7: Sample of a letter requesting information about a preexisting condition.

such conditions, but any questionable case should be referred to the supervisor, medical review department, or a consultant for review.

Refer to the ABC Contract. According to this plan, if the claimant was effective when the plan became effective 1/1/81, the preexisting exclusion will not apply to that person. If the claimant was not effective on the plan effective date of 1/1/81, the exclusion would apply.

Example: Claimant effective 2/1/91 and a claim is received for a diagnosis of diabetes for the date of service 3/1/91. Diabetes is a chronic condition; therefore, it is possibly preexisting. An investigation must be pursued in the manner previously indicated so that the claim file can be properly documented to substantiate the claims decision. Let's examine the claim form. Does it list the following: the date of the first treatment for the condition? Was the treatment prior to the effective date? If so, the condition is possibly preexisting because persons with some diabetic conditions require insulin injections or pills on a daily basis.

If not, is there a name of a referring physician? If so, write to that physician and request treatment information. If the first treatment date is not indicated, write to the physician who submitted the claim and to the claimant, requesting the following information:

- The names of all physicians seen between 12/1/90 and 3/1/91 (this covers the 90-day period prior to the effective date of coverage, up to and including the current treatment date).
- The names and dates of all prescriptions written during this same period of time.
- The names of all other medical providers referred to or from and the dates of treatments during this period of time.

The objective of this questioning is two-fold.

1. To determine whether treatment commenced during the 90-day period of time prior to the effective date of the plan, 3/1/91.
2. To determine whether a 3-month period of time has intervened in which the claimant did not receive treatment (determine whether the 3-month treatment free period provision applies).

Once the claimant has been covered under the plan for 12 consecutive months, the preexisting exclusion no longer applies whether or not the condition was preexisting.

On a plan that includes a specific money limit for preexisting conditions, it is not necessary to pend the claims and request information. However, the allowable amounts that have been provided under the plan must be tracked so that once the specified limit has been reached for each condition, the preexisting inquiry can be initiated.

Properly applying preexisting limitations takes experience. Remember what is being investigated and what the plan provisions allow or do not allow. Also, request assistance at the beginning of the process until you are familiar with the application of the various provisions. In so doing you will not delay the claim unnecessarily.

Possible Preexisting Conditions

The following is a list of conditions by body system that are potentially preexisting.

CARDIOVASCULAR SYSTEM
Abnormal ECG
Aneurysm
Arteriosclerosis/ASHD
Coronary disease
Dyspnea
Edema
Enlarged heart
Fibrillation
Heart disease/ASHD
Heart failure
Heart murmurs
Hemophilia
High blood pressure
Irregular pulse
Leukemia
Pacemaker
Rapid pulse
Stroke/CVA

ENDOCRINE SYSTEM
Adrenal disorders
Diabetes
Elevated blood sugar
Hyperglycemia
Pituitary disorders
Thyroid disorders (except hypothyroidism)

GASTROINTESTINAL SYSTEM
Colostomy/ileostomy
Duodenal ulcer
Esophageal disorders
Gastric ulcer
GI hemorrhage
Liver disorders
Pancreas disorders
Peptic ulcer
Regional enteritis
Regional ileitis
Ulcerative colitis

GENITOURINARY SYSTEM
Albuminuria
Congenital GU disorders
GU stone
Hematuria
Hydronephrosis
Hysterectomy
Kidney disorders
Nephrectomy
Nephritis
PID
Prostatic disorder
Pyelitis
Pyelonephrosis
Pyonephrosis
Sexually transmitted diseases
Toxemia/eclampsia
Unlisted or undiagnosed

NERVOUS SYSTEM
Autism
Cerebral palsy
Headaches
Mental retardation
Down's Syndrome
Multiple sclerosis
Parkinson's disease
Psychoses
Seizure disorders
Severe neuroses
Suicide (attempted)
Syncopy/vertigo
Tremors

RESPIRATORY SYSTEM
Asthma
Bronchiectasis
Chronic bronchitis
Constrictive pulmonary disease
Emphysema
Obstructive pulmonary disease
TB/TBC

MISCELLANEOUS CONDITIONS
Arthritis
Back disorders, disc, sacro
Bone/joint disorders
Cancer
Cataracts
Eye disorders
Glaucoma
Gout
Hodgkin's lymphoma
Impaired vision
Lupus erythematosus
Lymph node disorders
Mastoiditis
Meniere's disease, labyrinthitis
Muscular dystrophy
Osteomyelitis
Otitis media
Regional disorders
Skin cancer
Spinal curvature
TB
Tumors, malignant
Tumors, benign

NONPHYSICAL CONDITIONS
Alcoholism
Drug addiction

Mandates

Some states have laws or mandates on their books that require certain services to be offered, or providers to be covered by insurance companies within those states.

Following is a list of state-mandated benefits, providers, and persons covered as of June 1991. For more complete and current information for your state, contact your state's Department of Insurance.

Benefits

Alcoholism Treatment: AL, AK, AR*, CA*, CO*, CT, FL, GA*, HI, IL, KS, KY*, LA*, ME*, MD, MA, MI, MN, MS, MO, MT, NE, NV, NJ, NM*, NY, NC, ND, OH, OR, PA, RI, SD, TN, TX, UT, VT, VA*, WA, WV, WI.
Ambulance Transportation: CT, LA, MS, NV, OK.
Ambulatory Surgery: AZ, AR, FL, HI, KY, MI, MN, MO, OK.
Antiabortion: CO, CT, ID, KY, ND, PA.
Breast Reconstruction: AZ, CA, FL*, IL, MI, MN, NV, NJ, NY, WA.
Cleft Palate: CO*, ID, IN, LA, MD, MN, NC.
Diabetic Education: CA*, LA*, OR, WI.
Drug Abuse Treatment: AL, AK, AR*, CA*, CT, FL, GA*, HI, KS, LA*, ME, MD, MI, MN, MO, MT, NV, NY*, NC*, ND, OR, PA, RI, TN*, TX, UT*, VA*, WI.
Home Health Care: AZ, CA*, CO*, CT, FL, KY*, ME, MD, MA, MT, NM, NY, RI, TX*, VT, WA*, WI.
Hospice Care: CO*, CT, MD*, MI*, NV, NY, WA*.
In Vitro Fertilization: AR, CT*, HI, MD, MA, RI, TX*.
Long-Term Care: KY, OR, WV.
Mammography Screening: AK, AZ, AR*, CA, CO, CT, FL, GA*, HI, IL, IN*, IA, KS, KY, ME, MD, MA, MI, MN, MO, MT, NV, NH, NM, NY, ND, OK, PA, RI, SD, TN, TX, VT, VA, WA, WV, WI.
Maternity: CA*, CO, CT, GA, HI, ME, MD, MA, MN, MO, NV, NY, ND, OH, OK, OR, TN, TX, VA, WI.
Mental Health Care: AR*, CA*, CO, CT, FL, GA*, HI, IL*, KS, KY*, LA*, ME, MD, MA, MN, MO, MT, NH, NY*, ND, OH, OK*, OR, TN*, VT, VA*, WA, WV, WI.
Orthotic Prosthetic Care: CA*, CT, FL*, MD, MI, OR.
Prescription Drugs: CT, ME, ND*.
Rehabilitation Services: CT*, LA*, ME*, MA, WV*.
Second Surgical Opinion: MD, NJ*, NY, PA.
TMJ Disorder: KY, MN, NV, NM, ND, TX, WA*, WV*.
Well Child Care: AR*, CA*, CT, FL, HI, MA, MN, MO*, MT, NY, PA, RI, UT, VA*, WI.

Providers

Acupuncturist: CA*, NV, NM, OR.
Chiropractors: AL, AK, AZ, AR, CA, CT, DE, FL, GA, IL, IN, IA, KS, KY, LA, ME, MD, MA, MI, MN, MS, MO, NE, NV, NJ, NM, NY, NC, ND, OH, OK, PA, RI, SC, TN, TX, UT, VA, WA*, WI.
Dentists: AL, AK, AZ, AR, CA, CT, HI, IN, IA, KS, LA, ME, MD, MA, MN, MS, MO, MT, NE, NV, NJ, NM, NY, OH, OK, OR, PA, TN, TX, WI.
Licensed Health Professions: AR, IL, IN, MD, SD, UT, WY.
Naturopath: AK, CT.
Nurses (RNs): CO, IA*, NV, NJ, NY, ND, PA, WA.
Nurse Midwives (CNMs): AK, AZ, CO, CT, DE, FL, LA, MD, MA, MN, MS, NE, NV, NJ, NM, NY, ND, OH, OK, PA, RI, SD, UT, WA, WV.
Nurse Anesthetist (CRNAs): AZ, CO, KS, MD, MN, MS, ND, PA, SD.
Nurse Practitioners: AK, AZ, CO, CT, DE, MD, MN, MS, NH, ND, OR, PA, SD, WA.
Nurse Psychiatric: CA, CO, CT, ME, MD, MA, NV, ND, VA, WV.
Occupational Therapist: AK, CA, CT.
Optometrists: AL, AK, CA, CT, DE, FL, GA, IL, IN, IA, KS, ME, MD, MA, MN, MS, MO, MT, NE, NV, NJ, NM, NY, OH, OK, OR, PA, SC, TN, TX, UT, VA, WI.
Oral Surgeons: IL, MI, NH.
Osteopaths: AK, AR, IL, MD, NE, NV, NM, OH, OK, PA, TX, VA.
Physical Therapists: AK, CT, NJ, NM, NY, PA, VA, WY.

*** Denotes that insurance companies within this state must offer this benefit. However, they are not required to be covered under a standard policy, merely to have a policy (usually with a higher premium), which can be added to the regular insurance policy.**

Podiatrists: AL, AZ, AR, CA, DE, FL, IL, IN, KS, MD, MA, MN, MO, NE, NV, NM, NY, OH, OK, PA, SC, TN, TX, UT, VA, WA, WI.
Professional Counselors: AR, CA, MT, NH, TX, VA.
Psychologists: AL, AR, CA, CO, CT, GA, HI, IL, IN, KS, LA, ME, MD, MA, MN, MS, MO, MT, NE, NV, NH, NJ, NM, NY, NC, ND, OH, OK, OR, PA, SD, TN, TX, UT, VA, WY.
Public and Other Facilities: AZ, AR, CA, CT, FL, ID, IN, ME, MD, MI, MN, MS, MT, NE, NC, OH, OR, PA, TX, WA, WI, WY.
Social Workers: CA, CO, CT, IL, KS, ME, MD, MA, MI, MT, NV, NH, NY, ND, OR, SD, TN, TX*, UT, VA.
Speech/Hearing Therapist: AR, CA, MO, TN, TX, VA.

Persons Covered

Adopted Children: AZ, AR, FL, GA, IL, IN, KS, MA, MN, MT, NV, NM, ND, OK, SD, UT, VA, WY.
Continuation/Dependents: AR, CA, CO, CT, GA, IL, IA, KS, KY, ME, MD, MN, MO, NE, NV, NH, NM, NY, NC, ND, OK, OR, RI, SC, SD, TN, TX, UT, VT, WA, WV, WI.
Continuation/Employees: AR, CA, CO, FL, HI, ID, IL, IA, KS, KY, LA, ME, MD, MN, MO, MT, NE, NV, NH, NY, ND, OK, OR, TN, TX, UT, VT, WA, WV, WI.
Conversion to Nongroup: AZ, AR, CA, CO, CT, IL, IA, KS, KY, ME, MD, MA, MN, MO, MT, NE, NV, NM, NY, NC, ND, OH, OR, PA, RI, SC, SD, TN, TX, UT, VT, VA, WA, WI, WY.
Dependent Students: CT, GA, LA, NE, ND.
Handicapped Dependents: AZ, AR, CA, CT, FL, GA, HI, ID, IL, IN, LA, MD, MA, MI, MN, MS, MT, NH, NJ, NM, NY, NC, ND, OH, PA, SC, SD, TN, TX, UT, VT, VA, WA, WI, WY.
Newborns: AL, AK, AZ, AR, CA, CO, CT, FL, GA, HI, ID, IL, IN, IA, KS, KY, LA, ME, MD, MA, MN, MS, MO, MT, NE, NV, NH, NJ, NM, NY, NC, ND, OH, OK, OR, PA, SC, SD, TN, TX, UT, VT, VA, WA, WV, WI, WY.
Noncustodial Children: CT, FL, ME, MT, ND, OR, UT, WY.

Summary

Acts of third parties and subrogation can drastically alter the way a claim is paid and who is responsible for the claim payment. Preexisting conditions account for one of the highest dollar amounts of claims paid incorrectly, costing insurance companies thousands of dollars. The Health Claims Examiner must understand these concepts and when they come into play.

Assignments

Complete Questions for Review.
Complete Exercise 5-1.

Questions for Review

Directions: Answer the following questions without looking back into the material just covered. Write your answers in the space provided.

1. Why are Acts of Third Parties and Subrogation provisions included in many benefit plans? ________________
____
2. Under ____________________________, the plan advances money to the injured person with the understanding that if the claimant is successful in obtaining reimbursement monies from a third party, the plan will be reimbursed.
3. Under ____________________________, the plan has an obligation to pay a benefit under the contract, but a subrogated right for a portion of the recovery that the claimant may obtain from a third party.
4. Improperly handled claims for preexisting conditions are a common source of complaints and lawsuits. (True or False) ____________________________
5. An examiner should not notify the member and the provider of the delay of a claim. (True or False) ____________________________

If you were unable to answer any of the questions, refer back to the section and then complete the answers.

Exercise 5-1

Directions: Indicate whether or not the following situations would warrant a preexisting investigation and why.

1. Thomas is covered under the ABC Corporation plan. His effective date of coverage is 1/1/81. He received treatment for chronic allergies on 12/15/80, and a claim was received for services rendered on 1/25/81. ______________________________
2. Gerald is covered under the Ninja Enterprises plan. His effective date of coverage is 7/4/89. He received treatment for a finger laceration on 4/23/92. ______________________________
3. Adam is covered under the XYZ Corporation plan. His effective date of coverage is 4/14/83. He received treatment for leukemia on 3/15/83, and a claim was received for this same diagnosis for services rendered on 5/15/94. ______________________________
4. Alyse is covered under the Ninja Enterprises plan. Her effective date of coverage is 11/1/93. She received treatment for diabetes on 7/1/93, and a claim was submitted for services. ______________________________
5. Sebastian is covered under the ABC Corporation plan. His effective date of coverage is 2/15/91. A claim with a diagnosis of hypertension is received with a date of service of 2/20/91. ______________________________

6

Cost-Containment Programs

In this chapter you will learn:

- To identify cost-containment programs and describe their implementation.

Until the tremendous growth in health care costs triggered the need for new approaches, plan sponsors had been concerned primarily with improving employees' access to quality medical care. As a result of the increased health care costs of the last 10 years, many employers have been struggling to provide adequate care for their employees at an affordable cost. As a result, a variety of programs have been developed to slow down the rate of increase in both the premiums and the cost of health care.

Some of the more popular methods used in trying to slow down spiraling health care costs include the following:

- Preadmission Testing (PAT)
- Precertification of Inpatient Admissions
- Utilization Review (UR)
- Second Surgical Opinion (SSO) Consultation
- Preferred Provider Organizations (PPO)
- Health Maintenance Organizations (HMO)

Preadmission Testing

Preadmission testing consists of routine laboratory and x-ray tests performed on an outpatient basis prior to a scheduled inpatient admission. PAT was designed to reduce the duration of elective hospital confinements. This benefit is appropriate for scheduled, nonemergency hospital admissions that require the standard prerequisite testing prior to surgery. As a rule, this type of testing is restricted to a period of 3 to 7 days prior to admission. Additionally, some plans limit the place of testing to either the hospital where the surgery is performed or the patient's regular provider of services.

No payments under PAT are made for preadmission tests that are repeated during the hospitalization or whose results are rejected by the physician as unreliable. Since preadmission testing generally serves to reduce costs, most plans offer an incentive to the member to use PAT by paying these charges at a higher coinsurance rate than regular testing or hospital-related services.

Precertification of Inpatient Admissions

To precertify means to get preapproval for admission on elective, nonemergency hospitalizations. Contact is made either to the plan administrator or to some other entity sanctioned to determine the necessity of the admission. Most often, these entities are composed of a specialized corps of nurses working under the direction of a physician. The nurses deal directly with the physician's office and the facility to determine whether the admission is necessary and whether the number of days of care is medically necessary. If the patient stays longer than the approved number of days, the additional days of care may not be paid for or the usual payment may be reduced by a percentage specified in the plan document. The objective of this program is to prevent unnecessary admissions and to get the patient out of the hospital as soon as is medically appropriate.

Some programs provide for precertification only (prior to or on the day of hospitalization). Other programs provide for a complete approach to managing the care, which entails a utilization review program.

Utilization Review

As previously indicated, precertification or a prospective review determines the need and appropriateness of the recommended care. A complete UR program contains the following three components:

1. Precertification (prior to) or prospective review.
2. Concurrent review (during the confinement).
3. Retrospective review (after termination of confinement).

Concurrent review determines whether the estimated length of time and scope of the inpatient stay is justified by the diagnosis and symptoms. This review is conducted periodically during the projected length of stay. If the length of stay exceeds the criteria or if there is a change in treatment, the matter is referred to the medical consultant for review. This consultant at no time dictates the method of treatment or the length of stay. These decisions are left entirely to the patient and the attending physician. However, the consultant is entitled to inform the patient, physician, and facility that the continued stay exceeds the approved number of days and may not be covered by the plan as medically necessary. It is then the patient's responsibility to decide what course to take.

Retrospective review is used to determine after discharge whether the hospitalization and treatment were medically necessary and covered by the terms of the benefit program. This type of review may be used as a substitute for admission and concurrent reviews when the failure to notify the UR program of an admission prevents the regular review procedures. However, the main drawback to the retrospective review is that the patient and providers are not notified about the services that will not be covered until after they have been provided. The best programs always work most effectively when the patient is notified beforehand that he or she will be primarily responsible for payment of services. This approach deters the member from incurring unnecessary expenses.

Second Surgical Opinion Consultations

Surgical claims represent the second highest categorical cost to benefit plans (hospitalization ranks first). The United States has the world's highest rate of surgical treatment because neither the physician nor the patient has any financial incentive to consider less expensive alternatives.

About 80% of all surgeries can be considered as "elective." That is, they are not required because of a life-threatening situation. The objective of an SSO is to eliminate elective surgical procedures that are classified as unnecessary.

Unnecessary surgery is that which is recommended as an elective procedure when an alternative method of treatment may be preferable for a number of reasons, including:

- The surgery itself may be premature, taking into consideration all pathologic indications.
- The risk to the patient may not justify the benefits of surgery.
- An alternative medical treatment may be superior for both medical and cost-effective reasons.
- A less severe surgical procedure may be preferable under the circumstances. Or, no medical or surgical procedure may be necessary at all.

In this program, the plan participant consults an independent specialist to determine whether the recommended elective surgical procedure is advisable. This process is not intended to interfere with the patient-physician relationship nor to prevent the participant from receiving necessary elective operations.

This program may be administered in one of two ways:

1. A mandatory program requires the patient to obtain an SSO for specified procedures, or there is an automatic reduction or denial of benefits. (For an example of this type of program, see the Ninja Enterprises contract in the Student Exercise Manual.)
2. A voluntary program encourages participants to have an SSO, but there is no automatic reduction of benefits if the patient does not comply. In both approaches, the SSO and related tests are usually paid at 100% so that the patient will not have any out-of-pocket expenses for conforming with the program.

In the last 5 years, the SSO program has met with much criticism because it has not effectively reduced the number of elective surgeries. One of the main reasons for this ineffectiveness is that physicians are reluctant to tell a patient that a surgery is not necessary. This attitude stems from the growing number of malpractice lawsuits. For example, if a physician states that a patient does not need surgery and a sudden emergency situation arises that is related to the original need for surgery, the physician may be held liable under a malpractice suit. Consequently, many plans are abandoning the SSO plan provision.

Managed Care

Managed care is a strategy for reducing or controlling health care costs by tightly monitoring and restricting the use and cost of services. With this type of system, the insurer manages the delivery of health care and controls costs by emphasizing primary and preventive care services. Managed care plans use quality assurance and utilization review to ensure the appropriate delivery of care. Preferred providers organizations, HMOs, and point-of-service plans are examples of managed care plans.

Preferred Provider Organizations

A Preferred Provider Organization is a group of health care providers who agree to provide services to a specific pool of patients for an agreed fee (contractual). PPOs include doctors, dentists, hospitals, and any provider group that contracts with another entity to provide services at competitive fees.

PPO packages may involve contractual agreements for a limited number of health care services or for a full range of inpatient and outpatient medical services. Because the PPO group has agreed to specified benefits, they usually have their own utilization review committees or guidelines to reduce the amount of testing performed, hospitalizations, and other services.

In some cases, a health plan may continue to offer a standard indemnity coverage but also offers special PPO arrangements in which the PPO provider is paid more quickly and at a higher percentage rate than non-PPO providers. In such a case, the plan participant saves money because out-of-pocket expenses are also reduced.

Many PPO providers are available. Some are good and some are not. The benefits of a PPO provider compared with a non-PPO provider vary greatly from plan to plan. However, generally both the patient and the plan reduce costs by being members of a good PPO.

Some of the advantages for the patient associated with being in a PPO are:

- Reduced health care costs with no restriction (or with only a minimal restriction) of freedom of choice of providers. Reduced health care costs mean reduced out-of-pocket expenses.
- Less paperwork in filing claims because the PPO submits the claim directly to the payor and payment is made directly to the PPO.
- Generally, provision only of services that are medically necessary because there is usually a formal utilization review program.

Some of the advantages to the provider associated with being in a PPO are:

- Increased patient volume.
- Prompt claim payment.
- Reduced financial risk due to automatic assignment of benefits.
- Active participation in local cost-containment efforts.

Some of the advantages to the Benefit Plan associated with being in a PPO are:

- Reduced health care cost.
- Better utilization control.

Health Maintenance Organizations

A Health Maintenance Organization is a type of prepayment policy in which providers agree to charge HMO members for their services in accordance with a fixed schedule of rates. The HMO member (insured) may pay a certain portion of the charge at the time services are rendered, and the balance is either directly billed to the HMO or included in the monthly fee that the HMO pays the provider for participating.

If services are available through the HMO but the insured does not go to the HMO provider, either the benefit will be reduced or the member will be entirely responsible for payment of care received. Any services provided outside the HMO network must be preapproved by the HMO to be covered. If services are not approved, the HMO will not pay anything toward the charges.

The main difference between a PPO and an HMO is that an HMO provider receives a monthly fee based on capitation (number of covered plan members), whereas a PPO provider is paid only when a member is treated. A disadvantage of the HMO arrangement is the limitation of the patient's freedom of choice of physicians. In addition, the location of the HMO facilities may be limited or inconvenient for many plan members.

Exclusive Provider Organizations

In the Exclusive Provider Organization, the patient must select a primary care giver and can use only physicians who are part of the network or who are referred by the primary care physician. EPO physicians are paid as service is rendered, after which they get a capitation or utilization bonus from the carrier.

Gatekeeper PPO

In the Gatekeeper PPO, the member chooses a family provider or physician and must see him or her before being referred to a specialist. The specialist may or may not be within the network. In essence, the family physician is the "gatekeeper" to alternate services and can choose to refer the patient or not.

Physician Hospital Organizations

A Physician Hospital Organization is an organization of physicians and hospitals that bands together for the purpose of obtaining contracts from payor organizations. The PHO bargains as an entity for preferred provider status with various payors. The organization also refers clients to each other.

Management Service Organizations

A Management Service Organization is a separate corporation set up to provide management services to a medical group for a fee. Individual physicians and providers contract with the MSO for services. An MSO may be owned by a single hospital, several hospitals, or investors.

Managed Competition

Managed Competition is an evolving reform plan that uses some government intervention to create a competitive market for health care. Employers, particularly small businesses, band together in purchasing groups to increase their bargaining strength. Insurance companies, doctors, and other providers also join forces to offer comprehensive benefit packages.

This model of health care delivery has been embraced by the Clinton administration. This delivery system focuses on shifting competition in the health insurance market from risk (insuring individuals who are healthy instead of those with preexisting conditions) to price. Under this model, a national health board would set the standards for a minimum benefits package and adjust the risks among Accountable Health Partnerships (AHP), which would function as both providers and insurers of health care services. Large businesses would act as sponsors and would be able to buy insurance directly from the AHP. Small businesses and individuals would have to go through a Health Insurance Purchasing Cooperative (HIPC). (HIPCs are entities that would purchase health care benefit packages on behalf of small employers and individuals.) These entities would be set up to offer a menu of plans from which to choose. For individuals with low incomes, the federal government would foot the bill for the basic benefits package.

Medical Case Management

Medical Case Management is the process of evaluating the effectiveness and frequency of medical treatments by reviewing to determine whether the care that is being rendered or that is going to be rendered is appropriate. When a situation arises in which the potential for high claims payment exists based on the diagnosis or the type of services needed by the claimant, the case is generally referred to the Medical Case Management Department. The MCM (in some instances, an outside company performs this function) reviews these cases and tries to minimize the company's loss by finding alternative solutions to providing patient care. This may necessitate providing the patient with equipment or care that is normally not covered under the plan, but based on the circumstances it is more cost-effective and beneficial to the patient to make these provisions. MCM often concentrates on high dollar claims involving inpatient hospital confinements. Less costly alternatives such as hospice, nursing home, and home health care with discounted nursing or equipment are explored.

An important goal of MCM is to save costs for the insured, the patient, the account, the health care providers, and the administrator. Even more important, this process can result in higher quality care.

Under most plans, MCM is a voluntary process. To be successful, the cooperation of the patient and family is important.

Situations that may indicate possible claims for MCM are included in Appendix 6-1; however, the health claims examiner should watch for certain factors. These include:

1. Pattern of repeated hospital admissions (or two within 6 months).
2. Outpatient therapies of more than 6 weeks (including nursing services).
3. Home care by an RN of more than 4 hours per day.
4. Skilled nursing care in an extended care facility of more than 6 weeks.
5. Any hospital interim bill (excessive length of stay).
6. Any terminal or progressive disease requiring long-term skilled care.

Use experience and common sense to identify claims that are unusual and may become "catastrophic" by virtue of chronicity or immediately high cost.

Summary

The cost of health care coverage in general is increasing faster than any other segment of service or commodity in our society. In general, although overall inflation has been very low in the last few years, the medical inflation rate, particularly as it relates to health insurance has increased by double digits. Because of these factors, it is essential to the survival of the health insurance industry that cost-containment provisions be implemented to help reverse this trend.

Assignments

Complete the Questions for Review.

Questions for Review

Directions: Answer the following questions without looking back into the material just covered. Write your answers in the space provided.

1. List six of the more popular methods used in trying to slow down spiraling health care costs.
   a. Preadmission Testing PAT
   b. Precertification of Inpatient admissions
   c. Utilization Review (UR)
   d. Second Surgical Opinion (SSO) consultation
   e. Preferred Provider Organizations (PPO)
   f. Health Maintenance Organizations (HMO)
2. Preadmission testing is routine laboratory and x-ray tests performed on an outpatient basis prior to a scheduled inpatient admission.
3. To precertify means to get preapproval for an admission on an elective, nonemergency hospitalization.
4. List the two ways that second surgical opinion programs may be administered.
   a. mandatory program
   b. voluntary program
5. A Health Maintance Organization is a type of prepayment policy in which providers agree to charge HMO members for their services in accordance with a fixed schedule of rates.

If you were unable to answer any of the questions, refer back to the section and then complete the answers.

Appendix 6-1

Potential Medical Case Management Claims

The following list consists of diagnoses that are potentially medical case management claims. This list is intended to be used for training and reference purposes only, since the particular company or plan guidelines may differ from those stated.

Section 1: Potential medical case management claims listing by condition are as follows:

Neonatal Patients
- Premature birth
- Hydrocephalus
- Respiratory distress and in ICU over 1 week
- Meningomyelocele
- Bronchopulmonary dysplasia
- Major or multiple congenital anomaly

Obstetric Patients
- Expected multiple birth of three or more infants
- Previous history of neonatal ICU-confined infant
- Bleeding during pregnancy
- Toxemia (hypertension) requiring hospitalization during pregnancy

Transplant/Dialysis Patients
- Heart, liver, or bone marrow transplant
- Organ rejection
- Cardiomyopathy
- Biliary atresia
- Renal failure

Neurologic Patients
- Brain tumors
- TIA (transient ischemic attack)
- Closed head injury
- Unconsciousness (any cause)
- Cerebral aneurysm or AV malformation
- Meningitis or encephalitis
- Reye's syndrome
- Anoxic encephalopathy
- Guillain-Barré
- Quadriplegia
- Paraplegia
- Chronic stroke
- Multiple sclerosis (MS)
- Amyotrophic lateral sclerosis (ALS)
- Alzheimer's disease

Psychiatric Conditions
- Anorexia nervosa
- Adolescent adjustment reaction
- Manic depression; bipolar disorder
- Schizophrenia
- Sexual abuse
- Chemical dependency
- Depression with or without suicide attempt

Cardiovascular Conditions
- Ruptured abdominal aortic aneurysm
- MI (heart attack)
- Intractable angina
- Peripheral vascular disease, with pending amputation

Respiratory Conditions
- Respirator dependency (any cause)
- Emphysema
- Chronic bronchitis or asthma

Malignancy Patients
- Multiple surgeries
- Radiation treatments
- Cancer in children
- Chemotherapy
- Acute leukemia
- Aplastic anemia
- Kaposi's sarcoma

Other Diagnoses
- AIDS
- Lupus
- Any condition causing paralysis

Traumatically Injured Patients
- Thermal burns or frostbite
  - Child over 10%
  - Adult over 20%
- Crash injuries
- Amputations
- Multiple trauma or fractures
- Spinal cord injury

Section II: Potential medical case management claims by ICD-9 codes are as follows:

Medical Cases	ICD-9 CM Code	Description
High-risk mothers	640.x—644.0	Complications of pregnancy
	646.x—648.x	
	760—779	Perinatal conditions
Other	344.x	Other paralytic syndrome
	045.x	Poliomyelitis and other viral diseases of central nervous system
Highly suggestive of AIDS	031.0	Pulmonary infection by *Mycobacterium*
	112.0*	Candidiasis of mouth (thrush)
	112.4	Candidiasis pneumonia
	112.5	Systemic candidiasis
	112.81—112.89*	Candidiasis of other sites
	114	Coccidioidal meningitis
	114.0	Pulmonary coccidioidomycosis
	114.9	Coccidioidomycosis, unspecified
	115.0—115.9	Histoplasmosis
	130.0	Toxoplasmosis encephalitis
	130.3—130.9	Toxoplasmosis of other sites
	136.3	*Pneumocystis carinii* pneumonia
	173.9	Kaposi's sarcoma
	279.3	Deficiency of cell-mediated immunity
	279.3	Unspecified immunity deficiency
	279.9	Unspecified disorder of immune system
	279.10	Immunodeficiency with predominant T-cell defect, unspecified

Medical Cases	ICD-9 CM Code	Description
	279.19	Other
	780.6*	Fever of unknown origin
	785.6*	Lymphadenopathy
	790.8*	Viremia, unspecified
Traumatic brain injury	850.x—854.x	Various types of head injury
	800.x—804.x	Skull fracture
	780.0	Coma and stupor
Nontraumatic brain injury	191.x	Brain tumors
	293.x	Transient organic condition
	294.x	Other organic psychotic conditions
	310.x	Mental disorders due to organic brain damage
	348.x	Brain conditions
	349.x	Other and unspecified diseases of CNS
Spinal cord injury	952.x	Spinal cord injury without evidence of spinal bone injury
	805.x—806.x	Fracture of neck and trunk
	827.x—828.x	Fracture of neck and trunk
	336.x	Diseases of spinal cord
Stroke	342.x	Hemiplegia
	430	Subarachnoid hemorrhage
	431	Intercerebral hemorrhage
	432	Other unspecified intracranial hemorrhage
	433.x	Occlusion and stenosis of cerebral arteries
Multiple fractures	733.81	Malunion (fx)
	733.82	Nonunion (fx)
Burns	940.x—949.x	Burns
High-risk infants	343.x	Infantile cerebral palsy
	741.x	Spina bifida
	742.x	Other congenital anomalies of the nervous system
	644.2	Early onset of delivery

***These codes appear frequently with AIDS-related complex (ARC) or AIDS. However, these codes also appear with a substantial number of non-AIDS-related illnesses. "X" denotes the entire range of subset numbers describing variations on the particular diagnosis.**

7

Usual, Customary, and Reasonable Fees

In this chapter you will learn:

- To determine the correct unit value of the procedure code billed.
- To determine the appropriate conversion factor as indicated by geographic region and status of provider.
- To accurately calculate customary and reasonable allowances.

Benefit plans define covered expenses as charges for the following services and supplies: those that are medically necessary for the treatment or diagnosis of an injury or illness; those that are ordered or prescribed by a licensed provider; and those that do not exceed the usual, customary, and reasonable (UCR) fee generally charged by like providers in the same geographic area for the same procedure.

There are several sources that compile and publish UCR data for surgical, medical, laboratory, and x-ray services in the United States. Using this data or compiling their own data, third party administrators and insurance companies determine the UCR allowances for their plans or clients. Monies in excess of UCR are not considered to be an allowable expense under the plan and are therefore excluded from all benefit calculations.

UCR is based on the procedure performed, the geographic location (zip code area) of the provider of services' office, and the date the service was performed.

UCR is usually applicable only to professional services or to hospital billings that give CPT/RVS codes. Individually, some administrators are establishing daily UCR amounts for hospital services.

Not all procedures have UCR. For instance, new procedures, experimental procedures and very unusual, complex procedures may not have an established UCR amount. UCR can be established only when enough procedures of a particular type have been performed in a geographic area to allow for an "average" or "usual" amount to be determined. Usually, a minimum of 50 operations is required to provide even a rough estimate of the amount that should be considered as usual.

There are several reasons why a UCR amount will not be available, including:

- The CPT code is a BR (By Report) procedure. The value of this service is based on the operative report because the service is too unusual or variable to be assigned a unit value.
- The code entered is an RNE (Relativity Not Established) procedure. This indicates new or infrequently performed services for which sufficient data have not been collected to allow establishment of a relative value.
- The code entered is not listed in the most recent Current Procedural Terminology (CPT) book because it is a new procedure.

UCR Definitions

This section includes definitions of some of the terms most commonly used by medical billers, health claims examiners, and health care providers in determining UCR.

Conversion Factor—a dollar amount determined for a specific service type or a particular region. Each region may have a unique set of conversion factors, and each service type may be assigned a specific conversion factor.

Usual, Customary and Reasonable—an amount usually charged by most providers within a geographic region for a specified service.

Modifier Codes—two-digit numerical codes attached to a CPT code to indicate special circumstances for that particular service. This may mean that the unit value or UCR amount should be increased or decreased because of those special circumstances.

Procedure Code—five-digit numerical code used to designate medical services according to a standardized, industry-accepted method; usually reflected in a CPT manual.

Region—the geographic region of the country that is assigned a specific conversion factor. More expensive cost-of-living areas are assigned higher conversion factors than less expensive cost-of-living areas. Some states or cities are divided into multiple, different regions, whereas other states or cities may have only one area or may even be combined with other states or cities.

Type of Treatment—the type of service performed, which is usually classified by the following categories: surgery, medical, x-ray, laboratory, and anesthesia.

Unit Value—a numerical value assigned by a relative value study to a procedure code. The unit value is multiplied by the conversion factor to determine the UCR allowance or a basic allowance.

Resource-Based Relative Value Study

The studies that assign unit values to a particular procedure are called relative value studies (RVS). These studies take into consideration the time involved in a service rendered, the skill required to deliver a service, the severity of the patient's condition generally involved, the risk to the patient, and the medicolegal risk to the physician. The most commonly used are the California RVS, Fifth Edition Revised, the 1989 Florida RVS, Resource Based Relative Value Study (RBRVS), and the Health Insurance Association of America Surgical Prevailing Healthcare Charges System (referred to as HIAA).

Currently, the HIAA System is used to determine UCR for surgical charges only, but it is being expanded to include laboratory, x-ray, and medicine. The system tracks actual charges submitted by providers throughout the nation and compiles this information to be used by many insurance carriers in determining their allowable amounts.

The method used for payment to providers was historically payment-based. Payment of reasonable charges was based on profiles and prevailing rates in geographic areas. With the passage of OBRA 90-Public Law 101-608, major changes for physician payment reform took place. One of these changes was the replacement of historic payment basis, with a fee schedule for physician payment. This fee schedule is to be based on relative value units that reflect the resources required to provide a service. OBRA 90 declared that after January 1, 1992, and each year thereafter, a fee schedule must be established for all physician services in all geographic areas. The fee schedule will be based on national uniform relative values for all physicians without respect to area of specialization. The relative value units (RVUs) represent the total RVS for components of the schedule.

Components of resource-based RVS (RBRVS) include:

- Physician Work Component—reflects the resources required to furnish the professional service including the time and the intensity of effort.
- Overhead or Practice Expense Component—reflects customary practice expenses such as rent, salaries, staff, equipment cost, and so on.
- Malpractice or Professional Liability Component—reflects the risk inherent in providing various procedures. This component does not reflect any specialties but reflects that some procedures are performed routinely by physicians with specialty training in the procedure.

The RVS are to be adjusted for various locales by a Geographic Adjustment Factor. The Geographic Adjustment Factor is calculated by the following:

Geographic Practice Cost Indices (GPCI) are factored by each RBRVS component to reflect the different cost of each component in various locales where services are provided. These include GPCI for physicians' work, GPCI for practice overhead, and GPCI for professional liability coverage.

The weighted sum of each GPCI equals the Geographic Adjustment Factor.

The following formula is used to determine the total unit value for all procedures. RBRVS values are published in the Federal Register by HCFA. To determine the fee schedule or payment for a provider, the formula is:

Work = RVU x GPCI
\+
Overhead = RVU x GPCI
\+
Malpractice = RVU x GPCI

Calculating UCR

UCR calculation is the process of determining the fee usually charged by similar providers for the same procedure in the same geographic area during a specified time period.

Conversion Factors

In determining UCR, the listed procedure unit value is multiplied by the plan's appropriate conversion factor or factors. Often there are separate conversion factors for medicine, surgery, DXL, and anesthesia charges.

The CPT code for the procedure determines the appropriate conversion factor, not the description of the service. The ranges by conversion factor categories are:

Medicine	90701-99499
Anesthesia	00100-01999
Surgery	10040-69979
DXL	70010-89399

The conversion factor is a dollar amount based on the geographic area in which the provider practices. For instance, Los Angeles may have a surgical conversion factor of $50.64, whereas Bismarck, North Dakota's surgical conversion factor may be $28.00 (refer to the Usual Customary and Reasonable Conversion Factor Report on page 104 of the Student Exercise Manual).

Example:

Tonsillectomy, 42842, RVS, Procedure Unit Value = 16.39

Geographic conversion factor for San Francisco (zip code 940XX) is $39.54. To determine UCR for this procedure, multiply the RVS 16.39 unit value by the conversion factor of $39.54 (for 940XX, San Francisco). The total UCR amount is $648.06.

On a Basic-Major Medical plan, two limits must be calculated:

1. Basic allowance.
2. Total plan allowance or Major Medical allowance.

The basic benefit usually has one dollar conversion factor specified in the plan document. Consequently, all providers, regardless of their geographic location or when the service is performed, receive the same basic allowance for a specific procedure. Also, the basic allowance is usually paid at 100%.

Conversely, the UCR allowance under Major Medical is not normally specified in the plan document because it is usually upgraded periodically in accordance with inflationary factors.

Refer to the contract for XYZ Corporation. As indicated, this is a Basic-Major Medical plan. For office visits, the specified conversion factor is $7.50 and for DXL it is $7.00. For Major Medical, no conversion factors are indicated because these factors are contingent to date and geographic location. Therefore, the factors will keep changing over time.

Basic Allowance

To calculate the Basic payment:

1. Look up the procedure code and determine the relative unit value that applies to the procedure for the specified schedule.
2. Multiply the RVS unit value by the plan basic conversion factor. (In the case of XYZ, it would be $7.00 for DXL or $7.50 for office visits.)

The resulting figure will be the amount payable at 100% under basic benefits.

Major Medical UCR

To calculate the Major Medical UCR limit:

1. Look up the procedure code and determine the relative unit value that applies to the procedure for the specified schedule.
2. Multiply the RVS unit value by the plan (or Major Medical) conversion factor based on:
   a. The specific time period during which the services were provided;
   b. The geographic location of the provider (using the first three digits of the zip code).
   c. The type of service being performed, eg, surgery, medical.

The figure arrived at will be the maximum amount allowed under the plan. "Allowed" does not necessarily mean the same as "paid."

Amounts over the Major Medical UCR allowance are not considered covered by the Plan. Amounts below the UCR amount are applied toward all of the plan limitations, including the deductible and coinsurance. The amounts not covered by the plan are the patient's sole responsibility.

Normally, if the provider's charge exceeds the UCR allowance by more than 20% or 25%, a Peer Review (consultant) may be required. In this case, a copy of the operative report (eg, for a surgery) or other documentation will be required for the claim to be reviewed for possible additional allowance.

Special Services

The services in the procedure code range of 99000—99199 are considered special services. Regardless of the type of service provided, the UCR calculation is based on the medicine conversion factor category. This classification may vary from administrator to administrator.

UCR Modifications

Remember that the addition of modifiers will alter the percentage of the UCR that is allowed. There will also be adjustments based on whether or not there were multiple or asterisk procedures. For standard adjustments on modifiers, consult the CPT book. For those modifications not listed, the adjustment will vary according to the insurance carrier's policy and the contract provisions.

Fee Schedules

Some plans have done their own calculations of the amount payable for particular services. These amounts are listed on what is commonly called a fee schedule. Fees are assigned according to the particular CPT code, and this is considered the allowable amount for that particular procedure.

If a fee schedule is used, the claims examiner must look up the appropriate code to obtain the allowed amount. This eliminates the need for numerous calculations and can speed up the process of claims examining. However, the compensation with the schedules is the same in a large city as it is in outlying areas.

Summary

The concept of Usual, Customary, and Reasonable charges allows a payor to determine allowable charges based on what is considered to be a usual and reasonable charge for a given service performed in a given area. This prevents the paying of excessive benefits to doctors who may charge high fees on their bills. UCR allows for the payment of higher rates in areas in which there is a higher cost of doing business (ie, building costs, personnel) and lower rates in areas in which there is a lower cost of doing business.

Assignments

Complete the Questions for Review.
Complete the UCR exercises 7-1 to 7-5.

fee schedule - usually basic only plan (dental) set rate for CPT codes - insurance companies offer multiple

Questions for Review

Directions: Answer the following questions without looking back into the material just covered. Write your answers in the space provided.

1. What does UCR mean? usual, customary & reasonable
2. What is UCR based on? procedure performed, zipcode, date service was provided on
3. Explain why a procedure may not have a UCR allowance.
   new procedures, experimental procedures, very unusual complex procedures may not cause usually about 50 procedures have to be done before they come up with an average
4. Define the following words:
   a. Conversion factor dollar amount determined for a specific service type or a particular region
   b. Unit value numerical value assigned by a relative value study to a procedure code
   CPT code ← c. Procedure code 5 digit numerical code used to designate medical services according to a standardized industry accepted method
   d. Region geographic region of the country that is assigned a specific conversion factor
   e. Modifier codes 2 digit numerical codes attached to a CPT to indicate special circumstances for a particular service
5. How do you calculate Major Medical UCR? (1) Look up procedure code & determine Relative Unit Value (2) Multiply RVS unit value by the plan conversion factor
6. How do you calculate the basic allowance? (1) Look up procedure code & determine Relative Unit Value (2) Multiply RVS unit value by plan basic conversion factor
7. The maximum amount allowed under the plan will always be the amount paid. (True or False) False
8. Are amounts in excess of the UCR allowance considered covered by the plan? NO
9. What is the procedure code range for special services? 99000 - 99199 (Not on test)
10. What do BR and RNE stand for and what is the difference between them?
    BR - by Report - value of service is based on the operative report because the service is too unusual or variable to be assigned a unit value
    (both same reason)

If you were unable to answer any of the questions, refer back to the section and complete the answers.

RNE - Relativity Not Established
new or infrequently performed services for which sufficient data have not been collected to allow establishment of a relative value

Exercise 7-1

Directions: Using your Conversion Factor Report, list the Surgery, Medicine, DXL, and Anesthesia conversion factors for the following zip codes.

Zip Code	Surgery	Medicine	DXL	Anesthesia
1. 12345	________	________	________	________
2. 75839	________	________	________	________
3. 98023	________	________	________	________
4. 78593	________	________	________	________
5. 03464	________	________	________	________
6. 89456	________	________	________	________
7. 21438	________	________	________	________
8. 63545	________	________	________	________
9. 85679	________	________	________	________
10. 00615	________	________	________	________
11. 54632	________	________	________	________
12. 76385	________	________	________	________
13. 94612	________	________	________	________
14. 27893	________	________	________	________
15. 93480	________	________	________	________

Exercise 7-2

Directions: Using your Conversion Factor Report, list the Surgery, Medicine, DXL, and Anesthesia conversion factors for the following zip codes.

Zip Code	Surgery	Medicine	DXL	Anesthesia
1. 36845	________	________	________	________
2. 40267	________	________	________	________
3. 52455	________	________	________	________
4. 87754	________	________	________	________
5. 14543	________	________	________	________
6. 31778	________	________	________	________
7. 94345	________	________	________	________
8. 67845	________	________	________	________
9. 02845	________	________	________	________
10. 24176	________	________	________	________
11. 54378	________	________	________	________
12. 43127	________	________	________	________
13. 68575	________	________	________	________
14. 49956	________	________	________	________
15. 78239	________	________	________	________

Exercise 7-3

Directions: Using your XYZ contract, calculate both basic and plan UCR. Use the conversion factor for zip code 94325.

Description	Proc. Code	Units	Basic	Plan
1. Diathermy with paraffin bath				
2. Limited OV with actinotherapy				
3. Manipulation				
4. Electrocardiogram, complete				
5. Pulmonary stress testing (DXL)				
6. Heart electroconversion				
7. Gonioscopy (Med)				
8. Medical Psychoanalysis				
9. Biofeedback for high blood pressure				
10. EEG (DXL)				
11. F/up consultation for complications of diabetes				
12. Injection of penicillin				
13. Brief initial ER exam for severe congestion				
14. Extensive exam for new patient w/severe arthritis				
15. Intermediate eye exam				

Exercise 7-4

Directions: Using your ABC contract, calculate the plan UCR. Use the conversion factor for zip code 90020.

Description	Proc. Code	Units	Plan
1. Diathermy with paraffin bath			
2. Limited OV with actinotherapy			
3. Manipulation			
4. Electrocardiogram, complete			
5. Pulmonary stress testing (DXL)			
6. Heart electroconversion			
7. Gonioscopy (Med)			
8. Medical Psychoanalysis			
9. Biofeedback for high blood pressure			
10. EEG (DXL)			
11. F/up consultation for complications of diabetes			
12. Injection of penicillin			
13. Brief initial ER exam for severe congestion			
14. Extensive exam for new patient w/severe arthritis			
15. Intermediate eye exam			

Exercise 7-5

Directions: Using your Ninja contract, calculate the plan UCR. Use the conversion factor for zip code 38100.

Description	Proc. Code	Units	Plan
1. Diathermy with paraffin bath			
2. Limited OV with actinotherapy			
3. Manipulation			
4. Electrocardiogram, complete			
5. Pulmonary stress testing (DXL)			
6. Heart electroconversion			
7. Gonioscopy (Med)			
8. Medical Psychoanalysis			
9. Biofeedback for high blood pressure			
10. EEG (DXL)			
11. F/up consultation for complications of diabetes			
12. Injection of penicillin			
13. Brief initial ER exam for severe congestion			
14. Extensive exam for new patient w/severe arthritis			
15. Intermediate eye exam			

8

Claims Administration

In this chapter you will learn:

- To understand the job responsibilities of a Health Claims Examiner.
- To understand the process of administering claims.

The claims examiner's job entails a wide variety of administrative duties to ensure proper claims handling. In this chapter, we will address the importance of the following: verification of coverage and eligibility, accurate claim file documentation, investigation, referrals, and pending claims. Company guidelines vary from payor to payor, so please review your company guidelines upon employment.

Maintenance of Claim Files

When a claim is received by a payor, the department (the name of the department varies from company to company) documents the receipt of the claim usually via a microfilm medium that copies the claim and assigns it a claim number, which includes the date. The date is used to keep all claims received in chronologic order so that the oldest mail can be processed first. After the claim has been documented as received, it is routed to the claims processor for handling.

When a claims payor does not have a computerized processing system, the physical claims must be kept for ready access by examining personnel. Although manual filing systems may vary, they usually entail the maintenance of family files, patient files, or batch files.

Family Files

Family files are folders of claims that are kept for each family of claimants. The claimants/patients are usually identified by the same subscriber identification number. This identification number is used to group the members of a family together into a single file or folder. Most companies use the member's social security number as the identification number.

Within the family folder, each member's information and claims are grouped separately. This grouping is based on the calendar year in which the charges were incurred, the date the expenses were processed, and whether the claim is completed or pending for additional information.

Therefore, each member will have a separate interfamily subfile for each calendar year. Within this subfile, completed claims are usually arranged with the claim processed earliest in a calendar year placed at the bottom of the file and the claims processed later in the year placed at the top. In addition, there may be a separate correspondence subfile and a separate pending claim file by year, or there may be only one of each of these subfiles for each member with all years combined together. However, as with the completed claims, the correspondence or pending claims are usually arranged chronologically so that those received the earliest are placed at the bottom and those received later are placed at the top of the stack.

Patient Files

An alternative to having family files is to have patient files. With this type of filing system, there is only one patient per file. Claims for the patient for all years are kept in the same file. Therefore, unlike the family files, in which the entire family file is accessed when a claim or phone call is received for a family member, only a single member's file is accessed. Correspondence and pending claims are kept separate from completed claims, and all information is arranged chronologically according to the date of handling.

Unfortunately with the individual patient file, it is difficult for the examiner to see trends, fraud, overutilization, and other abuses being practiced by a family or provider, since the information is scattered in multiple files. However, patient files tend to be neater and easier to handle than family files.

Batch Files

Batch files are batches of claims grouped together according to the date they were processed and the person who processed them. Every claim processed by an individual each day is placed in the same folder or secured together with rubber band and filed. The claims are placed in order by claim number. Pending claims and correspondence are usually kept in separate files. When a pended claim is completed, it is placed in the batch file based according to the date of completion.

With the batch system, when claims for one person need to be accessed, multiple batch files must be accessed as well. This process tends to be labor-intensive. In addition, as with patient files, trends and abuses cannot be easily recognized by examining personnel.

Claim File Documentation

Documentation is the orderly organization and communication of important facts that can be used to furnish decisive evidence of claim handling or processing. Documenting the claim file with pertinent information is an important job of the claims examiner. If the claim cannot be processed upon receipt, the claim file must be documented as to the disposition of the claim. The most common reason why a claim cannot be processed is that additional information is needed from the provider or the member. The claims examiner's responsibility is to indicate in the claim file the information requested and the date of the request. The date that the follow-up letter should be sent, in the event that the information is not received within a certain amount of time, should also be included in the claim file.

This documentation enables the examiner to refresh his or her memory at a future date. Since you may not be the person that follows up on the claim or receives the information requested, be sure that the documentation is understandable and that it provides concise, informative and pertinent information. Refrain from marking claim documents unnecessarily, since this may be very confusing to others reviewing the claim at a later date. Proper documentation should have the following attributes:

- Clean claim files. Never include any derogatory references to the member. Never write down personal remarks. Likewise, there should never be any reference to ethnic origin unless that information is relevant to the case. Always keep your points objective. Do not underline negative facts or information unless you also underline positive information.
- Document the files properly and show the basis for your decision. Careless or poorly worded claim files can give an appearance of bad faith or a conscious disregard of the claimant's rights. The representative not only must be fair and reasonable but must also create a claim file that shows fairness, reasonableness, and factual accuracy when read by a jury. Always correctly record the basis for all claim decisions. Such a practice should also force you to carefully consider your action before taking that action and to discover and correct errors before any serious damage has occurred.
- Be careful when using words of the trade. Sometimes such words or phrases may be taken out of context and used to give a bad connotation. Be especially aware of words that may have a double meaning, especially if taken out of context.
- Give initial, factual information to an attorney involved on behalf of the claimant, if there is one involved. If the attorney requests further information, questions concerning the extent and nature of that information should be discussed with a member of your firm's legal department or a supervisor before responding to the attorney. All information or copies of documents should be clearly documented in the file.

  Some firms retain specialists to handle attorney claims. In such cases, the case should be referred immediately to the specialist. Nothing should be said or sent to the attorney regarding the case unless it is directed by the specialist. Since the handling of these claims differs significantly from office to office, always request clarification on the handling of such claims prior to taking any action.
- All information regarding the claim should be put in writing. This means that phone conversations should always be documented and summarized in writing. This is often done on a form called a Telephone Information Sheet. A sample copy of a Telephone Information Sheet is shown as Figure 8-1. Also, keep to the facts with what you have to say about a case or an individual and express no opinion either in oral or written communication.
- Be careful when asked to furnish information. Information furnished by a doctor or other provider with regard to a claim may be privileged

ANY INSURANCE CARRIER, INC.
0123 Any Drive, Anywhere, USA 12345 • (800) 555-1234

Date ______________________
Claim Identification ______________________
____
____
____
____

Telephone Information Sheet

Person making inquiry: ______________________
Person supplying information: ______________________
Telephone Number: ______________________
Briefly state information received or desired: ______________________
____
____
____
____
____
____
____
____
____
____
____

Indicate additional handling, if any: ______________________
____
____
____

This form, when completed, should be placed in the claim file.

Figure 8-1: Sample Telephone Information Sheet.

information. If medical information is requested by the claimant, normally the claimant should be advised to contact the provider directly. The fact that the claimant is a patient of the provider does not necessarily entitle him or her to the information that has been furnished.

Claim Investigation

Claim investigating is making a detailed inquiry to verify facts pertaining to a claim submitted. When a claim is received, the minimal information that should be obtained is a diagnosis, and the age, marital status, and student status (if applicable) of the claimant. Reasons for investigation may include possible preexisting conditions, fraud, work-related injuries, and coordination of benefits. When making your request for information, be as specific as possible regarding the type of information needed. Request information in a way to get narrative answers rather than yes or no answers. Avoid sending several requests for different information to the same provider or member. Request all information at once so that claims are not delayed unnecessarily. Always attach an Authorization to Release Information with your request.

Referrals

Upon receipt of the information requested, you may find that the claim decision is beyond your level of expertise or authorization. When this occurs, the claim must be referred and reviewed by a technical claims person. This person may be a lead examiner, supervisor, medical review person, or consultant. This referral process ensures that there is a consistent approach to unusual situations and maintains an avenue of communication to higher levels in the case of sensitive issues. Following is a list of claims that are usually referred to technical personnel:

- Lawsuits, legal actions, or legislation issues. An attorney letter may be received demanding payment or making reference to insurance law, a summons or Notice of Complaint, or receipt of other lawsuit notification correspondence.
- Providers who have been flagged. Flagged providers are those who have been identified as being questionable; therefore, special handling is required. Some reasons why providers are flagged are questionable billing practices, overuse of certain benefits (eg, chiropractic services, biofeedback), new providers pending state approval to perform qualified services (eg, surgi-center).
- Fraud. Providers have submitted claims in which indications of fraud have been identified and the claims are pending for verification.

When claims are received for the above situations, a referral form should be completed and routed to the appropriate department. It is important that copies of all documents, letters, and forms be sent along with the referred claim. Figure 8-2 shows an example of a claims referral form.

Pended Claims

Pended claims are claims that have not been completely adjudicated or closed. These claims may require follow-up investigation so that correct and prompt liability decisions can be made, which comply with legislative or regulatory requirements for fair claim handling.

When requesting information, make sure that you request all the information needed to complete processing of the claim to ensure that an additional delay does not occur. A letter notifying the insured and the provider that the claim payment will be delayed must be sent. Many companies use a standard form letter requesting further information. Figures 8-3 and 8-4 show two standard request forms.

The first follow-up date should be scheduled 3 to 4 weeks after the original request. If the requested information is not received within the scheduled follow-up period, send a second notice letter with follow-up

Claim Office Referral Sheet

To		From	Date
Policy #	Soc. Sec. #	Employee's Name	Dependent's Name
Claimant's Eff. Date	Term Date	Patient's Age	Provider of Service

Reason for Referral

____
____
____
____
____
____

Attachments:

( ) ❑ Denial/ ❑ Attorney Letters	( ) ❑Preop Photos	( ) ❑Policy/ ❑Booklet Page
( ) Special Correspondence	( ) Op/Anesthesia/Path Report	( ) Billings
( ) ❑ Hospital/ ❑ Dr. Records	( ) X-rays	( ) Other________

Please make sure that all material referenced in any appeal letters (insured/provider/attorney) are enclosed with this file.

Reply:

____
____
____
____
____
____

____
Signature Date

Figure 8-2: **Sample Claim Referral Form.**

ANY INSURANCE CARRIER, INC.
0123 Any Drive, Anywhere, USA 12345 • (800) 555-1234

Control No. ______________________

Name ______________________

Please refer to the paragraph checked below.

❑ Careful attention is being given to this claim. We will write you further about it in a short time.

❑ As you requested, we are returning the ______________________

❑ Please let us know whether this claimant has returned to work and if so, when. ______________
If not, does total disability still exist? ________ Will proofs of claim be submitted? ______________
Information as to the claimant's present condition will be appreciated.

❑ Please have the ____________ statement completed and return the attached form to us.

❑ Consideration of further benefits can be given only after we receive the ______________________

____

____

❑ The attached furnished our first knowledge of this claim. Will you please arrange for submission of the required proofs of claim if this is properly covered under our insurance.

Figure 8-3: Sample Request for Additional Information Letter.

ANY INSURANCE CARRIER, INC.
0123 Any Drive, Anywhere, USA 12345 • (800) 555-1234

Request Form

❑ Medical ❑ Dental

Please return requested information to:

❑ First Request
❑ Second Request
❑ Third and Final Request

Insured: ______________________ Date: ______________________

Patient: ______________________

WE NEED YOUR HELP

BEFORE WE CAN PROCESS YOUR CLAIM, WE WILL NEED THE ADDITIONAL INFORMATION CHECKED BELOW

❑ Please complete in full the member portion of the claim form. ❑ Dental (employee section).

❑ Itemized Statements from: ______________________

❑ Copies of other Insurance Payments from: ______________________

❑ Full Time Student Eligibility Form Request: Please have the Registrar of the College/University that __________ ______________________ attends complete the attached Student Eligibility Form for the ______________________ Semester/Quarter.

❑ Other: ______________________

❑ THE FOLLOWING EXPENSES WILL BE HELD UNTIL THE ABOVE REQUESTED ITEMS ARE RECEIVED IN THIS OFFICE: ______________________

❑ We have attempted on ______________ to obtain the above necessary information to properly process your claim. As of this date it has not been received. The file will now be considered closed until such time the information is received and proper evaluation can be given your claim.

Thank you,

Figure 8-4: Sample Request for Additional Information Letter.

scheduled for 3 to 4 weeks. If the requested information is not received within 60 days, it may be necessary to close the claim. Send a final letter advising the insured and the provider that "because information requested has not been received, the claim is being closed. If the information is received within a reasonable length of time we will be happy to reopen the claim." If the company has a statute of limitations on filing a claim, this information should be indicated in the letter: "We are unable to process claims received more than 6 months after the date of service. If information is submitted prior to this time, we will be happy to reopen the claim."

Claims Examiner's Responsibilities

The conduct of all claims personnel is extremely important. Claims personnel are more visible because most of the public interfaces with either the customer service representative or directly with claims processing personnel. The public's opinion of the payor is based solely on their contacts with claims personnel. Therefore, it is important for examining personnel to establish basic principles and to adhere to them. The claims examiner's guiding philosophy should be to provide timely, competent, fair, and friendly claims service to all members.

A proposed workflow model is illustrated in Figure 8-5. Reviewing this model periodically will ensure that you have taken the basic steps toward proper claims processing. Keep in mind that this is a basic outline, and the specifics may vary from company to company.

When mail comes in, it is opened, sorted, and stamped with the receipt date. If the mail is a response to a pended claim, the letter is matched with the original claim.

The claims examiner then enters the claims and processes them, pends them, or refers them for review.

If the claim is to be processed (column one), it is either paid or denied, according to the terms of the contract. A check or statement is then generated. The claim is stored in a daily batch with the file copy. The clerk then mails out the check or statement and files the file copy.

If additional information is needed, the claim is pended (column two). A letter is generated by the system or the claims examiner manually fills out a form letter identifying the additional information needed. The pended claim is stored in the pend file for 30 days. If a response has not been received by that time, a follow-up letter is sent. A maximum of two follow-up letters should be sent. If the reply has not been received within 30 days of the last follow-up letter, the pended claim should be processed and denied for lack of sufficient information.

If the claims examiner is unable to make a decision based on his or her own expertise, the claim is referred for review (column three). Many insurance companies have a listing of certain types of claims that should be referred for review. These claims are then reviewed for appropriateness. The reviewer informs the claims examiner of the action to be taken, and the claim is processed accordingly. Reviewing the consultant's decision helps to improve the claims examiner's expertise.

Since the examiner's main responsibility is to determine the payor's obligation in accordance with policy provisions and to discharge those obligations fairly and promptly, each examiner is expected to have exemplary integrity and to demonstrate forthrightness in dealings with the public. The following is a list of nine guiding principles to assist the examiner in adopting a professional claims philosophy:

1. Know the plan provisions of the contracts you are responsible for handling.
2. Be sure you understand the application of the provisions. If you are not sure, ask before processing.
3. Conduct claim investigations that reflect a prompt and diligent search for the facts.
4. If additional information or clarification is required, review the claim and ask for all information required at one time. Re-pending claims and asking for additional information is extremely irritating to members.
5. Conclude each claim, large or small, on the basis of its own merits, in the light of the facts, the law,

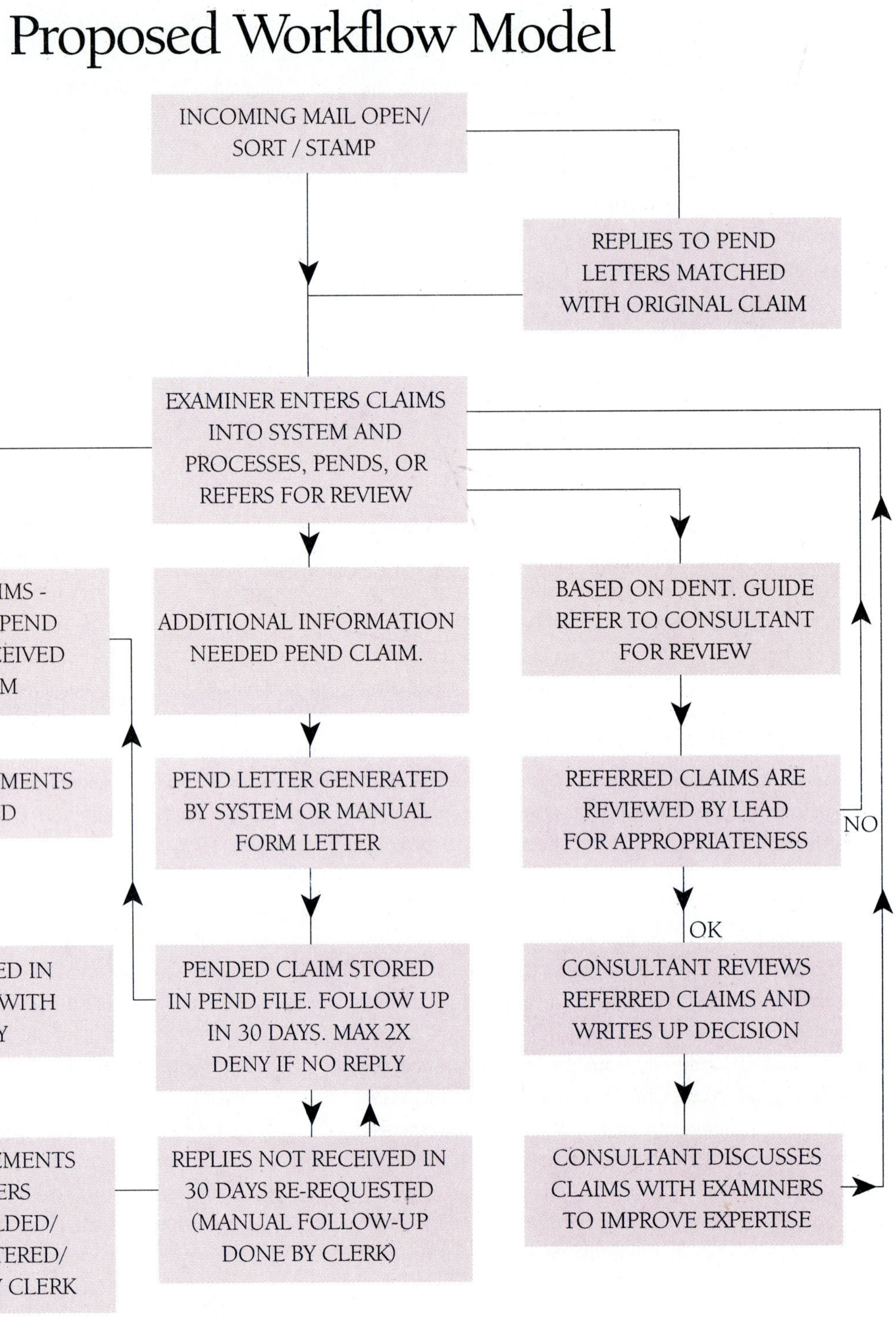

Figure 8-5: **Sample Workflow Model.**

and the coverage afforded.

6. Give a prompt, courteous, and forthright explanation to each claimant about the company's position with respect to the claim.
7. Respond promptly when a response is indicated to all communications from policyholders, claimants, attorneys, and other involved persons. (Or refer the claim promptly to the designated person responsible for responding in those situations.)
8. Seek and support new methods designed to provide improved claims service.
9. Suggest or help establish procedures and practices to:
    a. Prevent misrepresentation of the pertinent facts or policy provisions.
    b. Avoid unfair advantage by reason of superior knowledge.
    c. Maintain accurate claim records as privileged and confidential.

Claim Processing

In the following paragraphs, we will discuss coverage and guidelines for processing claims. These guidelines are generalized, and company guidelines will always supersede any of the guidelines discussed in this chapter. Use the guidelines when processing the claims in the workbook with this course. To ensure success in the claims processing portion of this chapter, review UCR before attempting to process claims if more than 2 months has elapsed since taking the UCR portion of the Health Claims Examiner/Medical Biller course.

Claim Analysis

A skill of primary importance in a good claims examiner is a thorough and systematic process for analyzing claims. The same process is used on each claim no matter how simple or complex. This is what develops consistency and accuracy. The following model may be used in the development of an individual systematic approach. Identify the issues involved in the claim. There may be many issues, including the following eight:

1. Eligibility
    a. Has the policy lapsed for nonpayment of premiums?
    b. At the time of service, was the patient currently enrolled under the plan?
    c. If a dependent, is the patient within the proper age limit. If not, is the patient a full-time student or otherwise within the extended age limit?
    d. Have all eligibility requirements set forth in the policy been met?
    e. Was any material misrepresentation made in the original application for coverage?
2. Possible other coverage
    a. Is an injury involved? If so, do you have the date, place, and circumstances of the injury on file?
    b. Is there evidence of other insurance? Could TPL be involved?
    c. Is the injury work-related? If so, Worker's Compensation coverage applies.
    d. Does the patient have other insurance that might cover these services?
3. Determine what the policy/plan language provides:
    a. What is the definition of total disability?
    b. What is the contract definition of accident and sickness?
    c. What plan provisions could apply to this claim? What plan limitations and maximums could apply to the claim?
    d. Is a preexisting limitation on the plan and how is it applied?
4. Is there any information missing from the claim which is necessary for determination of payment (diagnosis, patient, provider licensing, etc.)?
5. Obtain all relevant facts. Request all missing information or documentation at one time. Thoroughly investigate all available data. Don't pend a claim again and again and keep asking questions that should have been asked initially, all at once.
6. Make an honest evaluation of the facts and the

plan benefits. Seek assistance from supervisors or lead examiners when necessary, before, not after, pending or denying a claim.

7. Keep the member informed. Each time a claim is pended or denied, a letter must be sent. In addition, usually every 30 days a follow-up letter should be sent on a claim remaining pended.
8. No decision is final. If benefits are denied, there should always be an opportunity for reevaluation of the claim if new or different information is received.

Good Claims Practice

Consider the following five guidelines when processing claims:

1. Fully analyze the claim initially. Consider all possible basis for acceptance or denial. Look for a way to pay a claim, not deny it. Often, an initial review of a claim will reveal clear and obvious grounds for denial. Sometimes the obvious grounds disappear later when the denial is questioned. Always clearly document the grounds for denial. Resist the natural temptation to deny a claim without a complete investigation and without considering all other possible grounds for acceptance.
2. Thoroughly investigate and document the facts within the claim file. This may be one of the most important steps that each examiner needs to take before paying or denying a claim. The lack of a proper investigation or documentation has probably resulted in more bad faith charges than any other individual factor.
   a. Investigate and thoroughly document all aspects under investigation before taking a position on the status of the claim.
   b. After investigation, evaluate the facts in an impartial and objective manner. If the facts are technical or if the decision appears close, seek assistance from a lead examiner or supervisor.
   c. Verify the authenticity of the data. Is the person providing the information a qualified provider or other qualified person?
   d. Never rely on incomplete or ambiguous claim forms or inspection reports.
   e. Consider all policy provisions.
3. Handle claims promptly and keep claimants informed.
   a. Give priority to delayed/pended claims/cases.
   b. Resolve conflicting evidence or information promptly.
   c. Do not withhold or delay payments in hope of a compromise.
4. Make proper use of medical evidence.
   a. Always contact the doctor to clear up any medical questions concerning the claimant.
   b. When a second medical opinion is required, the proper selection of an independent medical examiner is very important. A specialist should be chosen for the specific disease or injury. The medical examiner must always be provided with all the claimant's relevant medical information and records, whether they are favorable or unfavorable. Also, the examiner cannot provide a correct conclusion unless the correct questions are asked. Sometimes asking the correct questions is the most difficult part of preparing a case for review.
5. In keeping with good claim practices, vigilance for excessive charges must be maintained. Some doctors will indicate a long list of diagnoses to match up the wide variety of tests given with a diagnosis, so that the patient is covered by the insurance carrier. Some situations to watch for are:
   a. High charges, a long list of diagnoses, and no subsequent visits.
   b. Multiple diagnoses involving multiple bodily functions.
   c. Services described in very technical and nonstandard medical terminology, especially in connection with exotic extensive medical testing.
   d. Vague or ambiguous diagnoses.
   e. Diagnoses involving extensive testing, beginning with hyper- or hypo- (eg, hypoglycemia, hypercholesterolemia, hypomineralism).

f. Bills that appear to be preprinted or that include wordy descriptions of services either on the bill or enclosed with the bill.

These are only a few of the instances that should alert the attention of a good claims examiner. Medical records should be requested to investigate the patient's history and chief complaints, the tests performed, and their results.

In questionable cases, use common sense and seek advice early. Often a second opinion or different point of view can clarify the situation. Don't hesitate to seek the opinions of your supervisor or lead examiner. Two areas in which help is often needed is in questioning preexisting conditions and usual and customary charges. Your responsibility is to make decisions, but prudent decisions come with time and experience. Until you have the experience, consider asking questions as a part of your learning and training experience.

Payment Worksheet

Whenever claims are processed manually, a payment worksheet must be completed by the examiner, which explains to the member how the benefits on the claim were calculated. Although worksheets vary from company to company, the general format and requirements remain the same. The worksheet that you will be using to process the claims in your workbook is explained on the following pages (see Figure 8-6).

Header Information

The header area is where the member and plan identification information are indicated. It is composed of the following fields:

1. Eligible Employee—The insured or employee's full name.
2. Company—The name of the employer or company.
3. Social Security Number—The insured or employee's social security number.
4. Patient—The patient/claimant's name.
5. Relationship—The relationship of the patient to the insured.

The following information should be filled in after completing the claim payment worksheet:

6. Accident Benefit—Amount of accident benefit year to date.
7. Lifetime Max—Amount of lifetime maximum to date.
8. Deductible—Amount of deductible, year to date.
9. Carryover Deductible—Amount of deductible carried over from the previous year.
10. Coinsurance—Amount of coinsurance paid year to date.

Claim Data Information

The body of the worksheet is where the billed services are itemized indicating the amount allowed for each service, the amount excluded, and at what percentage the amount allowed is payable. It includes the following 18 fields:

1. Procedure/Type of Service—The applicable CPT code or English language description of service.
2. Dates of Service—Date of service for the particular charge being coded out.
3. Billed Amount—The total amount of the charges for the services indicated on this single line of coding.
4. Excluded Amounts*—The amount of charges for this single line of coding that are not allowable under the plan. An explanation should be placed under Denial Reasons (asterisk reference).
5. Allowed—The amount remaining after the excluded expenses are subtracted from the total charge.
6. Basic 100%—The amount of the allowable expense that is payable at 100%. If there are multiple applicable plan percentages for a single charge, the allowable should be broken up based on the amount payable at each specific percentage.
7. Maj Med %—The Major Medical amount allowed after any higher benefits such as basic have been subtracted.
8. %—Any additional applicable percentage rate that may apply to an allowable amount. This can be due to OOP maximums, SSO not done, etc.

Payment Worksheet

Eligible Employee:	Accident Benefit: (19 ___)
Company:	Lifetime Max:
Social Security Number:	Deductible: (19 ___)
Patient:	Carryover Ded: (19 ___)
Relationship:	Coinsurance: (19 ___)

Procedure Type of Service	Dates of Service	Billed Amount	Excluded Amounts*	Allowed	Basic 100%	Maj Med ____%	____%
Remarks:		Totals:					
		Deductible:					
		Amount Subject to Coinsurance:					
		Coinsurance:					
		Amount Subject to Adjustment:					
		Adjustment (See Remarks):					
		Payment Amount:					

*Denial Reasons
1.
2.
3.
4.
5.
6.

Payees
1.
2.
3.
4.
5.
6.

Figure 8-6: **Payment Worksheet.**

9. Totals—The totals of all amounts within that column.
10. Deductible—The amount of the charges applied to the plan deductible.
11. Amount Subject to Coinsurance—Amount payable at the plan coinsurance rate after any deductible is taken.
12. Coinsurance—The coinsurance rate that is the patient's liability.
13. Amount Subject to Adjustment—The amount that would need to be adjusted because of COB, overpayment, or any other type of adjustment.
14. Adjustment (see Remarks)—The actual adjustment being made.
15. Payment Amount—The final payment that would be paid by the plan.
16. Remarks—This space is used to explain the type and reason for any adjustments being made.
17. Denial Reasons—A reason for the denial, which must be explained to the member whenever a charge or portion of a charge is not covered under a plan. The reason should be entered in this area.
18. Payees—Up to six payees entered per claim. This normally includes a maximum of providers and the employee.

Processing the Claim

Now that you know the claims examiner's responsibilities and the basic guidelines used to process a claim, let's go step by step through the processing of a medical claim using the payment worksheet just described and the guidelines just covered.

After it has been determined that the claim is filled out properly, the patient is covered, the provider is appropriate, there is no other insurance, and the services are covered, it is time to begin processing the claim.

The first step is to determine the allowable amount for the service or procedure. Using the Relative Value Study listed in the back of the workbook, locate the unit value for the CPT code assigned to the service provided. The unit value for the procedure is located in the right-hand column titled Total RVUs.

Next, determine the conversion factor for the procedure from the UCR Conversion Factor Report. Using the first three numbers of the zip code of the provider, locate the type of service. Each of four categories is listed next to the zip code location. The categories are:

1. Surgery
2. Medicine
3. X-ray/Lab
4. Anesthesia

Multiply the appropriate conversion factor by the unit value for the procedure. Remember the appropriate category is determined by the CPT code, not the description of service. This gives you the allowable amount. However, if the billed amount is less than the allowable amount, the billed amount is considered to be the allowable amount.

Completing the Claim Payment Worksheet

The claim payment worksheet is equivalent to an explanation of benefits. A copy of this form will be sent to the insured to explain the benefit payment for the claim. Therefore, each section should be filled out completely to decrease the possibility of confusion on the part of the claimant.

The claim payment worksheet used for this course is intended to be an example only. It contains the information in much the same format as other insurance carrier payment forms. This worksheet and the guidelines for completing it are to be used for training and reference purposes only, since the particular company or plan worksheets and guidelines may differ.

Complete the information regarding the patient and the insured first. This information is contained in the box in the upper left-hand corner of the payment worksheet.

Next, each CPT code should be listed in the first column on the claim payment worksheet. Only codes that are the same should be combined together, otherwise list one service per line, regardless of whether this means using more than one claim payment worksheet.

List the date(s) of service in the second column and

the amount that the provider billed in the third column. Next, skip to the fifth column (Allowed) and enter the allowed amount as figured above. Subtract the allowed amount from the billed amount. The resulting figure is the excluded amount that goes in the fourth column. Remember, if the allowed amount is greater than the billed amount, the billed amount will be the allowable amount. Therefore, the excluded amount will be $0.00.

Make sure that you also enter a denial reason on the corresponding line in the denial reasons section. Usually, a brief explanation such as "$21.83 Not covered—charge exceeds amount covered by your plan" is sufficient. If the service is not covered, the corresponding code (or description) and an explanation should be listed in the same manner (ie, $300.00 Not covered—cosmetic services are not covered by your plan).

If the plan has a basic allowance, the unit value should be multiplied by the basic allowance listed in the contract. For example, if the contract stipulates that the basic allowance for an office visit is $7.00 and the service has a unit value of 1.0, then the basic allowance is $7.00. The basic allowance amount should be placed in the sixth column (Basic 100%). The basic allowance is subtracted from the allowed amount and the remainder is placed in the seventh column.

After all the charges have been figured individually, the total for each column is added up and placed at the bottom of the column. Check your totals for accuracy by adding the allowed amount to the excluded amount. The total of these two figures should match the billed amount on the claim. Likewise, the sixth and seventh columns added together should equal the allowed amount.

If the contract allows different percentages depending on the type of service (eg, basic services paid at 100%, major medical at 80%, and so on), then all services with a similar copayment amount should be placed together in a single column. There is an additional, eighth column to allow for varying percentages.

Figuring the Benefit Payment

Now calculate the actual benefit payment. At the top of each payment column (columns 6 through 8), place the coinsurance percentage amount that applies to the figures in that column.

Check the contract for the deductible amount and the Beginning Financials for any previously paid deductible amounts.

- Has the deductible for this individual been satisfied?
- Does the deductible combine the medical plan with a dental plan (the plans are integrated)?
- If so, has the deductible been satisfied under the medical or dental portion of the contract?
- Has the family deductible been satisfied?
- Is there any carryover deductible from the previous year?

Using the latter questions and information, calculate the deductible that should be applied to this claim. The amount of the deductible is placed across from the word deductible in the first column in which benefits are payable at less than 100% (deductible is not taken from basic benefits). If the deductible remaining is more than the amount of the column, the amount of the column should be placed in the deductible box and any remaining amounts carried over to additional columns with less than a 100% coinsurance amount.

Subtract the deductible amount from the total of the column. The remaining amount is the portion that is subject to coinsurance.

Multiply the amount subject to coinsurance by the insured's portion of the coinsurance amount (the remaining amount needed to reach 100%). For example, if the plan's coinsurance amount is 80%, then the insured's responsibility is 20%. Next, ask the following questions:

- What is the maximum coinsurance amount listed in the contract?
- Has this coinsurance limit been met?
- If the individual coinsurance limit has not been met, has the family coinsurance limit been met?

If any coinsurance limits have been met, the coinsurance amount should be adjusted accordingly. For example, if the individual coinsurance limit is $1500 and $1495 has been paid by the individual, the coinsurance amount is $5.00. The correct coinsurance amount goes in the next space labeled coinsurance.

Now subtract the coinsurance amount from the amount subject to coinsurance. The remaining balance is the amount subject to adjustment and goes in the next column. Then ask:

- If there is other insurance, what is the amount paid by the other insurance company?
- Are there any other reasons why there would be an adjustment on this claim?
- If so, what is the proper adjustment amount?

If there is an adjustment, the amount of the adjustment should be placed in the following box labeled "Adjustment (see remarks)," and an explanation should be placed in the remarks box to the left.

The adjustment is then subtracted from the amount subject to adjustment, and results are written in the payment amount (following box). The payment amount from each column should be added together, and the resulting payment amount placed in the box immediately to the right of the words "Payment Amount." This is the amount of the benefits being paid by the insurance carrier.

Note: If any individual or family deductible or coinsurance amounts have been met with this claim, an asterisk should be placed beside the deductible or coinsurance amount and a notation made in the remarks box (eg, 1992 Family deductible has been met).

ERISA

Federal ERISA requirements affect all claim denials. The ERISA Right of Review statement must be included with every claim denial and on every EOB where all or part of a claim is denied. The following is wording that may be used:

> If you disagree with our decision on your claim, you have the right by law to request that your claim be reviewed by your plan administrator. This request must be made in writing within 60 days of receipt of this notice. If you wish, you may submit your written comments and views. Please consult your plan's claim review procedures. See your employer on any other ERISA questions.

Payees

Now all that is left is to determine to whom to make out the check and to update the financial history. Look back on the claim form. Benefits may be assigned to the provider of services by the member. The assignment must bear the member's written signature on a form that authorizes benefits payable directly to the provider of service. An assigment or authorization to pay benefits is a statement usually included on the claim form, which permits the member to authorize the administrator to pay benefits directly to the person or institution who provided the service. The examiner is required to honor all valid assignments made by the member.

When reviewing a claim, note whether an assignment has been made. If payment is made because of failure to honor an assignment and benefits are released to the member, the provider of service can also request payment, and payment must be made to the provider as well. The incorrect payment made to the member must be recouped, and this will be covered in Chapter 21. Ensuring that all valid assignments are honored is a basic part of good claim handling.

When processing a claim, ask yourself, did the insured authorize payment directly to the provider of services or is there a mandatory assignment of benefits?

- If not, the payee would be the insured.
- If so, check the billed amount from the claim and the amount (if any) that the patient/insured has already paid. If the difference between the billed amount and the amount that the patient or insured paid (balance due) is more than the benefit payment amount, the payee would be the provider of services. If the difference between the billed amount and the amount that the patient or insured paid (balance due) is less than the benefit payment amount, the payee would be the provider of services up to the balance due. Any remaining funds would then be paid to the insured.

Updating History

Updating the payment history is vitally important to ensure that proper benefit payments are calculated. Each preceding question that related to previous payments of deductibles, coinsurance amounts, satisfaction of individual or family limits, accident benefits, and others will change with the processing of each claim.

On our payment worksheet, the updated history appears in the upper left-hand corner of the sheet.

If claims are processed by computer, the computer should handle the updating of the history for you.

If accident benefits were paid on this claim, add the payment amount of the accident benefits to any previous accident benefit amounts paid on this individual in this calendar year. The amount goes on the first line along with the current year.

The amount of the benefits paid under Major Medical should be added to all previous benefits paid. If the plan has a calendar year maximum rather than a lifetime maximum, the amount of the benefits paid should be added to all previous benefits paid during that calendar year. The result should be placed in the lifetime maximum space on the next line. Usually, basic benefits on Basic and Major Medical plans do not apply to lifetime paid amounts. Check the contract to see whether there are separate maximums for Basic and Major Medical payment amounts. If the plan calls for a calendar year maximum, the word lifetime should be replaced by the words "calendar year" and the current year should be included.

The amount of any deductibles calculated on this claim should be added to any previously paid deductible amounts and the result placed in the deductible space with the current year.

If any of the dates of service on this claim fall within the last 3 months of the calendar year and the contract includes a carryover provision, the amount of deductible paid on these services should be placed on the line labeled "carryover deductible," along with the year. If there is more than one date of service and if some are in the last 3 months and others are not, the deductible amount should be taken from the amount or amounts of the services in the order in which they are received. For example:

An exam and x-ray were performed on 9/18/93. Two moles were found and an appointment was made to remove them on 10/10/93. The billed amount for the exam and x-ray was $40.00, and all of it was allowed (the UCR amount was higher than the billed amount). The allowed amount for the mole removal was $120.00. The patient had previously satisfied $25.00 of the $100.00 deductible. The total paid deductible amount would be $75.00 on this claim. Forty dollars of the deductible would be for the first two services and $35.00 would be for the two moles removed. Therefore, $35.00 would be considered the carryover deductible amount.

Finally, add the amount listed on the coinsurance line with any previous coinsurance amounts for the calendar year. The total, along with the year, should be placed on the coinsurance line of the financial history box. You have now completed payment on this claim.

Computing Stop Loss

Many Major Medical contracts have a provision that provides for a greater reimbursement percentage (usually 100%) following the payment of a certain dollar amount for a calendar year period. This provision limits the amount of money that the member/patient is responsible for on allowable charges. Of course, such a provision would apply only toward "allowable" charges. Expenses not allowed under the plan, such as UCR excess amounts and noncovered expenses, would not be applied toward the stop loss. The patient would remain entirely responsible for their payment.

An example of such contract wording follows:
80% of the first $5000 100% thereafter.

Example 1
The plan coinsurance rate is 90%.
Stop loss is $6000.
Major Medical paid to date for the year is $5200.
Claim: $2000 eligible under Major Medical.

Step 1. Subtract the amount in Major Medical paid to date for the year from the plan's stop loss limit.

$6000.00
– 5200.00
$ 800.00

$800.00 is 90% of the amount that must be considered by the payor to max the stop loss for the year.

Step 2. Calculate the amount that $800.00 is 90% of to determine the amount of eligible charges subject to the coinsurance stop loss limit.

$800.00 divided by .90 = $888.89

$888.89 will be covered at 90% to meet the stop loss limitation.

Step 3. Figure the total payment on the claim by doing the following:

A. Subtract the amount covered at 90%, $888.89, from the allowable charges on the claim to determine the amount that will be paid at 100% because the stop loss limit has been met.

$2000.00
– 888.89
$1111.11 = Payable at 100%

B. Multiply $888.89 by the plan's coinsurance rate of 90% to determine the amount payable by the payor.

$888.89
x .90
$800.00 (see Step 2)

C. Add the amount payable at 100% to the amount payable at 90%.

$1111.11
+ 800.00
$1911.11 = Total amount payable on this claim

Step 4. The plan's stop loss has now been met. Subsequent allowable charges will be payable at 100% (there are some exceptions on some plans). Some types of expenses, such as nervous and mental, remain at a specific coinsurance rate regardless of whether the coinsurance limit has been met.

Note: To determine the member's out-of-pocket amount, subtract the amount paid at 90%, $800.00, from the amount subject to the coinsurance rate, $888.89.

$888.89
– 800.00
$88.89 = Member's responsibility, OOP.

Example 2

The plan's coinsurance rate is 80%.
Stop loss is $6000.
Major Medical paid to year is $5700.
Claim: $2000 eligible under Major Medical.

Step 1. Subtract the amount applied to the Major Medical stop loss limit to date.

$6000.00
– 5700.00
$300.00

Step 2. Calculate the amount that $300.00 is 80% of to determine the amount of eligible charges subject to the coinsurance stop loss limit.

$300.00 divided by .80 = $375.00

$375.00 will be covered at 80% to meet the stop loss limitation.

Step 3. Figure the total payment on the claim by doing the following:

A. Subtract the amount covered at 80%, $375.00, from the allowable charges on the claim to determine the amount that will be paid at 100% because the stop loss limit has been met.

$2000.00
– 375.00
$1625.00 = Payable at 100%

B. Multiply $375.00 by the plan's coinsurance rate of 80% to determine the amount payable by the payor.

$75.00
x .80
$300.00 (see Step 2)

C. Add the amount payable at 100% to the amount paid at 80%.

$1625.00
+ 300.00
$1925.00 = Total amount payable on this claim

$375.00
– 300.00
$ 75.00 = Member's out-of-pocket amount on this claim

Step 4. The plan's stop loss has now been met. Subsequent allowable charges are payable at 100% (there are some exceptions on some plans). Some types of expenses, such as nervous and mental, remain at a specific coinsurance rate regardless of whether or not the coinsurance limit has been met.

Example 3

The plan's coinsurance rate is 70%.

Stop loss is $5000.

Major Medical paid to year is $4000.

Claim: $4500 eligible under Major Medical (Total submitted charges: $5000).

Step 1. Subtract the amount applied to the Major Medical stop loss limit to date.

$5000.00
– 4000.00
$1000.00

Step 2. Calculate the amount that $1000.00 is 70% of to determine the amount of eligible charges subject to the coinsurance stop loss limit.

$1000.00 divided by .70 = $ 1,428.57

$1428.57 will be covered at 70% to meet the stop loss limitation.

Step 3. Figure the total payment on the claim by doing the following:

A. Subtract the amount covered at 70%, $1428.57, from the allowable charges on the claim to determine the amount that will be paid at 100%, since the stop loss limit has been met.

$4500.00
– 1428.57
$3071.43 = Payable at 100%

B. Multiply $1428.57 by the plan's coinsurance rate of 70% to determine the amount payable by the payor.

$1428.57
x .70
$1000.00 (see Step 2)

C. Add the amount payable at 100% to the amount paid at 70%.

$3071.43
+1000.00
$4071.43 = Total amount payable on this claim

$1428.57
– 1000.00
$ 428.57 = Member's out-of-pocket amount on this claim

Step 4. The plan's stop loss has now been met.

Quick Reference Formulas

Plan UCR

Unit value x plan conversion factor = plan UCR

Anesthesia: Time units + procedure unit value x plan conversion factor

(TU + UV) x CF = ANES. ALLOW.

Multiple Surgery: 100% of the basic or UCR allowance for the major procedure.

Noncovered Charges

Total charges minus allowable amounts (UCR).

TC – UCR = NC

Basic Allowance

Procedure unit value x basic conversion factor.

UV x BCF = BASIC

Major Medical Allowance

Plan Major Medical UCR allowance minus basic allowance.

MM UCR –BASIC = MM ALLOWABLE

Major Medical Payment

Plan UCR minus basic allowance minus applicable deductibles multiplied by plan coinsurance rate.

(UCR – BASIC) – DEDS x % = MM PAYMT

Total Payment

Major Medical payment plus basic payment.

MM + BASIC = TP

Processing Drug Claims

Many health plans cover expenses for prescription drugs. However, these drugs must often meet the following three criteria:

1. They must be prescribed by the member's physician. This physician must be duly licensed and able to prescribe medications in the state in which the prescription was issued.
2. They must be prescription medications (ie, they must, by law, require a prescription from a licensed physician for their dispensation).
3. They must be prescribed to treat a disease, bodily injury, or a mental or nervous disorder.

Some plans may cover prescriptions that do not meet the above criteria. These can include antacids, eye and ear medications, compounded dermatologic preparations, or other medications. If these drugs are listed, they will be specifically indicated in the policy.

Nonprescription drugs are generally not covered under the provisions of a contract. In addition, some prescription drugs may not be covered. These can include:

- Contraceptives prescribed for contraception.
- Dietary supplements, health foods, or vitamins (including prenatal vitamins).
- Appetite suppressants.

The *Physician's Desk Reference* should be consulted to determine whether a drug is a prescription or a nonprescription drug.

Handling Prescription Claims

Prescription drugs can be issued on an outpatient or inpatient basis. For the guidelines regarding payment for inpatient drugs (including those issued for take-home), see Chapter 14.

For outpatient drug claims, certain guidelines should be followed. These include the following nine:

1. A valid claim form must be on file showing the eligible diagnosis for which the drugs are being issued. This form shows that the patient was under the care of a physician for the covered diagnosis when the prescription was issued. After a valid claim form has been accepted, it is not necessary for a new claim form to accompany each drug claim as long as the patient is still under the doctor's care and the diagnosis is still valid. For example, if the diagnosis is of a chronic nature, drugs will often be refills of earlier prescriptions.
2. The pharmacy bill, receipt, or pharmacy statement for each prescription must accompany the request for payment.
3. All drug receipts or pharmacy bills must show the prescription number, the name of the physician, the name of the patient, the date of issuance, and the amount charged. If any of these items are omitted, the validity of the prescription should be checked prior to payment of the claim. Some receipts may also list the type of drug. This is helpful for determining whether the drug is a prescription drug or an over-the-counter drug.
4. The drugs must be appropriate for the condition being treated, the amount of time since the first diagnosis of the condition, and the amount of drug prescribed. For example, persons suffering from a serious heart disease or diabetes may require large amounts of drugs over an extended period of time, whereas a patient suffering from an ear infection would require a small amount of drugs over a much shorter period of time.
5. If prescriptions are questionable, further information should be obtained from the prescribing physician, not from the patient. Causes for review include:

   a. The amount of the prescription expense is not appropriate to the condition being treated.

b. The drugs are generally used to treat conditions that are not covered under the policy (eg, exogenous obesity, contraception).
c. The claim is for contraceptive medications. If the woman is over the age of 45, many doctors prescribe contraceptive medications for hormone imbalance. Some plans may cover contraceptives issued for these reasons, but not for contraceptive reasons.
d. A large number of prescription claims is submitted at one time. This may indicate claims being submitted for prescriptions that were issued to more than one person.
e. The prescription or information on any claim appears to have been altered.

6. If a receipt or statement is received for more than one drug, care should be taken to determine which drugs are covered and which are not. Often several types appear on the same claim.
7. Plan provisions should be checked to determine which drugs are covered and which are not. Also drugs issued for a noncovered diagnosis should be denied as noncovered. For example, morphine would be covered for heart surgery but not for cosmetic surgery.
8. Check the licensure of the prescribing doctor. In many states, physicians, dentists, podiatrists, and psychiatrists are allowed to prescribe medications. However, chiropractors, naturopaths, optometrists and psychologists are not. These doctors may suggest or dispense nonprescription medications, food supplements, or vitamins. However, since these items are not generally covered under the plan, no benefits would be payable. If the drug appears to be a prescription drug, but the physician indicated is not a physician, dentist, podiatrist, or psychiatrist, further investigation is warranted.
9. Finally, check the appropriate coverages for drug claims. Most prescription drugs are covered under Major Medical benefits and would be processed according to the general guidelines given in the Major Medical contract. However, there may be specific plan provisions on medications. Care should also be taken to check the exclusions listed in the policy because this is where several exclusions to types of drugs and diagnoses will be listed.

Red Book and Blue Book

Some plans have a separate drug subcoverage. Drugs on these plans are often paid according to a set price schedule, regardless of the amount charged by the pharmacy or dispensing physician. These schedules are often based upon the Drug Blue Book or the Drug Red Book. These two books list the wholesale prices of drugs.

Often the plan provisions will specify payment at 150% or 175% of the Drug Blue Book or Drug Red Book price. Typical wording of the contract often reads as follows:

a. Eligible expenses are X% (150% or 175%) of the Red Book or Blue book plus ($1.50, $1.35, or $1.65), or the charge, whichever is less.
b. Coverage is limited to (31-day, 90-day, 100-day) supply, except for maintenance drugs, which are limited to a (100-day) supply.
c. Benefits are payable at (50%, 75%, or 100%).

To find the correct payment amount, first determine the manufacturer of the drug. If the drug manufacturer is not listed, the information should be looked up using the *Physician's Desk Reference*. The least expensive generic drug should be used to calculate benefits.

Determine the charge for the smallest quantity listed, then determine the price per unit. The unit may be indicated in quantification by tables, by ounces, or by some other measurement. If the drugs are listed in metric units and the prescription is issued in nonmetric units, the metric units must be converted to nonmetric units (or vice versa). Metric conversion tables can be found in most medical dictionaries.

You then multiply the price per unit times the number of units dispensed. This is the wholesale price for the drug. This wholesale price should be multiplied by the X% (150% or 175%) indicated by the plan. Then, add any amount indicated as $A ($1.50, $1.35, or $1.65). If this amount is more than the amount charged, the amount charged should be used. If not, this amount is considered the allowable amount. This allowed amount is then paid at the (50%, 75%, or 100%) amount at which benefits are payable.

Summary

We have covered several important responsibilities of the claims examiner, including some basic guidelines that apply to each duty. By applying these guidelines, the examiner will establish a practice that will enable him or her to routinely make clear and concise claim decisions.

Assignments

Complete Questions for Review.

Questions for Review

Directions: Answer the following questions without looking back into the material just covered. Write your answers in the space provided.

1. Name the three types of manual claim files that may be used in a claims processing system.
   a. Family
   b. Patient
   c. Batch.
2. If the claim cannot be processed upon receipt, the claim file must be pend + investigated.
3. Referrals should be made for which three types of claims?
   a. law suits
   b. fraud
   c. flagged
4. Briefly explain the pended claim follow-up procedure.
   diary 3-4 weeks then send 2nd request
5. Why is it important to update payment history? make sure proper payment is made

If you were unable to answer any of the questions, refer back to the section and then complete the answers.

9

Fraud

In this chapter you will learn:

- To understand what constitutes fraud and the procedures to follow when fraud is suspected.

Fraud is defined in Webster's Dictionary as "deception to cause a person to give up property or something of lawful right." Fraud is synonymous with deceit, trickery, cheat, and imposter. Schemes for gain involve almost every conceivable form of deception, from a subtle omission of fact to the most flagrant lie.

Fraud can be perpetrated by anyone and involves every type of claim. Doctors, lawyers, hospitals, claimants, beneficiaries, and claims handlers working for an insurance company are capable of committing fraud. It is estimated that millions of dollars annually are paid out by the health benefits industry on fraudulent claims. Regardless of who or how the expenses are submitted for payment, the overall impact on claim payments, premiums, administrative costs, and other expenses is devastating.

Forms of Fraud

Fortunately, most claims are legitimate and forthright. Therefore, a claims examiner should not automatically assume fraud. However, awareness of the possibility is necessary to properly recognize and detect those instances of fraud. The two major areas of fraud concern are:

1. Internal fraud, which involves the employees of the company against which the fraud is perpetrated. The employee may act alone or with another or other employees.
2. External fraud, which involves people outside the company that it is directed against. Claims personnel are often the innocent parties through whose routine claim paying activities the fraud is discovered.

Fraud can assume many different shapes and forms and is as limitless as the creativity of the human mind. Some forms are more obvious than others. With training and experience, a competent examiner develops a sense about claims that do not appear "just right." In such cases, the examiner needs to listen to that sense and take steps to explore such a possibility. The following scenarios may be of assistance in identifying fraudulent situations:

- A member is covered for group hospital benefits as both an employee and a dependent. This fact is concealed to avoid COB.
- A prospective insured has been receiving medical treatment for hypertension. This question is answered negatively on an application for life insurance in an effort to obtain coverage not otherwise available or at a more favorable premium rate.
- A member has a condition that requires prescription medication. Dates on the bills are altered and photocopies plus the originals are filed to receive multiple payments for the same charges.
- An employee photocopies another claimant's bills, replacing the actual claimant data with his or her own. The bills are marked paid and the fake claims are submitted as his or her own.
- The insured's attending physician signs a return to work release. Discarding this, the insured shops for another doctor who will extend disability.
- The insured stages an intentional injury to appear accidental.
- A worker strains his back lifting a TV set at home. The next day, coworkers find the insured lying at the bottom of a flight of stairs complaining of back pain. A Workers' Compensation claim for loss of wages and medical expenses is filed.
- The member's spouse sustains a stroke and requires constant custodial care at home. The member's stable, chronic condition suddenly becomes acute, thus rendering the member unable to continue working and enabling the member to remain home and care for the spouse.

Although the list of potential fraud situations is endless, an attitude of alertness and thorough and conscious efforts can curb the success of the various scenarios.

The following four procedures can assist in establishing a case of fraud and subsequent successful prosecution.

1. If the file is out of the ordinary in any way or contains discrepancies, be inquisitive. Try to determine why file statements or circumstances con-

flict with expected conclusions. The claim should be filed in a timely manner. Information about other insurance, the how, when, and where of the accident, and the names and addresses of all attending physicians and witnesses should be freely available from the claimant. Appearance of undue anxiety or anger on the part of the claimant or beneficiary for a prompt payment could be a fraud indicator. Any alteration of a claim form or bill is to be questioned.

Sometimes routine, in-depth file reviews of original claim files disclose questionable elements or trends. Suspicious elements should not be ignored and should be pursued and developed.

A questionable element in one area of a claim file often points to further discrepancies in other areas, until an entire series of payments may be found to have been made but not owed. Follow through on all leads and clues. Be sure claims are handled promptly. Use tact in pursuing possible fraud indicators.

Attempts to recognize and deal with fraud are a basic part of an overall philosophy of good claim practices. There is not only a contractual obligation to properly handle possible fraudulent situations, but a social obligation as well. Like any other crime, insurance fraud is detrimental to society in many ways, including the influence it may have in increasing the overall price of benefit coverage.

2. Although investigation of fraudulent claims may be thorough and complete and the documentation may seem irrefutable, fraud is often difficult to prove in court. In some cases, depending on the nature of the fraud, the insurance company or administrator may be hesitant to prosecute because of the possibility of a countersuit on the charge of libel. This does not mean that efforts to resolve fraudulent claims should be restricted. Rather, this emphasizes the need for in-depth investigation and development of a complete, accurate claim file so that any fraud case that is prosecuted will be as solid as possible. Thorough investigation increases the chances that the case will be prosecuted in the courts, that prosecution will be successful, and that the occurrence of countercharges for libel will be reduced.
3. Although each examiner must recognize and investigate each case of potential fraud, actual and overall control should be retained by management. In the process of prosecuting fraud, many persons have certain definite responsibilities. Cooperation among and between several different departments is essential. Communication plays a critical role in the investigation process.
4. In identifying possible fraud, some "indicators" may help to isolate situations. No single indicator is necessarily suspicious, nor is it evidence that fraud has occurred. The examiner must assume an identity of an investigator and put all of the facts and indicators together to see whether fraud is actually present. Following are some indicators that have been put into categories for easier reference.

Fraud Indicators

Indicators associated with the claimant or insured (employee) are as follows:

- Claimant is overly "pushy" and demanding of a quick claim settlement.
- Claimant is unusually familiar with insurance terminology or claims procedures.
- Claimant handles business in person or by phone, apparently avoiding use of the mail. (Using the mail for such purposes is a federal felony.)
- Attorney or claimant is willing to accept less than the actual claim estimate just to help out and resolve the matter quickly.
- Insured/claimant contacts the insurance agent to verify coverage or extent of coverage just prior to loss.
- Attorney representation is coincident with or shortly after injury date and threatens a bad-faith lawsuit unless the carrier or administrator agrees to settle quickly.

- No police report was made or only an over-the-counter report occurred, when police would usually investigate the actual scene.
- Claimants or witnesses use post office box or hotel addresses.
- Claimant has multiple policies covering the same loss.
- Unwitnessed, one-car or hit-and-run accidents.
- Medical treatment is declined at the time of the accident, but injured party is later hospitalized for "extensive" injuries.
- History of previous loss with similar treatment exists, or the same doctor or attorney repeatedly handles medical or lost earnings claims following minor accidents.
- Claimant has a history of numerous past questionable claims.
- Trends can be observed on billing statements or treatments by providers that appear to show excessive charges. These may include same fees and treatment regardless of condition, differences between amounts billed to patient, and amounts on claim forms.

Claim Processing and Claim Inflation Indicators

During claim review, "discrepancies" seem to exist. Often, these are "flags" that should warn the examiner to go over the claim papers more thoroughly or to check past history in depth. Rather than being obvious, these indicators are often "seen" only after a number of payments have occurred. Things to look for include:

- A minor accident produces major accident costs, lost wages, and so on.
- Medical bills indicate routine treatment being provided on Sundays, holidays, or usual doctor's day off.
- Summary medical bills are submitted without itemization of office visits or treatments.
- Photocopies of medical, prescription, or dental bills; third or fourth generation bills especially suspect. Photocopies of claim forms contain alterations or corrections.
- Receipts or bills are submitted without provider's letterhead.
- Several different typefaces, handwritings, or colors of ink are on claim forms or bills.
- Unusually high number of treatments are noted for relatively minor conditions. Such ailments persist for weeks or months.
- Insurance effective or employment commenced just a short time prior to the claim.
- Condition is diagnosed subjectively as "nausea," "fatigue," "inability to sleep," "headaches," "low back pain," "sprain," "whiplash," and so on.
- Patient's statement that services were not received as shown on the billing.
- Provider accepts claim payment as payment in full for services rendered, regardless of the billed amount.
- Unassigned benefits are seen on large medical claim amounts with questionable evidence to support payment in full and with a claim form as the only information submitted. Supporting bills are seldom, if ever, included.
- Incorrect or incomplete forms are submitted. For example, there are questionable signatures from providers (ie, doctor's name is signed "Doctor J. Jones" instead of "J. Jones, MD").
- Unusual or unfamiliar medical terms, misspelled medical words, or a nonexistent diagnosis are found.
- Improbable, impossible treatment or unlikely surgery (eg, second appendectomy, bilateral procedure questionable) is listed.
- Doctor's specialty is not related to patient's diagnosis (eg, male treated by Ob-Gyn specialist, severe heart problem treated by chiropractor).

Insurance Speculation Indicators

Insurance speculation means buying insurance or coverage for the purpose of making a profit. It may include "staging" a fake death or accident to make claims under more than one policy. Collusion with others may occur. Things to look for are as follows:

- An attorney demand or threat of lawsuit even before a claimant files a claim.
- Claims reported late.
- Instant pressure from the claimant or provider to pay fast.

- Multiple hospital indemnity coverages held by claimant or combined hospital, medical, accident, and hospital indemnity policies.
- Denial or omission of information about other insurance coverage.

Other Indicators of Fraud

Indicators pointing to employee embezzlement usually apply to employees within or even outside the claim operation. Access to claim files is usually involved. Things to look for include:

- Payee name or address does not match claim form, bills, or other pertinent material.
- Change in lifestyle or lifestyle is inconsistent with expected income level.
- Undocumented claim file actions are found such as voids, reversals, reissued payments by employee.
- Provider bills and claim forms do not match explanation of benefits; unusual payee, questionable assignment/nonassignments are noted.
- Claim payments are split by examiner to allow payment to be within "dollar authorization levels."
- No documentation is located for many payments on a claimant's file. System production records and manual counts of work do not match, with claim papers missing from daily correspondence files.
- Overutilization of certain benefits: claims are for hospitalization or extensive treatment indicating total disability, and claimant was not observed to have been absent or ill from work.
- Pattern of accident claims by an individual or family is found.
- Alteration of bills is made for other family member's expense, to allow payment under another member's history to avoid deductible, and so on.

Investigation

Investigation means "an organized effort to discover the facts or truth of the matter."

Legitimate claims should be paid promptly and in accordance with scheduled allowances. The handling of such claims should reflect a positive service attitude. The same amount of effort and determination should go into the denial of every illegitimate claim. The claims examiner cannot accomplish this purpose without exercising investigative efforts whenever claim discrepancies occur.

During review of every claim, the examiner must be alert to items that do not "look right." Because most claims are payable without further question, it is only necessary to investigate claims that raise questions.

Although investigation of facts takes time, it is absolutely necessary to properly document the claim file. Threats of contacting a State Department of Insurance or threat of lawsuit should not deter continued investigation as long as the examiner and his or her supervisor are relatively sure that the claim investigation is justified. No delays can be unaccounted for. The claimant or the provider should be kept well informed of the claim's status regarding what has been requested and what items are necessary or outstanding, in order to complete the processing of the claim. Be aware of legal time standards required in responding to claimants and in communicating regularly during investigation.

Be candid with persons inquiring about the claim to a point. Do not hesitate to let him or her know that the claim needs further research to determine the validity of the facts presented. Avoid words that can be damaging to a case, such as "crook," and "thief"; never make accusations (see Table 9-1).

Table 9-1: Investigation Terminology

Words to Avoid	Word to Use
Investigation	Clarification of charges, services, etc
Fraud	Incomplete or omitted information
Lied	Inconsistency in information reported
Any other derogatory remark or term	"It appears that..."

Prompt, cautious contact with information sources is essential in every investigation. When possible fraud indicators are present, a greater degree of caution must be exercised and the source of suspected fraud must be taken into account when various contacts are made.

Remember that all plans have the right to investigate and confirm the validity of the submitted information.

Inside Sources of Fraud

Whenever a company's employees within or outside the claim processing area appear to be involved in questionable activity, the claims examiner should contact his or her supervisor, personnel director, or others in management.

Under no circumstances should the matter be discussed with anyone other than management personnel in a secluded area. It is then up to management to decide how the matter will be handled.

Outside Sources of Fraud

Whenever insureds, members, claimants, or other persons (not including the provider of service) appear to be involved in fraud, careful contact with providers of services should be made. These contacts involve the verification of dates, type of services rendered, and amounts charged to the patient. Verification of disability and accident-related information is also included. The use of an outside investigator may be required to expedite the contact. All contact should be documented in writing. If possible, the information should be requested in writing, and the reply should also be given in writing with the name and title of the person supplying the information.

When providers of services appear to be involved in fraud, careful contact with the member/claimant should be made. Limit verification to dates and types of treatment and to amounts of charges for those services. Avoid discussion regarding diagnoses. As previously indicated, all information requested and received should be documented in writing whenever possible.

Building the Claim File

The following five steps should be taken to build the evidence in a claim file.

1. Carefully document all discrepancies, conflicting facts, omissions. Do not write on any of the original submitted claim documents. Make notes on a note pad or separate pieces of paper.
2. Make a written record of pertinent points of phone conversations. Summarize conflicting facts that were obtained by phone and note any new information carefully. Include dates of conversations, names, and phone numbers of contacts.
3. Place all documents in the order in which they occurred or were received. Keep a log that clearly shows the dates of all communications and whom they were with.
4. Retain the envelopes on all documents mailed to the office. Attach it to the back of the documentation received.
5. Coordinate the investigation with the insurance company's or administrator's legal department or counsel.

Checkpoint for Spotting Provider Fraud and Insurance Abuse

Every claims examiner should be aware of the possibility of fraud and briefly check each claim for fraudulent indicators. The following checklist should alert you to the need for further investigation, although one or more of these factors does not prove that fraud exists. Look carefully for the following situations:

- When the insured lists "no insurance coverage" on hospital admission forms.
- When the insured does not assign benefits on inpatient hospital bills.
- When proof of accident or illness includes photocopies of documents, forms, or bills with altered dates or receipts with serialized numbers.
- When prescription bills submitted for payment are consecutively numbered.
- When claimants say that the insurance company is being billed for services not received or treatment not provided.
- When claims are submitted for injuries not reported or not witnessed.
- When you notice the doctor's portion of the bill or claim form has erasures or strikeovers.

Summary

Submission of fraudulent claims has hit epidemic levels due to a recessed economy. Payments for fraudulent claims cost administrators millions of dollars annually.

One of the qualities of a good claims examiner is the ability to use good judgment in making claim decisions. Fraud is a very sensitive issue, and the guidelines we have just covered should be practiced along with your company guidelines to ensure accurate and fair claims decisions.

Assignments

Complete the Questions for Review.

Questions for Review

Directions: Answer the following questions without looking back into the material just covered. Write your answers in the space provided.

1. What are the two main areas of fraud concern?________________________________

   a. ____

   b. ____

2. ______________________ involves people outside the company against which it is directed.
3. __________ is fraud that involves the employees of the company against which the fraud is perpetrated.
4. A claims examiner should avoid words that can be extremely damaging to a case. (True or False) ________
5. Prompt, cautious contact with information sources is essential to every investigation. (True or False) ______

If you were unable to answer any of the questions, refer back to the section and then complete the answers.

10

Physician's Services

In this chapter you will learn:

- To identify services that fall within the medical/physician's services 90000 code range of the CPT.
- To understand how the physician's services section is broken down, when codes should be used, and which providers may bill using these codes.
- To properly code and process physician's services claims.

The most common services billed by a physician are office and hospital visits. We will review and discuss some specific physician's services and basic guidelines and coverage for these services.

When referring to medical services, there are three basic categories:

1. Professional services
   a. Surgical
   b. Nonsurgical
2. Facility services
3. Miscellaneous services

Professional services are those performed by a licensed individual such as a medical doctor, nurse, or chiropractor. Facility services are those provided by a "place," for example, a hospital or clinic. Equipment usage and room fees (eg, operating room, x-ray equipment) are considered facility expenses. Miscellaneous services are all other types of expenses not included in the previous categories. For example, prescriptions, medical equipment (wheelchairs, crutches), and ambulance expenses all are considered miscellaneous types of expenses.

Custodial Care (99321—99333)

Custodial care is primarily for the purpose of meeting the personal daily needs of the patient and can be provided by personnel without medical care skills or training. For example, custodial care includes assistance with walking, bathing, dressing, eating, and other activities. Skilled nursing personnel are not required for this nonmedical type of care, which is commonly referred to as "meeting the daily living needs" of the patient. Most plans do not provide coverage for these types of services and for those that do, payment is very limited. If there is a question whether care is custodial, copies of the provider's nursing notes or the Admit and/or Discharge Summary reports should be requested.

Emergency Department Services (99281—99288)

When a patient goes to the outpatient or emergency department of a hospital, a physician is usually in attendance who has a contract to provide professional care at the facility. The contracting physician's charges may appear on the hospital bill or may be billed separately. Many hospitals have two types of outpatient departments: the emergency room (ER) and outpatient medical clinics.

When a billing is received from a hospital for clinic charges, there is often a room charge for the use of the facility and a separate physician charge. The coding of these types of claims varies greatly from payor to payor, so the handling procedures need to be clarified. However, there are two main handling procedures:

1. CPT services are coded separately and subjected to usual, customary, and reasonable (UCR) and
2. Generic or UB-92 (hospital claim codes that are covered in Chapter 14) codes are used and not subjected to UCR.

The following rules provide some common handling suggestions:

- If a hospital is billing for professional component charges separately from the actual lab or x-ray charges, combine the two together because they represent one total service.
- Physician treatment charges (professional fees) may be coded separately from other fees. This will depend on whether or not the payor is cost-conscious. If coded separately, the charge is usually subject to UCR, whereas if not coded separately, it will not be subject to UCR.
- Stat fees should also be combined with the actual laboratory or x-ray charges.

These guidelines vary from company to company, so verification must be requested.

If the patient wants to have his regular physician in attendance and the physician is called in from outside the hospital to provide services, code 99056 should be used. If the patient visits the outpatient clinic of a facility, regular office visit coding should be used, since a clinic is conceptually the same as an office. That is, the same doctors see the same patients, visits are scheduled the same as in an office, the treatment provided is the same as what would be provided in an office, and so on. In essence, the physician is using the facility as his office.

Consultations (99241—99263)

Usually, a consultation is provided by a specialist who has been requested to provide an opinion only. The specialist examines the patient at the request of another physician. He or she may request diagnostic services and may make therapeutic recommendations to the referring physician. However, the specialist does not usually take over the day-to-day treatment or management of the patient. In fact, to qualify as a consultation, the consulting physician cannot be responsible for the regular management of the patient.

If the physician subsequently assumes responsibility for the routine care of the patient, the services should be coded as visits and not consultations even if billed as consultations. (The initial consultation would be allowed as such.) If the consultant is seeing the patient, in addition to the regular attending physician, 99231—99233 should be used.

Second Surgical Opinion Consultations (99271—99275)

A second opinion is designed as a benefit to the patient by confirming the need for surgeries that have a reputation for being done needlessly. Many plans provide a special benefit called an SSO Benefit, which provides 100% payment on services provided by a second, independent specialist whom the patient consults prior to the scheduling of an elective, nonemergency surgery. Normally, for an SSO benefit to be payable, the following requirements must be satisfied:

- The second or third opinion physician must be totally uninvolved with the original recommending physician. Therefore, he or she cannot be part of the same medical group and will often be picked by the administrator, medical management firm, or payor.
- The consultation must be completed prior to the scheduling of the surgery.
- The second opinion physician cannot perform the recommended surgery.

Depending on the plan, failure to obtain an SSO may result in:

- Complete denial of all charges for the surgery and related services.
- Application of a special, reduced coinsurance. For instance, instead of paying 80% of the expenses, 50% would be paid. Noncompliance penalties vary substantially.
- No change of benefits. In this case, the SSO is considered to be a benefit for the member and is not used to penalize for noncompliance.

Immunizations (90700—90749)

Immunizations are considered to be preventive treatment. Therefore, usually an active illness or disease is not present. Consequently, many plans do not cover such routine services except under five special circumstances:

1. 90724—Influenza virus—may be covered for senior citizens who have a history of respiratory illness.
2. 90726—Rabies—may be covered as active treatment of an animal bite.
3. 90732—Pneumococcal—may be covered for

young or older patients with a history of respiratory illness.

4. 90703—Tetanus toxoid—may be covered when provided due to an injury such as stepping on a nail. Some firms code this injection as 90782 rather than 90703.
5. The state in which the plan operates may have mandated laws that specify that all plans must provide specific levels of routine care for children. In such a case, the plan may be obligated to provide such benefits.

Nervous/Mental Care and Treatment (90801—90899)

Nervous/mental care and treatment includes:

- Psychotic and neurotic disorders
- Organic brain dysfunction
- Alcoholism
- Chemical dependency

The language description on the claim form generally indicates "psychotherapy," "individual therapy," or "group therapy." The ICD-9 coding is usually in the range of 290.00—319.00. The providers of service are usually medical doctors (typically psychiatrists) or clinical psychologists.

If one of the following providers is indicated, most benefit plans require a referral by an MD:

- Marriage, Family and Child Counselor (MFCC)
- Licensed Clinical Social Worker (LCSW)
- Master of Social Work (MSW)

These CPT codes are used only when psychiatric counseling or therapy is provided. If such therapy is not provided, even if the service is performed by one of the above licensed providers, a different code range should be used.

Most plans pay a reduced benefit for this type of treatment. There may be a limit on the number of visits per year or per lifetime, along with a dollar limit per visit, per calendar year, or per lifetime. Also, many plans cover only certain provider licensing. Therefore, read the plan document carefully before processing any psychiatric care claims.

Biofeedback (90900—90915)

Biofeedback is training an individual to consciously control automatic, internal body functions. For instance, through conscious control, some body rhythms that control the constriction of blood vessels or the beating of the heart can be increased or decreased. This type of treatment can be used for a variety of illnesses or symptoms. A common use is for the control of intractable pain.

Biofeedback is controversial in that its effectiveness is very hard to prove or disprove. In addition, it does not cure anything. Instead, it is used as a tool in dealing with the symptoms of a condition, not in its treatment. Most plans do not cover biofeedback treatment, or if it is covered, it is very limited and only for certain diagnoses.

Dialysis (90918—90999)

Dialysis is a maintenance procedure used for End-Stage Renal Disease when the kidneys cease functioning. Notice that this is not really a treatment because it is only handling the functions normally performed by the body (however, it is still referred to generically as "treatment"). For a patient with this disease to survive, the blood-cleansing function must be performed artificially by one of three processes currently available:

1. Hemodialysis
2. CAPD—continuous ambulatory peritoneal dialysis
3. Transplantation of a new kidney.

Most hemodialysis is performed at private dialysis centers. A small percentage of the patients have a machine in their own home. The fees for dialysis are usually billed on a monthly basis. When coding, either the actual dates of service should be indicated or a monthly from/through date is used. Normally, the only time you see these bills is for the first 18 months of treatment. After that, Medicare becomes the primary payor (refer to the Medicare section for additional information). If the dialysis is performed in an acute facility, you may be billed separately for the facility fees and the physician fees. Remember, the CPT codes are to be used only on physician's services. Dialysis treatment runs about $5000 per month.

CAPD is performed by the patient at home. The peritoneum of the stomach is used to cleanse the blood. Surgery is required for the implantation of catheters and the construction of the internal bag (made of the peritoneum) to hold the dialysate fluids. Monthly supplies must be purchased, and there will be monthly examination charges by the attending physician. This type of treatment runs about $2000 per month. Transplants are coded in accordance with the surgery section of the CPT.

Ophthalmology (92002—92499)

Ophthalmology care is provided either by an optometrist or an ophthalmologist (MD). Most health plans do not cover routine vision care services related to the refraction and subsequent prescription of glasses or contact lenses. If they are covered, the benefits are usually very limited in both the dollar allowance and the time restraints and are often provided under a separate vision care plan or benefit. Therefore, always be sure to verify plan benefits before processing a vision claim. Also be aware that not all vision care is routine. Some vision care is essential for the proper care and treatment of eye diseases. Most payors have a listing of payable diagnoses, but even then the important point will be in what type of services are being provided. Prescriptive services for glasses or contact lenses are still considered routine (except possibly if the lens of the eye has been removed, as in cataract surgery).

Orthoptics is a retraining of the muscles that control vision. Some plans allow for this therapy for certain conditions such as strabismus and binocular vision. If the plan does allow the therapy, it is usually very limited and may require a second opinion from an ophthalmologist.

Speech Therapy (92507—92508)

Speech therapy must be for the correcting of speech that has been impaired because of sickness or injury and occurred while the individual was insured under the plan. The services must also be performed by a qualified practitioner. Conditions such as restoration of speech ability after a stroke or throat surgery would be covered. However, speech therapy for conditions such as stuttering or congenital deafness would not be covered.

If you are unsure of the underlying need for the speech therapy services, the claim should be referred to a specialist for further review.

Cardiovascular (92950—93981)

This is a very large section, and it is heavily used by the examiner. The following codes are some of the more commonly billed services:

93000	EKG
93010	EKG Interpretation Only
93015	Cardiovascular Stress Test
93224	24-hr EKG Monitoring

As a rule, the codes from 93000 through 93350 and 93600 through 93981 are considered to be DXL (Diagnostic X-ray and Laboratory) expenses. Codes 93501 through 93545 are considered surgical procedures.

With careful consideration, the proper code can be determined. It is usually easier to start with the code supplied by the provider (if any) and then verify it for accuracy.

Physical Medicine (97010—98929)

Physical Medicine is the manipulation and physical therapy associated with the nonsurgical care and treatment of the patient. The most common form of physical medicine is chiropractic manipulation of the spine (theoretically, any joint can be involved). The chiropractor's scope of practice is limited in most states. For instance, in California, chiropractors are not allowed to draw blood or prescribe prescription medicines. The limitations vary by state.

Chiropractic care and billing used to be limited to manipulation of the spine and x-rays. Now, chiropractors use many different physical therapy modalities. Consequently, there has evolved an intense monitoring and restricting of payment for chiropractic services. Such restrictions may limit the number of visits per year, per month, or per condition, along with specifying daily money maximums or limiting the number of modalities that may be performed in a single visit. A wide variety of techniques have emerged to handle the overutilization of chiropractic care. As a result, it is important to check the coverage, as the administrative policies vary from payor to payor.

Many chiropractors use an accident diagnosis, 84x.xx series, for billing purposes. Unless an accident or injury has actually occurred with a date, place, and circumstance indicated, the coding should be changed to reflect a noninjury skeletal condition, (72x.xx). (This varies by administration.) Situations that should warrant further review include:

- Possible overutilization.
- Over three physical medicine visits in a week.
- Over 12 visits in a month.
- Over 3 months and at least 34 visits of physical medicine visits.
- Second provider of physical medicine on the same day
- Over four physical medicine codes per day.
- More than one initial office visit by the same physician.
- Claims when the only physical medicine charges are for modalities or massage (97010—97039 procedure codes). Modalities are a method therapy, usually physical (ie, massage).
- Claims for use of an orthion table or orthion therapy.

If a particular claim appears to be excessive, the attending physician should be contacted and the following information obtained:

- An outline of the therapy program recommended.
- A list of goals to be achieved through the program.
- A narrative description of how the physician sees each procedure being performed as working toward one or more of the goals listed.

If the physician's reply justifies the use of therapy, frequency, and duration, process the claim. It takes time and skill to be able to interpret or determine necessity of services rendered. Therefore, if you are not sure what action should be taken after compiling the information necessary to make a claims determination, refer the information to a claims specialist. Any of these limitations would depend on the individual contract and the administrator policy. Please check with your administrator before processing this type of claim.

Maintenance Therapy

Maintenance therapy is a repetitive service rendered to maintain a level of function with no other neurologic function or other function gained. Maintenance services must be considered under standard practice of medicine and must be skilled. Most payors don't cover services for maintenance therapy or for therapy in which there is no improvement in the patient's condition.

Summary

Physician's services includes a wide array of services from treating a patient in the office to providing services in an emergency room setting or at a skilled nursing facility.

Physician's services charges may be billed by a variety of practitioners. Learn to identify the covered providers, and use these guidelines to determine whether the charges billed are covered services.

Assignments

Complete the Questions for Review.

Complete the billing of the Physician's Services claims in the Student Exercise Manual and process Physician's Services claims 3-1 to 3-15 using the guidelines just covered. Remember, company guidelines always supersede the guidelines provided here.

Questions for Review

Directions: Answer the following questions without looking back into the material just covered. Write your answers in the space provided.

1. If the diagnosis is for psychiatric care, regardless of the service provided, codes 90801—90899 are used. (True or False) True
2. What are dialysis services? maintenance procedure used for End-Stage Renal Disease when the kidneys cease functioning
3. Custodial care is usually a covered service. (True or False) False
4. The three types of end stage renal disease treatment are:
   a. Hemodialysis
   b. CAPD - continuous ambulatory peritoneal dialysis
   c. Transplantation of new kidney
5. Antibiotics, when administered in an injection, are usually what type of injection? ______
6. Consultations are usually provided by a specialist who has been requested to provide an opinion only
7. A clinical psychologist requires a referral from an MD. (True or False) False
8. A Skilled Nursing Care Facility provides this type of care. medical type of care
9. A second opinion physician can be in the same medical group as the surgeon. (True or False) False
10. What type of care is usually provided by an RPT? ______

If you were unable to answer any of the questions, refer back to the section and then complete the answers.

* Christian Scientist practioner
providers recognized by both insurance + medacare
treats by prayer
Christian Church of Scientology

11

X-ray and Laboratory Services

In this chapter you will learn:

- To identify services that fall within the DXL 80000 CPT codes.
- To identify common diagnostic tests performed in a physician's office.
- The normal range of specific DXL test values.
- How this section is broken down, when codes are to be used, and which providers may bill using these codes.

Radiology and laboratory charges are charges that may be billed by a physician, an independent laboratory, or a free-standing radiology facility. In this chapter we will discuss some of the basic guidelines used in determining whether laboratory and radiology services billed are covered. We will also cover some of the guidelines for processing laboratory and radiology charges.

X-ray and Laboratory Services

Laboratory examinations consist of the analyzing of body substances to determine their chemical or tissue type makeup. Body fluids or tissues are collected and are either run through analyzing machines or looked at under a microscope to identify any abnormal substances or tissues.

There are basically two types of x-ray and laboratory charges: diagnostic x-ray/lab and medical management x-ray/lab. Diagnostic charges are for initial testing to confirm a diagnosis or to rule out other diagnoses. The physician orders the appropriate lab tests to confirm or rule out this diagnosis. Medical management x-ray/lab charges are charges that are incurred to control or manage a diagnosis (eg, monitoring blood glucose levels on a patient with diabetes).

Laboratory tests are considered covered charges and may be payable under an x-ray and laboratory benefit. This benefit pays for the x-ray and laboratory test up to the policy maximum necessary to diagnose or manage a condition, as long as the expense is not payable under another Basic benefit (eg, inpatient hospital, preadmission testing, accident). The laboratory benefit is also not payable for charges incurred in connection with any examination or test that is not necessary or incident to the establishment of a diagnosis for an injury or illness.

The XYZ plan has a Basic benefit that covers a maximum of $200 per calendar year for x-ray/lab charges.

Automated Laboratory Charge

Automated laboratories offer their services primarily to doctors' offices. Usually, the doctor's office is furnished with all the necessary supplies for securing samples of blood and urine and with lab sheets indicating which tests are to be performed on which specimens. Lab reports are received from the laboratory within 3 days. The doctor is billed, usually monthly, for this service.

Panel tests are composed of multiple tests that are combined and run from one specimen. These tests can be requested from one or two specimens and cost substantially less than one test ordered separately from one specimen. These services are very sophisticated, highly computerized, and usually very reliable. CPT codes 80002–80092 refer to various types of panel tests. The number of tests performed determines which code to use. Doctors are allowed to bill for the collection of the specimen, a venipuncture if the specimen is blood, and the handling charge for packaging the specimen. See Appendix 11-1 for a list of common lab tests.

It is not uncommon for providers to do what is known as "unbundling" when billing. Unbundling is when a provider bills separately for each test performed even though all the tests came from the same specimen and were done simultaneously. In this circumstance, the provider gets significantly more money for doing nothing additional. When a bill is received "unbundled," the examiner needs to rebundle it (see Appendix 11-2: Laboratory Profile Index). An example of unbundling is shown in Table 11-1.

Table 11-1: Unbundling

Bill from Doctor	CPT/RVS Code	Charges	Coding by Examiner/Charge	
Albumin	82040	$15.00		
Calcium	82310	20.00		
Chlorides	82435	25.00		
Cholesterol	82465	25.00		
Creatinine	82565	15.00		
Glucose	82947	10.00		
Potassium	84132	15.00		
Sodium	84295	15.00		
BUN	84520	30.00		
Uric acid	84550	25.00		
		$195.00	80010	$195.00

In Table 11-1, all the billed charges should be combined and coded under one panel code. Benefits would then be determined based on the one code.

Papanicolaou (Pap) Smear

A Papanicolaou or "Pap smear" is a diagnostic laboratory test for detecting the absence or presence of infection, viruses, trauma, or cancer. Expense for Pap smear is eligible when one of the following six conditions exists:

1. The result of the Pap smear is abnormal.
2. A previous cancer of the cervix, uterus, or vagina has been present or is presently being treated.
3. The patient complains of symptoms referable to the female reproductive system.
4. The results of a Pap smear taken in the last 12 months was abnormal.
5. Signs or symptoms are present which, in the physician's opinion, are reasonably related to a gynecologic disorder.
6. The physical examination indicates any abnormal findings of the vagina, cervix, uterus, ovaries, or adnexa.

Usually, routine Pap smears performed in conjunction with a routine physical examination are not covered unless the contract specifically indicates coverage or the state mandates coverage.

Component Charges

Whenever a lab or an x-ray test is performed, two distinct services are actually performed:

1. The first service is the taking of the specimen or x-ray. This charge should include the expense for the personnel performing the test and the cost of the necessary equipment. This is called the technical component and is denoted by adding modifier -27 to the CPT code.
2. The second service is the interpretation or the reading of the results of the test. This is called the professional component and is denoted by adding modifier -26 to the CPT code.

An independent pathologist or radiologist often bills separately for the interpretation report. This interpretation-only charge is a professional component (PC) charge. To figure the cost of an x-ray or lab test, the PC charge (if billed separately) needs to be added to the base or technical charge (the charge for performing the test). Sometimes, both the base charge and the PC charge are billed by the same provider but are broken down into separate charges (not uncommon on hospital bills). When coding the claim, the two charges should be combined and coded as one charge. If the professional component and the technical component are performed by different providers, they are not to be combined and coded as a single expense. In such a case, these separate charges should be coded and paid separately.

A professional component charge ranges from 25% to 40% of the cost of the actual test. If an RVS lists the code with the -26 modifier attached, the unit value is not to be decreased. (For training purposes, contracts that do not state a professional component percentage have had their claims computed at 40% of UCR.)

Summary

X-ray and laboratory services are essential in determining the patient's problems, ruling out illnesses, and managing illnesses or injuries. It is now possible to perform certain tests in the privacy of one's home (eg, pregnancy and glucose level tests).

We have discussed only some of the rules and guidelines used to process charges received for laboratory and radiology services. These guidelines should enable you to identify covered services and determine the correct processing procedures for services that are covered.

Assignments

Complete the Questions for Review.

Complete billing of the DXL claims in the student exercise manual and process DXL claims 4-1 to 4-15 using the guidelines just covered.

Questions for Review

Directions: Answer the following questions without looking back into the material just covered. Write your answers in the space provided.

1. What is the numeric range of the CPT laboratory panel codes?
2. What are panel tests?
3. What is unbundling?
4. What are professional and technical components?
5. What does modifier -26 denote?

If you were unable to answer any of the questions, refer back to the section and then complete the answers.

Appendix 11-1

Common Laboratory Tests

Following is a list of frequently used laboratory tests, the common conditions for which they are performed, and the normal adult values. This list is intended to be used for training and reference purposes only.

Tests: Adult Normal Values

Acid Phosphatase
1.0–4.0 King-Armstrong U/dL
0.5–2.0 Bodansky or Gutman U/dL
0.0–1.1 Shinowara U/mL

Significantly elevated levels are nearly always indicative of metastatic cancer of the prostate.

Moderately elevated values are found in:
Acute pancreatitis
Acute renal impairment
Alcoholism
Any cancer that has metastasized to the bone
Barbiturate use
Cancer of the liver or bile duct
Cholecystitis/cholelithiasis
Congestive heart failure (CHF)
Hepatitis
Hyperparathyroidism
Multiple myeloma
Paget's disease

Albumin
Protein – Negative or 2–8 mg/dL
Urine – 10–100 mg/24 hr
Common diagnoses:
Acute and chronic renal disease
Ascites
Cardiac disease
Hyperthyroidism
Negative nitrogen imbalance
Nephritis
Severe anemias and leukemia

Alkaline Phosphatase
1.5–4.5 U/dL (Bodansky method)
4.3 U/dL (King-Armstrong method)
15.35 U/mL (Shinowara-ones-Reinhart)
Common diagnoses:
Bone disease
Hyperparathyroidism
Infectious mononucleosis
Liver disease

Ammonia (40–110 mg/100)
Common diagnoses:
Azotemia
Cor pulmonale
Erythroblastosis fetalis
Liver disease
Pericarditis
Postoperative test for estimating the success or patency of portacaval shunt
Pulmonary emphysema

Amylase (60–200 Somogyi U/100 mL)
Common diagnoses:
Liver disease (hepatitis, cirrhosis)
Pancreatitis
Pancreatic calculi
Parotitis (mumps)
Perforated peptic ulcer (but not usually done for those conditions because diagnosis is evident without this test)

Antinuclear Antibody (ANA) – Negative
Common diagnoses:
Anaplastic carcinomas or lymphomas
Rheumatoid arthritis
Scleroderma
Systemic lupus erythematosus

Antistreptolysin-O-Titer (ASO) – 200 IU or less than 160 Todd U. Levels are age-dependent.
Used to detect recent or present Streptococcus infection. Aids in diagnosis of rheumatic fever and acute glomerulonephritis.

Batonite (Batonite Flocculation Test)
Common diagnosis:
Rheumatoid arthritis

Bilirubin; Icterus Index (Serum)
Total bilirubin 0.3–1.3 mg/dL
Direct conjugated 0.1–0.4 mg/dL
Free indirect unconjugated 0.2–0.18 mg/dL
Newborn 1–12 mg/dL
Icterus Index
Normal serum level 4–6 U
Common diagnoses:
Bilirubin elevations accompanied by jaundice:
Hepatocellular causes:
Cirrhosis
Infectious mononucleosis
Viral hepatitis
Obstructive causes:
Calculi
Cancer
Hemolytic jaundice:
Erythroblastosis fetalis
Pernicious anemia
Sickle cell anemia
Transfusion reactions
Elevation of nonconjugated bilirubin in:
Hemolytic anemia
Hemorrhagic pulmonary infarcts
Trauma in the presence of a large hematoma
Elevation of conjugated bilirubin in:
Cancer of the head of pancreas
Choledocholithiasis
Dubin-Johnson syndrome
Elevation of both conjugated nonconjugated bilirubin (with the conjugated levels more elevated) in:
Cholestasis secondary to drugs
Cirrhosis
Hepatic metastasis
Hepatitis
Lymphoma

Bilirubin (Urine) – Negative (0.02 mg/dL)
Common diagnoses:
Liver disease due to infections or toxic agents
Obstructive biliary disease

Bleeding Time
Duke's method—less than 8 min (usually 1–6 min)
Ivy's method—2 to 9.5 min
Common diagnoses:
Presurgical test for coagulability of blood (commonly used for T&A)
DIC
Hemophilia
Leukemia

Blood Culture – Negative
Common diagnoses:
All diseases causing bloodstream infection or suspected bloodstream infection

Blood (Red Cell Count)
Men 4.2–5.4 million/mm^3
Women 3.6–5.0 million/mm^3
Common diagnoses:
CBC and listed parts: RBC, WBC, Hgb, HCT, diff
Anemias
Infections
Leukemias
Polycythemia
Routine in practically all diseases

Blood Urea Nitrogen (BUN) (10–15 mg/100 mL)
Common diagnoses:
Chronic gout
Dehydration
GI hemorrhage
Kidney disease
Liver failure
Nephrotic syndrome
Shock

Blood Sugar (See Glucose.)

Bone Marrow
Common diagnoses:
All blood diseases: leukemia, anemia, Hodgkin's disease

C-Reactive Protein (Trace Amounts)
Any titer is significant for:
Acute rheumatic fever

Bacterial and viral infections (acute)
Myocardial infarction
Pneumonia
Postcommissurotomy syndrome
Sometimes present in the following:
Nephritis
Pericarditis
Pyelitis
Rheumatoid arthritis

Calcium
($Ca2+$) – 9.0–10.6 mg/dL
4.5–5.3 mEq/L
Common diagnoses:
Addison's disease
Kidney stones and renal insufficiency
Osteogenesis imperfecta
Osteoporosis and osteomalacia
Parathyroid disease
Rickets
Tetany

Carbon Dioxide Combining Power (Alkaline Reserve)
– 53–76 vol%
Common diagnoses:
Alkalosis } Many disease states can
Acidosis } cause these conditions.
Diabetes
Heart disease (congestive failure)
Tetany

Carcinoembryonic Antigen (CEA)
– 2.5–3.0 ng/mL
Common diagnoses:
Cancer (liver, pancreas, prostate)
Inflammatory bowel disease
Cirrhosis

Carotene (50–300 U/100 mL)
Common diagnoses:
Vitamin A deficiency (night blindness)

Chloride (Cl) – 95–105 mEq/L
Common diagnoses:
Addison's disease
Dehydration
Diabetes
Heart disease
Kidney disease
Severe vomiting and diarrhea

Cholesterol
120–290 mg% at age 30
135–315 mg% at age 40
150–340 mg% at age 50
Common diagnoses:
Arteriosclerosis or atherosclerosis
Diabetes
Heart disease
Liver disease (obstructive jaundice)
Nephrosis
Pancreatitis
Pernicious anemia
Thyroid
Tuberculosis

Cholesterol Esters (70–78% of above)
Common diagnoses:
Jaundice
Liver disease
Conditions as above

Cholinesterase (0.5–1.3 ph U)
Common diagnoses:
Acute infections
Amoebic hepatitis
Anemia
Cirrhosis
Congestive heart failure
Dermatomyositis
Hepatitis–viral
Liver abscess
Liver disease
Metastatic cancer of liver
Myocardial infarction
Nephrotic syndrome
Obstructive jaundice

Coagulation Time (3–7 min)
Common diagnoses:
Blood diseases

Cold Agglutinins (0–8)
Values above 16 are significant.
Common diagnoses:
Atypical pneumonia
Congenital syphilis
Cirrhosis
Lymphatic leukemia
Malaria
Peripheral vascular disease
Severe hemolytic anemia

Complement Fixation Tests (Wassermann and others)
– Negative
VDRL
Kolmer
Eagle
Hinton

Complement fixation tests other than the latter are used in diagnosis of Weil's disease (rickettsial disease), virus diseases (rabies, arborvirus, echovirus, and coxsackievirus), coccidioidomycosis, mumps, smallpox, lymphogranuloma venereum, toxoplasmosis, syphilis.

Coombs' Tests – Negative
Common diagnoses:
Hemolytic disease of newborn (erythroblastosis fetalis) for determination of RH sensitivity.

Copper – 70–140 μg%
Common diagnoses:
Wilson's disease (hepatolenticular liver degeneration)

Creatine (0.1–0.4 mg%)
Common diagnoses:
Kidney disease

Creatine Phosphokinase (CPK)
Men 5–35 μg/mL
Women 5.25 μg/mL
Common diagnoses:
Delirium tremens
Myocardial infarction
Progressive muscular dystrophy
Pulmonary infarction

Creatinine Clearance (70–160 mL/min)
Common diagnoses:
Kidney disease

Electrophoresis Pattern: Protein and Lipoprotein
Common diagnoses:
Anemias—sickle cell, thalassemia (Mediterranean or Cooley's anemia)
Cardiac disease
Cardiovascular renal (CVR)
Liver disease
Multiple myeloma
Renal disease
Vascular disease

Electrolytes (Sodium, Chloride, Potassium)
(See individual tests.)

Erythrocyte Sedimentation Rate (ESR)
0–20 mm/hr depending on patient's sex, age, and test methodology.
Common diagnoses:
Collagen diseases
Infections
Rheumatoid arthritis

Fibrinogen (0.2–0.4 g%)
Common diagnoses:
Blood diseases (particularly hemorrhagic conditions) for example: Hemophilia
Defibrination syndrome
Hereditary fibrinogenemia
Liver disease or damage (liver function test)
Thrombocytopenia

Flocculation (Kline, Kahn, VDRL, and others)
Negative
Common diagnoses:
Syphilis

Folic Acid (Folate) (5.9–21.0 μg/mL
Common diagnoses:
Celiac disease
Chronic dialysis
Hemolytic anemia
Liver disease
Megaloblastic anemia

Glucose Sugar (70–110 mg/dL)
Common diagnoses:
Cushing's disease
Diabetes
Hypoglycemia
Pancreatic disease (tumors/cysts in pancreas tail)

Glucose Tolerance Test (GTT)
Fasting blood sugar (FBS):
Below 100 mg/100 mL
30 min 155 mg/100 mL
1 hr 165 mg/100 mL
2 hr 140 mg/100 mL
3 hr 80 mg/100 mL
Common diagnoses:
Diabetes
Hypoglycemia

Hematocrit (HCT) (Part of CBC)
Men 40–54/100 mL
Women 37–47/100 mL
Common diagnoses:
Anemia
Cirrhosis
Leukemia
Polycythemia

Hemoglobin (Hgb) (Part of CBC)
Men 14–16.5 g/100 mL
Women 12–15 g/100 mL
Newborn 14–12 g/100 mL
Common diagnoses:
Anemia
Chronic obstructive pulmonary disease (COPD)
Cirrhosis
Congestive heart failure (CHF)
Hemorrhage

Heterophile Antibody Agglutination (Monospot)
Negative
Common diagnoses:
Infectious mononucleosis

Icteric Index (See Bilirubin.)

Iodine (Protein-Bound Iodine [PBI]) (4.0–8.0 μg/dL)
Common diagnoses:
Acute and chronic thyroiditis
Hyperthyroidism
Hypothyroidism
Myxedema
Nephrosis

Iron (Fe) (50–150 μg/dL)
Common diagnoses:
Anemia
Conjunctival pallor
Decreased hemoglobin in red cells
Lowered vitality
Pale complexion
Retarded development

Iron Binding Capacity (TIBC) (250–450 mg/dL)
Common diagnoses:
Anemias of all kinds
Hepatic disease
Polycythemia vera

Lactic Dehydrogenase (LDH) (150–450 U)
Common diagnoses:
Acute leukemia and chronic granulocytic leukemia
Heart disease, particularly myocardial infarction, pericarditis, congestive failure
Hemolytic crises
Liver disease (metastatic cancer, hepatitis, cirrhosis, obstructive jaundice)
Myeloblastic and sickle cell anemia

Other conditions: delirium tremens, progressive muscular atrophy, renal disease, mononucleosis, myxedema

Latex Immobilization (RA Test) – Negative
Common diagnoses:
Arthritis, particularly rheumatoid arthritis

LE Test – Negative
Common diagnoses:
Hepatitis (certain types)
Lupus erythematosis
Rheumatoid arthritis
Scleroderma

Lead – Negative
Common diagnoses:
Lead poisoning

Leucine Aminopeptidase (LAP) (50–220 U)
Test done on blood, serum, and urine
Common diagnoses:
Cancer of pancreas
Leukemia
Lymphomas

Lipase (up to 1.5 U/mL)
Common diagnoses:
Acute cholecystitis
Cancer of pancreas
Pancreatitis (acute and chronic)

Lipids (Total) (450–1000 mg/dL)
Common diagnoses:
Arteriosclerosis and atherosclerosis
Biliary disease (liver, gallbladder, and duct)
Diabetes mellitus
Heart disease
Idiopathic disease of lipid metabolism
Ketosis due to nephrosis and glomerulonephritis
Pancreatitis
Thyroid disease

Magnesium (Mg^{2+})
1.8–3.0 mg/dL
1.5–2.5 mEq/L
Common diagnoses:
Chronic pancreatitis
Cirrhosis
Hemodialysis
Hypo- or hyperparathyroidism
Renal failure, chronic renal disease

Papanicolaou (Pap) Smear
Class I is negative.
Class V is conclusive for malignancy of the female genital tract.
Common diagnoses:
Cancer

Partial Thromboplastin Time (PTT) (30–45 sec)
Common diagnoses:
Anticoagulant therapy
Coagulation defects (hemophilia, DIC)
Liver disease

Platelet Count (15,000–350,000/mm^3
Common diagnoses:
Acute infection
Anemia (pernicious, aplastic, hemolytic)
Cancer
Leukemia
Polycythemia vera

Phosphate/Inorganic Phosphorus (P) (PO_4)
Adult 2.5–4.8 mg/dL
Child 3.5–5.8 mg/dL
Common diagnoses:
Addison's disease
Hypocalcemia
Hypo- or hyperparathyroidism
Renal insufficiency

Potassium (K^+), Serum (3.8–5.0 mEq/L)
Common diagnoses:
Diarrhea, vomiting
Diuretic administration
Liver disease
Primary aldosteronism
Pyloric obstruction
Renal tubular acidosis
Severe burns
Steroids

Proteins, Albumin, and Globulin; A/G Ratio (Serum)
Total 6–8 g/dL
Albumin 4–4.5 g%
Globulin 1.5–3 g%
A/G ratio 1.5:1–2.5:1
Common diagnoses:
Cancer
Collagen disease
Dehydration
Diarrhea
Liver disease
Rheumatoid arthritis

Prothrombin Time (PT)
11–16 seconds or 100%
Common diagnoses:
Anticoagulant therapy
Liver disease
Salicylate intoxication (aspirin)
Vitamin K deficiency

Rapid Plasma Reagin (RPR) – Negative
Common diagnosis:
Syphilis

RA Test (Latex Immobilization) – Negative
Common diagnosis:
Arthritis, particularly rheumatoid arthritis
(See Latex Immobilization.)

Red Cell Fragility
Common diagnoses:
Anemias, particularly congenital hemolytic anemia and other hemolytic anemias
Hereditary spherocytosis
Iron deficiency anemias
Jaundice
Liver diseases
Polycythemia vera
Postsplenectomy anemia
Sickle cell anemia
Thalassemia (Cooley's anemia or Mediterranean anemia)

Reticulocyte Count (Retic)
Adults 0.5–1.5% of total erythrocytes
Children 0.5–4.0% of total erythrocytes
Infants 2–5% of total erythrocytes
Common diagnoses:
Anemias (pernicious, hemolytic, iron-deficiency)
Hemolytic disease of newborn
Leukemia
Radiation therapy
Test of treatment response or results in pernicious anemia

RH Antibody Titer Test – Negative
Normally done as part of total blood typing procedure.

Pregnancy: If mother is RH-negative and father is RH-positive, test is done periodically throughout pregnancy to determine titer and the occurrence of any increase in titer during pregnancy.

Newborn: Test is done to determine RH type of infant to watch for or diagnose erythroblastosis fetalis.

Rheumatoid Factor (RA Factor)
Negative (1:20)
Common diagnoses:
Rheumatoid arthritis
Lupus erythematosis
Endocarditis
Disease affecting the liver, lung, or kidney

Sedimentation Rate (SR; Sed Rate)
See erythrocyte sedimentation rate (ESR).

SGOT (5–40 U/mL)
Common diagnoses:
Acute renal disease
Liver disease–particularly liver necrosis, hepatitis, cirrhosis, metastatic cancer, obstructive jaundice
Myocardial infarction (coronary thrombosis)

SGPT (5–35 U/mL)
Common diagnoses:
Essentially the same as for SGOT, but more specifically:
Liver congestion due to heart failure or hepatic vein thrombosis

Liver tumor, infection, congestion, toxic hepatitis
Metastatic liver cancer
Obstructive jaundice
Viral hepatitis
Acute pancreatitis } SGOT more value
Myocardial infarction } in these cases.

Smears for Parasites – Negative
Common diagnoses:
Amoebiasis and all other intestinal parasites
Diarrhea possibly caused by parasitic disease
Flukes (schistosomiasis) blood smears
Malaria–blood smears

Sodium (NA) (Serum)
136–142 mEq/L in adults under 65 years of age
132–140 mEq/L in adults over 65 years of age
Common diagnoses:
Addison's disease
Diabetic acidosis
Excessive sweating accompanied by large amounts of water by mouth
Febrific (fever) diseases
GI disturbances—vomiting and diarrhea
Heart disease
Kidney disease—severe nephritis
Pyloric obstruction
Severe burns

Sugar (See Glucose; Glucose Tolerance.)

Sulfonamide Level
Common diagnoses:
Infections of all kinds that are being treated with sulfonamides

Thyroid Function Tests
Thyroid tests can be done alone or in combination

T4 (Gycolumn)	5.0–11.0 μg/dL
T4 (Murphy-Pattee)	6.0–11/8 μg/dL
Free T4	0.9–2.3 μg/dL
T3 (resin uptake)	25–35%
T4 uptake	10–26 μg/dL
Free thyroxine index	0.9–2.3 μg/dL

TSH (thyroid-stimulating hormone less than 5 U/mL
Common diagnoses:
Endocrine diseases
Graves' disease
Hypo- and hyperthyroidism
Infertility
Myocardial infarction

Triglycerides (40–150 mg/100 mL)
Common diagnoses:
Hyperlipoproteinemia
Liver disease
Myocardial infarction
Pancreatitis

Thromboplastin (See PTT.)

Tubular Reabsorption of Phosphate Test (TRP)
78% on normal diet
85% on low phosphate diet
Common diagnoses:
Metabolic bone disease, particularly if related to parathyroid disturbance
Parathyroid disease
Children suspected of having excessive growth hormone activity (pituitary gland such as achromegly, gigantism)
Chronic renal insufficiency

Typing: Blood ABO and RH
Common diagnoses:
Anemias from any cause (hemorrhage, cancer, leukemia, and so on)
Blood transfusions—involved in great number of diseases
Newborn—suspected erythroblastosis

Urea Nitrogen (See Blood Urea Nitrogen.)

Urea Clearance (See Blood Urea Nitrogen.)
Common diagnoses:
Same as for urea nitrogen, but more specific in nephrotic disorders

Uric Acid
Serum: Male 7–8.5 mg/100 mL
Female 3.0–7.5 mg/100 mL
Urine: Male 2.1–7.8 mg/dL
Female 2.0–6.4 mg/dL
Common diagnoses:
Gout
Kidney disease
Leukemia
Lead poisoning
Liver disease
Polycythemia
Toxemia of pregnancy

Urinalysis (UA) – Negative
One of the most useful indicators of health and disease, especially helpful in the detection of renal or metabolic disorders.

Vitamin A (65–275 U/100 mL)
Common diagnoses (aids in differential diagnosis of jaundice):
Hyperfolliculosis—involves hair follicles
Jaundice hyperkeratosis—vitamin A (carotene) in excess causes pseudojaundice
Keratomalacia—involves cornea of the eye
Liver disease: hepatitis, cirrhosis
Vitamin A deficiency disease, particularly "night blindness" or deficiency in carotene
Xerophthalmia—eye disease

Volume
Blood Volume 55–80 mL/kg
Plasma Volume 30–45 mL/kg
Common diagnoses:
Congestive heart failure
Polycythemia vera
Severe blood loss as in shock, burns, hemorrhage

White Blood Count (WBC)
5000–10,000 mm^3
Common diagnoses:
Infections—to establish whether infection is present and to determine clinical response to treatment
Many other diseases: cancer, leukemia, anemias, leukopenias and agranulocytosis, allergies
Routinely done as part of complete blood count in practically all diseases

Zinc Sulfate Turbidity (2–9 U)
Common diagnoses:
Hyperglobulinemia
Liver disease: cirrhosis, jaundice

Appendix 11-2

Laboratory Profile Index

Following is a list of laboratory tests normally performed in a particular laboratory panel test. It is intended to be used for training and reference purposes only. The list includes:

- Chemfile combinations
- Allergy profiles
- Anemia profiles
- Arthritic profiles
- Coronary profiles (including lipid profiles)
- Electrolyte profile
- Endocrinology profiles (including hormone and thyroid profiles)
- Hepatitis profiles
- Immunology profiles
- Liver profiles
- Prenatal-obstetric profiles (including TORCH profile)
- Toxicology profiles
- Tumor markers

Chemfile Combinations

CPT Code 80019

Test	Group	Broader group
LDH	Necrosis Infarction	Hepatic
SGOT	Necrosis Infarction	Hepatic
Bilirubin, total		Hepatic
Bilirubin, direct (if total is 1.7 or above)		Hepatic
SGPT		Hepatic
GGTP (gamma-glutamyltranspeptidase)		Hepatic
Total protein		Hepatic
Albumin		Hepatic
Globulin		Hepatic
A/G ratio		Hepatic
Alkaline phosphatase		Hepatic; Bone and joint
Calcium	Parathyroid disease	Hepatic; Bone and joint
Phosphorus	Parathyroid disease	Hepatic; Bone and joint
Uric acid	Gout	Bone and joint
Urea nitrogen (BUN)	Kidney	
Creatinine	Kidney	
BUN creatinine ratio	Kidney	
Glucose	Diabetes	
CO_2	Electrolytes	
Chloride	Electrolytes	
Sodium	Electrolytes	
Potassium	Electrolytes	
Triglycerides	Lipid metabolism	
Cholesterol	Lipid metabolism	
Iron	Anemia	
Ferritin (if iron is below 20)	Anemia	

Reflex "+A" Option (added to any 80019 Chemfile combination)
Lipid phenotyping (if chol or trig is significantly high)
PLUS
Protein electrophoresis (if A/G ratio is reversed)
Reflex "+B" Option (added to any 80019 Chemfile combination)
HDL cholesterol

CPT Code 80019
Chemfile (CPT Code 80019) plus:
STS Qualitative } Syphilis
STS Quantitative }

CPT Code 80019
Chemfile (CPT Code 80019) plus:
Urinalysis

CPT Code 80019
Chemfile (CPT Code 80019) plus:
T_4 (RIA) Thyroid

CPT Code 80019
Chemfile (CPT Code 80019) plus:
Platelet count
WBC
RBC
Hemoglobin Hemanalysis
Hematocrit
Mean corpuscular volume
Mean corpuscular hemoglobin
Mean corpuscular hemoglobin concentration

CPT Code 80019
Chemfile (CPT Code 80019) plus:
Complete blood count (includes platelet count and differential)

CPT Code 80019
Chemfile (CPT Code 80019) plus:
All of the other options EXCLUDING and B

Allergy Profiles
RAST Allergy Testing
CPT Code 86003

Grasses
g1 Sweet vernal grass
g2 Bermuda grass
g3 Orchard grass (cocksfoot)
g4 Meadow fescue
g5 Perennial rye grass
g6 Timothy
g7 Common reed
g8 June grass (Kentucky blue)
g9 Red top (bent grass)
g10 Johnson grass
g11 Brome grass
g12 Cultivated rye
g13 Velvet grass
g14 Cultivated oat pollen
g15 Cultivated wheat pollen
g16 Meadow foxtail

Weeds
w1 Common ragweed (short)
w2 Western ragweed
w3 Giant ragweed (tall)
w4 False ragweed
w5 Wormwood (sagebrush)
w6 Mugwort (sagebrush)
w7 Ox-eye daisy
w8 Dandelion
w9 English plantain
w10 Lamb's quarter
w11 Russian thistle
w12 Goldenrod
w15 Scale

Epidermals
e1 Cat epithelium
e2 Dog epithelium
e3 Horse dander
e4 Cow dander
e5 Dog dander
e6 Guinea pig
e7 Pigeon droppings

Hymenoptera Venom
i1 Honeybee
i2 White-faced hornet
i3 Yellow jacket

i4 Paper wasp
i5 Yellow hornet
i100 Cockroach

Trees

t1 Maple (box elder)
t2 Alder
t3 Birch
t4 Hazelnut
t5 Beech
t6 Mountain cedar
t7 Oak
t8 Elm
t9 Olive
t10 Walnut
t11 Sycamore
t12 Willow
t14 Cottonwood
t16 White pine
t102 Mesquite

Foods

f1 Egg white
f2 Milk
f3 Codfish
f4 Wheat
f5 Rye
f6 Barley
f7 Oat
f8 Corn
f9 Rice
f10 Sesame seed
f11 Buckwheat
f12 Pea
f13 Peanuts
f14 Soybean
f15 White bean
f17 Hazelnut
f18 Brazil nut
f20 Almond
f23 Crab
f24 Shrimp
f25 Tomato
f26 Pork
f27 Beef
f31 Carrot
f33 Orange
f35 Potato
f40 Tuna
f44 Strawberry
f45 Baker's yeast
f47 Garlic
f75 Egg yolk
f81 Cheddar cheese
f82 Cheese mold
f83 Chicken
f85 Celery
f86 Parsley
f87 Melons
f100 Lettuce
f105 Chocolate
f108 Onion

House Dust

h1 House dust (Greer)
h2 House dust (Hollister-Stier)

House Dust Mites

d1 *Dermatophagoides pteronyssinus*
d2 *Dermatophagoides farinae*

Molds

m1 *Penicillium notatum*
m2 *Cladosporium herbarium*
m3 *Aspergillus fumigatus*
m4 *Mucor racemosus*
m5 *Candida albicans*
m6 *Alternaria tenuis*
m7 *Penicillium G*
m8 *Penicillium V*

Allergy Testing: Regional Inhalant Profiles

CPT Code 86005 Southern California Profile

Bermuda grass
June (Kentucky blue)
English plantain
Russian thistle
Olive tree, oak tree
Alternaria
House dust (H-S)
Dust mite (*D farinae*)
Cat epithelium
Dog epithelium

CPT Code 86005 Northern California Profile

Bermuda grass
Perennial rye grass
Russian thistle
Mugwort (sagebrush)
Olive tree, oak tree
Alternaria
House dust (H-S)
Dust mite (*D farinae*)
Cat epithelium
Dog epithelium

CPT Code 86005 Southwest (Arid) Profile

Bermuda grass
Johnson grass
Western ragweed
Lamb's quarter
Cottonwood tree, oak tree
Alternaria
House dust (H-S)
Dust mite (*D farinae*)
Cat epithelium
Dog epithelium

CPT Code 86005 Midwest Profile

Timothy
June grass
Short ragweed
Russian thistle
Oak tree, maple tree
Alternaria
House dust (H-S)
Dust mite (*D farinae*)
Cat epithelium
Dog epithelium

Anemia Profiles

CPT Code 80002 Anemia Profile #1

Folic acid
Vitamin B_{12}

CPT Code 80003 Anemia Profile #2
Folic acid
Vitamin B_{12}
Iron binding capacity (includes total iron)

CPT Code 80006 Anemia Profile #3
CBC (includes platelet count)
Reticulocyte count
Iron binding capacity (includes total iron)
Ferritin
Folic acid
Vitamin B_{12}

Arthritic Profiles

CPT Code 80007 Arthritic Profile #1

RA factor	
Total protein	
Albumin	Nutrition and Infection
Globulin	
A/G Ratio	
Sed rate	
Alkaline phosphatase	Bone and Joint
Calcium	
Phosphorus	
Uric acid	Gout

CPT Code 80072 Arthritic Profile #2

RA factor	
C-reactive protein	Inflammation
Sed rate	Infection
Streptozyme (antistreptococcal antibody titer)	
Uric acid	Gout
Calcium	Bone and Joint
Phosphorus	

CPT Code 80072 Arthritic Profile #3

CPT Code 80007 with ANA Fluorescent

CPT Code 80072 Arthritic Profile #4

RA factor	
C-reactive protein	Inflammation
Sed rate	Infection
Streptozyme (antistreptococcal antibody titer)	
Uric acid	Gout
Calcium	Bone and Joint
Phosphorus	
HLA-B27	Seronegative arthropathy (ankylosing spondylitis, Reiter's disease)

Coronary Profiles

CPT Code 80002 Coronary Risk #1
Cholesterol
HDL cholesterol
Cholesterol/HDL risk ratio

CPT Code 80004 Coronary Risk #2
Triglycerides
Cholesterol
HDL cholesterol
LDL cholesterol (by calc.)
LDL/HDL risk ratio

CPT Code 80004 3
Coronary Risk #3
Triglycerides
Cholesterol
Apolipoprotein A-I
Apolipoprotein B
Apolipoprotein A-I/apolipoprotein B ratio

CPT Code 80061 Coronary Risk #4

Triglycerides	VLDL
Cholesterol	Lipoprotein phenotyping by electrophoresis (includes Fredrickson's classification)
HDL cholesterol	
LDL cholesterol (by calc.)	
LDL/HDL risk ratio	

CPT Code 80061 Lipid Phenotype Profile
Cholesterol
Triglycerides
Lipoprotein phenotyping by electrophoresis (includes Fredrickson's classification)

IgA, IgG, IgM quantitative
Rheumatoid factor
Antinuclear antibody (ANA)
Anti-DNA (if ANA positive with titer 1:80 or higher)

CPT Code 80004 Autoimmune Profile
Antimitochondrial antibody
Smooth muscle antibody
Parietal cell antibody, IFA
Antinuclear antibody (ANA)
Anti-DNA (if ANA positive with titer 1:80 or higher)

CPT Code 80004 Humoral Immunity Profile
Serum protein electrophoresis (IG level and paraprotein)
IgA, IgG, IgM quantitative

CPT Code 80009 Lupus Profile
Antinuclear antibody (ANA)
Antimitochondrial antibody
Smooth muscle antibody
Parietal cell antibody, IFA
Thyroid microsomal antibodies
Anti-ENA (anti-SM and anti-RNP)
SSA/SSB
Complement C4
Anti-DNA (if ANA positive with titer 1:80 or higher)

CPT Code 80006 Autoantibody Profile
Thyroid microsomal antibodies
Thyroglobulin autoantibodies
Antimitochondrial antibody
Parietal cell antibody, IFA
Smooth muscle antibody
Rheumatoid factor
Antinuclear antibody (ANA)
Anti-DNA (if ANA positive with titer 1:80 or higher)

CPT Code 80002 Lymphoid Cancer Subtyping
Leukemia and lymphoma
Subtyping: classifies lymphoid malignancy according to lymphocyte subset involved
Includes:
T- and B-lymphocyte quant.
B-lymphocyte subset quant.
Heavy chains: IgA, IgM, IgG, IgD
Light chains: kappa and lambda

LIVER Profiles

CPT Code 80008 Liver Profile #1
LDH
SGOT
Bilirubin, total
Bilirubin, direct (if total is 1.7 or above)
SGPT
GGTP (gamma-glutamyltranspeptidase)
Total protein
Albumin
Globulin
A/G ratio
Alkaline phosphatase

CPT Code 80009 Liver Profile #2
LDH
SGOT
Bilirubin, total
Bilirubin, direct (if total is 1.7 or above)
SGPT
GGTP (gamma-glutamyltranspeptidase)
Total protein
Albumin
Globulin
A/G ratio
Alkaline phosphatase
Hepatitis B surface antigen

Prenatal Profiles

CPT Code 80055 Prenatal-Ob Profile #1
WBC
RBC
Hemoglobin
Hematocrit
Mean corpuscular volume
Mean corpuscular hemoglobin
Mean corpuscular hemoglobin concentration
Differential
Platelet count
STS (serologic test for syphilis)

Blood, type and Rh irregular antibody screen and titer (if Rh (d) negative)

CPT Code 80055 Prenatal-Ob Profile #2

CPT Code 80055 with rubella, IgG

CPT Code 80055 Prenatal-Ob Profile #3

CPT Code 80055 with routine irregular antibody screen and titer

CPT Code 80090 TORCH
Toxoplasma, IgG
Rubella, IgG
CMV, IgG
Herpesvirus types 1 and 2

Toxicology Profiles

CPT Code 80100 Urine Drug Screen #1
Amphetamines
Barbiturates
Benzodiazepines
Cocaine (as benzoylecgonine)
Methadone
Methaqualone (Quaalude)
Opiates (codeine, morphine)
Phencyclidine (PCP)
Propoxyphene (Darvon)

CPT Code 80100 Urine Drug Screen #2
Urine drug screen (CPT Code 80100) plus:
Alcohol, urine

CPT Code 80100 Urine Drug Screen #3
Urine drug screen (CPT Code 80100) plus:
Marijuana (cannabinoids), urine

CPT Code 80100 Urine Drug Screen #4
Urine drug screen (CPT Code 80100) plus:
Marijuana (cannabinoids), urine
Alcohol, urine

CPT Code 80100 Urine Drug Screen #5
Urine drug screen (CPT Code 80100) plus:
Marijuana (cannabinoids), urine
Includes positives confirmed by GC-MS (qualitative)

CPT Code 80100 Urine Drug Screen #6
Urine drug screen (CPT Code 80100) plus:
Marijuana (cannabinoids), urine
Alcohol, urine
Includes positives confirmed by GC-MS (qualitative)

CPT Code 80102 Comprehensive Drug Analysis: Coma Panel
This analysis is valuable when drug overdose is possible or suspected, but the causative agent is unknown and other data available to the physician are insufficient to permit definite treatment. The study includes qualitative analysis for the types of drugs listed below and blood quantitations of the drugs marked with an asterisk (*):

Analysis Performed

Amphetamines
Dextroamphetamine (Benzedrine)
Methamphetamine (Desoxyn)

Analgesics
Acetaminophen (Tylenol)
Salicylate (Aspirin)

Antidepressants
Amitriptyline (Elavil)
Desipramine (Norpramine)
Doxepin (Sinequan)
Imipramine (Tofranil)
Nortriptyline (Aventyl)

Antihistamines
Diphenhydramine (Benadryl)
Phenylpropanolamine (Dietac)

Miscellaneous drugs
Cocaine (as Benzoylecgonine)
Marijuana (cannabinoids)
Phencyclidine (PCP)
Phenytoin (Dilantin)

Narcotics
Codeine
Hydromorphone (Dilaudid)
Meperidine (Demerol)
Methadone (Dolophine)
Morphine (Heroin)
Oxycodone (Percodan)
Norpropoxyphene
Pentazocine (Talwin)
Propoxyphene (Darvon)

Phenothiazines (as Metabolites)
Chlorpromazine (Thorazine)
Perphenazine (Trilafron)
Trifluoperazine (Stelazine)
Thioridazine (Mellaril)

Barbiturates
Amobarbital (Amytal)
Butabarbital (Butabell, Butisol)
Butalbital (Fiorinal)
Pentobarbital (Nembutal)
Phenobarbital (Luminal)
Secobarbital (Seconal)

Benzodiazepines
Chlordiazepoxide (Librium)
Diazepam (Valium)
Flurezepam (Dalmane)
Oxazepam (Serax)

Cardiacs
Lidocaine (Xylocaine)
Quinidine/quinine

Sedatives and Hypnotics
Ethchlorvynol (Placidyl)
Ethinamate (Valmid)
Glutethimide (Doriden)
Meprobamate (Equanil)
Methaqualone (Quaalude)
Methocarbamol (Robaxin)
Methyprylon (Noludar)
Carisoprodol (Soma)

Volatiles
Acetone
Ethanol
Isopropanol
Methanol

CPT Code 80102 Urine Drug Screen–Expanded
This qualitative analysis is similar to the Comprehensive Coma Panel; however, it is only performed on urine. It is a rapid analysis designed for the detection of drugs in the overdose situation. The drugs listed here are detected as either their parent compound or their urinary metabolite.

Analysis Performed

Amphetamines
Dextroamphetamine (Benzedrine)
Methamphetamine (Desoxyn)

Analgesics
Acetaminophen (Tylenol)
Salicylate (Aspirin)

Antidepressants
Amitriptyline (Elavil)
Desipramine (Norpramine)
Doxepin (Sinequan)
Imipramine (Tofranil)
Nortriptyline (Aventyl)

Miscellaneous Drugs
Cocaine (as Benzoylecgonine)
Marijuana (cannabinoids)
Phencyclidine (PCP)
Phenytoin (Dilantin)

Narcotics
Codeine
Hydromorphone (Dilaudid)
Meperidine (Demerol)
Methadone (Dolophine)
Morphine (Heroin)
Oxycodone (Percodan)
Norpropoxyphene

Antihistamines
Diphenhydramine (Benadryl)
Phenylpropanolamine (Dietac)

Barbiturates
Amobarbital (Amytal)
Butabarbital (Butabell, Butisol)
Butalbital (Fiorinal)
Pentobarbital (Nembutal)
Phenobarbital (Luminal)
Secobarbital (Seconal)

Benzodiazepines
Chlordiazepoxide (Librium)
Diazepam (Valium)
Flurezepam (Dalmane)

Cardiacs
Lidocaine (Xylocaine)
Quinidine/quinine

Pentazocine (Talwin)
Propoxyphene (Darvon)

Phenothiazines (as Metabolites)
Chlorpromazine (Thorazine)
Perphenazine (Trilafron)
Trifluoperazine (Stelazine)
Thioridazine (Mellaril)

Sedatives and Hypnotics
Ethchlorvynol (Placidyl)
Ethinamate (Valmid)
Glutethimide (Doriden)
Meprobamate (Equanil)
Methaqualone (Quaalude)
Methocarbamol (Robaxin)
Methyprylon (Noludar)
Carisoprodol (Soma)
Oxazepam (Serax)

Volatiles
Acetone
Ethanol
Isopropanol
Methanol

Tumor Markers

CPT Code	Test
82105	Alpha-Fetoprotein (Nonpreg)
84999	Alpha Subunit
84702	Beta Subunit (RIA), Quant
83520	CA 15-3
83520	CA 19-9
83520	CA 125
82378	Carcinoembryonic Antigen (CEA)
84153	Prostatic Specific Antigen (PSA)

12

Surgery

In this chapter you will learn:

- The definition of surgery.
- To list the four general classifications of surgical procedures.
- To process surgery claims.
- To identify possible cosmetic procedures.
- To define pre- and postoperative care and to determine when it is included with surgery.
- To apply surgical guidelines as they relate to maternity and cosmetic procedures.

Surgery is defined as that branch of medicine that treats diseases, injuries, and deformities by operative or invasive methods. Although surgery usually involves cutting, cutting does not have to be involved for a procedure to be considered surgery. The surgery concept is anything that involves removing, altering, repairing, entering, or the carrying out of any other invasion of the body. Therefore, insertion of a tube into a person's throat does not involve cutting but is considered surgical in nature because it invades the body.

Most benefit plans cover only surgeries that are necessitated by disease or injury. In other words, the procedure must be considered medically necessary to repair or improve function or diagnose an illness. In addition, because a procedure is listed in the surgery section of the CPT does not mean that the procedure is allowable under a benefit plan nor does it mean that it will necessarily be coded as a surgical procedure. The coding of procedures varies from company to company.

Surgical Procedures

In general, surgical procedures can be classified as one of the following types:

- Diagnostic
- Therapeutic
- Reconstructive
- Cosmetic

Diagnostic procedures are those performed to determine the presence of disease or the cause of the patient's symptoms. One of the most commonly used forms of diagnostic surgery is the endoscopic procedure. This type of procedure involves making a small incision on the exterior part of the patient's body in the area near the organ or space being examined. Then, a very small instrument, called a scope, is inserted through the incision into the body cavity. The surgeon can then look through the scope and see the interior condition of the examination area. If desired, pictures or a video may be taken of the area. Examples of diagnostic procedures include bronchoscopy (31622), gastroscopy (43234), and sigmoidoscopy (45330).

Therapeutic procedures are performed to remove or correct the functioning of a body part that is diseased or injured. As a rule, failure to perform the therapeutic procedure results in either the patient's loss of life or a progressive functional decline.

A removal, repair, or manipulation may be involved in the correction of the abnormally functioning organ. Some cutting is usually required. However, with continual medical advances, more and more procedures are being performed without cutting or with very minimal incisions. Examples of therapeutic procedures are liver transplant (47135), craniectomy (removal of tumor of the brain) (61510), and appendectomy (44950).

Reconstruction is performed to rebuild or restore aesthetically a part of the body that was damaged or defective as a result of an illness or injury. Reconstruction is necessary to return the body to its normal or near-normal appearance and may or may not affect the functioning of the organ/area. Even though reconstruction may be necessary for purely cosmetic reasons, it is considered eligible under most plans as long as it is necessitated as a result of a disease or injury occurring while the patient was covered under the plan. If the injury or illness occurred prior to the date that the patient was covered under the plan, the repair may be considered cosmetic, not reconstructive. Examples of reconstructive procedures are rhinoplasty (surgical correction of the external appearance of the nose; 30400–30450) and breast augmentation/reconstruction (after a mastectomy resulting from breast cancer; 19324–19499).

Cosmetic procedures are those procedures performed solely to improve the appearance of a part and are not usually covered by benefit plans. If the procedure is functional in nature, cosmetic exclusions do not apply. For example, a scar revision is performed as a result of a contracture of a scar received in an accident. The release of the contracture is considered functional in nature, although the appearance of the scar would also be significantly affected.

Situations may arise in which it is difficult to ascertain whether a procedure should be considered cosmetic or reconstructive. In these instances, a professional opinion is required. For examples, refer to the section entitled Possible Cosmetic Procedures.

General Guidelines

The following guidelines will assist you in the processing of surgery claims.

Surgery in a Physician's Office

Billings for surgery performed in a physician's office are often itemized for each charge incurred such as the surgery, local anesthesia, medication, surgical trays, and dressings.

Generally, the charge made by the physician for surgery includes performing the surgical procedure, administering local anesthetic (if required), and all routine follow-up care. The charge for surgery always includes:

- The immediate preoperative visit.
- The surgical procedure.
- Local anesthesia (eg, topical, digital block).
- Routine follow-up care (visits) provided within the follow-up days listed in the RVS.

Nonroutine follow-up visits due to complications or other reasons may be billed and considered separately from the original surgical charge. Medical supplies, medications, x-rays, facility fees, and other services are usually considered and covered (or not covered) separately.

Preoperative Care

The immediate preoperative visit in the hospital or elsewhere is generally necessary to examine the patient, complete the hospital records, and initiate the treatment program. Charges for these procedures are included in the surgical allowance. However, a separate allowance may be warranted for preoperative services in the following circumstances:

- When the preoperative visit is the initial visit (eg, in an emergency), and prolonged detention or evaluation is required to prepare the patient or to establish the need for surgery.
- When the preoperative visit is a consultation.
- When procedures that are not usually part of the basic surgical procedure (eg, bronchoscopy prior to chest surgery) are provided during the immediate preoperative period.
- When a procedure could normally be performed in the office, but under certain circumstances requires hospitalization (eg, patient's age, condition). See modifier code -22.

Follow-up Days

Follow-up days are the days immediately following a surgical procedure during which a doctor must monitor a patient's condition in regard to that particular procedure. The RVS lists unit values for surgical procedures that include the surgery, local anesthesia, and the normal, uncomplicated follow-up care associated with the procedure for the time period indicated in the section titled Follow-up Days.

Complications or other circumstances requiring additional or unusual services concurrent with the procedure or procedures, or during the listed period of normal follow-up care, may warrant additional charges on a fee-for-service basis. However, unless the physician specifically indicates unusual circumstances, it should be assumed that the follow-up care is routine. Regardless of how the physician bills, all visits occurring within the listed follow-up days should be combined with the surgical charge. The following are categories of follow-up care:

- Follow-up care for diagnostic procedures (eg, endoscopy, injection procedures for radiography) includes only care that is related to recovery from the diagnostic procedure itself. Care of the underlying condition for which the diagnostic procedure was performed or other accompanying conditions is not included and may be charged for separately in accordance with the services rendered.
- Follow-up care for therapeutic procedures generally includes all normal postoperative care. Complications, exacerbations, recurrence, or the pres-

ence of other diseases or injuries requiring additional services concurrent with the surgical procedure(s) or during the indicated period of normal follow-up care may warrant additional charges coded and allowable separately.

When additional surgical procedure(s) are carried out within the listed period of follow-up care for a previous surgery, the follow-up periods will run concurrently through their normal termination.

Separate charges for routine follow-up care should be added to the surgical charge and the total compared with the UCR fee for the procedure performed.

For example:

Procedure: 40808, 10 f/u days

Description	Date	RVS/CPT Codes	Charge
Office visit	4/1	99213	$ 25.00
Surgery	4/3	40808	350.00
F/up hsp visit	4/4	99221	25.00
F/up hsp visit	4/5	99231	25.00
F/up office visit	4/10	99213	30.00
			$455.00

Based on administrative practices, the preoperative visit may or may not be considered part of the surgery charge. In the latter example, and unless you are told otherwise, assume that the preoperative visit is part of the surgery charge. Therefore, $455 would be compared against the plan's UCR limitation for the surgery.

Asterisk Procedures

Asterisk procedures are surgical procedures denoted by an asterisk to the left of the CPT code, which require special handling. If an asterisk (*) follows a CPT code, the following six rules apply:

1. The listed value is for the surgical procedure only.
2. Pre- and postoperative care is to be added on a fee-for-service basis.
3. When the (*) procedure is carried out at the time of an initial (new patient) visit and this surgery constitutes the major services at that visit, procedure number 99025 is listed in lieu of the usual initial visit as an additional service (under CPT).
4. When the (*) procedure is carried out at the time of an initial or other visit involving significant identifiable services (eg, removal of a small skin lesion at the time of a comprehensive history and physical examination), the appropriate visit is coded in addition to the (*) procedure and its follow-up care (under CPT and RVS).
5. When the (*) procedure is carried out at the time of a follow-up (established patient) visit and this procedure constitutes the major service at that visit, the service visit usually is not coded separately (under CPT and RVS).
6. When the (*) procedure requires hospitalization, the appropriate hospital visit is coded in addition to the (*) procedure and its follow-up care (under CPT).

By Report Procedures

Some procedures are so unusual or variable that it is impossible to determine a standard UCR or unit value allowance. These procedures are called By Report (BR) procedures. The RVS may refer to these procedures as Relative Value Not Established (RNE). BR and RNE procedures have to be referred to a professional review unit, a supervisor, or a consultant for review to determine the allowance. For proper review, a copy of the operative report is required. The anesthesia record may also be needed. If the operative report is not submitted with the claim, the claim should be pended and a copy requested before referral.

Multiple or Bilateral Procedures

Multiple procedures are more than one surgical procedure performed during one operative session. Bilateral procedures are surgeries that involve a pair of similar body parts (eg, breasts, eyes).

There are two main types of multiple or bilateral procedures:

1. Same time, different operative field, incision, or orifice: When more than one surgery is performed during the same operative session but through a different orifice (opening) or incision or in a different operative field, 100% of the actual charge or UCR (or scheduled amount) is allowable for the major procedure and 50% of UCR (or actual charge, whichever is less) is allowable for each additional procedure.

Bilateral procedures follow the same rules as multiple procedures performed through different incisions. Multiply the UCR allowance for the single procedure by 150% or 1.5. If there is an established bilateral procedure code, that code would be allowable at 100% only because the units have already been assigned at 1.5 times the units of the single procedure.

2. Same time, same operative field, incision or orifice: Usually, when multiple procedures are performed during the same operative session through the same incision, orifice, or operative field, the additional procedures are considered to be incidental.

An incidental procedure is one that does not add significant time or complexity to the operative session. In such a case, the allowable amount will be that of the major procedure only. No additional amount will be allowable for the extra procedures.

However, if the additional procedures are not incidental, the rules for handling multiple procedures previously explained would be applied. That is, the major procedure would be considered at 100% of UCR and the lesser at 50%.

For example, suppose that the following bill is received from the provider:

	Billed Amt	UCR
Tonsillectomy (42821)	$600.00	$600.00
Eustachian tube inflation (69400)	300.00	200.00

Following the rules previously indicated, 100% of the major procedure plus 50% of the lesser procedure would be allowed. Therefore, the allowable amount in this example would be:

100% of $600	$600.00
+ 50% of $200	$100.00
Total allowance	$700.00
Total billed amt	$900.00
Less allowed amt	−700.00
Member's responsibility	$200.00

It is important to look at the total billing so as not to penalize the patient for the way the physician bills. For example, suppose the same procedures as above were billed in the following way:

	Billed Amt	UCR
Tonsillectomy (42821)	$300.00	$600.00
Eustachian tube inflation (69400)	600.00	100.00
	$900.00	$700.00

By referring to the RVS, you can determine that the major procedure is the tonsillectomy, which allows 16.39 units, whereas 69400 (eustachian tube inflation) allows only 1.39 units. Therefore, using the multiple surgery rules but following the doctor's billing, you can determine the allowable to be:

100% of $600 up to the actual charge of	$300.00
50% of $200 or the actual charge, whichever is less	+100.00
Total allowance would be	$400.00

As shown, this calculation would be financially detrimental to the patient solely because the doctor's office did not properly allocate the expenses. Therefore, when expenses are improperly allocated, a "global approach" should be used. The total billed amount should be compared with the total UCR amount. In our example, the total UCR amount is $700 versus the total billed amount of $900. The objective is to deny amounts in excess of the global UCR.

100% of UCR	$600.00
Plus 50% of UCR for the 2nd procedure	+100.00
Total correct allowance	$700.00

Therefore, even though the doctor billed incorrectly, when you use the global approach, $700 would be allowable toward the total billed amount of $900, and the patient would not be penalized by being allowed only $400.

Some insurance companies use HCFA guidelines. When multiple surgeries are performed and the additional procedures are not incidental, HCFA guidelines are to allow:

Major procedure: 100% of UCR or the billed amount, whichever is less

2nd procedure: 50% of UCR or the billed amount, whichever is less

3rd through 5th procedures: 25% of UCR or the billed amount, whichever is less

Multiple procedures (more than two) are often referred to Consultants or Professional Review Departments, which consist of medical doctors and nurses, for analysis prior to payment. The Consultants or Review Department may give alternative instructions based on the actual operative report. Check with the administrator for guidelines for multiple surgeries before processing for payment.

Block Procedures

Block procedures are multiple surgical procedures performed during the same operative session, in the same operative area, and usually in the integumentary system. The objective of these codes is to handle multiple repetitions of the same service. A block procedure consists of a primary code and subsequent modifying codes. For example:

11100 is for biopsy of skin, subcutaneous tissue or mucous membrane, single lesion.

11101 is for each separate/additional lesion.

Therefore, if a bill was received for the removal of five lesions, the total allowance would be based on the following unit factors:

1.24	Units for the first lesion
2.6	Units total for lesions 2, 3, 4, and 5 (4x.65)
3.84	Total units allowed

For another example of a block procedure, see codes 11200—11201.

Maternity Expenses

Most plans provide coverage for maternity-related expenses on the same basis as any other illness. Some plans, however, limit or exclude maternity-related expenses for either the spouse or the dependent children or occasionally for the subscriber/member. The services normally provided in maternity cases include all routine, antepartum care (prior to delivery), delivery, and all routine, postpartum care (after delivery). The maternity procedure codes are based on this premise unless the specific code indicates otherwise. Therefore, if the doctor breaks up his or her bill into different segments, the charges should be combined and lumped together under the single appropriate code. This would apply unless the patient sees different doctors for antepartum care and for delivery or for any other combination. In such a case, the benefits would be broken up in a way to compensate the doctors appropriately for their services.

Antepartum care (prenatal) includes:

- Initial and subsequent history.
- Physician's exams, usually 1 per month for the first 8 months, then weekly during the 9th month.
- Weight, blood pressure, urinalysis (monthly or weekly).
- Fetal heart tones.
- Maternity counseling on food requirements, vitamins, and related items.

Delivery includes:

- Vaginal delivery (with or without episiotomy, forceps or breech delivery).
- Cesarean delivery.

Postpartum care (after delivery) includes:

- Postdelivery hospital visits.
- Postdelivery office visits (usually 1 or 2 routine check-ups) during the first 6 weeks following delivery.

Maternity Billing Procedures

Maternity cases are usually billed in a unique manner. Most Ob-Gyn physicians require full payment from the patient before the delivery date. Conversely, most benefit plans will not process the claim for any benefits until after the delivery. Therefore, the patient often has a substantial, initial out-of-pocket amount. The following are some of the more common maternity billing procedures:

- Lump sum billings: When a lump sum charge (a single, all-encompassing charge) is made for total obstetric care, the charge should be coded and processed under the appropriate CPT/RVS code for total obstetric care.
- Itemized billings after delivery: When charges for antepartum care, delivery, and postpartum care are itemized by the physician, the charges should be combined into one charge and processed under the CPT/RVS code for total obstetric care. Charges for routine ultrasonography may or may not be covered by the plan. Usually, these charges are considered and coded separately from obstetric care. Charges for lab studies, especially

urinalysis, are usually considered part of the complete care unless the physician indicates medical necessity for services beyond routine care. (Routine lab expenses may be coded and allowable separately. This varies by payor.)

- Predelivery billings: When a physician bills for the total obstetric care prior to delivery (based on monthly installments, eg, 80% of the charge by the 7th month), the plan may deny the claim and ask the doctor to rebill after delivery. Other plans may consider payment on the part of the services that have been provided as of the date of the billing. Clarification needs to be requested.
- Two or more physicians (unrelated, not in the same medical group): If two or more physicians are involved in the total obstetric care of a patient (usually one performs the delivery and the other provides the antepartum or postpartum care), each physician's charge should be processed separately for the services rendered. CPT code 59410 is for a vaginal delivery only (including in-hospital postpartum care). For antepartum care only (up to three office visits), use the appropriate office visit code range of 99201—99205 for the initial visit and 99211—99215 for subsequent visits. Antepartum care beyond three visits should use CPT code 59425 or 59426. 59430 is for postpartum care only.

Other Maternity-Related Procedures

The following are other types of maternity billings that you may encounter:

- Artificial insemination is the introduction of semen into the vagina or cervix by artificial means. Some plans consider this a covered expense, and some do not since it is not treatment of a disease condition.
- Amniocentesis/chromosomal analysis is the transabdominal perforation of the uterus for the purpose of withdrawing amniotic fluid surrounding the fetus. The chromosomal analysis is the diagnostic study performed on the fluid to study the number and structure of the chromosomes to see whether any abnormalities are present.

An amniocentesis/chromosomal analysis is performed:

- To identify genetic defects of the fetus.
- To determine whether the fetus has attained an adequate state of gestation.
- To determine the sex of the fetus.

Charges for amniocentesis and chromosomal analysis are usually covered if the attending physician can demonstrate the medical necessity of the testing for the patient, such as a family history of specific genetic defects, maternal age of greater than 35 years, and so on. The use of these tests to determine fetal sex alone is not covered by most plans.

In utero fetal surgery has made it possible to perform surgery on a fetus while it is in the mother's womb and also to remove the fetus from the womb, perform surgery, and return it to the womb with the pregnancy continuing to term. If the surgery is covered, it is probably covered as the mother's expense as a complication of pregnancy.

In vitro fertilization is the fertilization of the ovum within a test tube. Charges for in vitro fertilization may be covered. Refer to the plan for verification.

Abortion is the premature expulsion of an embryo or nonviable fetus. There are three different types of abortions:

1. A spontaneous abortion occurring naturally.
2. A therapeutic abortion intentionally induced because the life of the mother would be endangered if the pregnancy were allowed to continue to term.
3. An elective abortion intentionally induced to terminate an unwanted pregnancy.

Coverage for abortions varies greatly from plan to plan. Spontaneous and therapeutic abortions are covered by most plans. Elective abortions are often excluded from consideration. In addition, some plans may pay for certain services for spouses and then exclude these services for dependent children. Therefore, read the plan document carefully before processing these types of expenses.

Delivery with Tubal Ligation

Not all plans cover sterilization. For those plans that do not cover sterilization, the expense for a tubal ligation, regardless of when it is performed, would be denied as not a covered expense.

When the plan provides coverage for sterilization procedures and a tubal ligation is performed during the same operative session as that for a vaginal delivery, the UCR fee (or the surgeon's fee, whichever is less) for the delivery would be allowable at 100% and the sterilization fee would be allowable at 50% of UCR.

When a sterilization procedure is performed during the same hospitalization as that for a vaginal delivery but not in the same operative session, 100% of the fee or UCR would be allowable for each procedure.

When a tubal ligation is performed during the same operative session as that for a cesarean section or intra-abdominal surgery, the C-section should be processed under the appropriate CPT/RVS code and the tubal under CPT code 58611. The UCR for both the C-section and the tubal ligation should be allowable at 100%, since the relative value for 58611 has already been reduced.

Vaginal delivery with:	
Tubal ligation	59400–100%
During same operative session	58605–50%

Vaginal delivery with:	
Tubal ligation	59400–100%
Not during same operative session	58605–100%

C-section delivery with:	
Tubal ligation	59510–100%
During same operative session	58611–50%

C-section delivery with:	
Tubal ligation	59510–100%
Not during same operative session	58605–100%

Cosmetic Surgery

Cosmetic surgery is a surgical procedure performed solely to improve appearance and is usually not covered by benefit plans.

To properly handle possible cosmetic claims, become familiar with the terminology. The following are some of the more common cosmetic procedures and are therefore not usually covered. However, each claim should be investigated and evaluated on an individual basis. The primary intent of each procedure must be established to determine whether the procedure is cosmetic or reconstructive.

Although some procedures are cosmetic in nature, they may also be performed for functional reasons. For instance, a blepharoplasty is the removal of excess skin and fat from the eyelids. Certainly, removal of excessive skin and fat improves the person's appearance. However, most plans cover blepharoplasty when the skin overhang is so extensive that it interferes with the patient's peripheral vision. Therefore, the fact that a cosmetic procedure is performed does not necessarily mean that it is considered solely cosmetic.

When the restorative or cosmetic nature of the procedure is not obvious, claim investigation must be initiated with a careful review of the following documentation:

- Hospital admission history and physical.
- Operative report.
- Pathology report.
- Pre- and postoperative photographs.
- A narrative report from a referring physician, if available.

Preoperative and Postoperative Photographs

Providers routinely take preoperative and postoperative photographs. These photos are sometimes needed to determine whether a surgery was cosmetic in nature.

To request photographs, use a standard request for additional information form letter. The operative report for the procedure should be requested at the same time.

When the operative report and photographs are received, they should be compared with the claim to determine the reason for the surgery. If the surgery appears to be cosmetic in nature, the claim, along with the photographs and any reports, should be forwarded to a consultant for review.

Cosmetic Procedure Guidelines

Following are three general guidelines regarding cosmetic surgeries:

1. Cosmetic surgery done purely for cosmetic reasons is not covered. However, cosmetic surgery after an accident, injury, or surgical procedure may be covered (eg, breast reconstruction after a mastectomy).
2. When there is an underlying condition, the surgery is not considered cosmetic, regardless of the nature of the surgery (eg, removal of a scar if there is an underlying disease).
3. When processing a surgical claim, determine the primary reason for the surgical procedure. If the treatment is due to injury or disease, the surgery is not considered cosmetic.

Possible Cosmetic Procedures

Following is a list of procedures that can be considered cosmetic in nature. These are some of the more common surgeries that might be questioned as to their being cosmetic or not. Keep in mind that numerous other procedures and services would fall under a cosmetic heading. This sample list is for training purposes only, and the individual plan guidelines should be consulted prior to processing a surgery claim.

Blepharochalasis—A condition in which the skin of the eyelids sags. In severe cases, the peripheral vision may be impaired.

Blepharoplasty—Surgical repair of the eyelids. This surgery is done to correct blepharoptosis, which is a drooping of the upper eyelid (see Figure 12-1). This condition may cause impairment of peripheral vision. The surgery may be of the upper lid only, the lower lid only, or both upper and lower lids. Surgery of both lids requires the use of modifier -50.

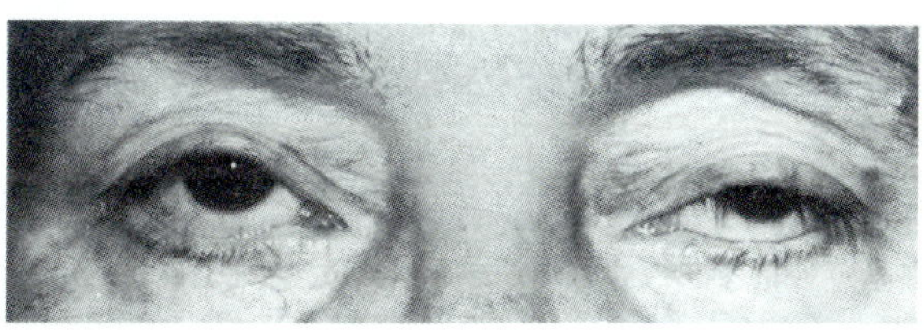

Figure 12-1: Blepharoptosis.
Smith: Ophthalmic Plastic and Reconstructive Surgery, St. Louis,1987, Mosby.

When blepharoplasty is done on the upper lid, the removal of the fat decreases the bulging lid, relieving the patient of a perpetual "tired look" about the eyes and thus imparting a more youthful appearance. The diagnosis most often listed on the claim is blepharochalasis, which means "acquired atrophy of the skin of the upper eyelid as in aging."

Blepharoplasty may also be done for ptosis, which is an abnormal downward displacement of the eyelid due to muscle weakness, eyelid trauma, facial nerve paralysis, or loss of innervation. As this condition worsens, vision is progressively impaired by the tissue obstructing the pupil. The operative report for treatment of functional blepharoptosis will describe structural rearrangement such as palpebral muscle shortening, resection of the part of the upper lid including the tarsal plate, nerve and muscle transplantation, and facial sling.

Vision impairment is the only condition for which an upper lid blepharoplasty would be considered noncosmetic. Lower lid blepharoplasties are nearly always considered cosmetic. The documentation required to assess visual impairment includes at least one of the following:

- Results of a tangent screen examination.
- Results of a confrontation test.
- Results of perimeter testing.

The latter tests measure the patient's peripheral vision and support the medical record and preoperative photos in establishing the functional need for surgery.

Claims received for lower lid blepharoplasty are usually purely cosmetic. The surgery consists of removing the herniated fat pads in the lower lid and excising the redundant skin. Three conditions in which a blepharoplasty of the lower lid may be indicated and not considered cosmetic are:

1. Ectropion—A condition in which the margin of the upper or lower eyelid turns outward. When the lower lid is involved, involuntary tearing often constitutes the most annoying symptom. Surgery consists of removing a portion of the inside of the lid to cause the eyelid to turn inward. This is a functional correction.

2. Entropion—A condition in which the margin of the upper or lower eyelid turns in, causing the eyelashes to rub against and irritate the eyeball. If a secondary infection occurs, scarring of the cornea may ensue with subsequent loss of vision. Therefore, correcting the condition in the early stages of development is important. Surgery consists in cutting away a portion of the inside of the eyelid in a way that causes the eyelid to turn outward. This is a functional correction.

3. Lid lesions—Most often a chalazion that is a cyst-like mass resulting in chronic inflammation of the meibomian gland in the eyelid. This may also be called a meibomian or tarsal cyst. Another lesion is a hordeolum or sty, which is an infection of the eyelash and is associated with whitish pus under the skin. When medical treatment fails to alleviate the condition, surgery may be done to remove the affected area. Tumors constitute the third type of lesion that might require surgical care.

In a blepharoplasty, the pockets of fat in the upper and lower lids beneath the skin are removed. The ellipse of skin has to be cut off to elevate the drooping eyebrow. The margins are sewn together, with the final suture line lying with the eyebrow's upper hairline. The redundant skin of the lower lid is undermined, and the excess fat is removed along with the redundant skin. The wound is then sutured with fine silk.

The suture line in the upper eyelid partially coincides with the old; the one in the lower lid is disguised by the eyelashes. The rest of the two sutures coincide with the natural creases about the eyes.

Breast augmentation—Surgical enlargement of the breast by use of implants. Implants can come in many various types but are most often gel- or fluid-filled sacs.

Breast prosthesis—An artificial sac implanted in the chest muscles to replace or enlarge the breast. Many types of prostheses are available.

Breast reconstruction—A procedure in which an implant is placed under the skin or muscle of the chest wall to restore the contour of a missing breast. This procedure is usually eligible when it is used to restore the appearance of patients who have had a mastectomy due to cancer, fibroadenoma, or fibrocystic breast disease. Claims submitted for breast reconstruction should include the diagnosis of the underlying disease and the date of the previously performed mastectomy. In cases of breast cancer, only those charges submitted for reconstruction of the removed breast are considered eligible expense. Charges submitted for reduction mammoplasty on the unaffected side (to make the unaffected breast appear similar in size and shape to the reconstructed breast) are considered cosmetic and are usually not eligible.

Asymmetry is a condition in which the breasts are grossly dissimilar in size, shape, or arrangement on the chest wall. Since a slight discrepancy in the breasts is normal, the condition must be severe to be considered functional (see Figures 12-2 and 12-3).

Breast reduction—Surgical procedure to reduce the size of the breast. This may be covered in extreme cases (usually when over 1 pound of fat is removed on each side).

Chemical peel or chemical abrasion—This has the same effect as dermabrasion except that caustic chemicals such as phenol or trichloracetic acid (TCA) are used. The technique creates a superficial chemical burn which, when healed, has flattened fine wrinkles and tightened the skin. This is considered purely cosmetic.

Cheiloplasty—Surgery of the lips. The lips, like the skin and mucous membranes of other parts of the body, are subject to precancerous and cancerous lesions. These lesions most often occur in fair-skinned persons with a long history of exposure to sunlight.

A common precancerous condition is known as *hyperkeratosis,* a condition in which the mucosa of the lip becomes paler, thinner, and more fragile with numerous cracks and fissures. Gradually, ulcerations appear, which continue to break down and heal. Treatment consists of removing all of the involved lip surface and advancing the inner lining of the lip to cover the defect. This procedure is called *lip stripping and resurfacing* and is considered medically necessary.

A cheiloplasty can also be done to make the lips narrower, to enlarge thin lips, and to create a "cupid's bow" (the dip in the edge line of the upper lip). When done for these reasons, cheiloplasty would be consid-

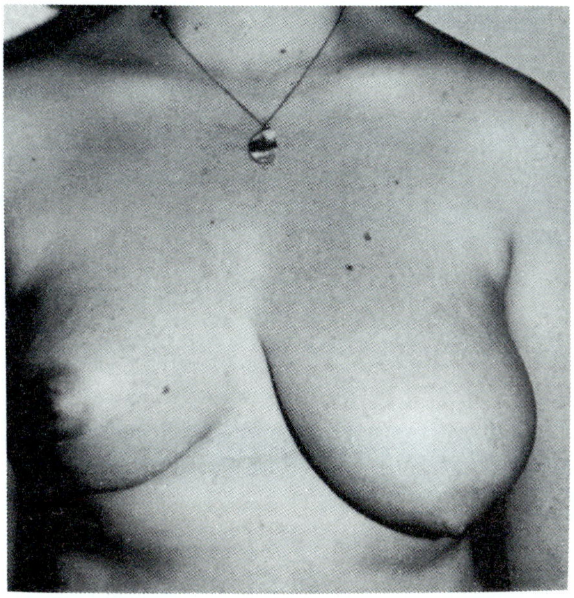

Figure 12-2: Breast asymmetry.
Jurkiewicz: *Plastic Surgery Principles and Practice*, St. Louis,1990, Mosby.

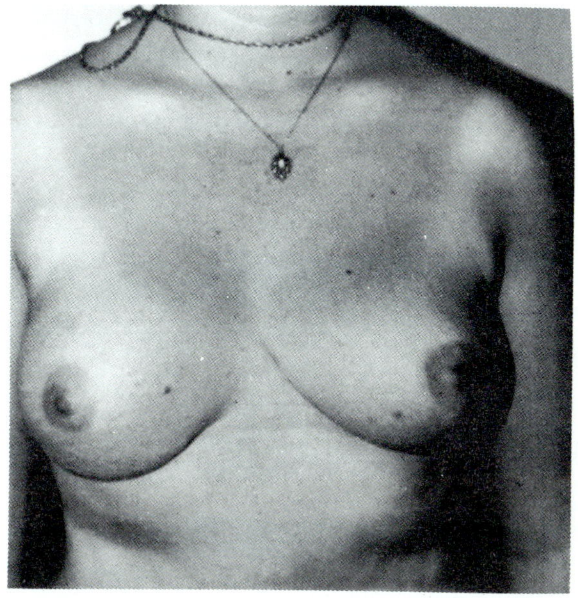

Figure 12-3: Symmetry achieved by surgery.
Jurkiewicz.

ered cosmetic.

Cleft lip and palate—A birth defect in which the two sides of the face fail to unite properly in the early stage of prenatal development, resulting in a fissure or split in the lip and/or palate (roof) of the mouth. A cleft lip may occur unilaterally (Figure 12-4) or bilaterally. An incomplete cleft lip occurs when a bridge of skin connects the cleft and noncleft sides (Figure 12-5). If a skin bridge does not exist, the cleft is complete. Deformity of the nose usually accompanies a cleft lip in the form of a distortion and displacement of the lower lateral nasal cartilage.

Surgery to correct a cleft lip and/or palate is scheduled when a child is old enough to tolerate the procedure safely, usually at about 10 weeks of age with a weight of about 10 pounds and a hemoglobin of 10 g. By that time, the tissues are large enough to allow accurate repair. Further correction of the nasal deformity, often with simultaneous revision of minor lip irregularities, may be done when the child is older and final

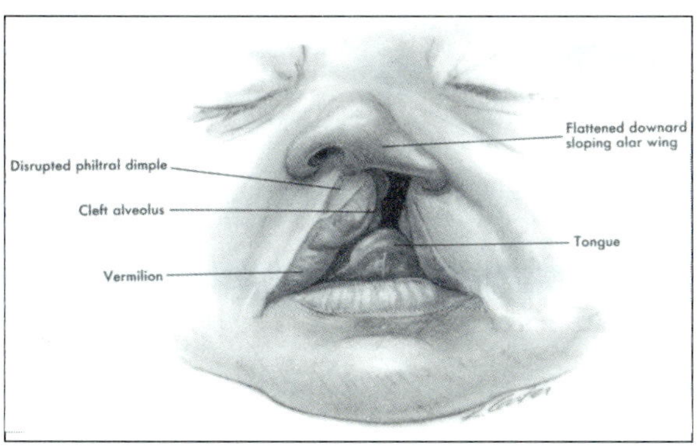

Figure 12-4: Unilateral cleft lip.
Jurkiewicz.

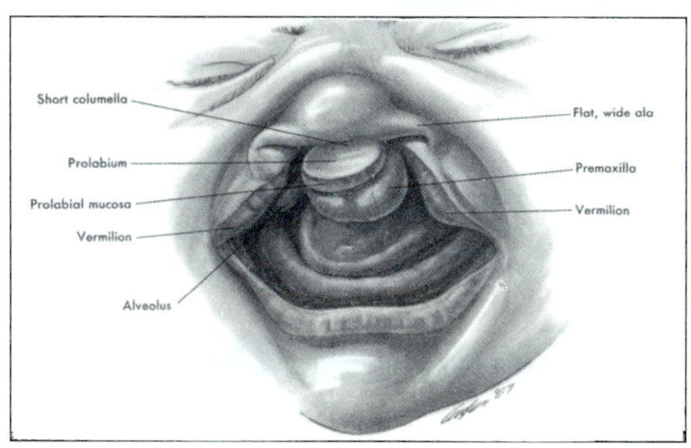

Figure 12-5: Bilateral cleft lip.
Jurkiewicz.

surgery may be delayed until adolescence to allow for full maturity of the facial features. Services to correct this congenital defect are considered functional.

However, claims for services related to cleft lip (and possibly palate) repair in persons older than adolescent age should be reviewed for possible purely cosmetic repair and not functional repair of the defect.

Collagen or zyderm injections—Zyderm is a medical grade of collagen (taken from cows), which is injected into fine lines or small defects in the skin. It is a temporary measure, which plumps up the indented areas making them appear less pronounced. Usually, supplemental injections must be performed about every 6 to 9 months. Collagen injections are strictly cosmetic.

Congenital anomaly—A birth defect. Depending on the defect, a congenital abnormality may or may not be covered by a plan.

Dermabrasion—A procedure using abrasive materials (sandpaper, emery paper, or wire brushes) to remove acne scars, birthmarks, fine wrinkles, or other skin defects. When the skin grows back, the surface irregularities have been smoothed away. Although this is considered a cosmetic procedure, check the plan guidelines because it may be covered to restore the skin to the appearance of a presickness state. Some plans may cover dermabrasion for cases of severe acne.

Deviated nasal septum—A condition in which the dividing wall between the two nasal cavities is deflected (turned) away from the center of the nose.

Electrolysis epilation—Removal of hair by destruction of the hair follicle (root) with an electric current. This is considered the only method of permanent removal of hair currently available. For women, the usual diagnosis submitted is hirsutism, which is a condition of adult male hair growth in a female. Electrolysis does not treat the underlying condition, which is a hormonal imbalance and is therefore considered purely cosmetic.

Gynecomastia—A swelling of the breast tissue in the male. If an underlying hormonal disease has been ruled out, the condition is treated by removing a small section of the breast tissue. This may be considered eligible under some plans.

Hair transplantation—Moving healthy hair follicles from one location on the body to another location—usually the head. Alopecia areata is a condition in which patchy areas of baldness occur. Alopecia means the absence of hair from areas where it normally occurs. Male pattern baldness (androgenic alopecia) is loss of hair from the crown of the head. This occurs in about 30% of adult males. A few medications have been shown to assist in regrowing hair in some instances. Transplantation does not treat the condition, only the symptoms and is therefore usually considered purely cosmetic.

Hypertrophied/macromastia breasts—An abnormal enlargement of the female breasts caused by hormonal factors or obesity. The condition may require a mastectomy when the weight of the breast tissue causes physical complaints. Among the symptoms present are shoulder, neck, and back pain; numbness of the hand and arm caused by the bra straps compressing the brachial plexus (the group of nerves in the area between the neck and shoulder that innervate the arm); and chronic inflammation of the skin of the opposed surfaces (intertrigo). Documentation to substantiate the functional nature of this procedure includes pre- and postoperative photos, admission history and physical examination information including the patient's height and weight, discharge summary, operative report, and pathology report.

Each administrator has its own guidelines. Therefore, all claims involving hypertrophied breasts should be researched prior to payment after verification of the applicable guidelines.

Keloid—A thick scar resulting from excessive growth of fibroid tissue. Any open wound can develop keloid scarring. Therefore, this scarring may occur following surgery. Keloid scar surgery is not usually considered cosmetic.

Lipectomy—The surgical removal of fatty tissue. Common in women over 50 or persons who have lost a large amount of weight. Redundant skin and tissue hanging from the upper arms is known as the "bat wing" deformity. Bat wings do not present any impairment to the function of the arms, and such surgical removal of the redundant fatty tissue and hanging skin is purely aesthetic.

In some persons, excess fat accumulates predominantly on the hips, buttocks, and thighs. This condition is referred to as "riding breeches syndrome." Like bat wing deformity, no functional impairment is involved. The removal of this fatty tissue may be accomplished by standard surgical technique (incisional approach) or by liposuction, which consists of "sucking" out the fatty tissue through a vacuum tube inserted through small incisions. Regardless of the method used, the surgical reduction of hips, thighs, and buttocks is considered cosmetic.

Mammoplasty—Surgery to reduce (reduction mammoplasty) or enlarge (augmentation mammoplasty) the size of the breast.

Amastia or *amazia* is defined as the congenital absence of mammary tissue. These terms refer to masculine breast characteristics in an adult female. Amastia can be unilateral (one-sided) or bilateral (two-sided).

Hypomastia or *hypomazia* is defined as abnormal smallness of the mammary gland and, like amastia, it can affect one or both breasts. In cases in which one breast is normal and the other is markedly small or absent, asymmetry results. Augmentation mammoplasty is performed for both of these conditions.

Mastectomy—Excision or amputation of the breast, usually required as a result of a malignant disease. This is not the same as a reduction mammoplasty. The three types of mastectomies are:

1. *Radical mastectomy* is the removal of the breast tissue (mammary gland), pectoral muscles, axillary lymph nodes, and associated skin and subcutaneous tissue. This procedure is used for the treatment of cancer but may result in the partial loss of arm movement. Usually, radical mastectomy is followed by reconstructive surgery to restore the appearance of the remaining tissue.
2. *Modified radical mastectomy* is the same as the radical procedure except that the pectoral muscles are left intact. This procedure can usually be performed in the earlier stages of cancer (stage I or II). Modified radical mastectomy is also usually followed by reconstructive procedures.
3. *Subcutaneous mastectomy* is a technique in which most of the breast tissue is removed but the skin and areola are preserved. Unlike the other two methods, immediate reconstruction can usually be done by inserting a Silastic prothesis into the subcutaneous pocket left by the excision of the breast tissue or under the pectoralis major muscle. Subcutaneous mastectomy and reconstruction for multipathology breasts (eg, fibrocystic disease, fibroadenoma) consists of removing the mammary tissue and inserting a prosthesis (implant) under the remaining skin to maintain the breast contour. The surgery is used to treat chronic mastitis in patients who experience incapacitating breast pain or those who have repeated breast biopsies of the cystic nodules to rule out cancer.

To determine the medical necessity of a mastectomy, the documentation requested from the physician should include a history of removal of the lumps or repeated aspirations of the cysts as well as the laboratory results of the previous biopsies.

Mentoplasty/genioplasty—Surgery to change the size and shape of the chin with an implant. This procedure is done for a small (microgenic) or moderately receding chin in persons in whom there is no underlying effect with the jaw itself. A small incision is made under the chin and a silicone implant is inserted, giving increased prominence to the chin.

Otoplasty—Plastic surgery to change the position or configuration of the ear or ears. The most common deformities that require an otoplasty are:

- **Protruding or lop ears**—Ears normally set at about a 25-degree angle from the skull. They may protrude due to cartilage deformities to such an extent that they form a right angle to the side of the head. In lop ears, the ear is bent upon itself (see Figure 12-6 a & b). Prominent ears are usually caused by a lack of definition of the antihelical fold. This defect is referred to in the diagnosis and operative report.

  The best age to perform corrective surgery for these conditions is about 13 to 14 years, when the ear has attained almost maximal growth. However, because of the emotional and psycho-

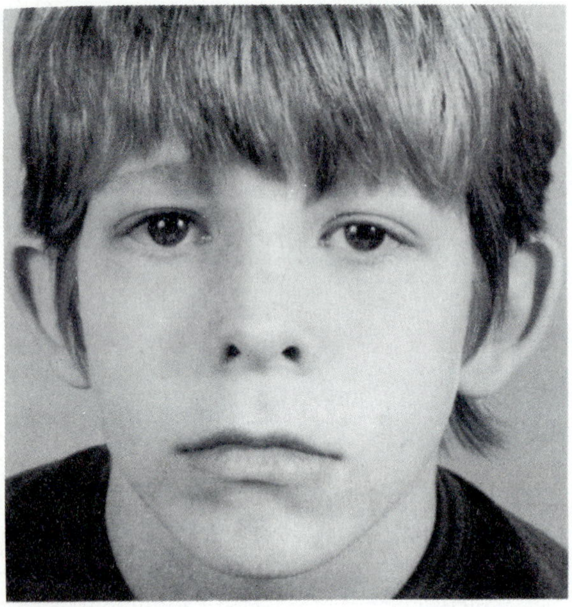

Figure 12-6a: Lop ears (before surgery).
Jurkiewicz.

logical problems associated with these conditions, surgery may be done before the child reaches school age. This surgery is usually considered cosmetic.

- Microtia—A congenital defect characterized by a small, malformed, malpositioned ear remnant. A hearing deficit is almost always present in affected children. Repair begins at age 5 or 6 years and is performed in a series of surgeries. The surgery is considered reconstructive.

Palatoplasty—Plastic surgery of the palate, usually to correct a cleft palate.

Panniculectomy—Removal of a sheet or layer of fatty tissue. This procedure is most often done to remove excess fatty tissue from the abdomen.

"-Plasty"—The surgical suffix that means to mold or to shape.

Ptosis—Drooping or sagging of an organ or part.

Removal of tattoos—This procedure is always considered cosmetic.

Rhinoplasty—Cosmetic repair of the external part of the nose to change its size or shape. This procedure does not involve the internal functioning of the nose,

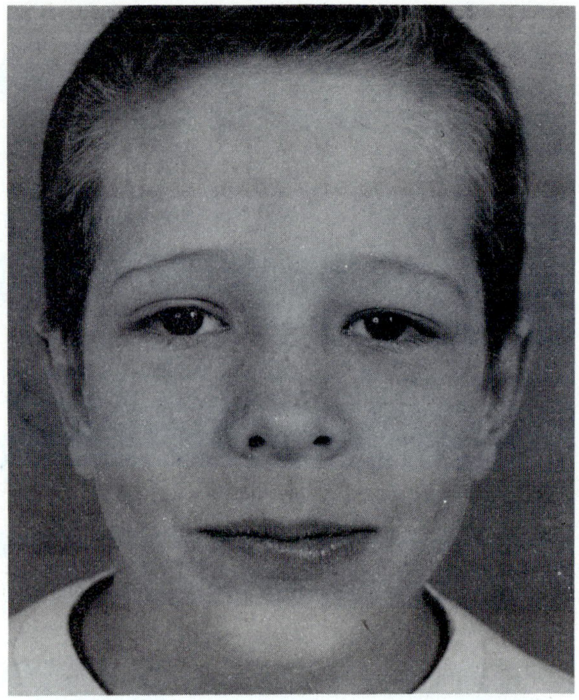

Figure 12-6b: Lop ears (after surgery).
Jurkiewicz.

although it is performed entirely within the nose to prevent scarring.

A rhinoplasty consists of five major steps:

1. Elevating the skin from the bony and cartilaginous dorsum.
2. Removing the hump or lowering a prominent dorsum.
3. Narrowing the nasal pyramid to compensate for the flatness caused by the hump removal.
4. Shortening the nose if necessary.
5. Modeling the tip or lower cartilaginous complex to proportions consistent with the previous steps.

Key words to look for in determining whether surgery on the nose is cosmetic are "modifications of alar cartilages" and "lowering the dorsum." It is never necessary to modify the alar cartilages or lower the dorsum other than for cosmetic reasons. It is also never necessary to do alar base excisions for functional reasons. In fact, this constricts the airway and is against the principle of improving air flow.

Rhinoplasties are often combined with a septoplasty or submucous resection. Therefore, proper claim investigation is essential to determine whether and what part of the nasal procedure is necessary to correct a functional defect versus what part is for purely cosmetic purposes.

The test used to document airway obstruction is called a *rhinomanometry*. It is the measurement of the airflow and pressure within the nose during respiration, and the resistance or obstruction is calculated. Unfortunately, this test is not often performed.

The structures of the nose responsible for airway obstruction are the septum and the nasal turbinates. The septum is made up of the downward projection of the ethmoid bone at the back, the vomer bone at the bottom, and the triangular shaped septal cartilage. It divides the nasal cavity (internal nose) into two wedge-shaped cavities.

An accident can displace the septal cartilage where it meets the vomer or ethmoid bones, causing one side of the nasal cavity to become narrower and to obstruct the airway.

Rhytidectomy—Surgical removal of wrinkles. This procedure is usually cosmetic unless it interferes with the normal function of a body part.

Rhytidoplasty (facelift)—Removal of facial wrinkles. Wrinkles are related to an absorption of subcutaneous fat, a decrease in the thickness and elasticity of the skin, and a failure in adherence of the skin to the deeper tissues—all processes that are part of the normal physiology of aging. This is possibly one of the most graphic examples of a purely cosmetic procedure.

Senile ptosis of the eyelids—A condition in which the skin of the eyelids sags or droops. This may cause vision impairment.

Septoplasty—Surgical correction of a deviated nasal septum. This involves only the internal functioning of the nose and is usually covered. Septoplasty or submucous resection of the septum involves undermining the mucous membrane that covers the septum. This procedure is also referred to as "raising the mucoperichondrial and mucoperiosteal flaps." The cartilage is then cut into at its base so as to allow it to be moved over and straightened.

Septum—The dividing wall between the two nasal cavities.

Submental lipectomy—Removal of fat deposits under the chin. The region under the chin (submental region) and the neck often requires special attention. A submental lipectomy through a separate incision may be required to remove the fat deposits beneath the chin, thus correcting double chins. Suturing and repositioning of the neck muscle (platysma) is done to obliterate jowls.

Submucous resection—Removal of a portion of the nasal septum.

TMJ surgery—Osteoplastic surgery of the jaw for prognathism (projection of the jaw(s) beyond the projection of the forehead), micrognathism (abnormal smallness of jaws), and other variations may be cosmetic or functional, depending on the degree of malocclusion.

Turbinates—Bony projections from the side walls of the internal nose. The purpose of the turbinates is to warm and moisten air. Each nasal cavity is divided into three passageways by the turbinates. A submucous resection of the turbinates consists of undermining the mucous membrane that covers them and removing a portion of the bone, thereby enlarging the nasal passageway. A submucous resection is a functional correction and is therefore an eligible expense.

Wart and mole removal—Moles and warts are discolorations of the skin which protrude above the normal skin elevation. Often warts and moles are associated with other diseases and conditions, especially cancer. Therefore, many plans will cover the removal of warts and moles.

Obesity Surgery

Exogenous obesity is obesity caused by overeating. Treatment for this condition is not considered treatment of a disease and is usually not covered by most plans until the level of obesity reaches a point at which it is life threatening. Most administrators have defined this level as being 100 pounds or 30% over the weight considered optimal for a person of a particular height and bone frame.

Endogenous obesity is obesity caused by an internal malfunction usually hormonal (eg, thyroid disorder). Treatment for this type of obesity or for the underlying cause is considered treatment of a disease and is eligible under most plans. This is a comparatively rare condition.

Most administrators require the following documentation to be submitted before the scheduled treatment for review:

- Current weight and height.
- Frame type (small, medium, large).
- History of weight loss in the past (eg, what diets have been tried, what level of success).
- Concurrent medical complications such as high blood pressure, diabetes.
- Family history of obesity or other health problems.

The following three procedures are the most common procedures used to combat exogenous obesity:

1. Gastric balloon/garren gastric bubble—A procedure in which a balloon is inserted into the stomach, thus giving the impression of being "full." Since many overweight people do not eat because they are hungry but because of habit or compulsion, this has not been an effective method. In addition, many complications, including death, have resulted from this procedure. Therefore, it is no longer considered an accepted medical practice.
2. Gastric bypass—A procedure in which the stomach is bypassed, allowing for food to empty directly into the large intestine. The theory behind this procedure is that the food, nutrients, and fats are not thoroughly broken down and digested, resulting in fewer calories being accessible to the body for storing. Therefore, weight is lost. This is usually considered to be a permanent procedure, although it can be revised. See CPT codes 43844, 43846.
3. Gastric stapling—A procedure in which a portion of the stomach is stapled off so as to reduce the size of the stomach. This procedure decreases the amount of food that may be eaten at a single meal. See CPT code 43843.

All procedures for obesity involving surgery have side effects. Some of the side effects for some people may be so severe that the procedure will have to be reversed. Therefore, only the severely obese should consider any of these methods of treatment.

The alternatives to surgery include the following services that are usually not covered under benefit plans:

Special diets and dietary supplements
HCG (human chorionic gonadotropin) and vitamin injections
Acupuncture
Appetite suppressants
Biofeedback
Hypnosis
Hospital confinements for weight reduction
Exercise programs
Health centers, weight loss centers, or other similar programs
Diet books and instructions

Co-Surgeons

Under some circumstances, two surgeons, usually with similar skills, may operate simultaneously as primary surgeons performing distinct, separate parts of a total surgical service. For example, two surgeons may simultaneously apply skin grafts to different parts of the body or two surgeons may repair different fractures of the same patient.

Different plans and different administrators handle co-surgeons differently. There are no set rules. Therefore, when a claim is received for co-surgeons, plan guidelines or administrative guidelines have to be referred to before processing. Usually co-surgeon procedures are referred to a consultant, supervisor, or Medical Review Department before processing.

Assistant Surgeons

Extensive surgeries require a primary surgeon and an assistant surgeon. The assistant surgeon may do the closing of the operative wound, hemostasis of the wound edges, and suturing of vessels. The job of the assistant surgeon is to assist the primary surgeon as required. Since the assistant surgeon is not the physician primarily responsible for the patient, the UCR allowance is considerably less than that for the surgeon.

The first consideration is that the complexity of the surgical procedure must medically require an assistant (see Appendix 12-1 Assistant Surgeon Procedures on page 167). Obviously, an assistant surgeon would not be covered for minor surgery such as acne surgery (CPT code 10040).

As a rule, the following guidelines may be used in determining whether an assistant is required:

- The place of service is either an inpatient or outpatient hospital, or a surgicenter. Seldom are major surgeries performed in an office.
- Usually, follow-up days are listed in the RVS for the procedure. Services without follow-up days are not complex enough to require an assistant.

The allowance for an assistant surgeon is 20% of the surgery allowance (UCR). Modifier -80 is used to designate the assistant surgeon's fee.

Example:

Procedure 20205 has a unit value of 10.0. The conversion factor is \$8.50. Therefore, 10 units x \$8.50 = \$85.00, 20% of \$85.00 = \$17.00.

Based on the previously stated guidelines, \$17.00 would be considered UCR.

Summary

Surgery charges may be the most complicated charges you will encounter. That is why there are so many guidelines covering surgery, multiple surgery, and cosmetic surgery. If for any reason you are unsure, request the opinion of a senior examiner or technical person.

The use of an assistant surgeon always depends on the medical necessity of the procedure performed. Using these guidelines and the Assistant Surgeon Procedures list will enable you to determine whether the assistant surgeon is necessary and what portion of the charges are covered.

Assignments

Complete the Questions for Review.

Complete billing of the Surgery and Multiple Surgery claims in the Student Exercise Manual and process claims 5-1 to 5-15 and 6-1 to 6-10 in the Exercise Manual using the guidelines covered.

Complete billing of the Assistant Surgery claims in the Student Exercise Manual and process Assistant Surgery claims 7-1 to 7-15.

Questions for Review

Directions: Answer the following questions without looking back into the material just covered. Write your answers in the space provided.

1. Define surgery. branch of medicine that treats diseases, injuries + deformities by operative or invasive methods

2. Are cosmetic surgical procedures usually covered by benefit plans? (Yes or No) no

3. What are the four types of surgical procedures? (List and define.)

   a. Diagnostic - procedures are those performed to determine the presence of disease or the cause of the patients symptoms

   b. Therapeutic - procedures are performed to remove or correct the functioning of the body part that is diseased or injured

   c. Reconstructive - performed to rebuild or restore aesthetically a part of the body that was damaged or defective as a result of injury or illness

   d. Cosmetic - procedures performed solely to improve the appearance of a part + are not usually covered by ins.

4. What does the physician's charge for surgery performed in the office generally include? performing the surgical procedure, administering the anesthesia, and all routine follow up care

5. Identify two situations that would warrant separate payment for preoperative care.

   a. when preoperative visit is a consult

   b. Procedures that are not usually part of the basic surgical procedure are provided during the immediate preoperative period

6. What does the surgical unit value include? the surgery, local anesthesia, the normal, uncomplicated follow-up care associated with the procedure for the time period indicated in the section titled follow up days

7. When is follow-up care allowed separately? complications or other circumstances requiring additional or unusual services concurrent with the procedure or during the listed period of normal follow up care

8. What are asterisk procedures? are surgical procedures denoted by an asterisk to the left of CPT code, which require special handling

9. What are By Report procedures and what other term may be used to indicate these procedures? Procedures so unusual or variable that it is impossible to determine a standard UCR or unit allowance. Relative Value not Established (RNE) BR and RNE

10. What services are normally provided in maternity cases? all routine, antepartum care delivery, & all routine, postpartum care

11. What are therapeutic procedures? procedures performed to remove or correct the functioning of a body part that is diseased or injured.

12. What is the difference between a cosmetic procedure and a reconstructive procedure? cosmetic - performed solely to improve appearance of a part Reconstructive - to rebuild or restore part of body that was damaged as a result of injury or illness

13. What is a blepharoplasty? surgical repair of eyelid. may be upper lid only, lower lid only, or both upper + lower lid

14. Define lump sum billing in relation to maternity charges. a single, all encompassing charge. Its made for total obstetric care

15. When would charges for amniocentesis or chromosomal analysis usually be covered? if attending physician can show its medically necessary for testing the patient. family history of specific genetic defects - over age 35

16. What is cheiloplasty? surgery of the lips

17. Are collagen injections a cosmetic procedure? yes

18. What is the name of the surgical procedure for reduction or enlargement of the breast? Mammoplasty
19. What is the name of the surgical procedure for excision or amputation of the breast? Mastectomy
20. What is a deviated nasal septum? a condition in which the dividing wall between the 2 nasal cavities is turned away from the center of the nose
21. An extensive surgery requires an assistant surgeon without a primary surgeon. (True or False) False
22. Major surgeries are normally done in the doctor's office. (True or False) False
23. Modifier 80 is used to designate the assistant surgeon's fee.
24. The allowance for an assistant surgeon is 20% of the surgery allowance.
25. Would an assistant surgeon be required for acne surgery? No

If you were unable to answer any of the questions, refer back to the section and then complete the answers.

Appendix 12-1

Assistant Surgeon Procedures

The following is a list of surgical procedures by CPT code for which an assistant surgeon is considered NOT necessary. These procedures use an assistant surgeon in fewer than 5% of these surgeries performed in the United States. This is a partial list and is intended to be used for training and reference purposes only, as the particular company or plan guidelines may differ from those guidelines stated. Each company or plan will generally provide its own similar list. However, the list may run several hundred codes in length.

11921	26516	46700	63308
17108	27358	52510	63746
19328	27619	54110	64862
21616	27831	54430	65155
23020	28290	54645	66605
24101	30140	55040	67101
24105	30520	55680	67311
24110	30620	56304	67875
24351	31502	58880	68505
25295	33470	59821	69631
25909	36469	61106	69670
26037	37700	61556	
26358	42220	62142	

13

Anesthesia

In this chapter you will learn:

- To define the four methods of anesthesia administration.
- The anesthesia CPT code ranges (10000–69999).
- To identify anesthesia modifiers.
- To calculate anesthesia benefits (both base and time units).

Anesthesia is the artificially induced loss of feeling and sensation with or without loss of consciousness. The four kinds of anesthesia administration methods are:

1. General anesthesia
2. Regional anesthesia
3. Intravenous (IV) sedation
4. Acupuncture

General Anesthesia

General anesthesia produces a state of unconsciousness. It may be brought about by inhalation of drugs such as ether, nitrous oxide, and ethylene or by drugs administered intravenously such as sodium pentothal. General anesthesia produces preliminary excitement, replaced by a loss of voluntary control. Loss of consciousness occurs when the anesthetic reaches the brain, with hearing being the last sense to be lost. Most major operations, particularly on the upper abdomen, chest, head, and neck, are performed under general anesthesia. A number of side effects may accompany general anesthesia, many of which cannot be controlled or predicted. General anesthesia is considered more dangerous than other forms of anesthesia. Therefore, anesthesiologists have one of the highest malpractice insurance rates.

Prior to surgery requiring general anesthesia, the anesthesiologist usually meets with the patient to assess his or her general health and record age, weight, concurrent medical problems, family history, and other pertinent data. Anesthesiologists are reluctant to administer general anesthesia to patients who are extremely obese or who have blood pressure or respiratory problems because they have the highest risk factors.

General anesthesia can be used in outpatient surgery. However, it requires a prolonged postoperative recovery period (usually 2 to 4 hours) and therefore is commonly reserved for use in a facility setting (outpatient hospital, surgicenter). The administration of general anesthesia in a doctor's or dentist's office is considered very dangerous, although some specialists do so routinely.

Regional Anesthesia

Regional anesthesia is the loss of sensation of a part of the body due to the interruption of nerve conduction. While regional anesthesia is in effect, the patient remains conscious. This method is adequate for many operations and is considerably less dangerous than general anesthesia. Regional anesthesia can be safely performed on an outpatient basis. The three types of regional anesthesia are topical, local, and nerve block.

Topical anesthesia is applied directly to the surface of the area to be anesthetized. The conjunctiva and mucous membranes of the mouth, throat, urethra, and bladder are examples of areas that are most effectively anesthetized by a topical application.

Local anesthesia affects only a localized area. The drug is directly introduced by injection into the skin and subcutaneous tissues. The anesthesia injection wears off very quickly; therefore, only short procedures can be performed painlessly. Superficial biopsies, mole excisions, and suturing of lacerations are the most common procedures performed with a local anesthesia.

For a **nerve block anesthesia,** a drug is injected close to the nerve so that the nerve impulses are interrupted, thereby producing a loss of sensation.

Spinal anesthesia is a special type of nerve block. The spinal nerves are blocked in either the subarachnoid or the epidural space. The term **spinal anesthesia** generally refers to nerves blocked in the subarachnoid space. **Epidural anesthesia** refers to the nerves blocked in the epidural space. Another type of spinal anesthetic is a **saddle block.** This is so named because the injection produces a loss of feeling in the region of the body that corresponds to the area that makes contact with a riding saddle (buttocks, perineum, and thighs). Spinal anesthesia was formerly used frequently for normal deliveries. Now, it is mainly used on operations within the peritoneal cavity and on the lower extremities.

Intravenous Sedation

Intravenous (IV) sedation is a medication composed of a sedative and a painkiller administered intravenously.

A semiconscious state is produced. A common mixture is meperidine (Demerol) and diazepam (Valium). This type of anesthesia is often used in dental surgical procedures and in many diagnostic procedures such as bronchoscopy and esophagogastroduodenoscopy in which the surgical invasion is obtained through an existing orifice. This type of anesthesia is commonly referred to as "twilight sleep."

Acupuncture

Acupuncture is an ancient Chinese procedure in which fine needles are inserted into various points in the body to relieve pain and to regulate and improve body functions. There are more than 1000 acupuncture locations on the body. A different effect is produced in each location or combination of locations. Sometimes only one needle is necessary; sometimes many. The patient remains awake and can talk during the procedure. Acupuncture works similarly to the way in which nerve block anesthesia works. Although this type of anesthesia is popular in China, it is not used extensively in America.

Handling Procedures

An anesthesiologist may be classified as either a hospital staff anesthesiologist (employed by the hospital) or an independent anesthesiologist (self-employed or not employed by the hospital). Charges made by a hospital for the services of a staff anesthesiologist are usually covered as a hospital ancillary expense.

Charges by an outside anesthesiologist vary according to the plan provisions, but are usually covered under either a separate (Basic) anesthesia benefit or Major Medical. When processing, do not confuse the professional anesthesia expense with the charges that may appear on a hospital bill. The anesthesia charges on a hospital bill are for the actual anesthesia drug, the anesthesia machine, and other associated supplies.

RVS Ground Rules

The CPT code range for anesthesia is 00100—01999. The RVS may use 00100—01999 or 10000—69999 (same as surgery). Anesthesia unit values are listed in the RVS for procedures that require that anesthesia be administered by an anesthesiologist. Remember that local anesthesia is never allowable separately. Therefore, anesthesia benefits are those that are allowed on procedures that require more than a local anesthesia. These units (for all schedules) are used when:

- The anesthesia is personally administered by a licensed physician.
- The physician remains in constant attendance during the procedure for the sole purpose of rendering the anesthesia service.

Basic/Base Units

The basic or base anesthesia units are designed to allow for the usual pre- and postoperative care, the administration of the anesthesia, and the administration of fluids or blood incident to the anesthesia or surgery.

Remember that the surgical unit values include surgery, local infiltration, and digital block or topical anesthesia.

Time Units

The length of time that a person is under anesthesia determines the amount of money that will be considered allowable for the procedure. Anesthesia time begins when the anesthesiologist starts to physically prepare the patient for the induction of anesthesia in the operating room area (or its equivalent). The time ends when the anesthesiologist is no longer in constant attendance, usually when the patient is ready for postoperative supervision.

For the first 4 hours, time units are computed by allowing 1.0 time unit for each 15 minutes, or if less than 15 minutes, 1.0 unit is allowed for spans between 5 and 15 minutes. After 4 hours, 1.0 unit is allowed for each 10 minutes, or if less than 10 minutes, 1.0 unit is allowed for spans between 5 and 10 minutes. The reason for this is that the risks of injury or adverse effects significantly increase with time. Therefore, extra compensation is provided for extended anesthesia time.

For example, if the anesthesia time were 50 minutes, a total of 4.0 time units would be allowed: 1.0 unit for every 15 minutes = 3.0 units plus 1.0 unit for the additional 5 minutes. Therefore, the same number of units would be allowed for a 50-minute procedure, a 55-minute procedure, or a 1-hour procedure.

Many anesthesiologists bill the time according to the military clock, that is, by a 24-hour standard. When using military time, do not worry with converting to the regular clock. The regular time is unimportant. Instead, concentrate only on determining the time units involved. For instance:

(1) 13:15 to 14:25 = 1 hour = 4.0 units
14:15 to 14:25 = 10 min = 1.0 unit
1 hr 10 min = 5.0 units

(2) 15:20 to 18:25 = 3 hours = 12.0 units
18:20 to 18:25 = 5 min = 1.0 unit
3 hr 5 min = 13.0 units

Anesthesia Time	Units of Occurrence
5 min - 19 min	1 unit
20 min - 34 min	2 units
35 min - 49 min	3 units
50 min - 1 hr 4 min	4 units
1 hr 5 min - 1 hr 19 min	5 units
1 hr 20 min - 1 hr 34 min	6 units
1 hr 35 min - 1 hr 49 min	7 units
1 hr 50 min - 2 hr 4 min	8 units
2 hr 5 min - 2 hr 19 min	9 units
2 hr 20 min - 2 hr 34 min	10 units
2 hr 35 min - 2 hr 49 min	11 units
2 hr 50 min - 3 hr 4 min	12 units
3 hr 5 min - 3 hr 19 min	13 units
3 hr 20 min - 3 hr 34 min	14 units
3 hr 35 min - 3 hr 49 min	15 units
3 hr 50 min - 4 hr 4 min	16 units
4 hr 5 min - 4 hr 14 min	17 units
4 hr 15 min - 4 hr 24 min	18 units
4 hr 25 min - 4 hr 34 min	19 units
4 hr 35 min - 4 hr 44 min	20 units
4 hr 45 min - 4 hr 54 min	21 units
4 hr 55 min - 5 hr 4 min	22 units
5 hr 5 min - 5 hr 14 min	23 units

Calculating Anesthesia

The anesthesia allowance is calculated by adding the basic units to the time units and multiplying that amount by the conversion factor. This procedure applies to all schedules.

	Basic Unit Value for the procedure
+	Time Unit Value
+	Modifier unit value (if applicable)
	Total anesthesia value

Total anesthesia value × plan/Basic Conversion Factor = Anesthesia basic allowance or plan UCR

Multiple Procedures

On anesthesia claims with multiple procedures, the basic units for the major procedure (the procedure with the greatest number of basic units) are the only basic units allowed. The basic units for the secondary procedure are not taken into account. The additional expense is accommodated by allowing the extra time units necessitated for completion of the multiple procedures.

Modifiers

Anesthesia services are recognizable on a claim by the two-digit modifier code that follows the procedure code or by the time shown somewhere on the claim. Physical status modifiers are represented by the initial P, followed by a single digit from 1 to 6.

P1: A normal healthy patient

P2: A patient with mild systemic disease

P3: A patient with severe systemic disease

P4: A patient with severe systemic disease that is a constant threat to life

P5: A moribund patient who is not expected to survive without the operation

P6: A declared brain-dead patient whose organs are being removed for donor purposes

Optional modifiers denote special conditions. The following are the valid anesthesia two-digit modifier codes (for additional information, consult your CPT):

- 22: Unusual services
- 23: Unusual anesthesia
- 32: Mandated services
- 47: Anesthesia by surgeon
- 51: Multiple procedures, but not bilateral
- 75: Concurrent care, services rendered by more than one physician

Qualifying Circumstances

Many anesthesia services are provided under particularly difficult circumstances, depending on factors such as extraordinary condition of the patient, notable operative conditions, and unusual risk factors. This section includes a list of important qualifying circumstances that make a significant impact on the character of the anesthesia service provided. These procedures would not be reported alone, but as additional procedure numbers qualifying an anesthesia procedure or service. More than one may be selected.

99100 Anesthesia for patient of extreme age, under 1 year or over 70 years

99116 Anesthesia complicated by use of total body hypothermia

99135 Anesthesia complicated by use of controlled hypotension

99140 Anesthesia complicated by emergency conditions. Most plans require emergency conditions to be specified. Treatment is considered emergency treatment when its delay would lead to a significant increase in the threat to life or body part.

Miscellaneous

Epidural anesthesia is often provided during labor for normal deliveries. Time tends to run 4 or more hours. Some administrators provide their own rules, and some plans do not cover anesthesia during labor at all. Therefore, verify the guidelines that apply to the plan you're processing (also see Chapter 12).

General anesthesia is usually administered when shock therapy is provided. Many plans do not cover it for this purpose or may have special handling guidelines. Verify before processing.

A standby anesthetist may be asked to be available while diagnostic procedures are performed on a patient who may require emergency surgery. If the anesthesiologist is not rendering treatment, administering anesthesia, monitoring vital signs, and so on, but is merely making a charge for being available, the charge is usually not a covered expense. However, verify first before processing.

Summary

Anesthesia plays an important role in patient care. Anesthesia in certain situations has been shown to help the patient to recover more rapidly than if anesthesia were not used.

The guidelines we have just covered will enable you to process anesthesia charges, no matter what method or type of anesthesia is given. There is almost always an anesthesia charge when major surgery is performed and you as the claims examiner are responsible for processing these charges. Use the preceding guidelines to calculate anesthesia time and to identify the provider of services (anesthesiologist, nurse anesthetist, or surgeon).

Assignments

Complete the Questions for Review.
Complete billing of the Anesthesia claims in the Student Exercise Manual and process Anesthesia claims 8-1 to 8-10, using the guidelines covered.

Questions for Review

Directions: Answer the following questions without looking back into the material just covered. Write your answers in the space provided.

1. What are the four methods of anesthesia administration?
   a. General anesthesia - completely unconscious
   b. Regional anesthesia - specific area numbed otherwise know whats going on
   c. Intravenous IV sedation - semi-conscious state - twilight sleep - don't feel anything
   d. acupuncture needles to relieve pain
2. What is the CPT code range for anesthesia? 00100 - 01999
3. What is the RVS code range for anesthesia? 00100 - 01999 or 10000 - 69999
4. The total anesthesia unit values consist of basic and time units.
5. Most plans cover anesthesia for shock therapy. (True or False) [False circled]

If you were unable to answer any of the questions, refer back to the section and complete the answers.

14

Hospital Services

In this chapter you will learn:

- To identify hospital room-and-board charges from hospital ancillary charges.
- To break away hospital room-and-board charges from hospital ancillary charges.
- The different levels of care and different types of rooms within a hospital.
- The advantages of preferred provider organization (PPO) networks.

Hospital services are those services performed in a hospital setting. The term is used generically to refer to charges billed by a hospital, urgent care center, surgicenter, alternative birthing center, or similar institution. This chapter deals with the various types of facilities available, their billing formats, and general handling guidelines.

The term "hospital" means an institution that meets most of the following:

- It mainly provides medical treatment to inpatients.
- It provides treatment only by or under a staff of physicians.
- It provides care by registered nurses 24 hours per day.
- It maintains facilities for diagnosis.
- It maintains a daily medical record for each patient.
- It complies with all licensing and other legal requirements.
- It maintains permanent facilities for surgery.

Most carriers have a file of established hospital, surgicenters, skilled nursing facilities, or birthing facilities that are licensed to treat patients in the state where they practice business. Occasionally, a new facility opens and, when claims are received, the information must be requested and verified to determine whether the facility is eligible for payment.

Hospital services are covered under the hospital benefits portion of the contract. Whether the contract is a Basic/Major Medical plan or a Comprehensive Major Medical plan, hospital charges are a covered benefit. The following are typical hospital expenses:

- The daily room-and-board charge of a hospital
- The charges for outpatient emergency treatment of illness and injuries
- The charge for outpatient surgery
- The charges for medical services and supplies during confinement, excluding private duty nursing
- The charge for administration of anesthesia
- The ambulance care if billed through the hospital
- The charges for lab tests and other services performed by an outside facility at the hospital's request.

UB-92 Billing Form

The Uniform Bill-92 (UB-92) is intended to be used by hospitals or other hospital-type facilities for inpatient and outpatient billing. The data elements and the design of the form were determined by the National Uniform Billing Committee. This form was designed to provide the basic data needed by most payors to adjudicate most of their claims. The objective was to accommodate a wide range of needs while eliminating the need for attachments. For further information regarding the UB-92 billing form, see Chapter 19 of Volume I.

Inpatient Hospital Claims

On inpatient hospital claims, the provider of service is a facility that provides inpatient care. This may be an acute care facility, a skilled nursing facility, a custodial care facility, or a similar facility.

For inpatient care, the patient has to be admitted into the hospital and stay for a period of time, usually a minimum of 24 hours. There must be a room-and-board charge. A hospital room-and-board charge is similar to that for staying in a hotel. That is, the day entered is paid but not the day discharged as long as the discharge time is prior to the required check-out time. The UB-92 form should always indicate admission and discharge dates.

When coding inpatient hospital claims, the CPT or RVS books are not used unless the billing has itemized some charges according to valid CPT/RVS codes. Each payor has its own coding guidelines. Therefore, before a claim can be coded for processing, the payor-specific codes must be obtained. Most payors break up the bills according to:

- Room and board charges
- Ancillary charges
- Take-home prescriptions
- Professional fees for exams, surgery, and so on

Providers of service use revenue codes in box 42 of the UB-92 form to indicate or identify the specific accommodation, ancillary service, or billing calculation (see Chapter 19 of Volume I).

Room and Board

Hospitals have a variety of rooms available, which include but are not limited to:

- Private—a single-occupancy room. The extra cost for a private room is not covered by most plans.
- Semiprivate—a double-occupancy room. Most plans cover the cost of a semiprivate room. The cost may vary based on the type of floor on which the room is located. That is, a semiprivate room in a burn ward may cost more than a semiprivate room in a maternity ward because of the increased level of care required.
- Ward—a room with three or more beds. A ward is also covered by most plans. Aside from county hospitals, many facilities no longer offer this type of room.
- Nursery—a large room for newborn babies. Twenty or 30 babies may be in a nursery.
- Specialized units—areas in which special monitoring equipment and a higher ratio of nurses to patients are required. These units are established for extremely ill or terminal patients with different illnesses or injuries that require more acute, intensive care. Specialized units tend to be considerably more expensive than other units. Normally, this type of room may cost $700 or more per day. Examples are the Intensive Care Unit (ICU), Coronary Care Unit (CCU), and Definitive Observation Units (DOU).

Telemetry charges (specialized observation equipment) may be billed separately from the base room-and-board amount. In addition, nursing charges may also be billed separately. If so, the telemetry charges and nursing charges should be combined with the base room-and-board amount to obtain the actual room-and-board charge.

To code the room-and-board amount, the number of days in the hospital is determined by counting the day of admission but not the day of discharge. If there is a charge for the day of discharge, the facility will have to be contacted to see why the last day is being charged. Usually, the charge will be for a late discharge. In this case, the late discharge is covered if it was caused or ordered by the attending physician. A late discharge for the patient's convenience is not a covered expense.

Each type of room accommodation is coded on a separate line, and the quantity (number of days) applies to that type of room only. Also, if either the type of room (semiprivate, private, or other) or the per-day-charges are different, even if the room type is the same, separate lines of coding are required. For instance, the following claim is received:

5/1, 5/2	Semiprivate $250.00 per day
5/3, 5/4	Semiprivate $275.00 per day

In this case, the two different semiprivate room rates must be coded on two different lines, with the number of services shown on each line as two (unless 5/4 is the discharge date). If the charge per day was the same for all of the semiprivate rooms, only one line of coding would be required with the number of services as four. Remember that the day of the discharge is not charged nor counted.

Check for the following revenue code ranges on the UB-92 for room-and-board expenses:

110–119	140–149	170–179
120–129	150–159	200–209
130–139	160–169	210–219

Ancillary Expenses

Ancillary expenses are miscellaneous services or supplies that are provided by the hospital on an inpatient or outpatient basis, which are necessary for the medical care or treatment of an individual. The most common charges include x-rays, lab fees, pharmacy, med-surgical supplies, operating room expenses, surgery room supplies, recovery room time, anesthesia supplies, occupational therapy, and inhalation therapy. All these expenses can be combined under a single line of coding for ancillary expenses. The only items that may be separated and coded on a different line are charges for personal, noncovered items, doctor's emergency room examination charges, other professional exam charges, or other expenses that may be limited by the plan. This does not include professional component charges (unless specified by the plan).

Take-Home Prescriptions

Often doctors in a hospital setting prescribe medications to be taken after the patient is released from the hospital. These medications may be dispensed by the hospital pharmacy and the charges included on the hospital bill. The medications are often covered under Major Medical benefits rather than standard hospital benefits. For this reason, these items are usually billed and coded separately, since they are not considered to be hospital expenses and may be subject to other plan provisions.

Professional Fees

Bills for doctors, anesthesiologists, technicians, and other hospital professionals are often included on the hospital bill rather than billed separately on a HCFA 1500. These bills are broken away from the regular hospital bill and paid under the normal plan provisions as if they had been billed on a HCFA 1500. Therefore, it is important to go through the itemized billing and determine whether the charges were for materials, equipment, and overhead (rendered by the hospital), or for professional services (rendered by an individual).

Personal Items

The following items are considered to be personal items and are not usually covered by a benefit plan. These charges may have to be coded separately or they may be combined with other ancillary charges and then denied with an appropriate explanation indicating that they are not covered under the plan. This handling procedure varies from payor to payor.

Barber expenses	Personal hygiene kit
Videotaping of birth	Birth certificate and photographs
Cot rentals	Patient requested room transfer
Lotion	Television
Telephone	Toothbrush, toothpaste, mouthwash
Guest trays	Slippers
Gift shop expenses	

Most hospitals automatically issue an admission kit to incoming patients. An admission kit usually includes an emesis basin, carafe, cup, lotion, tissue, and mouthwash. Some plans administratively allow for one kit. Additional kits are not covered. This type of kit may also be called a maternity kit, Ob-Gyn kit, hygiene kit, patient comfort kit, and other names. Therefore, if items such as mouthwash and toothpaste are billed separately in addition to a kit, they are not usually covered charges. (Even if a kit is not billed, these types of charges are not usually allowable.)

Outpatient Hospital Claims

The outpatient provider of service is a hospital facility (the title may be Hospital or Medical Center, Surgicenter, Birthing Center) in which there are no room-and-board charges. Commonly, "come-and-go" or outpatient surgery is performed in the outpatient department because an inpatient admission is not medically necessary. An outpatient hospital facility may have two departments:

1. The emergency room
2. Outpatient clinics

There may be facility charges such as emergency room usage fees, examination room usage charges, operating room expenses, and recovery room expenses. In an outpatient setting, ancillary expenses include everything except professional fees for examinations, surgery, and other professional services.

Clinic charges should be treated as an office visit as far as coding for the physician. The actual facility usage fee is not coded with or considered a professional fee. It is coded separately.

The charges generally submitted are for lab or x-ray services, pharmacy or durable medical equipment (revenue code ranges 250–259, 290–299, 300–309, 310-319, 320–329, 330–339, 340–349, and 350–359).

Miscellaneous Facilities

Many other types of treatment centers may be classified as facilities. Usually, they are designed to handle specialized treatment programs such as psychiatric care, alcoholism, and emergency care. The following is a sampling of other types of facilities in existence.

Day Care Centers

As the name implies, day care centers provide treatment during the daylight hours with the patient being released at night. The converse of this are centers that allow the patient to pursue a normal routine during the day such as working, and be treated at the center and maintained there overnight. Generally, these types of centers are for treatment of mental and nervous disorders.

A great disparity is seen in the handling of these claims from payor to payor. Usually, the following is required by the examiner to determine whether the treatment or the facility is eligible for benefits:

- A complete review of the facility must be made including:
  - —Staffing—the type of licensing required for the staff.
  - —Type of billing—how the bills are broken down, whether they are inclusive, itemized, and so on.
  - —Type of state or federal licensing the facility has.
  - —The facility's primary purpose (custodial care, active treatment, or other).
  - —A detailed description of the type of treatment including length of each treatment, licensing of person actually performing the treatment, ancillary services, and other pertinent data.

Often, senior examiners may handle day care claims to ensure that the proper correspondence is prepared and mailed; then they review the documentation when a reply is received. Prior to any denial of benefits, all plan provisions and limitations must be verified.

Urgent Care Centers

An urgent care center is a facility that follows professionally recognized standards to provide urgent or emergency treatment. Many plans have specialized benefits to handle this type of center. An urgent care center generally meets the following eight requirements:

1. Mainly provides urgent or emergency medical treatment for acute conditions.
2. Does not provide services or accommodations for overnight stays.
3. Is open to receive patients every day of the calendar year.
4. Has a physician trained in emergency medicine, nurses, and other supporting personnel specially trained in emergency care on duty at all times.
5. Has x-ray and laboratory diagnostic facilities, emergency equipment, trays, and supplies available for use in life-threatening events.
6. Has a written agreement with a local acute care inpatient facility for the immediate transfer of patients who require more intensive care than can be furnished at an outpatient facility, has written guidelines for stabilizing and transporting such patients, and has immediate and reliable direct communication channels with the acute care facility.
7. Complies with all state and federal licensing and other legal requirements.
8. Is not the office or clinic of any physician.

Generally, a medical emergency exists when:

- Severe symptoms occur. The symptoms must be severe enough to cause a person to seek immediate medical aid regardless of the hour of the day or night.
- The severe symptoms must occur suddenly and unexpectedly. A chronic condition in which subacute symptoms have existed over a period of time usually does not qualify as a medical emergency. However, symptoms that become severe enough to require immediate medical aid may qualify as a medical emergency.
- Immediate care was secured. Usually, a medical emergency would not be considered to exist if medical care is not received immediately after the appearance of acute symptoms. A telephone call to a doctor does not fulfill this requirement if the actual examination and treatment are deferred until the next day.

The administration of the urgent care benefit varies greatly. Therefore, refer to the provisions prior to taking any action on such a claim.

Surgicenters

Ambulatory surgical centers (surgicenters) are equipped to perform surgery on an outpatient basis. These centers may be freestanding or attached to a major acute care facility. Surgicenters provide financial savings by avoiding admission into an inpatient facility. An ambulatory surgical facility is a specialized facility that meets all eight of the professionally recognized standards indicated below:

1. Provides a setting for outpatient surgeries.
2. Does not provide services or accommodations for overnight stays.
3. Has at least two operating rooms and one recovery room; all the medical equipment needed to support the surgery being performed; x-ray and laboratory diagnostic facilities; and emergency equipment, trays, and supplies for use in life-threatening events.
4. Has a medical staff that is supervised full time by a physician including a registered nurse when patients are in the facility.
5. Maintains a medical record for each patient.
6. Has a written agreement with a local acute care facility for the immediate transfer of patients who require greater care than can be provided on an outpatient basis.
7. Complies with all state and federal licensing and other legal requirements.
8. Is not an office or clinic for any physician.

Usually, plans provide benefits on a global basis, covering the facility room usage charges, supplies (eg, anesthesia gases, medications, trays) on the same basis as inpatient hospital services. However, as with other benefits, coverage provisions vary greatly.

Alternative Birthing Centers

Alternative birthing centers (ABC) are outpatient care centers that provide special rooms for routine deliveries. As a rule, these centers provide quiet, nontraditional types of home-style rooms, which are designed to allow the parents to be together and participate in the birthing experience.

Often, a nurse practitioner rather than a physician is in attendance. The mother and child should go home within 5 to 12 hours after the delivery. As with other types of outpatient facilities, the following six or similar requirements are necessary for a facility to qualify as a birthing center:

1. Does not provide services or accommodations for overnight stays.
2. Has a medical staff that is supervised full time by a physician. A registered nurse is also in attendance when patients are in the facility.
3. Maintains a medical record for each patient.
4. Has a written agreement with a local acute care facility for the immediate transfer of patients who require greater care than can be provided on an outpatient basis.
5. Complies with all state and federal licensing and other legal requirements.
6. Is not an office or clinic for any physician.

Most confinements at an ABC should not exceed a 24-hour period without the transfer to an acute care facility. If the stay exceeds 24 hours, charges should be referred for investigation as to the medical necessity of the continued stay.

Rehabilitation Facilities

Rehabilitation facilities specialize in long-term, postsickness, or postinjury care. Rehabilitative treatment rather than active medical care is provided. This treatment is designed to return a patient to a normal or more normal state. Rehabilitative care is designed for those who are left paralyzed, deformed, handicapped, or otherwise not totally functional as a result of an accident, injury, or illness such as a stroke or spinal cord injury.

Many plans provide for some type of rehabilitative care. The limitations are usually based on a point at which progress ceases and the condition or status of the patient is stabilized. Many plans, however, do not provide any benefits for rehabilitative treatment. This type of care is very similar to convalescent care, although generally care at a rehabilitation facility is more aggressive than that provided in a convalescent facility.

Convalescent Hospitals

Convalescent facilities are usually considered to be midrange facilities, which provide nonacute care for persons recovering from an acute illness or injury. Usually, admission into a convalescent facility must commence within a specified number of days following a discharge from an acute care facility. The care provided must be active treatment, not custodial care. The institution generally must meet all seven of the following requirements to be considered an eligible convalescent facility:

1. Is primarily engaged in providing skilled nursing care to sick or injured persons as inpatients under 24-hour supervision of a physician or registered nurse.
2. Has on duty at all times a registered nurse, licensed vocational nurse, or skilled practical nurse. A registered nurse must be on duty at least 8 hours a day.
3. Is not, other than incidentally, a place for drug addicts, alcoholics, mentally ill persons, or senile or mentally deficient persons.
4. Maintains a medical record for each patient.
5. Has a written agreement with a local acute care facility for the immediate transfer of patients who require greater care than can be provided in a non-acute care facility.
6. Complies with all state and federal licensing and other legal requirements.
7. Is not an office or clinic for any physician.

Many plans provide very limited convalescent care benefits. However, always verify that the care being provided is not custodial. Some rehabilitative services may be provided and may be billed separately or included on a global basis (no breakdown).

Nursing Homes

Nursing homes specialize in custodial care, that is, care that is primarily for the purpose of meeting the personal needs of the patient and that could be provided by personnel without professional skills or training. Custodial care may include assistance with walking, bathing, dressing, eating, and other activities. Most plans do not provide custodial care coverage or, if they do, payment is limited. If there is a question whether or not care is custodial, copies of the provider's nursing notes and admission or discharge summary should be requested.

Hospice Care

A hospice is generally held to be a health care program providing coordinated services in the home. Usually, such care is provided only for persons suffering from a terminal condition, generally with a life expectancy of 6 months or less. The hospice concept is based on the following principles:

- The beneficiaries of the program are both the terminally ill person and his or her family.
- An interdisciplinary team is required to serve the patient, which includes nurses, social workers, psychologists, clergy, volunteers, and other professionals.
- The alleviation of pain and suffering is emphasized rather than the treatment of the illness.
- Support is provided for all family members to help offset emotional pain.

Hospice care is billed in a variety of methods. One billing may be provided by a hospice agency, which is then responsible for paying other providers. Another method may be that of separate bills from the various providers. Usually, such services include the rental of beds, commodes, and other equipment, along with various medications and supplies required to care for a terminally ill person. For hospice care to be covered, the contract usually specifies such benefits.

Summary

Hospitals provide a sterile environment to have medically necessary services and treatments, surgical or otherwise. They also provide a serene environment in which to recover.

The foregoing is by no means a complete list of all available facilities but provides a guide for the most common types of facilities that you'll encounter when processing claims. Most plans and payors have specific handling guidelines that should be checked before processing.

Assignments

Complete the Questions for Review.
Complete billing of the Hospital Claims in the Student Exercise Manual and process Hospital Claims 9-1 to 9-25, using the guidelines.

Questions for Review

Directions: Answer the following questions without looking back into the material just covered. Write your answers in the space provided.

1. Define hospital services: services performed in a hospital setting
2. What type of claim form is used to bill for hospital services? Uniform Bill - 92 (UB-92)
3. Name the four categories of hospital charges that most payors use:
   a. Room + board charges
   b. ancillary charges (mis.)
   c. Take home prescriptions
   d. Professional fees for exams, surgery etc (CPT)
4. Name the five varieties of hospital rooms.
   a. Private - single occupancy
   b. Semi - Private - double occupancy
   c. Ward - 3 or more beds
   d. Nursery - large room for new borns usually about 30 babies
   e. Specialized units
5. What are ancillary services? miscellaneous services or supplies that are provided by the hospital on an inpatient or outpatient basis which are neccessary for the medical care + treatment of the patient
6. Name three items that may be considered personal items.
   a. video taping of birth

b. Personal hygiene kit

c. Toothbrush, toothpaste

7. What are the two departments of an outpatient hospital facility?

a. emergency room

b. Outpatient clinics

8. What are urgent care centers? a facility that follows professionally recognized standards to provide urgent or emergency treatment

9. What are surgicenters? are equipped to perform surgery on an outpatient basis

10. What does the abbreviation ABC stand for? alternative Birthing Center

If you were unable to answer any of the questions, refer back to the section and then complete the answers.

15

Coordination of Benefits

In this chapter you will learn:

- To define and explain the purpose of coordination of benefits.
- The order of benefit determination rules and right of recovery.
- To recognize and investigate potential COB situations involving a claim.
- To compute the correct secondary benefit and benefit reserve.
- To understand the differences between primary and secondary carriers.
- To determine COB benefits as they apply to PPO and HMO plans.

Coordination of benefits (COB) is a process that occurs when two or more group plans provide coverage on the same person. Coordination between the two plans is necessary to allow for payment of 100% of the allowable expenses but no more. This process was developed in response to a growing problem of overinsurance. **Overinsurance** occurs when a person is covered under two or more policies and is eligible to collect an accumulation of benefits that actually exceeds the amount charged by the provider. The purpose of COB is to allow coverage and usually payment of 100% of allowable expenses without allowing the covered member or members to "make" money over and above the total costs for care.

In response to the diversity of handling procedures used by various carriers and administrators in coordinating coverages, the National Association of Insurance Commissioners (NAIC) developed a standardized model for COB administration. Most benefit plans follow this model, but it is not mandatory. Therefore, the plan provisions must be checked prior to processing COB claims, since the handling procedures will vary according to whether or not the NAIC guides are used.

Definitions

To process COB claims correctly, the following definitions must be understood:

Group Plan—a form of coverage with which coordination of benefits is allowed. A plan may include:

- Group, blanket, or franchise insurance policy or plan if not individually underwritten.
- Health maintenance organization or hospital or medical service prepayment policy available through an employer, union, or association.
- Trusteed policy or plan, union welfare policy or plan, multiple employer policy or plan, or employee benefit policy or plan.
- Governmental programs (Medicare) or policies or plans required by a statute, except Medicaid or Medi-Cal.
- "No fault" auto policy or plan. (Applies to some plans only. The plan must specify whether or not this is applicable.)

Primary Plan—the benefit plan that determines and pays its benefits first without regard to the existence of any other coverage.

Secondary Plan—the plan that pays after the primary plan has paid its benefits. The benefits of the secondary plan take into consideration the benefits of the primary plan and may reduce its payment so that only 100% of allowable expenses are paid.

Allowable Expense—any necessary, reasonable, and customary item of medical or dental expense, at least partly covered under at least one of the plans covering the person for whom a claim is made. Items that are excluded by the secondary plan, such as dental services and vision care services, would not be considered allowable. Conversely, amounts that are limited under the secondary plan would be considered allowable (the entire charge). For example:

- Each plan provides a limit of $35.00 per visit for outpatient psychiatric care. The psychiatrist charges $50.00 per visit. As long as the $50.00 is within one of the two plan's UCR guidelines, the entire $50.00 would be considered an allowable expense under COB.
- Based on the primary plan's UCR guidelines, the amount allowed for a surgery is $1200. The secondary plan's UCR for the same surgery is $1000. When coordinating, the secondary plan would allow the greatest amount allowed by at least one of the plans.

Therefore, the allowable amount when coordinating would be $1200. Bear in mind that this amount has nothing to do with how the secondary plan calculates its usual payment. You will see how the two amounts interact later.

Claim Determination Period—usually a calendar year. It does not include any part of a year before the effective date of duplicate coverage under the secondary plan. It does include any remaining amount during a calendar year occurring after the termination date of the primary plan. As long as the secondary plan is not terminated, COB continues to be performed even though there is no longer multiple coverages.

Normal Liability (NL)—the amount payable under the secondary plan's provisions without regard to any other coverage (what would regularly have been paid if there were no other insurance). This is not necessarily the amount that will actually be paid.

Example: The secondary plan pays 80% of UCR after a $100.00 deductible. The first claim is paid as follows:

Charge	$200.00
Deductible	100.00
OIS paymt	160.00
#2 NL	80.00
#2 Actual paymt	40.00

Credit Reserve (benefit credit, credit savings, etc.)—a cumulative amount within a claim determination period that is derived from the amount of funds that a plan has saved by being the secondary carrier. The credit reserve does not carry over from one calendar year to another. Each year, the balance begins at $0.00. A running total is kept for each separate determination period (calendar year).

Example: Same benefits as above.

Charge	$200.00
Deductible	100.00
OIS paymt	160.00
#2 NL	80.00
#2 Actual paymt	40.00
#2 CR	40.00

CR = NL – AP, or $80.00 – $40.00 = $40.00 in savings.

Insular COB—COB applied separately to medical and dental charges. All savings are kept separate.

Global COB—COB applied to both medical and dental charges combined. All savings are kept intermingled.

EOB—a letter of explanation of benefits from a payor indicating how a member's benefits have been applied in response to the submission of a claim for services. The EOB indicates deductibles, coinsurance amounts, nonallowable amounts, UCR limitations, and so on. An EOB is required by law to be generated on each claim submission showing the disposition of the claim (eg, how it was paid, denied, pending for additional information).

OIS = other insurance

Order of Benefit Determination Rules

Before standardized coordination rules were adopted by the benefits industry, a person covered under two policies could collect full benefits from both. Thus, the individual could actually make a profit by being sick. Since each plan would prefer to pay as the secondary payor, it became necessary to develop rules to determine when a plan should pay as primary, secondary, and so on. The 14 rules determining the order of payment are referred to as the Order of Benefit Determinations (OBD) and are explained below:

1. The plan without a COB provision will be primary to a plan with a COB provision.
2. When a plan does not have OBD rules, and as a result the plans do not agree on the OBD, the plan without these OBD rules will determine the order of payment.
3. The plan that covers an individual as an employee will be primary to a plan that covers that individual as a dependent.
4. If an individual is an employee under two plans, the primary plan is the one under which the employee has been covered the longest.
5. If an employee is an active employee under one plan and a retiree (or laid off) under another, the active plan will pay as primary.

The parent birthday rule, explained in #6 and 7 which follow, affects the OBD for dependent children of parents who are living together and married (not divorced or legally separated).

6. The plan of the parent whose birthday (based on month and day only) occurs first in the calendar year is the primary plan.
7. When both parents' birthdays are the same (based on month and day), the benefits of the plan that covered one parent the longest is the primary plan.

For dependents of legally separated or divorced parents and those whose parents have remarried, the order of benefits determination is based on the following rules:

8. The plan of the parent specified as having legal

responsibility for the health care expense of the child is the primary plan.

For dependents of separated parents with no court decree:

9. The plan of the parent with custody is prime.
10. The plan of the step-parent with whom the child resides is secondary.
11. The plan of the natural parent without custody is tertiary.
12. The step-parent (if any) who does not reside with the child has no legal right to declare dependency. Therefore, no coordination should be performed because the child is probably not an eligible dependent under the plan.
13. For joint custody, with no additional responsibility designation, the plan of the parent whose coverage has been in effect the longest would be the primary payor. However, this rule may vary by administrator. Some parents pay costs on a 50/50 basis, thereby sharing equally in the health care risk.
14. A few rare plans don't use the birthday rule as previously described. These plans generally use the old gender rule. The plan covering the male employee is primary, and the plan covering the female employee is secondary.

Right to Receive and Release Information

Certain facts are needed to determine and apply the appropriate COB rules. Therefore, plan representatives have the right to decide which facts are required and to obtain the needed facts from, or give the facts to, any other organization. The plan need not notify or get the consent of any person to do this. In addition, each person claiming benefits under a plan must give the facts required to properly process a claim. However, it is also important to realize that most providers of care do not release any information to a payor without a signed release from the member. Information should be requested or released to others only when absolutely necessary to determine benefits under the plan. The unnecessary request for or release of information could be a violation of the right to privacy, which is punishable by law. Therefore, request only what is necessary, and routinely request a written authorization from the member to release information.

Facility of Payment

A payment made under another plan may include amounts that should have been paid by the secondary plan. If it does, there are two options:

1. Payment may be made to the member, with a letter of notification sent to the primary carrier. In this case, the primary carrier would be responsible for recovering payment from the member.
2. The secondary plan may reimburse that amount to the organization or plan that made the initial incorrect payment, thus allowing that payor to recover the overpayment. In such a case, the amount reimbursed to the initial payor will be treated as if it were a benefit paid under the secondary plan. The secondary payor will not have to pay that amount again to either the member or the provider of service. The term "payment made" includes providing benefits in the form of services, in which case payment made means reasonable cash value of the benefits provided in the form of services.

Right of Recovery

If the amount of the payments made by the plan is more than it should have paid under the COB provision, the plan may recover the excess from one or more of the following:

- The person or persons it has paid or on behalf of whom it has paid.
- Other insurers/plans.
- Other organizations.

The "amount of the payments made" includes the reasonable cash value of any benefits provided in the form of services.

Miscellaneous Guidelines

Following are some miscellaneous guidelines:

- The difference between the cost of a private hospital room and the cost of a semiprivate room is not considered an allowable expense unless the patient's stay in a private room was medically necessary either as generally accepted medical practice or as specifically defined in the plan.
- Items of expense under coverages such as dental care, vision care, prescription drug, or hearing aid programs may be excluded from the definition of allowable expense. A plan that provides only benefits for such items may limit its definition of allowable expense to like items.

This means that a medical plan may have COB with medical expenses only, and a dental-only plan may limit COB to other dental plans only.

An item of expense covered under the primary plan may be considered an allowable expense under the secondary plan even though that plan does not provide such a benefit. For example:

The primary plan covers routine examinations. The secondary plan excludes routine examinations. This expense may be considered an allowable expense. This COB rule varies widely from payor to payor. As previously indicated, some payors do not consider excluded expenses as allowable; others do. Therefore, the COB provisions and administrative handling rules must be verified. (Remember that we're talking about the amount considered allowable under COB, not the amount used to determine the secondary plan's normal liability.)

Health Maintenance Organizations

A health maintenance organization (HMO) is a type of prepayment plan in which providers agree to charge members for their services in accordance with a fixed schedule of rates. The HMO member (insured) may pay a specified co-payment at the time the service is rendered or may not be required to pay anything. The patient and the doctor are never involved in having to complete claim forms for submission to a payor. Instead, the HMO is billed directly, or the HMO pays a monthly retainer fee to the physician for membership plus other specified fees.

If the required medical services are available through the HMO but the insured does not go to an HMO provider for the treatment, he or she may be held entirely responsible for all the expenses.

Prepayment plans are included in the definition of the type of policies to which COB provisions apply. However, many HMOs do not have COB provisions, although more are starting to incorporate the COB concept because of the spiraling costs of medical care.

An example of an HMO is Kaiser Permanente. Kaiser provides a prepayment policy for hospital and professional medical services at no cost or at a small fee, as long as the member goes to a Kaiser facility. Subsequently, the HMO provides the member with a "reasonable cost statement," which represents what would have been charged to a nonmember. If the HMO does not have a COB provision, the HMO would be considered the primary payor. To coordinate benefits, a request must be made for receipts or statements showing the actual "out-of-pocket" expense. The secondary plan would pay no more than the amount that would be considered the allowable expense. If the HMO does have a COB provision, the regular OBD determination rules should be applied.

Preferred Provider Organizations

As previously covered, preferred provider organizations (PPOs) are special arrangements in which members are responsible for expenses based on specific contractual UCR arrangements. Some services may be covered in full, and some may not be covered at all. Usually, COB will apply to PPO claims. The main difference between going to a regular provider and going to a PPO provider is reflected in the patient's liability. That is, if the member goes to a PPO provider, the member is not responsible for any amounts in excess of the PPO contractual UCR amount.

Also, depending on the payor, the plan, and the PPO, the secondary payor may not be held responsible for any amounts in excess of the contractual PPO amount, even though the secondary payor is not a party to the contract. This handling is based on the premise that if the member is not responsible for anything over the PPO rate, then neither is the secondary plan. Once again, this handling varies.

A PPO EOB usually specifically states the member's responsibility. By referring to the appropriate field on the EOB, the secondary carrier can tell what amount to use to determine the allowable expense. Anything in excess of the patient's liability amount is not considered allowable.

If the member does not go to a PPO provider, the member is responsible for all the charges including the amounts in excess of the primary plan's UCR. In addition, most plans penalize their members for not going to PPO providers by reducing the plan's payment (eg, the coinsurance percentage paid by the plan is reduced from 80% to 70%).

Civilian Health and Medical Programs of the Uniformed Services

The Civilian Health and Medical Programs of the Uniformed Services, also known as CHAMPUS, provides a comprehensive program of health care benefits for active-duty and retired services personnel, their dependents, and the dependents of deceased military personnel.

CHAMPUS is secondary to all other insurance or health policies except Medicaid and CHAMPUS supplemental insurance. However, because many services are provided free of charge or with only a minimal fee, many examiners never see a CHAMPUS EOB.

Recognizing the Presence of Dual Coverage

The possibility that a claimant may have dual coverage is indicated in the following two examples:

1. The greatest likelihood of dual coverage occurs when the spouse is employed. Claim forms usually request the name of the employee's spouse and the name and address of the spouse's employer. The claim form defines what is meant by other group insurance and asks the claimant to designate which type of other insurance exists.
2. Even when the claimant states that there is no other coverage, additional inquiries should be made in the following instances:

- In claims that involve married female employees or their dependents, often the husband also has group coverage on the family.
- The claim form indicates that the male spouse is not employed. Under the policy held by the spouse's previous employer, extended benefits or a provision for the continuation of insurance (COBRA) may be available.
- The claim is for a dependent child, but the area on the form requesting other insurance information has been left blank.
- Notations on the hospital bills or claim papers show that some other insurer/plan has paid benefits or that there is other employment within the family.
- The claimant does not assign hospital benefits. This may indicate that the claimant has used other benefits to pay the provider and thus does not want a duplicate payment to be made (to the provider).
- It is known from a group's local sources that a patient is covered under another plan.
- Photocopies of bills are submitted. Usually, the original is submitted, and a copy is kept by the member. The originals may have been submitted to another payor.
- The provider charges for the completion of a claim form, but the submitted form was not received from the provider. The charge may have been for completing a form for another payor.
- Requests for information are received from other policyholders/plans or insurers.
- The occupation of the claimant or spouse of a dependent suggests coverage through a union or some other professional affiliation.

- A hospital or surgeon's bill makes reference to other coverage.
- A bill showing a substantial credit or adjustment to the account.
- The claim submitted is the first maternity bill for the subscriber's spouse. In such a case, the wife may have been regularly employed until her pregnancy, and benefits may be available through the extension of benefits provision of her previous policy.
- The claim is submitted on another carrier's claim form, or an EOB is attached.
- A duplicate coverage inquiry (DCI) is received. This is an industry-approved form designed to establish the existence of other coverage.
- An HMO requests reimbursement for the value of service provided to one of their patients.
- Claims history shows COB payments in the past, but claims began being paid as primary with no explanation. Or, claims history shows claims paid as secondary and others paid as primary with no explanation.

Pursuit of details pertaining to other coverage can be through a variety of sources. If the claim form indicates that the insured's spouse is employed and includes the name and address of the spouse's employer, contact that employer to determine whether there is other group coverage.

If the claim form does not indicate the name and address of the spouse's employer, request the missing information from the subscriber.

Additional sources of information regarding the existence of dual coverage include:

- Files from hospital admissions.
- City directories listing members of a family, their occupations, and places of employment.
- Information cards compiled by the Benefits Office for local employer plans.

COB Worksheet

The COB worksheet is used to help calculate the proper benefits when there is COB between more than one health plan. Figure 15-1 is a sample COB worksheet. To begin, calculate the allowable amount that would be paid on this claim if there was no other insurance company. Then, follow the instructions below:

Place the patient's name and the year that services were rendered in the box on the top of the COB calculation sheet.

1. Enter the total allowable amount (not the amount paid) for all previous claims in this year for this patient.
2. Enter the total allowable amount on this claim.
3. Add lines 1 and 2 to obtain the total allowable amount during this year for this patient.
4. Enter the total amount that other insurance companies have paid on claims for this patient during this year. This information can be obtained from the EOB sheets prepared by other insurance companies.
5. Enter the total amount that other insurance companies have paid on this claim.
6. Add lines 4 and 5 to obtain the total amount of other insurance available during this year for this patient.
7. Subtract line 6 from line 3.
8. Enter the normal liability amount for this insurance company for all previous claims for this patient during this year.
9. Enter the normal liability amount for this insurance company for this claim.
10. Add lines 8 and 9 to obtain the normal liability for this insurance company for this patient during this year.
11. Enter line 7 or line 10, whichever is less.
12. Enter the amount of actual payments that this insurance company made on all previous claims for the patient during the year.
13. Subtract line 12 from line 11. This is the actual payment that should be made on this claim.
14. Enter the amount of credit reserve for all previous claims for this patient for this year. The credit reserve is the difference between the normal liability and the actual amount paid.
15. Enter the amount of credit reserve for this claim.
16. Add lines 14 and 15 to obtain the total credit reserve.

Coordination of Benefits Calculation Worksheet

Patient's Name: ____ Year: __________

1. Total allowable amount previous claims (line 3 on prior COB Calculation Worksheets) __________
2. Total allowable amount this claim __________
3. Total allowable year to date (line 1 plus line 2) __________
4. Total other insurance available previous claims __________
5. Total other insurance available this claim __________
6. Total other insurance available year to date (line 4 plus line 5) __________
7. Difference between line 3 and line 6 __________
8. Normal liability previous claims (line 10 on prior COB Calculation Worksheets) __________
9. Normal liability this claim __________
10. Total normal liability year to date (line 8 plus line 9) __________
11. The lesser of line 7 or 10 __________
12. Actual payments made previous claims __________
13. Actual payments this claim __________
14. Credit reserve previous claims __________
15. Credit reserve this claim __________
16. Total credit reserve __________

Figure 15-1: **Coordination of Benefits Calculation Worksheet.**

Summary

Coordination of benefits is necessary to ensure that when charges are covered by more than one carrier total payment does not exceed more than 100%. These guidelines should be considered whenever there is the possibility of dual coverage or a third party payor. Learn to identify the possible existence of another payor by applying the guidelines and rules we have just covered.

Assignments

Complete the Questions for Review.
Complete COB exercise 15-1.
Complete billing the remaining COB claims in the Student Exercise Manual, and process COB claims 10-1 to 10-15 using the guidelines covered.

Questions for Review

Directions: Answer the following questions without looking back into the material just covered. Write your answers in the space provided.

1. Define COB. ______
2. What is the purpose of COB? ______
3. The ______ is the benefit plan that determines and pays its benefits first without regard to the existence of any other coverage.
4. The ______ is the plan that pays after the primary plan has paid its benefits.
5. What are the rules that determine the order of benefit payment? ______
6. Spell out HMO and describe what an HMO is. ______
7. What does CHAMPUS stand for? ______
8. The plan without a COB provision is secondary to a plan with a COB provision. (True or False) ______
9. Define Global COB. ______
10. ______ applies separately to medical and dental charges. All savings are kept separate.

If you were unable to answer any of the questions, refer back to the section and then complete the answers.

Exercise 15-1

Directions: Using the following information, complete a COB calculation worksheet.

1. Total submitted expenses = $1600.00. Primary carrier, A, considers the allowable amount to be $1450.00 and has made a payment of $1160.00 on this claim. Secondary carrier, B, considers the allowable amount to be $1495.00. Both plans calculate benefits at 80%. Neither carrier has made any previous payments or had any previous allowable amounts.

2. Total submitted expenses = $1200.00. Primary carrier, A, considers the allowable amount to be $1000.00 and has made a payment of $800.00 on this claim. Secondary carrier, B, considers the allowable amount to be $1200.00. Both plans calculate benefits at 80%. Use previous allowable amounts, payment amounts, and credit reserve amount from Worksheet #1.

3. Total submitted expenses = $1400.00. Primary carrier, A, considers the allowable amount to be $1400.00 and has made a payment of $1120.00 on this claim. Secondary carrier, B, considers the allowable amount to be $1200.00. Plan A calculates benefits at 80%. Plan B limits payment to 50% of the allowable amount to a calendar year maximum of $500.00. $450.00 has already been paid out. Use previous allowable amounts, payment amounts, and credit reserve amount from Worksheets #1 and #2.

16
Medicare

In this chapter you will learn:

- The purpose of the Social Security Administration's Medicare Department.
- About TEFRA and DEFRA and their relevance to claims processing.
- Medicare eligibility requirements.

Medicare is the Federal Health Insurance Benefit Plan for the Aged and Disabled, Title XVIII of Public Law 89-97 of the Social Security Act. This program is for people 65 years of age or older and certain persons who are totally disabled.

Social Security Administration (SSA) offices throughout the United States take applications for Medicare, determine eligibility, and provide general information about the program. The actual processing of the claims is administered by many different insurance companies, usually one or two within each state. Consequently, as an examiner, you will see a diversity in the application or denial of benefits and in the explanation of benefits forms.

TEFRA/DEFRA

The Tax Equity and Fiscal Responsibility Act of 1982 (TEFRA)—and amendments to it—has redirected the financial responsibility for medical coverage of active employees age 65 years and older and their spouses age 65 years and older. When this federal program was introduced, it was determined that Medicare would be the primary payor for persons who have reached their 65th birthday, regardless of employment status.

Initially, TEFRA regulations did not apply to spouses over age 65 of active employees who were under 65 years of age. The Deficit Reduction Act of 1984 (DEFRA), effective January 1, 1985, amended TEFRA so that now spouses, age 65 years and older, of active employees who are under 65 can elect their primary coverage, either Medicare or the private group plan.

The employers affected by these Acts are those who regularly employ 20 or more workers for each working day in at least 20 weeks of the current or preceding calendar year. Employees of such employers must be offered coverage under the group plan on the same basis as other employees. An election form choosing the primary plan must be completed and signed by each employee who is or becomes affected.

If coverage is chosen under the employer's group plan, the group plan will be the primary payor on all medical services and Medicare will be the secondary coverage. If coverage under the group plan is rejected and Medicare is chosen, the employee/spouse by law can be covered only by Medicare. The group plan will not provide secondary coverage.

Obviously, employers with fewer than 20 employees are exempt from the TEFRA/DEFRA regulations, and Medicare is the primary carrier for their active employees and spouses age 65 years or older. Medicare is also primary for all retired employees and for active employees and their spouses under age 65 who are totally disabled with conditions other than end-stage renal disease (ESRD).

After it has been determined that the group plan is subject to TEFRA/DEFRA, it becomes necessary to determine the individual's eligibility for Medicare.

Medicare Eligibility

Medicare eligibility is based on three guiding principles:

1. Age
2. Disability
3. ESRD

An individual is eligible for Medicare coverage on the first day of the month in which he or she reaches age 65 years. Persons born on the first day of the month are eligible on the first day of the month preceding their birth date.

Example:

Birthday: June 15, eligible for Medicare on June 1

Birthday: June 1, eligible for Medicare on May 1

Medicare coverage for totally disabled persons begins on the first of the 25th month from the date approved for Social Security Disability or Railroad Retirement benefits. Those covered include disabled workers of any age, disabled widows between the ages of 50 and 65, disabled beneficiaries age 18 and over who receive Social Security benefits because of disability prior to age 22, the blind, and railroad retirement annuitants.

End-stage renal disease (ESRD) is the condition in which a person's kidneys fail to function. As a result, the patient needs dialysis treatments (refer to Chapter 10 for a review of this type of service). Because of the many problems associated with ESRD, patients are considered to be totally disabled, even though some persons with this disease continue to work. As a result, the following special rules apply to ESRD patients.

The employer's group health plan is the primary payor for the first 18 months after a patient (under age 65) with ESRD becomes eligible for Medicare. This 18-month period begins based on the earlier of:

- The month in which a regular course of renal dialysis is initiated.
- The month in which the patient is hospitalized for a kidney transplantation.

Medicare is the secondary payor during this 18-month period but will revert to the primary status beginning with the 19th month. As a general rule, all services under a dialysis program are Medicare assigned.

Providers of Service

Providers of services and medical equipment suppliers under Medicare must meet all licensing requirements of the state in which they are located. To be a participating provider under the Medicare program, they must meet additional Medicare requirements before payments can be made for their services. Medicare does not pay for the following care received in nonparticipating facilities:

- Hospital care
- Skilled nursing facility
- Home health agency
- Hospice
- Outpatient rehabilitation
- Dialysis facilities
- Ambulatory surgical centers
- Independent physical therapists
- Independent occupations therapists
- Clinical laboratories
- Portable x-ray suppliers
- Rural health clinics

The Two Parts of Medicare

The two parts to the Medicare program are A and B. The services covered are as follows:

1. Part A is considered the basic plan or hospital insurance, which covers facility charges for acute inpatient hospital care, skilled nursing, home health care, and hospice care.
2. Part B is the medical (supplementary, voluntary) insurance, which covers doctors' services, outpatient hospital services, home health care, outpatient speech and physical therapy, and durable medical equipment.

Part A

Eligibility

The two parts of the Medicare program have different eligibility requirements. Part A is automatic upon enrollment for the following:

- All persons age 65 years and over, if entitled to (a) monthly Social Security benefits or (b) pensions under the Railroad Retirement Act.
- All persons who have reached age 65 prior to 1968, whether or not under the Social Security or Railroad Retirement Programs.
- Workers who reached 65 in 1975, or subsequently, *and* have 20 quarters of Social Security work credits, if female, or 24 quarters of Social Security work credits if male.

Effective July 1, 1973, all persons age 65 and over who are not otherwise eligible for Part A may enroll by paying the full cost of such coverage, provided that they also enroll in Part B.

Certain exclusions such as members of subversive organizations and aliens who have not been permanent US residents for 5 years are applicable.

Benefits

As previously indicated, Part A is the hospital insurance portion of Medicare. There is a deductible that is taken from the first admission. If the patient is out of the hospital for at least 60 consecutive days (including the day of discharge), a new benefit period begins and another inpatient deductible would be taken if readmitted. (This is known as the period of renewal.) For 1994, the Part A deductible is $696.

If a member remains in the hospital for an extended period of time, additional copayments are required. Medicare deducts the copay amount from the billed amount and then pays the amount in excess of the copay. The 1994 inpatient hospital copayments are as follows:

- 1st to 60th day = Deductible only, no additional copayment.
- 61st to 90th day = $174/day.
- 91st to 150th day= $348. These days are known as the 60-day Lifetime Reserve. These do not renew. Once used, they are gone.

For skilled nursing facilities (SNF), there is a separate copayment schedule and requirement. To be eligible for this benefit, the two following conditions must be met:

1. A doctor must certify the necessity of skilled nursing and rehabilitative care on a daily basis. Custodial care is not covered nor is occasional rehabilitative care.
2. The Medicare intermediary must approve the stay.

The 1994 SNF copayments are as follows:

1st to 20th day = No copayment. Since admission is usually from an acute care facility, during which time the deductible was met, 100% of the allowable is generally paid by Medicare.

21st to 100th day = $87.00 Coinsurance/copay per day.

The maximum number of allowable hospital days is 100 per calendar year. These deductibles and copayments are adjusted upward each calendar year based on inflation.

Psychiatric inpatient hospital care is covered for a maximum of 190 days per lifetime of the member. These days do not renew. The only applicable deductible is the inpatient hospital deductible of $696 for 1994. There are no other copayments. Also, the facility must be a participating Medicare provider for the patient to be covered.

Care at foreign facilities is generally not covered. However, some qualified Canadian or Mexican hospitals may qualify for coverage during emergency situations. All such bills should be submitted to Medicare for consideration.

Part-time home health care may be covered under the following circumstances:

- The care needed includes intermittent skilled nursing care, physical therapy, or speech therapy.
- The patient is confined to the home.
- A doctor prescribed the care and sets up a home health plan.
- The home health agency is a participating provider.

Medicare will not cover the following services:

- Full-time nursing care in the home.
- Drugs and biologicals.
- Meals delivered to the home.
- Homemaker services.
- Blood transfusions.

Hospice care may be covered under the following circumstances:

- A doctor certifies that the patient is terminal.
- The patient chooses to receive care from a hospice instead of standard Medicare benefits (inpatient).
- Care is provided by a Medicare certified hospice program.

Special benefit periods and payments apply to this benefit. If additional clarification is required, refer to a Medicare handbook.

Part A insurance does not cover the following services:

- Replacement fees for the first three pints of blood.
- Personal convenience items.
- Private duty nurses (inpatient).
- Private room difference, unless it is determined to be medically necessary.

Part B

Part B is the supplementary medical insurance that covers doctors and outpatient hospital services. It is considered a supplemental plan because each participant must pay a stipulated amount each month for the benefits. The monthly premium is adjusted each year based on inflation.

The rules, limits, and maximums under this coverage are subject to change every year. In addition, certain types of services are covered under some circumstances but not under others. Therefore, it is less confusing to have a general idea of the most common benefits and not become overly concerned with the details. Normally, the claims examiner will not be concerned with Medicare except when it is the primary payor. In such circumstances, the explanation of benefits is needed to process the claim. The following briefly summarizes some of the more common benefits. For more specific rules, refer to a Medicare booklet or carrier.

Benefits

The 1994 yearly deductible is $100, which has a 3-month carryover provision. After the deductible has been satisfied, generally 80% of the approved charge is paid. Services covered by Part B of the Medicare program are as follows:

- Manual manipulation of the spine for subluxation demonstrated by x-rays.
- Nonroutine podiatric care.
- Dental care for surgery of the jaw/related structures and fractures of facial bones.
- Some nonroutine optometry services.
- Outpatient hospital services.
- Outpatient physical/speech therapy—1994 maximum, $750.
- Independent clinical laboratory/x-ray services.
- Ambulance transportation.
- Some durable medical and prosthetic equipment.
- Outpatient treatment of mental illness.
- Home health care.

Doctors' services *not* covered by Part B are as follows:

- Routine physical examinations and related diagnostic, x-ray, and laboratory services (DXL).
- Routine foot care.
- Eye or hearing examinations for eyeglasses or hearing aids.
- Immunizations (exceptions may be pneumococcal and hepatitis B).
- Cosmetic surgery (some exceptions).

Approved or Reasonable Charges

Medicare payments are based on what the law defines as "reasonable charges," which are the amounts approved by the Medicare carrier based on what is considered reasonable for the geographic area in which the doctor practices. Because of the way that the approved amounts are determined and because of high rates of inflation in medical care prices, the approved amounts are often significantly less than the actual charges billed by providers. The charge approved by the carrier is the lowest of either of the following: the charge billed by the provider or the prevailing charge (based on all the customary charges in the locality for each type of service) as determined by Medicare.

Since the participating provider must write off the amounts that are more than the approved amount, many providers have refused to participate in Medicare. Unfortunately, the member, who is often on a fixed income, is then held responsible for a large portion of the billed amount.

Medicare Assignment of Benefits

Medicare assignment of benefits has no involvement as to whom the claims examiner will make payment. A participating provider must agree to accept assignment on all Medicare claims. By doing this, the payment goes directly to the provider from Medicare, rather than to the member. In addition, the provider has agreed to accept the amount approved by the Medicare carrier for the covered services. The patient is not responsible for any amount over the approved amount. In such a case, the secondary carrier is also not responsible for the amount in excess of the approved amount.

Physicians Who Accept Medicare Reimbursement

When a physician agrees to accept Medicare assignment for a bill, Medicare pays the physician directly for that bill. The physician may bill the patient only for any deductibles or coinsurance that Medicare has deducted from the assigned bill. As a result, the total fee that physicians may receive from Medicare and from beneficiaries for an assigned bill is limited by what Medicare deems an appropriate fee for the particular service or procedure (the Medicare "allowance").

To encourage physicians to accept assignment, the Medicare allowance is higher for physicians who agree to accept assignment for all bills for Medicare-eligible persons. These physicians are called *participating physicians*. Thus, participating physicians agree not to practice *balance billing*, that is, charging patients for more than Medicare allows.

The phrase "participating physician" can be confusing because physicians who sign these agreements are not the only ones who treat Medicare patients. Physicians who treat Medicare-eligible patients but who decide whether to accept assignment on a case-by-case basis are called *nonparticipating physicians*. In exchange for the freedom to make this choice for each patient, nonparticipating physicians receive only 95% of the reimbursement that participating physicians receive from Medicare. For example, if the Medicare allowance for a procedure is $100 for participating physicians, the allowance for nonparticipating physicians would be $95. Therefore, if the patient's deductible had been paid, a participating physician would receive $80 from Medicare (80% of $100), and a nonparticipating physician would receive $76 from Medicare (80% of $95). Although the participating physician is not allowed to charge the Medicare patient more than the $20 copayment, the nonparticipating physician has no such restriction. However, if the nonparticipating physician agrees to accept assignment for that bill, he or she can bill the patient only for $19 ($95 minus $76).

A New Procedural Requirement

The least significant of the new Medicare changes took effect on October 1, 1990, requiring all physicians who treat Medicare patients—both participating and nonparticipating—to complete the paperwork on behalf of their patients. Previously, only participating physicians were responsible for filling out Medicare claim forms. Physicians may not charge for filling out the forms. If they fail to file a claim form within 1 year of performing the service, they can be fined up to $1000.

Restrictions on Balance Billing

Beginning on January 1, 1991, the most important Medicare changes took effect. Balance billing by nonparticipating physicians was strictly limited. (Of course, limits had no effect in states such as Massachusetts, where balance billing is prohibited by law. In New York, the limits affected only office and home visits, since New York has limits on balance billing for all other services. Also, participating physicians are not affected, since they were not allowed to balance bill Medicare patients for any services.

As of January 1991, nonparticipating physicians were not allowed to charge Medicare patients more than 25% over the Medicare allowance for nonparticipating physicians for that particular procedure or service. (OBRA '90 increased the limit for evaluation and management services from 25% to 40% for 1991 only.) In 1992, the limit was lowered to 20%. In 1993, balance billing was restricted to no more than 15% over what Medicare allows. This restriction is sometimes referred to as *capitation*. Following are some examples of how this rule affects the payment of claims.

Example 1: Provider accepts assignment.

A.

Billed charge	$42.00
Approved amt	$35.00
Medicare pays	$35.00 to ded = 0
Member pays	$35.00

B.

Billed charge	$90.00
Approved amt	$75.00
Medicare pays	$20.00 to ded +
	$44.00 (80% of $55.00)
Member pays	$31.00 (ded + 20% of $55.00)

C.

Billed charge	$480.00
Approved amt	$400.00
Medicare pays	$320.00 (80% of $400.00)
Member pays	$ 80.00 (20% of $400.00)

Example 2: Provider does not accept assignment.

A.

Billed charge	$42.00
Approved amt	$33.25
Medicare pays	$33.25 to ded = 0
Member pays	$38.24 (ded + $4.99 balance billing allowed)

B.

Billed charge	$90.00
Approved amt	$71.25
Medicare pays	$20.00 to ded + $41.00 (80% of $51.25)
Member pays	$44.94 (ded + 20% of $51.25 + $10.69 balance billing allowed)

C.

Billed charge	$480.00
Approved amt	$380.00
Medicare pays	$304.00 (80% of $380.00)
Member pays	$133.00 (20% of $380.00 + $57.00 balance billing allowed)

There are a variety of ways in which group health plans coordinate their payments with Medicare when Medicare is primary and the group plan is secondary. The most common methods in use include the following:

- Nonduplication of Medicare.
- Maintenance of benefits.
- Coordination of benefits.
- Medicare supplemental coverage.

Nonduplication of Medicare

Calculation of benefits under the nonduplication approach is the same as with COB except that allowable expenses are those that are listed as covered expenses under the group plan. To compute benefits under this approach, use the following four guidelines:

I. Regular group benefits are computed. Apply all eligibility requirements, deductibles, limitations, and maximums.

II. If Medicare assigned, the Medicare-approved amount is used as the base.
   A. Subtract the amount paid by Medicare from the Medicare-approved amount.
   B. Compare the balance with the plan's normal liability (the amount determined in step I).
      1. If the normal liability amount is equal to or greater than the balance amount, the balance is paid by the plan.
      2. If the normal liability amount is less than the balance, the normal liability amount is paid.

III. If the claim is not Medicare assigned, the base is the lesser of the plan's eligible expense or Medicare's approved amount plus the capitation percentage (balance billing limit). Rather, the amount eligible or approved under the plan is used as the base.
   A. Subtract the amount paid by Medicare from the plan's approved amount (calculated in step I).
   B. Compare the balance with the group's normal liability (the amount determined in step I).
      1. If the normal liability amount is equal to or greater than the balance amount, the balance is paid by the plan.
      2. If the normal liability amount is less than the balance, the normal liability amount is paid.

IV. The credit reserve is calculated, based on the difference between the plan's liability (calculated in step I) and the amount actually paid by the plan.

Following are three examples of calculation of benefits using the nonduplication of Medicare benefits approach:

Example 1:

Plan benefits: $100.00 deductible, $65.00 satisfied to date. 85% payable for doctor's expenses, and 100% for diagnostic x-ray and lab to $100.00 per calendar year maximum. Amount over $100.00 is not covered.

Charges on 1st claim submitted. Nonassigned claim.

Submitted charges
$ 25.00 Office visit
$150.00 Lab
$ 10.00 Dispensed meds
$185.00

Normal liab (#1)
$ 0.00 Pd, $25.00 to ded (OV)
$100.00 Pd, $50.00 N/C (Lab)
$ 0.00 Pd, $10.00 to ded (Meds)

Medicare pay (#2)
$ 0.00 Pd, $25.00 to ded
$ 75.00 ded @ 80%
$ 0.00 Paid, not covered

$ 185.00	Charge
– 60.00	Medicare/primary payor
125.00	Balance due
–100.00	Plan/secondary payor
25.00	Out-of-pocket to patient

Example 2: Same plan benefits as in #1. Nonassigned claim.

Submitted charges
$300.00 Surgery
$ 36.00 OV
$ 48.00 X-ray
$384.00

Normal liab (#1)
$255.00 Pd, 85% of $300.00
$ 29.75 Pd, 85% of $36.00
$ 0.00 Max DXL paid
$284.75

Medicare approved
$237.50
$ 28.50
$ 38.00
$304.00

Medicare pay (#2)
$201.88 Pd, 85% of 237.50
$ 22.80 Pd, 80% of 28.50
$ 38.00 Pd, 100% of 38.00
$262.68

$ 384.00	Charge
–255.08	Medicare payment
$ 128.92	Balance due
–128.92	Plan payment
0	Out-of-pocket to patient

$ 284.75	Plan's normal liability
–128.92	Actual payment
$ 155.83	Plan credit reserve

Example 3: Same Plan benefits as in #1. Assigned claim.

Submitted charges
$300.00 Surgery
$ 36.00 OV
$ 48.00 X-ray
$384.00

Normal liab (#1)
$212.50 Pd, 85% of $250.00
$ 25.50 Pd, 85% of $30.00
$ 0.00 Max DXL pd
$238.00

Medicare approved
$250.00
$ 30.00
$ 40.00
$320.00

Medicare pay (#2)
$200.00 Pd, 85% of 250.00
$ 24.00 Pd, 80% of 30.00
$ 32.00 Pd, 80% of 40.00
$256.00

$ 320.00	Medicare-approved charge
–256.00	Medicare payment
$ 64.00	Balance due
– 64.00	Plan payment
0	Out-of-pocket to patient

$ 238.00	Plan's normal liability
– 64.00	Actual payment
$ 174.00	Plan credit reserve

Maintenance of Benefits

Maintenance of benefits refers to a provision in many group health plans that allows the person who has Medicare to "maintain" the same group benefits as members who do not have Medicare. Benefit credits are not established. To determine the payable benefits under this provision, follow the five procedures indicated below:

1. Compute the regular basic or Major Medical benefits that would be payable in the absence of Medicare (line-for-line calculation). Apply all eligibility requirements, deductibles, limitations, and contractual maximums.
2. Determine the amount payable by Medicare.
3. If #1 is greater than #2, pay the amount of the difference.
4. If #2 is greater than #1, no payment will be issued by the plan.
5. Credit reserve is not maintained.

Example 1: Plan benefits: $150 deductible, none satisfied to date. 85% payable for doctor's expenses and diagnostic x-ray and lab. 80% for meds.

Charges on 1st claim submitted. Not Medicare assigned.

Submitted Chg	**Normal Liab (#1)**
$ 25.00 OV	0.00 Pd $25.00 to ded
$150.00 Lab	$125.00 ded, $25.00 @ 85%
$ 10.00 Disp meds	$ 10.00 @ 80% MM
$185.00	$ 29.25

Medicare Pay (#2)

0.00 pd, $25.00 to ded
$75.00 ded, $75.00 @ 80%
$0.00 not covered
$60.00

Since the payment made by Medicare is greater than the normal liability under the plan, no additional payment will be made by the plan.

$ 185.00	Charge
– 60.00	Medicare payment
$ 125.00	Out-of-pocket to patient

Example 2: Same plan benefits as in #1. Not Medicare assigned.

Submitted Chg	**Normal Liab (#1)**
$36.00 OV	$36.00 @ 85% = $30.60
$48.00 X-ray	$48.00 @ 85% = $40.80
$84.00	$71.40

Medicare Appr	**Medicare Pd (#2)**
$28.50	$28.50 @ 80% = $22.80
$38.00	$38.00 @ 80% = $30.40
$66.50	$53.20

Since the normal liability for the plan, $71.40, is greater than Medicare's payment, $53.20, a payment will be issued for the difference between the two, or $18.20 ($71.40–$53.20).

$ 84.00	Charge
–53.20	Medicare payment
$ 30.80	Balance due
–18.20	Plan payment
$ 12.60	Out-of-pocket to patient

Example 3: Same plan benefits as in #2. Medicare assigned.

Submitted Chg	**Normal Liab (#1)**
$36.00 OV	$30.00 @ 85% = $25.50
$48.00 X-ray	$40.00 @ 85% = $34.00
$84.00	$59.50

Medicare Appr	**Medicare Pd (#2)**
$30.00	$30.00 @ 80% = $24.00
$40.00	$40.00 @ 80% = $32.00
$70.00	$56.00

Since the normal liability for the plan, $59.50, is greater than Medicare's payment, $56.00, a payment will be issued for the difference between the two, or $3.50 ($59.50–$56.00).

$ 70.00	Medicare-approved amount
–56.00	Medicare payment
$ 14.00	Balance due
– 3.50	Plan payment
$ 10.50	Out-of-pocket to patient

Example 4: Same benefits as above. $150.00 deductible, deductible satisfied. 85% payable for doctor's expenses and diagnostic x-ray and lab. Medicare assigned. Fill in the blanks.

Submitted Chg	**Normal Liab (#1)**
$36.00 OV	$ @ 85% =
$48.00 X-ray	$ @ 85% =
$84.00	$

Medicare Appr	**Medicare Pd (#2)**
$30.00	$30 @ 80% = $24
$40.00	$40 @ 80% = $32
$70.00	$56

$	Allowable charge
– 56.00	Medicare payment
$	Balance due
–	Difference between Medicare payment and plan liability
$	Out-of-pocket amount for patient

Under maintenance of benefits, when a group plan and Medicare are both providing benefits on the same expenses, the total benefits provided should equal what the benefit would have been under the group plan alone as if the member did not have Medicare (except that Medicare assignment must be taken into consideration).

Regular group benefits are provided for charges covered by the group plan but not covered by Medicare at all.

Coordination with Medicare

COB with Medicare is calculated as with any other COB claim. Allowable expenses are based on the amount approved by Medicare on an assigned claim or the amount approved by the plan or Medicare, whichever is greater, on a nonassigned claim. Also, as with other COB claims, allowable expenses are considered those payable in whole or part by one or both plans. Benefit credit reserve is established and used to cover allowable expenses.

Example 1: Plan benefits: $150.00 deductible, none satisfied to date. 85% payable for doctor's expenses and diagnostic x-ray and lab.

Charges on 1st claim submitted. Not Medicare assigned.

Submitted Chg	**Normal Liab (#1)**
$ 25.00 OV	0 Paid $25 ded
$150.00 Lab	$125 ded $25 @ 85%
$ 10.00 Disp meds	$10 @ 80% MM
$185.00	$ 29.25

Medicare Pd (#2)

0 Paid $25 ded
$75 ded 75 @ 80%
0 not covered
$ 60.00

$ 185.00	Charge
– 60.00	Medicare payment
$ 125.00	Balance due
– 29.25	Plan payment
$ 95.75	Out-of-pocket to patient

Example 2: Same plan benefits as in #1. Not Medicare assigned.

Submitted Chg	**Normal Liab (#1)**
$36.00 OV	$36 @ 85% = $30.60
$48.00 X-ray	$48 @ 85% = $40.80
$84.00	$71.40

Medicare Appr	**Medicare Pd (#2)**
$28.50	$28.50 @ 80% = $22.80
$38.00	$38.00 @ 80% = $30.40
$66.50	$53.20

$ 84.00	Charge
– 53.20	Medicare payment
$ 30.80	Balance due
– 30.80	Plan payment
$ 0	Out-of-pocket to patient

$ 71.40	Plan liability
– 30.80	Actual payment
$ 40.60	Credit reserve

Example 3: Same benefits as above. $150.00 deductible, deductible satisfied. 85% payable for doctor's expenses and diagnostic x-ray and lab. Medicare assigned. Fill in the blanks.

Submitted Chg	Normal Liab (#1)
$36.00 OV	$ @ 85% =
$48.00 X-ray	$ @ 85% =
$84.00	$

Medicare Appr	Medicare Pd (#2)
$30.00	$30.00 @ 80% = $24.00
$40.00	$40.00 @ 80% = $32.00
$70.00	$56.00

$	
– 56.00	Medicare payment
$	
– ______	Plan payment
$	Out-of-pocket to patient
$	Normal liability
– ______	Actual payment
$	Credit reserve (if applicable)

Medicare Supplement

Supplements are separate plans written exclusively for Medicare participants. A supplement plan may be written with any optional benefits the policyholder wants. Common options are as follows:

- Physicians' services—Covers Part B deductible and 20% coinsurance for reasonable charges. "Reasonable charges" means that amounts reduced by Medicare because of prevailing fees are not covered under the plan even though the plan's prevailing fee may be higher than that of Medicare when the bill is assigned. If the bill is not assigned, the plan's UCR or Medicare's UCR is the amount allowable, whichever is greater.
- Hospital services—Covers Part A deductible and may or may not cover the various copays not covered by Medicare.
- Nursing care, prescriptions, nonreplaced fees on the first three pints of blood—may also be covered.

With the changes in Medicare, supplemental plans have become more flexible. Therefore, the benefits can be complex and comprehensive or very basic.

Estimating Medicare Coverage

Sometimes a member is entitled to Medicare but has not enrolled. In this circumstance, many policies specify that the group plan will "estimate" what Medicare would have paid if the person had been enrolled properly. The policy may specify instead that benefits will be reduced only when the member is actually enrolled in Medicare. In this situation, the regular plan benefits will be provided and the Medicare payment will not be estimated.

To estimate the Medicare payment, use the following as a guide:

Hospital: Part A

1. Provide full benefits toward the Medicare deductible and coinsurance amounts.
2. Provide regular group benefits for services or items covered by the group plan but not covered by Medicare.

Professional: Part B

1. Determine the plan's UCR for the billed charges.
2. The UCR amount is considered the estimated Medicare-approved amount.
3. Multiply 80% of the estimated approved amount (#2). This is your estimated Medicare payment.
4. Take the estimated Medicare payment (#3) and

subtract that amount from the regular plan benefit amount.

5. Follow the rules in #3 and #4 on the preceding page to determine whether or not the plan will provide any payment.
6. If #1 above is greater than #2, pay the amount of the difference.
7. If #2 is greater than #1, no payment will be issued by the plan.

Diagnosis-Related Group Billing

Effective October 1, 1983, Medicare instituted diagnosis-related group (DRG) payments for inpatient hospital claims. Under DRG, a flat rate payment is made, based on the patient's diagnosis rather than the hospital's itemized billing. If the hospital can treat the patient for less, it keeps the savings. If treatment costs more, the hospital must absorb the loss. Neither Medicare nor the patient is responsible for the excess amount.

Exceptions

Provisions have been made for cases atypically expensive (based on the diagnosis) because of complications or an abnormally long confinement. Known as outliers, these cases will be reimbursed on an itemized or cost percentage basis rather than DRG. The bill from the hospital must indicate that it is an outlier.

Exclusions

Excluded from DRG are long-term care, children's care, and psychiatric and rehabilitative hospitals. Also excluded are hospitals located in the states of Maryland, Massachusetts, New Jersey, and New York. These states have obtained waivers from DRG. Waivers and exclusions are subject to change, and you should consult your state department of insurance for updated information.

DRG Benefit Payment Calculations

As shown in the following examples, the maximum liability under a plan consists of only the following expenses:

- Those covered by the plan.
- Those that the insured is legally obliged to pay.

Example 1: Itemized hospital bill exceeds Medicare DRG allowance.

Hospital bill	$8700.00
DRG allowance	$7000.00
Medicare payment	$6372.00 (DRG, $628 ded)
Patient's responsibility	$ 628.00
Hospital write-off	$1700.00

Although the Medicare DRG allowance is less than the itemized hospital bill, the insured is legally obligated to pay only the $628 Part A deductible. Therefore, exclude the difference between the itemized hospital billed amount and the DRG allowance as not covered, no legal obligation to pay. The plan's benefits would be based on the total charges of $7000, with the $1700 reflected as not covered because it exceeds DRG allowance.

When coding out the claim, different firms may handle the coding differently. However, frequently the actual billed amount for room and board is used and then the difference between that amount and the actual billed charges is used for the miscellaneous amount.

Example 2: Medicare DRG allowance exceeds itemized billed amount.

Hospital bill	$ 8,700.00
DRG allowance	$10,000.00
Medicare payment	$ 9,372.00
Patient's responsibility	$ 628.00

Although the Medicare payment exceeds the itemized hospital bill, the insured is legally obligated to pay the $628 Part A deductible. Handling of this type of billing also varies. Sometimes the DRG amount may be used as the billed amount or the actual billed amount may be used by manipulating the Medicare paid amount. Check the office guidelines before processing the claim.

Summary

Medicare is administered through the Health Care Financing Administration. Each year, rules and guidelines for payment and covered charges are established. Claims examiners must keep abreast of the changes in the Medicare system. This can be accomplished by subscribing to the Medicare bulletin that is usually published by the fiscal intermediary for Medicare in the local area. Other agencies conduct seminars in various locations. Contact the fiscal intermediary for these agencies and their locations. By attending seminars, using the Medicare bulletins, and applying the guidelines we have covered in this chapter, claims examiners will establish a consistent approach to processing Medicare claims, which will result in competent and accurate claim decisions.

Assignments

Complete the Questions for Review.
Complete billing the remaining Medicare claims in the Student Exercise Manual and process Medicare claims 11-1 to 11-15.

Questions for Review

Directions: Answer the following questions without looking back into the material just covered. Write your answers in the space provided.

1. What is Medicare? Federal Health Insurance Benefit Plan for aged and disabled
2. On what three criteria is Medicare eligibility based?
   a. Based on age
   b. Based on disability
   c. Based on end stage renal disease
3. Medicare Part A is considered the basic plan or hospital insurance.
4. Medicare Part B is the medical insurance that covers doctors' services, outpatient services, and so on.
5. What does it mean when a provider accepts assignment of benefits in relation to Medicare? The provider receives payment directly from Medicare. The provider has agreed to accept the amount approved by the Medicare carrier for the services covered. The patient isn't responsible for any amount in excess of the approved amount

If you were unable to answer any of the questions, refer back to the section and then complete the answers.

17
Medicaid

In this chapter you will learn:

- Medicaid eligibility requirements.
- What the HIPD form is and how to use it.

Medicaid is not a health insurance program. The Federal Medicaid program was established under Title XIX of the Social Security Act of 1965. The purpose of this program is to provide the needy with access to medical care. By law, Medicaid is always secondary to private group health care plans. If Medicaid inadvertently pays primary, it will exercise its right of recovery and seek reimbursement from the private plan. Again, the private plan by law is required to process Medicaid's request for reimbursement and pay back Medicaid the monies it paid the Medicaid provider.

The regulations governing eligibility under the Medicaid program are complex. Individuals may be entitled to coverage due to medical, family, or fiscal situations. The fact that the individual has private insurance does not preclude him or her from being eligible for Medicaid benefits.

The Medicaid program does not process its own claims. Medicaid contracts with an organization to act as the fiscal intermediary, similar to Medicare. The intermediary processes the claims according to specifications set forth by the Medicaid program.

The rates under Medicaid are based on the results of reimbursement studies conducted by the Department of Health Services. Reimbursement for hospital inpatient services are based on each facility's "reasonable cost" of services as determined from audit cost reports and annual limitations on reimbursable increases in cost.

Providers are not allowed to bill or submit a claim to the Medicaid beneficiary for any service included in the program's scope of benefits except to collect money from a patient's private health care coverage prior to billing Medicaid. There is a 3-year statute of limitations from the date of service for recovery. In addition, there is a 3-year subrogation right.

For a claimant's services to be covered under Medicaid, the claimant must be a Medicaid beneficiary and the provider must be an approved Medicaid provider. To be an approved provider, the provider of services must agree to accept Medicaid's determination of approved amounts as binding. That is, similar to Medicare's approved amount on assigned claims, the provider is not allowed to bill the patient for any amount not approved by Medicaid. In recent years, many providers have dropped out of the Medicaid program because their allowances and payments are extremely low, even lower than those provided by Medicare.

Health Insurance Payment Demand

The Health Insurance Payment Demand (HIPD) is a bill that lists the health care services paid by the Medicaid program on behalf of a person who has indicated that he or she has other health care coverage benefits available. Insurers/plans are to reimburse the Medicaid program for these services to the extent of the plan's available benefits or the amount paid by Medicaid, whichever is less. If the private plan is not liable for a particular service, the reason for this must be explained on the HIPD, along with indications of what was paid.

The HIPD is a computer-generated list that includes the following:

- The patient's name
- The policyholder name
- The policy number
- The provider
- The diagnosis
- The treatment provided
- The dates of services
- The charges
- Payments previously made by Medicaid on each service

The HIPD is usually accompanied by a cover letter (see Figure 17-1). The forms may differ from state to state, but they usually contain similar information.

In addition to the cover letter, the State's Recovery Unit will also supply the HIPD Processing Form, which is used by the payor when responding to an HIPD. It is completed by the carrier and then sent to Medicaid with the state's copy of the HIPD. A sample of the front of this form is shown in Figure 17-2.

Return Address

Attention: Claims Manager

Warning! Enclosed is confidential information. This information is provided to you so that you may determine the liability of your company or your health insurance carrier to repay the Medicaid program on behalf of the individual listed. This is pursuant to State Code Sections 100XX et seq., 140XX.XX, or 141XX. Any person may be subject to civil or criminal penalties for disclosure, publication, or other use, or for permitting or causing this confidential information to be disclosed, published, or used except as necessary to accomplish the above-mentioned purpose or with specific written permission from the Medicaid beneficiary, personal representative, or guardian (if a minor).

Enclosed are Health Insurance Payment Demands (HIPDs) for claims for health care services paid by the Medicaid program for individuals who indicate that they have health care coverage with your organization.

Payment to the extent of your contractual obligation is now due. Medicaid should be reimbursed for all amounts that it has paid as shown on the following form. When making payment on this claim, please indicate the HIPD number and the patient's Medicaid number on your check. Mark the amount of payment for each service on the state copy of the HIPD. If a service or services are not covered, a complete explanation of the reason for nonpayment should be indicated on the enclosed HIPD Processing Form. The HIPD Processing Form may be reproduced for use within your office.

If you are unable to identify the claimant as an insured policyholder under your plan, mark the HIPD 4a and return. If you need additional information to locate the claimant or confirm eligibility, list the precise information needed. Additional information that would facilitate future HIPD processing (ie, group name, policy #), which is not listed on the HIPD, may be noted under response #4d (Other) on the HIPD Processing Form.

If this HIPD should be sent to another department or location, indicate the appropriate department and the complete address and return the HIPD to us. We will update our files with the proper information.

All policyholders that provide coverage for the claimant listed are indicated under the claimant's name. This information is for use in coordinating benefits with other health insurance carriers.

Thank you for your cooperation. If you have any questions, please write us at the address indicated above.

Sincerely,

Jane Doe, Chief
Health Insurance Unit
Recovery Branch

Figure 17-1: **Sample HIPD Cover Letter.**

Health Insurance Payment Demand (HIPD) Processing Form

Please Return State Copy of HIPD to:

Please feel free to write on the HIPD. In addition, complete the appropriate information below and return with the HIPD.

Patient Name (Medicaid Beneficiary): ____________________ Medicaid #: ____________

HIPD Number(s) (From the upper right-hand corner of the HIPD): ____________________

HIPD Billing Date(s) (From the upper right corner of the HIPD): ____________________

❑ 1. The enclosed check(s) for $________ represents payment of our liability under this policy. For any charges considered ineligible, see Number 3 below.

❑ 2. Charges previously considered (if additional space is needed, please use reverse side).

Payee ____________________ Amount $ __________ Date__________

Address ____________________ Date(s) of Service ____________

Payee ____________________ Amount $ __________ Date__________

Address ____________________ Date(s) of Service ____________

3. Claimant is ineligible due to:

❑ a. Claimant's policy is no longer in effect. Termination date: ____________________

❑ b. Claimant was not covered on date of service. Coverage date(s) __________ to __________

❑ c. Claimant's group was not insured on date of service. Coverage date(s) __________ to __________

If liable carrier is known, provide complete name and address: ____________________

❑ d. Claimant was not a covered dependent on date of service. Explain: ____________________

❑ e. Services are not covered expenses under the policy. Why?

❑ Policy does not cover convalescent care. ❑ Policy covers in-hospital services only.

❑ Policy does not cover drugs, vision, etc. ❑ Other ____________________

❑ f. Maximum benefit of $ __________ per __________ (time period) has been exhausted.

❑ g. Charges do not exceed policy deductible. Deductible is $ __________ per __________ .

❑ h. Other reasons (specify) ____________________

4. This HIPD is being returned or processing is being delayed due to:

❑ a. We are unable to identify individual/group as our insured. We need: ____________________

❑ b. Dual coverage is indicated. We need: ____________________

❑ c. Additional information is needed on the following service(s): ____________________

❑ d. Other (specify) ____________________

Figure 17-2: Sample HIPD Processing Form.

Handling Procedures

When an HIPD is received, the following eight procedures will assist in its handling. (Item numbers that follow refer to the numbers on the front side of the sample HIPD Processing Form). (Reason codes are the numbered items on the back side of the sample HIPD Processing Form.)

1. Determine whether or not the patient is eligible under the indicated plan. If not, complete item #3. If the information provided on the HIPD is incomplete and you are unable to identify the member or patient, complete item #4.
2. Determine whether the indicated charges were previously paid under the plan. If so, no payment is due Medicaid. Complete item #3 or #4 and enter the reason code (3a, 4c, and so on) in the Insurance Paid Amount column of the HIPD.
3. If no payment has been made for the charges in question, calculate the normal plan benefits. Do not request an attending physician's statement because the HIPD constitutes sufficient proof of loss.
4. Usually, a line-by-line comparison is made between the amount paid by Medicaid and the amount payable under the private plan. However, it is also possible to do a total-by-total comparison. To do this, subtract the amounts paid by Medicaid for expenses not covered by the private plan from the total Medicaid payment.
5. Pay the lesser of:
   a. The normal private plan benefit or
   b. The total Medicaid payment, as adjusted in item #4. The payment by the private plan to Medicaid should never exceed the total adjusted Medicaid payment. The draft should be made payable to Health Care Deposit Fund.
6. If payment has previously been made, complete item #2. If some or all of the charges are not covered under the terms of the plan, complete item #3 or #4.
7. Send the completed HIPD Processing Form, the state copy of the HIPD, and the benefit draft (if benefits are payable) to the Health Recovery Bureau for your state.
8. Retain one copy of the HIPD in the claim file.

After payment has been made to Medicaid as just outlined, the plan's full liability has been discharged. This is true even if the payment made is less than the payment that would have been made in the absence of Medicaid.

These instructions apply only if the HIPD has been received. If the claims file indicates that the claimant is eligible for Medicaid, but the state has not submitted an HIPD, any charges received should be handled in the usual manner. When processing an HIPD billing, all plan provisions except the timely filing limitations apply.

Summary

Medicaid guidelines vary from state to state. Medicaid bulletins are produced to assist you in interpreting the rules for coverage and to determine which charges are covered by Medicaid. These manuals are available to Medicaid providers and are primarily used by billers. However, they may be helpful to the claims examiner. Contact your Medicaid intermediary for copies of these manuals.

Assignments

Complete the Questions for Review.

Questions for Review

Directions: Answer the following questions without looking back into the material just covered. Write your answers in the space provided.

1. What is the purpose of the Medicaid program? Provide the needy with access to medical care
2. By law, Medicaid is always primary to private group health insurance plans. (True or False) False
3. In what situation are providers allowed to bill or submit a claim to the Medicaid beneficiary? To collect money from a patients private health care coverage prior to billing medicaid
4. The Health Ins Payments Demand (HIPA) is a bill that lists the health care services paid by the Medicaid program on behalf of a person who has indicated that he or she has other health care coverage benefits available.
5. For a claimant's services to be covered under Medicaid, the claimant must be a Medicaid beneficiary and the provider must be an Approved Medicaid provider.

If you were unable to answer any of the questions, refer back to the section and then complete the answers.

18

Podiatric Surgery

In this chapter you will learn:

- Common foot conditions and surgical procedures.
- To process podiatric surgery claims.

Podiatry is an area of medicine that provides services for the feet. The services are usually provided by a podiatrist with the professional designation, DPM, Doctor of Podiatric Medicine.

The joints of the feet are very complex. When surgery is performed, the claims that are received by the claims examiner will also be complex. In this chapter we will discuss some of the procedures performed on the foot and some guidelines that have been established regarding payment of podiatry claims.

General Guidelines

Because of the complexity of podiatry claims, most administrators have special handling guidelines for podiatric care and for podiatric surgery. Many plans have provisions that place a UCR limitation and a daily maximum on podiatric claims. In addition, most of these claims may also be referred for review prior to payment.

The UCR fee allowance for podiatric surgery is determined on the same basis as any other surgical procedure. The most common problem in determining the correct UCR allowance is the excessive detail in which the surgery is sometimes described. At times, the podiatrist describes and bills each procedure independently, even though some procedures are incidental to the major operation performed. Refer to Chapter 12 for further information on multiple, bilateral, and incidental surgeries. The following four handling procedures may be helpful in identifying the correct breakdown of the surgeries performed:

1. Separate the procedures performed on each foot. The foot that has the most or major surgery is identified as the primary foot.
2. List the independent procedures and identify the metatarsal or phalange on the M-P joint by digit (eg, great toe #1, second toe #2).
3. Determine whether more than one procedure has been performed on one joint, one toe, or adjacent parts of the foot. If this is identified, no additional allowance is made for secondary procedures, because all such procedures are to be considered incidental (part of the major procedure).
4. After all the independent procedures for both the primary and secondary foot have been identified, the correct CPT surgical procedure code can be located.

Surgical Coding

To select the correct procedure code, identify the diagnosis and the required procedures necessary to correct the medical problem. For example, a bill with a diagnosis of "hammertoe" may list service for an arthroplasty, a capsulotomy, and a tenotomy with a separate charge for each procedure. The benefit for correction of the diagnosis, repair of hammertoe (CPT code 28285), should be allowed. No additional allowance is available for each separate procedure because they are included in the hammertoe repair procedure code. The following eight rules are important to consider when determining correct surgical codes:

1. Only one bunion surgery is allowable per foot.
2. Only one bone operation is allowable per toe.
3. Only one capsulotomy/tenotomy is allowable per metatarsal.
4. No increase is allowable for K wires (stabilizing wires placed in the foot). These are considered a necessary part of the procedure and do not warrant an extra benefit.
5. Generally one operation is allowable per incision.
6. Taylor's bunion is not a bunion.
7. Unna's boot (gauze soaked in zinc oxide) is considered part of the surgery itself and does not warrant an additional allowance. When the boot is used for treatment of leg ulcers, additional benefits can be allowed.
8. Flexible casts are nothing more than a tape or bandage and do not warrant a casting benefit.

Remember that these are general guidelines only. The actual administration of podiatric claims varies greatly among companies.

Conditions of the Foot and Treatment Procedures

The following are explanations of common foot conditions and some of the procedures performed to treat or correct problems.

Foot surgeries usually involve some incision of the skin and, in some cases, of the bone also. Skin heals in phases. In the first phase, skin grows together, which allows stitches to be removed. The scar may look slightly inflamed. Some redness and swelling are normal. After about 6 months, the scar blends with the surrounding skin. However, scarring varies according to the individual.

Bone also heals in phases. A bone-like "cement" forms first, which bridges the affected bone and enables it to bear some weight. Later, this extra bone dissolves. The healing process varies from person to person and also depends on the health and age of the person.

Ligaments are flexible bands of fiber joining bone to bone. Joints are where two bones meet. Thirty-three complex joints in each foot permit flexibility.

Bunions

A bunion is an enlargement of a bone in a joint at the base of the big toe. Bunions are most often inherited. Contrary to what many people believe, bunions are not caused by tight shoes, although tight-fitting shoes can aggravate them.

The simplest bunion procedure is the Silver procedure. The Silver procedure does not involve any surgery in the first metatarsal interspace; all other bunion procedures do.

The McBride procedure is performed to remove the bump on the outside of the first metatarsal, remove the sesamoid, and sever the abductor and short tendon. If tenotomies are not performed, the procedure is a Silver.

Reverdin or Reverdin and Green bunionectomy involves the removal of the bunion on the outside of the first metatarsal and a wedge osteotomy of the first metatarsal to bring the toe into proper alignment.

The Austin, Reverdin, Peabody, Mitchell, Wilson, and Rue bunionectomies all involve some kind of osteotomy in the head of the metatarsal and all have the same procedure code of 28296. A metatarsal base osteotomy is a valid second procedure with a CPT code of 28306.

The Akin osteotomy involves the removal of a cylindrical wedge of the proximal phalanx of the great toe and is closed with a screw, wire, or pin. This cylindrical wedge can be taken from either the distal or proximal end of the phalanx. If done with the Akin bunionecto-

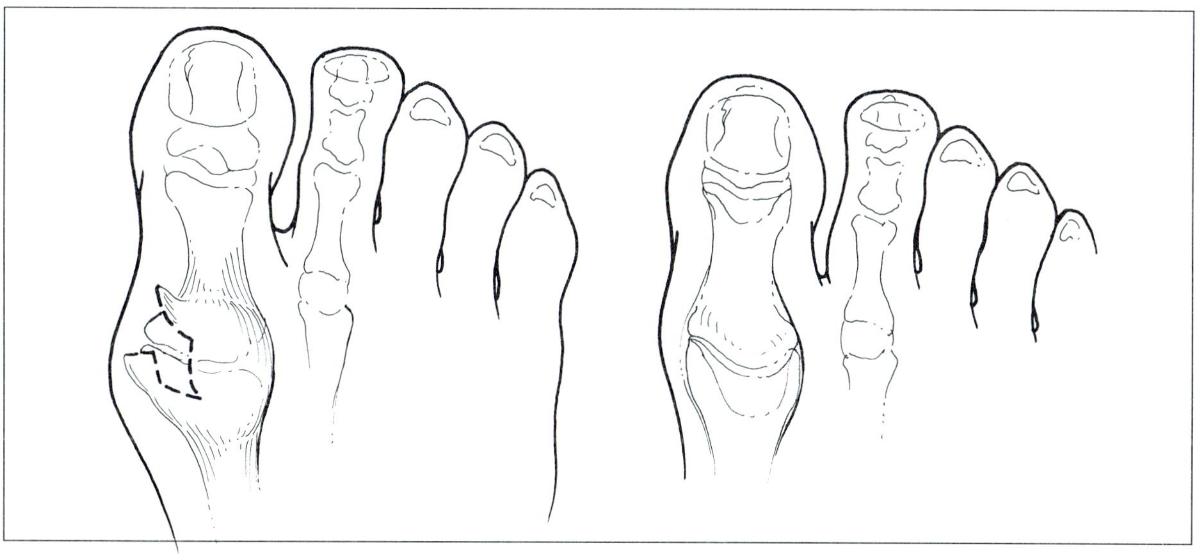

Figure 18-1: Positional bunionectomy.

my, the procedure code is 28298. When the Akin osteotomy and bunionectomy are performed at the same time, there should be one surgery per foot.

The Keller bunionectomy with Silastic implant involves the removal of a bunion from the first metatarsal and excision of the head of the proximal phalanx with insertion of the Silastic head into the end of the phalanx so that it forms a new gliding joint.

Positional Bunions

A positional bunion develops when a bony growth on the side of the metatarsal bone enlarges the joint, forcing the joint capsule to stretch over it. As this growth pushes the big toe toward the others, the tendons on the inside tighten. This then forces the big toe further out of alignment. The bunion presses against the shoe, irritating the skin and causing increased pain.

In treatment of a positional bunion (positional bunionectomy), the bump is removed (Figure 18-1). A wedge of the joint capsule may also be removed to reposition it. Tight tendons may also have to be released. A special wooden shoe or a splint may be required for about 3 weeks postoperatively.

Structural Bunions

A mild structural bunion occurs when the angle between the first and second metatarsal bones increases to a point at which it is greater than normal. The increased angle of the metatarsal makes the big toe bow toward the other toes. This is usually an inherited tendency. Treatment of a structural bunion (structural bunionectomy) involves repositioning the bone (Figure 18-2). A splint or a special shoe may be required for about 6 weeks postoperatively.

A structural bunion becomes severe when the angle between the metatarsal bones of the first and second toes grows greater than the angle of a mild structural bunion. The big toe bows toward the others, sometimes causing the second and third toes to buckle.

For a severe structural bunion, a base osteotomy may be performed to remove a wedge of bone so that the metatarsal can be repositioned. Tiny K wires or

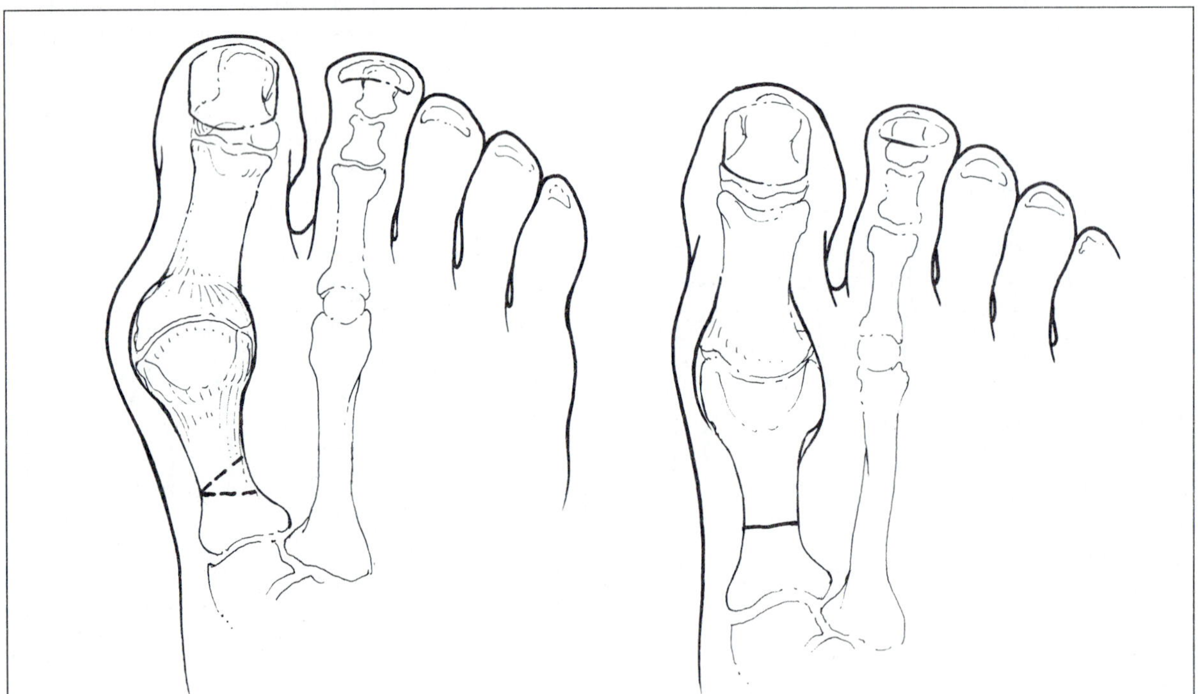

Figure 18-2: **Structural bunionectomy.**

screws may be used to stabilize the bone.

The foot and ankle may be immobilized with a cast; no weight should be placed on the foot for several weeks.

Degenerative Disease

Degenerative disease is not a bunion, but it is often associated with bunions. This is because an untreated bunion can increase wear and tear on the joint of the big toe, break down the cartilage, and pave the way for degenerative diseases such as arthritis, osteoarthritis, and rheumatoid arthritis.

Treatment of degenerative conditions involves removal of all bunions; the degenerated joint is then removed and replaced with a Silastic (plastic) implant. A splint or a special shoe may be worn for several weeks. However, the ability to walk may return within 1 or 2 days after surgery.

Taylor's Bunionectomy

Taylor's procedure is not a bunion operation, but the removal of a small bone portion of the fifth metatarsal. It is often done with an osteotomy. When the portion of the fifth metatarsal is removed, it may accompany an incidental removal of the outside of the first phalanx.

Hammertoes

Hammertoes are inherited muscle imbalances or abnormal bone lengths that can make the toes buckle under, causing their joints to contract. Subsequently, the tendons shorten. A flexible hammertoe is one in which the buckled joint can be straightened manually with the hand. These may progress and become rigid over time. Corns, irritation, and pain are common symptoms. Rigid hammertoes are fixed and cannot be manually straightened. Corns, irritation, pain, and loss of function may be more severe in rigid than in flexible hammertoes.

Surgical Repair

There are two different types of hammertoe repair: simple and radical. Regardless of the procedure, only one hammertoe operation is allowable per toe. Some of the more common hammertoe repair procedures are tenotomy, capsulotomy, osteotomy, arthroplasty, and arthrodesis.

A tenotomy and capsulotomy are performed to release the buckling and the top and bottom tendons. The joint capsules may also have to be cut (see Figure 18-3). When a tenotomy and capsulotomy are performed on the same joint, only one operation is allowable per joint.

When an osteotomy is done in conjunction with a tenotomy and capsulotomy, the additional procedure is incidental.

Arthroplasties and osteotomies on the same digit are generally the same procedure. In other words, one surgery is necessary to perform the other, with the latter fee covering the arthroplasty.

When an arthrodesis is being performed, only one operation is allowable per toe. The fusion may be accomplished by either screw or pin. CPT coding is determined by the procedure and the appropriate toe on which the procedure was performed. The joint most commonly fused is the second joint; occasionally, the distal joint is fused (there is no additional complexity for fusion of the distal joint).

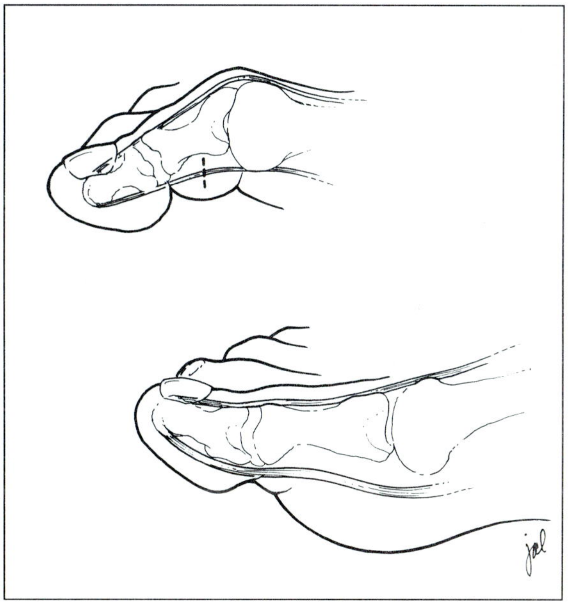

Figure 18-3: Tenotomy and capsulotomy.

Triple arthrodesis is an operation to fuse the three bones on the ankle joint. Multiple osteotomies are performed, and then the area is packed with bone chips and fixed in a stationary position with either pins or staples and placed in a cast for 3 to 6 months.

An arthroplasty is a procedure in which a portion of the joint is surgically removed and the toe is straightened. The resulting gap will fill in with fibrous tissue. Removal of the joint and fusion of the bones constitute an alternative treatment.

The fifth (little) toe may curl inward beneath the 4th toe, so that the nail faces outward. This inherited problem results in corns and pain. A derotation arthroplasty is performed to remove a wedge of skin and bone to uncurl (derotate) the toe. A bandage, splint, and sometimes a surgical shoe are required for several weeks following surgery.

Plantar Calluses

A metatarsal plantar callus occurs when the metatarsal bone is longer or lower than the others so that it hits the ground first at every step, with more force than it is equipped to handle. As a result, the skin under this bone thickens and becomes hardened into a callus. The callus causes irritation and pain. The treatment is a V osteotomy in which the metatarsal bone is cut in a V shape. The end of the bone is then lifted and aligned with the other bones. The V shape holds the bone in its new position, preventing it from rocking to the left or the right.

A fifth metatarsal plantar callus is caused by walking improperly on the outside of the foot. The extra pressure may cause the skin under the bone to thicken causing irritation and pain.

Dwyer Osteotomy Surgical Procedure

The Dwyer procedure is the treatment for a deformity of the calcaneus or large heel bone. It consists of a wedge resection of a portion of the calcaneus bone and is closed with staple, pin, or screw fixation.

A dorsal osteotomy is performed by removing a small wedge of bone from the top (dorsal) side of the base of the fifth metatarsal bone. This elevates the bone and relieves pressure on the callus. The bone is then fixated with tiny wires or screws.

Bone Spurs

A spur is a bony overgrowth on a bone. Bone spurs have a variety of causes and usually result in pain, interfere with the use of the foot, and detract from its appearance.

A heel spur is an overgrowth on the heel bone. It may be stimulated by muscles that pull from the heel bone along the bottom of the foot. High-arched feet are especially apt to have excessively tight muscles in this area.

Treatment of bone spurs involves releasing the band of tight muscles to relieve the stress. The bone spur is then surgically removed (see Figure 18-4). Crutches may be required for up to 2 weeks after surgery to avoid weight bearing on the foot.

A bone spur may occur alone or with a hammertoe, usually resulting in pain and interfering with the use of the foot. An overgrowth under the toenail can press up into the tissue underneath the growth plate, deforming the nail above. This is especially painful when shoes are worn.

Common Surgical Procedures

The most common exostosis (bony growth) on the foot is the heel spur. In most cases, surgery is the most

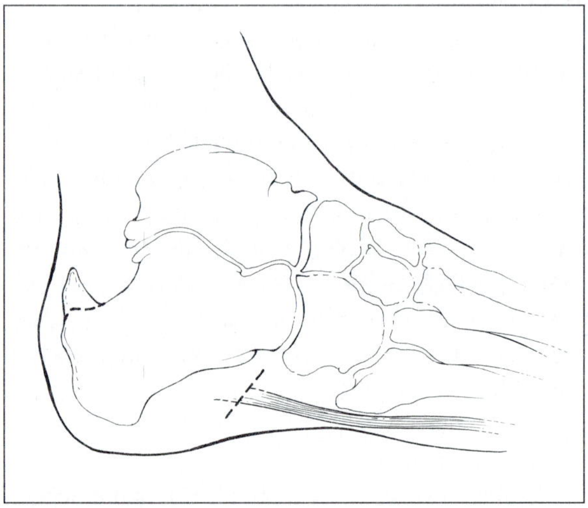

Figure 18-4: **Treatment of bone spur.**

effective way to treat a heel spur. A plantar fasciotomy performed at the same time as a surgery for heel spurs is an incidental procedure, since a fasciotomy must be done to cut through the area before the heel spur is located. In many cases, the use of an orthosis (an orthopedic appliance) is as effective as the surgery.

Treatment for subungual exostosis is performed to smooth down the spur with a tiny rasp. The rasp resembles a dental burr and is inserted through a small incision.

Ingrown Toenails

A nail is ingrown when one or both corners or sides of the nail grow into the skin of the toe. Irritation, redness, an uncomfortable sensation of warmth, swelling, pain, and infection can result.

Surgical Procedures

Removal of a nail margin can be done with or without the excision of the root or matrix. To allow surgical benefits for the total excision of the nail and matrix, it must be indicated that the root and matrix are being permanently removed. Excision of subungual exostosis is sometimes used to describe the removal of one or two margins. This is not a separate procedure.

On a partial ingrown toenail, only one or two sides grow into the skin. The treatment is a partial matrixectomy in which a wedge of the nail and the underlying nail bed are removed. The nail portion can be surgically removed with a scalpel or by chemical means. This is a simple, brief procedure.

In severe cases of ingrown toenail, the whole nail grows into the skin on all sides. This is called a completely ingrown toenail. Usually, significant pain is present. Treatment is a total matrixectomy in which the nail and growth plate are removed either surgically or chemically (see Figure 18-5). The body then produces a "false nail," that is, tough skin that mimics a real nail. This false nail usually grows in within a few months after the surgery.

Warts

Warts are caused by a virus and are contagious. They often grow in groups and spread to the fingers and other areas of the body. Warts occurring on the soles of the feet are called plantar warts, which are painful and may affect walking. Usually, these warts grow on the soles, but may occur on the toes or on the top of the foot. Treatment entails scooping out the wart with a curette, a spoon-shaped surgical instrument. The base is then cauterized (burned either electrically or chemically) to discourage regrowth.

Neuromas

A neuroma is a tumor arising from the connective tissue of nerves. Although there are four interspaces, neuromas most often occur in the second interspace. Neuromas are commonly bilateral, but rarely does more than one occur on the same foot or in the first interspace.

If any other surgical procedure is done on the first toe or on the M-P joint of the second, third, fourth, or fifth toes, no additional allowance is available for removal of neuromas from the adjacent interspace. This procedure should not call for any increased allowance for microsurgery.

When a nerve is pinched between two metatarsal bones (usually the third and fourth metatarsal), enlargement of the nerve may occur. Abnormal bone

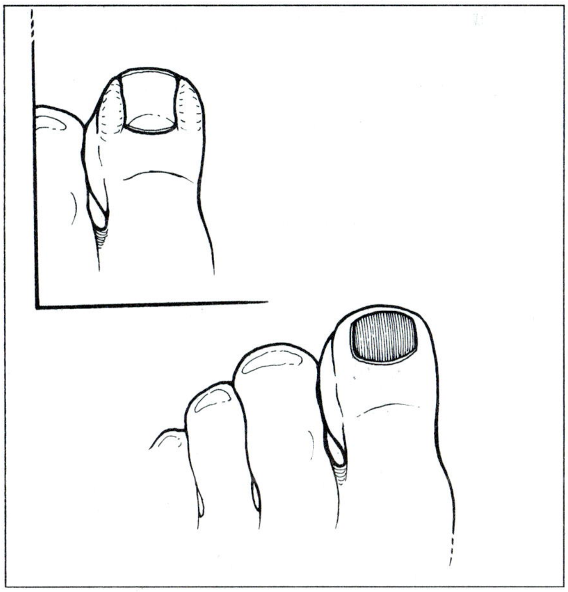

Figure 18-5: **Treatment of ingrown toenail.**

structure contributes to the cause, but too-tight shoes can aggravate the condition. The treatment is to remove a small portion of the nerve. As a result, this area is permanently numbed.

Ganglions

Ganglions are fluid-filled sacs that may grow on a joint capsule or tendon (see Figure 18-6). The location and size vary. The cause is unknown. Ganglions cause irritation, swelling, and pain when they press against nerves.

Treatment involves excision of the ganglion by separating it from the surrounding tissues. If not removed completely, a ganglion may grow back.

Miscellaneous

High-arched feet (pes cavus) are caused by an imbalance of muscles and nerves and is often inherited. High arches can cause various problems such as foot, heel, ankle, or tendon pain and calluses. Treatment depends on the specific problems. Usually, surgery or an orthosis is prescribed.

Flat feet (pes planus) are also hereditary and are caused by a muscle imbalance. Feet with low, relaxed arches may create problems such as hammertoes and bunions; arch, foot, and leg fatigue; calf pain; and an overly tight heel cord (which makes the foot even flatter). Loose joints move too freely causing pain and instability. Surgery and orthoses may also be used to treat this condition. Orthotic devices are prescribed–custom-made arch supports that fit inside most shoes and "bring the floor up to your feet." To make this support, a plaster impression of the feet is made. The orthotic device is made of leather, plastic, or other material, depending on the particular foot problem based on the impression.

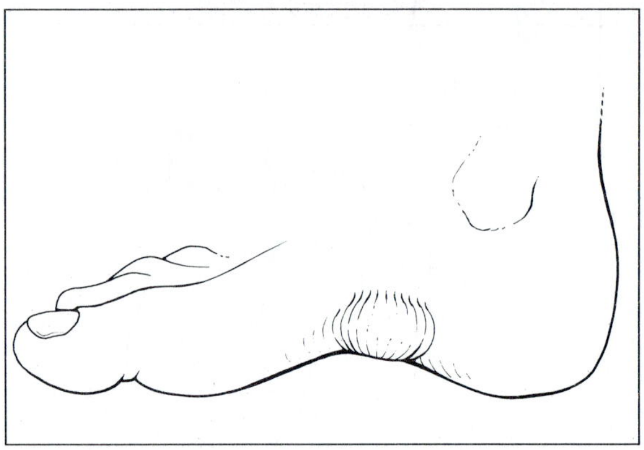

Figure 18-6: Ganglion.

Assistant Surgeon

Because of the complexity of the bones, joints, and tendons in the foot, many podiatric surgeries that are performed on an inpatient basis require an assistant surgeon. However, some surgeries performed in a doctor's office may also require an assistant surgeon.

It is generally accepted medical practice to allow an assistant surgeon when doing soft tissue work. The exception to this is for ingrown toenails. Multiple or bilateral procedures may also require an assistant surgeon.

Single-toe procedures for excision of bone and simple hammertoe procedures usually do not warrant the use of an assistant surgeon.

When allowed, the assistant surgeon's benefits are paid according to the standard policy provisions for assistant surgeons.

Referrals

Because of the difficulty in determining allowable expense and the correct surgical allowance, questionable claim situations should be referred to a supervisor, review department or consultant.

Following are some guidelines or situations that may warrant a consultant's review:

- Charges for insertion or removal of K wire.
- Microsurgical repair of nerves.
- Serial surgery. (Serial surgery is surgery on several individual toes or joints with one surgical procedure being performed in a single operative visit, eg, surgery on one toe followed by the surgery on another toe 1 week later, followed by still other

surgeries after that. Or, it is surgery on one joint, followed by surgery on a different joint of the same toe at a later date.) It can last days, weeks, or even months.

- Fragmented fees billed at 100% for each procedure. This situation may also include misrepresented procedure codes.
- Vascular studies (eg, temperature gradient studies, Doppler studies, or plethysmography). These tests can be considered medically necessary in certain situations or for certain conditions (eg, diabetes, peripheral vascular disease). Test results and the patient's history are needed for review.
- Possible unnecessary services or procedures. These can include:
  - Use of nitrous oxide anesthesia.
  - Operating room charge for office surgery.
  - Preoperative sedatives.
  - Use of power equipment steroid injections or arthrocentesis on the day of the surgery.
  - Rental of TENS unit.
  - More than two postoperative x-rays. The exception is in the case of major bone surgery and delayed bunion surgery.

When referring a claim for review, the claims examiner should request all necessary documentation before referring the claim. Necessary documentation includes the operative report and the patient diagnosis and history as well as the claim. In addition, diagnostic tests, before and after photos, x-rays, and the physician's daily office notes may also be necessary for review on some claims.

If a claim is sent for referral, the claims examiner should first make a determination and payment on any and all services that are not being questioned. Written notification should accompany the payment regarding which services are being held pending a consultant's review.

When the consultant's review is received, some services may be allowed and others denied. The claims examiner should verify the plan guidelines and benefits, and make a payment determination on the claim.

The consultant's report and the name, address, and phone number of the consultant are the property of the company and should never be shown to the claimant. This information should be retained as part of the claim file.

Summary

The charges for podiatry services vary from simple to complex. These guidelines will assist you the examiner in identifying podiatry services. They will also enable you to determine which podiatry services are covered and which services have limitations.

Because podiatry surgery guidelines vary from company to company, check with the administrator before processing these types of claims.

Assignments

Complete the Questions for Review.

Questions for Review

Directions: Answer the following questions without looking back into the material just covered. Write your answers in the space provided.

1. What is podiatric surgery?____

2. Define ligaments. ____

3. How many complex joints are in the foot? ________________________________

4. How many bunion surgeries are allowed per foot? ____________________________

5. What is an orthotic device?____

If you were unable to answer any of the questions, refer back to the section and then complete the answers.

19

Ambulance Expenses

In this chapter you will learn:

- To identify ambulance services billings and determine benefits payable.
- To process ambulance claims.

Ambulance expenses are charges billed for transporting an injured or ill person to a medical facility. Ambulance services are not considered professional or hospital services.

When ambulance services occur and charges are received, investigate to determine whether the charges are eligible for coverage under the insured plan. Under most plans, charges must be from a professional ambulance service; private automobiles, taxicabs, or similar vehicles are not covered.

Guidelines for Coverage

Below are some guidelines for ambulance coverage:

- Charges for ambulance services are covered only when either emergency or inpatient hospital charges are also made. An exception would be in the case of an insured who is dead on arrival at the hospital.
- The ambulance must be medically necessary and not only for patient convenience.

Benefits are payable when transfer to another hospital is medically necessary. For example, if one hospital does not have the facilities to treat the patient's medical condition, the patient will be transferred to the closest hospital with appropriate facilities.

An ambulance expense is covered under Major Medical, basic ambulance, and basic hospital under the following conditions:

- Transportation is medically necessary.
- Transportation is provided by a professional ambulance/paramedic service.
- Transportation is to the nearest facility capable of treating the patient.
- Transportation is provided from one facility to another when the necessary treatment cannot be obtained from the first hospital.
- Transportation home from a facility is provided if the patient is unable to travel in an upright position. Exceptions such as this are plan-dependent, so refer to the plan provisions before processing.
- Transportation to a facility if the claimant is dead on arrival, even though no treatment or charges are incurred at the facility.

Basic benefits usually designate a maximum allowable/payable amount for:

- Each trip to and from a facility.
- All trips made during a period of disability.
- All expenses incurred during a calendar year.

The plan provisions indicate which limitations apply. Major Medical plans usually designate a maximum allowable/payable amount for each trip based on usual and customary guidelines. Expenses commonly billed by an ambulance service include:

- Base call charge. This is the amount automatically charged for the ambulance to respond to a call even if the patient is not subsequently transported.
- Oxygen and oxygen supplies.
- Mileage.
- Linens.
- Emergency response charge. This is an extra expense, in addition to the base charge, which may be added if the patient's condition is severe enough that resuscitation efforts or other types of stabilization measures are required.
- Paramedic response charge. If paramedics rather than emergency medical technicians (EMTs) are used, an extra expense may be added on.

Air Ambulance

Air medical transport may be covered (1) if the facility in the area where the patient is injured cannot manage the patient's condition and it is medically necessary to transfer by air to a tertiary facility more equipped to treat the patient or (2) if ground transport time would be prolonged and thus compromise the patient's medical status. Coverage will be limited to the regular air ambulance charge for transportation to the nearest facility in the area that can handle the case.

Under a Basic plan, all trip or per disability limitations apply. A few Basic plans may have a special allowance designated to cover air medical transport. However, many plans do not cover this type of service, regardless of the reason required. The cost of air ambulance ranges upward from a base charge of about $800 and is usually based on an hourly rate.

When a person is taken ill while traveling, he or she may want to be transferred to a hospital near home or to be treated by a specific specialist in another city, even though the city where he or she is currently located has qualified specialists in the same field. In these instances, ambulance expenses are not covered, regardless of whether an air ambulance or a conventional ambulance is used. This is because the transportation is not considered "medically necessary."

Charges for commercial or private airplane transportation, regardless of the reason required, are usually not covered.

Paramedics

Paramedics are specially trained emergency medical personnel who render emergency treatment at the scene of the injury or illness. They are trained in advanced life support, whereas EMTs are trained in basic life support. There are significant differences in educational requirements and certification of a paramedic compared with those of an EMT. Consequently, when a paramedic is required, an additional fee is usually charged.

Paramedic fees may be covered under an ambulance benefit or may be strictly allowable under Major Medical. The plan provisions should stipulate the handling of this expense.

Mobile Intensive Care Unit

A mobile intensive care unit is a life support vehicle equipped to provide care to critically ill patients who require transportation to a hospital or from one hospital to another. It is designed to serve as an extension of an intensive care unit of a hospital.

The staffing of this unit usually involves a registered nurse and several other allied health professionals. The fees are in the same range as that of an air ambulance. Such charges may be covered if they are determined to be medically necessary in lieu of regular ambulance service.

Van Transportation Unit

Many companies provide nonemergency transportation of the disabled to doctors' offices or hospital facilities. Van transportation units are specially equipped to handle wheelchairs and patients who are unable to get in or out of a regular vehicle. As a rule, it is required that the patient be able to sit in an upright position. The driver may have very basic medical training, such as cardiopulmonary resuscitation (CPR), but is generally not able or equipped to handle acute patients. This type of transportation is not covered by most plans because it is not considered medically necessary.

Summary

Ambulance expenses are expenses that are incurred to transfer an injured or sick person to a medical facility. These expenses are not considered professional or hospital services. Learning to identify and process claims for these services takes skill and practice and will be learned with time and practice.

Assignments

Complete the Questions for Review.

Questions for Review

Directions: Answer the following questions without looking back into the material just covered. Write your answers in the space provided.

pd under

1. Name the three different types of benefits that may cover ambulance expenses.
   a. Basic ambulance
   b. " hospital
   c. Major Medical
2. The base call charge is amount automatically charged for the ambulance to respond to a call even if the patient isn't transported
3. If a person is injured while on vacation, most plans will pay to have the patient transported to the nearest facility to his or her home, even if there is no other reason for the transfer. (True or False) ______
4. In an emergency, taxicab fees would be covered since the transportation was medically necessary. (True or False) ______
5. Name the two circumstances in which air ambulance charges may be covered under a plan.
   a. facility in the area where the patient is injured isn't able to care for patient, + is medically necessary
   b. ground transportation would be prolonged + thus compromise the patients medical status

If you were unable to answer any of the questions, refer back to the section and then complete the answers.

20

Durable Medical Equipment

In this chapter you will learn:

- To define and explain what qualifies as durable medical equipment.
- To identify DME services billings and to determine benefits payable.
- The common criteria for equipment covered under the DME provision.

Durable medical equipment (DME) is an item that can be used for an extended period of time without significant deterioration; that is, it can stand repeated use. Therefore, an item that can be rented and returned for re-use would meet the requirement of durability. Medical supplies of a disposable nature, such as incontinent pads and surgical stockings, would not qualify as durable. (However, these items may be covered under the plan as medical supplies.)

Medically oriented equipment is primarily and customarily used for medical purposes; that is, it is designed to fulfill a medical need. Therefore, it is generally not useful in the absence of an illness or injury. For example, an air conditioner may be used in the case of a heart patient to lower room temperature and reduce fluid loss. However, since the primary and customary use is nonmedical in nature, an air conditioner cannot be considered medical equipment. If the item could be used in a regular manner in the absence of a diagnosis, it is probably nonmedical in nature.

DME Billing Procedures

Most plans allow for the purchase or temporary rental of equipment and supplies when prescribed by a physician. However, certain requirements must be satisfied before authorizing payment.

Basically, three tests must be applied to items billed as DME in determining whether or not the items may be covered under a plan:

1. Does the item satisfy the definition of DME?
2. Is the item reasonable and necessary for the treatment of an illness or injury or for improvement of the functioning of a malformed body member?
3. Is the item prescribed for use in the patient's home?

Only when all three conditions are met will the item be covered by the plan.

Reasonable and Necessary

An item may meet the definition of DME and yet not be covered by the plan. Two things to be considered are:

1. Reasonableness. This evaluates the soundness and practicality of the DME approach to therapy, including such factors as:
   a. Is the need for the unit based on failures of other less costly approaches?
   b. Have more conservative means been attempted?
   c. What benefits will be derived from the unit?
   d. Do the benefits justify the expense?
2. Necessity. Equipment is necessary when it is expected to make a meaningful contribution to the treatment of the patient's illness or injury or to the improvement of the functioning of a malformed body part. Physicians tend to prescribe equipment based on a variety of reasons including:
   a. Familiarity. The physician is familiar with a particular piece of equipment. Other less expensive, more effective means of treatment or equipment may be available.
   b. Current popularity. As with clothes fashions, treatment and equipment popularity runs in cycles. Patients may even request the use of some pieces of equipment because it is hyped by the news media or some other medium. The particular equipment may not be the best or least expensive treatment available.
   c. Monetarily beneficial. Some equipment suppliers provide monetary inducements to physicians who use their equipment. Therefore, some physicians may routinely prescribe certain equipment based on this factor.

Even with a physician's prescription, it may be necessary to refer the claim to a consultant for review prior to payment or approval for purchase.

Patient's Home

For DME to be purchased or temporarily rented, the equipment must be prescribed for use in the home. Therefore, any facility that meets at least the minimum requirements of the definition of a hospital or skilled nursing facility is usually excluded from consideration.

A patient's home can be considered, but not limited to:

- His or her own home/apartment/dwelling.
- A relative's home.
- A home for the elderly.
- A nursing home.

Oxygen

Many plans cover the use of oxygen under DME. Even though the oxygen itself is not durable, the canister in which the oxygen is contained and transported is durable, and it therefore falls under the category of DME.

Remember that these are general guidelines only. The specific requirements may vary from payor to payor.

Billing Requirements

All claims for DME should be documented with the following information:

- A description of the equipment prescribed by the physician. If the item is a commonly used item, a detailed description may not be necessary. However, with new equipment, it is important to try to obtain a marketing or manufacturer's brochure, which indicates how the item is constructed and how it functions.
- A statement of the medical necessity of the equipment. This should be in the form of a prescription showing the imprinted name, address, and telephone number of the prescribing physician. The related diagnosis should also be indicated.
- An indication as to whether the item is to be rented or purchased and the rental or purchase price.
- The estimated length of time that the equipment will be needed. This information will aid in the analysis of whether a rental or a purchase is more economical.
- An indication as to where the equipment will be used and for how long.

Rental versus Purchase Determinations

The following four steps will assist in determining the most cost-efficient means of reimbursement.

1. Determine the period of time in months in which the item will be medically required from the information provided by the attending physician.
2. Multiply the number of months by the monthly rental fee. (This must be obtained from the supplier. Do not include the costs of perishable supplies, batteries, electrodes, and so on).

Estimated length of use in months
x monthly rental fee
= total estimated equipment rental fee

- Request the supplier's purchase price for the equipment. Compare the purchase price to the calculated total estimated rental fee obtained in step #2.
- If the total estimated rental fee is less than or equal to the purchase price, allow for the rental. If the rental fee is greater than the purchase price, rental is allowed up to but not exceeding the purchase price. Purchase of the item is not required. However, both the member and the supplier need to be notified that an expense that is higher than the purchase price will not be allowed under the plan.

Repairs, Replacement, and Delivery

Repairs are covered when necessary to make the equipment functional. If the expense for repairs exceeds the estimated cost of purchasing or renting new equipment for the remaining period of medical need, payment is limited to the lower amount. Verify manufacturer's warranties before payment of repair fees.

Replacements are usually covered in cases of irreparable damage or wear or when the patient's physical condition has changed. Replacement due to wear or changes in the patient's physical condition must be supported by a current physician's order. Replacements due to loss may or may not be covered, depending on the circumstances. Usually, replacement is not covered when disrepair results from a patient's carelessness. Other reasons for repair or replacement may be covered based on the plan provisions.

Charges for delivery of the DME and oxygen are usually covered.

Prosthetic Devices

Prosthetic devices are designed to replace a missing body member or to restore some function to a paralyzed body member.

Prosthetic devices include the making and application of an artificial part medically necessary to replace a lost or impaired body part or function, such as an artificial arm or leg, obturator, urinary collection and retention systems, or other loss.

Covered expenses associated with prosthetics include:

- Shipping and handling as part of the purchase price.
- Temporary postoperative prostheses.
- Replacement charges when replacement is due to a change in the patient's physical condition. (Children often need replacement prostheses every 6 to 12 months depending on their growth rate and other factors.) Replacement is not covered for wear and tear.

Medical/Surgical Supplies

Perishable medical/surgical supplies may be covered under the plan if the items can be used only by the patient and are medically necessary in the treatment of the illness or injury. Medical and surgical supplies include:

- Disposable, nondurable supplies and accessories required to operate medical equipment or prosthetic devices.
- Necessary drugs and biological items put directly into equipment (such as nonprescription nutrients).
- Initial and replacement accessories essential for operating medical equipment.
- Supplies furnished and charged by a hospital, surgical center, or physician as part of active therapy, such as ace bandage, cast, cervical collar.

Do not include items or supplies that could be used by the patient or a member of the patient's family for purposes other than medical care.

Questionable items should be referred to your supervisor or other designated person with the following information:

- Patient's diagnosis.
- Prescription from attending physician.
- Product description, literature, and prices.

See Appendix 20-1 for a list of DME and coverage guidelines. This list is provided as a guide only. Actual administration may vary from company to company.

Summary

Durable medical equipment includes medical-surgical equipment that can stand repeated use, is not useful in the absence of illness or injury, and is prescribed by a physician. In addition, the item must be necessary and reasonable for treatment of the illness or injury or to replace an injured or lost bodily function and must be appropriate for home use.

In addition to the cost of the item, charges are also covered for shipping, handling, and postage of the item, which is considered a part of the purchase price. Necessary repairs to purchased equipment (if the equipment is not covered under warranty) are also covered. However the cost of repairs is not covered for rented equipment. Broken rental equipment should be returned to the supplier for repair or replacement.

Charges are not usually covered for modification of the structure of the patient's home (including wiring, plumbing, or structural modifications), the installation of the equipment, or modifications to transportation vehicles.

Assignments

Complete the Questions for Review.

Complete billing the remaining Miscellaneous claims in the Student Exercise Manual and process Miscellaneous Claims 12-1 to 12-15 using the guidelines covered.

Questions for Review

Directions: Answer the following questions without looking back into the material just covered. Write your answers in the space provided.

1. What three tests must be applied in determining whether items billed as DME may be covered under a plan?

   a. ______________________________

   b. ______________________________

   c. ______________________________

2. All DME claims should be documented with the following information:

   a. ______________________________

   b. ______________________________

   c. ______________________________

   d. ______________________________

   e. ______________________________

3. Repairs are covered when necessary to make the equipment ______________________________.

4. Replacements are usually covered in cases of irreparable damage or because of ______________________________.

5. ____________________ are designed to replace a missing body member or to restore some function to a paralyzed body member.

If you were unable to answer any of the questions, refer back to the section and then complete the answers.

Appendix 20-1

Durable Medical Equipment and Coverage Guidelines

The following is a list of commonly billed DME items and coverage guidelines. This list is intended to be used for training and reference purposes only, since the particular company or plan guidelines may differ from the guidelines stated.

Item	Description	Coverage Guidelines
Action bath hydro massage	See Whirlpool.	Rx required. Refer for medical review.
Adjust-a-Bed	Lounger	Not covered. Comfort item.
Aero-massage	See Whirlpool.	See Whirlpool.
Aero-pulse surgical leggings	Nonreusable support leggings	Rx required following surgery.
Air conditioner	Recirculates and cools in home	Not covered. Environmental control equipment.
Air-fluidized bed	Institutional equipment	Not covered. Not for home use.
Air purifier	Electronically cleans house environment	Not covered. Environmental control equipment.
Allergy-free items	Not primarily medical	Not covered. Preventive in nature, nondurable.
Alternating pressure pad	Prevents pressure sores in bed- or wheelchair-confined person.	Rx required when ordered for treatment of decubitus ulcers or when person is susceptible to ulcers.
Ankle weights	As exercise equipment For postoperative care	Not a covered medical expense. Covered only when prescribed in a postop situation to return function (eg, knee surgery).
Apnea monitor	Monitors apnea (cessation of breathing) episodes in infants.	Medical documentation of condition necessary. Rx required.
Aqua-matic K-pad	Heating pad	Not covered. Comfort item, nondurable medical equipment.
Aqua-matic K-thermia	Warm water system	Used only in institutions or acute care facility. Not covered.

Item	Description	Coverage Guidelines
Aqua massage pump	Same as Whirlpool	See Whirlpool.
Aqua-whirl	Same as Whirlpool	See Whirlpool.
Arch supports	Removable in-shoe support. See Orthotics.	Not covered. Nondurable medical equipment.
Arterio Sonde	Automatic blood pressure monitor	Covered as home blood pressure monitoring device.
Artificial kidney	Home hemodialysis unit	Covered for chronic renal disease; ancillary supplies essential to medical use may also be covered. Refer to medical review.
Astromatic bed Astropedic bed Comfort-a-bed	Comfort bed. Not medical equipment.	Not covered. Comfort item.
Autolift (bathtub)	Bathtub lift	Possible convenience item. Rx required, patient's weight and statement of medical necessity; refer for medical review.
Backtrak (Cotrell)	Home back traction unit	Not covered.
Barbells	As exercise equipment. For postop rehabilitation	Not a covered medical expense. Covered only if prescribed in a postop situation to return function.
Bathtub rail and seat	Attached to bathtub for patient assistance	Rx required or statement of medical necessity. Covered for paraplegics, quads, or stroke patients.
Beautyrest adjustable bed	Not a hospital bed, not primarily medical	Not covered. Convenience item. See Hospital bed (standard).
Bed bath	Hygienic equipment	Convenience item. Not treating disease or injury.
Bedboard	Provides firm support under mattress	Not covered. Not treatment of disease or injury.

Item	Description	Coverage Guidelines
Bed lift	Sling, either manual or electronic; lifts person to and from bed	See Bathtub rail and seat. Rx required, patient's weight and statement of medical necessity.
Bed lounge (power or manual)	Not a hospital bed	Convenience item (power or manual). Not covered. See Hospital beds (standard).
Bed mattress	Standard mattress for adjustable hospital bed	Covered when hospital bed is allowed.
Bedpan	Hospital type	Covered for bed-confined or immobilized patients.
Bed siderail	Attached to hospital bed, protective device, often standard bed equipment	Covered if person is bed-confined, or if condition of vertigo, seizure, or neurologic disorder is present; also covered for small children.
Bed (oscillating type)	Swings back and forth	Not covered for home use. Institutional equipment.
Bell & Howell Master	Speech teaching machine, training aid	Not covered.
Bendix-type oxygen concentrator	Concentrates room air oxygen to a therapeutic level	Rx required. Covered for person with severe breathing impairment.
Bennett IPPB machine	Intermittent positive-pressure breathing	Rx required. Covered for person with severe breathing impairment.
Bicycle (standard)		Not covered.
Bicycle (stationary)	For cardiac medical exercise program only	Refer for medical review.
Bidet	Hygienic toilet item	Not primarily treatment of disease or medical condition. Not covered.
Bimler appliance	Orthodontic dental appliance, corrects tongue thrust	Not covered.
Bi-osteogenic electromagnetic treatment system	Electrical currents used to treat nonunion fracture	Covered to treat fractures. Medical documentation required.

Item	Description	Coverage Guidelines
Bird respirator	IPPB Machine for respiratory therapy	Rx required. Covered for person with severe breathing problem.
Blood pressure cuff	Measures blood pressure; necessary for home management	Covered with documented diagnosis of hypertension; also used with home hemodialysis units.
Body braces (back, foot, leg, arm)	Supportive devices	Rx required. Covered if durable and necessary.
Bra (Jobst Surgical)	Support item following surgery	Initial bra only following postsurgical reconstruction and mastectomy.
Braille teaching aid	Training and vocational equipment	Not covered.
Breast pump	Assists mother in breastfeeding; may be either manual or electric.	Not covered. Elective device for patient comfort.
Canes	Straight, quad, ambulatory aids	Covered for ambulatory impairments.
Cardiac phone monitor	Telephone-relayed EKG reporting devices	Charges covered within physician's office fee.
Cast guards	A waterproof (usually plastic) coverlet for casts	Covered for all covered casting procedures.
Cast shoes (fracture boot)	A wood or rubber-based shoe with canvas sides to support casts in ambulation	Covered with documentation by diagnosis.
Catheter	Medical supply item, not reusable	For bed-confined or similarly disabled persons; for urinaray retention problems.
Centrifuge Readocrit	Blood testing equipment	Rx required. Covered for person on home dialysis.
Cervical collar	Neck support item	Covered for appropriate diagnosis, such as cervical sprain.
Cervical pillow	Neck support item	Covered for appropriate diagnosis, such as cervical sprain.
Colostomy supplies (bags and accessories)	Used after ostomy procedures	Covered for colostomy patients, postrectal surgery.

Item	Description	Coverage Guidelines
Commode	Bedside toilet chair	Covered for bed- or wheelchair-confined person.
Computerized equipment for mobility and speech	For paraplegics	Not covered.
Contact lens (bandage)	Protects cornea following surgery or injury	Rx required.
Contact lens (orthokeratology)	Myopia or refractive	Refer for medical review.
Corset	Supportive item	Covered with appropriate diagnosis such as thoracic sprain.
Crutches	Ambulatory aids	Covered for ambulatory impairments.
Cushion-lift power seat	Assist person in/out of seat	Covered for person with hip, knee arthritis, or other neuromuscular conditions.
Dehumidifier	Room or central system type	Not covered. Environmental control equipment.
Deluxe padding	Comfort item, special order for wheelchairs, other seating	Not covered.
Denis Browne splint or bar	Metal support to maintain and correct adduction	Covered for child with clubfoot or metatarsus deformity, (includes 1 pair of shoes).
Dextrometer/glucometer/ diabetic supplies	Measures blood sugar levels	Rx required. For diabetic treatment.
Diabetic supplies	Supportive items	For medical management only.
Dialysis equipment	Artificial kidney	Covered for chronic renal disease. See hemodialysis.
Diapulse machine	Diathermy machine	Not covered for home use.
Diathermy equipment	Heat treatment	Not covered for home use.
Disposable sheets and bags	Supplies	Not covered. Nondurable medical equipment.

Item	Description	Coverage Guidelines
Ear molds	Prevents water from entering inner ear canal	Refer for medical review.
Eas-o-matic Bed Spring	Comfort item, not adaptable to hospital bed	Not covered. See Hospital bed (standard).
Eaton E-Z Bath	Bathtub seat	See Bathtub rail and seat.
Egg-crate pad (mattress)	Portable pad for preventing bedsores	Rx required. For treatment of decubitus ulcers.
Elastic stocking (Jobst type)	Supportive, medical item following surgery	Rx required. Covered postsurgical expense or for diagnosis of circulatory problems.
Electra-Rest Bed	Not a hospital bed	Not covered.
Electrocardiocorder	Diagnostic equipment	Covered only as part of physician diagnostic charge.
Electrostatic air purifier machines	Air cleanser, environment control apparatus	Not covered. Environmental control equipment.
Elevators	Convenience item	Not covered.
Emesis basin	Basin for vomitus, fluids	Covered expense for home bed-confined patients.
Enema supplies	For stimulating lower colon activity	Rx required.
Enuresis equipment	Monitors and training devices for involuntary urination	Not covered.
Enurtone	Training device for enuresis	Not covered.
Ergometer	Tension measuring device for stationary bicycle	See Bicycle (stationary).
Esophageal dilator	To open esophagus	Used only by physician. Not covered for home use.
Exercise equipment	Not primarily medical	Not covered.

Item	Description	Coverage Guidelines
Exercise pad	Flat soft surface	Not covered.
Exercycle	Stationary bicycle	Rx required. For cardiac patients in active program. See Bicycle (stationary).
Face mask (oxygen)	Necessary for oxygen therapy	Covered when oxygen therapy is required.
Face mask (surgical)	For contagious diseases, isolation care	Rx required.
Flowmeter (oxygen)	Oxygen regulator	Covered when oxygen therapy is required.
Fluidic breathing assistor	Positive-pressure machine	Covered when IPPB care is necessary.
Foundation garment	Padding, bras, etc	Not covered. Check under specific items such as Corsets.
Freika pillow splint	Maintains adduction	Covered for small child with hip disorder.
Gatchboard	Bedboard	Not covered.
Gel flotation pad and mattress	Treats and prevents pressure sores	Covered for treatment of decubitus ulcers.
Glideabout chair	Chair with small wheels	Rx required. Covered in lieu of wheelchair.
Glucometers	Measures blood sugar levels	Rx required. For medical management of covered conditions.
Gravitronics gravity device (boots and traction)	Antigravity treatment for back condition	Not generally accepted medical practice.
Hand-D-Jet	Portable whirlpool machine	See Whirlpool.
Hand-E-Vent	Similar to IPPB machine; manual respiratory therapy	Rx required. Covered for severe respiratory impairment.
Hearing aid	To assist hearing	No coverage when specifically excluded by policy.

Item	Description	Coverage Guidelines
Heating lamp	External thermal applicator	Not covered outside hospital setting.
Heating pad	Applies external heat	Not covered. Nondurable medical equipment.
Hemodialysis equipment	Artificial kidney device for blood filtering	Rx required. For chronic renal disease.
Holter monitor	24-hour cardiac measurement	Used only in physician's office. Charges payable within office fee as billed by physician.
Hospital bed (electric)	Power multipurpose bed	Rx required. May be necessary when person is required to self-change bed position. Refer for medical review.
Hospital bed (standard)	Multilevel positioning bed	Rx required. For bed-confined person who requires frequent position changes.
Hot tub	Thermal bath home spa systems	Not covered.
Hoyer lift (hydraulic)	Hydraulic patient lift	Rx required. Generally a convenience for lifting person from bed to wheelchair, etc. Patient's weight and statement of medical condition necessary. Refer for medical review.
Humidifier (component of oxygen equipment)	Adds moisture to oxygen	Covered when oxygen therapy unit is covered.
Humidifier (room or central)	Environment control	Not covered. Environmental control equipment.
Hydrocollator heating unit	Applies local external heat	Rx required. Expense should be incurred through physician's office.
Hydro-jet whirlpool bath	Comfort whirlpool	See Whirlpool.
Hypodermic needles and supplies, hypospray	Administration of intramuscular, intradermal injections	Rx required. For medical management of covered condition.
Incontinence pads	Nondurable, disposable supply	Covered only for postsurgical urinary conditions for 1 month.

Item	Description	Coverage Guidelines
Infusion pump	Stimulates constant infusions of medication subcutaneously or intra-arterially	Rx required. Refer to medical review.
Insulin pump	Artificial pancreas function surgically implanted	Procedure still investigational. Submit records for medical review.
Inhalator	Respiratory assistance	Rx required.
IPPB machines	For respiratory therapy	Rx required.
Iron lung	External respirator	Covered for respiratory paralysis.
Irrigation kit	For hygienic use	Covered for respiratory paralysis, wound drainage, etc. 60 days rental.
Jacuzzi portable pump	For use in bathtubs	Rx required. Refer for whirlpool medical review.
Jobst Hydro Float	Special flotation cushion	Covered for prevention or treatment of decubitus ulcers.
Jobst pneumatic appliance and compressor (pump)	Pneumatic full-limb appliance that maintains surface pressure	Rx required. Covered for intractable edema, postradical mastectomy, etc. Refer for medical review.
Jobst Fabric Support (hose, sleeves, stockings)	Nonreusable items, antiembolism hose	Rx required. For circulatory conditions, pre- and postop situations.
Lambs wool pad	Soft padding, deluxe item, nondurable	Covered for bed sores, etc.
Laser equipment (any kind)	High-intensity light source	Covered service only in physician's office.
Lattoflex spring base	Not a hospital-type bed	Not covered. Comfort item.
Lenox Hill knee brace	Supportive orthopedic device	Rx required. Charges based on individual custom-ordered appliance.
Leotards	Tight body apparel	Not covered.
Life-O-Gen tank	Portable oxygen	Rx required. Covered for persons with respiratory impairment.

Item	Description	Coverage Guidelines
Limb-O-Cycle	Exercise equipment	Not covered.
Linde Oxygen Walker	Portable oxygen system	Rx required. Covered for persons with respiratory impairment.
Lumex chair table	Like a rollabout chair	Covered in lieu of regular wheelchair.
Lymphedema pump	Appliance that maintains surface pressure	Rx required. Covered for intractable edema of extremity.
Mask devices	To mask out ringing in ears	Refer for medical review.
Mask (oxygen)	Used to deliver oxygen	Covered for persons who require oxygen.
Massage devices	Comfort item	Not covered.
Massage pillow	Comfort item	Not covered.
Mattress (medical)	For use with hospital bed	Covered when hospital bed is allowed.
Maxi-Mist Machine	Delivers medicines as mist to be inhaled	Rx required.
Medasphere portable oxygen unit	Portable oxygen system	Covered when oxygen is necessary with exercise or walking.
Medcolator	Physical therapy equipment	Not covered.
Medi-Cool refrigerator	For cooling medication	Not covered.
Medi-Jector (injection gun)	Delivers insulin without use of needles. Convenience item	Not covered.
Micronaire environmental control	Equipment to control environment; air purifier	Not covered. Environmental control equipment.
Milwaukee back brace	Supportive orthopedic brace	Rx required.
Mobile geriatric chair	Wheelchair with smaller than normal wheels	Covered in lieu of regular wheelchair.
Nebulizer	Delivers medicine in mist form for inhalation	Covered for respiratory impairment.

Item	Description	Coverage Guidelines
Neck halter	Supportive device	Rx not required.
Nolan bath chair	For assistance in bathtub	Rx required. Possible convenience item. Statement of medical necessity. See Bathtub rail and seat.
Nonvocal communication system	Daily living assistance system, electronic	Not covered.
Obturator	Oral prosthesis	Rx required. Cleft palate prosthesis.
Orthopedic shoes	Custom shoes	Not covered.
Orthosis (cash)	Adjustable back brace	Rx required.
Orthotics (foot stabilizers)	Acrylic arch supports	Covered only when dispensed by physician and when not excluded for policy provisions.
Osci Lite	Heat lamp	Not covered.
Oscillating bed	Alternating motion bed	Not covered for home use.
Ostomy bags	Used after ostomy procedures	Covered postsurgically.
Ottobock cosmetic stockings	Covers existing prosthesis	Not covered. Nondurable medical equipment.
Overbed tables	For use with hospital bed. Comfort item	Not covered.
Oxygen	Compressed gas or liquid in tank	Rx required.
Oxygen concentrator	Condenses oxygen from room air	Rx required. Covered for persons with severe respiratory impairment.
Oxygen humidifier	Adds moisture to oxygen before inhalation	Rx required. Used in conjunction with oxygen tank system.
Oxygen regulator	Measures oxygen flow	Covered when oxygen unit is allowable.
Oxygen tent	Plastic overbed cover	Rx required.

Item	Description	Coverage Guidelines
Oxygen tank (spare)	Precautionary supply	Not covered.
Pace Trac	Pacemaker monitor	Rx required. Refer for medical review.
Poli-Axial knee cage brace system	Lightweight supportive athletic knee cage and brace; very costly	Not covered. Athletic support device.
Paraffin bath unit (portable and standard)	Wax immersion of affected joints	Covered for home use for arthritis patients.
Parallel bars	Exercise equipment	Not covered.
Penile implant	Inflatable penile prosthesis	Covered for those with diabetes, spinal cord injury, vascular disease, hypertension, postsurgical impotence.
Penile monitor	Electronic measuring device	Covered only in hospital under medical supervision.
Percusser	Striking instrument used to perform percussion	Refer for medical review.
Phonic Mirror Handi-Voice	Electronic device that produces words by pressing buttons	Not covered.
Pogon buggy (stroller type)	Adaptive wheelchair for child	Covered for nonambulatory child who requires more support than standard wheelchair provides.
Pollen extractor	For home environment use air purifier	Not covered. Environmental control equipment.
Portable oxygen system	Transportable	Rx required.
•Regulated (adjustable flow rate)		Rx required.
•Preset (one flow rate)	For general use	Not covered.
Portable room heater	Environmental control	Not covered.
Posture support chairs	Comfort item	Not covered.
Posturpedic mattress	Special mattress	Covered only when hospital bed is allowable.

Item	Description	Coverage Guidelines
Pressure-Eze pad	Alternating pressure pad	Covered for treatment of decubitus ulcer.
Pressure leotard	Form-fitting apparel	Not covered.
Pulmo-Aide	Medicated nebulizer system	Covered for upper respiratory disease.
Pulse tachometer	Electronic pulse reader	Not covered.
Reading lamp	For home use	Not covered.
Rib belt	Supportive elastic item	Rx not required. Covered for appropriate diagnosis such as rib injury.
Sacro-Ease car seat	For auto use	Not covered.
Sanitation equipment	For environmental use	Not covered.
Sauna bath	Comfort item	Not covered.
Scolitron stimulator	For curvature of the back, similar to TENS unit	Refer for medical review.
Seat lift	Seat that raises and lowers person in and out of chair	Rx required. For arthritis or other degenerative type diseases when the person is ambulatory.
Selectron air purifier	Air cleaner for environmental control	Not covered. Environmental control equipment.
Shoe wedging	Sole modification	Rx required.
Shoes	Wearing apparel item	Not covered. See Orthopedic shoes.
Sitz bath	Moist heat application	Not covered for home use.
Sleek seat	Supportive chair for atonic child	Rx required. For children with atonic muscle condition.
Spectrowave machine	Diathermy machine	Not covered for home use.
Speech teaching aids	Education devices	Not covered.

Item	Description	Coverage Guidelines
Sphygmomanometer	Blood pressure equipment	Covered with documented diagnosis of hypertension; also used with home hemodialysis units.
Spircare incentive breathing device	Usually shows pulmonary function	Not covered.
Stairglide	Home elevator system	Not covered.
Stand alone	Device that allows a paraplegic to stand unassisted. Comfort item	Not covered.
Standing table	Special table for use in standing position.	Not covered.
Stethoscope	Blood pressure monitor equipment	Covered only with home blood pressure monitoring program.
Stimulators (TENS)	Electronic pulse	Rx required. Refer for medical review.
Stryker flotation pad and mattress	Gel flotation pad treats and prevents pressure sores	Rx required.
Suction machine	Removes secretions from airway, etc	Rx required. Must have qualified person in home to handle machine.
Sun lamp	Thermal application to skin	Not covered.
Superpulse machine	Diathermy machine	Not covered for home use.
Surgical stockings and leggings	Support apparel, antiembolism hose	Rx required. See Jobst fabric.
Telemedic II	Telephone cardiac monitor	Covered only when done in physician's office.
Telephone arm	Attaches to receiver, comfort item	Not covered.
Thermo-Jet	Whirlpool pump	See Whirlpool.
Thermometer (clinical)	Measures temperature	Not covered.
Thermophore fomentation device	Heat applicator, external heat source moist heating pad	Not covered. Nondurable medical equipment.

Item	Description	Coverage Guidelines
Tilt table	Adjustable exercise table	Not covered.
Toilet seat (raised)		Rx required. Hip replacement surgeries. See Seat lift for other conditions.
Traction device	Weighted device for physical therapy	Rx required.
Trapeze bar	Supportive device used for lifting self in hospital bed	Rx required. For use with a standard hospital bed only.
Treadmill devices	Home walking exercise unit	Rental covered with Rx and appropriate cardiac diagnosis.
Truss	Hernia support	Rx not required. Covered with appropriate diagnosis.
Tub chair	Bathtub use. Comfort item	Not covered.
Twister cable medical review	Pediatric orthopedic	Rx required. Refer for medical device.
Ultrasound machine	Sound waves applied to muscles, tendons, etc.	Covered only in physician's office. Not for home use.
Ultraviolet equipment	Directs ultraviolet light to body areas	Covered for persons with psoriasis when medical necessity is documented and home use approved by physician.
Urinal (autoclaveable hospital type)	Not a comfort item	Rx not required. Covered for bed-confined able person.
Vaporizer	Delivers water mist to limited area in home	Not covered. Does not dispense medication as a nebulizer does.
Vasculating bed	Special hospital bed providing movement	Not covered for home use.
Vision therapy training aids	For adjunctive home use with vision therapy program	Not covered.
Walker	Ambulatory aid	Rx not required.
Water bed	Comfort item	Not covered. See standard adjustable hospital bed.

Item	Description	Coverage Guidelines
Water pressure pad and mattress	Treats and prevents pressure sores (hospital bed type)	Rx required.
Weighted quad boot	Physical fitness equipment	Not covered. See ankle weights.
Wheel-o-Vater	Home elevator	Not covered.
Wheelchair		
• Regular manual standard model		Rx not required if documented by diagnosis.
• Electric type		Rx required. Person must require independent mobility.
• Accessories and repair to function	Rubber wheel linings, ball bearings, batteries, seat pad	Rx required. Covered when appropriate and only when policy provisions do not exclude. Convenience items or modifications not functional in nature such as color coordination, deluxe padding, and trays are not covered expense.
• Travel type		Covered in lieu of regular wheelchair.
Wheelchair insert	For small child, when chair seat does not fit	Rx not required.
Whirlpool pumps	Portable units for home use in baths	Rx required. Refer for medical review.
Wigs and toupees	Cosmetic application for conditions of alopecia (hair loss)	Refer for medical review.

21

Adjustments

In this chapter you will learn:

- The various types of adjustments and how to apply them.

An adjustment is the reprocessing of a claim to correct prior errors. Although the terminology may vary from company to company, the concepts behind each type are basically the same. The four basic types of adjustments are:

1. Statistical adjustment—An adjustment that changes the claim data (eg, procedure coding, type of benefit paid, diagnosis) but does not increase or decrease the original claim payment.
2. Supplemental adjustment—An adjustment that increases the original claim payment. A statistical adjustment may also be involved (often but not always), since the original claim coding may have caused the incorrect payment.
3. Full credit adjustment—An adjustment that completely reverses a claim payment because the original submission should not have been paid at all.
4. Partial credit adjustment—An adjustment that partially reverses a claim payment. The original claim was overpaid.

Statistical Adjustment

A statistical adjustment changes claim data but does not increase or decrease a claim payment. As the name implies, this type of adjustment is required to correct historical data only. The original payment is not affected by the corrected data.

The following are some of the more common reasons for requiring a statistical adjustment:

- The claim was processed under an incorrect member identification (ID) number.
- The claim was processed on an incorrect claimant but on the correct ID number.
- The claim payment was issued to an incorrect provider of service. The provider's tax identification number or social security number was input incorrectly, or a totally wrong provider was paid. If the provider paid was in the same medical group, a statistical adjustment may be sufficient. However, if a completely separate and unaffiliated provider was paid, a full credit adjustment is probably required with a new payment issued to the correct provider.
- The claim was processed under an incorrect group number, but the payment remains the same.
- The claim was erroneously denied; charges should have been applied to the deductible. (No payment will be made even when processed correctly.)
- Charges were applied to the deductible but should have been denied.

Supplemental Adjustment

A supplemental adjustment is performed to increase an original claim payment. Often, a supplemental adjustment is required because the original claim was coded incorrectly. Therefore, a statistical adjustment is usually involved, but the changes are such that a payment or an additional payment will result. The following are some of the more common reasons why a supplemental adjustment may be required:

- The original claim was erroneously denied when benefits should have been paid.
- Charges were applied to the deductible in error; benefits should have been paid. This usually occurs when the deductible applies to specific types of expenses, but not to all types.
- Some benefits were paid, but additional benefits should have been paid.
- Late charges are received.
- Corrected billing or other information is received.
- The claims examiner or adjuster applied incorrect benefits.
- The examiner coded the diagnosis or procedure incorrectly, thus causing an incorrect UCR allowance or other limitation.

Full Credit Adjustment

A full credit adjustment completely reverses the original claim payment. Usually, this type of adjustment is not performed until the original monies paid out have been returned in full to the payor. When an incorrect provider is paid and the money is returned, many companies consider this to be a full credit adjustment with a subsequent payment remitted to the correct provider. Regardless of whether or not a subsequent corrected payment is issued, the original payment is received back in the claims office and is reversed in the system. Following are some reasons why a full credit adjustment may be required:

- A duplicate claim is received and paid in error.
- The member is not eligible for benefits under the plan.
- Claim benefits are applied incorrectly, or plan limitations are not adhered to.
- An incorrect provider is paid who is unaffiliated with the correct provider of service.

Partial Credit Adjustment

A partial credit adjustment partially reverses a claim payment. In this case, part of the original payment is correct and part is incorrect. The common reasons why partial credit adjustments are performed include:

- When a greater payment was made on a claim than what should have been made according to the plan provisions and limitations.
- Because the claims examiner applied benefits incorrectly either through incorrect coding, duplication of payment, inappropriate application of benefits, or some other error.

Collecting Overpayments

Even the best claims examiners may make errors. When this happens, an overpayment of benefits may occur. Under most circumstances, every attempt should be made to recover overpayments when they are discovered. However, there are times when recovery of overpayments are not feasible nor cost-effective. The following are guidelines only and apply to situations in which overpayment recovery should not be attempted:

- The overpayment is under $25.00.
- The overpayment occurred more than 12 months ago and is under $200.00.
- The claimant is deceased and the overpayment is under $200.00.

There are normally three ways to obtain reimbursement of an overpayment.

1. Deduct the overpayment from future benefits of the family member for whom the overpayment occurred. You cannot deduct an overpayment on one family member's claim from benefits due on another family member's claim unless specifically requested by the insured and confirmed in writing. It is not necessary to obtain permission to deduct benefits for the member for whom the overpayment occurred, but advise the claimant of the circumstances of the overpayment and the method that will be used for recoupment.
2. Arrange with the insured for lump sum payment or establish a payment plan to recoup the overpayment.
3. Obtain reimbursement from a third party, usually another carrier where COB is involved.

Remember that benefits cannot be taken from charges that have been assigned to the provider of services.

When a refund is received or offered, accept or pursue all such refunds, regardless of the amount of the overpayment or the time that had elapsed since the overpayment occurred.

Summary

Remember that most adjustments affect the monies that the subscribers, members, or providers receive. This is always a sensitive situation. Therefore, always be sure that an adjustment is necessary and is done correctly so that a third or fourth adjustment is not required.

Follow the procedures established by the payor for handling adjustments, and give the affected parties adequate notification. Failure to follow such procedures significantly increases the likelihood of subsequent ill will, legal action, and so on. If in doubt, request assistance before making an adjustment.

Assignments

Complete the Questions for Review.

Questions for Review

Directions: Answer the following questions without looking back into the material just covered. Write your answers in the space provided.

1. List the four basic types of adjustments.
   a. ______________________________
   ____
   b. ______________________________
   ____
   c. ______________________________
   ____
   d. ______________________________
   ____
2. A ______________________ adjustment changes claim data but does not increase or decrease a claim payment.
3. A ______________________ adjustment is performed to increase an original claim payment.
4. A ______________________ adjustment reverses the original claim payment.
5. A ______________________ adjustment partially reverses a claim payment.

If you were unable to answer any of the questions, refer back to the section and then complete the answers.

22

Dental Terminology

In this chapter you will learn:

- To interpret the meaning of dental terms, including prefixes, suffixes, and root words.

About 75% of all medical terms are derived from Latin and Greek prefixes, suffixes, and roots. A **prefix** is the portion of the word found at the beginning of a term (ie, *endo*—meaning within, -dontics meaning teeth = *endo*dontics meaning within the teeth). Prefixes alter the root word by adding a number (bi- two), a direction, (ab- away from), a location (endo- within), or a description (dis- bad).

A **suffix** is the portion of the word found at the end of a term (ie, gingi- meaning gum, *itis* meaning inflammation = gingiv*itis* meaning inflammation of the gums). Suffixes also alter the root word, usually by indicating a state of being (-itis).

A **root** is usually found in the center of a term and identifies the organ or body part involved.

In dental terminology, and less often in medical terminology, it is possible to combine a prefix and suffix to form a word, even though no root word is involved (as in gingivitis). Table 22-1 presents a list of prefixes and suffixes used in dental terminology. Medical Billers and Health Claims Examiners should become familiar with the prefixes and suffixes to help in accurate billing and processing of dental claims.

Following is a list of common dental terms and procedures. Medical Billers and Health Claims Examiners should become familiar with these terms to help them accurately bill and process dental claims.

Table 22-1: Dental Prefixes and Suffixes

Prefix/Suffix	Meaning
ab-	away from, not
-al	pertaining to
-algia	pain
alveol-	tooth socket
an-, a	without, not
ante-	in front of, before
antr-	cavity
apic, apex-	tip of the root, top
arthr-	joint
auto-	self
bi-	two
benign	mild, not cancerous
bucc-	cheek
calc-	stone
-centesis	punctured
cephal-	head
cervic-	neck
cid-	falling
condyle	knob on the end of a bone
cut-	skin
de-	down from
dent-	teeth
-desis	binding, fixation
doch-	duct, tube
dys-	bad
-ectomy	surgical removal
en-	in
end-	inside, within
esthesia	sensation
ex-	out, from
fistul-	pipe, tube
fistule	pipe, tube
fren-	fold of skin
frenul-	fold of skin
gemin-	twin, double
gen-	originate, produce

Common Dental Terms and Procedures

Abrasion—Wearing away of the surfaces of the teeth as a result of their use in chewing.

Abscess—A collection of pus in a cavity formed within the tissue of the body.

Absorption—The process of sucking up, taking in, and assimilating certain substances, such as fluids and other suitable matter, by the skin, mucus membranes, blood vessels, or lymphatics.

Abutment—A tooth used to support or stabilize one end of a prosthetic appliance, such as a dental bridge.

Accretion—An accumulation of foreign matter, such as

Prefix/Suffix	Meaning
gingiv-	gum
gloss-	tongue
gnath-	jaw
grad-	step, stage
gram-	record
hemi-	half
hyper-	above, more than normal, excessive
hypo-	under, beneath, deficient
infra-	beneath, below
inter-	between
intra-	within
-ist	one who practices
-itis	inflammation
labi-	lip
later-	side
lig-	tie
lingu-	tongue
lith-	stone
-lysis	loosening, set free, destruction
macr-, macro-	large
mal-	bad
malign-	bad
mandibul-	lower jaw
maxillo-	upper jaw
menisc-	pad, disc
-ment	a way of
micr-	small
myel-	marrow, spinal cord
neo-	new
occlud, occlus-	close
odont-	tooth
-odyn-	pain
-ologist	a specialist in the study of
-ology	study of
or-	mouth

Prefix/Suffix	Meaning
os-, oss-	bone
ost-, oste-	bone
-osis	any condition
-ostomy	create a new opening or passageway
-otomy-	cut into, incision
palat-	roof of mouth
pan-	all
parotid	near the ear
path-	disease
peri-	about, around
-pexy	suspension, fixation
physio-	nature
-plasia	developing, development
plast-	plastic repair
post-	behind, in back of
pre-	in front of, before
pro-	in front of, before
pulp	juicy tissue
quadr-	four
radi-	ray
radic-	root
retro-	backward
sial-	saliva
sinus	hollow space
stom-, stomat-	mouth, opening
sub-	under, beneath, below
temporal	on side of skull
top-	place
trans-	through, across, beyond
traum-	wound, injury
tri-	three
-trophy	development
uni-	one
vestibul-	entrance
-vulse	twitch, pull
zygomatic/malar	cheekbone

tartar on the surface of a tooth or decayed matter within a cavity.
Acid-etch—In restorative dentistry, a method of etching the tooth enamel with an acid to provide an adhesion of composite filling material to the tooth's surface.
Acrylic—A synthetic thermoplastic substance resembling clear glass, but lighter in weight, which permits passage of ultraviolet rays and is used in making dental prostheses and temporary artificial eyes.
Acrylic Resins—Plastic restorative materials used in making dentures and crowns and as filling material.
ADA—American Dental Association.
Adaptic—Type of filling (composite); recommended for class I, III, and V restorations.
Adduct—To move toward the center or midline.
Adhesives—In restorative dentistry, a compound used after the acid-etch to provide an adhesion between the composite and the tooth surface.
Adjunctive Treatment—Supplementary and additional therapeutic procedures.
Adjustment—An alteration or modification that may be required on a tooth or a denture (after it has been placed in the mouth). Occlusal adjustment is a form of modification.
Align—To position properly in relation to another object or objects.
Alloy—The product of fusion of two or more metals; a silver alloy combined with mercury to produce an amalgam for restoration of destroyed tooth structure.
Alveolalgia—Pain in the alveolus or tooth socket following tooth extraction. It may involve osteitis or dry socket.
Alveolar—Pertaining to an alveolus.
Alveolar Osteitis—A painful condition caused by loss of the blood clot or from an infected clot; commonly referred to as "dry socket."
Alveolectomy—Shaping of the dental ridges by removal of prominences of bone and excess of soft tissue, usually in preparation for construction of a prosthetic appliance.
Alveolotomy—Incision into a tooth socket.
Alveolus—Bone cavity or a socket in which the root of a tooth is held by the periodontal ligament.
Alveoplasty—Surgical excision or revision of the alveolar process to restore a normal contour. It may range from simple alveolectomy in conjunction with extractions to necessary reconstruction of the ridge in preparation for dentures.
Amalgam—An alloy of mercury with any other metal. The compound of a basal alloy of silver and tin with mercury, used for restoring teeth. Copper and zinc are usually added as modifying metals to the basal alloy.
Amputation (Root)—Excision of the root portion of a tooth. It is usually performed on a multirooted tooth to eliminate a root that cannot be treated.
Analgesia—Reduction or loss of sensibility to pain without loss of consciousness.
Anesthesia—Loss of sensation.

Block—Anesthesia produced by injecting an anesthetic solution into the nerve trunks supplying the operative field, called *regional block*, or by infiltrating close to the nerves, called *infiltration block*, or by wall of anesthetic solution injected about the field, called *field block*. In all the following methods, the nerve conduction is blocked, and painful impulses fail to reach the brain.

General—Loss of sensation with loss of consciousness.

Infiltration—Anesthesia induced by the injection of the anesthetic solution directly into the tissues that are to be anesthetized.

Local—Anesthesia limited to a local area.

Regional—Local anesthesia.

Anesthetics—Drugs that produce loss of feeling or sensation either as local or general anesthesia.
Angle's Classification—A classification of the forms of malocclusion as established by Edward Hartley Angle, an American orthodontist.

Class I—The normal anteroposterior relationship of the lower jaw to the upper jaw. The mesiobuccal cusp of the maxillary first permanent molar occludes in the buccal groove of the mandibular first permanent molar.

Class II—The posterior relationship of the lower jaw to the upper jaw. The mesiobuccal cusp of the maxillary first permanent molar occludes mesial to the buccal groove of the mandibular first permanent molar.

Class III—The anterial relationship of the lower jaw to the upper jaw with possible subdivision. The mesiobuccal cusp of the maxillary first permanent molar occludes distal to the buccal groove of the mandibular first permanent molar.

Ankyloglossia—Partial or complete fusion of the tongue to the floor of the mouth.

Ankylosis—Fixation or true bony union between bones or a tooth to the jaw; abnormal immobility of a joint.

Anodontia—Failure of tooth formation; congenital absence of teeth.

Anomaly—Any deviation from the normal; any organ or part existing in an abnormal form, structure, or location.

Antagonist—A tooth in the upper jaw that articulates with a tooth of the lower jaw, or vice versa.

Anterior—Situated in front; dentally, referring to the teeth at the front of the mouth, ie, central incisors, lateral incisors, and first bicuspids.

Anterior Posterior Dysplasia—An abnormal fit of the maxilla and mandible to each other or to the cranial base.

Anteversion—In dentistry, the forward tipping or tilting of the teeth or other structures of the oral cavity.

Antibiotic—A drug that inhibits or destroys bacterial growth. When correctly used, antibiotics can inhibit or destroy microorganisms.

Antiseptic—A pharmaceutical substance that stops or inhibits the growth of microorganisms.

Aperture—An opening.

Apex—The terminal end of a cone; a conical end; the terminal end of a root of a tooth.

Apexification—Removal of dental pulp and treatment of the apex with calcium hydroxide resulting in stimulation of growth of the cementum, which promotes apical closure. It is normally performed in a young patient whose apex is incompletely formed. Root canal therapy is usually performed for an older person.

Apical—Pertaining to the apex or conical endings of the roots of the teeth.

Apical Foramen—The opening at the end of a root of a tooth through which the tooth receives its nerve and blood supply.

Apices—Plural form of apex.

Apicoectomy—The excision or resection of the apex of a tooth root, usually following root canal therapy.

Apicostomy—A surgical opening through the mucoperiosteum and alveolar bone for access to the apex of a tooth root.

Aplasia—Lack of origin or development.

Appliance—In dentistry, a device used to replace missing parts, to provide function, or to perform a therapeutic purpose. Dental protheses, splints, orthodontic appliances, and obturators are examples of appliances.

Craniofacial—Used to reduce and immobilize mandibular or midfacial fractures. Attachments may be external or internal, by means of wires, pins, bars, or headcaps. Holes may be drilled through the craniofacial bones to facilitate placing wires or other attachments.

Crozat—A removable orthodontic appliance.

Fixed—An appliance attached to the teeth by cement or by adhesive materials.

Fracture—Device for reduction or fixation of fractures. Pins, screws, and other types of fixation are used in replacing or realignment of fractures parts.

Hawley—A removable appliance usually made to fit in the palate against the lingual surfaces of the teeth and used as a retainer after the teeth have been aligned. There are numerous forms and uses.

Arch—Any object that is curved, like an arc.

Arch, Dental—The curving structure formed by the crowns of the teeth in their normal position, or by the residual ridge after loss of the teeth. The inferior dental arch, or arch of the mandible, is formed by the lower teeth, and the superior dental arch, or arch of the maxilla, is formed by the upper teeth.

Arch Retainer—An appliance to prevent collapse of the dental arch.

Arch Wire—In orthodontics, the main wire framework, which is attached to bands and passes around the entire dental arch, on the lingual surface or facial surface or both, and which serves as the frame of attachment for finger springs.

Artificial Teeth—A denture or bridgework; dental prostheses composed of two materials—porcelain or plastic. The former is a hard, baked vitreous material with specific properties. The latter is a less hard, more resilient material with different characteristics and indicated uses.

Attrition—The normal or abnormal loss of teeth structure to the friction caused by physiologic or pathologic forces interacting between the teeth and an abrasive substance, object, or other tooth; also called *abrasion*.

Autogenous Bone Graft—A bone graft obtained from another part of the same person's body to induce new bone formation in a defect.

Axis—A real or imaginary line passing through a body or part, such as the vertical axis of a tooth.

Backing—A piece of metal, usually gold, that backs up an artificial bridge or tooth and to which the tooth is soldered or otherwise attached.

Band—In orthodontics, a metallic attachment that surrounds and is cemented on the tooth, used to anchor archwires to the teeth.

Bar—A connector of two or more parts. It may be used for removable partial dentures, for fixed prostheses to provide additional strength, and for splinting in treatment of fractures of teeth and jaws.

Basal Bone—The bone-like tissue of the mandible and maxilla, other than the alveolar process.

Base—A protective material, such as a cement, placed over the pulpal area of the tooth (pulp not exposed) to reduce irritation and thermal shock to the pulp. In dentures, the portion of the prostheses that is supported by the alveolar ridge, it is generally made of acrylic resin, unless metal is required to provide strength. Part of a denture that replaces the normal contours of the soft tissues and supports the artificial teeth.

Baseplate—A temporary form to represent the base of a denture that is used for making maxillomandibular (jaw) relation records and for arrangement of the teeth.

Bell-crowned—Pertaining or referring to a tooth crown that is largest at the occlusal surface and tapers to the gum, usually used on incisors and bicuspids.

Bicuspid—Having two cusps, as in bicuspid teeth, a premolar.

Bifurcate—Fork; divided into two branches; having two roots.

Bifurcation—Anatomic area where roots divide into a two-rooted tooth.

Bilateral—Having two sides. Any partial denture having a major connector is said to be bilateral, ie, one on each side.

Bite—The force with which the teeth close and crush food is called the strength of the bite, or simply, the bite; also, a plastic impression in the relationship of the upper and lower teeth in occlusion. This force is measured with a gnathodynamometer.

Bite, closed—A condition in which the upper teeth close too far over the lower, and usually bite into the roof of the mouth.

Bite, cross. See Cross-Bite.

Bite Guard—An appliance that covers the occlusal and incisal surfaces of the teeth. It is used to stabilize the teeth or to provide a flat surface for unobstructive movement of the mandible.

Bite, open—A condition in which the upper and lower incisors do not occlude.

Bite Plane—An appliance that covers the palate and is designed to provide resistance to the mandibular incisors where there is contact.

Bite Raising—The process of increasing the distance between the occlusal surfaces of the teeth. It may be accomplished by placing appliances or gold inlays or crowns.

Bite Wing Radiograph—An x-ray that shows the crowns of the upper and lower teeth and a portion of the roots and supporting bone.

Bleaching—A technique that restores a discolored tooth to its natural color.

Bone, alveolar—A portion of the alveolar process that surrounds the roots of the teeth; a thin plate of bone to which the periodontal ligament is attached. It is pierced by many small openings that transmit blood, lymph vessels and nerves to the periodontal ligament.

Bracing—Resistance to displacement in a lateral direction.

Bracket—In orthodontics, an attachment that is either welded or soldered to a band (except a molar band), which is the means by which arch wires are secured to bands.

Bridge—A partial denture; bridgework.

Fixed—Bridge that is permanently attached to its abutments.

Removable—Denture that may be removed by the wearer, although held firmly in place.

Removable Fixed—Bridge that may be removable by the dentist (not by the patient) without mutilation of any of its parts.

Bridgework—An appliance made of artificial crowns of teeth to replace missing natural teeth.

Broken Stress Bridge—A fixed bridge that includes a rigid connector at one end and a nonrigid connector, or stress breaker, at the other end.

Bruxism—The unconscious habit of gnashing or grinding the teeth, often limited to the sleeping period sometimes occurring during mental or physical concentration or strain.

Buccal—Pertaining to the cheek. The buccal surface of a tooth is a surface next to the cheek.

Buccal Frenum—The string-like tissue that attaches to the cheeks to the alveolar ridge in the bicuspid region.

Buccolingual—From the cheek toward the tongue with the buccolingual diameter of the crown of a molar tooth.

Butterfly—A removable acrylic partial denture for the temporary replacement of front teeth; sometimes referred to as a flipper, or provisional partial, or temporary bridge.

Calcification—The act of depositing calcific matter or calcium salts during growth. Bones and teeth become calcified. Also, pathologic calcifications occur in several parts of the body.

Calculus—A hard calcareous concretion deposited on the surface of the crown or root of a tooth; tartar.

Salivary—Calcareous deposits in the duct of a salivary gland or on the surface of the teeth, which originate from the salivary secretion.

Serumal—Calcareous deposits formed about the teeth by exudation from diseased gums.

Canal, root—The opening through the center of the long axis of the root of a tooth from the crown to the apex, which under normal conditions contains a root portion of the dental pulp.

Canine—The teeth corresponding to the long teeth of a dog, usually referred to as cuspids.

Cantilever—A dental prostheses that has one or more abutments at one end and the other end being unsupported.

Cap—A substance or structure designed to cover the exposed pulp of the tooth.

Capping—A covering, as with the cap. A term applied to the operation of placing a covering over an exposure of the pulp of a tooth.

Direct Pulp—Direct pulp capping provides a direct contact between the material used and the pulp.

Indirect Pulp—Indirect pulp capping is application of the material to vital or diseased dentin.

Care—The total of diagnostic, preventative, treatment, and restorative services rendered by a licensed dentist.

Adequate—May denote repair of oral damage and the placing of the mouth in a condition to prevent deterioration. Also, it may denote the most desirable treatment for an individual but frequently refers to the substitution of a less costly but satisfactory type of service.

Comprehensive—All dental services indicated for the restoration and maintenance of oral health. It sometimes includes, but more often excludes, dental care for cosmetic reasons.

Emergency—Any dental services for unexpected and urgent conditions, such as toothache, acute infection, hemorrhage, accidental injury to teeth and supporting structures, and broken dentures. Sometimes it is inaccurately used to mean any dental service between scheduled recall visits.

Initial—Services required for dental needs existing at time of enrollment in a planned dental care; frequently called mouth rehabilitation.

Maintenance—Service required to maintain oral health after the backlog of dental needs has been met.

Minimum—Generally, oral treatment of acute conditions of teeth and gums.

Caries—A molecular depth of bone or teeth, corresponding to ulceration in the soft tissue.

Of the Teeth—A localized, progressive molecule disintegration of the teeth, beginning with the solution of the enamel lactic and pyruvic acids. The acids break down and remove the inorganic constituents of the enamel and dentin, and the unsupported organic matrix is gradually removed, leaving the so-called "cavity of decay."

Interproximal—Caries of the surfaces of the teeth in contact with each other.

Cariogenic—Conducive to caries.

Carious—Affected with or of the nature of caries.

Cast—The positive reproduction of the mouth or teeth in plaster or similar material, upon which a prosthetic appliance is constructed.

Cavity Classifications

Class I—Cavities beginning in structural defects such as pits and fissures.

Class II—Cavities in proximal surfaces of bicuspids and molars.

Class III—Cavities in proximal surfaces of cuspids and incisors that do not involve the incisal edge.

Class IV—Cavities in proximal surfaces of cuspids and incisors involving the incisal angle.

Class V—Cavities of the gingival third of the labial, buccal, or lingual surfaces of the teeth.

Class VI—Cavities on the incisal edges and cusp tips of the teeth.

Cavity Liner—A substance that is placed on the walls of the cavity before insertion of a restoration.

Cement—In dentistry, an adhesive filling material used for cementing bridges, crowns, and inlays. It is used also as a temporary filling material in certain instances.

Acrylic Resin—A type of autopolymerizing acrylic used as a restorative material.

Copper Phosphate—Zinc phosphate cement to which copper oxide has been added; thought to impart germicidal qualities to the cement created.

Base—Used for insulation in deep cavity preparation.

Germicidal—Copper or silver salts added to destroy bacteria.

Sealer—Used for filling root canals.

Silicate—Commonly used to fill cavities in the anterior teeth; made of powdered kaolin, quartz, lime, and magnesium mixed with liquid phosphoric acid.

Zinc Phosphate—Commonly used to seal gold inlays and crowns into place on the teeth and used as a base under metallic restorations.

Zinc Oxide Eugenol—A sedative cement used as a temporary filling or as a base under restorations, where sedative treatment of the tooth is indicated.

Cementoenamel Junction—The portion of the tooth at which the cementum and the enamel join.

Cementosis—The same as hypercementosis, which refers to excessive formation of cementum on the tooth roots. (Hypocementosis relates to reduced or insufficient cementum.)

Cementum—The hard calcified tissue that covers the anatomic root of a tooth. It is formed by cementoblast and arranged in layers that cover the root dentin.

Central Ray—The x-ray located in the center of the bundle of x-rays that make up the useful beam.

Cephalometrics—A scientific study of the measurements of the head.

Ceramco—Trade name for the combination of porcelain with metal used in restorations of fixed prosthetics.

Cervical—Pertaining to the neck or cervix of a tooth.

Cervical Anchorage—In orthodontics, a strap of elastic tape with wire hooks that fits around the back of the patient's neck and is used in a situation in which a force from outside the mouth is desirable to move teeth distally.

Cervical Line—The neck of a tooth; the cementoenamel junction.

Cervicogingival—The space between the gingiva and the enamel of the tooth crowns; or the space between the gingiva and the cementum in cases in which the gingiva has receded.

Chamber—An enclosed area.

Pulp—Pulp cavity or space in the coronal position of the tooth, containing the pulp.

Relief—A recess in a denture to reduce or eliminate pressure from the corresponding area of the mouth.

Clasp—The metal part of a partial denture.

Arm—The portion of the clasp that extends from the body of the clasp out to the end of the clasp.

Cleft Lip—A congenital cleft or defect in the upper lip, usually due to failure of the median nasal and maxillary process to unite.

Cleft Palate—A congenital defect due to failure of fusion of embryonic facial process, resulting in a fissure through the palate. It may be complete, extending through both hard and soft palates into the nose, or it may be any degree of incomplete, or partial, cleft.

Cohesive—Uniting together, or characterized by cohesion. In dentistry, a property of annealed gold (foil or crystal) that causes separate particles to stick to one another as they are welded, when placed in contact with each other by a heavy hand or mallet pressure.

Coil Spring—A small wire spring wrapped around the main arch wire in an orthodontic appliance, which is used as a force to pull teeth together or to push them apart.

Cold Cure—Usually relates to denture relining not requiring laboratory service.

Collar—A small part of the root of a denture tooth.

Complete Denture—One that replaces all teeth in an arch.

Composite—A plastic restorative material that blends resin and quartz crystal with a catalyst.

Compressive Strength—The greatest compressive force that can be applied to material before it ruptures.

Concrescence—The union of two teeth, after eruption, by fusion of the cementum surfaces.

Concretion—In dentistry, a deposit on the surface of a tooth. Also, a calculus.

Condensation—In dentistry, the packing of a restorative material into the prepared cavity of a tooth.

Condyle—The rounded, knuckle-shaped process of the mandible, which forms a joint at the temporal bone.

Condylectomy—Surgical removal of a condyle.

Contact Point—The surface of a tooth that touches the surface of an adjacent tooth.

Coping—A thin metal covering over a prepared tooth, which is used as a base for the construction of a crown.

Coronal—Pertaining to the crown of a tooth.

Coronoid—Shaped like the beak of a crown, as the coronoid process of the mandible.

Coronoid Process—The more anterior process on the superior border of the ramus.

Correction of Occlusion—The correction of malocclusion by elimination of disharmony of occlusal contacts. It may be performed by means of many different methods, depending on the degree of severity, from selective spot grinding to gnathologic evaluation with subsequent treatment to correct any disharmonies.

Crest Ridge—The projecting ridge of the alveolar process that surrounds the teeth.

Cross-Bite—Bite in which the jaws may be in normal relationship when closed, but the buccal cusp of the upper molars bite into the buccal cusp of the lower molars.

Crown—Top part of anything; any structure like a crown.

- Anatomic—Portion of a tooth covered by enamel.
- Artificial—A cap of metal, plastic, or porcelain process to cover the portion of the tooth that projects beyond the gum line.
- Clinical—The portion of the tooth exposed beyond the crest of the gingiva.
- Complete—The crown that covers the entire clinical crown.
- Of a Tooth—The part covered with enamel.
- Dowel—A complete crown that replaces the entire coronal portion of the natural tooth, which is retained by a post extending into the root canal.
- Faced—A metal crown with a tooth-colored material on the labial or buccal surface.
- Full Veneer—A dental restoration that covers in its entirety the part of a tooth exposed to the oral environment.
- Jacket—A term generally used to indicate complete veneer crowns that are made entirely of porcelain or acrylic resin.
- Shell—A metal cap designed to fit a prepared tooth. It is usually preformed and reproduces the natural crown.
- Three-quarter—A dental restoration that covers all of the tooth exposed to oral environment except the labial or buccal surface.
- Crozat Appliance—A removable orthodontic appliance.

Curettage—Scraping or removal of diseased tissue with a curet.

- Apical—Curettement of diseased tissue in the periapical area on the apical portion of the tooth, without removal of the root tip.
- Gingival—Débridement of a pathologic, or diseased, gingival attachment to eliminate edema, inflammation, and pocket formation.

Infrabony Pocket—The removal of a soft tissue inflammation located within and around an infrabony defect. Débridement and cleaning of the root surface of the pocket.

Root—Removal of accretions on the root's surface by débridement and cleaning, providing a more suitable environment for development of healthy tissues.

Subgingival—Débridement of the entire pocket and epithelial subjacent connective tissues, performed to eliminate the inflammatory process.

Cusp—A pronounced elevation or point on the surface of a tooth, especially on the occlusal surface.

Cuspid—A cuspid or canine tooth with one point or cusp.

Cyst—Sac containing fluid, bladder.

DDS—Doctor of Dental Surgery.

Débridement—Removal of diseased or devitalized tissues and foreign materials.

Debris—Soft-formed material loosely attached to the surface of a tooth as a refuge from the drilling of a cavity.

Decalcification—Withdrawal or removal by acid of mineral salts of bone or other calcified substance.

Decay—Decomposed structures; caries or other carious lesions of the teeth.

Deciduous—Term used to identify primary dentition.

Def Rate—Similar to the DMF rate but used for primary dentition (baby teeth). Although lower case letters are used, the symbol (d) standing for decayed primary teeth indicated for filling and the symbol (f) for filled primary teeth have the same meaning as DMF. The symbol (e) stands for decayed teeth indicated for extraction; missing teeth are not counted for this rate.

Dens in Dente—A developmental anomaly of a tooth, usually involving the upper lateral incisors. The invagination of the tooth enamel in the dental papilla gives the appearance of a tooth within a tooth.

Dental—Pertaining to the teeth.

Dental Floss—Fine string pulled between the teeth to aid the mechanical cleaning of interproximal surfaces of the teeth.

Dental Hygienist—A person licensed to clean and polish teeth and to instruct in the fundamentals of oral hygiene.

Dental Laboratory Technician—A person trained to perform certain mechanical operations that are necessary in preparing dental appliances and restorations for placement in the mouth.

Dental Pulp—The soft vascular tissue that fills the pulp chamber and the root canals of a tooth and is responsible for its vitality. It consists of connective tissue, blood vessels, and nerves.

Dental Senescence—Deterioration of the teeth and associated structures, due to the aging process.

Dentate—Having teeth.

Dentifrice—A substance, as a paste or a powder, used in the mechanical cleaning of teeth.

Dentin—The calcified tissue that forms the major part of the tooth. Dentin is related to bone, but differs from it in the absence of included cells. It is covered by enamel over the crown of the tooth, and by the cementum over the roots.

Dentinogenesis Imperfecta—Hereditary disturbance that affects the development of dentin.

Dentistry—The profession that is concerned with the prevention, diagnosis, and treatment of diseases of the teeth and adjacent tissues, and the restoration of missing dental and oral structures.

Operative—The phase or branch of dentistry concerned with the preservation of the natural teeth and its supporting structures and with the restoration of loss of tooth structure to a state of normal function and esthetics.

Preventive—The phase or branch of dentistry dealing with prevention of dental diseases by prophylactic and educational methods.

Prosthetic—The phase or branch of dentistry that deals with the replacement of missing teeth or oral tissues by artificial means; also called prosthodontics.

Dentition—The process of teething; the eruption of teeth in the alveolar ridge. Also, the character and arrangement of the teeth.

Deciduous—The 20 teeth which erupt first and are later replaced by the permanent teeth.

Mixed—The complement of teeth in the jaw after eruption of some of the permanent teeth, before all the deciduous teeth are shed.

Permanent—The 32 teeth that erupt after the deciduous teeth are lost.

Dentulous—Having teeth, as opposed to edentulous, not having teeth.

Denture—The natural or artificial teeth of a person considered as a unit.

Artificial—The complete artificial replacement of either the upper or lower teeth.

Butt—Denture with almost no flange, designed because of full lips, leaving no room for additional thickness of the denture flange.

Duplicate—Usually refers to a second denture that is a copy of the existing denture.

Duplication—Usually refers to a jump case or rebasing of the denture; also known as duplicating or rematerial. Rebasing is the replacement of the base of the denture of deterioration or tissue changes. Duplication can be misleading because occasionally the term is used to mean a spare set. Because of many uses, it is advisable to ask for explanation of service.

Full—Replacement of the complete dental equipment of either jaw.

Immediate Full—Denture constructed to permit some natural teeth to remain in the mouth during its fabrication. When the remaining teeth are removed, the denture is inserted; hence, the patient is never without teeth of some kind.

Implant—A substructure usually made of cast metal, which is implanted over the alveolar ridge and under the soft tissues. Posts extend through the gingival tissues to support a denture. There may also be extensions into the bone for support.

Overlay—Complete denture that fits over one or more retained natural teeth. Ideally, it provides a more comfortable fit and retention because of the attachment to the teeth. It is used in both the upper and lower jaws, but more frequently placed in the mandible. The preparation consists of performing root canal therapy on the remaining teeth and placing a small gold cap or crown. An alternate method is to perform root canal therapy and then cut the tooth off at the level of the alveolar ridge. Attachments are then inserted into the root canal and used to provide support to a denture.

Remote—Denture placed following the healing of an extraction site; may also be the replacement of an existing denture.

Diagnostic Services—Procedures such as x-rays, clinical examinations, biopsies, blood tests, study models, and other vitality tests, which assist the dentist in determining the conditions present and the treatment required.

Die—An exact reproduction in metal of any object or cast.

Inlay—An exact reproduction of a prepared tooth in high-strength dental stone or metal.

Distal—Away from the median line of the face following the curve of the dental arch. The surfaces of the teeth most distant from the median line are called *distal surfaces*.

DMD—Doctor of Dental Medicine.

DMF Rate—For an individual, the number of permanent teeth (or for a group, the average number) that are (d) decayed, (m) missing, or indicated for extractions, and (f) filled. A tooth both filled and decayed is counted only as decayed. The DMF rate is a measure of accumulative effects of caries and a useful means for comparing the lifetime of caries' experience of a group of comparable age.

Dolder Bar—Bar used to connect crowns for stabilization and reduce stress in anterior fixed prosthetics. The bar is attached to the abutments.

Double Lingual Bar—A type of lower partial denture that includes a secondary, or auxiliary bar in addition to the lingual bar.

Dowel Post and Pins—Cast metal or manufactured strengthening device, placed in a tooth to provide retention for a crown.

Duct—A passage with well-defined walls.

E Clasp—A bar-type clasp that is shaped like the letter "E."

Edentulous—Without teeth.

Elongation—Abnormal elongation of a tooth on a dental x-ray film by improper positioning of the x-ray machine in relation to the x-ray film in the patient's oral cavity.

Embrasure—Space between the sloping proximal surfaces of the teeth. The opening may be toward the cheek (buccal), the lips (labial), or the tongue (lingual).

Enamel—The vitreous covering tissue of the anatomic crowns of the teeth, consisting of enamel rods or prisms and a cementing interrod substance. It is cleavable along the general direction of the rods.

  Rods—The calcified column or prism, with an average diameter of 4 mm; extends in a wavy pattern through the entire thickness of the enamel and is generally perpendicular to the surface of the tooth.

  Mottled—A defect in the enamel structure of the teeth manifesting as chalky white, yellow-brown, or black discolorations. The enamel may be pitted. The affected areas may vary in size and degree, depending on the severity of the causative factor.

Encirclement—A clasp that extends more than halfway around a tooth to provide a secure attachment; provides encirclement.

Endodontics—The branch of dentistry that deals with the diagnosis and treatment of diseases of the dental pulp and periapical tissues.

Endopost—A cast post designed to fit into the endodontically treated root canal of a tooth to provide strength and stability.

Epithelium—Cellular structure arrangement or membrane that covers a service or lines the cavity—the layer of cells forming the epidermis of the skin.

  Enamel—Ameloblasts that form the dental enamel of the developing tooth.

  Gingival—Epithelial covering of the gingival tissue.

  Pocket—Cellular structure that lines the gingival or periodontal pockets.

  Sulcular—Stratifying squamous epithelium covering the soft tissue walls of the gingival sulcus or crevice.

Epulis—Solitary tumor-like lesion developing from the periosteum of the maxilla or mandible, appearing clinically as a circumscribed swelling beneath the gum.

Equilibrate—To be in balance; to balance.

Equilibration—Maintenance of the equilibrium, as a pressure.

  Occlusal—Modification of the occlusal form by grinding for equalizing occlusal stress, producing simultaneous occlusion contact, or harmonizing cuspal relations.

Equilibrium—Perfect balance. The condition made possible by complete synchronization and harmony among all vital factors.

Erosion—Wearing away or loss of tooth structure by chemical process without known bacterial action, usually beginning in the enamel at the neck of a tooth.

Eruption—The act of breaking up, appearing, or becoming visible; the appearance of a tooth through the gums.

Esthetics—Harmony of form, color, and arrangement.

Etch and Polish—Removal of portions of enamel, usually performed on primary teeth followed by etching and polishing of the tooth areas.

Ethical—Pertaining to standards of right and wrong.

Ethics—A system of moral principles and ideas of human behavior.

  Dental—The principles of professional conducts; duties a dentist owes to self, colleagues, patients, and fellow man.

Exfoliation—A peeling and shedding of a horny layer of skin or of a tooth.

  Normal time—The time at which a primary tooth is expected to become loose and fall out of a child's mouth.

Exodontia, Exodontics—The art and science of extraction of teeth.

Exostoses—Bony outgrowths from the surface of a bone, as localized enlargements of outer cortical plate of the maxilla and mandible.

Extension of Prevention, Dental—Extending the margins of a cavity preparation to remove incipient carious lesions to areas of the tooth that are either self-cleansing or readily cleansed. Such extensions are to prevent the recurrence of caries at the margins of the restorations.

Extracoronal—The external coronal portion of a natural tooth.

Extraction—Removal of a tooth from the oral cavity.

  Serial—Extraction of selected teeth over a period of time.

  Simple—Uncomplicated removal of a tooth.

  Surgical—Removal by means of surgical methods,

usually involving the turning of a flap or removal of bone.

Extraoral—Outside the mouth.

Extrude—To force (in dentistry) a tooth out of its normal occlusal position. It may be due to absence of opposing occlusal force, in which the contacting tooth in the opposite arch is missing.

Extrusion—Hypereruption of a tooth from its socket; movement of tooth out of the natural occlusal plane.

Eyetooth—A canine tooth of the upper jaw; bicuspid.

Facial—Pertaining to the face; the surface of the tooth or appliance nearest to the lips or cheeks; used synonymously with the words *buccal* and *labial*.

Facing—A manufactured porcelain piece that simulates a natural tooth.

Festoon—Carvings in the base material of an artificial denture, simulating contours of the natural tissues being replaced by the denture.

Fibroblast—Connective tissue cells found in fibrous tissue, fundamental to all healing processes.

Filling—Material used in closing cavities in carious teeth; also, the process of inserting, condensing, shaping, and finishing a filling.

Finger Spring—A small wire attachment soldered to the main arch wire that acts as a spring force to move teeth in an orthodontic appliance.

Fissure—A groove or cleft; a fault in the enamel of a tooth caused by imperfect union.

Flange—The part of the denture or saddle that extends on the facial or lingual from the ridgecrest to the periphery.

Flap—Massive tissue partly detached by a knife or blunt instrument in dentistry, the raising of the gingival mucosa from the alveolar bone to secure access to an underlying area. Sometimes, a flap procedure is used to remove a broken or retained root. It is frequently required as a result of periodontal disease.

FLC—Full line or finished crown.

Flipper—A provisional partial or temporary bridge.

Floss—Waxed or unwaxed silk or nylon thread, used to clean the interproximal surfaces of the teeth. It may also be used as ligature to secure a rubber band to the teeth.

Fluoridation—The addition of fluoride to the water supply of a community as an aid to the control of dental caries.

Fluoride—A salt of hydrofluoric acid. Fluorides in drinking water are effective in preventing tooth decay.

Fluoride, topical—The direct application of a solution of fluoride (usually 2% sodium fluoride) to the crowns of the teeth for preventing dental caries; usually carried out at the ages of 3, 7, 10, and 13 years.

Foramen—A natural opening in a bone or other structure.

Apical—An aperture at or near the apex of the root of a tooth, giving passage to the blood vessels and nerve supply in the pulp.

Mandibular—The opening on the medial aspect of the vertical ramus of the lower jaw or mandible approximately midway between the mandibular and gonial notches; may be located posterior to the middle of the ramus. It contains inferior alveolar vessels and inferior alveolar nerves.

Foreshortening—Term used in dental radiology denoting the abnormal shortening of a tooth or teeth on a dental x-ray film.

Formocreosal—A solution used in root canal therapy and in treatment of dental pulp.

Fossa—A pit, hollow, depression.

Dental—A round or angular depression in the surface of a tooth, occurring mostly in the occlusal surfaces of the molar and also in the lingual surfaces of the incisors.

Frenectomy—Excision of the mucous membrane attaching the cheeks and lips to the mucosa of the maxilla or mandible; excision of the lingual frenum attaching the tongue to the floor of the mouth and alveolar ridge.

Frenotomy—Division of any frenum, especially for tongue-tie.

Frenum—A fold of integument or mucous membrane that checks or limits the movements of any organ.

Labial—The fold or tissue that connects the lip with the gingiva at a point normally in the median line.

Lingual—The fold of tissue that connects the tongue to the gingiva and the floor of the mouth in the median line.

Full Mouth X-Ray—X-ray of the mouth equaling 16 bite wings.
Furcation—The tooth area where roots branch out. Bifurcation relates to two roots; trifurcation relates to three roots.
Germination—The division of a single tooth germ or bud that produces double or twin crowns on a single tooth.
Gerodontics—Practice of dentistry as it pertains to aged patients.
Gigantism—Macrosomia; excessive growth.
Gingiva—The part of the gum that surrounds the tooth and lies close to the crest of the alveolar ridge.
  Free—The part of the gingiva about the neck of a tooth that is not closely opposed to or attached to the tooth's surfaces.
Gingival—Of or pertaining to the soft tissues of the gum and the tooth.
  Crevice—The narrow opening sulcus between the circumferential soft tissue of the gum and the tooth.
  Cuff—The most coronal portion of the gingival tissue immediately surrounding the tooth to where it attaches to the tooth.
  Curettage—Débridement of a pathologic (diseased) gingival attachment. The objective is elimination of edema, inflammation, and pocket formations.
  Margin—The most coronal portion of the gingiva surrounding the tooth.
  Morphology—The form, shape, or profile of gingival tissues.
  Papillae—Extensions or projections of gum tissue in the interproximal areas between the teeth.
  Stimulation—Application of frictional activity to the gingival tissue to stimulate circulation and increase keratinization of the surface epithelium.
  Sulcus—A crevice, group, or pocket in the gingiva; a trough formed by the attachment of the gingiva to the surface of the tooth.
Gingivectomy—The surgical excision from supported gingival tissue to the level where it is attached, creating a new gingival margin, apical and posterior to the old.
Gingivitis—Inflammation of the gingival tissue; may be caused by pressure or contact by dentures, metallic poisoning, desquamative conditions, faulty restorations, dietary deficiency, herpesvirus, hormonal imbalances, malopposed teeth, bacterial invasion, organic malfunction, or pregnancy.
  Desquamative—Inflammation of the gingiva, but not a pathologic entity; may be associated with a biologic stress.
  Hemorrhagic—Characterized by bleeding, particularly associated with ascorbic acid deficiency.
  Herpetic—Inflammation due to presence of herpes virus.
  Hormonal—Associated with an endocrine imbalance.
  Necrotizing Ulcerative—Inflammation with narcosis of the intradental papilla, ulceration of the gingival margins, pain, and offensive odor; an acute gingivitis that is sometimes chronic.
  Pregnancy—Gingival enlargement due to hormonal imbalance during pregnancy; inflammatory hyperplasia of the gingiva during pregnancy.
Gingivoplasty—The procedure by which gingival deformities are reshaped and reduced to create a normal and functional form; surgical contouring of the gingival tissues.
Gingivosis—A degenerative condition of the gingiva and connective tissue of uncertain origin. It is a noninflammatory disease with many phases: edema of the interdental papilla progressing to the marginal and attached gingiva, profuse bleeding progressing to necrosis, recession, and resorption.
Gingivostomatitis—A form of oral inflammatory disease that involves both the gingiva and portions of the remaining oral mucosa. Herpetic gingivostomatitis is caused by invasion of herpesvirus, which usually occurs in children.
Glossitis—Inflammation of the tongue.
Gnathology—The science of the masticatory system, including physiology, functional disturbances, and treatment.
Gold—A noble metal used extensively in dentistry, considered superior because of its malleability; may be used in the pure state or alloyed.
Gold Foil—Pure gold rolled into a thin sheet compacted into a cavity. The gold is annealed, then packed

loosely into a prepared cavity, condensed, and polished. The restoration is built to harmonize with existing occlusal anatomy. It is a direct gold filling in contrast to an inlay in which an impression is made and an exact form is made and cemented in. The three types are:

Matte—Not developed by chemical prescription; a noncohesive form that may be used in combination with cohesive gold.

Sheet—Original type, which was 24-karat gold, rolled into thin sheets and then cut; a disappearing art.

Gold Dent—A combination of matte gold and cohesive made into globules.

Granuloma—A small mass of granulated tissue containing bacterial deposits found on the root of a tooth or in an edentulous area of the jaw after the removal of a tooth.

Groove—An elongated depression, as in the surface of a tooth; also, the portion of a cast that corresponds to the periphery of the impression.

Gum—The mucous membrane and underlying connective tissue covering the alveolar processes and necks of erupted teeth.

Guttering—Shaping bone to remove dead tissues as a result of osteomyelitis.

Halitosis—Fetid odor of the breath due to poor oral hygiene, periodontal disease, sinusitis, tonsillitis, or bronchopulmonary disease.

Hard Palate—The approximate two-thirds of the anterior section of the palate, composed of relatively hard and unyielding tissue.

Hay Rake—A device used with children, which is fixed temporarily to the upper teeth to break undesirable habits such as thumb or lip sucking.

Heel–Denture—The posterior extremities of a denture. It corresponds with the retromolar pad area of a lower denture and the tuberosity area of an upper denture.

Hemisection—The surgical division of a tooth for purposes of facilitating removal of the ensuing fragments or allowing salvage of one part of the tooth that is relatively free of disease. Root canal therapy may be necessary on other roots of the tooth before hemisection is performed.

Herpes—A form of blister-like elevation appearing in clusters on the skin; an inflammatory skin disease.

Labial (Cold Sore)—Herpes simplex occurring on the lips caused by herpesvirus.

Simplex—A viral infection appearing on the face or genital regions with resulting itching and localized hyperemia. The lesions dry up and form a yellowish crust that normally disappears in 10 or 14 days, depending on care.

Zoster—An acute and painful viral disease that affects the cerebral ganglia and posterior nerve roots. Lesions or vesicles appear on the skin over the infected area. Oral lesions occur on the tongue, soft palate, cheek, and the gingival tissues.

Horseshoe Denture—A partial upper denture from which the palate is omitted. In edentulous cases, a horseshoe denture is termed a *roofless denture*.

Hutchinson's Teeth—Congenitally malformed, peg-shaped incisors with incisal edges narrower than the middle part or notching of the incisal edges. Primary dentition is not affected.

Hygienist—A person trained and licensed by the state to perform dental prophylaxis under the direction of a licensed dentist.

Hypercementosis—Extensive formation of cementum on the roots of the teeth.

Hyperkeratosis—The most common white lesion in the oral cavity. A benign lesion that may be elevated or flat and is in the form of a thickened layer of keratin. It may be associated with a cause such as lip biting, or its cause may be obscure. The lesion usually disappears within 2 to 3 months if the cause is eliminated.

Hyperplasia—Excessive growth of normal cells in the normal tissue arrangement of an organ; may have a hereditary or inflammatory cause.

Denture—Enlargement of tissues caused by trauma to the soft tissues from dentures or other injuries.

Dilantin—Caused by the use of dilantin therapy.

Hypocalcification—Reduced calcification; a condition that produces opaque white spots on tooth enamel; may be a hereditary anomaly affecting the dentition, both primary and permanent. The enamel peels off, exposing the dentin and giving a yellow appearance to the teeth.

Hypoplasia—With dental enamel, it is a defective or

incomplete development. When it is a hereditary anomaly, a thin layer of hard enamel covers the dentin, giving a brownish appearance to the teeth.

I Clasp—Roach-type clasp shaped like an I.

Immediate Abutment—The metal abutment in a three-abutment bridge. With a bridge extending from one cuspid to a second molar with a second bicuspid present.

Immediate Denture—A complete or partial denture made before the natural teeth are extracted. It is inserted at the time the teeth are extracted.

Immediate Surgical Splint—Metal, acrylic resin, or modeling compound, fashioned to retain teeth that have been replanted, are unmovable, or have fractured roots; may also be a temporary denture after extraction of teeth. It is an appliance for the protection of a surgical site.

Impacted Tooth—Commonly, any tooth that is positioned or wedged against another tooth, bone, or soft tissue, preventing it from erupting normally.

Impingement—Overcompaction, displacement, or compression. It may be the result of pressure from a unit of a removable prosthesis or traumatization of the periodontal membrane, caused by occlusal force on a tooth.

Implants—Dental implants are made of metal or other foreign material and are placed into or on the alveolar bone, to provide support.

> Endosseous—May be a single metal post inserted into the alveolar bone to support an artificial crown that replaces a missing natural tooth; may also be a metal blade to support one or more artificial crowns or to support a metal crown that would serve as an abutment for a fixed bridge. There are many types and shapes of implants.
>
> Subperiosteal—Used for support of dentures in which there is sufficient resorption of the alveolar ridge. The gingival tissue is open along the alveolar ridge, and impressions are made. A metal prosthesis is made from this impression and the tissues open again to permit placing the implant that creates an artificial ridge. Extensions from the metal saddle extend above the gingival tissue for denture attachments.

Impressions—A negative reproduction of the teeth or tissues of the mouth. A positive reproduction is made from the impression and used in the preparation of restorations such as crowns, fixed and removable prosthetics, and appliances. They are also used for diagnostic purposes.

> Plaginate—A relationship impression taken in combination of quick-set, plaster, and alginate.
>
> Relationship—Impression taken to establish the relationship of abutment teeth.

Incisal—Pertaining to the cutting edges of incisors and cuspid teeth.

Incisor—A cutting tooth; one of four front teeth of either jaw.

Infrabulge—The formation of a crown that is cervical to the clasp guideline, survey line, or height of contour.

Initial Centric—A centric determination made by the dentist, usually without the use of mechanical aids, which is fairly accurate and is commonly used in the final process in establishing true centric.

Inlay—A dental restoration shaped to the form of a cavity and inserted and secured with cement.

Intercuspation—The cusp tooth fossa relationship of the opposing upper and lower posterior teeth.

Intercusping—A correct occlusion of the cusp of the teeth of one jaw with a corresponding impression in the occlusal surfaces of the teeth in the opposite jaw.

Interdigitation—Enclosure of the posterior teeth, the striking of the cusp of one denture fairly into the occluding sulci of the other denture.

Interproximal—Between the proximal surfaces of the adjacent teeth.

Intraoral—Inside or within the mouth.

Ionization—The process of ionizing; use of an electric current to ionize medication within a root canal; also used in treatment of sensitive teeth.

Jacket—A term commonly used in reference to an artificial crown composed of fired porcelain or acrylic resin, eg, porcelain jacket crown, acrylic resin jacket crown, especially of the anterior six teeth are crowned.

Jaw—Either the maxilla or the mandible.

Jumpcase—See Denture Duplication.

Labial—Pertaining to the lips. It is the surface of an anterior tooth opposite the lips.

Labial Bar—The metal bar (major connector) used to

connect the right and left side of a lower partial denture. It is contoured to the labial tissue anterior to the lower teeth.

Labiolingual—From the lips toward the tongue, as a labiolingual diameter of the central incisor.

Lamina Dura—The inner bony wall of the tooth socket. It shows up as a fine white line around the root of a tooth in a dental x-ray.

Lateral (Incisor)—An anterior tooth located just distal to the central incisors; the second tooth from the midline.

Ligature Wire—A fine wire used to tie the main arch wire into the bracket of an orthodontic appliance on the bands or the teeth.

Lingual—Pertaining to the tongue; the surface of a tooth or prosthesis next to the tongue.

Lingual Bar—The metal bar (major connector) on the lingual surfaces of the teeth connecting the right and left sides of a lower partial denture. It is contoured to the lingual tissue behind and below the anterior teeth.

Luxation—Detachment of a tooth from its socket as a result of trauma or pathologic progress; may be partial or complete.

Macrodontia—Abnormally large teeth.

Macrognathia—Abnormally large jaws.

Malalignment—Displacement; not in normal alignment.

Malar Process—The bony extensions of the temporal and maxillary bones that unite with the zygomatic process to form the zygomatic arch; sometimes called the *cheekbone*.

Malocclusion—Any deviation from normal occlusion of the teeth, usually associated with abnormal development and growth of the jaws.

Mandible—The lower jaw.

Mandibular—Pertaining to the mandible.

Marginal Ridge—A ridge or elevation of enamel forming the margin of a surface of a tooth; specifically, one of the mesial or distal borders of the lingual surfaces of anterior teeth and the occlusal surfaces of posterior teeth.

Mastication—Chewing food at the first stage of digestion.

Maxilla—The bone of the skull that supports the upper teeth. Commonly, the term is used to name the upper jaw with its teeth when present and associated with soft tissues.

Maxillae—The bones of the upper jaw.

Maxillary—Referring to the maxilla, or upper arch.

Maxillofacial—Relates to the jaws and the face.

MDS—Master of Dental Science.

Median—The middle; situated or placed in the middle of the body or in the middle of a part of the body.

Megadontism—The condition that results in abnormally large teeth.

Mental Protuberance—A triangular elevation forming the prominence of the chin.

Mesial—The surface of a tooth which, in normal occlusion, is nearest the midline.

Mesioclusion—Occlusion of the teeth in which the mesial buccal cusp of the upper first molar interdigitates between the lower first and second molars.

Mesiodens—Accessory or supernumerary tooth, which may be erupted or unerupted, and located between the maxillary central incisors.

Mesiodistal—From mesial to distal, as the mesiodistal diameter of the lower first molar.

Mesioversion—In the oral cavity, indicative of a closer than normal position to the median plane, or midline of the jaw. When in reference to the maxilla or mandible, the jaw is anterior to its normal position.

Macrodontia—Abnormally small teeth.

Micrognathism—Abnormal smallness of jaws; lack of normal development.

Midline—The imaginary dividing line through the middle of an object or space.

Migration—The movement of a tooth or teeth out of the normal position. It is usually caused by loss of supporting structures.

Milk Teeth—Primary or deciduous teeth (so-called because of their white or milky appearance).

Mineralize—The precipitation of calcium and other salts into an organic matrix, to form a hard deposit such as a dental calculus.

Mobility—The degree of looseness of a tooth, as a result of loss of part or all of the attachments and supportive structures.

Molars—The three teeth in each quadrant that are

located distal to the second bicuspids. They are used for grinding.

Morphology—The branch of biology that deals with structure and form. It includes the anatomy, histology, and cytology of the organisms at any stage of its life history.

Mottled Enamel—A dappled condition of the enamel of the teeth caused by ingestion of too high concentrations of fluorides or drugs such as tetracycline during the formative period.

Mucobuccal Fold—The junction between the cheek and the mucous membrane of the upper or lower jaw.

Mucogingivoplastic Surgery—Procedures designed to correct or modify defects in the morphology and the position of the soft tissues surrounding the teeth.

Mucoperiosteum (Mucoperiosteal Tissue or Periosteum)—A layer of connective tissues that covers the outer surfaces of bone. Periosteum in the oral cavity is covered with gingival tissue and is significant to periodontics.

Mucositis—Inflammation of the mucous membrane.

Mucous Membrane—The soft tissue covering or lining of the mouth.

Mulberry Molars—Congenitally malformed molars. The occlusal surfaces are narrow and there is hypoplasia of the enamel.

Multirooted—A tooth with two or more roots.

Nasion—The part of the skull located at the midpoint of the nasofrontal suture at the root of the nose; the junction of the nasal bones with the frontal bone. It is a landmark in clinical prosthetics.

Neutroclusion—Occlusion of the teeth in which the mesiobuccal cusp of the upper first molar interdigitates with the buccal groove of the lower first molar.

Nitrous Oxide—A colorless gas used in dentistry as a general anesthetic with the performance of uncomplicated operations; also called *laughing gas* and *nitrogen monoxide*.

Nonprecious Metals—Material developed for use in all types of restorative procedures that are less precious than gold and other precious metals.

Obturator—An appliance designed to fill in a cleft palate defect. It is usually held in place with clasps or splinted to the teeth.

Occlude—To close, specifically so that the cusps of the posterior teeth fit together.

Occlusal—The chewing or masticating surfaces of the bicuspids and molars.

Balance—Contact relationship of the biting surfaces of the teeth; simultaneous contacts; equilibrium of mastication.

Equilibration—The process of refining and perfecting the occlusion.

Film—X-ray exposures made on larger films than those used for the periapical and bite wing exposures. The film is placed in the occlusal plane and held in position by the teeth in occlusion. It is used to augment the other exposures.

Guard—A removable dental appliance usually constructed of acrylic resin, which covers one or both dental arches to protect the teeth from the damaging effects of bruxism and other occlusal habits.

Rest—The part of a clasp that lies on the occlusal surface of the tooth.

Surface—The grinding, chewing, or masticating surface of molars and bicuspids.

Occlusion—A closing or shutting up; the state of being closed or shut; the full meeting or contact in a position of the rest of the masticating surfaces of the upper and lower teeth—erroneously called "articulation."

Odontalgia—Toothache.

Odontalysis—Examination of the teeth.

Odontectomy—Surgical extraction of a tooth.

Odontexesis—Cleaning the teeth, including thorough scaling.

Odonthemodia—Treatment of sensitive teeth.

Odontinoid—A tumor composed of tooth substance.

Odontoblast—Connective tissue cells that line the surface of the dental pulp adjacent to the dentin. During the tooth development period, these cells have much to do with the formation of dentin.

Odontoma—An odontogenic tumor composed of enamel, dentin, cementum, and pulp tissue; an anomaly such as dens in dentes or enamel pearl.

Odontomy (Prophylactic Odontomy)—Surgical cutting into a tooth for removal of precarious pit and fissures, with subsequent restoration.

Odontrophia—Imperfect development of the teeth.

Onlay—A cast occlusal restoration that covers the entire incisal or occlusal surface of the tooth, frequently used to restore lost tooth structure and restore the vertical dimension.

Opacity—The condition of being impervious to light.

Opaque—Not transparent; not letting light through.

Open Bite—A condition that prevents the anterior mandibular teeth to achieve proper occlusal relationship to the maxilla; more than the correct amount of jaw opening. Cause may be fractures, dislocations, abnormal tongue habits, or genetic or developmental abnormalities. It involves failure of the anterior maxillary teeth to occlude normally with the mandible.

Operative Dentistry—The branch of dentistry primarily concerned with restoring carious, diseased, or damaged natural teeth to a satisfactory state of health.

Operculum—Cover or lid, such as a tissue over the crown of a tooth.

Oral—Pertaining to the mouth.

- Habit—A frequently repeated practice that may produce injury to teeth and their attachments, the temporal mandibular musculature, or other structures. Oral habits include bruxism, tongue thrust, lip or cheek biting, and biting on hard objects.
- Hygiene—The laws of health as applied to the mouth.
- Pathology—The study of diseases of hard and soft tissues of the mouth.
- Surgery—The branch of surgery dealing with the operative procedures as related to the teeth and jaws.

Orthodontics—The branch of dentistry concerned with the detection, prevention, and correction of abnormalities in the positioning of the teeth in relationship to the jaws.

Orthodontist—A dentist who has met all requirements to qualify as a specialist in the practice of orthodontics.

Orthopantomograph Film—An extraoral view of the teeth and associated structures on a single, continuous film. It is similar to a panorex film.

Osseous Tissue—Bone tissue.

Osseous Surgery (Periodontal)—Surgical correction or therapeutic treatment performed to eliminate osseous deformities and create a more favorable environment; removal of diseased and defective bone tissue.

Ostectomy—The excision of bone; in periodontics, the excision of bone around the teeth or tooth roots to remove pockets or to provide a physiologic form.

Osteitis—Inflammation of the bone.

Overbite—Vertical overlap of the upper teeth over the lower teeth; overlapping of the mandibular incisors by maxillary incisors.

Overjet—The horizontal overlap of the upper teeth over the lower teeth; projection of maxillary incisors beyond the mandibular incisors.

Overlay—An inlay or splint that fits over the biting or grinding surface of a tooth.

Palatal—Of or pertaining to the roof of the mouth.

Palatal Bone—The bone that forms the posterior portion of the hard palate.

Palate—The roof of the mouth, consisting of a hard anterior part and a soft movable part. The palatal structures separate the mouth from the nasal cavity.

Palatine—Of or pertaining to the palate.

Palliative Treatment—Treatment that relieves pain or prevents a condition from becoming worse, but does not cure it.

Panoramic—A term applied to any one of several techniques for making an x-ray picture of all the teeth and contiguous structures on a single film.

Panorex—See X-Ray.

Pantograph—An instrument used for occlusal tracing as a part of extensive equilibration.

Papilla—A small, nipple-shaped elevation or protuberance.

- Intradental—The gingiva filling the intradental spaces between two teeth. It is partly free and partly attached to the gingival tissues.
- Of Tongue—Finger-like elevations on the surface of the tongue.

Partial Denture—A prosthesis replacing one or more, but not all, natural teeth and associated structures; may be removable or fixed, unilateral, or bilateral.

PCP—Plaque Control Program.

Pedodontics—The specialty of children's dentistry. It includes training the child to accept dentistry, restoring and maintaining the primary, mixed, and permanent dentitions, applying preventive measures for dental

caries and periodontal disease, and preventing, intercepting, and correcting various problems of occlusion.
Peg Laterals—The lateral incisors that are peg-shaped due to a developmental disturbance.
Periapical—Tissues surrounding the apex of a tooth.
Pericoronal—The tissues surrounding the crown of a natural tooth.
Pericoronitis—Inflammation of the tissues over a partially erupted tooth or surrounding the crown of an erupted tooth. It frequently involves an erupting third molar, and there may be infection in the area.
Periodontal Membrane—The fibers between the alveolar bone and the tooth that holds the tooth in its socket; a modified periosteum.
Periodontics—The science of examination, diagnosis, and treatment of diseases affecting the periodontium.
Periodontitis—Inflammation of the periodontium that may cause alterations of the periodontal process. It may be caused by environmental or systematic factors.
Periodontium—Collectively, the tissues that surround and support the tooth.
Periodontoclasia—Condition characterized by inflammation accompanied by degenerative and retrogressive changes in the periodontium.
Periodontosis—Degeneration of the periodontium; a noninflammatory condition. With resorption of the alveolar bone, loosening and migration of the teeth occur. It is a rare disease, usually occurring in young people.
Periosteum—A layer of connective tissue, which is a tough, fibrous membrane that covers the outer surface of all bone and varies in thickness in the different areas of the bone.
Permanent Teeth—The teeth that replace the primary teeth.
PFC—Porcelain face crown.
Pin Pontic—A pontic with a long pin porcelain facing. Metal pins are embedded in a porcelain facing and extend out of it lingually. The pins fit into a customized cast metal backing that finishes the occlusal surface.
Pinlay (Pinledge)—A thin cast inlay that depends in part on small parallel pins that fit into the prepared tooth for its retention. Pinledge crowns are modified three-quarter crowns gaining retention from cast pins.
Pit—An indentation; a depression.
Pivots—Elevations, usually artificially developed, on the occlusal surface of natural or artificial posterior teeth to induce mandibular rotation. The term may also be used in reference to dowel pins. Pivots may or may not be adjusted.
PJC—Porcelain jacket crown.
Plane—A term used to describe an ideal, flat surface, which intersects solid body and extends in various directions.

Axial—A hypothetical plane that parallels the long axis of an object.

Bite—An appliance that covers the palate and has an incline or flat plane at the anterior border. It provides resistance to the mandibular incisors when there is contact.

Occlusal—A plane established by the occlusal surfaces of the bicuspids and molars of both the upper and lower jaw in opposition. In orthodontics, a line between two points that represents one-half of the incisal overbite and one-half of the cusp height of the posterior molars.

Plaque—An accumulation of bacteria and debris on the tooth's surfaces.
Plastic—In dentistry, the capacity to be moved. A restorative material, ie, amalgam, cement, gutta-percha, and resin, which is soft at the time of insertion and may be shaped or molded before it hardens or sets.
Plastic Fillings—See Restorations.
Pocket—A space or pocket between the affected tooth and the diseased epithelium; diseased gingival tissues with resulting discoloration, retraction from the root, bleeding and presence of exudate. Depth of the pocket would be limited by the epithelial attachment at the apex of the root.
POH—Personal oral hygiene.
Polishing—The act of buffing and shining the teeth.
Pontic—The part of a fixed bridge that is suspended between abutments and replacing a missing tooth; an artificial tooth in a removable denture.
Porcelain—A tooth-colored, sand-like material; used for inlays, facings, crowns, pontics, and denture teeth. It fuses at high temperatures to form a hard substance

much like enamel in appearance. Dental porcelain is a fuse mixture that is glass-like.

Post—In partial denture work, the minor connector that attaches the clasp body to the framework; an upright, metal device that extends into a tube tooth to retain it; in restorative dentistry, a metal projection in crowns to give strength. It may extend into the root of a pulpless tooth, or it may extend through the root into the alveolar bone.

Post and Core—A single cast unit that provides strength and restores lost structure. It is placed into the tooth, followed by the permanent exterior restoration, usually a crown.

Postdam Area—The soft tissues along the junction of the hard and soft palate where pressures can be applied for retention of a denture. Special provision is designed into the denture for the purpose of sealing against the resilient soft tissue in the palate.

Posterior Teeth—All teeth located distal to the cuspids; a tooth having an occlusal surface.

Postpermanent Dentition—Teeth that erupt after the loss of permanent dentition. It is a rare condition and these teeth are usually impacted accessory teeth that erupt following the insertion of dentures.

Predeciduous Dentition—Teeth that precede the primary dentition. It is a rare condition in which teeth are present at birth or erupt after birth. They are not fully developed and consist only of enamel or enamel and dentin.

Premolars—Bicuspids.

Primary Stress-Bearing Area—The area of the mouth that is suited to withstand heavy stress from wearing dentures.

Primary Teeth—The first teeth to erupt in childhood.

Primate Spaces—In primary dentition, spaces mesial to maxillary cuspids and distal to mandibular cuspids.

Process—In anatomy, a marked prominence or projection of a bone. In dentistry, a series of operations that convert a waxed pattern of a dental appliance into a permanent restoration composed of some relatively indestructible material.

Alveolar—The part of the bone that surrounds and supports the teeth in the maxilla and the mandible.

Condyloid—The posterior process on the ramus of the mandible that articulates with the mandibular fossa of the temporal bone.

Coronoid—The anterior part of the upper and ramus of the mandible, to which the temporal muscle is attached.

Maxillary—The irregular-shaped bone forming one-half of the upper jaw. The upper jaw is made up of two maxillas.

Palatine—One of four shelf-like extensions of the embryonic upper jaw that give rest to the premaxillary palate.

Prognathic—A protrusive relationship of the jaws to the head.

Prognathism—Facial disharmony due to prominence or projection of one or more jaws, occurring most frequently in the mandible.

Prophylactic Odontotomy—The technique of opening and filling structural imperfection of enamel to prevent dental caries.

Prophylaxis—Prevention of disease by removal of calculus, stains, and other extraneous material from the teeth; cleaning of the teeth by a dentist or dental hygienist.

Prosthesis (plural, prostheses)—An artificial replacement of one or more natural teeth or associated structures; replacement of a part of the body.

Prosthetic—Pertaining to prostheses.

Prosthodontics—The branch of dentistry concerned with restoration and maintenance of function by replacement of natural teeth.

Provisional Splinting—A therapeutic appliance placed to assist with healing, repair, or cure. It may serve as a temporary stabilization for mobile teeth.

Proximal Surface—The surface of a tooth that is next to another tooth; usually, the mesial or distal surface, unless the tooth is rotated.

Pulp—Highly vascular and innervated connective tissue, which fills the pulp chamber and root canals. "Vitality" of pulp refers to the health of the pulp. When there is degeneration or the pulp has been removed, the tooth is termed nonvital.

Pulp Canal—See Root Canal.

Pulp Capping—See Capping.

Pulp Chamber—The space in the coronal portion of

the tooth occupied by the pulp.

Pulpectomy—Complete removal of either vital or inflamed pulp from the chamber and root canal. The term is not appropriate in reference to necrotic pulp tissue.

Pulpotomy—Removal of dental pulp in the coronal portion of the tooth; removal of exposed vital pulp to retain a healthy pulp in the root. It may be partial or complete.

Pyogenic—Pus-producing.

Pyorrhea—Flow of pus from the periodontal wound; an outdated term replaced by "periodontitis" or "periodontal disease."

Quadrant—One-fourth of the two dental arches; one-half of each arch.

Radectomy—Surgical removal of a part of a tooth root.

Radiculalgia—Neuralgia of the nerve roots.

Radicular—Pertaining to the tooth root.

Radiograph—A picture produced on a sensitive surface by a form of radiation other than light; an x-ray or gamma-ray photograph. It produces a shadow image.

Ramus—The ascending part of the mandible from the angle to the condyle.

Reattachment—The readaptation of the gingival and underlying tissues to the root surface of a tooth.

Rebase—Placement of the denture base material without changing the occlusal relations of the teeth; adding to the denture base to compensate for altered tissues.

Recalcification—See Remineralization.

Reline—Resurface the tissue-borne areas of a denture with new material.

Remineralization—The use of calcium hydroxide or similar materials as a treatment prior to placing a temporary restoration.

Remote Denture—See Denture.

Replantation (Reimplantation)—The replacement of natural teeth that have been dislodged or removed, either accidentally or unintentionally; reinsertion of a natural tooth to the alveolar socket.

Resin—A term commonly used to indicate organic substances that may be solid or semisolid, translucent or transparent. Resins are named according to their chemical composition, physical structure, and means for activation or curing. Examples are acrylic resin, autopolymer resin, synthetic resin, styrene resin, and vinyl resin.

Resorption—Loss of substance. Alveolar resorption is loss of substance or structure; reduction in size or residual alveolar ridges; destruction of bone. Primary tooth roots are reabsorbed as a part of normal shedding.

Rest—An extension of the prosthesis that provides support.

Restoration—Restoring natural or ideal contour and function. The term relates to fillings, inlays, crowns, bridgework, partial and complete dentures, and restoration of contour and function as a result of disease and other factors.

Retained Root—A root or part of a root, remaining soft or hard tissue.

Retainer—An abutment tooth in a fixed bridge that may be in the form of an inlay or a partial or full crown; a removable prosthesis, a clasp, attachment, or device used for fixation or stabilization. In orthodontics, an appliance to maintain the altered position of the teeth and jaws until they stabilize.

Retention—In removable prostheses, a resistance to force or movement. In orthodontics, an appliance used to maintain the teeth in the position to which they have been moved for harmonious relationship. The necessary procedure in a cavity preparation to prevent loss or displacement of a restoration.

Retrognathism—A disharmony as a result of one or both jaws being posterior to normal facial relationships.

Retrograde Amalgam—Amalgam filling placed into the apex of a tooth root; also called *retrofilm* or *reverse amalgam*. It would normally follow some form of endodontic therapy.

Retroversion—Indicated teeth or associated structures that are posterior to the generally accepted standard.

Ridge Bar—A splint or lingual bar that connects abutments.

Roach Clasp—See Clasp.

Root—The anatomic part of a tooth, normally within the alveolar bone, and attached to it by the periodontal ligament.

Root Amputation—Removal of one or more roots of a

multirooted tooth. Also, see Apicoectomy.

Root Canal—The space within the root of a tooth, containing nerves and blood vessels. They connect the pulp chamber with the apex of the root.

Root Canal Therapy—Endodontic therapy; treatment of a tooth having a damaged pulp, or associated with periapical disease. It is normally performed by completely removing the pulp, sterilizing the pulp chamber and root canals, and filling those spaces with a sealing material.

Root Planing—The smoothing of roughened root surfaces by the use of scalers and curets.

Root Resection—Removal of all or part of the tooth root. See Root Amputation.

Rotated Teeth—Teeth rotated out of normal position. The laterals and bicuspids are the most frequently rotated.

Rugae—The irregular ridges in the mucous membrane covering the anterior part of the hard palate.

Saliva—The digestive secretions from the salivary glands into the mouth. It assists in chewing and preparing the food for digestion by moistening the food and lubricating the mouth. It initiates digestion of starches; it aids in excretion of waste products and regulation of water balance.

Sanitary Pontic—A conical-shaped pontic that has been contoured to provide a sanitary environment.

Scale—To remove calculus (tartar) and stains from the teeth with a scaler and other special instruments.

Sealer—A material used to fill the space around silver or gutta-percha points as a part of root canal therapy.

Secondary Dentin—Dentin formed on the inner walls of the pulp cavity after the tooth is fully formed; a protective mechanism whereby the pulp seeks to protect itself from injury. It may be the result of disturbances or irritation and stimulation of the odontoblasts.

Secondary Stress-Bearing Area—An area of the mouth not suited for bearing a major part of the pressure under a denture; a relief area in an upper denture.

Sedative—Drugs or any other means of producing a calming effect.

Semiprecious—Materials developed for dental restorations that have a lesser amount of precious metal.

Semiridge Bridge (Broken Stress Bridge)—A fixed bridge in which one of the connections between the units is composed of a male/female joint that reduces the effect of stress.

Septic Alveolus (Dry socket)—Pain from breakdown or loss of the blood clot from a tooth socket following extraction.

Shell Crowns—See Crowns.

Shell Teeth—Teeth having a form or dentinogenesis imperfecta; lack of root development and the pulp chambers wider than normal.

Sialolithiasis—Salivary gland or duct stones.

Sialolithotomy—Incisions of a salivary gland or duct to remove stones.

Silica—One of the three major ingredients in dental porcelain; provides stiffness and hardness.

Sinus—A cavity, a canal or passage, recess or hollow space.

Alveolar—A pathologic cavity in the alveolus connecting with either the oral or nasal cavity.

Maxillary—The bony cavity in the body of the maxilla. In dental x-rays, the floor of the sinus may be seen above the alveolar process. Occasionally, the apices of the teeth including the cuspid and posterior teeth may extend into the sinus.

Sinusotomy—Incision into a sinus cavity.

Socket—An alveolus in the alveolar process that holds the roots of a tooth.

Sodium Fluoride—A solution applied topically to the teeth and used in drinking water as a caries preventive agent; also used with kaolin and glycerin as a desensitizing agent for hypersensitive dentin.

Space Maintainer—A fixed removable appliance placed to maintain space created by the premature loss of one or more teeth. It may also be used to create space by moving teeth apart while holding the space open.

Space Obtainer—An appliance used to increase the space between two teeth.

Space Regainer—A fixed removable appliance to move a displaced tooth into proper position; commonly used for the first permanent molar.

Splint—An appliance constructed of metal, acrylic resin, or modeling compound, designed to retain teeth in position.

Acrylic resin biteguard—An appliance for immobilizing teeth, eliminating the effect of traumatic oral habits by covering the occlusal and incisal surfaces of the dental arch.

Cross-arch bar—A metal bar that united one or more teeth in one side of the arch to teeth on the opposite side; also used to stabilize weakened teeth against lateral forces.

Fixed—A fixed prosthesis used for treatment of periodontal disease, designed to prevent adverse occlusal forces and maintenance of good gingival health. It stabilizes and immobilizes the teeth and may also replace missing teeth.

Gunning's—a maxillomandibular splint used with maxillofacial surgery.

Inlay—A casting to provide retention or support to one or more approximating teeth. This may include two inlays soldered together or a single casting spanning the approximating teeth.

Intradental—A splint applied to the teeth on the labial and/or lingual surfaces to provide points for attaching mandibular and/or maxillofacial traction and/or fixation.

Provisional—A therapeutic appliance designed to assist in healing, repair, and cure of periodontally involved teeth. It is semifixed and may consist of connected full crowns to stabilize the teeth during the mandibular movements. Materials used are acrylic resin, metal, and combinations of both.

Surgical—A thin acrylic or metal form that fits the contour of the alveolar ridge and is used after surgery. The function is to protect the surgical area during healing.

Splinting—Stabilizing or immobilization of periodontally involved teeth. Splinting may be accomplished with acrylic resin biteguards, orthodontic band splints, wire ligation, provisional splints, and fixed prostheses.

Stannous Acid Fluoride—A more recently developed form of fluoride, applied topically in a single treatment.

Stayplate (Flipper)—An acrylic partial, with or without wire clasps, which replaces one or more teeth; used as a temporary replacement until a more permanent prosthesis is prepared.

Steele's Facing—A pontic having a prefabricated backing combined with an acrylic or porcelain grooved facing.

Stressbreaker—An attachment that is incorporated into a removable partial denture or fixed bridge work to relieve pressure on the abutment teeth.

Study Models—See Diagnostic Casts.

Subgingival Curettage—See Gingival Curettage.

Supernumerary Tooth—A tooth in excess of the regular or normal number.

Supraocclusion—Abnormal overlap of a dental arch or group of teeth over the opposing arch or group of teeth.

Surfaces—Tooth surfaces.

Buccal—Pertaining to or adjacent to the cheek.

Distal—Away from the median plane of the face, following the curvature of the dental arch.

DLG—The distal lingual groove, which normally extends to the occlusal.

E—The external gingival surface.

Facial—The same as labial or buccal, external surface or next to the face.

Incisal—Cutting surface of anterior teeth.

Labial—Same as facial, but toward the mouth and lips.

Lingual—Pertaining to or adjacent to the tongue.

Mesial—Toward the center of the median line of the dental arch.

Occlusal—The masticating or grinding surfaces of molars and bicuspids.

Proximal—The surface nearest the adjacent tooth.

Tartar—See Calculus.

Temporal Bone—The irregular-shaped bone at the side and base of the skull.

Temporomandibular Joint—The joint formed by the condyle for the mandible and the temporal bone.

TMJ Syndrome (Costen's Syndrome)—The symptoms associated with malfunction of the temporomandibular joint, frequently caused by loss of molar support or absence of occlusal balance.

Three-Quarter Crown—See Crowns.

Tinker Bridge—A fixed bridge involving the use of sanitary pontics.

Tissue Bar—A lingual bar connecting crowns for the purpose of stabilizing or reducing stress. They are placed adjacent to the gingival tissues.

Tissue-borne—A partial denture is referred to as a "tissue-borne" when most or all of the masticatory stresses are borne by the soft tissues of the mouth.
Tissue Conditioning—A method of correcting tissue irritation occurring from the wearing of dentures. An impression-type material is placed in the saddle of the denture and, with the denture in place, a displacement of this material indicates any corrections necessary to eliminate distortion from pressure on the tissue. This procedure is more complicated than the usual adjustment.
Tooth-borne—A partial denture is referred to as "tooth-borne" when most or all of the masticatory forces are carried by the abutment teeth.
Traumatogenic Occlusion—A malocclusion that is injurious to the teeth or associated structures; an injury in the periodontal tissues produced by an occlusal pressure.
Treatment Partial Denture—A denture used for a limited time during the transition from normal dentition to complete dentures. It may be the same or similar to a stayplate, thumbplate, splitplate, or butterfly partial, which is also known as a *flipper*. It may be used during a healing period or for esthetics before a permanent denture is constructed.
Trial Baseplate—The temporary foundation used in established maxillomandibular relationship for arrangement of the teeth in a denture, consisting of the baseplate and the occlusal rim.
Trifurcation—The area where roots divide into a trirooted tooth.
Truss Bar—The metal piece placed across the edentulous space between two bridge abutments, on which the pontic is constructed.
Tube Tooth—An artificial tooth containing a vertical channel in which a pin or metal post is placed to secure the tooth to a denture base.
Tuberosity—The posterior aspect of the maxillary alveolar process. It may appear as a normal bone curving upward, or it may be in the form of a bridge.
Unerupted Tooth—Tooth that has not broken through the bone or gingival tissue.
Vault—In the oral cavity, the palate or roof of the mouth; a prepared cavity in the bone for placing an implant.
Veneer Crown—See Crowns.
Vertical Dimension—The vertical height of the face with the teeth in occlusion; vertical relationship; the degree of jaw separation when teeth are in contact. This measurement is usually made from the tip of the chin to the base of the nose.
Vestibular Space—Space in the oral cavity bounded by the teeth and gums and externally by the lips and cheeks.
Vestibule—The part of the oral cavity that lies between the teeth and the gingiva or between the residual alveolar ridge and the lips and cheeks.
Vestibuloplasty—Revision of the vestibule; frequently performed to accommodate the placing of dentures.
Vitality—Presence of vital dental pulp in the mouth.
Vitality Test—A test using thermal electrical or mechanical stimuli to determine the vitality of the dental pulp.
X-ray—Roentgen-ray; called x-ray by the discoverer because of its enigmatic character. It has also been named roentgen-ray to honor Dr. Wilhelm C. Roentgen and to identify this form of radiation. The term x-ray is more commonly used.

Bitewing—Both upper and lower teeth shown on one film.

Extraoral—Film held outside the mouth and recording larger areas than is possible with smaller film; used to detect cysts and tumors and used with orthodontic treatment.

Full Mouth—Usually consists of 14 periapical films plus bitewings.

Occlusal—An intraoral film showing the lingual surfaces of the teeth in a portion of the palate.

Panorex—An extraoral film that provides a continuous view of the teeth and associated structures. It is used for orthodontics and for detection of fractures, temporomandibular joint disease, cysts, and tumors. It is also taken with the unit having a swinging arm that moves from one side of the arch to the other.

Periapical—So named because it records the entire tooth including the apex of the root and some of the surrounding bone tissues.

X-ray Film—A shadowy negative that provides a means of diagnostic evaluation.

Summary

We have covered some of the common prefixes, suffixes, terms, and procedures that you will see frequently when receiving dental charges. Familiarize yourself with these; by doing so you will be able to correctly identify dental services and procedures and determine whether the services are a covered dental benefit.

Assignments

Complete the Questions for Review.
Complete Terminology Exercises 22-1 to 22-5.

Questions for Review

Directions: Define the following prefixes, suffixes, and terms without looking back into the material just covered. Write your answers in the space provided.

Prefixes and Suffixes

1. mal- ______________________________
2. apex- ______________________________
3. -itis ______________________________
4. labi- ______________________________
5. arthr- ______________________________
6. -desis ______________________________
7. gloss- ______________________________
8. -antr ______________________________
9. lingu- ______________________________
10. bucc- ______________________________

Terms:

11. Anesthetics ______________________________
12. Plane ______________________________
13. Abrasion ______________________________

14. Abutment

15. Pontic

16. Rebase

17. Bridge

18. Bruxism

19. Caries

20. Plaque

21. Impacted tooth

22. Maxilla

23. Median

24. Onlay

25. Splint

If you were unable to answer any of the questions, refer back to the section and then complete the answers.

Exercise 22-1

Directions: Match each term in column 1 with the term in column 2 that is closest to its meaning without looking back in the text.

	Column 1	Column 2
________	1. Calculus	A. Gum
________	2. Primary	B. Cleaning
________	3. Cuspid	C. Composite
________	4. Radiograph	D. Top
________	5. Resin	E. Premolar
________	6. Caries	F. Tartar
________	7. Bridgework	G. Bad breath
________	8. Bicuspid	H. Groove
________	9. Pulp canal	I. Deciduous
________	10. Crown	J. X-ray
________	11. Prophylaxis	K. Canine
________	12. Gingiva	L. Removal
________	13. Fissure	M. Cavities
________	14. Extraction	N. Root Canal
________	15. Halitosis	O. Partial denture

If you were unable to answer any of the questions, refer back to the section and then complete the answers.

Exercise 22-2

Directions: Match each prefix or suffix in column 1 with the term in column 2 that is closest to its meaning without looking back in the text.

	Column 1	Column 2
________	1. fistul-	A. Falling
________	2. -pexy	B. Tongue
________	3. retro-	C. In front of, before
________	4. ante-	D. Development
________	5. -ectomy	E. A way of
________	6. pan-	F. Jaw
________	7. -trophy	G. Duct, tube
________	8. cid-	H. Surgical removal
________	9. -ology	I. Half
________	10. lingu-	J. Pipe, tube
________	11. gnath-	K. Study of
________	12. top-	L. Suspension, fixation
________	13. doch-	M. All
________	14. hemi-	N. Backward
________	15. -ment	O. Place

If you were unable to answer any of the questions, refer back to the section and then complete the answers.

Exercise 22-3

Directions: Define the following prefixes and suffixes without looking back in the text.

1. apex-____________________
2. dys- ____________________
3. -ostomy ____________________
4. infra-____________________
5. -vulse ____________________
6. stom- ____________________
7. -lysis ____________________
8. end- ____________________
9. fren- ____________________
10. calc- ____________________
11. bucc- ____________________
12. labi- ____________________
13. -itis ____________________
14. odont- ____________________
15. -plasia ____________________

If you were unable to answer any of the questions, refer back to the section and then complete the answers.

Exercise 22-4

Directions: Fill the correct dental term in the space provided without looking back in the text.

_______________ 1. A dental restoration shaped to the form of a cavity and then inserted and secured with cement.

_______________ 2. Tissues surrounding the apex of a tooth.

_______________ 3. Doctor of Dental Medicine.

_______________ 4. A collection of pus in a cavity formed within the tissue of the body.

_______________ 5. Any deviation from normal occlusion of the teeth, usually associated with abnormal development and growth of the jaws.

_______________ 6. Pertaining to the mouth.

_______________ 7. The joint formed by the condyle for the mandible and the temporal bone.

_______________ 8. The hard, calcified tissue that covers the anatomic root of a tooth. It is formed by cementoblast and arranged in layers that cover the root dentin.

_______________ 9. Doctor of Dental Surgery.

_______________ 10. An accumulation of bacteria and debris on the tooth's surfaces.

_______________ 11. American Dental Association.

_______________ 12. Complete removal of either vital or inflamed pulp from the chamber and root canal. The term is not appropriate in reference to necrotic pulp tissue.

_______________ 13. The three teeth in each quadrant that are located distal to the second bicuspids and are used for grinding.

_______________ 14. The branch of dentistry concerned with restoration and maintenance of function by replacement of natural teeth.

_______________ 15. The anatomic part of a tooth, normally with the alveolar bone, and attached to it by the periodontal ligament.

If you were unable to answer any of the questions, refer back to the section and then complete the answers.

Exercise 22-5

Directions: Define the following terms in the space provided without looking back in the text.

1. Crown: ______________________________

2. Fluoride: ______________________________

3. Intraoral: ______________________________

4. Prophylaxis: ______________________________

5. Bilateral: ______________________________

6. Amalgam: ______________________________

7. Quadrant: ______________________________

8. Space maintainer: ______________________________

9. Endodontics: ______________________________

10. Full mouth x-ray: ______________________________

11. Partial denture: ______________________________

12. Root canal: ______________________________

13. Overbite: ______________________________

14. Mucous membrane: ______________________________

15. Primary teeth: ______________________________

If you were unable to answer any of the questions, refer back to the section and then complete the answers.

23

Anatomy and Physiology of the Mouth

In this chapter you will learn:

- To name the parts of the tooth and its supporting structures.
- To identify the teeth by numbers and locations.
- The difference between primary and permanent teeth.

Dentists provide services not only for the teeth, but also for their surrounding and supporting structures. Therefore, it is necessary for the Dental Claims Examiner to understand the structure and formation of the entire oral cavity or mouth.

The Oral Cavity

The oral cavity (cavum oris) is an oval-shaped cavity (see Figure 23-1). Technically, it consists of two parts, the vestibule and the mouth cavity. The vestibule is the outer, smaller portion surrounded by the lips, cheeks, gums, and teeth. The mouth cavity consists of the area surrounded by the alveolar arches and the teeth. In other words, the vestibule is the area between the teeth and the cheek or the teeth and the lips, and the mouth cavity is everything inside the teeth. The oral cavity stops at the lips in front, the palate on the top, the cheeks on the sides, the tongue on the bottom, and the oropharynx at the back. The oral cavity does not include the nose, the sinuses, the palates, the nasopharynx, or the laryngopharynx.

The mouth is primarily responsible for the introduction of air, food, and other substances into the body. It is also used for vocalization and speech. The opening of the mouth is connected to the pharynx and the larynx at the back of the mouth.

The process of digestion is begun immediately when food enters the mouth. The teeth break down the food by chewing. In addition, salivary glands secrete saliva, which helps to chemically break down foods and also provides moisture to the mouth.

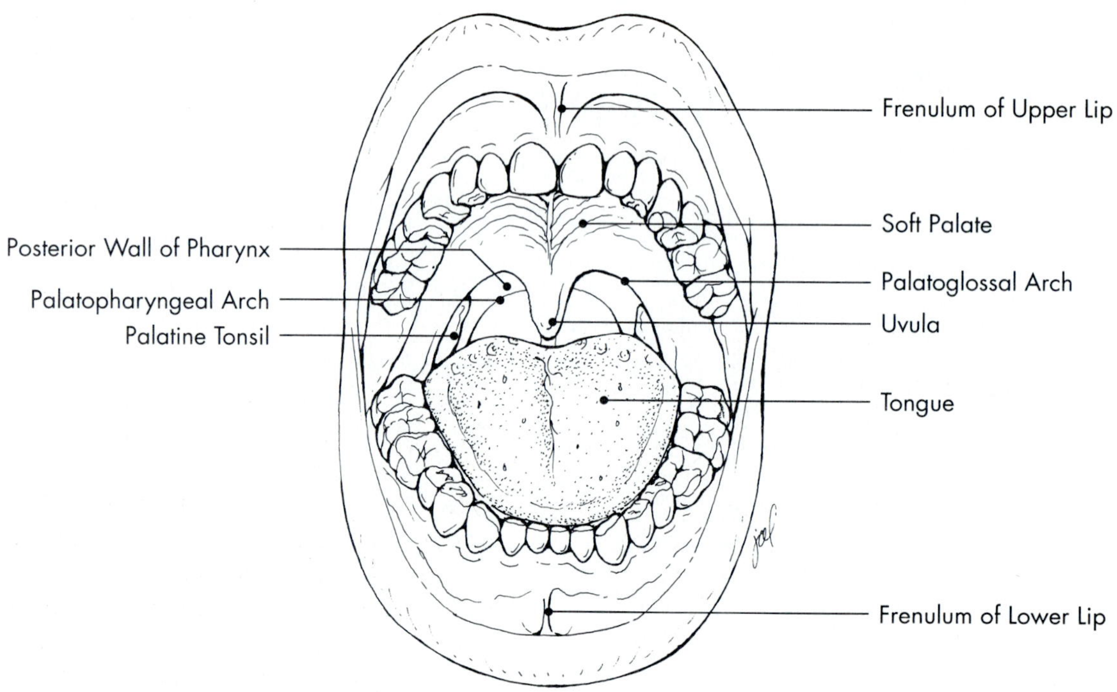

Figure 23-1: The Oral Cavity.

Saliva and Salivary Glands

Saliva consists of salivary amylase and mucus. Salivary amylase is an enzyme that helps to break down food molecules. Mucus is a liquid containing mucin, leukocytes, inorganic salts, epithelial cells, and water. It is secreted by the mucous membranes and glands that line the mouth. The purpose of mucus is to moisten the food and ease the friction as it passes down the esophagus and into the stomach.

Three main pairs of salivary glands supply saliva to the mouth: the parotids, the submandibulars, and the sublinguals. The parotid gland is located beneath the temporomandibular joint, just in front of the ear. Saliva is conveyed to the mouth by the parotid duct. The opening of the parotid duct is on the inside of the cheek, across from the second molar; it can be felt with the tongue.

The submandibular glands are located under the mandible, below the bottom molars. The sublingual gland is located below the floor of the mouth. Both the submandibular glands and the sublingual glands secrete saliva through duct openings on the floor of the mouth under the tongue.

The Palates

The hard and soft palates form the roof of the mouth. The hard palate is toward the front and is so named because it is a hard, bony structure. It is formed by portions of the maxillary and palatine bones. The soft palate is in the rear portion of the mouth and is composed mostly of muscle. The purpose of the soft palate is to prevent foods or liquids from entering the nasal cavity. The opening for the nasal cavity is directly behind the soft palate. The soft palate is aided in this endeavor by the uvula, the small muscular projection that is suspended in the center, posterior portion of the mouth.

The Tongue

Although the tongue is generally not treated under dental services, it is helpful to understand its basic function and how it relates to the surrounding structures in the mouth. The tongue is a muscular organ that lays on the floor of the mouth and continues partway into the pharynx. The tongue consists of a body and a root. The body of the tongue resides in the mouth, and the root extends down the pharynx. Its purpose is to assist in the chewing and swallowing of food and the formation of speech or other sounds.

The surface of the tongue is covered with mucous membrane. Mucous membrane also attaches the tongue to the floor of the mouth, the side walls of the pharynx, and the epiglottis. In addition, the tongue is attached by muscles to the mandibular bone in front, the hyoid bone below, the styloid process behind, and the palate (roof of the mouth) above. A fold (frenulum linguae) runs down the center of the tongue. In addition, the frenulum is a mucous membrane that connects the tongue to the floor of the mouth. There is also a frenulum of the upper and lower lip, which are mucous membranes connecting the lips to the maxilla and mandible.

Papillae

The surface of the tongue is covered with papillae (tiny nipple-like protuberances), which consist of several types:

Filiform papillae are very slender and are situated at the end of the tongue.

Fungiform papillae are broad and flat papillae and resemble a fungus. They are found mostly in the rear central portion of the tongue.

Circumvallate papillae are the large bumps found near the base of the tongue, at the back of the mouth. They are arranged in a V shape.

Gustatory papillae possess a taste bud. They may be either filiform, fungiform, or circumvallate. Not all papillae contain taste buds at any given time.

Taste buds are sensory end organs that help carry the sensation of taste to the brain. They are located on the sides of the papillae and on the epiglottis, the soft palate, and portions of the pharynx. When chemical stimuli (such as food) comes in contact with the taste buds, they produce nervous impulses that are carried by means of the lingual and glossopharyngeal nerves to the brain. This produces one of four basic taste sensations: sweet, bitter, sour, and salty.

The lingual nerves carry nerve impulses from the

taste buds on the front two-thirds of the tongue. The glossopharyngeal nerves carry nerve impulses from the posterior one third of the tongue. The average life-span of a taste bud cell is about 10 days. They are constantly dying off and being replaced by new taste bud cells.

The Gums

The gum, or gingiva, is the firm but soft tissue that surrounds the alveolar process and the mandibular and maxillary bones. It also covers the connecting area between the teeth and bone, thus helping to keep out food particles and bacteria as well as to keep the teeth in place. The gingiva is made up of connective tissue that is covered by mucous membrane.

The alveolar process is the portion of the mandible or maxilla that contains the tooth socket. The word *alveolar* comes from the Latin word meaning "small hollow or cavity."

Normal healthy gums are pink, but they may become red, white, or black when injured or diseased.

The Jaw

The jaw consists of two bones. The upper fixed (nonmovable) bone is the **maxilla**. It is actually made up of two maxillae, which form the skeletal base of most of the upper face, the roof of the mouth, the sides of the nasal cavity and the floor of the orbit (the portion of the skull that contains and protects the eyeball).

The lower jaw is called the **mandible**. The lower jaw is nonfixed (movable), which allows for not only biting and chewing food, but for speech, vocalization (speech and sound), and opening and closing the mouth. The lower jaw is hinged to the upper jaw by a sliding joint called the **temporomandibular joint**. The temporomandibular joint is the only joint in the skull that is synovial, that is, containing synovia.

Synovia is a colorless liquid that lubricates the joints, bursae, and tendon sheaths; it is secreted from synovial membranes. Synovial joints are prone to irritation and inflammation. They are also associated with arthritis, rheumatic fever, and other connective tissue disorders, emotional states, and malocclusional disorders.

Because of the complexity of the problems and the various forms of treatments (many still experimental), disorders of the temporomandibular joint (more often called temporomandibular joint dysfunction or TMJ) are often regarded as a combined medical and dental problem. For further information regarding this disorder, see Chapter 25.

Diseases of the Mouth

Following is a list of the more common diseases of the mouth that may require the services of a dentist:

Gingivitis—Inflammation of the gums. It may include swelling, redness, pain, bleeding, or difficulty in chewing. Possible causes are improper dental hygiene, dentures or dental appliances that fit improperly, or improper occlusion (closure) of the teeth. Occasionally, gingivitis accompanies upper respiratory infections or diseases such as scurvy or metallic poisoning.

Periodontitis—Inflammation of the periodontal tissues. It may be caused by bacteria, calcium deposits, or food particles that collect between the tooth and the gum. If not treated, the infection may spread to the bone, possibly causing loss of the teeth. Periodontitis is the primary cause of tooth loss in people over the age of 35 years.

Periodontosis—Any degenerative disease of the periodontal tissue.

The following are also diseases of the mouth. However, since they are generally treated by a medical doctor rather than a dentist, they will be given only brief mention here.

Stomatitis—Inflammation of the mouth. This can include cold sores, fever blisters, or canker sores.

Cheilitis—Inflammation of the lips.

Cheiloschisis—A deep groove in the lip. It is also known as a harelip or a cleft lip.

Cleft palate—A deep fissure of the palate. It may involve the soft palate, the hard palate, the lip, or all three.

Ankyloglossia—A shortened frenulum of the tongue, preventing proper movement of the tongue.

Sialodentitis—Inflammation of a salivary gland.

The Teeth

Humans have four types of teeth: incisors, canines, premolars, and molars (Figure 23-2). Canines are referred to as cuspids, with premolars called bicuspids and molars called tricuspids. The premolars and molars are considered the posterior teeth, and the incisors and canines are the anterior teeth.

Incisors are located at the front of the mouth and have a sharp edge that is used for biting. The normal adult has eight incisors, four on the top and a matching set of four on the bottom.

Behind the incisors are the cuspids. Cuspids are used for tearing or piercing, and the normal adult has four, one behind each set of incisors. Behind the cuspids are the premolars (bicuspids), which have two (bi-) cusps or grinding protrusions. Behind those are the molars (tricuspids), which have three cusps. The normal adult has eight premolars (two behind each canine) and twelve molars. However, the third molars, or wisdom teeth, may never appear (erupt).

Numbering the Teeth

The normal adult has 32 teeth. Accordingly, these teeth are numbered 1 through 32, beginning with the third molar on the upper right side of the mouth (see Figure 23-3). The upper teeth are the maxillary teeth, numbers 1 through 16. The lower teeth are the mandibular teeth, numbers 17 through 32.

Tooth	Maxillary Teeth
1	Right third molar
2	Right second molar
3	Right first molar
4	Right second premolar
5	Right first premolar
6	Right canine
7	Right lateral incisor
8	Right central incisor
9	Left central incisor
10	Left lateral incisor
11	Left canine
12	Left first premolar
13	Left second premolar
14	Left first molar
15	Left second molar
16	Left third molar

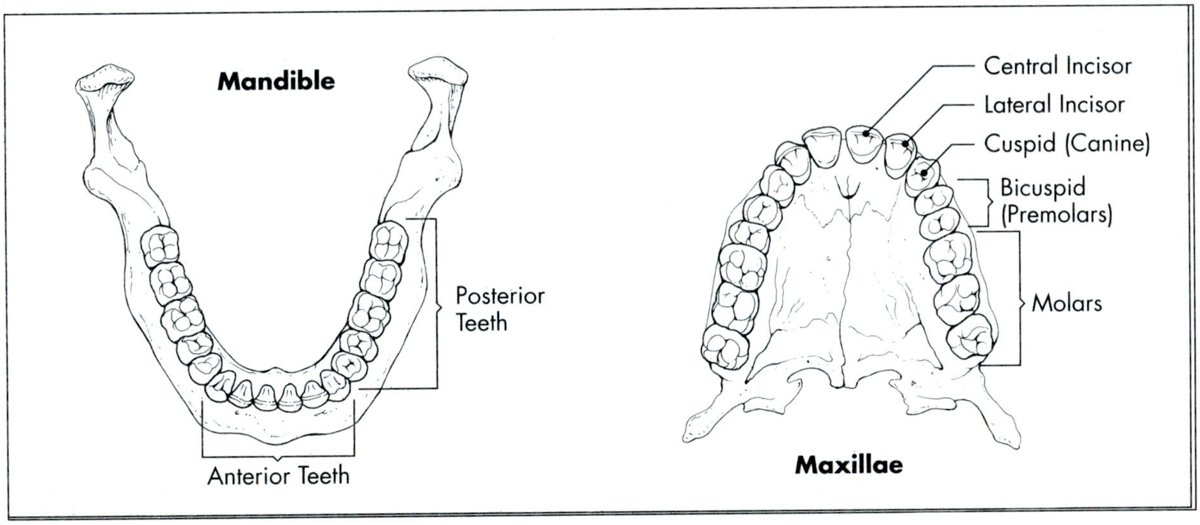

Figure 23-2: Types of teeth and positions in arch.

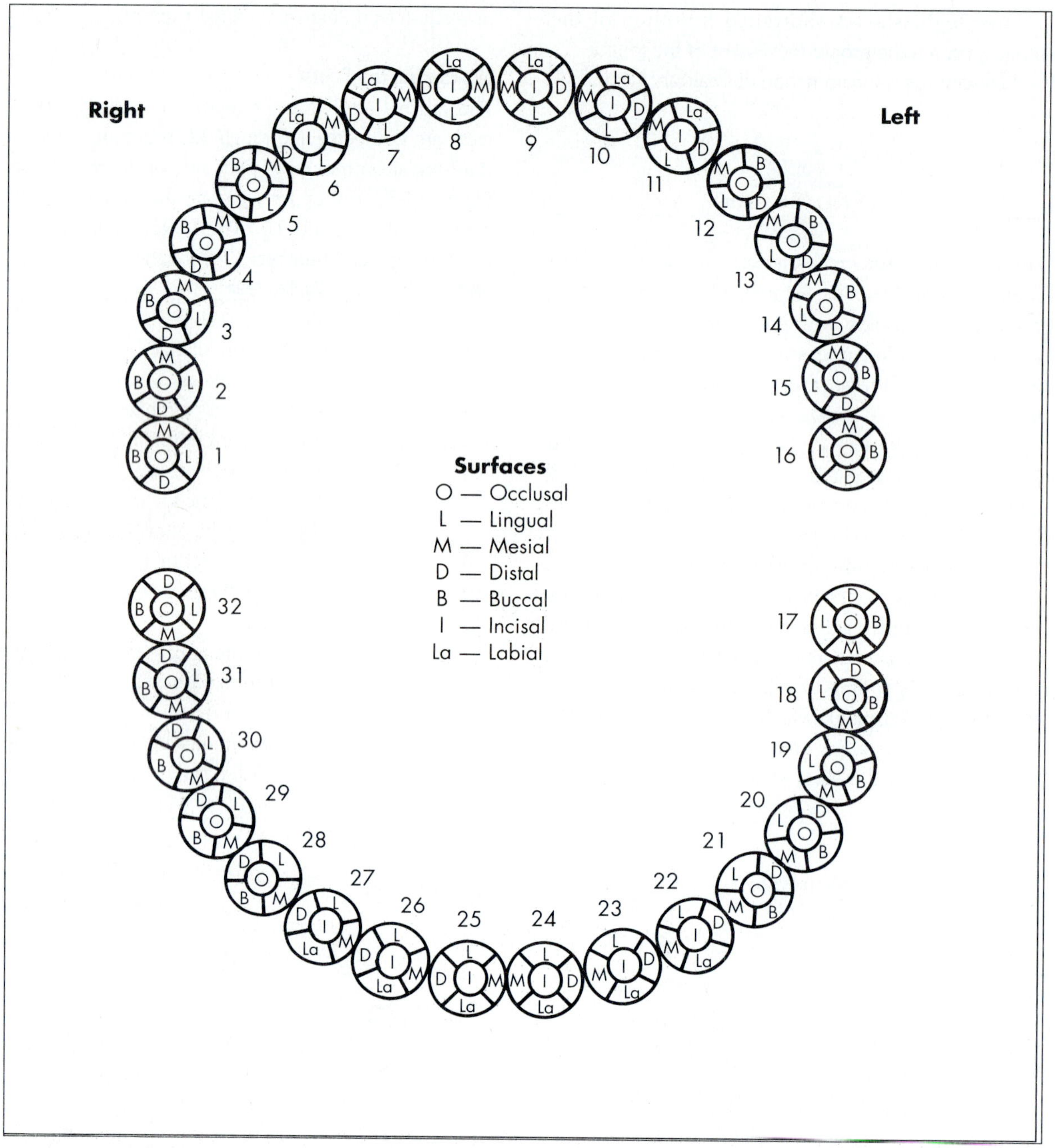

Figure 23-3: Universal System of tooth numbers and surfaces.

Tooth	Mandibular Teeth
17	Left third molar
18	Left second molar
19	Left first molar
20	Left second premolar
21	Left first premolar
22	Left canine
23	Left lateral incisor
24	Left central incisor
25	Right central incisor
26	Right lateral incisor
27	Right canine
28	Right first premolar
29	Right second premolar
30	Right first molar
31	Right second molar
32	Right third molar

The primary or deciduous teeth number to 20 and apply to children. However, the deciduous teeth are lettered rather than numbered to avoid confusion with the adult numbering system. Figure 23-4 shows the lettering of the primary teeth, beginning on the maxillary right and ending on the mandibular right. Note that there are no premolars or third molars in the deciduous set of teeth.

Tooth	Maxillary Tooth
A	Right second molar
B	Right first molar
C	Right cuspid
D	Right lateral incisor
E	Right central incisor
F	Left central incisor
G	Left lateral incisor
H	Left cuspid
I	Left first molar
J	Left second molar

Tooth	Mandibular Tooth
K	Left second molar
L	Left first molar
M	Left cuspid
N	Left lateral incisor
O	Left central incisor
P	Right central incisor
Q	Right lateral incisor
R	Right cuspid
S	Right first molar
T	Right second molar

Some dental services are billed according to the section of the mouth that is treated. Most frequently, this involves periodontal (gum) treatment, but it may also apply to the application of sealants. (For more information regarding these procedures, see Chapter 24.)

The mouth may be divided into either quadrants or sextants. Please refer to Figures 23-5 and 23-6. Quadrants are named and abbreviated in the following manner:

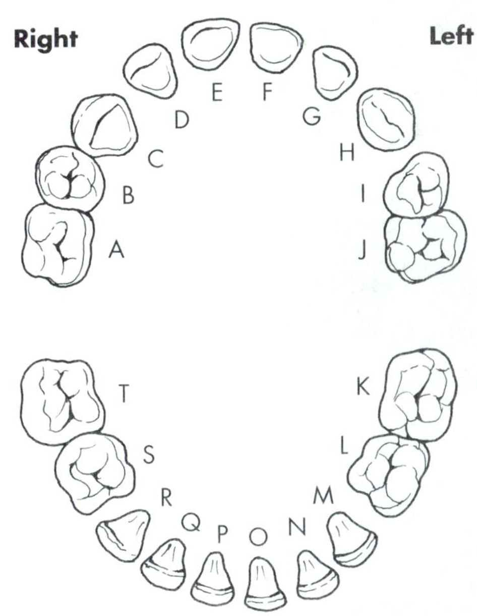

Figure 23-4: **Placement of primary, or deciduous, teeth.**

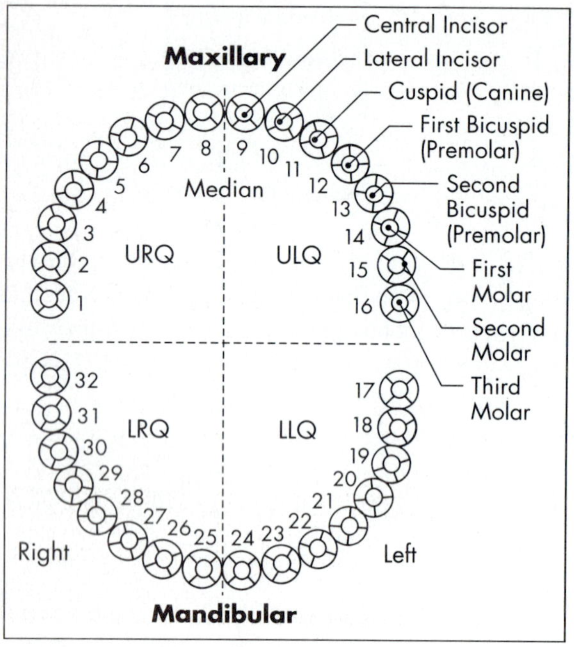

Figure 23-5: Quadrants.

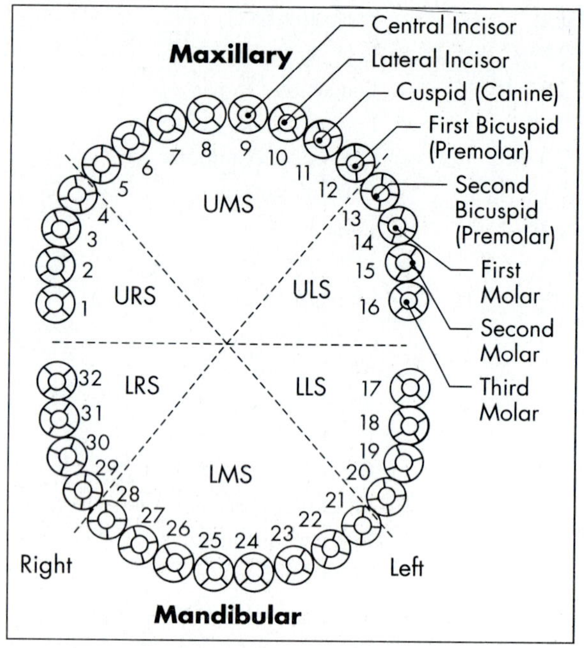

Figure 23-6: Sextants.

URQ Upper Right Quadrant
ULQ Upper Left Quadrant
LRQ Lower Right Quadrant
LLQ Lower Left Quadrant

Sextants are named and abbreviated in the following manner:

URS Upper Right Sextant
UMS Upper Middle Sextant
ULS Upper Left Sextant
LRS Lower Right Sextant
LMS Lower Middle Sextant
LLS Lower Left Sextant

The Structure of the Teeth

Each tooth is divided into three parts: the crown, the neck, and the root. The crown is the portion of the tooth that shows above the gum. The neck is the portion covered by the gum, which links the crown to the root. The root is the portion that is embedded in the bone (see Figure 23-7).

The extreme center of the tooth is called the pulp cavity. This cavity contains the tooth nerves, veins, and arteries that allow essential blood flow into the tooth. The root canal is the portion of the pulp chamber that carries the blood vessels from the tooth socket to the tooth itself. The pulp is made up of connective tissue that contains a network of capillaries. The capillaries supply blood nourishment to the tooth. The pulp also contains lymph vessels and nerve fibers. Surrounding the pulp is the dentin (sometimes called the ivory), which forms the bulk of the tooth. The apex of the tooth is the terminus or end of the root. The root canal connects the pulp chamber with the apex.

In the root and neck of the tooth (the portion below the gum line), the dentin is covered with cementum.

Cementum is a bone-like material. Although hard, it is not in the same category as the enamel or the dentin. The cementum forms a junction with the enamel to seal off the exposed portion of the tooth (the crown). The cementum is actually a part of the periodontium or supporting structure of the tooth, since its main func-

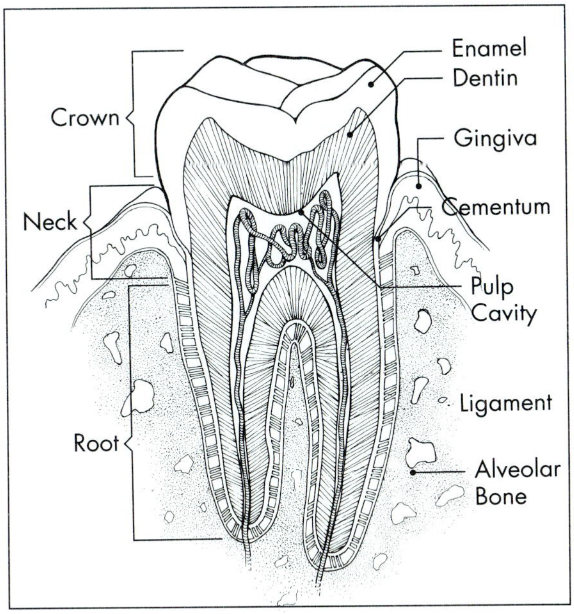

Figure 23-7: Structure of the tooth.

tion is neither biting, chewing, or tooth nourishment.

In the crown of the tooth (the portion above the gum line), the dentin is covered with enamel, which is smooth and white. This is the hardest substance in the human body.

For functional purposes, the tooth is often classified into two parts: the hard part and the soft part. The hard part of the tooth consists of the enamel, the dentin, and the cementum. The main purpose of the hard part is chewing and biting. The soft part of the tooth includes the pulp and the periodontal membrane. The periodontal membrane lines each tooth socket and covers the root of the tooth. The entire periodontal membrane acts as a bond between the cementum and the jawbone (mandible or maxilla). The main purpose of the soft part of the tooth is tooth nourishment.

Cementum, dentin, and enamel are composed chiefly of proteins, calcium carbonate, calcium phosphate, and magnesium phosphate. Calcium and phosphorus are constantly being washed away and replaced. For this reason, the human diet must contain enough calcium and phosphorus to ensure the health of the teeth.

Surfaces of the Teeth

Each tooth has five surfaces. These surfaces differ, depending on whether the tooth is a posterior tooth (premolar or molar) or an anterior tooth (incisor or canine).

Surfaces that appear on all the teeth are the lingual (Li), which is the surface nearest the tongue; the mesial (M), which is the surface nearest the midline (an imaginary line drawn between the maxillary centrals and the mandibular centrals); and the distal (D), which is the surface farthest away from the midline. Posterior teeth have two additional surfaces consisting of the buccal (B), which is the surface nearest the cheek, and the occlusal (O), which is the biting surface. Anterior teeth also have two additional surfaces consisting of the labial (La, L), which is the surface on the anterior teeth nearest the lip, and the incisal (I), which is the biting edge or surface (see Figure 23-8).

The surface names of the primary teeth are the same as for adult teeth. Also, note the tooth surfaces shown in Figure 23-3.

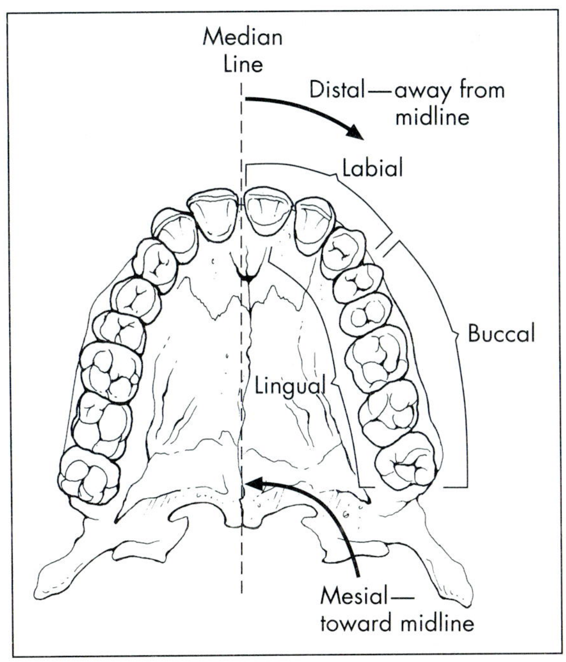

Figure 23-8: Median line and tooth surfaces.

Growth and Development of Teeth

All teeth, including permanent teeth, begin their development before birth. Calcification of the deciduous teeth takes place just before and just after birth. That is why it is important that the mother's diet contain high amounts of calcium, phosphorus, and vitamin D. Without these vital nutrients, the teeth remain soft and are prone to decay. Permanent teeth calcify during infancy and childhood, necessitating the need for high amounts of calcium, phosphorus, and vitamin D in children's diets.

As a general rule, teeth erupt from the midline toward the back. The exception is the first molar, which usually erupts third in the deciduous teeth and first or second in the permanent teeth. The deciduous teeth normally erupt by the time a child is 2 years old. By the time a person reaches 17 to 24 years of age, the full set of permanent teeth is in place. Table 23-1 shows the order and general time of eruption.

Table 23-1: Eruption of Teeth

Deciduous	Erupts (Months)
Central incisor	6–8
Lateral incisor	7–12
Canine	16–20
First molar	12–16
Second molar	20–30

Permanent	Erupts (Years)
Central incisor	6–8
Lateral incisor	7–10
Canine	9–13
First premolar	9–12
Second premolar	10–13
First molar	5–7
Second molar	10–13
Third molar (wisdom)	17–23

Diseases of the Teeth

Following is a list of common diseases and conditions of the teeth that may require the services of a dentist:

Bruxism—Grinding of the teeth. It refers to grinding other than chewing and often occurs at night. If it continues, it can cause abnormal wear on the teeth.

Edentulous—Without teeth.

Dentalgia—A toothache or pain in the tooth. It usually indicates another existing condition such as a dental cavity or a periodontal problem.

Dental plaque—A mass of microorganisms that grows on the exposed portions of the teeth and may spread under the gum line. It is the cause of dental caries and periodontal disease. Calcified dental plaque is called calculus. Most dental plaque can be removed by brushing and by using dental floss. Calculus may need to be removed by a dentist or dental hygienist. Such cleaning of the teeth is called prophylaxis.

Dental caries or cavities—Holes or decayed portions in a tooth. They are caused by the progressive decalcification of a tooth. Decalcification begins when food particles, fluid, or bacteria adhere to the tooth and break down the insoluble calcium salts into soluble salts. The calcium is then washed away and a cavity forms. Proper brushing and use of dental floss can greatly assist in removing food particles and bacteria. Topical application of fluoride while the teeth are still forming (usually prior to age 17 or 18 years) has also proven effective. After a cavity has begun forming, all bacteria must be removed from the hole and the cavity filled. If the cavity is not treated, it may spread into the pulp of the tooth, causing inflammation and abscess. In such a case, root canal treatment may be necessary, or the tooth may need to be extracted. Following are the three categories of cavities:

1. Simple cavities—Involve only one surface of a tooth.
2. Compound cavities—Involve two surfaces of a tooth.
3. Complex cavities—Involve three or more surfaces of a tooth.

Cavities are classified according to the surface(s) of the tooth, the type of surface (smooth or occurring in a pit or fissure), and a numerical grouping. The most common numerical grouping is Black's Classification System, as follows:

Class 1	Caries beginning in structural defects of the teeth, such as fissures or pits.
Class 2	Caries in the proximal surfaces of (the space between) bicuspids and molars.
Class 3	Caries in the proximal surfaces of cuspids and incisors that do not involve removal or restoration of the incisal angle.
Class 4	Caries in the proximal surfaces of cuspids and incisors that do require removal or restoration of the incisal angle.
Class 5	Caries in the top third (gingival third, not pit cavities) of the labial, buccal, or lingual surfaces of the teeth.
Class 6	Caries of incisal edges and cusp tips of the teeth.

For further information regarding treatment of cavities, refer to Chapter 24.

Summary

The primary purpose of the mouth is the ingestion of food, the intake of air, and vocalization. The breakdown of food begins as it enters the mouth. The teeth aid in the digestive process by chewing and breaking down food particles. Further chemical breakdown of food particles is accomplished by the addition of saliva.

Each tooth consists of a crown, a neck, and a root. The tooth itself is made up of dentin, enamel, pulp, and cementum. Each tooth is numbered, and each surface of the tooth is labeled. This eliminates confusion and helps to pinpoint the exact tooth and area where procedures have been performed.

The most common diseases of the teeth are dental caries or cavities. However, teeth can also fall victim to dentalgia, dental plaque, and bruxism.

Assignments

Complete Questions for Review.
Complete Exercises 23-1 to 23-5.

Questions for Review

Directions: Answer the following questions without looking back into the material just covered. Write your answers in the space provided.

1. What is the primary purpose of the mouth? ______

2. Are deciduous teeth numbered or lettered? ______

3. In the permanent tooth numbering system, what tooth is number 1? ______

4. What is the palate? ______

5. What are the seven surfaces of the teeth and their abbreviations? ______
   a. ______
   b. ______
   c. ______
   d. ______
   e. ______
   f. ______
   g. ______

If you were unable to answer any of the questions, refer back to the section and then complete the answers.

Exercise 23-1

Directions: Label the surfaces of the teeth on Figure 23-9A and B. The teeth are shown from the inside of the mouth with the midline being to the left.

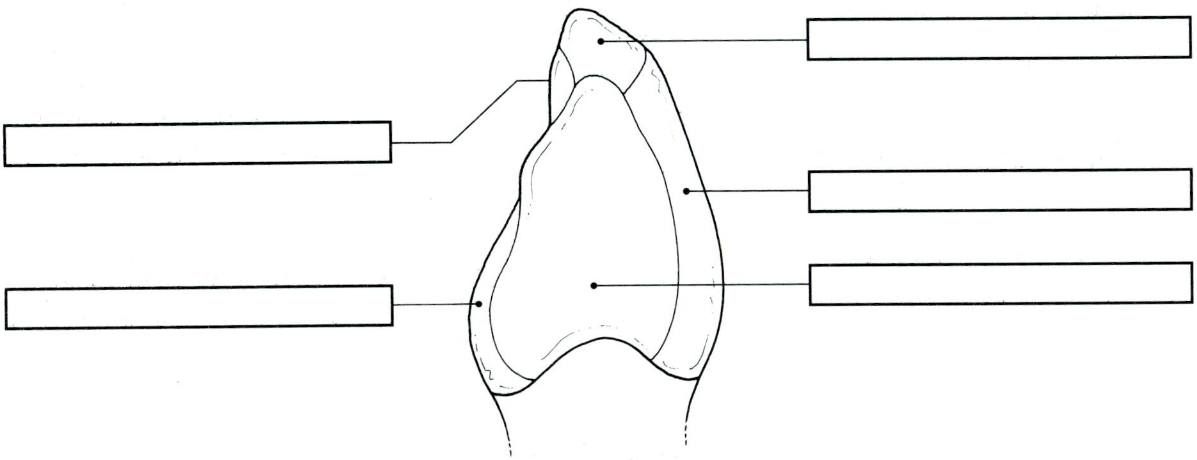

Anterior Tooth

Figure 23-9A: Anterior Tooth

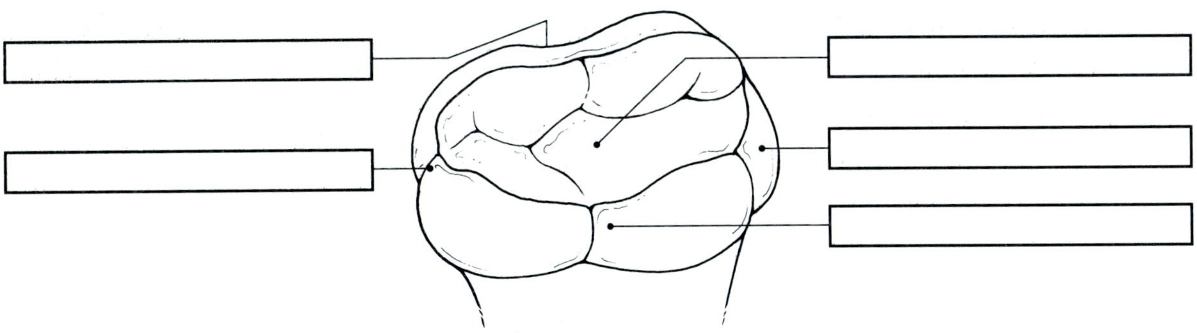

Posterior Tooth

Figure 23-9B: Posterior Tooth

Exercise 23-2

Directions: Number the teeth in Figure 23-10.

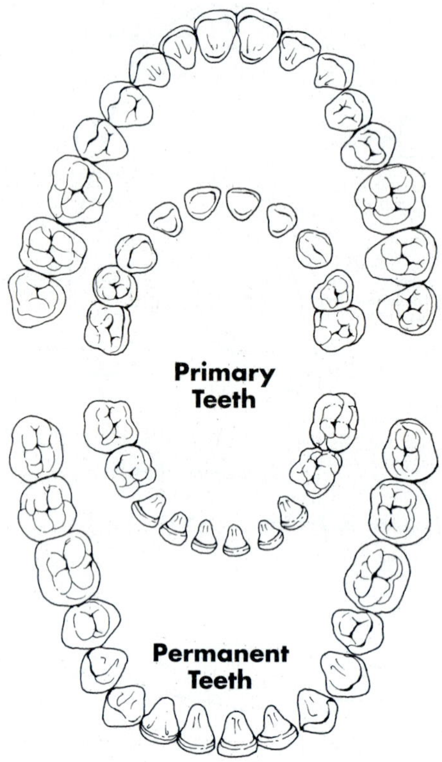

Figure 23-10: The teeth.

Exercise 23-3

Directions: Place the names of the teeth on the line next to them in Figure 23-11.

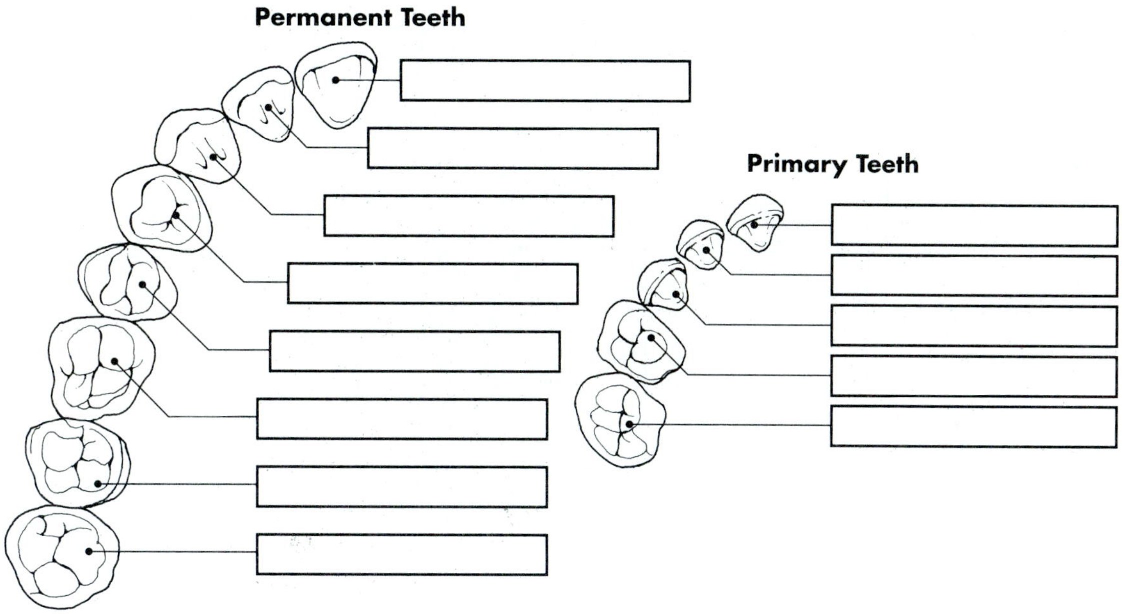

Figure 23-11: The teeth.

Exercise 23-4

Directions: Label the parts of the tooth in Figure 23-12.

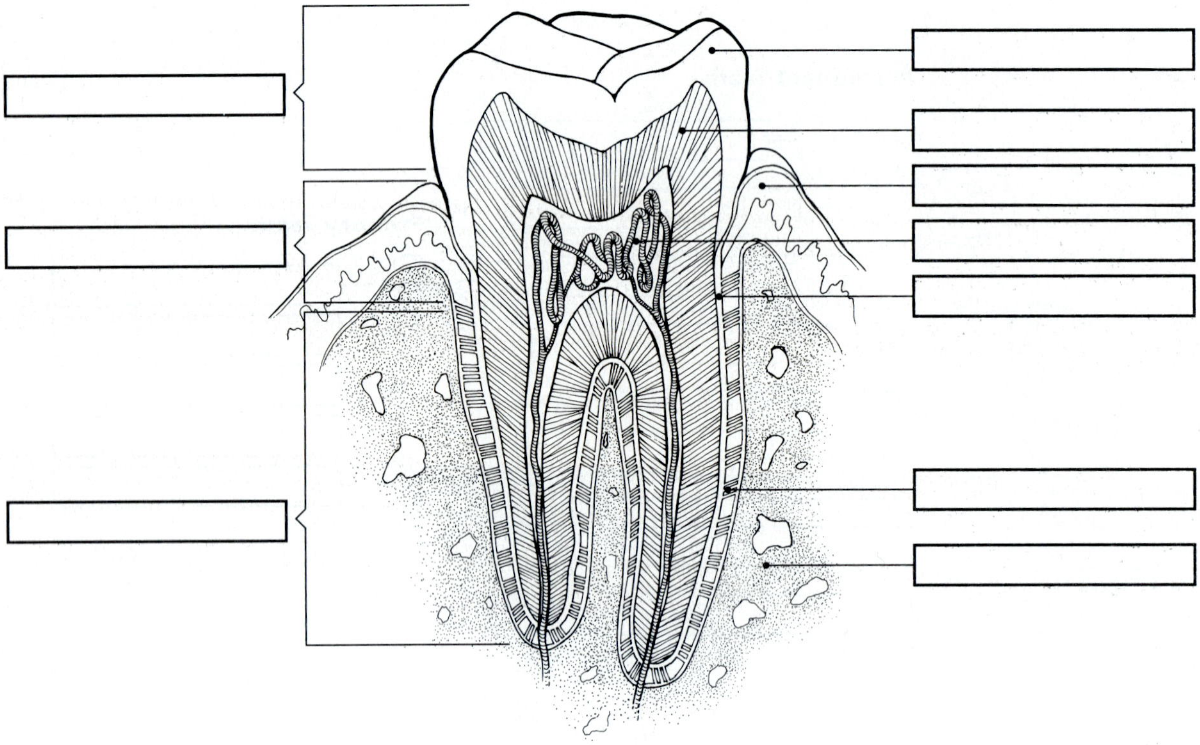

Figure 23-12: The tooth.

Exercise 23-5

Directions: Divide the teeth into quadrants and sextants in Figures 23-13 and 23-14.

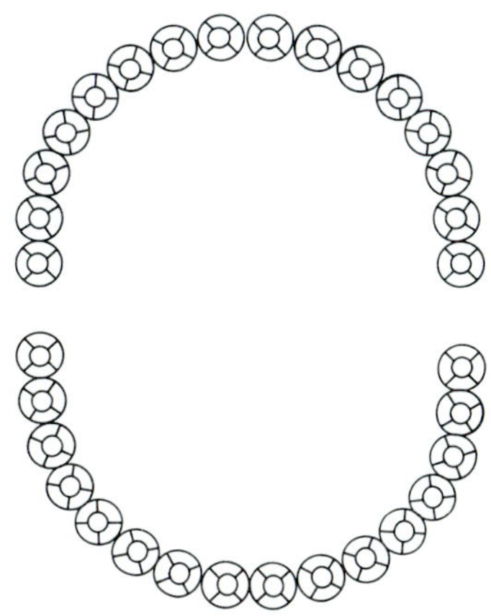

Figure 23-13: Quadrants.

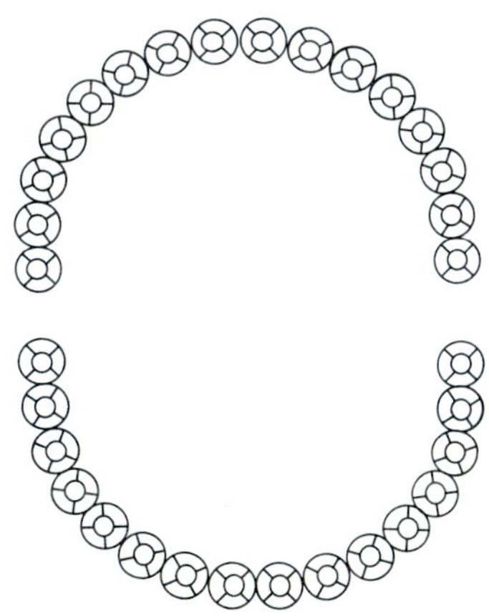

Figure 23-14: Sextants.

24
Dental Services and Coding

In this chapter you will learn:

- To identify the different types of dental services performed.
- To identify services that fall within certain ranges to determine the types of services rendered.
- How codes are broken down and when specific codes should be used.

The terms Dentistry and Dental are derived from the Latin word *dens,* meaning teeth. Dentistry is officially that department of the healing arts that is concerned with the teeth, the oral cavity (mouth), and its associated structures. This includes diagnosis, treatment, restoration, and replacement of missing portions or parts. It also includes surgical procedures performed in and about the inside of the mouth or oral cavity.

Dental Professionals

Dentists are doctors who have received a Doctor of Medical Dentistry (DMD) degree. Other recognized titles and degrees include:

DDS Doctorate in Dental Surgery (DMD and DDS are graduate degrees)
FACD Fellow of American College of Dentists
FAGD Fellow of the Academy of General Dentistry
FICD Fellow of the International College of Dentists, an English degree with international recognition
MDS Master of Dental Science

Diplomas are also awarded to dentists who have met the criteria for certification as a specialist in a chosen field. For the purposes of this book, we will use the term dentist to refer to all of the above.

Dental Treatment

In dentistry, the following four pathologic conditions require treatment:

1. Tooth decay
2. Tissue or periodontal disease
3. Trauma to teeth (including loss of teeth) or supporting structures
4. Development diseases such as cysts, tumors, and abscesses

Services are also performed in dentistry for other than existing pathologic conditions. Some of these services (such as prophylaxis, x-rays, fluoride treatments, and repair of dentures and bridgework) are specifically included as covered dental services under most plans, but are usually subject to limitations.

Other services may be performed, not for a pathologic condition but primarily for cosmetic or similar reasons, or they may be elective procedures of the patient or dentist. Although the particular type or category of service that is received might be covered under the plan, benefits are usually not provided for services performed for cosmetic or similar purposes or for elective services. An example would be the placing of crowns on healthy teeth that require no restoration. That is, the crowns are placed to improve the appearance of the tooth such as color or shape.

Dental Coding

In 1969, the American Dental Association (ADA) created a coding system that also served to categorize dental services. This system also established a uniform nomenclature for all dental services. The ADA listing uses a four-digit coding system and classifies procedures under certain categories. Services (and thus their codes) are defined based on the type of treatment provided. Following is a list of the 10 ADA categories. Most dental plans separate services into similar classifications.

1. Diagnostic—Routine services designed to assist in the diagnosis and planning of required treatment.
2. Preventive—Routine services designed to prevent decay, gum disease, and so on, through the care of the dental structures before disease has occurred.
3. Restorative—Treatment involving the use of fillings or crowns to save or restore dental structures.
4. Endodontics—Treatment of dental pulp or other internal structures of the teeth.
5. Periodontics—Treatment of the tissues surrounding and supporting the teeth.
6. Prosthodontics, removable—Replacement of the natural teeth through the use of a removable appliance(s).

7. Prosthodontics, permanent—Replacement of the natural teeth through the use of a permanent appliance(s).
8. Oral surgery—Treatment on the internal structures of the mouth limited to the dental structures and surrounding tissues.
9. Orthodontics—Correction or prevention of poorly or misaligned teeth.
10. Adjunctive general services—Miscellaneous services, treatments not listed elsewhere.

It is important to know what type of service is being performed in order to code it properly. Not all plans, insurers, or dental offices code claims according to the ADA code list. Many have developed their own version of the list. However, most of these lists are based on the format of the ADA code list.

The main differences that may often be noted include:

- Dental visits and anesthesia services are given their own section because these services are the most often rendered. Some dental lists also include a section for drugs. The ADA list includes all these services under the heading of Adjunctive Dental Services.
- Many insurance carrier or plan lists omit codes in areas that they do not routinely cover. Such areas usually include orthodontic services and fractures and dislocations.

Regardless of the differences, it is important for the Dental Biller and the Dental Claims Examiner to become familiar with the types of services because nearly all dental code lists fall under categories similar to the ADA list.

In the following sections we will discuss the treatments covered under each ADA category and list the appropriate codes. It will be helpful to compare this section with the Dental Code List in Appendix 24-1.

Diagnostic

Diagnostic procedures are those that are necessary to properly determine the most appropriate course of treatment for the patient's condition. The services that usually fall within this category are discussed in the following text.

Clinical Oral Examination

A clinical oral examination is the examination of the mouth by a dentist. Oral examinations are broken into three classifications: initial oral examinations (to indicate the first time a patient is seen), periodic oral examination (to indicate any examinations other than the first), and emergency oral examinations (to indicate emergency examinations).

Radiographs

Radiographs are x-rays of the mouth and teeth. The first code is for a full-mouth set of x-rays (0210). Following that are intraoral mouth x-rays (0220–0240) and extraoral mouth x-rays (0250–0260). Intraoral x-rays are taken with the film placed inside the mouth. Extraoral x-rays are taken with the film placed outside the mouth. Bitewing x-rays have separate listings for one film, two films, three films, four films, and each additional film. Bitewing x-rays show the relationship of the teeth in two opposing dental arches.

In addition, occlusal x-rays are larger x-rays (2.5 x 3 inches), which show the floor of the mouth and the palate. An occlusal x-ray shows the lingual (next to the tongue) side of the teeth and a portion of the palate. Its purpose is to aid in locating impacted teeth, bone fractures, cysts, and salivary duct disorders.

In each case, coding is made by the number of films taken. The first film would be coded individually; any additional films taken would be listed under the additional code(s). For example, refer to Appendix 24-1. If a dentist were to take six bitewing x-rays, the appropriate codes would be 0274 for the first four films and 2 x 0275 for the additional two films.

In many plans, there are limitations regarding the number of bitewing or other x-rays that may be taken during a given period of time. The plan should always be checked for such limitations. In addition, many plans have a full-mouth x-ray limitation. This means that if the dollar amount payable for the total number of x-rays taken individually exceeds the dollar amount payable for a set of full-mouth x-rays, the allowable amount would be based on the full-mouth x-ray allowance because the dentist could have taken an entire x-ray series to see all tooth structures.

Certain conditions may require posteroanterior and lateral skull and facial bone survey films. These are usually covered only under orthodontic services or TMJ conditions. These films include the following:

- Posteroanterior and lateral skull and facial bone survey films. This set of films shows the architecture, size, density, contouring, and positioning of the skull bones. One film shows height and width, and a second shows height and depth. When used together, they provide a nearly three-dimensional picture. Various views can be selected, including the Towne View, the Waters View and the Basal View. This is usually covered only under orthodontic services or TMJ conditions.
- Sialography. This x-ray allows inspection of the salivary glands and ducts. A radiopaque medium (radioactive dye) is injected and enables the x-ray to show any obstructions or blockages (stones) in the salivary glands or ducts. This examination is most often performed by an otorhinolaryngologist (ear, nose, and throat specialist) in a hospital setting. It is usually performed only for a saliva problem or for a suspected cyst or tumor of the salivary glands.
- Temporomandibular joint film. The TMJ film allows inspection of the temporomandibular joint and its function. It is usually covered only when TMJ is a covered benefit or when there are orthodontic problems.
- Panoramic maxilla and mandible film (Panorex). This is a large x-ray that shows all the teeth, the surrounding alveolar bone, the sinuses, and the TMJ all on one film. It helps to show tooth spacing or crowding as well as impacted teeth and jaw fractures. Periodontists use panoramic x-rays to determine the condition of the supporting structures of the teeth. Most plans consider it the same as a full-mouth x-ray and subject to the same guidelines. It is usually covered once every 3 years.
- Cephalometric film. This is an extraoral x-ray done with a cephalometer. The cephalometer is an instrument that holds the patient's head in position while at the same time measuring the bony structure of the head. The cephalometric film provides the greatest dimensional accuracy. It is used in conjunction with orthodontics or TMJ disorders and is usually covered under orthodontic or TMJ conditions.
- Intraoral x-rays include periapicals, bitewings, full-mouth series, and occlusal x-rays. Extraoral x-rays include Panorex and cephalometrics.
- Code 0390 is the catch-all code for any other diagnostic radiographs that have been taken.

Laboratory Tests and Other Services

Occasionally, laboratory tests are needed to help determine a specific disease or patient condition. These tests include the following:

Complete blood count
Urinalysis
Hemoglobin
Hematocrit
Bacteriologic studies for determination of pathologic agents
Caries susceptibility tests
Histopathologic examination
Pulp vitality tests

Laboratory tests are often covered under medical plans as well as dental plans, and specific policy guidelines should be consulted to ensure proper payment.

Diagnostic casts and photographs may also need to be taken in order to diagnose the patient's condition. Diagnostic casts (models) duplicate the structure of the mouth. They are also called study models and working models. The only difference between a study model and a working model is how they are used. Study models are studied to assist in determining diagnoses and treatments. They are also used by orthodontists to record and evaluate problems or conditions that need treatment. Working models are used to aid in fabricating restorations, crowns, and fixed and removable prosthetics. Since a working model is an integral part of fabricating restorations, normally no additional allowance is given beyond that for the procedure itself. Diagnostic casts are usually covered only under orthodontic services or TMJ conditions.

Diagnostic photographs are colored photographs of the oral cavity and are used to show various conditions of the teeth and mouth structures. They are also used to show pre- and postoperative conditions. Diagnostic photographs are generally used in conjunction with orthodontic treatment. Many payors do not cover this procedure because they feel it is merely evidence for the dentist's files, not a diagnostic procedure.

Code 0490 is the catch-all code for miscellaneous tests that were not specifically in the previous text.

Many plans do not cover any laboratory services or casts and photographs under dental services, with the exception of diagnostic casts and photographs, which may be covered if the dental plan covers orthodontic care and treatment. Some services may be covered under the medical plan.

Preventive

Preventive services are designed to assist in preventing the development of diseases of the dental structures. If disease is treated in the early stages, it prevents the disease from spreading to other teeth and structures within the mouth. Dental plans usually cover preventive services because it is less expensive to pay for a small treatment now than for a larger treatment later.

Dental Prophylaxis

Prophylaxis is the removal of bacterioplaque, calculus, stains, and other potentially harmful materials from the teeth by superficial scaling and polishing as a preventive measure for the control of local irritational factors.

The first step involves using a scaler to scrape off the built-up calculus (a whitish-yellow chalky substance, also called plaque) from beneath the gum line, then polishing the teeth with an abrasive mixture (a type of pumice).

There are two ADA codes for prophylaxis: one for adults and one for children. Age 14 years is usually considered to be the dividing line between adults and children. Many dental plans cover a limited number of prophylaxis treatments (generally no more than two per year), and some pay for prophylaxis for children, but not for adults.

Fluoride Treatments

Fluoride treatments are the application of a topical fluoride substance to the teeth. The three types of fluoride are stannous, acid, and sodium. All three types can be obtained in either liquid or gel form. Sodium fluoride is usually applied in four treatments. Acid and stannous fluoride are usually applied in a single treatment. Stannous fluoride is the most commonly used. The only difference in the fluoride treatments is in the chemical make-up of the fluoride compound. Stannous fluoride contains tin, acid fluoride contains acid, and sodium fluoride contains salt.

The enamel surface of the teeth is soft in children and grows harder as the teeth mature. Fluorides help to harden the enamel more quickly, thus helping to prevent cavities. When a child reaches about age 14, the enamel has completely hardened. This is one reason why adults usually get fewer cavities than children. Because fluoride is much less effective after the teeth have matured, most plans cover fluoride treatments only up to a certain age, usually ages 14 to 19. While the teeth are immature, the surface is soft and allows for the absorption of the fluoride. After maturity, this is no longer possible. Therefore, fluoride treatment usually is not covered for adults. For children, one treatment every 6 months is generally allowable.

Fluoride treatments are coded according to the type of fluoride used and whether or not the treatment includes a prophylaxis.

Other Preventive Services

Occasionally, a dentist provides preventive services other than those already mentioned. These may include dietary planning for the control of dental caries, oral hygiene instruction, and training in preventive dental care. These are considered educational services and thus are generally not covered under most plans.

In addition, a fairly new procedure is the application of **sealants**, which consist of a plastic-like coating that is placed on a healthy tooth to prevent decay. Sealants are coded per quadrant or per tooth. These preventive measures are normally used on children, since the posterior teeth often have fissures (cracks) or pits (holes) during their developmental stage. The application of sealants prevents bacteria, fluids, or food particles from lodging in the fissures or pits, thus preventing cavities. Although the teeth are healthy, the benefits of this type of service are becoming better known and many plans are starting to cover this service.

Note that data indicate that 87% of sealants applied to a tooth are likely to be retained after a period of 2 years. For this reason, excessive sealant application (more than once every 4 or 5 years to the same tooth surface) should be questioned.

Space Management Therapy

Space management is the placement of wires or a retainer (either permanent or temporary) in the mouth to prevent the wrongful movement (known as drifting) of teeth into a space where a tooth has been lost. This type of treatment may be covered for children (usually up to age 18) but usually not for adults. Some of the common names for this appliance are stayplates or flippers.

When a deciduous tooth is lost prematurely, space maintainers not only serve to hold the remaining teeth in place, but also prevent the space from being closed and prevent malocclusion with the opposing teeth. Patients with space maintainers should be examined regularly by a dentist. Adjustment of the maintainers or removal may be required. If a space maintainer is left in place longer than necessary, damage to the teeth can result.

Coding is according to the type (unilateral or bilateral) of maintainer placed and whether or not the appliance is fixed or removable. In many plans, the use of these procedures includes all adjustments and follow-up visits necessary for a specified period of time.

Occasionally, it is necessary to re-cement a space maintainer.

Restorative

Restorations are procedures used to restore a natural tooth. They serve two purposes: to restore the dental structure after removal of the diseased portion and to make the tooth appear normal.

Charges/payments for restorations are based on:

- The number of surfaces of the tooth restored.
- The type of material used in the restoration.

Fillings

Filling restorations include a base, polishing, and local anesthetic. The types of materials used for fillings include:

- Amalgam—A silver-colored material composed of a mixture of mercury, silver, tin, copper, and zinc. This is the most durable material but is not aesthetically desirable. It is most appropriate for occlusal surfaces and other surface fillings on posterior teeth. Amalgam is the most inexpensive type of filling material.
- Composite—A plastic white material blended with resin and quartz crystal. This is the second most durable material, about 75% as durable as that of amalgam restorations. Composite is not considered appropriate for occlusal surfaces or for other surfaces of posterior teeth because of its reduced strength. Plans normally consider benefits for placement on anterior teeth and labial and incisal surfaces. Composite fillings should be coded as plastic or acrylic fillings.
- Plastics/acrylics—Synthetics are not as durable as composites. Many plans either limit or exclude payment for plastics. If used, they are appropriate only on the labial surfaces of the anterior teeth. Although plastic or acrylic restorations match natural teeth and are not complicated to perform, they have a tendency to expand with heat, to shrink during curing, and to discolor. They do not wear well and have a low strength and surface hardness. These restorations are also subject to recurrent decay around the filling.
- Silicate—A synthetic porcelain powder (also

called synthetic porcelain or silicate cement) composed of silicate, aluminum, and a flux of either sodium or calcium fluoride. Silicate can be mixed to match existing teeth and therefore is used mainly on the anterior teeth. It is less desirable than other fillers because it is brittle, is unable to absorb shock, discolors easily, and has a tendency to shrink or dissolve slowly. Silicate restorations generally last less than 5 years.

- Gold foil—comes as a 4-inch sheet of very thinly pressed gold. Gold restorations are appropriate for cavities covering one, two, or three surfaces. Gold restorations are more time-consuming to perform.
- Gold and metal alloys—A combination of one or more different metals. Gold is usually the most desirable fillings because of its resistance to corrosion, ability to be adapted closely to cavity walls, and extreme density (if properly condensed) and because it maintains a high polish and does not dissolve in saliva or other mouth fluids. Gold is generally more expensive than other restorative materials. It also is not as aesthetically appealing, is difficult to manipulate, can be extremely soft (compared with other filling materials), and has a high level of thermal conductivity.

  Often gold is mixed with other metals to increase strength. When mixed with copper, it becomes stronger, but it tends to corrode and lose its high polish much faster. Platinum and palladium add strength and hardness to gold as well as help to whiten the material. Palladium is a less expensive substitute for platinum. Zinc mixed with gold reduces the melting range and helps the gold to combine with any oxides present.
- Miscellaneous synthetic filling materials—May be known under a variety of trade names.
- Acid etch—A procedure, not a filling material. Because of its use during the cavity-filling procedure, it is often lumped together with filling materials. Acid etch is often referred to as an adhesive because it helps to bond the filling material to the tooth. It provides a far more durable bond than regular composites. Acid etch is generally used with acrylics and with composite resins. However, it is usually used only on the labial surfaces of the anterior teeth where the adhesion of filling material is difficult and an aesthetic appearance is desired. The acid etch technique (with composite or acrylic resins) has allowed for restoration of teeth that may not previously have been saved or may have required more extensive work (crowns, inlays, or onlays). Such teeth include fractured teeth, developmental defects, and eroded areas among others.

Amalgam, composite and plastic/acrylic are the most commonly used materials for restorative procedures. The basic procedure for filling dental cavities, or caries, is shown in Figure 24-1. (For further information on dental cavities, see Chapter 23.) Figure 24-1 shows the decay of the tooth. This is caused by insoluble calcium salts being broken down into soluble salts and being washed away. The breakdown of these salts is caused by bacteria that have attached to the tooth or lodged in a hole or fissure.

To treat the cavity, the dentist must first remove all bacteria and diseased material from it to prevent the bacteria from continuing to grow after the cavity has been filled. The hole is then treated with a cavity liner or varnish. Cavity liners line the inside of the cavity and form a barrier against irritation from the zinc phosphate and silicate cements that are used in the filling material. Cavity liners also reduce the sensitivity of the dentin. Cavity varnishes are applied in several thicknesses and help to reduce acid diffusion from the restorative cements into the dentin. They also insulate the pulp from shock due to thermal changes. Finally, the cavity is filled with one of the filling materials previously listed.

Tooth restorations or fillings may involve multiple surfaces. However, only one restoration is generally allowable per tooth.

The following are examples of single restorations (may be multiple surfaces, but only one restoration per tooth):

M	1 surface
MO	2 surfaces
MOL	3 surfaces

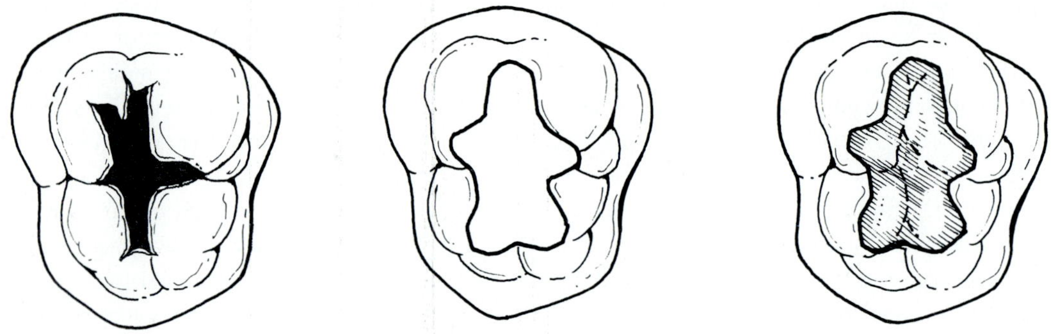

Figure 24-1: Basic procedure for filling dental caries.

MODB	4 surfaces
MODBL	5 surfaces

Examples of multiple restorations:

MOD, B	3 surfaces and 1 surface
MOD-B	3 surfaces and 1 surface
MD	2 single surface restorations
ML, DL	2 single surface restorations if performed on anterior teeth with the exception of teeth #6 and #11; this is because the anterior teeth are so narrow that an M or a D cannot be performed without going into the L surfaces. An ML or DL filling is really only one surface. In such a case, regardless of how the dentist bills it, only one surface should be allowable.

Coding for tooth restorations is based on the type of filling used, the number of surfaces, and the type of tooth (primary, permanent, anterior, posterior, and so on).

Pin retention is the insertion of a small, thin needle-like pin into the remaining tooth structure to provide extra support for the restoration. Occasionally, a pin retention is done when no restoration was provided. In this case, the pin retention, exclusive of the restoration code, should be used under either the amalgam or acrylic restoration headings.

Inlays and Onlays

An inlay is a gold alloy or porcelain casting that lies on the occlusal surface of the patient's cusps (the pronounced elevation or edge of the tooth). An onlay is also a gold alloy casting that lies on the occlusal surface but covers one or more cusps. Inlays and onlays are used to restore lost tooth structure and vertical dimension. Vertical dimension (height) allows for proper occlusion with the opposing teeth. One of the main differences between inlays/onlays and fillings is that fillings are formed within the cavity, whereas inlays and onlays are shaped in a mold and then cemented onto the tooth.

Application of an inlay requires two separate visits to the dentist: the first for drilling the cavity and making an impression of the hole to be filled and the second for cementing the inlay into place after its manufacture. Inlays also require that enough of the tooth be cut away to make an impression of the cavity to be filled.

Inlays have declined in popularity in the last few years. More frequently, a complete crown is provided. As a rule, most plans require that an inlay procedure be referred to a consultant for approval. An inlay can be applied without an onlay, but an onlay cannot be applied without an inlay. Therefore, if you receive a bill for an onlay only, assume that an inlay was also performed and code accordingly.

Crowns

A crown is a covering that is placed on a tooth. Crowns are required when a tooth has lost so much of its structure that a filling would not be stable. This means that the disease has progressed to the point where the decay is so large that there is very little, if any, supporting structure to hold a filling.

Crowns can be used strictly for cosmetic purposes. For instance, when a tooth may require treatment and a filling would be appropriate, the patient may prefer a crown to a filling because it appears more natural-looking. Perhaps the tooth in question is off-color or crooked. By applying a crown, the color and the position of the tooth can be improved in addition to treating the disease.

The following are the different types of crowns:

- Full crowns. These crowns cover the entire top of the tooth and extend to just below the gum line. A cast preparation is formed and then placed over a tooth on which the four outside surfaces (lingual, facial, mesial, distal axial) have been filed toward each other to form a rounded point. Several full crowns connected together and placed over several adjacent teeth can be used to help to stabilize those teeth.
- Full veneer crowns. These crowns are similar to full crowns, but they have a thin layer of acrylic resin or porcelain bonded to the surface of the crown. They replaced nearly the entire tooth and are placed over a "stump" that has been made of the natural tooth.
- Partial crowns. Similar to full crowns, partial crowns do not cover all the surfaces of the tooth. The surfaces involved are usually the occlusal or incisal, the lingual, and the proximal. Partial crowns are never done in a series, but are single unit restorations.
- Partial veneer crowns. Also called three-quarter veneer crowns, partial veneer crowns do not completely cover the tooth. They are cast metal and cover only that portion of the tooth that needs restoring. Three-quarter crowns also serve as abutments for a fixed bridge.
- Porcelain-faced crowns. These crowns have porcelain inlayed or veneered onto the buccal or labial surface.
- Seven-eighths crowns. These crowns are usually placed on the molars to serve as bridge abutments. Their purpose is to strengthen the tooth to help it withstand the added stress of the bridge.
- Steel crowns. These crowns are noncast (preformed) crowns that are usually made of stainless steel.

Dental plans cover a crown only when less drastic (and less expensive) methods of treatment are not appropriate. That is, if a filling can correct the problem, then a filling, not a crown, would be the appropriate treatment. Remember that the patient or dentist can use whatever treatment is desired. However, the amount allowable would be based on the necessity of services rendered.

There are permanent crowns and temporary crowns. When a crown is required, the dentist makes a model of the mouth (or arch). Then, a match of the surrounding teeth using a color chart is determined. The patient's natural tooth is then filed down until it resembles a spike. A temporary crown is placed on the diseased tooth while the model is sent to a dental laboratory for casting (some dental offices perform the casting in house). A cast is made from the model from the material ordered by the dentist in a color matching the patient's surrounding teeth. The finished crown is then given to the dentist for application and fitting. The patient usually returns for the "seating" (placement) of the finished crown. Normally, the patient has to return to the dentist several times for adjustments to the vertical height of the crown so that it fits comfortably and is in alignment with the surrounding teeth.

The types of permanent crowns are:

- Full cast (gold).
- Three-quarter gold.
- Porcelain veneer (porcelain on the outside and a designated metal frame on the inside, which may be gold, nonprecious metal (alloy) or semi-precious metal).

Temporary crowns are usually constructed of stainless steel. The temporary is precast instead of being made specifically for the patient.

As a rule, porcelain crowns are the most expensive crowns. They may be covered only on the anterior teeth. However, since this material has become the most accepted material for crowns, porcelain crowns may be allowable even on posterior teeth. Usually, the nonprecious frame is allowable on posterior teeth. The semiprecious or gold frame is allowable on anterior teeth. At one time, most plans were written with the provision that only gold crowns would be covered on posterior teeth. That was because years ago, gold was the least expensive material. However, now many plans will allow whatever material is the least expensive on the posterior teeth.

Crowns must be prepped and the natural tooth prepared while the patient is covered under the plan. However, many plans allow for the actual seating to take place after coverage has terminated if it is within 30 days of the termination date. The plan provisions must be checked for this exception.

Stainless-steel crowns are usually covered on deciduous teeth; however, regular crowns are not usually allowable on deciduous teeth because they will be lost as the child matures.

If properly prepared, a crown should last a minimum of 5 years. Therefore, if a replacement is requested on a crown that has been in place for less than 5 years, a review by a consultant is usually required. If the replacement is necessitated because of poor workmanship by the dentist, the original dentist may be expected to redo the restoration at no extra charge. This approach varies greatly by administrator.

Many plans monitor crowns to see whether more than one crown per arch or quadrant is being performed, since the underlying reason may be cosmetic, not functional. Also, crowns on teeth that are abutments (teeth used to support or stabilize one end of a prosthesis and lie next to an area of a missing tooth) to dentures are also monitored for necessity.

Crowns are coded according to the type of material used in the crown. This may be a single type of material or a combination of materials.

Other Restorative Services

It may become necessary to re-cement a loosened inlay or crown. The codes for re-cementing are dependent on whether the procedure is for an inlay or a crown.

Medicated or sedative fillings are temporary fillings to help relieve pain. As a rule, they may not be covered. The final restoration only may be the covered expense. For further information regarding this, see Chapter 27.

Other restorative services include crown buildup (to build up a crown to match the height of other teeth) and a labial veneer (a cosmetic procedure that coats the tooth. This can be done to match the color of other teeth or to whiten the teeth.) The veneer is seldom covered by plans.

Endodontics

Endodontic treatment deals with the diagnosis and treatment of diseases of the internal structures of the teeth, pulp, and periapical tissues. The most common type of endodontic treatment is a root canal procedure. Benefit payments for endodontic procedures include all x-rays and office visits. Additional charges for these services are denied if billed with endodontic procedures.

Pulp Capping

Another type of endodontic treatment is pulp capping. Pulp capping is the placing of a covering over an exposed tooth pulp. Pulp capping is done only on children because after a tooth matures, the pulp is occluded and becomes a root instead. Some doctors bill pulp caps consistently on adults. As a rule, the treatment is considered a sedative filling instead of a pulp cap. A dental consultant has to review the x-rays to determine the legitimacy of the billing.

There are two types of pulp caps: direct and indirect. A direct pulp cap is directly in contact with the material used (often calcium hydroxide) and the pulp. In an indirect pulp cap, the treatment material is placed on the vital or diseased dentin and not directly on the pulp.

Recalcification or remineralization is similar to a pulp cap. In this type of treatment, calcium hydroxide or a similar material is placed in the tooth prior to placing a temporary restoration. If this is done on permanent teeth, a consultant normally should review the x-rays, since it is usually appropriate only on deciduous teeth.

Pulpotomy and pulpectomy consist of complete and partial removal, respectively, of the pulp and are appropriate only on deciduous teeth. There are two types of pulpotomies: vital and therapeutic. If the provider does not indicate which type was performed, it is usually safe to assume it was a vital pulpotomy.

Root Canals

A root canal is the removal of the entire root pulp, the sterilizing of the chamber, and the filling of the chamber with sealing material. This is performed when a tooth has an infected or damaged pulp. There are two types of root canal therapy: conventional (traditional) and Sargenti. The Sargenti treatment is done in one seating. The conventional treatment usually takes three treatments. In the conventional treatment, the chamber is sterilized and then allowed to settle before filling. This allows the dentist to be sure that all of the infection is cleared up before the final step—that of placing a crown on the tooth. Today, the conventional style is highly preferred over the Sargenti method, and many consultants will question the appropriateness of the Sargenti when submitted because it is essential that the infection be completely cleared before the crown is placed. After the crown is placed, it cannot be removed without ruining it. It is possible to drill through the top of the crown to reach the canal but this is certainly not desirable.

Table 24-1 will assist in identifying whether or not the dentist is billing correctly. If a root canal is performed, all the roots have to be cleaned and filled even if they are not all infected. This is because the infection will inevitably spread and because, as previously stated, once a crown is placed, it is not desirable to have to remove it for any reason. By treating all the roots, this possibility is minimized.

Root canals are coded according to the type of root canal that is done. If the Sargenti method was used, the code depends on the number of roots involved in the therapy. A root canal not done by the Sargenti method is coded according to the type of tooth, anterior, premolar, or molar.

The process of a root canal leaves a cavity in the tooth that must be filled. All root canal codes do not include the final restoration. Therefore, a corresponding restoration should be billed and coded for each root canal performed. In the Sargenti method, the restoration is done on the same day and should be included on the same billing form. In a non-Sargenti

Table 24-1:
Usual Number of Root Canals for Each Tooth

Tooth #	Permanent Tooth Name	Usual # of Canals
1	Upper right 3rd molar	3
2	Upper right 2nd molar	3
3	Upper right 1st molar	3
4	Upper right 2nd bicuspid	1
5	Upper right 1st bicuspid	2
6	Upper right cuspid	1
7	Upper right lateral incisor	1
8	Upper right central incisor	1
9	Upper left central incisor	1
10	Upper left lateral incisor	1
11	Upper left cuspid	1
12	Upper left 1st bicuspid	2
13	Upper left 2nd bicuspid	1
14	Upper left 1st molar	3
15	Upper left 2nd molar	3
16	Upper left 3rd molar	3
17	Lower left 3rd molar	3
18	Lower left 2nd molar	3
19	Lower left 1st molar	3
20	Lower left 1st bicuspid	1
21	Lower left 2nd bicuspid	1
22	Lower left cuspid	1
23	Lower left lateral incisor	1
24	Lower left central incisor	1
25	Lower right central incisor	1
26	Lower right lateral incisor	1
27	Lower right cuspid	1
28	Lower right 1st bicuspid	1
29	Lower right 2nd bicuspid	1
30	Lower right 1st molar	3
31	Lower right 2nd molar	3
32	Lower right 2nd molar	3

method, the restoration is not completed until a subsequent visit and may be billed on a separate claim form.

Apexification

Apexification is performed on the permanent tooth of a young person when the apex of the tooth is incompletely formed. It is a series of treatments, wherein the pulp is removed and the apex is treated with a solution of calcium hydroxide. This procedure stimulates growth of the cementum and helps to form apical closure.

Often apexification is done prior to root canal therapy. Apexification treatment occurs in a series of visits and can last from 6 to 18 months.

Periapical Services

Other types of periapical treatments include:

- Apical curettage—Scraping but not excision of the apex.
- Apicoectomy—Excision of the apex of a root (usually considered medical, not dental). An apicoectomy is coded depending on whether or not it was performed with other endodontic procedures. The coding method is per root. Therefore, if two or more roots were done, the code (and RVS unit values) should be multiplied accordingly.
- Endodontic implants—The placement of an implant through the tooth and into the jaw. It is used to stabilize a loose tooth. Many administrators consider endodontic implants to be experimental; therefore, services are referred to a consultant for review.
- Retrograde filling—Amalgam filling placed into the apex of a root. This usually follows an apicoectomy.
- Root resection—Cutting off a portion of the root, usually because of disease or decay.

Other Endodontic Procedures

Other endodontic procedures may include:

- Bleaching of discolored teeth—A cosmetic procedure to whiten the teeth. As such, it is not covered by most dental plans.
- Canal preparation and fitting of preformed dowel or post—The drilling of a canal and the inserting of a post or dowel into the canal.
- Hemisection—Cutting an organ in half.
- Surgical procedure for isolation of tooth with a rubber dam—Use of a thin rubber tissue by the dentist to seal off the tooth from saliva in the mouth. It also protects the patient from dental instruments, assists in the elimination of saliva and other fluids, and helps to keep the gingiva out of the way. Often, payors will not cover this procedure.
- Recalcification (perforations, root resorption)—The restoration of calcium salts to the teeth.

Periodontics

Periodontal treatment is the diagnosis and treatment of diseases affecting the periodontium, the tissues that surround and support the teeth. This includes the gingiva, cementum, and periodontal membranes. Periodontal procedures are usually performed by a dentist, periodontist, or oral surgeon. Periodontal treatment is one of the most highly abused areas of dental care. For this reason, many administrators have very stringent periodontal guidelines together with heavy consultant review.

Some periodontal care is considered oral surgery, whereas other treatments are considered strictly dental. To be effective, some periodontal treatments must be used in conjunction with or followed up by other adjunctive treatments. Such in-depth training is best done at the administrator level instead of in this general training guide.

Surgical Services

Surgical services to the periodontium include:

- Free soft tissue grafts—Soft tissue grafts that do not involve the use of a pedicle.
- Gingival curettage—The intentional surgical removal of the inner soft tissue wall of the gingival pocket. It is usually performed with local anesthetic. Access is through the pocket opening and no flap is performed (see item that follows).

Many plans consider gingival curettage to be medically necessary if performed by a licensed provider, but limit treatment to one occurrence per year per quadrant.

- Gingivectomy (the surgical removal of diseased gum tissue) or gingivoplasty (the surgical correction of the gingiva margin or edge).
- Gingival flap procedure—The movement of masses of partially detached tissue from one area to an adjacent area—in this case, the gum. The flap is not fully detached so that it retains its own blood supply during transfer. Flap procedures are often used for covering the end of a bone after a resection.
- Mucogingival surgery—Surgery involving the mucous membranes and the gums.
- Osseous grafts—Transplants involving the bone.
- Osseous surgery—Surgery involving the bone.
- Pedicle soft tissue grafts—Grafts that involve a pedicle. (A pedicle is a narrow, stem-like projection that attaches the graft to a blood or nutrient supply.)
- Periodontal pulpal procedures—Surgical procedures that involve the periodontal pulp.
- Vestibuloplasty—Surgery involving the vestibule of the mouth.

Gingivectomy or gingivoplasty, mucogingival surgery, and osseous surgery can be used for single tooth procedures, multiple tooth procedures, or full quadrant procedures. Check the tooth numbers on the claim to determine how many teeth were affected by the procedure. Benefits will be allowed according to the number of teeth involved.

Adjunctive Periodontal Services

The following are additional periodontal services:

- Athletic mouth guard fabrication—Making of an appliance that fits over the teeth and protect them from harm during rough athletic activity (eg, football, boxing).
- Occlusional adjustment—An adjustment to allow proper occlusion (closing) of the teeth.
- Scaling (thorough removal of calculus and bacterioplaque from the crowns and all root surfaces of the teeth) and root planing (a more definitive form of scaling to smooth roughened root surfaces [cementum] and to remove deep, heavy plaque). The ADA describes and codes scaling and root planing as one procedure, since both procedures must be done at the same time.
- Code 4340—For scaling and root planing of the entire mouth (more than 12 teeth) during one appointment. This may be performed before or after a routine prophylaxis.
- Code 4341—For definitive scaling and planing per quadrant per appointment. The entire mouth should be done. This code should be used with a comprehensive approach to a more complicated or advanced case of periodontal disease.
- Special periodontal appliances (including occlusal guards)—Special appliances that may be required to aid in the treatment of periodontal diseases.
- Splinting—The attaching together of multiple teeth with wire or some other supportive material. In advanced cases of periodontal disease, the teeth become loosened in their sockets due to the loss of supporting tissue. In an effort to salvage the teeth, multiple teeth may be "splinted" together. This provides a wider base so that if one tooth moves, all teeth must move. To move several teeth requires significantly more pressure than to move a single tooth. Consequently, there is less movement in teeth splinted together. There are two types of splinting:

1. Intracoronal (provisional), in which the teeth are wired together.
2. Extracoronal, which is considered a permanent treatment wherein crowns or inlays are placed on the subject teeth and soldered together.

Many plans limit coverage for splinting, and a consultant review should always be provided.

- Tooth movement for periodontal purposes—Allows the teeth to be moved so that the dentist may treat the periodontal tissues underneath.

Description of Case Patterns

Gingivitis and periodontitis are usually classified

under a case pattern section that lists the disease and the appropriate treatment under one ADA code.

- Case pattern modifiers (by report)—For use when extenuating circumstances accompany a specific case pattern.

All the following treatments and procedures are included under one code. If treatment is listed or billed separately, all services should be combined under the single code.

Treatment includes: all necessary diagnostic procedures, training in personal preventive dental care, mouth preparation procedures, occlusal adjustment, surgical procedures (involving flap entry and osseus procedures, complex procedures, and so on), routine finishing procedures, and posttreatment evaluation.

- Type I gingivitis—Shallow pockets, no bone loss.
- Type II early periodontitis—Moderate pockets, minor to moderate bone loss, satisfactory topography.
- Type III moderate periodontitis—Moderate to deep pockets, moderate to severe bone loss, unsatisfactory topography.
- Type IV advanced periodontitis—Deep pockets, severe bone loss, advanced inability patterns (usually cases involving missing teeth and reconstruction).

Other Periodontic Procedures

Preventive periodontal procedures (periodontal prophylaxis) include:

- Perioprophylaxis (also referred to as a periorecall or periodontal maintenance)—Performed following the completion of comprehensive periodontal treatment. The patient returns within 12 months (usually at 3-month intervals) for posttreatment evaluation and further preventive care. Periodontal scaling and possibly root planing and polishing of the teeth may be necessary at this time as well as reinstruction in preventive oral hygiene procedures.
- Unscheduled dressing change—Used when a dentist other than the treating dentist performs a dressing change.

Prosthodontics

Prosthodontics is the branch of dentistry concerned with restoration and maintenance of function by the artificial replacement of missing natural teeth. It covers the initial preparation and installation of bridges and dentures.

On all claims involving prosthodontics, the examiner needs to determine:

- Which teeth, if any, are congenitally missing.
- The tooth number of any and all teeth being replaced, plus the date of extraction or loss of each tooth.
- Whether any other teeth are missing in the arch and whether they are being replaced.
- For a replacement prosthesis, the date of installation of the prior prosthesis.

Many policies require that the prosthesis replace "natural" teeth. The following are not considered natural teeth:

- Tooth roots, when the condition of the tooth was such prior to the effective date of coverage.
- Congenitally missing teeth.
- Diastema (space between two adjacent teeth)

The following teeth do not require replacement and are usually not covered:

- Third molars that occupy the third molar position.
- Any tooth that is not in functional occlusion, that is, any tooth that is not opposed by another tooth in the opposite arch.

For example, a denture is replacing numbers 14 and 15 teeth. Numbers 18 and 19 (in the opposite arch) are also missing but not being replaced. As number 14 and 15 teeth will not oppose teeth or a prosthesis, their replacement will serve no function and thus, cannot be considered for coverage. The charges for all prosthetics (and therefore the coding and billing) include:

- The initial preparation of the teeth for a prosthetic.
- Study models.
- Fitting of the prosthesis.
- Initial installation of the prosthesis.
- All adjustments required within 6 months of the installation.

Prosthodontics—Removable

Full and partial dentures are prosthetic appliances. The following sections explain the types of dentures and give general guidelines concerning them.

Full Dentures

Full dentures are appliances that replace all of the patient's natural teeth. The types of complete (full) dentures are (see Figure 24-2):

- Immediate permanent—Made before all the natural teeth have been extracted. After extractions, it is placed immediately before the healing is complete.
- Immediate temporary—Constructed of temporary material; has anterior teeth and posterior biting blocks (not true artificial teeth).
- Overdentures—Fabricated to fit over the remaining teeth. Usually, two natural teeth per arch remain in the mouth to provide support. Root canals, posts, copings, and crowns are performed on the remaining teeth to provide the necessary strength to support the overdenture.
- Regular permanent—Made following all extractions and healing of the tissues or for replacement of an existing denture.

Full dentures are coded according to the location (upper or lower) and whether they are complete or immediately placed.

Full dentures for patients under age 35 and fixed bridges on patients under age 16 should normally be reviewed by a consultant for appropriateness.

Complete denture codes range from 5110 to 5140. Partial denture codes range from 5211 to 5294. Relines, tissue conditioning, and adjustments for 6 months after the initial placement of the dentures are usually considered part of the basic denture procedure. Therefore, additional payments are not allowed.

Partial Dentures

Partial dentures are used to replace missing teeth (see Figure 24-3). For a partial denture to be used, enough structurally sound natural teeth must be available to anchor the partial denture. If the patient has advanced periodontal disease, bone disease, or other conditions, a partial denture may not be able to be used. A partial denture may be either fixed or removable. A fixed partial is usually called a bridge.

The types of removable partial dentures are:

- Permanent—Used when only a few, scattered teeth need replacement.
- Temporary—Temporary replacement. This is usually not covered except after periodontal

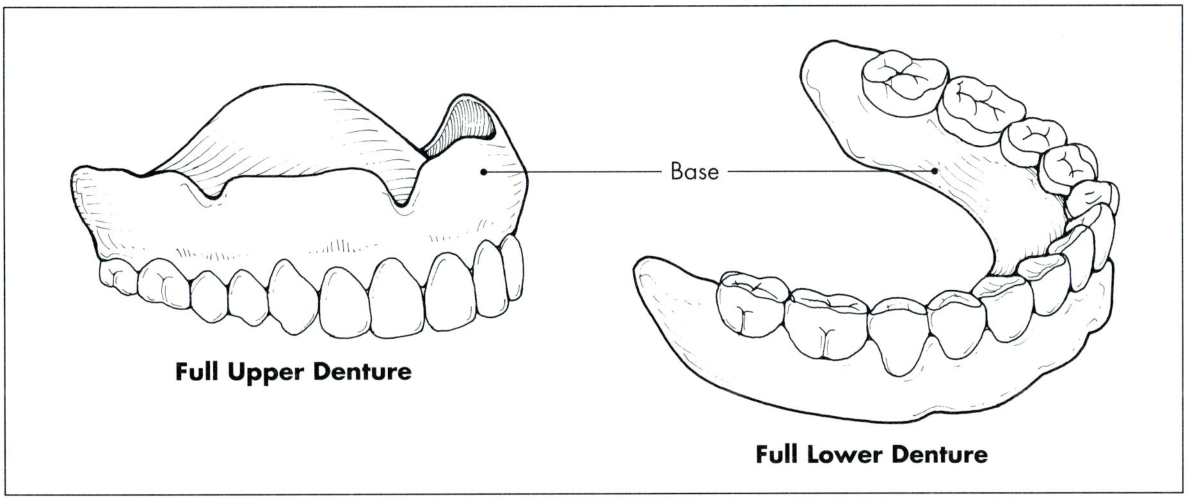

Figure 24-2: Full dentures.

work. A consultant review is generally required.

- **Unilateral partial**—Replaces only one tooth. A partial is usually constructed "symmetrically," that is, one or two teeth are being replaced in each quadrant of the arch. When teeth are missing in only one quadrant, a fixed bridge is usually used, depending on the circumstances of the missing teeth. If only one tooth is missing in one quadrant, a unilateral partial can be used.

The charge for a partial denture includes:

- All teeth.
- The base, which is a pink-colored plastic and metal and lies against either the palate or the alveolar ridge (bottom of the mouth).
- Two rests and two clasps.
- All adjustments or relines required during the first 6 months following seating.

Many dentists routinely itemize their billing for partials showing a separate charge for each tooth, the base, and the clasps and rests. When processing or billing, all these charges should be combined and coded as one appliance. Additional clasps or rests are coded separately. All the teeth are always included, regardless of the number of teeth involved.

A palatal bar is the support that runs across the top of the palate (roof of the mouth). A lingual bar is the support that runs along the bottom of the mouth. Different codings reflect different materials used in the construction of the partial. Many plans specify that only certain materials, usually nonprecious or semiprecious materials, can be used in the construction.

Teeth numbers 7 and 10 are often not strong enough to support bridgework or partials. Therefore, care should be taken when approving these teeth for use as abutments. A consultant should review the x-rays and treatment plan prior to approval.

Partial dentures are coded according to the type of denture (complete or partial), their location (upper or lower), the materials (eg, acrylic, chrome), and the number of clasps used. The two codes most commonly used for partials are 5241 and 5261.

Additional Units for Partial Dentures

Use of these codes and additional allowance may be given if more teeth are being added to an existing partial. Code 5310 is for each additional clasp with rest. Code 5320 is for each additional tooth.

Adjustments to Dentures

Occasionally, a dentist has to adjust dentures because of changes in the mouth (often due to aging or disease). The codes within the 5410 to 5422 range are used to bill for these types of services.

Repairs to Dentures

Occasionally, it becomes necessary to repair or add

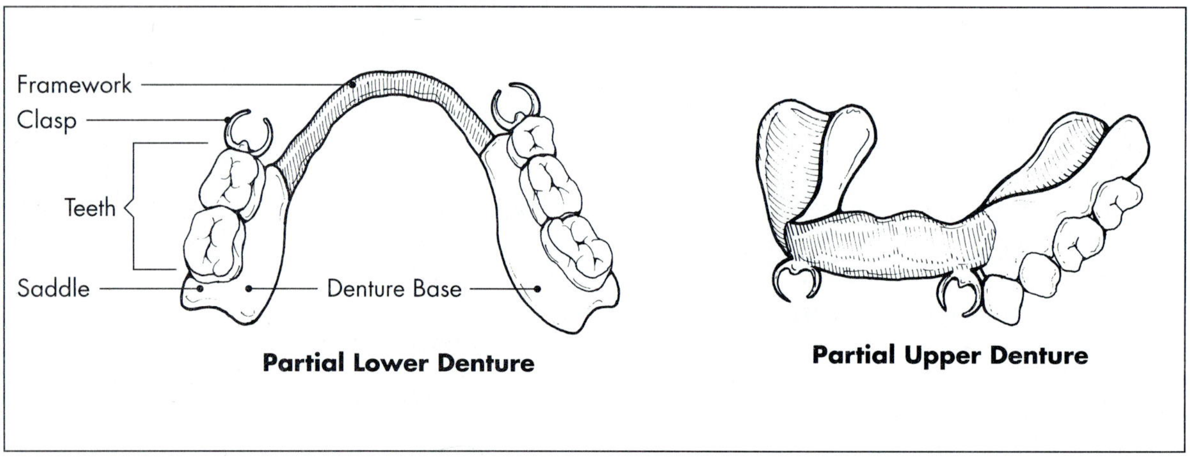

Figure 24-3: Partial dentures.

to a denture. The code range 5610 through 5690 is used to bill these types of services. These codes are used only when a new denture or partial does not have to be made, when a repair can be made, or when a tooth can just be added on. The codes are as follows:

5610 Repair broken complete or partial denture—no teeth damaged
5620 Repair broken complete or partial denture—replace one broken tooth
5630 Replace additional teeth—each tooth (this code should always be used with 5620)
5640 Replace broken tooth on denture—no other repairs
5650 Adding tooth to partial denture to replace extracted tooth—each tooth (not involving clasps or abutment tooth)
5660 Adding tooth to partial denture to replace extracted tooth—each tooth (involving clasps or abutment tooth)
5670 Reattaching damaged clasp on denture
5680 Replacing broken clasp with new clasp on denture
5690 Each additional clasp with rest

Denture Duplication

Denture duplication to replace a lost denture or to make a spare set is usually not a covered expense. Jump or rebase (5710 and 5720) is the replacement of the base of the denture because of deterioration or tissue changes. Jump or rebase may be covered depending on the circumstances. Since the teeth from the original denture are being reused and only the base material is being remade, the cost is considerably less than the cost of a completely new denture. However, since these three terms are used interchangeably, it is necessary that an explanation be obtained from the provider that clarifies which service is being performed.

Denture Relining

A reline is a soft material placed on top of the base to help prevent tissue damage to the patient's mouth. This makes the partial or denture more comfortable to wear. It is coded according to the type of denture (complete or partial) and where the relining procedure took place (in the office or the laboratory).

Other Prosthetic Services

Temporary dentures are sometimes used until the permanent dentures have been constructed. Tissue conditioning is a method of correcting tissue irritation resulting from the wearing of dentures. First, an impression-making type of material is placed in the saddle of the denture. Then, with the denture in place, displacement of this material will indicate any corrections that are necessary to eliminate distortion from pressure on the tissue. Tissue conditioning is more complicated than the typical adjustment.

As previously indicated, an overdenture is considered a full denture, although it is placed "over" two teeth in each arch left for support. Unlike a partial denture in which clasps are used to grab onto the abutment teeth, an overdenture has two holes left in it to allow it to slide over the two remaining teeth. Overdentures are coded as complete or partial.

Maxillofacial Prosthetics

Many of the following services are not performed frequently and therefore have a BR (By Report) or RNE (Relativity Not Established) unit value. However, they may be covered by some major medical plans. As a rule, most plans require that this type of procedure be referred to a consultant for approval. The codes are very seldomly seen by the medical biller or the claims examiner. For this reason, these procedures will not be discussed in depth. Many of the following prostheses are replaced because of damage to the bone or tissues relating to either disease or blunt trauma (eg, auto accident, being hit by an object). These procedures most often are performed by a dental surgeon or an orthodontist.

Extraoral Prostheses

The following prostheses are actually outside the oral cavity. Please note that these codes include 3-month maintenance of the patient and the prosthesis.

- Auricular prosthesis—A prosthesis in the auricle of the ear.

- Composite facial prosthesis—A prosthesis of the facial structure.
- Facial moulage—The making of a wax model of the face or a portion of the face or mouth. This is usually done in preparation for the making of a prosthesis.
- Nasal prosthesis—A prosthesis of the nasal cavity or nose.
- Ocular implant—An implant in the eye.
- Ocular prosthesis—A prosthesis of the eye (eg, glass eye).
- Orbital implant—An implant to the orbit (bony structure surrounding the eye).
- Orbital prosthesis—A prosthesis of the orbit (the bony structure around the eyeball).
- Prosthetic dressing—The dressing applied to the injured area before, during, or after the insertion of a prosthesis.
- Replacement prosthesis—Replacement or duplicate of an existing prosthesis. Often much of the measuring of the patient and the formation of molds has been done. Therefore, a replacement prosthesis usually costs less than an initial prosthesis.

Intraoral Prostheses

This section is divided into two subheadings, one for acquired defects and one for congenital defects. Congenital defects are those that a patient is born with. Acquired defects are those that develop after birth. Acquired defects in the field of dentistry are most often the result of disease or blunt trauma.

Acquired Defects

The following are intraoral prosthetics services performed for acquired defects:

- Refitting of obturator—The refitting or reforming of an obturator to better fit changes in the structure of the patient's palate. An obturator is an appliance designed to fill in the hole created by a cleft palate defect. It is usually held in place with clasps or splinted to the teeth. Two codes are used to bill for these services: code 5840 if the cleft of the palate was congenitally formed and code 5830 if the cleft is surgically formed.
- Mandibular resection prosthesis—A prosthesis to replace bone that was excised (cut out) during a mandibular resection. There are two codes depending on whether the prosthesis is a flange (lower, the part of the denture that extends from the embedded teeth to the border of the denture) or a denture (artificial teeth) prosthesis.

Congenital Defects

The following are intraoral prosthetics services performed for congenital defects:

- Feeding aid—A prosthesis used to assist in feeding a person with a congenital defect.
- Obturator—A prosthesis to cover the hole created by a cleft palate defect.
- Palatal lift prosthesis—A prosthesis that is made to lift the palate.
- Speech aid—A prosthesis used to help a person's speech. The two codes for speech aids depend on whether the prosthesis is for a child or an adult.
- Superimposed prosthesis—A prosthesis that is superimposed (placed) over another prosthesis.

Implants

Implant means to transfer or to graft something additional onto or into an existing surface. An implant may consist of a piece of tissue or bone, a pellet of medicine, a tube or needle containing radioactive material, and so on. Coding is either for a single or a complex implant.

- Subperiosteal implant—An implant located below the periosteum.
- Endosseous implant—An implant in the bone.
- Endodontic endosseous implant—An implant through the root and into the bone.

Treatment Prostheses

The following are prostheses that are generally removed after treatment.

- Docking device—A device to which something can be anchored or docked during treatment.
- Fluoride applicator—A plastic receptacle that is filled with fluoride and then fitted around the

teeth, allowing fluoride to be absorbed into the teeth. This is the most common treatment prosthesis used and it often accompanies billings for fluoride treatments.

- **Infant orthopedic appliance**—An appliance to help preserve and restore the skeletal function in infants.
- **Mandibular guide flange**—An implant below the denture line that helps to guide the mandibular bone.
- **Radiation carrier**—A device (usually a tube or needle) that contains a radioactive material.
- **Radiation shield**—A shield that protects a portion of the body from radiation.
- **Splint**—A device that holds a body part rigid or immobile.
- **Trismus appliance**—An appliance to aid in trismus. Trismus (often called lockjaw) is a motor disturbance of the trigeminal nerve.

Prosthodontics—Permanent

The term bridge or bridgework is usually used in reference to "fixed" or permanent partials. These are bridges that are permanently attached and seated in the patient's mouth. Whereas a partial is usually removed at night, a fixed bridge is never removed unless required by a dentist for repair.

Although there are many different types of bridge, the most common is a three-unit bridge. A three-unit bridge is composed of two abutment teeth and one pontic. An *abutment* is a tooth that is used to support or stabilize one end of a prosthetic appliance. A *pontic* is the part of a bridge that is suspended between abutments and replaces a missing tooth. It is also the artificial tooth in a partial denture. A pontic is the object that is made to look like a natural tooth. Using both definitions just indicated, the normal three-unit bridge (the number of units applies to the number of abutments plus the number of pontics involved in a bridge) is:

Abutment — pontic — abutment

Abutments are normally crowned. This is because either a bridge or a partial causes considerable wear and tear on the abutment teeth. Crowns provide the extra strength and support that is needed. The two most common types of bridges are:

1. **Fixed bridgework**—Made up of pontics (artificial teeth) and abutments (anchors).
2. **Cantilevered bridge**—Composed of one pontic and one abutment. Cantilevered bridges need to be reviewed by a consultant to determine appropriateness of treatment.

A bridge may also have double abutments. Double abutments are sometimes necessary when the abutting tooth is not very strong (such as lateral incisors 7 and 10) or when the bridge is cantilevered. However, some providers consistently bill for double abutments because it significantly increases the cost of the bridge. A bridge is charged and paid for based on the number of units involved. The allowance for an abutment is based on a crown charge, about \$400 to \$700 (depending on the area). The pontic charge tends to run about the same amount. Therefore, a three-unit bridge usually costs \$1200 to \$2000.

If a bridge is covered, the abutments are also automatically covered. If the bridge (replacement of missing teeth) is not covered, the abutment teeth must be evaluated by themselves to see whether they require crowning because of disease. If they are so decayed or diseased that crowns would be appropriate, without regard to a bridge the crowns will be paid for even though the pontic for the missing tooth would not be.

Bridge pontics and crowns (abutments) are coded based on the type of material used in the pontic or crown. Remember that each abutment and each pontic constitute a unit in a bridge. Therefore, you would bill a three-unit bridge as a pontic and two crowns.

Although the crown performed for a bridge is substantially the same as that provided for a stand-alone crown, a different code is used. For instance, 2751 is used for a stand-alone crown, whereas 6791 is used for a bridge crown.

Retainers

A retainer is a device used for maintaining the teeth and jaws in an appropriate position. Retainers are coded according to the number of surfaces (two, three, or more). If there was onlaying of cusps, code 6540 should be used.

Repairs

Occasionally, repairs are needed on fixed prosthodontics. Following is a list for coding of repairs:

6610 Replace broken pin facing with slotted or other facing
6620 Replace broken facing where post is intact
6630 Replace broken facing where post backing is broken
6640 Replace broken facing with acrylic
6650 Replace broken pontic

Other Removable Prosthetic Services

- Dowel pin—A metal pin used to stabilize the denture.
- Replacement bridge—A duplicate bridge made to replace an existing bridge.
- Precision attachment—A specially designed attachment used in fixed and removable prosthetics for attachment to the abutment teeth. It usually consists of a tongue and groove or male-female design.
- Stress breaker—A device incorporated into a denture to relieve excessive stress on the abutting teeth during chewing.

Oral Surgery

Oral surgery includes the operative procedures related to the teeth and jaws. Technically, surgery to the mouth is split into two sections:

1. Dental surgery—For treatment of the teeth and gums, such as extractions.
2. Oral surgery—For treatment of the jaw or parts of the mouth other than the teeth and gums, such as treatment of the joints and bones.

A dentist, oral surgeon, or physician may perform both oral and dental surgery. The type of surgery is defined by the procedure performed, not by the licensure of the person performing the service.

The distinction between oral and dental surgery is important because oral surgery may be covered under the medical portion of the plan, whereas routine extractions are not.

Oral surgery involves cutting into the oral tissues, opening up the area, cutting or removing objects from that area (either teeth or tissues/cysts), and then suturing (sewing) the area. The services that are considered surgical and are therefore usually covered under the medical portion of a plan include but are not limited to gingival curettage, gingivectomy, gingivoplasty, osseous surgery, gingival or soft tissue grafts, and osseous grafts. Following are some of the more common oral surgeries and exceptions.

Extractions

An extraction normally does not involve any cutting (except in a very superficial manner) or suturing. Therefore, extractions are not usually considered oral surgery. Usually, pincers are used to grab the tooth that is to be removed and the tooth is pulled out. The exception may be for impacted wisdom teeth (third molars).

Extractions include local anesthesia and routine postoperative care.

Surgical Extractions

Surgical extractions include local anesthesia and routine postoperative care.

Code 7210 is the surgical removal of an erupted tooth, which requires elevation of mucoperiosteal flap and removal of bone or section of tooth. This is usually not considered to be oral surgery. Therefore, this code is payable under dental, not medical.

Code 7220 is impaction that requires incision of overlaying soft tissue and the removal of the tooth.

Code 7230 is impaction that requires incision of overlaying soft tissue, elevation of a flap, and either removal of bone and tooth or sectioning and removal of the tooth.

Code 7240 is impaction that requires incision of overlaying soft tissue, elevation of a flap, removal of bone, and sectioning of the tooth for removal.

Code 7241 is impaction that requires incision of overlaying soft tissue, elevation of a flap, removal of bone, sectioning of the tooth for removal, or that which presents unusual difficulties and circumstances.

An impacted tooth is one that is positioned or wedged against another tooth, bone, or soft tissue and is prevented from erupting normally. When this occurs, the gum must be cut and the tooth removed, often by fracturing it into smaller pieces. The gum is then sutured closed. Usually, the three molars in each quadrant have a tendency to become impacted.

- Root extraction—Surgical cutting into the gum and removing the root. This situation may occur when a tooth is extracted and a part of the root breaks off and remains in the gum. This is usually considered a medical procedure.
- Oroantral fistula closure—An abnormal opening into the mouth cavity. This code is also used for antral root recovery. Most often, an oroantral fistula occurs when the root of an upper tooth has grown into the nasal cavity. When this tooth is extracted, an unnatural opening occurs between the oral cavity and the nasal cavity. Oroantral fistulas can also occur as a result of infection; however, it is still most often associated with the extraction of a tooth in which bacteria entered the hole left by the root and infection occurred. If an oroantral fistula occurs more than 6 weeks after the extraction of the tooth, some plans will cover the expense under medical benefits since the cause is usually bacterial.

Other Surgical Procedures

- Tooth reimplantation—Stabilization of accidentally evulsed or displaced tooth or alveolus.
- Tooth implantation—Placement of a tooth back into the same socket after it has been knocked out.
- Tooth transplantation—Moving a natural tooth from one location to another. As a rule, implantation is covered but transplantation is not. Of course, it depends on the circumstances and the plan provisions.
- Surgical exposure—The cutting of the gum and sometimes the attachment of wires to the crown of the unerupted tooth to assist in the eruption and proper alignment of the tooth. Often, this is done for orthodontic purposes. In such a case, it would be covered only if the plan has orthodontic provisions.

The following codes are considered oral surgery and are usually covered under the medical plan.

7285	Biopsy of oral tissue (hard)
7286	Biopsy of oral tissue (soft)
7290	Surgical repositioning of teeth

Alveoloplasty

Alveoloplasty is surgical preparation of a ridge for dentures. It is coded per quadrant, either in conjunction with extractions or without. Unless otherwise specified in the contract, alveoloplasties are covered under dental, not medical.

Stomatoplasty

Stomatoplasty is plastic surgery or repair of the mouth. The following codes include revision of soft tissue on ridges, muscle reattachment, tongue, palate, and other oral soft tissues. It is coded per arch as 7340 (uncomplicated) or 7350 (complicated). Complications include ridge extension, soft tissue grafts, and management of hypertrophied and hyperplastic tissue.

Surgical Excision

Surgical excision includes excision of reactive inflammatory lesions, scar tissue, or localized congenital lesions. It is coded as 7410 for a lesion up to 1.25 cm or 7420 for a lesion over 1.25 cm.

Excision pericoronal gingiva is an excision of the gums around a tooth.

Excision of Tumors

Tumors are abnormal (possibly cancerous) growths in the body. The coding for the removal of tumors depends on their size and whether they are benign or malignant.

Removal of Cysts and Neoplasms

A cyst is an enclosed pouch that contains fluid, semifluid, or solid material. A neoplasm is a new tumor or growth. The code depends on the size of the cyst or neoplasm and whether it is odontogenic (relating to the origin and formation of the teeth) or nonodontogenic. Code 7465 is used for procedures which involve the destruction of lesions by physical methods: electrosurgery, chemotherapy, and cryotherapy.

Excision of Bone Tissue

Removal of exostosis is the removal of a bony growth that arises from either the maxilla or mandible. It often involves the ossification (bone formation) of muscular attachments. An ostectomy is the surgical excision of all or part of a bone. A radical resection of mandible with bone graft is coded 7490.

Surgical Incision

An abscess is a collection of pus that results in disintegration or displacement of tissues. In such a case, the abscess needs to be opened and drained of pus, then cleansed and sutured closed. Abscesses are coded 7510 if they are intraoral (inside the mouth) and 7520 if they are extraoral (outside the mouth).

Code 7530 is used to bill for the removal of a foreign body, skin, or subcutaneous areolar tissue.

Code 7540 is used to bill for the removal of reaction-producing foreign bodies in the musculoskeletal system.

A sequestrectomy for osteomyelitis is isolation of a portion of bone due to inflammation. This procedure prevents the inflammation from spreading to the surrounding bone.

Maxillary sinusotomy for removal of tooth fragment or foreign body is the surgical removal of a tooth fragment or foreign body from the maxilla sinuses.

There are some remaining dental codes used for fractures and dislocations. Some administrators will use these codes, but most will use the codes provided in the CPT. Review all the ADA codes until you are familiar with them.

Orthodontic Services

Orthodontics is the branch of dentistry concerned with the detection, prevention, and correction of abnormalities in the positioning of the teeth in relationship to the jaw. The alignment deals with both vertical and horizontal positioning of the teeth.

The principle of orthodontics is that in order for a person to properly chew food, each tooth must have an aligned opposing tooth. This alignment provides for the proper occlusion.

Many plans do not provide orthodontia benefits. Therefore, if teeth are being extracted (it is common for the bicuspids to be extracted to make sufficient room in the mouth for proper tooth alignment) or if teeth are being crowned (to increase vertical dimension and thus provide proper occlusion) for orthodontic purposes, even though the specific services may be covered by the plan, the services would not be covered because of the purpose of the treatment. Other plans may provide orthodontia benefits but only for children, up to a specific age.

Orthodontic treatment is divided into three classifications. The classifications range from the lesser level of misalignment (malocclusion) to the greatest level.

A class I malocclusion is called a *neutroclusion*. This occurs when the upper and lower set of teeth come together normally, but the teeth themselves do not occlude properly (see Figure 24-4). A class II malocclusion is called a *distoclusion*. This occurs when the maxillary arch protrudes out from the mandibular arch. A class III malocclusion is called a *mesioclusion*. This occurs when the mandibular arch protrudes in front of the maxillary arch.

There are other services in which only very slight guidance is required and the level is not even classified. Coding is based on the classification or the type of guidance being provided.

Preventive Treatment Procedure

Preventive treatment procedures are broken into three classifications: minor treatment for tooth guidance, minor treatment to control harmful habits, and interceptive orthodontic treatment. In each case the coding depends on whether therapy uses a removable or a fixed appliance. Appliances that are necessitated because of harmful habits such as tongue thrust, bruxism (grinding of teeth at night), thumb and lip sucking are usually covered only under orthodontics.

Comprehensive Orthodontic Treatment

Comprehensive orthodontic treatment is broken into two classifications: treatment of the transitional dentition (primary teeth) and treatment of the permanent dentition (permanent teeth). In each case, the coding depends on the degree of malocclusion (misalignment).

8650 Treatment of the atypical or extended skeletal case

8750 Posttreatment stabilization

Autoreposition appliances are used in temporo-

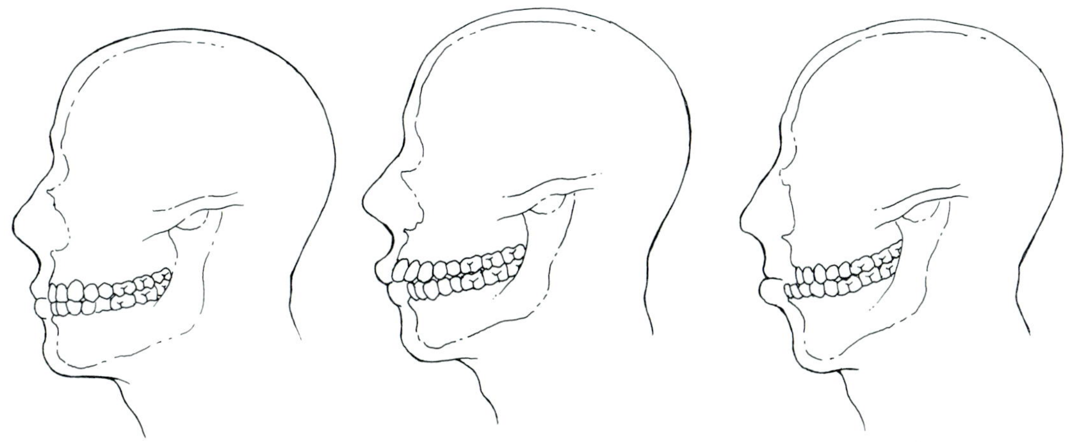

Figure 24-4: Classifications of Malocculusions.

mandibular joint (TMJ) treatment. Some orthodontic treatment is also done for this reason. TMJ is usually severely limited under most plans, but may be allowable if the plan has orthodontic coverage.

The total case fee is the amount charged by the provider for the entire orthodontic treatment program. This fee should include all diagnostic records, examinations, monthly fees, x-rays, including full-mouth x-rays, cephalometric tracings and photographs, and study models.

Most administrators will pay a portion of the total case fee (called the banding fee) upon activation of the orthodontic treatment. The remainder of the total case fee is paid on a monthly basis, and the provider must bill the monthly services charge as treatment is rendered. Some plans have provisions regarding the severity of the malocclusion for orthodontic benefits to be covered. If this is the case, the claim would need to be sent to the dental consultant for review. The average orthodontic case lasts 2 to 3 years.

Adjunctive General Services

A number of miscellaneous services are necessary for the care and treatment of dental conditions. The following will provide a guide for some of the more common ones.

Unclassified Treatment

Palliative treatment is emergency treatment performed to relieve pain or to prevent a condition from worsening. It is not a cure for the disease. Palliative is performed on an emergency basis. After treatment, the patient is directed to go to his or her regular doctor during office hours for treatment of the underlying condition causing the pain.

Anesthesia

Code 9210 is used for local anesthesia (not in conjunction with operative or surgical procedures). If another service is being performed, a local anesthesia is normally combined with the procedure and not allowable separately.

There are numerous types of anesthesia, as evidenced by the following codes:

9211 Regional block anesthesia
9212 Trigeminal division block anesthesia
9215 Local anesthesia
9220 General anesthesia
9230 Analgesia

9240 Intravenous sedation

General anesthesia is usually allowable for only limited services. Usually by administration or through plan provisions, it will be allowable only on procedures that are more definitive (such as oral surgery). Many people have an anxiety about going to a dentist. In such cases, the provider administers general, intravenous (IV) sedation, or "twilight sleep." IV sedation is usually allowable on the same basis as general anesthesia. Twilight sleep is a type of relaxation induced by the patient breathing gas. This may also be referred to as "laughing gas." Commonly, it is nitrous oxide. Many plans handle this on the same basis as a local anesthetic; that is, no additional allowance is provided and it may be combined with other procedures performed.

Professional Consultation

Code 9310 is used for diagnostic service(s) provided by a physician or dentist other than the practitioner providing the treatment. This code is also used for a second opinion. Often, the consulting provider is a specialist.

Professional Visits

These codes are used when a dentist visits a patient at the patient's home, at the hospital, at the office during regularly scheduled hours, or at the office outside of regularly scheduled hours.

Drugs

All drugs are coded as therapeutic drug injections or other drugs or medicaments.

Miscellaneous Services

These codes are used for services that do not fall into any other category. They are used to denote the application of desensitizing medications, any complications or unusual circumstances, the performance of an occlusion analysis, and the completion of a claim form.

Code 9999 is used for any services or procedures that do not have a code listed in the ADA code listing. It is classified as "unspecified" and usually requires the addition of a medical report describing the procedure.

Summary

Dentistry is officially that department of the healing arts that is concerned with the teeth, the oral (mouth) cavity, and its associated structures. This includes diagnosis, treatment, restoration, and replacement of missing portions or parts. Dentistry also includes surgical procedures performed in and about the inside of the mouth or oral cavity.

There are services in dentistry that are performed for other than existing pathologic conditions. Some of these services (such as prophylaxis, x-rays, fluoride treatments, and repair of dentures and bridgework) are specifically included as covered dental services under most plans, but are usually subject to limitations.

Other services are performed, not for a pathologic condition but primarily for cosmetic or similar reasons or at the election of the patient or dentist. Although the particular type or category of service that is received might be covered under the plan, benefits are usually not provided for services that are performed for cosmetic or similar purposes or at the election of the patient or dentist.

In 1969, the American Dental Association (ADA) created a coding system that also served to categorize dental services. This established a uniform nomenclature for all dental services. The ADA list uses a four-digit coding system and classifies procedures under certain categories. Services (and thus their codes) are defined based on the type of treatment provided. It is important to know what type of service is being performed to code it properly. Familiarity with the different types of dental services and their codes will help to ensure accurate dental coding.

Assignments

Complete the Questions for Review.
Complete the coding for Dental Claims 29-1 to 29-15 beginning on page 395.

Questions for Review

Directions: Answer the following questions without looking back into the material just covered. Write your answers in the space provided.

1. List the 10 ADA classifications of dental services.

   a. ______________________________

   b. ______________________________

   c. ______________________________

   d. ______________________________

   e. ______________________________

   f. ______________________________

   g. ______________________________

   h. ______________________________

   i. ______________________________

   j. ______________________________

2. What are diagnostic procedures? ______________________________

3. What are preventive procedures? ______________________________

4. What are cosmetic procedures? ______________________________

5. What are prosthodontics? ______________________________

6. What are restorative services? ______________________________

7. What are endodontic services? ______________________________

8. What are periodontic services? ______________________________

9. Under what ADA category do routine fillings fall? ______________________________

10. What are inlays and onlays and under what ADA category do they fall? ______________________________

If you were unable to answer any of the questions, refer back to the section and then complete the answers.

Appendix 24-1

Dental Code List

The following list of dental codes is intended to be used for training and reference purposes only, since the particular company or plan guidelines may differ from those stated. Please contact the American Dental Association or your State Department of Insurance for any changes or updates to this list.*

ADA Code	Unit Value	CFC	Description of Service
			Diagnostic (0100—0999)
			Clinical Oral Examination
0110	0.7	A	Initial oral examination
0120	0.5	A	Periodic oral examination
0130	0.8	A	Emergency oral examinations
			Radiographs
0210	1.4	A	Intraoral-full mouth series w/bitewings
0220	0.3	A	Intraoral-single, first film
0230	0.2	A	Intraoral-each additional film
0240	0.5	A	Intraoral-occlusal film each
0250	0.4	A	Extraoral-single, first film
0260	0.3	A	Extraoral-each additional film
0270	0.4	A	Bitewing-single film
0272	0.5	A	Bitewing-two films
0273	0.6	A	Bitewings-three films
0274	0.7	A	Bitewings-four films
0275	0.2	A	Bitewing-each additional film
0290	1.0	A	Posteroanterior and lateral skull and facial bone survey film
0310	1.8	A	Sialography
0321	2.0	A	Temporomandibular joint, film
0330	1.2	A	Panoramic-maxilla and mandible, film
0340	1.2	A	Cephalometric film
0390	BR	A	Diagnostic radiographs (by report)
			Labs and Other Tests
0401	0.6	A	Complete blood count
0402	0.3	A	Urinalysis
0403	0.3	A	Hemoglobin
0404	0.3	A	Hematocrit
0410	0.8	A	Bacteriologic studies for determination of pathologic agents

ADA Code	Unit Value	CFC	Description of Service
0420	0.6	A	Caries susceptibility tests
0450	1.2	A	Histopathologic examination
0460	0.5	A	Pulp vitality tests
0470	1.1	A	Diagnostic casts
0471	BR	A	Diagnostic photographs
0490	BR	A	Miscellaneous tests
			Preventive (1000—1999)
			Dental Prophylaxis
1110	1.0	A	Adults
1120	0.8	A	Children
			Fluoride Treatments
1201	1.1	A	Topical application of fluoride (including prophylaxis)-children
1210	1.1	A	Topical application of sodium fluoride-4 treatments (excluding prophylaxis)
1211	1.9	A	Topical application of sodium fluoride-4 treatments (including prophylaxis)
1220	0.3	A	Topical application of stannous fluoride-1 treatment (excluding prophylaxis)
1221	1.1	A	Topical application of stannous fluoride-1 treatment (including prophylaxis)
1230	0.3	A	Topical application of acid fluoride phosphate—1 treatment (excluding prophylaxis)
1231	1.1	A	Topical application of acid fluoride phosphate—1 treatment (including prophylaxis)
			Other Preventive Services
1310	BR		Dietary planning for the control of dental caries
1330	BR		Oral hygiene instruction
1340	BR		Training in preventive dental care
1350	0.6	A	Topical application of sealants—per quadrant
1351	0.5	A	Sealant—per tooth
			Space Management Therapy
1510	3.8	A	Fixed-unilateral type
1515	5.5	A	Fixed-bilateral type
1520	5.0	A	Removable unilateral type
1525	6.5	A	Removable bilateral type
1550	0.8	A	Recementation of space maintainer
			Restorative (2000—2999)
			Fillings, Inlays, Onlays, and Crowns
			Amalgam Restorations (Including Polishing)
2110	0.9	B	Amalgam-1 surface, primary
2120	1.2	B	Amalgam-2 surfaces, primary
2130	1.5	B	Amalgam-3 surfaces, primary
2131	1.8	B	Amalgam-4 surfaces, primary
2140	1.1	B	Amalgam-1 surface, permanent

ADA Code	Unit Value	CFC	Description of Service
2150	1.4	B	Amalgam-2 surfaces, permanent
2160	1.7	B	Amalgam-3 surfaces, permanent
2161	2.0	B	Amalgam-4 or more surfaces, permanent
2190	0.8	B	Pin retention-exclusive of amalgam
			Silicate Restorations
2210	1.2	B	Silicate cement per restoration
			Acrylic or Plastic Restorations
2310	1.3	B	Acrylic or plastic or composite resin
2330	1.3	B	Composite resin, anterior teeth-1 surface
2331	1.8	B	Composite resin, anterior teeth-2 surfaces
2332	2.3	B	Composite resin, anterior teeth-3 surfaces
2334	0.8	B	Pin retention-exclusive of composite resin
2335	2.5	B	Acrylic or plastic composite resin (involving incisal angle or 4 or more surfaces)
2337	1.9	B	Composite resin with ultra-violet, 1 surface
2338	2.6	B	Composite resin with ultra-violet, 2 surfaces
2339	3.1	B	Composite resin with ultra-violet, 3 surfaces
2340	0.6	B	Acid etch for restorations
2380	1.5	B	Composite resin, posterior, primary-1 surface
2381	2.0	B	Composite resin, posterior, primary-2 surfaces
2382	2.5	B	Composite resin, posterior, primary-3 surfaces
2385	2.0	B	Composite resin, posterior, permanent-1 surface
2386	2.5	B	Composite resin, posterior, permanent-2 surfaces
2387	3.0	B	Composite resin, posterior, permanent-3 surfaces
			Gold Foil Restorations
2410	5.0	C	Gold foil-1 surface
2420	6.5	C	Gold foil-2 surfaces
2430	8.0	C	Gold foil-3 surfaces
			Gold Inlay Restorations
2510	7.0	C	Inlay-gold, 1 surface
2520	8.5	C	Inlay-gold, 2 surfaces
2530	10.0	C	Inlay-gold, 3 surfaces
2540	2.0	C	Onlay-per tooth (in addition to above)
			Porcelain Restorations
2610	3.0	B	Inlay-porcelain
			Crowns (Single Restorations Only)
2710	3.0	C	Plastic (acrylic)
2711	2.5	C	Plastic-prefabricated

ADA Code	Unit Value	CFC	Description of Service
2720	11.0	C	Plastic with gold (high and medium noble)
2721	10.5	C	Plastic with nonprecious metal (base metal)
2722	10.7	C	Plastic with semiprecious metal (low noble)
2740	10.8	C	Porcelain
2750	12.0	C	Porcelain with gold (high and medium noble)
2751	11.4	C	Porcelain with nonprecious metal (base metal)
2752	11.8	C	Porcelain with semiprecious metal (low noble)
2790	11.8	C	Gold (full cast; high and medium noble)
2791	10.6	C	Nonprecious metal (full cast; base metal)
2792	11.0	C	Semiprecious metal (full cast; low noble)
2810	11.8	C	Gold (3/4 cast; high and medium noble)
2830	2.0	C	Prefabricated stainless steel-primary
2840	1.5	C	Temporary (fractured tooth)
2891	4.5	C	Cast post and core in addition to crown
2892	2.5	C	Prefabricated post and core in addition to crown
			Other Restorative Services
2910	0.8	C	Recement inlays
2920	0.8	C	Recement crowns
2940	0.8	B	Fillings (sedative)
2950	2.0	C	Crown buildup-including pins
2960	5.0	B	Labial veneer (laminate)
			Endodontic (3000—3999)
			Pulp Capping
3110	0.6	B	Pulp cap-direct (excluding final restoration)
3120	0.6	B	Pulp cap-indirect (excluding final restoration)
3220	1.2	B	Vital pulpotomy (excluding final restoration)
			Root Canal Therapy (Includes Treatment Plan, Clinical Procedures, and Follow-up Care)
3310	7.0	B	Anterior (excludes final restoration)
3311	6.5	B	Root canal therapy-1 (excluding final restoration), Sargenti
3320	8.5	B	Premolar (excludes final restoration)
3321	8.0	B	Root canal therapy-2 (excluding final restoration), Sargenti
3330	11.0	B	Molar (excludes final restoration)
3331	10.5	B	Root canal therapy-3 (excluding final restoration), Sargenti
3341	11.0	B	Root canal therapy-4 (excluding final restoration), Sargenti
3350	2.2	B	Apexification (treatment may extend over 6 to 18 months)

ADA Code	Unit Value	CFC	Description of Service
			Periapical Services
3410	8.0	B	Apicoectomy-performed as separate surgical procedure (per root)
3420	9.0	B	Apicoectomy-performed in conjunction with endodontic procedure (per root)
3430	3.0	B	Retrograde filling
3440	3.0	B	Apical curettage
3450	4.5	B	Root resection
3460	5.5	B	Endodontic implants
			Other Endodontic Procedures
3910	0.8	B	Surgical procedure for isolation of tooth with rubber dam
3920	3.5	B	Hemisection
3940	1.1	B	Recalcification (perforations, root resorption)
3950	1.4	B	Canal preparation and fitting of performed dowel or post
3960	BR	B	Bleaching of discolored tooth
			Periodontics (4000—4999)
			Surgical Services (Including Usual Postoperative Services)
4210	6.0	B	Gingivectomy or gingivoplasty-per quadrant
4220	2.0	B	Gingival curettage-per quadrant
4240	6.0	B	Gingival flap procedure
4250	8.3	B	Mucogingival surgery-per quadrant
4260	12.0	B	Osseous surgery (including flap entry and closure) per quadrant
4261	6.5	B	Osseous graft-single site (including flap entry, closure, and donor site)
4262	8.5	B	Osseous grafts-multiple sites (including flap entry, closure, and donor site)
4270	6.0	B	Pedicle soft tissue grafts
4271	6.5	B	Free soft tissue grafts (including donor site)
4272	11.5	B	Vestibuloplasty
4280	1.1	B	Periodontal pulpal procedures
			Adjunctive Periodontal Services
4320	2.0	B	Provisional splinting-intracoronal
4321	2.2	B	Provisional splinting-extracoronal
4330	1.1	B	Occlusal adjustment (limited)
4331	4.4	B	Occlusal adjustment (complete)
4340	10.0	B	Periodontal scaling and root planing-entire mouth
4341	2.5	B	Periodontal scaling and root planing-per quadrant
4350	8.0	B	Tooth movement for periodontal purposes
4360	8.0	B	Special periodontal appliances (including occlusal guards)
4365	BR	B	Athletic mouthguard fabrication
4370	BR	B	Case pattern modifiers (by report)

ADA Code	Unit Value	CFC	Description of Service
			Case Pattern Section
4500	BR		Type I Gingivitis—shallow pockets, no bone loss Treatment 1. All necessary diagnostic procedures 2. Training in personal preventive dental care 3. Mouth preparation procedures 4. Routine finishing procedures 5. Posttreatment evaluation
4600	BR		Type II Early periodontitis—moderate pockets, minor to moderate bone loss, satisfactory topography Treatment 1. All necessary diagnostic procedures 2. Training in personal preventive dental care 3. Mouth preparation procedures 4. Occlusal adjustment (if necessary) 5. Surgical procedures usually involving curettage or gingivectomy 6. Routine finishing procedures 7. Posttreatment evaluation
4700	BR		Type III Moderate periodontitis—moderate to deep pockets, moderate to severe bone loss, unsatisfactory topography Treatment 1. All necessary diagnostic procedures 2. Training in personal preventive dental care 3. Mouth preparation procedures 4. Occlusal adjustment 5. Surgical procedures usually involving flap entry and osseous procedures 6. Routine finishing procedures 7. Posttreatment evaluation
4800	BR		Type IV Advanced periodontitis—deep pockets, severe bone loss, advanced inability patterns (usually cases involving missing teeth and reconstruction) Treatment 1. All necessary diagnostic procedures 2. Training in personal preventive dental care 3. Mouth preparation procedures 4. Occlusal adjustment 5. Surgical procedures usually involving complex techniques 6. Routine finishing procedures 7. Posttreatment evaluation
			Other Periodontic Services
4910	1.4	A	Preventive periodontal procedures (periodontal prophylaxis)
4920	0.7	B	Unscheduled dressing change (by other than treating dentist)

ADA Code	Unit Value	CFC	Description of Service
			Prosthodontics, Removable (5000—5999)
			Complete Dentures (Including Routine Postdelivery Care)
5110	16.5	C	Complete upper
5120	16.5	C	Complete lower
5130	16.5	C	Immediate upper
5140	16.5	C	Immediate lower
			Partial Dentures (Including Routine Postdelivery Care)
5211	14.0	C	Upper—excluding clasps, acrylic base
5212	14.0	C	Lower—excluding clasps, acrylic base
5213	18.0	C	Upper—cast chrome base, with acrylic saddles, excluding clasps
5214	18.0	C	Lower—cast chrome base, with acrylic saddles, excluding clasps
5215	18.0	C	Upper—with 2 gold clasps with rests, acrylic base
5216	18.0	C	Upper—with 2 chrome clasps with rests, acrylic base
5217	18.0	C	Lower—with 2 gold clasps with rests, acrylic base
5218	18.0	C	Lower—with chrome clasps with rests, acrylic base
5230	20.0	C	Lower—with gold lingual bar and 2 clasps, acrylic base
5231	20.0	C	Lower—with chrome lingual bar and 2 clasps, acrylic base
5240	26.0	C	Lower—with gold lingual bar and 2 clasps, cast base
5241	26.0	C	Lower—with chrome lingual bar and 2 clasps, cast base
5250	20.0	C	Upper—with gold palatal bar and 2 clasps, acrylic base
5251	20.0	C	Upper—with chrome palatal bar and 2 clasps, acrylic base
5260	26.0	C	Upper—with gold palatal bar and 2 clasps, cast base
5261	26.0	C	Upper—with chrome palatal bar and 2 clasps, cast base
5280	4.0	C	Removable unilateral partial denture—1 piece gold casting, clasp attachments, per unit including pontics
5281	4.0	C	Removable unilateral partial denture—1 piece chrome casting, clasp attachments, per unit including pontics
5291	18.4	C	Full cast partial—with 2 gold clasps (upper)
5292	18.4	C	Full cast partial—with 2 chrome clasps (upper)
5293	18.4	C	Full cast partial—with 2 gold clasps (lower)
5294	18.4	C	Full cast partial—with 2 chrome clasps (lower)
			Additional Units For Partial Dentures
5310	1.7	C	Each clasp with rest
5320	BR	C	Each tooth
			Adjustments to Dentures
5410	0.8	C	Complete denture
5421	0.8	C	Partial denture (upper)
5422	0.8	C	Partial denture (lower)

ADA Code	Unit Value	CFC	Description of Service
			Repairs to Dentures
5610	1.7	C	Repair broken complete or partial denture—no teeth damaged
5620	1.9	C	Repair broken complete or partial denture—replace 1 broken tooth
5630	1.0	C	Replace additional teeth—each tooth
5640	1.7	C	Replace broken tooth on denture—no other repairs
5650	2.2	C	Adding tooth to partial denture to replace extracted tooth—each tooth (not involving clasps or abutment tooth)
5660	3.0	C	Adding tooth to partial denture to replace extracted tooth each tooth (involving clasps or abutment tooth)
5670	1.8	C	Reattaching damaged clasp on denture
5680	2.5	C	Replacing broken clasp with new clasp on denture
5690	1.8	C	Each additional clasp with rest
			Denture Duplication
5710	6.5	C	Rebase upper or lower complete denture
5720	6.5	C	Rebase upper or lower partial denture
			Denture Relining
5730	4.0	C	Relining upper or lower complete denture (office reline)
5740	4.0	C	Relining upper or lower partial denture (office reline)
5750	5.0	C	Relining upper or lower complete denture (laboratory)
5760	5.0	C	Relining upper or lower partial denture (laboratory)
			Other Prosthetic Services
5810	8.0	C	Denture—temporary (complete), upper
5811	8.0	C	Denture—temporary (complete), lower
5820	6.0	C	Denture—temporary (partial-stayplate), upper
5821	6.0	C	Denture—temporary (partial-stayplate), lower
5830	17.0	C	Obturator for surgically excised palatal tissue
5840	17.0	C	Obturator for deficient velopharyngeal function (cleft palate)
5850	1.6	C	Tissue conditioning
5860	16.5	C	Overdenture complete (by report)
5861	BR	C	Overdenture partial (by report)
			Maxillofacial Prosthetics
			Extraoral Prostheses (Including 3 Months' Maintenance)
5911	RNE		Facial moulage (sectional)
5912	RNE		Facial moulage (complete)
5913	RNE		Nasal prosthesis
5914	RNE		Auricular prosthesis
5915	RNE		Orbital prosthesis

ADA Code	Unit Value	CFC	Description of Service
5916	RNE		Ocular prosthesis
5917	RNE		Composite facial prosthesis
5918	RNE		Replacement prosthesis
5919	RNE		Prosthetic dressing
5920	RNE		Ocular implant
5921	RNE		Orbital implant
			Intraoral Prostheses (Acquired Defects)
5931	RNE		Surgical obturator
5932	RNE		Postsurgical obturator
5933	RNE		Refitting of obturator
5934	RNE		Mandibular resection (flange) prosthesis
5935	RNE		Mandibular resection (denture) prosthesis
			Intraoral Prosthesis (Congenital Defects)
5951	RNE		Feeding aid
5952	RNE		Pediatric speech aid
5953	RNE		Adult speech aid
5954	RNE		Superimposed prosthesis
5955	RNE		Palatal lift prosthesis
5956	17.0	C	Obturator
5957	RNE		Speech bulb
			Implants (Facial, Mandibular, Cranial)
5971	RNE		Single implant
5972	RNE		Complex implant
5973	RNE		Subperiosteal implant
5974	RNE		Endosseous implant (in the bone)
5975	5.0	B	Endodontic endosseous pin (through root and into bone)
			Treatment Prostheses
5981	RNE		Splint—per arch
5982	RNE		Surgical stent
5983	RNE		Radiation carrier
5984	RNE		Radiation shield
5985	RNE		Docking device—cone locator
5986	2.8	C	Fluoride applicator—per arch
5987	RNE		Trismus appliance
5988	RNE		Infant orthopedic appliance
5989	RNE		Maxillary inclined plane and/or maxillary occlusal table
5990	RNE		Mandibular guide flange

ADA Code	Unit Value	CFC	Description of Service
			Prosthodontics, Fixed (6000—6999)
			Fixed Bridges (Each Abutment and Each Pontic Constitute a Unit in a Bridge)
			Bridge Pontics
6210	11.8	C	Cast gold (high and medium noble)
6211	10.6	C	Cast nonprecious metal (base metal)
6212	11.0	C	Cast semiprecious (low noble)
6220	8.0	C	Slotted facing
6230	10.0	C	Slotted pontic
6235	9.0	C	Pin facing
6240	12.0	C	Porcelain fused to gold (high and medium noble)
6241	11.4	C	Porcelain fused to nonprecious metal (base metal)
6242	11.8	C	Porcelain fused to semiprecious metal (low noble)
6250	11.0	C	Plastic processed to gold (high and medium noble)
6251	10.5	C	Plastic processed to nonprecious metal (base metal)
6252	10.7	C	Plastic processed to semiprecious metal (low noble)
			Retainers
6520	8.5	C	Gold inlay—2 surfaces
6530	10.0	C	Gold inlay—3 or more surfaces
6540	2.0	C	Gold inlay—(onlaying cusps)
			Repairs
6610	2.5	C	Replace broken pin facing with slotted or other facing
6620	2.5	C	Replace broken facing where post is intact
6630	2.5	C	Replace broken facing where post backing is broken
6640	2.5	C	Replace broken facing with acrylic
6650	2.5	C	Replace broken pontic
			Crowns
6710	5.5	C	Plastic (acrylic)
6720	11.0	C	Plastic processed to gold (high and medium noble)
6721	10.5	C	Plastic processed to nonprecious metal (base metal)
6722	10.7	C	Plastic processed to semiprecious metal (low noble)
6740	10.8	C	Porcelain
6750	12.0	C	Porcelain fused to gold (high and medium noble)
6751	11.4	C	Porcelain fused to nonprecious metal (base metal)
6752	11.8	C	Porcelain fused to semiprecious metal (low noble)
6760	10.7	C	Reverse pin facing and metal
6780	11.8	C	Gold (3/4 cast; high and medium noble)
6790	11.8	C	Gold (full cast; high and medium noble)
6791	10.6	C	Nonprecious metal (full cast; base metal)
6792	11.0	C	Semiprecious metal (full cast; low noble)

ADA Code	Unit Value	CFC	Description of Service
			Other Prosthetic Services
6930	1.5	C	Replacement bridge
6940	2.8	C	Stress breaker
6950	5.8	C	Precision attachment
6960	3.0	C	Dowel pin—metal
			Oral Surgery (7000—7999)
			Extractions (Includes Local Anesthesia and Routine Postoperative Care)
7110	1.1	B	Single tooth
7120	1.1	B	Each additional tooth
			Surgical Extractions (Includes Local Anesthesia and Routine Postoperative Care)
7210	2.0	B	Surgical removal of erupted tooth requires elevation of mucoperiosteal flap and removal of bone or section of tooth
7220	2.5	B	Impaction that requires incision of overlaying soft tissue and the removal of the tooth
7230	3.6	B	Impaction that requires incision of overlaying soft tissue, elevation of a flap, and either removal of bone and tooth or sectioning and removal of the tooth
7240	4.2	B	Impaction that requires incision of overlaying soft tissue, elevation of a flap, removal of bone, and sectioning of the tooth for removal
7241	4.7	B	Impaction that requires incision of overlaying soft tissue, elevation of a flap, removal of bone, sectioning of the tooth for removal or presents unusual difficulties and circumstances
7250	2.0	B	Root recovery (surgical removal of residual root)
7260	8.0	B	Oroantral fistula closure (or antral root recovery)
			Other Surgical Procedures
7270	4.0	B	Tooth reimplantation or stabilization of accidentally evulsed or displaced tooth or alveolus
7271	8.0	B	Tooth implantation
7272	6.0	B	Tooth transplantation
7280	4.5	B	Surgical exposure of impacted or unerupted tooth for orthodontic reasons including wire attachments when indicated.
7281	3.5	B	Surgical exposure of impacted or unerupted tooth to aid eruption
7285	3.0	B	Biopsy of oral tissue (hard)
7286	2.2	B	Biopsy of oral tissue (soft)
7290	4.0	B	Surgical repositioning of teeth
			Alveoloplasty (Surgical Preparation of Ridge for Dentures)
7310	2.2	B	Per quadrant in conjunction with extractions
7320	3.2	B	Per quadrant not in conjunction with extractions

ADA Code	Unit Value	CFC	Description of Service
			Stomatoplasty (Including Revision of Soft Tissue on Ridges, Muscle Reattachment, Tongue, Palate, and Other Oral Soft Tissues)
7340	4.0	B	Per arch, uncomplicated
7350	BR	B	Per arch, complicated including ridge extension, soft tissue grafts, and management of hypertrophied and hyperplastic tissue
			Surgical Excision (Excision of Reactive Inflammatory Lesions — Scar Tissue or Localized Congenital Lesions)
7410	3.0	B	Radical excision—lesion diameter up to 1.25 cm
7420	6.0	B	Radical excision—lesion diameter over 1.25 cm
7425	1.7	B	Excision pericoronal gingiva
			Excision of Tumors
7430	3.0	B	Excision of benign tumor—lesion diameter up to 1.25 cm
7431	6.0	B	Excision of benign tumor—lesion diameter over 1.25 cm
7440	4.5	B	Excision of malignant tumor—lesion diameter up to 1.25 cm
7441	7.2	B	Excision of malignant tumor—lesion diameter over 1.25 cm
			Removal of Cysts and Neoplasms
7450	3.0	B	Removal of odontogenic cyst or tumor—up to 1.25 cm in diameter
7451	6.0	B	Removal of odontogenic cyst or tumor—over 1.25 cm in diameter
7460	3.0	B	Removal of nonodontogenic cyst or tumor—up to 1.25 cm in diameter
7461	6.0	B	Removal of nonodontogenic cyst or tumor—over 1.25 cm in diameter
7465	1.4	B	Destruction of lesions by physical methods: electrosurgery, chemotherapy, cryotherapy
			Excision of Bone Tissue
7470	4.5	B	Removal of exostosis—maxilla or mandible
7480	10.0	B	Partial ostectomy (guttering or saucerization)
7490	BR	B	Radical resection of mandible with bone graft
			Surgical Incision
7510	1.5	B	Incision and drainage of abscess—intraoral
7520	2.0	B	Incision and drainage of abscess—extraoral
7530	2.0	B	Removal of foreign body, skin, or subcutaneous areolar tissue
7540	2.0	B	Removal of reaction-producing foreign bodies, musculoskeletal system
7550	5.0	B	Sequestrectomy for osteomyelitis
7560	8.0	B	Maxillary sinusotomy for removal of tooth fragment or foreign body
			Treatment of Fractures (Simple)
7610	42.0	B	Maxilla—open reduction, teeth immobilized (if present)
7620	25.0	B	Maxilla—closed reduction, teeth immobilized (if present)
7630	42.0	B	Mandible—open reduction, teeth immobilized (if present)
7640	25.0	B	Mandible—closed reduction, teeth immobilized (if present)

ADA Code	Unit Value	CFC	Description of Service
7650	25.0	B	Malar or zygomatic arch—open reduction
7660	11.1	B	Malar or zygomatic arch—closed reduction
7670	25.0	B	Alveolus—stabilization to teeth, open reduction splinting
7680	53.0	B	Facial bones—complicated reduction with fixation and multiple surgical approaches
			Treatment of Fractures (Compound)
7710	42.0	B	Maxilla—open reduction
7720	25.0	B	Maxilla—closed reduction
7730	42.0	B	Mandible—open reduction
7740	25.0	B	Mandible—closed reduction
7750	33.0	B	Malar or zygomatic arch—open reduction
7760	19.4	B	Malar or zygomatic arch—closed reduction
7770	19.4	B	Alveolus—stabilization of teeth—open reduction splinting
7780	53.0	B	Facial bones—complicated reduction with fixation and multiple surgical approaches
			Reduction of Dislocation and Management of Other Temporomandibular Joint Dysfunctions
7810	28.0	B	Open reduction of dislocation
7820	5.6	B	Closed reduction of dislocation
7830	5.6	B	Manipulation under anesthesia
7840	4.2	B	Condylectomy
7850	4.2	B	Meniscectomy
7860	4.2	B	Arthrotomy
7870	2.8	B	Arthrocentesis
			Other Oral Surgery
			Repair of Traumatic Wounds
7910	3.3	B	Suture of recent small wounds up to 5 cm
			Complicated suturing (reconstruction requiring delicate handling of tissues, wide undermining for meticulous closure)
7911	5.6	B	Up to 5 cm
7912	8.9	B	Over 5 cm
7920	BR	B	Skin grafts (identify defect covered, location, and type of graft)
			Other Repair Procedures
7930	3.3	B	Injection of trigeminal nerve branches for destruction
7931	5.0	B	Avulsion of trigeminal nerve branches
7940	56.0	B	Osteoplasty (for orthognathic deformities)
7941	RNE	B	Osteotomy, ramus, closed
7942	RNE	B	Osteotomy, ramus, open
7943	RNE	B	Osteotomy, ramus, open with bone graft
7944	RNE	B	Segmented or subapical per sextant or quadrant

ADA Code	Unit Value	CFC	Description of Service
7945	RNE	B	Osteotomy, body of mandible
7946	RNE	B	Maxilla, total (Le Fort I)
7947	RNE	B	Maxilla, segmented
7948	RNE	B	Osteoplasty of maxilla or other facial bones for midface hypoplasia or retrusion (Le Fort II and III) without bone graft
7949	RNE	B	Same as above except with bone graft
7950	BR	B	Osseous, osteoperiosteal, periosteal, or cartilage graft of the mandible—autogenous or nonautogenous
7955	BR	B	Repair of maxillofacial soft and hard tissue defects
7960	3.3	B	Frenulectomy—separate procedure (frenectomy or frenotomy)
7970	4.4	B	Excision of hyperplastic tissue—per arch
7980	16.0	B	Sialolithotomy
7981	16.7	B	Excision of salivary gland
7982	19.4	B	Sialodochoplasty
7983	16.7	B	Closure of salivary fistula
7990	11.1	B	Emergency tracheotomy
7991	28.0	B	Coronoidectomy
7992	28.0	B	Eminectomy
7993	RNE	B	Alloplastic implant to maxilla and other facial bones
7994	RNE	B	Implant, chin, homologous, heterologous, or alloplastic
			Orthodontics (8000—8999)
			Preventive Treatment Procedure
			Minor Treatment for Tooth Guidance
8110	7.0	B	Removable appliance therapy
8120	8.3	B	Fixed or cemented appliance therapy
			Minor Treatment to Control Harmful Habits
8210	4.4	B	Removable appliance therapy
8220	5.6	B	Fixed or cemented appliance therapy
			Interceptive Orthodontic Treatment
8360	7.0	B	Removable appliance therapy
8370	8.3	B	Fixed appliance therapy
			Comprehensive Orthodontic Treatment
			Treatment of the Transitional Dentition
8460	BR		Class I malocclusion
8470	BR		Class II malocclusion
8480	BR		Class III malocclusion
			Treatment of the Permanent Dentition
8560	BR		Class I malocclusion

ADA Code	Unit Value	CFC	Description of Service
8570	BR		Class II malocclusion
8580	BR		Class III malocclusion
8650	BR		Treatment of the atypical or extended skeletal case
8750	BR		Posttreatment stabilization
			Adjunctive General Services (9000—9999)
			Unclassified Treatment
9110	0.8	B	Palliative (emergency) treatment of dental pain, minor procedures
			Anesthesia
9210	0.4	B	Local anesthesia (not in conjunction with operative or surgical procedures)
9211	0.9	B	Regional block anesthesia
9212	0.9	B	Trigeminal division block anesthesia
9215	0.4	B	Local anesthesia
9220	2.5	B	General anesthesia
9230	0.5	B	Analgesia
9240	1.5	B	Intravenous sedation
			Professional Consultation (Diagnostic Service Provided by Physician or Dentist Other Than Practitioner Providing Treatment)
9310	1.5	B	Consultation—per session
			Professional Visits
9410	1.0	B	House calls
9420	0.9	B	Hospital calls
9430	0.6	B	Office visit—during regularly scheduled office hours (no operative service performed)
9440	1.2	B	Office visit—after regularly scheduled office hours (no operative service performed)
			Drugs
9610	0.6	B	Therapeutic drug injection
9630	0.4	B	Other drugs or medicaments
			Miscellaneous Services
9910	0.6	B	Application of desensitizing medicaments
9930	1.0	B	Complications (postsurgical—unusual circumstances)
9950	11.0	B	Occlusion analysis (mounted case)
9960	NC		Completion of claim form
9999	BR		Unspecified (by report to be described by statement of attending dentist)

25

Temporomandibular Joint Dysfunction

In this chapter you will learn:

- What temporomandibular joint (TMJ) dysfunction is and possible treatments.
- To recognize and define terms related to diagnosis and treatment of TMJ.
- Which treatments are accepted and which are not accepted in the treatment of TMJ dysfunction.

Temporomandibular joint (TMJ) dysfunction is a manifestation of an abnormality of the joint where the lower jaw hinges to the upper jaw (the temporomandibular joint; see Figure 25-1). This manifestation can result from various conditions: a disease of the bones such as arthritis, an injury to the TMJ joint, a disintegrative wearing down of the joint socket (the hollow area where the lower joint actually fits into the upper jaw), rheumatic fever or other connective tissue disorders, malocclusion, and even anxiety, emotional problems, and stress.

Symptoms of TMJ can include tenderness and pain of the TMJ and surrounding areas, muscle spasms, limitation of movement, and clicking or grating sounds during chewing or speaking.

Coverage for TMJ

Because of the variety of causes of TMJ dysfunction, confusion often exists regarding how payment should be handled. If the disorder is caused by arthritis or rheumatic fever, it is due to illness and should fall under medical benefits. If it is caused by anxiety, stress, or emotional problems, it is a psychological problem and should be handled under psychological benefits. If the cause of TMJ dysfunction is malocclusion, it is a dental problem and falls under the dental benefits.

Even under dental benefits, categorizing TMJ dysfunction is confusing because some plans consider it to be a dental problem and some an orthodontic problem. If orthodontic services are not covered, TMJ bene-

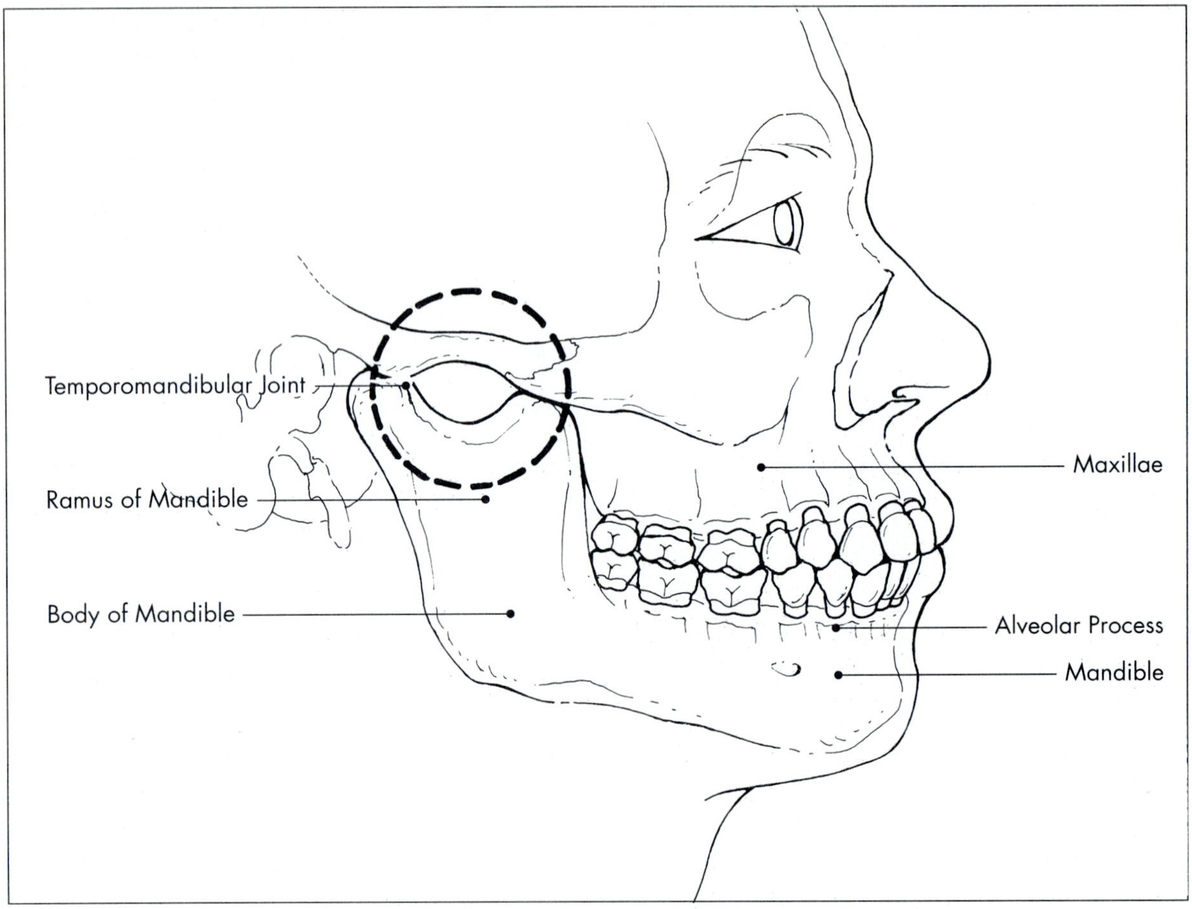

Figure 25-1: Dental skeletal structures.

fits may then be denied for this reason. Add to all this confusion the knowledge that some dental providers have overutilized the concept (often a patient has malalignment of the teeth, not TMJ dysfunction) in an effort to make the charges eligible under medical benefits rather than dental. Such an arrangement usually results in greater benefit payments because most medical plans have higher allowances and do not have the typical calendar year maximums that dental plans have.

As a result, most payors have adopted somewhat stringent guidelines regarding the payment of TMJ claims. Since treatment of TMJ is a very controversial subject, the following list shows some of the more common handling procedures. This is designed to provide guidance only. Remember that the handling of services vary greatly by payor. Therefore, the examiner needs to be aware of these differences and to recognize that special handling or guidelines may apply. Often, services and supplies must meet the following criteria to be payable:

- They must be recognized by the medical or dental profession as effective and appropriate treatment for TMJ dysfunction and its symptoms.
- They cannot be self-administered by the patient except with guidance by a licensed physician or dentist.

The following guidelines generally apply when processing TMJ claims:

- Services or supplies covered under medical plans when provided or prescribed by a dentist for TMJ dysfunction would be recognized as covered medical expenses if they were provided or prescribed by a physician for treatment of comparable forms of intractable pain not involving TMJ dysfunction.
- Services or supplies covered under dental plans with separate orthodontic benefits are those that are primarily or exclusively used to alter occlusion or reposition the lower jaw.
- Services or supplies not covered under medical plans or dental plans without separate orthodontic benefits are those specifically excluded under the contract or used to alter occlusion or reposition the lower jaw.

In other words, look at the services that have been rendered, not the TMJ diagnosis. For example, if surgery is performed and the surgery would normally be covered under medical benefits for other than a TMJ diagnosis, then the surgery is covered. If onlays or crowns are used to build up the teeth and reduce the malocclusion, these benefits would be covered under dental benefits if onlays or crowns are normally covered for other noncosmetic reasons.

If the exact cause of the TMJ disorder is proved, the following guidelines are used (often medical or dental review will be necessary before processing the claim):

- If the cause of the disorder is an accident, treatment is covered under both dental and medical plans.
- If the cause of the disorder is dental malocclusion (decayed, worn, or missing teeth), services are covered under dental benefits (if there is no exclusion for coverage of worn or missing teeth).
- If the cause of the disorder is congenital malocclusion (hereditary) or developmental (supernumerary teeth, teeth too large for the jaw), the plan should be consulted. If there is an exclusion for congenital or developmental problems, no benefits would be provided. If there is no exclusion, the services would be considered dental.

Some plans eliminate the confusion entirely by excluding TMJ services in their contract. In such a case, no benefits would be payable, regardless of the services rendered.

Appliances

An appliance is defined as any device or brace that includes banding or wiring used to reposition teeth, jaw joint, or lower jaw to restore normal occlusion. Appliances are often used in restoring normal occlusion to those with TMJ disorders. Examples of appliances include:

- Autorepositioning appliance.
- Bite splint.
- Bite guard.

- Orthopedic appliance.
- Orthodontic appliance.
- Mandibular orthopedic reposition appliance.

Claims Handling

Claims for appliances are usually referred to a dental consultant for review. Referral must include study models and all current x-rays that support the diagnosis.

If the consultant determines that current occlusion/malocclusion contributes to the patient's condition, benefits are usually paid only under orthodontic coverage unless the plan provides special TMJ coverage. If the plan does not have either type of coverage, benefits under medical or dental provisions (without orthodontic) are usually denied for "adjustments, correction, or altering of occlusion, jaw joint by any means, including appliances are excluded under the provisions of this plan." If the consultant determines that occlusion is not contributing to the patient's condition and there is radiographic evidence of degenerative joint changes, an appliance may be recommended and covered as an eligible medical expense. Of course, if the plan specifically disallows TMJ treatment, the services still will not be covered. TMJ handling procedures should always be discussed with your supervisor prior to processing.

Services and Supplies

The following is a list of services and supplies often associated with the treatment of TMJ disorders, their description, and general dental and medical benefit guidelines to be used in the processing of claims for these types of services and supplies. This list is intended as a general guideline only, and specific payor policies should be consulted.

Acupuncture—Insertion of needles into designated areas of the body to relieve or prevent pain. Dental benefits: Allowable only in lieu of general anesthesia for a covered surgical procedure. Acupuncture is covered under the dental plan if medical coverage is not available and is subject to applicable frequency limits. Medical benefits: Allowable only in lieu of general anesthesia for a covered surgical procedure.

Behavior modification and relaxation therapy—Educational training to modify behavior patterns and teach relaxation techniques. Dental benefits: Deny, not usually allowable. Medical benefits: Deny, not treatment of a disease or injury.

Biofeedback—Electronic devices used to monitor and control automatic body functions such as blood pressure, respiration. Dental benefits: Deny, not usually allowable. Medical benefits: Apply biofeedback guidelines.

Cranial manipulation—Chiropractic adjustment technique involving manipulation and realignment of skull bones. Dental benefits: Deny, not usually allowable. Medical benefits: Deny, not broadly accepted or recognized as effective or necessary treatment for TMJ.

Diagnostic examinations—Oral examination not including or related to a prophylaxis. Dental benefits: Cover under dental plans if no medical coverage available. Medical—Cover as a medical expense.

Diagnostic x-ray—Dental x-rays, x-ray of the jaw joint. Dental benefits: Cover under dental plans if no medical coverage available; subject to applicable frequency limits. Medical benefits: Cover as a medical expense.

Dry needling—See Acupuncture.

Electrogalvanic nerve stimulation/stimulators (EGS)—Same as transcutaneous electrical nerve stimulation (TENS) except that a different type of electrical current is used. Refer to discussions on TENS.

Holistic therapy—Hair analysis, fingernail analysis, vitamin therapy. Dental benefits: Deny, usually not listed as a covered expense. Medical benefits: Deny, not broadly accepted or recognized as effective treatment for TMJ.

Injections of muscle relaxants or other drugs—Any prescription item to treat muscle spasms; local anesthesia to relieve pain; and steroids to reduce inflammation. Dental benefits: Cover under dental plan if no medical coverage, unless specifically excluded. Medical benefits: Cover when prescribed or administered by a physician or dentist and not excluded by the plan.

Kinesiographic analysis—Measurement and analysis of muscle movement. Dental benefits: Deny, not necessary. Malfunctioning or spastic muscles can be recognized by direct observation or examination. Medical benefits: Deny, not necessary. Malfunctioning or spastic muscles can be recognized by direct observation or examination.

Mandibular repositioners—Stabilizing appliance to reposition the mandible. Dental benefits: Cover if orthodontic services are covered. Medical benefits: Deny, not covered.

Occlusal equilibration—Corrects minor malocclusion by selective grinding of teeth. This balances the bite and allows the lower jaw to relocate into proper position. Dental benefits: Considered orthodontic treatment; cover only under plans with orthodontic benefits. Medical benefits: Deny. Adjustments, correction, or altering of occlusion by any means including appliances are included as covered expense only under plans that provide orthodontic benefits.

Occlusal rehabilitation—Full-mouth reconstruction using crowns, fixed bridgework, or dentures to restore occlusion and proper relationship between the upper and lower jaw. Dental benefits: Considered orthodontic treatment. Cover only under plans with orthodontic benefits and only for noncosmetic purposes. Medical benefits: Deny. Adjustments, correction, or altering of occlusion by any means, including appliances, are included as covered expense only under plans that provide orthodontic benefits.

Oral surgery—Any surgical procedure necessary to remove, repair, revise, or reposition the TMJ such as meniscectomy, condylectomy, arthrectomy, high condylar shave, or joint implant. Dental benefits: Cover only when no medical coverage is available and oral surgery is listed as a covered dental expense. Medical benefits: Cover as a medical expense.

Physical therapy—Vapocoolant sprays, moist heat, massage, cold packs, exercise. Dental benefits: Deny, usually not considered a covered expense. Medical benefits: Deny. Physical therapy can be self-administered by the patient with instruction by a physician or dentist. Physical therapy does not require professional administration.

Prescription drugs—Any prescription item to treat muscle spasms. Dental benefits: Cover if benefits are payable for other prescription drugs. Medical benefits: Cover, payable as treatment of a physical condition, not a mental/nervous disorder.

Prosthetic appliances—Fixed or removable appliances (bridges, dentures, space maintainers). Dental benefits: Cover if prosthetic appliances are covered for other conditions. Medical benefits: Deny, not covered.

Splinting—Joining or tying the teeth for stabilization and immobilization or control of bad habits. Dental benefits: Cover if benefits are generally payable for splinting. Medical benefits: Deny, not covered.

Transcutaneous electrical nerve stimulation/stimulators (TENS)—Device used to apply electrical nerve stimulation to relieve TMJ pain. Dental benefits: Deny, usually not considered a covered expense. Medical benefits: Cover charges of a physician or dentist for office visits to administer or supervise TENS therapy for a maximum of 1 month for intractable pain only (8 to 12 visits, based on 2 to 3 visits per week, are reasonable). If TENS therapy is effective during the 1-month period, purchase or rental may be recommended. Allow benefits by following normal TENS guidelines limiting rental charges up to usual and customary purchase price of TENS unit.

Summary

Temporomandibular joint dysfunction is a manifestation of an abnormality of the TMJ joint. Since the causes of TMJ dysfunction can be many and varied, the treatment can also take a variety of forms. Some treatments fall under coverage for dental services; others are covered as medical services.

Because of the variety of payment options (and the past history of provider abuse in TMJ services), care should be taken to fully understand the terms of the contract and the TMJ policies of the payor.

Assignments

Complete the Questions for Review.

Questions for Review

Directions: Answer the following questions without looking back into the material just covered. Write your answers in the space provided.

1. What is TMJ dysfunction? ______________________________

2. Why have some dental providers overutilized the concept of TMJ? ______________________________

3. What are the claims handling procedures for TMJ appliances? ______________________________

4. What is the description for diagnostic examinations? ______________________________

5. Is holistic therapy usually a covered expense for TMJ? ______________________________

If you were unable to answer any of the questions, refer back to the section and then complete the answers.

26

Dental Claim Form

In this chapter you will learn:

- To understand the dental claim form and its proper use.
- To identify the minimum data requirements on a dental claim form.

There are two basic forms that dental providers use to bill claims. These forms are the American Dental Association (ADA) claim form and the Patient Information Sheet. The Dental Claim Form lists specific information regarding the patient and the services that have been or are going to be performed. The Patient Information Sheet contains information about the patient and dental coverage information.

The ADA Dental Claim Form

There are several versions of the ADA claim form currently in use; however, there is little difference among each of the versions. We will use the 1990 version of the claim form (see Figure 26-1). This claim form can be used as a billing statement for services performed, and also for a pretreatment estimate of services to be performed. However, at no time should services already performed be included with those for which the dentist or patient is seeking a pretreatment estimate.

Following is a list of the fields, their descriptions, and uses. The word "Same" as a description indicates that the description of the field is the same as the field name.

Field#	Field Name/Description
Blank	*Dentist's pretreatment estimate or dentist's statement of services performed.* The appropriate box would be checked depending on whether services have been performed. Only one box should be checked. Therefore, services previously performed and services to be performed should not be combined on the same form.
Blank	*Carrier name and address.* The name and address of the payor to whom this bill is being sent.
1	*Patient name.* The name of the patient appearing as first name, middle initial, and last name.
2	*Relationship to employee.* Check the appropriate box of self, spouse, child, or other. If other is checked, indicate the relationship of the patient to the employee or insured.
3	*Sex.* Check the box indicating the gender of the patient.
4	*Patient birthdate.* Enter the patient's birthdate as month, date, and year.
5	*If full-time student.* If the patient is a full-time student, enter the name of the school and the location (city) of the school.
6	*Employee/subscriber name.* Same.
7	*Employee/subscriber social security number.* Same.
8	*Employee/subscriber birthdate.* Enter the employee's or subscriber's birthdate as month, date, and year.
9	*Employer.* Indicate the full name of the company for which the employee/subscriber works.
10	*Group number.* Indicate the group or policy number.
11	*Is patient covered by another plan of benefits?* Indicate the name of any other medical or dental coverage that the patient may be covered under.

Note: Fields 12 through 15 are to be answered only if the patient has coverage by a second carrier.

Field#	Field Name/Description
12a	*Name and address of carrier(s).* Indicate the name and address of the carrier indicated in field 11.
12b	*Group number(s).* Indicate the group numbers of the policies indicated in 11.

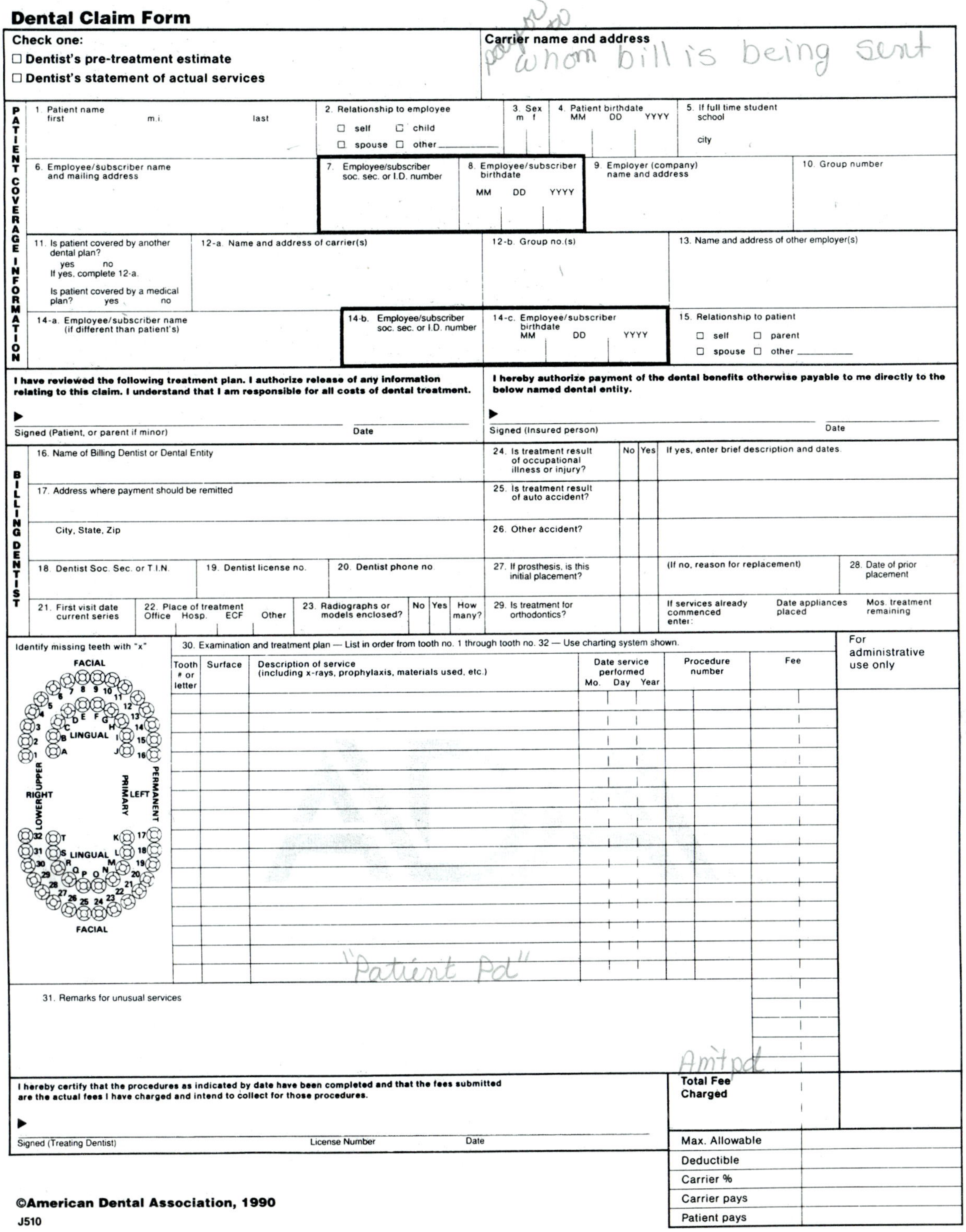

Dental Claim Form

Check one:
☐ Dentist's pre-treatment estimate
☐ Dentist's statement of actual services

Carrier name and address

PATIENT COVERAGE INFORMATION

1. Patient name first m.i. last
2. Relationship to employee ☐ self ☐ child ☐ spouse ☐ other
3. Sex m f
4. Patient birthdate MM DD YYYY
5. If full time student school city
6. Employee/subscriber name and mailing address
7. Employee/subscriber soc. sec. or I.D. number
8. Employee/subscriber birthdate MM DD YYYY
9. Employer (company) name and address
10. Group number
11. Is patient covered by another dental plan? yes no If yes, complete 12-a. Is patient covered by a medical plan? yes no
12-a. Name and address of carrier(s)
12-b. Group no.(s)
13. Name and address of other employer(s)
14-a. Employee/subscriber name (if different than patient's)
14-b. Employee/subscriber soc. sec. or I.D. number
14-c. Employee/subscriber birthdate MM DD YYYY
15. Relationship to patient ☐ self ☐ parent ☐ spouse ☐ other

I have reviewed the following treatment plan. I authorize release of any information relating to this claim. I understand that I am responsible for all costs of dental treatment.
Signed (Patient, or parent if minor) Date

I hereby authorize payment of the dental benefits otherwise payable to me directly to the below named dental entity.
Signed (Insured person) Date

BILLING DENTIST

16. Name of Billing Dentist or Dental Entity
17. Address where payment should be remitted
City, State, Zip
18. Dentist Soc. Sec. or T.I.N.
19. Dentist license no.
20. Dentist phone no.
21. First visit date current series
22. Place of treatment Office Hosp. ECF Other
23. Radiographs or models enclosed? No Yes How many?
24. Is treatment result of occupational illness or injury? No Yes
25. Is treatment result of auto accident?
26. Other accident?
27. If prosthesis, is this initial placement? (If no, reason for replacement)
28. Date of prior placement
29. Is treatment for orthodontics? If services already commenced enter: Date appliances placed Mos. treatment remaining
If yes, enter brief description and dates.

Identify missing teeth with "x"
FACIAL
LINGUAL
RIGHT LEFT
UPPER LOWER PRIMARY PERMANENT
FACIAL

30. Examination and treatment plan — List in order from tooth no. 1 through tooth no. 32 — Use charting system shown.

Tooth # or letter	Surface	Description of service (including x-rays, prophylaxis, materials used, etc.)	Date service performed Mo. Day Year	Procedure number	Fee

For administrative use only

31. Remarks for unusual services

I hereby certify that the procedures as indicated by date have been completed and that the fees submitted are the actual fees I have charged and intend to collect for those procedures.
Signed (Treating Dentist) License Number Date

Total Fee Charged
Max. Allowable
Deductible
Carrier %
Carrier pays
Patient pays

J510

Figure 26-1: Dental Claim Form.

13 *Name and address of employer.* Enter the name and address of the insured's or employee's employer indicated in 11.

14a *Employee/subscriber name.* If the employee or subscriber indicated in 11 is not the patient, list the employee's/subscriber's name here.

14b *Employee/subscriber social security number.* If the employee or subscriber indicated in 11 is not the patient, list the social security number here.

14c *Employee/subscriber birthdate.* If the employee or subscriber indicated in 11 is not the patient, list the birthdate here.

15 *Relationship to patient.* Indicate the relationship of the patient to the employee/subscriber listed in field 14a.

Blank *Release of information statement.* A patient must sign and date this box to authorize the provider (dentist) to release information to the payor.

Blank *Payment of benefits to provider.* A signature in this box authorizes the payor to pay the provider of services directly.

16 *Dentist name.* Same.

17 *Mailing address.* Enter the dentist's mailing address. Payments will be sent to this address.

18 *Dentist soc sec no or TIN.* Enter the dentist's social security number or taxpayer identification number.

19 *Dentist license no.* Same.

20 *Dentist phone no.* Same.

21 *First visit date current series.* Enter the date in which this series of treatments began (usually the date of the exam that initiated these treatments).

22 *Place of treatment.* Check the appropriate box for whether treatment was rendered at an office, a hospital, an intermediate (emergency) care facility, or other.

23 *Radiographs or models enclosed?* Indicate yes or no and the number of radiographs (x-rays) or models enclosed with the claim. These are generally enclosed to allow the claims examiner or review board to determine the necessity of services rendered. Radiographs or models will more often accompany a pretreatment estimate to assist the claims examiner in determining appropriate benefits.

Note: For questions 24 through 26, indicate yes or no. If yes, enter a brief description and the date(s).

24 *Is treatment the result of occupational illness or injury?* If yes, indicate any worker's compensation insurance information in fields 11 through 15.

25 *Is treatment the result of an auto accident?* If yes and there is a third party liability provision, indicate the automobile insurance coverage of all parties involved in the automobile accident in fields 11 through 15.

26 *Other accident?* For accidents other than by automobile. If yes and there is a third party liability provision (another person's or company's insurance, eg, homeowners), indicate this insurance coverage in fields 11 through 15.

27 *If prosthesis, is this initial placement?* If the answer is no (this is a replacement prosthesis), indicate reason for replacement.

28 *Date of prior placement.* If answer to 27 was no, the date of placement for the prosthesis being replaced should be entered here.

29 *Is treatment for orthodontics?* If the answer is yes and treatment has already commenced, enter the date appliances were placed and the months of treatment remaining.

30 *Examination and treatment plan.* List each treatment in order of tooth number (tooth 1 through tooth 32). For each service, indicate the following:

Tooth or letter number. Enter the tooth or letter number for the treatment described.

Surface. The surface letter for each surface of the tooth affected by the treatment.

Description of service. Include all x-rays, prophylaxis, materials used, and so on.

Date service performed. Same.

Procedure number. Enter the ADA procedure code for the service.

Fee. Enter the amount billed for the service. Remember to total the fees and place this amount in the "Total fee charged" box at the bottom of the column.

Note: If the patient made partial payment for the services rendered, the words "Patient paid" should appear at the bottom of the description box and the amount paid should appear at the bottom of the fee column. This payment should then be subtracted from the above fees and the balance due placed in the box labeled "Total fee charged."

For administrative use only. Leave blank.

31 *Remarks for unusual services.* Enter any remarks that clarify the services or use of materials in services above. Indicate tooth number or procedure code if necessary for clarification of the procedure being remarked upon. Any additional description needed for fields 24 through 29 can also be added here.

Dentist signature. By signing this form, the dentist indicates that those fees that have a date of service have been performed and that the charges are the actual charges for the services.

At the bottom of the form, there is space for the dental claims examiner to indicate the maximum allowable amount for the services, the deductible applied to this claim, the coinsurance percentage that the payor is responsible for, the amount the payor is responsible for, and the amount the patient is responsible for. Some payors also use the "For administrative use only" field to list the allowable amount of each service.

Patient Information Sheet

In addition to the ADA Dental Claim Form, a patient information sheet will need to be completed for each patient. These patient information sheets are created by each dentist or medical group. Therefore, the format varies widely from one dental office to another. However, the information contained on the patient information sheet is generally the same.

The dental patient information sheet is different from the medical patient information sheet. Whereas the medical information sheet carries basic identifying information on the patient, the insured, and the carrier, the dental information sheet requests specific information regarding the types and amounts of dental coverages.

The purpose of the patient information sheet is to determine the types and amounts of coverage on each individual patient prior to the rendering of services. It also informs the dental office of any procedures that are excluded or limited. This allows the dental office to estimate the coverage that the insurance payor will provide and to inform the patient of the remaining amount that they will be responsible for. Some dental offices require prepayment for services if the amount estimated to be not covered exceeds a specified dollar limit (eg, $100.00).

Since the patient information sheet is created by the dental office, it is by no means a determination of the exact benefits that a payor will reimburse. It is merely an estimate to help the dentist and the patient decide the monetary responsibility for the treatment sought.

The information generally found on a patient information sheet is as follows (see Figure 26-2).

Insured. List the name of the insured.

D O B. List the date of birth for the insured.

S S #. List the social security number for the insured.

Employer. List the employer for the insured.

Group/policy #. List the group or policy number under which the insured is covered.

Patient(s). List the name of the patient(s) for which treatment is planned.

Current date. List the current date.

Treatment Date. List the date treatment is planned.

Contact name. List the name of the person who was contacted at the insurance carrier.

Contacted by. List the name of the person who contacted the insurance carrier.

Insurance company name. Same.

Insurance company address. Same.

Telephone number. List the telephone number of the insurance carrier.

Effective date. List the date coverage became effective for the insured.

Current. Indicate whether or not the insurance is current.

Month to month. Indicate whether the insurance is month-to-month, quarterly, or annual premium payments. Most dental coverage is on a month-to-month basis. In such a case, care should be taken that the insured keeps his or her premium payments current throughout the term of the treatment. Otherwise, benefits may cease midway through the treatment process. It may be necessary to contact the payor several times during the course of extended treatment to ensure that coverage is still in place.

Coverage. Check each of the boxes for whom coverage is in force: self, spouse, dependents.

Fee schedule. Check the appropriate box as to whether the payor-allowable amount is determined by a UCR amount or an insurance fee schedule.

Authorization mandatory? Is preauthorization mandatory for services? If so, at what dollar limit is it necessary to obtain preauthorization for treatment?

Benefits: The following section is used to determine the benefits available.

Annual or lifetime maximum? Indicate whether there is an annual or a lifetime maximum amount.

Amount. Indicate the amount of the annual or lifetime maximum.

Available balance. Indicate the remaining balance available on the annual or lifetime maximum.

Preventive. Indicate the payor coinsurance percentage for preventive services.

Deductible. Indicate the deductible amount for preventive services.

Basic. Indicate the payor's coinsurance percentage for basic services.

Deductible. Indicate the deductible amount for basic services.

Major. Indicate the payor's coinsurance percentage for major services.

Waiting period. Is there a waiting period before these services come into effect? If so, indicate the amount of the waiting period here (eg, 3 months, 1 year).

Deductible. Indicate the deductible amount for major services.

Single crowns. Are single crowns covered? If so, are there any limitations regarding materials? A simple notation such as "no gold" will suffice.

Sealants. Indicate whether sealants are covered under the dental plan.

Age limit? If sealants are covered, is there an age limit (eg, only for children under age 14 can be written "-14" or "under 14").

Replacement of missing teeth prior to coverage. Indicate

Patient Information Sheet

Insured ______________________ D O B ______________________

S S # ______________________ Employer ______________________

Group/Policy # ______________________

Patient(s) ______________________

Current date ______________________ Treatment date ______________________

Contact name name of person contacted at ins carrier Contacted by person who contacted ins carrier

Insurance company name ______________________

Address: ______________________

Telephone number ______________________

Effective date ______________ Current ______________ Month to month ______________

Coverage: Self ______________ Spouse ______________ Dependents ______________

Fee schedule: UCR ______________ Ins fee schedule ______________ Authorization mandatory? ______________

BENEFITS:

Annual/Lifetime maximum? ______________ Amount ______________ Avail bal ______________

Preventive ______________________ Deductible ______________

Basic ______________________ Deductible ______________

Major ______________ Waiting period ______________ Deductible ______________

Single crowns ______________ Sealants ______________ Age limit? ______________

Replacement of missing teeth prior to coverage ______________________

Replacement of crowns and bridges ______________________

Replacement of partials and dentures ______________________

Prophylaxis ______________________

Scaling and root planing ______________________

FMX ______________________ Panorex ______________________

Specialist consultation ______________________

General anesthesia ______________________

Signature ______________________

Figure 26-2: **Patient Information Sheet**

whether or not the dental plan covers replacement of teeth that were missing prior to the beginning of coverage. Most plans will not cover this service.

Replacement of crowns and bridges. Indicate whether replacement of crowns or bridges are covered under this dental plan. Also, indicate whether there are any limitations to this coverage.

Replacement of partials and dentures. Indicate whether replacement of partials or dentures are covered under this dental plan. Also indicate whether there are any limitations to this coverage.

Prophy. Indicate any limitations on prophylaxis services. Often, dental plans limit coverage to twice in any 12-month period.

Scaling and root planing. Indicate whether scaling and root planing are covered under this dental plan. Also, indicate whether there are any limitations to this coverage.

FMX. Indicate any limitations on full mouth x-rays. Often, dental plans limit coverage to once every 3 years.

Panorex. Indicate any limitations on panorex (panoramic x-rays). Often, dental plans limit coverage to once every 3 years, if there is any coverage at all.

Specialist consultation. Indicate whether there is coverage for a specialist if the patient is referred by a dentist. Also, indicate whether the insurance carrier reserves the right to send the patient to a specialist for a consultation on diagnosis or proposed treatment.

General anesthesia. Indicate whether general anesthesia is a covered service under this dental plan. Also, indicate whther there are any limitations to this coverage (ie, only if patient is hospitalized).

Signature. Have the employee/insured sign the form at the bottom of the page.

Summary

The two forms used for billing dental services are the ADA Dental Claim Form and the dentist's patient information sheet. The patient information sheet helps the dentist to evaluate the coverage of services before initiating treatment or services. The ADA Dental Claim Form allows the dentist to either request a benefit determination on a proposed treatment plan or to report services already performed and request payment for those services.

Assignments

Complete the Questions for Review.

Claim form
Patient information sheet

Questions for Review

Directions: Answer the following questions without looking back into the material just covered. Write your answers in the space provided.

1. What is the purpose of the patient information sheet? to determine the types + amounts of coverage on each individual patient prior to the rendering of services. Also informs the dental offices of any procedures that are excluded or limited.
2. On the dental claim form, how would you indicate that the patient had made a partial payment for the services rendered? The words "patient paid" should appear at the bottom of the description box + the amount pd. should appear at the bottom of the fee column. This payment should be subtracted from the above fees + balance due
3. What does a signature in the "Payment of benefits to provider" box mean? authorizes the payor to pay the provider of services directly
4. What does the box "Month to month" denote on the patient information sheet? when premium payments are due
5. What does a dentist's signature on the dental claim form mean? indicates that those fees that have a date of service have been performed + that the charges are the actual charges for the services

If you were unable to answer any of the questions, refer back to the section and then complete the answers.

(2) placed in the box labeled "Total fee charged"

27

Dental Benefit Structures

In this chapter you will learn:

- To understand general policy guidelines for processing dental claims.
- To understand contract provisions.
- To identify the type of treatment as indicated by the provider.
- To identify contract limitations and exclusions.

The structure of dental plans is similar to the structure of medical plans. The dental portion of a plan is structured as a basic plan, a scheduled plan, or an integrated/nonintegrated comprehensive plan.

Initially, basic plans were developed to cover the most common illnesses or diseases. This left the patient without coverage for serious or catastrophic illnesses. To alleviate this problem, major medical plans were structured to provide coverage against catastrophic illnesses that were left uncovered by the basic plans. Finally, dental plans and vision plans were added to cover dental and optometry services.

Types of Dental Plans

Like medical plans, dental plans usually have coinsurance, deductibles, and limitations. However, the major difference between medical plans and dental plans is that dental plans encourage (and therefore usually cover) preventive care. In addition, many dental plans pay a higher amount of coinsurance for diagnostic and preventive services than for other services and may also include an "incentive plan," which encourages participants to make regular visits to their dentist.

Basic Plans

A basic dental plan pays dental benefits at 100% of either UCR or a scheduled amount. The UCR can be a set amount, or it can be a sliding scale based on when the service was performed and the geographic area of the provider performing the service. The scheduled amount is a set amount based on the procedure code. It is not contingent on a conversion factor nor the location of the provider. As a rule, a basic dental plan is kept entirely separate from an associated medical plan. That is, if there is a deductible, it is separate from the medical deductible. All dental limitations, exclusions, and maximums are kept separate and unique from the medical provisions. Usually, basic plans are easy types of dental plans to process because the exact allowances and procedures are specified in the plan documents.

Scheduled Dental Plans

In a scheduled plan, usually no conversion factors are involved. Instead, each ADA code has a specified dollar amount assigned to it. This dollar allowance applies to the procedure, regardless of where the provider is located or when the procedure is performed. The scheduled allowance never changes unless a plan change is approved to either lower or raise the allowance. Seldom if ever are only a few procedures adjusted; usually, there is an overall plan adjustment. Many payors consider a basic plan and a scheduled plan to be the same, and these terms are used interchangeably.

When a scheduled plan is involved, the scheduled allowance is programmed into the computer system so that the examiner simply enters the correct code. For manual claim computation, the examiner would check the schedule listing by code to determine the allowable amount. Deductibles are then subtracted from the scheduled allowances. However, like medical plans, if the scheduled amount exceeds the billed amount, the billed amount is the allowable charge. Generally, scheduled plans allow significantly less than current prevailing charges in most communities.

If a charge is submitted for a procedure that is not listed on the schedule, there are two handling methods:

1. The plan provisions may specify that unlisted procedures are not covered. Consequently, such expenses would be denied as not covered under the plan.
2. Unlisted procedures may be allowable (sometimes based on a consultant review). The amount allowable may be either a specified amount for unlisted procedures or current UCR (or some percentage of current UCR, or the amount billed). The provisions must specify which application to use.

Sometimes a basic dental plan is combined with a scheduled plan, resulting in a scheduled basic plan. In this case, the variations of the two types of plans will be applied as stipulated by the plan provisions.

Integrated Dental Plans

The ABC contract in Chapter 2 of the student exercise

manual is an integrated medical-dental plan. What this means is:

- There is only one deductible amount for the plan. Any amount applied on a dental claim applies toward satisfaction of the one deductible as does any amount applied on a medical claim. In this case, there is a $100.00 per person deductible, which can include both dental and medical charges.

  Notice that the family limit notated on the dental portion of the card is the same as that notated on the medical portion. This is because, as with the individual deductible, the family deductible limit can consist of both medical and dental charges. The first charges processed are the first charges applied toward satisfaction of both the individual and the family deductibles. The easiest way to think of this type of plan is that the limits are considered plan limits, not a medical or dental limit.
- As with the deductibles, the same logic applies to the coinsurance charges. On an integrated plan, the dental coinsurance percentage is usually the same as the medical coinsurance percentage, and amounts applied on dental claims apply toward the plan coinsurance limit as do amounts applied on medical claims.
- Dental payments apply toward the plan Lifetime Maximum amount. However, the dental portion of the contract usually has a separate calendar year maximum.
- Benefits are usually based on a UCR basis, with conversion factors, geographic location, and time performed being important.

Nonintegrated Dental Plans

The XYZ contract in Chapter 2 of the student exercise manual is a nonintegrated plan. That is, the dental benefits are applied entirely separate from the medical benefits. Each portion of the contract has its own deductible, coinsurance limits, and so on. Only dental charges can be used to satisfy the dental provisions, and only medical charges can be used to satisfy the medical provisions. Therefore, in contrast to an integrated plan, a nonintegrated plan does not have plan limitations; it has dental plan limitations and medical plan limitations with no mixing of the two. Usually, this type of plan uses conversion factors, geographic location, and time performed to determine allowances.

Understanding Dental Contracts

The benefits and structure of a dental contract are set up in much the same way as medical contracts, with the same types of considerations.

Definitions

Before understanding any medical or dental contract, it is important to understand some basic definitions. Following are some of the more common terms and their meanings:

Allowable amount—The maximum amount that a plan will pay for a specific procedure. If the billed amount is less than the allowable amount, then the billed amount is considered the allowable amount. The allowable amount is usually based on a table of charges or a UCR amount.

Carryover deductible provision—Amounts applied to the individual deductible during the last 3 months of the preceding year are "carried over" and applied to the individual deductible for the following year. The amount will not be applied toward satisfying the family deductible amount.

Child—The offspring of the subscriber or the subscriber's stepchild or legally adopted child.

Coinsurance percentage—The percentage that is applied to the allowable amount after all deductibles and other provisions have been satisfied.

Covered procedures—Procedures for which the payor has agreed to pay benefits, according to the provisions of the plan.

Disabled subscriber—A member who, because of illness or injury, is unable to work at any job for which he or she has been trained. To be totally disabled, a subscriber must be unemployed and currently unemployable.

Effective date—The date coverage begins under the plan.

Experimental procedures—Procedures that have been done in laboratory or animal research.

Investigative procedures—Procedures that have been performed on humans, but are not widely accepted by the medical community as proven and effective.

Generally, the plan is responsible for between 50% and 100% of the remaining amount, and the subscriber or patient is responsible for 0% to 50% of the remaining amount.

Maximum benefit amount—Fixed dollar amount. The payor will pay up to this amount in a given period of time (usually either a calendar year or a lifetime). After this amount has been reached, no more benefits are paid.

Plan—The contract between the employer and the carrier regarding the benefits and conditions of their agreement for insurance coverage. The plan specifies such things as the deductible, the coinsurance amount, exclusions, any limitations on coverage, and covered and noncovered procedures.

Spouse—The husband or wife as determined by a legally valid marriage between members of the opposite sex.

Subscriber—The insured employee. The insured must be enrolled in the plan at the time that services are rendered to be eligible for benefits. The terms "insured" and "member" are also used.

Usual, customary, and reasonable (UCR)—A process of calculating the usual, customary, or reasonable charges for a given procedure in a given area. The formula takes into account the varying amounts of overhead (eg, building expenses, malpractice insurance) that prevail in various cities. For example, a prophylaxis in Los Angeles would pay more than the same treatment on the same patient in Long Ridge, South Dakota. This would be due to the increased costs of doing business in Southern California (eg, higher building costs, higher wage scales for employees, higher insurance costs).

Covered Expenses

In general, benefits are paid for services that are covered by the plan. The date on which services are rendered is considered the date charges were incurred. Benefits are not payable for services that were performed or begun before the commencement of the plan. In addition, most expenses are subject to an allowable amount based on a table of charges or on what is considered UCR for the time and place of the services. (For further information see Chapter 7.)

Most dental contracts specifically list the services that are covered and those that are not covered. They also list the conditions (if any) that must be satisfied for treatment to be covered. These conditions can include:

- The person who may provide treatment (eg, licensed dentist, oral surgeon).
- Coverage of only the least expensive, adequate materials. If other more expensive materials are used, payment will be limited to the allowable amount of the least expensive adequate material.
- Personalized services or special techniques that are covered at the rate of standard techniques.

Deductible

Each insured, if applicable, must meet a deductible amount for covered services before any benefits are paid. Any amounts for services that are not covered under the plan or for charges exceeding amounts covered by the plan are not applied toward the deductible.

Extension of Benefits

As with medical plans, some circumstances allow for an extension of benefits beyond the time when benefits would usually cease or the insured would no longer be eligible for coverage. Extension can include the following reasons:

- An insured is totally disabled at the time coverage would normally end.
- An insured is confined in a hospital or skilled nursing facility and is considered totally disabled.

In such cases, benefits normally continue until the insured is no longer totally disabled, the maximum benefits have been paid, coverage commences under another plan, or 12 months have elapsed since the time coverage would have ended.

General Guidelines

Regardless of the method of classification, dental care and treatment provided by most plans is based on the premises covered in the following sections.

Is Treatment Covered or Excluded?

It is not enough to determine whether a disease or injury requires treatment. It must also be determined that the specific services, supplies, or treatment received or planned will correct the condition and restore the mouth to form and function. It must then be determined whether these services, supplies, or treatments are covered under the plan.

Covered services are limited to the listed individual services that will correct or eliminate the specific disease or injury in accordance with recognized professional standards of care. Services not listed or specifically excluded, even when such services are necessary to correct or eliminate disease or injury, may not be considered for coverage.

Covered services vary from plan to plan. Examples of services that may fall into this category are periodontal splinting (when specifically excluded), occlusal guards for bruxism (a preventive service not specifically listed), a crown placed on a tooth with only incipient decay (listed service, but service is not appropriate and rendered in accordance with recognized professional standards of care for the degree of decay present).

Is Treatment Appropriate to the Condition?

The proposed treatment should be appropriate in light of the total existing dental condition. Because so much of what happens in the mouth is interrelated, if part of a disease or injury is left untreated or some of the involved teeth are left untreated, the services provided may be rendered ineffective in a short time. Also, certain treatment approaches may be unrealistic when the total condition of the mouth is considered. Examples are (1) the placement of fixed bridgework where the abutment teeth are diseased and untreated and (2) unreasonable efforts to save teeth, especially for older people who are nearly edentulous.

Are the Services and Supplies of Acceptable Quality?

Materials as well as services are subject to poor quality. Material failure may result from poor laboratory fabrication or poor installation. Services failure may result from improper diagnosis, inadequate preparation, or poor mechanical skills. Examples of substandard quality are root therapy failure due to incomplete extraction of root pulp and denture or bridgework failure due to poor materials and fabrication.

What Is the Benefit Level?

One of the major problems in providing benefits for dental services is that in dentistry frequently more than one procedure, material, or technique may be used in accordance with recognized professional standards of care to correct or eliminate a disease or injury. Most dental benefit plans have been designed to provide benefits based on a certain level of care so that each insured person receives the same benefit level consistent with his or her needs.

The intent of dental plans is to provide benefits for covered services based on a level of dental care that is adequate (when determined in accordance with generally accepted professional standards) for treatment of the existing dental condition. This means that for benefits to be payable, the care and treatment must not be below acceptable standards of quality and appropriateness; it also means that benefits will not be payable for care and treatment that exceeds the level that is adequate and necessary.

Expenses for care above the adequate and necessary level are the patient's responsibility unless specifically listed as payable in the plan provisions.

Moreover, benefits for care above this adequate and necessary level will not be provided, regardless of whether they are provided as a result of the patient's or dentist's choice or the limited practice of the dentist or whether the services have already been provided. The patient or dentist is entirely free in the choice of level of care, but this choice will not affect the benefits payable; thus, the "alternate benefit" for adequate and necessary level of service is contractually allowable.

What Treatment Is Required?

Standard dental benefit plans provide benefits for services and supplies that are necessary for the treatment of disease or injury. Following are two examples of some standard wording that may appear in dental plans:

1. "Covered dental expenses are the reasonable charges that a subscriber is required to pay for necessary services received by a covered family member for the treatment of a nonoccupational injury."
2. "Covered dental expenses are the usual charges of a dentist that an employee is required to pay for services and supplies that are necessary for treatment of a dental condition, but only to the extent that such charges are reasonable and customary charges, as herein defined, for services and supplies customarily used for treatment of that condition, and only if rendered in accordance with accepted standards of dental practice."

These definitions are supplemented by additional provisions, exclusions, and limitations, both general and specific. Most plans contain provisions similar to one of the following general exclusions:

- "No insurance is afforded for care, treatment, services, or supplies that are not necessary for the treatment of the injury or disease concerned."
- "Covered dental expenses do not include and no benefits are payable for charges for services or supplies that are not necessary, according to accepted standards of dental practice."

The intent of dental benefit plans is to provide benefits for covered services and supplies that are necessary to eliminate or correct a dental disease or injury to restore the mouth to reasonable form and function. Not only must there be an existing disease or injury present that requires some treatment, but also the specific service received or planned must be required and the disease or injury must be covered under the plan.

Prosthetics

Many policies require that the prosthesis replace "natural" teeth. The following are not considered natural teeth:

- Tooth roots, when the condition of the tooth preexisted the effective date of coverage.
- Congenitally missing teeth.
- Diastema (space between two adjacent teeth in the same arch).

The following teeth do not require replacement and are usually not covered.

- Third molars (wisdom teeth) that occupy the third molar position.
- Any tooth that is not in functional occlusion, that is, not opposed by another tooth in the opposite arch.

For example, a denture is replacing tooth #14 and #15, but tooth #18 and #19 (in the opposite arch) are also missing but are not being replaced. Because tooth #14 and #15 will not oppose teeth or a prosthesis, their replacement will serve no function and thus cannot be considered for coverage.

Initial Installation

Most plans have a plan limitation called the "Missing and Unreplaced" rule. This rule limits coverage of the replacement of teeth that are lost while the patient was covered by the plan. If the prosthesis will replace teeth that were missing prior to coverage and teeth lost while insured, benefits usually are provided for the entire prosthesis unless it represents an unusual attempt to gain benefits for the teeth missing prior to coverage. If the plan does not have this limitation, benefits are payable (subject to all other policy limitations) for replacement of natural teeth whether or not they were extracted while covered. The way this provision works is:

If a tooth was missing prior to the effective date of coverage, bridgework, regardless of whether it is permanent or removable, will not be eligible for payment consideration under the plan. This would also include payment for crowns on the abutment teeth, unless the condition of those teeth is such that a crown would be appropriate treatment and covered because of an existing disease condition (decay).

For example, suppose that tooth #12 is missing and was extracted before the patient's effective date under the plan. Consequently, if the plan has a Missing and Unreplaced limitation, proceed with following:

Step 1. Determine whether or not the missing tooth is covered.

a. In this case, bridgework to replace tooth #12 would not be allowable (because the tooth was extracted prior to the effective date of coverage).

b. If the tooth was extracted (or lost) after the effective date of coverage, a replacement for that tooth would be covered. If the replacement of a missing tooth is covered, crowning of the abutment teeth (the natural teeth right next to the space where the tooth is missing) is also automatically covered. X-rays are not required to determine whether or not the abutment teeth are decayed.

Remember that if the missing tooth is covered, the abutment teeth are also covered.

Step 2. Determine whether or not the abutment teeth are covered.

a. If the missing tooth is not covered, then the abutment teeth need to be evaluated on their own merits. That is, are these teeth decayed and in need of restoration themselves? X-rays will be required to evaluate this.

b. If restoration is required, is a filling sufficient or is a crown necessary? As a rule, this determination has to be made by a dental consultant or an experienced claims person. If a crown is required, the abutment restorations are covered even though the missing tooth is not covered.

The following represents how these claims are generally handled. However, such handling procedures vary greatly from administrator to administrator:

- If x-rays do not accompany the claim and no other services reported on the claim would require obtaining x-rays and referral to the consultant, the bridgework should be denied completely as teeth missing prior to coverage. If the claimant or dentist feels that the abutment teeth require crowns for restorative purposes, it is necessary to resubmit for that purpose.
- If x-rays are submitted with the claim or if other procedures would require x-rays and referral to the consultant, ask the consultant whether the abutment teeth would require crowns for restorative reasons. If referral to the consultant is not otherwise required and the examiner can tell that a crown would be required, referral is not required. If crowns would be required, they should be benefitted as freestanding crowns, not as abutment.
- If x-rays are submitted with the claim and the consultant determines that crowns are not needed for restorative reasons, the abutments should be denied along with the pontics.

Another common dental plan provision that is often applicable to prosthetics is called an Alternative Benefit Provision. This provision determines the level of care/treatment that can be provided under the plan. Although other restorations are also affected by this provision, it is most frequently associated with prosthetics.

There are two basic types of dental programs that provide benefits based on a specific level of treatment:

1. Plans that have an alternate benefit provision.
2. Plans that do not contain an alternate benefit provision.

Note: All plans may not contain the exact wording "alternate benefit provision" or "alternate course of treatment." However, the cumulative wording contained in the provisions indicates the applicable type of philosophy.

The terminology "alternate benefit" will be used in the following sections when explaining benefit determinations to members and providers. This terminology has been widely misinterpreted by the dental community to mean that the plan is dictating the course of treatment that must be used. That is not the intent. The patient or the dentist can choose any method or materials for treatment. However, payment will be based only on what is determined to be the appropriate level of care.

Alternative Benefit Plans

Usually, an alternative benefit provision (ABP) plan contains wording similar to that indicated in the following:

"Alternate Treatment—If alternate services or supplies may be used to treat a dental condition, covered dental expenses will be limited to the services and supplies that are customarily used nationwide to treat the disease or injury and that are recognized by the profession to be appropriate methods of treatment in accordance with broadly accepted national standards of dental practice, taking into account the family member's total current oral condition."

The "limitations" section may contain examples such as:

"If a cast chrome or acrylic partial denture will restore the dental arch satisfactorily, payment based on the applicable percentage of the reasonable and customary charge for such procedure will be made toward a more elaborate or precision appliance that the patient and dentist may choose to use, and the balance of the cost remains the responsibility of the patient."

The policy may contain a separate section entitled "alternate services," "optional treatment," or "alternate treatment," which details the alternate benefit concept.

The alternate benefit provision has been designed to clearly describe the intent and benefit level of the plans in relation to the various approaches to dental treatment. In combination with the necessary treatment provision, the claims office will have the necessary contractual "tools" to effectively administer the benefits of their dental plans without interfering in the patient/dentist relationship.

If an alternate benefit determination is challenged, a detailed and conclusive proof from the dentist that an alternate procedure is inadequate would be required. Since professional dental judgment is necessary in such a challenge, the treatment and results of investigations need to be reviewed by a dental consultant.

Plans Without Alternate Benefit Provision

The benefit level for plans that do not contain an alternate benefit provision are controlled by application of the "necessary treatment" provision as well as the "appropriate" provision. As long as the treatment is not inappropriate in light of existing dental conditions, the service will be considered for coverage without regard to the relative costs of the various treatment methods.

Replacement Provisions

There are normally three provisions in a dental policy, one of which must be satisfied for a replacement prosthesis to qualify for coverage.

1. Additional extractions must occur while the patient is covered under the plan.
2. Five-Year Rule and Unserviceable.
   a. Under the 5-year rule, the former prosthesis must be at least 5 years old and unserviceable. The plan must specify any exceptions.
   b. Under some plans, the 5-year rule does not apply to replacement of an unserviceable prosthesis under certain conditions (the plan must specify what the conditions are). If this provision is waived, it is usually because the initial prosthesis was not installed under the current dental expense plan.
   c. "Unserviceable" is fairly constant under all policies. The intent of this requirement is that not only is the existing prosthesis unserviceable, but also it cannot "reasonably" be made serviceable by repair, reline, or replacement of specific parts. "Reasonably" means that the cost of making the prosthesis serviceable versus the cost of replacement makes repair an unreasonable economic choice.

   Detailed facts of the condition of the denture and the reason it cannot be repaired are required for all replacement dentures less than 6 years old. Dentures that are 6 years or older may be considered unserviceable by the examiner without investigation.
3. Immediate temporary denture and 12-month rule. For a prosthesis to qualify for replacement under this provision, both of the following requirements must be met.
   a. Immediate temporary denture: the existing prosthesis must be constructed of temporary material. Normally, this type of prosthesis is placed until tissue changes have stabilized. The intent of all plans is to provide dentures only once in any 5-year period, so usually a temporary is not covered.
   b. Twelve-month requirement: this requirement applies without exception whether or not the immediate temporary denture was installed

before or while insured. No exception is usually made under this requirement for replacement that takes place after 12 months have elapsed. When a temporary denture exceeds the 12-month limitation, the denture must meet either the additional extraction or 5-year/unserviceable provision to qualify for replacement benefits.

Any denture constructed of temporary material that is being replaced by a permanent denture can be considered "unserviceable" and in need of replacement. All other policy provisions must be met prior to determining benefits.

Office Visits

Office visits are generally eligible for coverage if they are for diagnostic purposes. Therefore, these visits are generally paid only when the office visit is billed alone or when it is billed with x-rays or prophylactic treatment. If an office visit is billed (on the same date of service) with any treatment other than prophylaxis or x-rays, it is usually not a covered benefit but is considered part of the normal service. It is presumed that a diagnosis and a plan of treatment were performed prior to the commencement of services.

Any charges for a follow-up review for treatment that occurs on the same day as the procedure is also considered an integral part of the procedure and should be included in the allowance for the procedure itself.

Care should be taken to ensure that this policy limitation is carried out correctly. A patient should not be penalized for failing to delay treatment for which there was no reason for delay. For example, if a cavity is discovered during a patient's routine 6-month check-up and the dentist fills the cavity at this time, the office visit should be allowable since it was for diagnostic purposes. Remember that if an office visit is billed with a prophylaxis or with x-rays, generally it is for diagnostic purposes.

Occasionally, the word "Consultation" will appear on a claim. A consultation is the same as an office visit, and the same limitations apply.

Cost Containment

Containing the costs that the carrier must pay is taken into consideration when writing a plan. Cost containment can include such provisions as predetermination (preauthorization), incentive plans and variable coinsurance, and others listed and explained in the following text.

Predetermination

Many dental plans stipulate that expenses over a certain amount are not covered unless an estimate of the cost of services is submitted to the insurance carrier prior to the beginning of treatment. Often, this limit is between $100 and $300. Many dental plans also require predetermination for orthodontics and prosthodontics, regardless of the estimated cost.

If predetermination is not obtained, often the plan will not pay more than the predetermination limit, regardless of the amount that would have been allowable for the services.

Predetermination encourages the insured to take an active part in containing the cost of his or her dental care while giving the insured a basis for determining whether the recommended treatment is appropriate. It also discourages dentists from overcharging or prescribing unnecessary treatment as a complete treatment plan, and the related costs must be submitted prior to the beginning of treatment.

Predetermination is not an authorization to perform the services, but merely a statement of what the plan will pay on the listed services. After the predetermination is received, the decision whether or not to authorize treatment is up to the patient. The patient must determine whether the treatment is worth the cost or whether other treatment may be warranted that would cost less money. The determination of benefits usually has a time limit (generally 90 days) during which it is effective. After that time, a new determination of benefits must be requested.

Payment example:

The plan states that predetermination must be obtained for all services over $300 or a limit of

$100 is payable. Dental services were charged at a rate of $400. The UCR allowance for the service is $430. The coinsurance is 70%, and all deductibles have been satisfied.

If predetermination was obtained, the plan would pay 70% of $400, or $280. The member would be responsible for $120.

If predetermination was not obtained, the plan would pay only the $100 limit. The member would be responsible for $300.

Incentive Plans

Incentive plans encourage regular dental care, thus decreasing the possibility that a minor problem will remain untreated until it becomes a major problem. Incentive plans usually work by increasing the coinsurance percentage for each year in which the insured saw a dentist. For example, during the first year of coverage the coinsurance may be paid at 70%. If the insured visited the dentist during that year, during the second year of coverage the coinsurance would be paid at 80%. If the insured visited the dentist the first and second year, the third year's coinsurance would be 90%. and so on. Usually, failure to visit a dentist (for any reason) during a given year will cause the loss of the increased coinsurance for the following year. In essence, the increased coinsurance is a reward for taking care of one's teeth.

In addition, the incentive programs may be limited by the type of coverage they provide. For example, many incentive programs apply only to preventive services and not to crowns, inlays, onlays, prosthodontics, and orthodontics.

Variable Coinsurance

Some dental plans vary the amount paid for different services. For example, they may pay 85% for preventive services, 65% for fillings and routine dentistry, 60% for prosthodontic services, and 50% for orthodontic services. This type of payment situation encourages the insured to seek treatment for a minor problem before it becomes a major one.

Preventive services can include not only regular diagnostic procedures (biannual check-ups), but also prophylaxis and even space maintainers to prevent drifting of teeth.

Annual Maximums

Dental plans often have an annual maximum rather than a lifetime maximum. Once the "calendar year" limit has been reached, additional services are not covered. Often, dental plan maximums are much lower than major medical maximums. The average dental plan maximum is $1000, whereas major medical maximums can often be as high as $1,000,000.

There are two exceptions to the annual maximum that are noteworthy:

1. If orthodontic work is covered, there is often a separate lifetime maximum. Some carriers allow only a portion of the lifetime maximum to be paid in any given year. This prevents someone from joining the plan, having expensive orthodontic work done, and then canceling the plan.
2. When dental coverage is integrated with medical coverage, then the dental coverage is often (but not always) considered part of the major medical lifetime maximums. In such a case, annual dental maximums are often eliminated.

Frequency Limitations

Many dental plans limit the frequency of certain treatments. For example, only one routine oral examination and bite-wing x-rays may be allowable during a 6-month period. The following are other common frequency limitations:

- Full-mouth x-rays may be allowable only once every 24 to 36 months.
- Prophylaxis may be limited to twice a year.
- The 5-year and unserviceable rule (see previous text under Replacement Provisions) will be in effect for crowns, jackets, gold or cast restorations, bridgework, and dentures.
- Appliances to control harmful habits are usually limited to a single appliance with no allowance made for repair or replacement.

Waiting Period

Many insurers include a waiting period within their

contract for certain dental services. This reduces the likelihood that payments will be made for preexisting conditions and that the insured will join the plan just to have expensive treatment covered. The waiting period can be anywhere from 3 months to 1 year. Services that may be subject to the waiting period include fixed or removable prosthetics and cast restorations.

Exclusions

It is not uncommon for dental plans to exclude treatment with a high potential for abuse. The following 17 services are generally not covered by dental plans:

1. Cosmetic dentistry or services for comfort or hygiene.
2. Replacement of lost or stolen appliances
3. Replacement of teeth that were missing before the insured joined the plan.
4. Treatment started before commencement of coverage under the plan.
5. Tooth implants.
6. Orthodontics may be covered by some plans with the payment of additional premiums.
7. Tooth wear. Over time, the surfaces of the teeth may be worn away due to bruxism or normal wear and tear on the teeth.
8. Charges over the allowable amount.
9. Charges covered by a Workers' Compensation plan.
10. Charges for which the insured would not be obligated to pay or for which there would be no charge if the patient were not insured.
11. Charges for treatment received in a US Government hospital or provided by a local, state, or federal government agency.
12. Charges for services that were rendered by a relative (whether by blood or marriage) or by someone who lives in the insured's home.
13. Charges for which a third party is liable or legally responsible.
14. Experimental procedures.
15. Dietary planning or oral hygiene instruction.
16. Wars or acts of God or those for which the underlying cause of the damage was due to nuclear energy.
17. Charges for filling out claim forms.

Some exclusions are listed under the heading "Exclusions" in a contract; however, others may be listed throughout the benefit provisions. It is important to read the contract carefully to determine the proper benefits.

Second Dental Opinion

Questionable services may need to be evaluated by an independent dentist prior to commencement of treatment. The second dentist is usually selected by the plan, and the patient is referred to this dentist.

The first dentist is usually sent a form to fill out, stating the condition and the proposed treatment. This form is then sent to the second dentist or is taken by the patient. The second dentist will complete the examination and provide a report. These reports help the plan to make a determination of the covered expenses and allowable amounts for the services.

Since the second dental opinion is sought by the plan, the responsibility for payment of the consultation rests solely with the plan. The member is not charged for the consultation.

Medical Review

Services that have a high abuse rate are often referred to a dental consultant or a dental prescreener prior to payment. The dental consultant determines the necessity of the procedures and determines payment accordingly.

Before sending a claim to the dental consultant, the claims examiner should gather all of the necessary information for the consultant to make the determination of benefits. These items include the claim, any operative reports, and all x-rays.

Most payors have an itemized list of services that should be sent to the dental consultant before processing. Services on this list can include the following 16:

1. Temporomandibular joint procedures or services.
2. By report or relativity not established (RNE) procedures.
3. Multiple fillings (five or more on one claim).
4. Crown restorations, buildups or posts, or any repairs to crowns.
5. Inlays and onlays.

6. Root canal therapy and apicoectomies.
7. Periodontal services.
8. Prosthodontics (partial dentures and bridges).
9. Multiple extractions (four or more on one claim).
10. Surgical extractions (including impactions).
11. Tests and pathologic exams.
12. Acid etch restorations.
13. Bonding or sealants.
14. Surgical procedures.
15. Palliative treatments
16. General anesthesia charges.

After review, the claim is returned to the claims examiner with the determination of benefits included. The claims examiner may then adjudicate the claim.

Required Participation

Many dental plans require a high participation rate among the eligible insureds in a plan. For example, a dental plan may require that 95% to 100% of the eligible employees in a company must take the dental plan for it to become effective for the entire group. If the participation level drops below the required percentage, dental coverage for all plan members is suspended.

Other dental plans require the employer to contribute 100% of the cost of the plan for their employees. This nearly ensures that 100% of the employees will enroll in the dental plan since there is no cost for coverage.

Late Enrollment Penalties

Often people delay enrolling in a dental program until they are in need of dental services. This allows them to gain benefits with little or no contribution into the plan. To help discourage this, some plans specify that if an employee enrolls more than 30 days after they are eligible to enroll, many benefits will be limited to 50% of the amounts otherwise payable. In addition, some plans drastically reduce the calendar year maximum during the first year. The maximum can go as low as $100.

Coordination of Benefits

Most dental plans carry a coordination of benefits clause, which states that benefits will be reduced if the member has other coverage (whether dental or medical) for services. Most plans stipulate that total benefits payable by both plans is not to exceed 100% of the charges.

Major Medical Coverage for Dental Procedures

Some procedures performed on the mouth or teeth are covered under dental plans, but may be covered under major medical plans. This holds true even though the services were performed by a dentist or an oral surgeon rather than an MD. These can include the following nine services:

1. Accidental injury to teeth (see section on dental accidents).
2. Surgery to remove impacted or unerupted teeth or to remove supernumerary teeth. Major medical generally pays in the case of tissue-impacted, partly bone-impacted, or totally bone-impacted teeth.
3. Jawbone surgery.
4. Tumors or cysts within the oral cavity.
5. Nasal, auricular, orbital, or ocular prosthesis.
6. Obturators or repair of cleft palate.
7. Complex, subperiosteal, or endosseous implants.
8. Lab charges such as urinalysis, hemoglobin, hematocrit, and complete blood count.
9. Repair of fractures of the mandible, maxilla, or facial bones.

If a specific service is covered under the major medical portion of the plan, then all related services (such as exams, x-rays) are also covered under the major medical plan.

Seven other services that may or may not be covered under a major medical policy include:

1. Emergency room benefits. If emergency services are necessary and a dentist is not available, benefits may be allowable under the medical plan.
2. Hospital and anesthesia benefits. If hospital confinement is necessary for dental services, some plans allow major medical coverage for the hospital expense. Anesthesia expenses are usually cov-

ered for services that require hospitalization. Generally, anesthesia charges are not covered for outpatient services. Hospital confinement may be necessary because of the severity of the condition or because of underlying factors. For example, if a patient has a history of hemophilia and unstable diabetes, because of the possible complications arising from the surgery, the hospital benefit is usually paid. When hospital benefits are covered under major medical, the physician's or dentist's fees are still covered under the dental plan.

3. Oral-antral fistulas. Oral-antral fistulas are unnatural openings between the oral and nasal cavities. If the opening occurs as a result of dental treatment (ie, tooth extraction where the root has penetrated the sinuses), then the services would be considered dental. However, if the opening is treated after a 6-week period, it may be considered a medical expense even though the cause was tooth-related. This occurs because the delayed closure is usually the result of disease or infection. If the fistula is not the result of a dental condition, the cause of the fistula should be indicated (eg, tumor, disease). In such cases, major medical benefits usually cover the services.
4. Gross misalignment of the jaws. Often, pretreatment study models and an operative report should be requested to assist in the determination of coverage.

   If the surgery is a covered expense, it is often covered under both medical and dental plans. Determination of coverage usually needs to be referred to a supervisor or a medical review committee.
5. Other surgical services. The following surgeries may be covered under dental or medical benefits, depending on the plan: reduction of fractures to the mandible or maxilla, tumors or cysts of the gums or mouth, alveolectomy (due to a nondental condition), cleft palate or similar medical condition, and nondental bone surgery.
6. Cobalt therapy-related services. Cobalt or x-ray therapy causes damage to the teeth and tissues of the oral cavity. Dental services that are necessary due to cobalt or x-ray therapy are generally covered as medical.
7. Prescriptions and injections. Prescriptions and injections that are generally covered for nondental services are usually also covered when prescribed by a dentist or oral surgeon.

Occasionally, an orthodontic appliance (eg, banding, braces) is used immediately before or after surgery. This appliance is often used as a splint. In this case, the appliance would be covered. However, care must be taken to ensure that the appliance is used for splinting purposes and not for orthodontic purposes. Appliances used for orthodontic purposes would not be covered unless specifically indicated by the contract.

If a dental service is covered under major medical, some payors convert the ADA codes into the appropriate CPT or HCPCS codes and then apply the appropriate UCR conversion. The specific company and plan guidelines vary widely regarding major medical coverage for dental services and should be consulted prior to claim processing.

Dental Accidents

Many carriers cover accidental injury to permanent natural teeth under medical benefits. For the injury to qualify as an accident, you should be able to place the exact date, time and place at which the accident occurred. However, damage due to chewing or biting is generally not considered accidental.

Under the provisions of most contracts, the teeth must be permanent natural teeth, which were in place prior to the accident. Often dentures, partials, or "nonnatural" teeth are excluded. In this case, if there was damage to a pontic and the adjoining abutment teeth, the abutment teeth would be covered but the pontic would not. However, if teeth were evulsed (knocked out) as the result of an accident, fixed or removable prosthetics may be covered as "required to alleviate the damage." Likewise, deciduous teeth are often not covered since they are not permanent teeth.

Some plans may restrict payment to "sound" natural teeth. The term "sound" natural teeth defines teeth that are in good condition, without substantial restoration, fractures, cracks, extensive decay, or damage due to periodontal disease. The "good condition" clause applies to not only the crown of the tooth, but also to the root structure and the supporting structures of the tooth.

If a plan contains the wording "sound natural teeth," the presence of a fracture, large restorations, and other serious conditions may be grounds for denial of the services. It may be necessary to obtain preaccident x-rays of the tooth or teeth to determine whether or not they would be considered "sound."

Temporary Restorations

Occasionally, temporary restorations may be needed during the course of dental treatment. The most common reasons for temporary restorations are:

- When the patient has extensive caries, and several treatments may be required. The dentist removes the decay and inserts a temporary filling to seal the hole. This prevents further decay from taking place.
- When caries are extensive, a temporary filling allows the formation of reparative dentin and seals the hole from exposure to bacteria. In this case, the temporary restoration may prevent the need for more extensive orthodontic treatment.
- Cavities may need to be sealed during endodontic therapy.

Generally, temporary fillings are not covered. They are considered a necessary part of permanent dental treatment and therefore are included in the allowable amount of the covered dental expense. Some dental services (eg, fixed restorations) normally involve several visits to the dentist over a period of time. Therefore, temporary fillings cover the prepared teeth during the fabrication of the restoration.

X-Rays

X-rays (also called radiographs) are taken because it is impossible to tell the extent of tooth damage by visual examination alone. X-rays are paid as diagnostic procedures, regardless of the licensure of the person performing the x-rays (ie, dentist, oral surgeon). X-rays are billed individually according to their type and whether they were intraoral or extraoral (inside the mouth or outside the mouth).

Fourteen or more films that are done on the same day are considered a full-mouth x-ray and should be paid at the full-mouth x-ray rate. In addition, any combination of individual x-rays with a combined RVS unit value greater than that of a full-mouth x-ray should be paid at the full-mouth x-ray rate.

Occasionally, the examiner needs to request x-rays of an insured's teeth from the dentist to aid in determining the extent of damage and the amount of benefits that will be covered.

X-rays may be needed to help determine whether the work is cosmetic, to assist in determination of benefits, to aid in determining preexisting conditions, to aid in determining degrees and types of impactions or supernumerary teeth, to locate and identify tumors, cysts, or abscesses of the mouth, to evaluate the need for orthodontic treatment, and to review damage as the result of an accident.

In general, the following nine situations or services require the requesting of x-rays:

1. By report or RNE procedures (usually).
2. Multiple fillings (usually five or more billed on the same claim).
3. Crown restorations or buildups or posts.
4. Inlays and onlays.
5. Root canal therapy and apicoectomies.
6. Periodontal services.
7. Prosthodontics (partial dentures and bridges).
8. Multiple extractions (usually four or more billed on one claim).
9. Surgical extractions (including impactions).

The claims examiner is not expected to be able to determine the need for services from the x-rays. Reading x-rays requires extensive training and experience. However, the claims examiner can make a cursory examination of x-rays and the benefits payable. In reviewing x-rays, claims personnel, as lay persons, can expect only to see where teeth are missing and to identify impacted teeth (but not the degree of impaction), malposed teeth, supernumerary teeth, mixed dentition, extensive caries, existing restorations, some forms of abscesses, and in some cases, evidence of need for orthodontics. It requires a professional consultant to read and interpret x-rays for other than the most evident condition.

A processor or analyst, on reviewing x-rays, can approve benefits, but a consultant's opinion is required for all denials that require a professional opinion. No person other than a consultant can recommend that benefits be reduced or denied unless the denial is based on plan limitations/exclusions. The following guidelines will assist in the use of x-rays to determine benefits:

- If caries appear on x-rays, benefits should be allowable for restorations (fillings).
- If the caries are deep or extensive, benefits are usually allowable for restorations or crowns.
- If teeth are missing, benefits should be allowable for prosthetics (either fixed or removable).
- If there are no teeth (the insured is edentulous), benefits are usually payable for full dentures.
- If several teeth are missing (especially several adjacent teeth), a consultant should review any planned bridgework.
- If there is extensive bone loss, restorative procedures or bridgework near the site of the bone loss should be evaluated by a consultant.
- If treatment is planned and the claims examiner is unable to see the need for any treatment, services should be evaluated by a consultant.

Remember that damage or decay is usually more extensive than that shown on an x-ray. For example, treatment or replacement may be recommended for an existing restoration or crown, but the decay is hidden beneath the restoration or crown on the x-ray (x-rays do not penetrate many crown and filling materials and therefore show up as dark spots on a radiograph).

Some materials do not show up on x-rays. In this case, a tooth that looks as if it needs treatment may already have been treated. As a general rule, if the sides are rough or irregular, restoration has not been done. Smooth sides usually indicate prior treatment.

X-rays belong to the dentist and should be returned as soon as possible, preferably within 1 week of receiving them. At no time should x-rays be held longer than 2 weeks without a letter or call to the dentist to explain the delay and request permission to hold the x-rays for a longer period of time. At all times, x-rays should be handled with care.

Orthodontic X-Rays

If a general dentist makes x-rays to determine the need for orthodontics, the x-rays would generally be covered even if orthodontic treatment was not covered. In this case, x-rays are used as a diagnostic tool to determine the need for orthodontic treatment. Policies that exclude orthodontic treatment would exclude all orthodontic services performed after the need for orthodontic services has been established, regardless of whether they were performed by the originating dentist or whether the insured was referred to an orthodontist for continued treatment.

To determine whether an x-ray is for the diagnosis of orthodontic treatment or a part of the orthodontic service, the following guidelines can be used:

- If the date of service for the x-rays is prior to the commencement of orthodontic services, x-rays should be allowable as diagnostic.
- If the date of service for the x-rays is after the commencement of orthodontic services, x-rays should be considered part of the orthodontic services.

Anesthesia

Anesthesia is usually required for most dental services other than x-rays, prophylaxis, and exams. The four types of anesthesia most commonly used for dental services are:

1. Local anesthesia.
2. Intravenous sedation.
3. Analgesia (nitrous oxide, twilight sleep).
4. General anesthesia.

Local anesthesia is the most commonly used anesthesia and is appropriate for nearly all dental procedures. Local anesthesia can be identified as local anesthesia (09210 or 09215), regional block anesthesia (09211), or trigeminal division block anesthesia (09212). The allowances for local anesthesia are included in the allowance for the basic procedure, so no additional payment is provided for this service.

Intravenous sedation (09240) and analgesia (09230) are usually allowable only for surgical extractions or for four or more simple extractions performed during the same visit (intravenous sedation renders the patient semiconscious). Many plans also allow intravenous and analgesic anesthesia for any dental services performed on a patient less than 12 years of age. No permit is required for analgesia or intravenous sedation.

If intravenous sedation or analgesia is performed for other than the previously mentioned services and on a patient above 12 years of age, the allowance for general anesthesia (if any) may be awarded.

Sedative Fillings

Medicated or sedative fillings are considered to be temporary. As a rule, they may not be covered; the final restoration only may be the covered expense. If the medicated or sedative filling is done on the same day as the final restoration, it is usually considered a base and is combined with the charge for the final restoration, since the final should include a base. The combined charge would then be subjected to any UCR limitation based on the coding for the final restoration. If the final restoration is a crown and not a filling, the medicated or sedative filling may be allowable separately. This varies by administrator.

Cosmetic Services

Remember that just because a particular service is cosmetic and "excluded," the cost of the noncosmetic, less expensive service would be allowable and that amount would be applied toward the cost of the more expensive service. Most plans are subject to the following exclusions:

- Cosmetic services, such as crowns that are not necessary because of disease or injury. This also includes the use of composite fillings on posterior teeth, bleaching of stains from the teeth, using crowns to straighten or align teeth in an arch, and so on.
- Precision attachments are usually excluded from consideration. They tend to be significantly more expensive than conventional clasps with no more usefulness.
- Characterization or personalization of dentures. Dentures can be custom-designed to include such features as staining or selected duplication of gold restorations that were present prior to the need for dentures.

Procedures that are considered wholly cosmetic include labial veneer (laminate) and bleaching of discolored teeth.

Unspecified and By Report Procedures

Unspecified procedures are codes that classify procedures that are not specifically listed in a section of the ADA code list. There is an individual code for each section of the ADA code list. These codes nearly always end in 99.

For example:

00999—unspecified diagnostic procedure

03999—unspecified endodontic procedure

By report (BR) or relativity not established (RNE) procedures are procedures for which a unit value has not been assigned. This is usually because a procedure is new or not performed often enough for sufficient data to be collected to establish a unit value.

Generally, the insurer places a dollar limit on unspecified and BR/RNE procedures. Any claims for unspecified or BR/RNE procedures that fall below this dollar limit are allowable as billed. Any claims that fall above this limit need to be sent to the review board to determine benefits. A common dollar amount is $100 to $150.

Summary

Although there can be multiple variations on all types of dental plans, as a rule, dental plans are easy to understand and apply. Missing and Unreplaced, Predetermination of Benefits, Alternate Course of Treatment and Five-Year Replacement Rule are universal and generally apply to most plans, regardless of whether the plan is basic, scheduled, integrated, or nonintegrated.

Read the plan provisions to find out how to apply the benefits and what type of plan it is.

Assignments

Complete the Questions for Review.

Read through the two dental contracts in Chapter 2 of the Student Exercise Manual and ensure your understanding of them.

Questions for Review

Directions: Answer the following questions without looking back into the material just covered. Write your answers in the space provided.

they are usually separate

1. On an integrated plan, dental charges can be applied to the medical calendar year deductible. (True or False) F
2. Usually, on a basic plan the fees are not dependent on conversion factor nor location of provider
3. What are the four types of anesthesia most commonly used for dental services?
   a. Local
   b. intravenous - surgical
   c. Analgesia - surgical
   d. General anthesia - Most common
4. On a scheduled plan, an unlisted procedure may be handled in the following two ways:
   a. Plan provisions may specify that unlisted procedures are not covered — deny
   b. sometimes allowed - based on a consultant review could be specified amount or a %
5. The charges for local anesthesia are included in the allowable amount for the procedure. (True or False)
   True

If you were unable to answer any of the questions, refer back to the section and then complete the answers.

28

Processing Dental Claims

In this chapter you will learn:

- How to apply dental conversion factors.
- To process dental claims, applying all contract provisions and limitations.

When a claim for dental services is received, it is the responsibility of the claims examiner to determine whether the claim received is eligible for payment. This entails several steps including verifying eligibility, determining whether services rendered are covered, identifying any limitations that may exist on coverage, and so on. After all preliminary investigation is complete, the processing of the claim can be completed.

Processing of dental claims occurs in much the same way as the processing of medical claims. Basic steps should be followed in each instance for the processing to be properly completed.

The Claim Form

First, determine the following:

1. Was the correct claim form used for the services provided?
2. Has the claim form been properly filled out?
3. Is all the information complete?
4. Did the patient authorize the release of information?

If the answer to any of the above is no, deny the claim or pend it and request additional information.

Eligibility

Next, determine the eligibility of the patient:

1. At the time of service, was the patient currently enrolled under the plan (check each listed date of service)?
2. If a dependent, is the patient within the proper age limit? If not within the normal age limit, is the patient a full-time student and within the extended age limit?
3. Is the plan currently in force (eg, have all premiums been paid)?
4. Have all eligibility requirements set forth in the contract been met?

If the answer to any of the previous questions is no, the claim is automatically denied since the patient was not insured at the time of service.

Other Insurance

Next, determine whether there is other coverage for the services rendered.

1. Does the patient have other insurance that might cover these services?
2. Is the claim related to Workers' Compensation?
3. Is the claim related to an accident? If yes, is there a third party that could be held legally responsible for the payment of the claim?

If the answer to any of the above questions is yes, try to determine the benefits that were paid by the other party.

Provider Authority

1. Who is the provider of service?
2. What is the medical degree of the provider of service? Is this a recognized medical degree for the type of treatment provided?
3. Is the provider's license number included on the form?
4. Is the place of treatment appropriate for the services rendered?

Coverage of Services

One of the most important parts of processing a claim is to determine whether services are covered. Ask yourself the following questions:

1. Are any of the services listed as excluded?
2. Was prior work done on the tooth that would exclude services?
3. Was there prior damage to the tooth that would

exclude services (eg, is tooth previously listed as missing)?

4. If there are limitations to the number of times that a service can be provided, has that limitation been met previously?
5. If the service is an office visit, is there an exam, prophylaxis, or x-rays, or was the service in conjunction with a treatment procedure?
6. Does missing and unreplaced apply?
7. Does the 5-year limitation apply for prosthetics?
8. Does the less than 6-month limitation apply for adjustments to appliances, prosthetics, or dentures?
9. Have calendar year or lifetime maximums already been reached for this patient?

Evaluating the Services

If it is determined that the services are covered, then go to the next step, evaluating the service that was performed:

1. Are tooth numbers consistent with surfaces (anterior and posterior teeth with anterior and posterior surfaces)?
2. Do the services match the codes?
3. Were any services performed on the same day as another service that would disallow one or the other of the services (ie, consultation/office visit billed with treatment)?
4. Do any other limitations apply (ie, for multiple x-rays; full-mouth series)?
5. Does the contract list specific provisions for the services provided (ie, orthodontic treatment is paid at 50%; second opinions are paid at 100%, and so on)?
6. Is a second opinion required for the services? If so, was a second opinion obtained? If a second opinion was required, but not obtained, what are the ramifications to the processing of the claim (are benefits reduced or denied)?

Processing the Claim

After it has been determined that the claim is correctly filled out, the patient is covered, the provider is appropriate, there is no other insurance, and the services are covered, begin processing the claim.

The first step is to determine the allowable amount for the service or procedure. Using the ADA Dental Code List on page 333, determine the type of service or conversion factor code (CFC). Types of service fall under three categories, and each is listed next to the unit value on the Dental Code List. The three types of service are:

A. Diagnostic and preventive services
B. All other services excluding gold restorations, crowns, and prosthetics.
C. Gold restorations, crowns, and prosthetics.

Next, determine the appropriate unit value for the service or procedure. The unit value is listed on the Dental Code List next to the codes.

Then, using the first three digits of the provider's zip code, look up the conversion factor in Appendix 28-1: Dental Prevailing Conversion Factors. Be sure to use the correct conversion factor according to the type of service or conversion factor code.

Multiply the conversion factor by the unit value for the procedure. This will give you the allowable amount. However, remember that if the billed amount is less than the allowable amount, the billed amount is considered to be the allowable amount.

Completing the Claim Payment Worksheet

The claim payment worksheet is equivalent to an explanation of benefits. A copy of this form will be sent to the insured to explain the benefit payment for the claim. Therefore, it is important that each section be filled out completely to reduce the likelihood of confusing the insured.

The claim payment worksheet used for this course is intended to be an example only. It contains the information in much the same format as other insurance carrier payment forms. This worksheet and the guidelines for completing it are to be used for training and reference purposes only, since the individual company or plan worksheets may differ.

Complete the information regarding the patient and the insured first. This information is contained in the box in the upper left-hand corner of the payment worksheet.

Next, list each code in the first column on the claim payment worksheet. Only codes that are the same should be combined; otherwise, list one service per line, regardless of whether this will mean using more than one claim payment worksheet.

List the date(s) of service in the second column and the amount that the doctor billed in the third column.

Next, skip to the fifth column (Allowable) and enter the allowable amount as figured above. Then, subtract the allowable amount from the billed amount. The resulting figure will be the excluded amount; write this in the fourth column.

Make sure that you also enter a denial reason on the corresponding line in the denial reasons section. Usually, a brief explanation such as "$21.83 Not covered—charge exceeds amount covered by your plan" is sufficient. If the service is not covered, the corresponding code (or description) and an explanation should be listed in the same manner (ie, $300.00 Not covered—orthodontic services are not covered by your plan.).

If the plan has a basic allowance, the unit value should be multiplied by the basic allowance listed in the contract. For example, if the contract stipulates that the basic allowance for office visits is $7.00 and the service has a unit value of 1.0, the basic allowance is $7.00. Place the basic allowance amount in the sixth column (Basic 100%). Note that if the contract is part of a medical contract, the medical basic allowances do not transfer to the dental plan. If basic allowances are not listed in the dental section, they do not apply.

Subtract the basic allowance from the allowable amount and place the remainder in the seventh column.

After all the charges have been figured individually, add up the totals for each column and place each total at the bottom of each column. Check your totals for accuracy by adding the allowable amount to the excluded amount. The total of these two figures should match the billed amount on the claim. Likewise, the sixth and seventh columns added together should equal the allowable amount.

If the contract allows different percentages depending on the type of service (eg, diagnostic services pay at 80%, restorative at 75%), then place all services with a similar copayment amount together in a single column. There is an additional, eighth column to allow for varying percentages.

Figuring the Benefit Payment

Now, begin figuring the actual benefit payment. At the top of each payment column (columns 6 through 8), place the coinsurance percentage amount that applies to the figures in that column.

Next, check the contract for the deductible amount and the beginning financials for any previously paid deductibles.

- Has the deductible for this individual been satisfied?
- Does the deductible combine with the medical plan (the plans are integrated)? If so, has the deductible been satisfied under the medical portion of the contract?
- Has the family deductible been satisfied?
- Is there any carryover deductible from the previous year?

Using the latter questions and information, calculate the deductible that should be applied to this claim. Place the amount of the deductible across from the word deductible in the first column, in which benefits are payable at less than 100% (deductible is not taken from basic benefits). If the deductible remaining is more than the amount of the column, place the amount of the column in the deductible column and carry over any remaining amounts to additional columns with less than a 100% coinsurance amount.

Subtract the deductible amount from the total of the column. This remaining amount is the portion that is subject to coinsurance.

Multiply the amount subject to coinsurance by the insured's portion of the coinsurance amount (the remaining amount needed to reach 100%). For example, if the plan's coinsurance amount is 80%, the insured's responsibility is 20%.

Next ask the following questions:

- What is the maximum coinsurance amount listed in the contract?
- Has this coinsurance limit been met?
- If the individual coinsurance limit has not been met, has the family coinsurance limit been met?

If any coinsurance limits have been met, the coinsurance amount should be adjusted accordingly. For example, if the individual coinsurance limit is $1500 and $1495 has been paid by the individual, then the coinsurance amount is $5.00. The correct coinsurance amount goes in the next space labeled coinsurance.

Subtract the coinsurance amount from the amount subject to coinsurance. The remaining balance is the amount subject to adjustment; place this amount in the next column.

Then ask:

- If there is other insurance, what amount is paid by the other insurance company?
- Are there any other reasons why there would be an adjustment on this claim?
- If so, what is the proper adjustment amount?

If there is an adjustment, place the amount of the adjustment in the following box labeled "Adjustment (see remarks)," and an explanation should be placed in the remarks box to the left.

Subtract the adjustment amount from the amount subject to adjustment, resulting in the payment amount (following box). Add the payment amount from each column and place the resulting payment amount in the box immediately to the right of the words "Payment Amount." This is the amount of the benefits being paid by the insurance carrier.

Note: If any individual or family deductible or coinsurance amounts have been met with this claim, place an asterisk beside the deductible or coinsurance amount and make a notation in the remarks box (eg, 1992 Family deductible has been met).

Payees

All that is left is to determine to whom to make out the check and to update the financial history. Look back on the claim form. Did the insured authorize payment directly to the provider of services?

- If not, the payee would be the member.
- If so, check the billed amount from the claim and the amount (if any) that the patient/insured has already paid.
- If the difference between the billed amount and the amount the patient or insured paid (balance due) is more than the benefit payment amount, the payee would be the provider of services.
- If the difference between the billed amount and the amount the patient or insured paid (balance due) is less than the benefit payment amount, the payee would be the provider of services up to the balance due. Any remaining funds would then be paid to the member.

Updating History

Updating the payment history is vitally important to ensure that proper benefit payments are calculated. Each of the previous questions that related to previous payments of deductibles, coinsurance amounts, satisfaction of individual or family limits, accident benefits, and so on, will change with the processing of each claim.

On our payment worksheet, the updated history appears in the upper left-hand corner of the sheet. If claims are processed by computer, the computer should handle the updating of the history for you.

If accident benefits were paid on this claim, add the payment amount of the accident benefits to any previous accident benefit amounts paid on this individual in this calendar year. Place the amount on the first line along with the current year.

Add the amount of the benefits paid to all previous benefits paid. If the plan has a calendar year maximum rather than a lifetime maximum, add the amount of the benefits paid to all previous benefits paid during that calendar year. Place the result in the lifetime maximum space on the next line. If the plan calls for a calendar year maximum, the word "lifetime" should be replaced by the words "calendar year," and the current year should be included.

Add the amount of any deductibles calculated on this claim to any previously paid deductible amounts, and place the result in the deductible space with the current year.

If any of the dates of service on this claim falls within the last 3 months of the calendar year and the contract includes a carryover provision, place the amount of deductible paid on those services on the line labeled carryover deductible, along with the year. If there is more than one date of service and some are in the last 3 months and others are not, the deductible amount should be taken from the amount(s) of the services in the order in which they are received.

For example:

An exam and x-ray were performed on 9/18/90. Two cavities were found and an appointment was made for filling them on 10/10/90. The billed amount for the exam and x-ray was $40.00, and all of it was allowable (the UCR amount was higher than the billed amount). The allowable amount for the filling was $120.00.

The patient had satisfied $75.00 of the $150.00 deductible. The total paid deductible amount would be $75.00 on this claim. Forty dollars of the deductible would be for the first two services and $35.00 would be for the two fillings. Therefore, $35.00 would be considered the carryover deductible amount.

Finally, add the amount listed on the coinsurance line with any previous coinsurance amounts for the calendar year. Place the total, along with the year, on the coinsurance line of the financial history box.

You have now completed payment on this claim.

Dental Form Letters

Occasionally, certain form letters are used during the processing of dental claims. These form letters are the same as those used for medical claims processing, so they have not been duplicated here.

Request for Additional Information

This form is used when more information is needed from the provider of services or the patient regarding the services that were performed or the necessity for those services. If there is any question on the claim, especially regarding the services, the patient identification, or other insurance that might be applicable, a request for additional information form should be completed and mailed out.

Third Party Liability

If the services were performed as the result of a work-related situation, Workers' Compensation should be paying the bill, not the patient's insurance carrier. In addition, if the patient was involved in an accident (especially an auto accident), another insurance carrier may be responsible for all or part of the bill. In this case, this would be the insurance carrier of the driver who caused the accident. In an accident that is not auto-related, negligence may be cited as a reason for another carrier to incur responsibility (eg, patient fell through a rotted stair and landed on jaw).

If any of the latter cases apply, the patient's payor may make payment on the claim; however, the payor usually requires the insured to sign a third party liability statement. In effect, this statement says that if any monies are paid by a third party on this claim, the patient's insurance carrier receives the money first. Only after the carrier has been reimbursed for any monies paid out will any additional monies revert to the patient or the insured.

Authorization to Release Information

Occasionally, no patient or insured signature is on file nor on the claim that authorizes the release of information to the payor. This authorization must be completed before a claim is sent in.

Often, an insurance carrier has a copy of an authorization to release information kept on file. This allows the carrier to receive the claim information without delay.

Handling Fraudulent Dental Claims

Occasionally, dentists and insureds submit fraudulent claims for processing. These fraudulent claims can include the following:

- Claims that have been submitted twice, either to the same insurer or to different insurers.
- Claims that have been submitted for services that were not actually rendered.
- Claims that have been altered to make it appear

that services were performed on a different date, patient, and so on.

The types of fraudulent dental claim situations are usually one of the following:

- Duplicate charges.
- Duplicate services.
- Altering dates of treatment.
- Reporting services that are not the same as those actually done.
- False information or rationale about diagnosis, treatment, condition of dentures, and so on.
- Submission of incorrect x-rays.

Fraud or mistakes are usually detected during the usual processing or review procedures prior to payment through the following nine ways:

1. Review of prior treatment against present treatment.
2. Completion or review of dental charts, checking prior work, existing work, and present or proposed work.
3. Verification of tooth numbers and positions.
4. Verification of dates of services and charges.
5. Checking for date of first visit and age of claimant.
6. Checking for erasures and changes of pen color, and other indications of changes.
7. Reviewing posttreatment x-rays.
8. Evaluating treatment plan by use of x-rays rather than rationale or facts supplied by the dentist. Rationale should be used to supplement x-rays and not as the sole determinant of benefits.
9. Verifying services with claimant.

There are several methods of determining whether misrepresentation has occurred. Before any steps are taken, the file should be reviewed by the supervisor and the dental consultant.

Postoperative x-rays should be obtained to show satisfactory completion of the work. This is not conclusive evidence one way or the other, since the wrong x-rays can be submitted.

Oral exams by outside dentists are the best method of determining what work has actually been performed. In cases involving large amounts, it may be helpful to request the examining dentist to take x-rays as a record of any discrepancies. It may also be wise to duplicate the preoperative x-rays before returning them to the attending dentist.

In a few instances, an on-site claim representative may examine the dentist's records. This method should be used judiciously and only for the purpose of verifying dates of treatment and whether duplicate services were rendered.

As with medical claim fraud, in all dealings with either claimants or dentists, it is important not to accuse anyone without adequate proof. Mistakes can easily be made in completing a claim form, and every effort should be made to rule this out. The Unit Supervisor and Claims Director should always be advised prior to taking any action.

The rules regarding documentation of the claim file, which were previously discussed in relation to medical claims, apply to dental claims also. Basically, if the information was not written down, the services are deemed not to have happened.

Summary

When a claim for dental services is received, it is the responsibility of the claims examiner to determine whether the claim received is eligible for payment. This entails several steps, including verifying eligibility, determining whether services rendered are covered, identifying any limitations that may exist on coverage. After all preliminary investigation is complete, the processing of the claim can be completed.

The basic steps just covered should enable you to process claims with the highest degree of accuracy and in the least amount of time.

Assignments

Complete the Questions for Review.

Complete Dental UCR Exercises 28-1 to 28-3.

Process Dental Claims 29-1 to 29-15 beginning on page 395, using the Beginning Financials and the guidelines covered in this chapter.

Questions for Review

Directions: Answer the following questions without looking back into the material just covered. Write your answers in the space provided.

1. What is the first thing that the claims examiner should check upon receipt of a claim form?
____
____
2. The claim payment worksheet is equivalent to an ______________________________
____
3. How do you determine the appropriate unit value for a dental service? ______________________________
____
4. How do you determine the allowable amount for a procedure? ______________________________
____
____
____
5. Why is it important to update the payment history upon completion of the calculation sheet?
____
____

If you were unable to answer any of the questions, refer back to the section and then complete the answers.

Exercise 28-1

Directions: Using the ADA Dental Code List on page 333 and the Dental Conversion Factor chart on page 394, calculate UCR for the following procedures. Use the conversion factor for zip code 94325.

Description	Proc. Code	Units	Conv. Factor	Amount
1. Adult prophylaxis	______	______	______	______
2. Gold inlay, one surface	______	______	______	______
3. Complete upper denture	______	______	______	______
4. Composite filling, tooth #28, 2 surfaces	______	______	______	______
5. Excise benign tumor, 1.45 cm	______	______	______	______
6. Bitewing x-rays, 5 films	______	______	______	______
7. Sodium fluoride treatment	______	______	______	______
8. Apical curettage	______	______	______	______
9. Upper bridge w/2 chrome clasps w/rests, acrylic base	______	______	______	______
10. Pulp vitality test	______	______	______	______
11. Amalgam filling, primary tooth #F, 3 surfaces	______	______	______	______
12. Single x-ray film	______	______	______	______
13. Extraction, tooth #21	______	______	______	______
14. Oral exam w/2 x-rays	______	______	______	______
15. Porcelain metal crown	______	______	______	______

Exercise 28-2

Directions: Using the ADA Dental Code List on page 333 and the Dental Prevailing Conversion Factor chart on page 394, calculate UCR for the following procedures. Use the conversion factor for zip code 90020.

Description	Proc. Code	Units	Conv. Factor	Amount
1. Adult prophylaxis	______	______	______	______
2. Gold inlay, one surface	______	______	______	______
3. Complete upper denture	______	______	______	______
4. Composite filling, tooth #28, 2 surfaces	______	______	______	______
5. Excise benign tumor, 1.45 cm	______	______	______	______
6. Bitewing x-rays, 5 films	______	______	______	______
7. Sodium fluoride treatment	______	______	______	______
8. Apical curettage	______	______	______	______
9. Upper bridge w/2 chrome clasps w/rests, acrylic base	______	______	______	______
10. Pulp vitality test	______	______	______	______
11. Amalgam filling, primary tooth #F, 3 surfaces	______	______	______	______
12. Single x-ray film	______	______	______	______
13. Extraction, tooth #21	______	______	______	______
14. Oral exam w/2 x-rays	______	______	______	______
15. Porcelain metal crown	______	______	______	______

Exercise 28-3

Directions: Using the ADA Dental Code List on page 333 and the Dental Prevailing Conversion Factor chart on page 394, calculate UCR for the following procedures. Use the conversion factor for zip code 93504.

Description	Proc. Code	Units	Conv. Factor	Amount
1. Adult prophylaxis	______	______	______	______
2. Gold inlay, one surface	______	______	______	______
3. Complete upper denture	______	______	______	______
4. Composite filling, tooth #28, 2 surfaces	______	______	______	______
5. Excise benign tumor, 1.45 cm	______	______	______	______
6. Bitewing x-rays, 5 films	______	______	______	______
7. Sodium fluoride treatment	______	______	______	______
8. Apical curettage	______	______	______	______
9. Upper bridge w/2 chrome clasps w/rests, acrylic base	______	______	______	______
10. Pulp vitality test	______	______	______	______
11. Amalgam filling, primary tooth #F, 3 surfaces	______	______	______	______
12. Single x-ray film	______	______	______	______
13. Extraction, tooth #21	______	______	______	______
14. Oral exam w/2 x-rays	______	______	______	______
15. Porcelain metal crown	______	______	______	______

Appendix 28-1

Dental Prevailing Conversion Factors

The following list of Dental Prevailing Conversion Factors is intended to be used for training and reference purposes only, since the individual company or plan guidelines may differ from those stated. Because all exercise manual claims are within the state of California, only California conversion factor codes are listed.

State: California

Area	Zip Codes	A. Diagnostic and Preventive	B. All Other Excl. Gold Restorations, Crowns, Prosthetics	C. Gold Rest., Crowns, and Prosthetics
Los Angeles, Long Beach, Code 900	900-918	40.00	41.75	37.25
San Diego, Code 920	920-921	34.00	36.50	33.00
San Bernardino, Riverside, Palm Springs, Code 922	922-925	35.00	36.50	31.75
Orange County, Code 926	926-928	40.00	41.00	35.00
Ventura, Santa Barbara, Code 930	930-931	35.75	38.25	33.50
San Francisco, Oakland, San Jose, Code 940	940-951	40.00	41.25	36.00
Sacramento, Stockton, Code 952	952-953, 956-958	35.75	35.00	30.75
Other California	932-937, 939, 954, 955, 959-966	35.75	35.25	31.00

29
Dental Claims

Dental Claims Beginning Financials

Claims 29-1 to 29-5

Plan - XYZ Corporation. Refer to Appendix 28-1 on page 394.

	MARIA	MAGGIE	MAEDEAN	MALCOLM
1990/DED	0.00	0.00	0.00	0.00
1990/PD	0.00	0.00	0.00	0.00
1991/DED	0.00	0.00	0.00	0.00
1991/PD	0.00	0.00	0.00	0.00

Claims 29-6 to 29-10

Plan - ABC Corporation. Refer to Appendix 28-1 on page 394.

	ORVILLE	OCTAVIA	ODELL
1990/DED	0.00	0.00	27.42
1990/COINS	0.00	0.00	0.00
1990/PD	0.00	0.00	0.00
1991/DED	0.00	0.00	27.42
1991/COINS	0.00	0.00	0.00
1991/PD	0.00	0.00	0.00
LT	0.00	4762.93	2763.99

Claims 29-11 to 29-15

Plan - XYZ Corporation. Refer to Appendix 28-1 on page 394.

	SALLY	SUSAN	SAMUEL	SANDRA
1990/DED	0.00	0.00	0.00	0.00
1990/PD	0.00	0.00	0.00	0.00
1991/DED	0.00	0.00	0.00	0.00
1991/PD	0.00	0.00	0.00	0.00

Attending Dentist's Statement

Claim 29-1

1. Patient Name	2. Relationship	3. Sex	4. Birthdate	5. FTS
Maria Murdock	Self	❑ M ☒ F	05/03/40	

5. Employee/Subscriber	7. Social Security No.	9. Name of Group
Maria Murdock	111-22-3333	XYZ Corporation

8. Employee Address	10. Employer Name
9876 Maraban Lane	XYZ Corporation
City/State/Zip: Montrose, CA 92318	

11. Group Number	12. Local	13. Are other family members employed? NO
112233		Address:

15. Is patient covered by another plan?	Name of plan	Union	Number
❑ Y ☒ N			

16. Dentist Name: Mable Miller, DDS

17. Mailing address: 1895 Myrtle Road

City/State/Zip: Montrose, CA 92309

18. Dentist TIN/SS#: 95-1234567

19. Lic. #: MM98234789

20. Dentist Phone No.: (818) 555-1234

21. Date of 1st Treatment: 04/28/90

22. Place of Treatment: Office

Is claim related to:	No	Yes	If yes, give date, etc.
24. Workers Comp	X		
25. Auto Accident?	X		
26. Other Accident?	X		
27. OIS?	X		
28. Initial Prosthetic?	X		Max Comp Dent
29. Date of Prior Placement:	More than 10 years		
30. Orthodontics?			Placement Date:
23. X-rays enclosed?		X	# 5

I authorize the release of information: Signature on file

I authorize payment of benefits to provider: Signature on file

Identify missing teeth with X

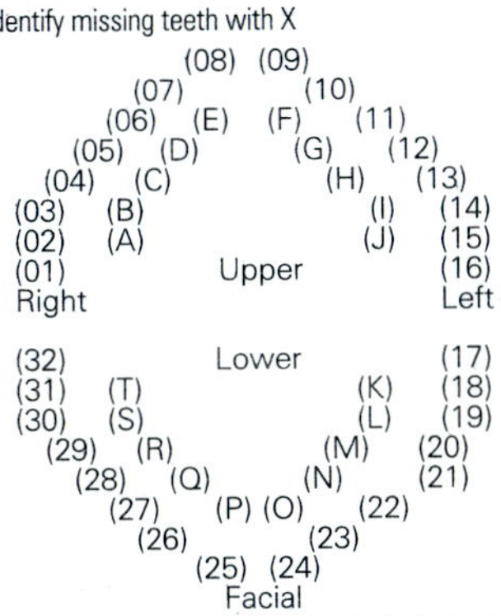

Tooth #	Surf	Description	Date	PRCDR Code	Fees
		Oral Exam/Office Visit	4/28/90		20.00
		X-Ray Single	4/28/90		10.00
		X-Rays additional (4)	4/28/90		24.00
	UR	Maxillary Tuberosity Reduc	5/12/90		150.00
	UL	Maxillary Tuberosity Reduc	5/12/90		150.00
21		Extraction	6/2/90		60.00
22		Extraction	6/2/90		55.00
		Upper Denture	8/4/90		600.00
		Partial Denture/Metal	8/4/90		500.00
		Teeth/Clasps-8 msg tth/2 cl	8/4/90		450.00
		Prophylaxis/Scaling	7/28/90		60.00

I hereby certify that the services listed above have been performed on the date(s) shown above, and that these are the charges that I actually charged.

Dentist's Signature *Mable Miller, DDS* Date

Total Fee	2079.00
Patient Paid	
Balance Due	

For official use only

I hereby certify that the foregoing statements including any accompanying statements are to the best of my knowledge true and correct.
Check: ☒ I do ❑ I do not authorize the administrator to pay directly to the named dentist or any other supplier of services any benefits otherwise payable to me, but not to exceed any of the charges by the dentist or any other supplier of services. I understand that I am financially responsible for any charges not covered by this authorization.

Employee's Signature *Maria Murdock* Date

Attending Dentist's Statement

Claim 29-2

1. Patient Name Maggie Murdock	2. Relationship Daughter	3. Sex ☐ M ☒ F	4. Birthdate 09/21/81	5. FTS
5. Employee/Subscriber Maria Murdock	7. Social Security No. 111-22-3333	9. Name of Group XYZ Corporation		
8. Employee Address 9876 Maraban Lane		10. Employer Name XYZ Corporation		
City/State/Zip Montrose, CA 92318				
11. Group Number 112233	12. Local	13. Are other family members employed? NO Address:		

15. Is patient covered by another plan? ☐ Y ☒ N	Name of plan	Union	Number

16. Dentist Name Mable Miller, DDS		Is claim related to:	No	Yes	If yes, give date, etc.
17. Mailing address 1895 Myrtle Road		24. Workers Comp	X		
		25. Auto Accident?	X		
City/State/Zip Montrose, CA 92309		26. Other Accident?	X		
		27. OIS?	X		
18. Dentist TIN/SS#	95-1234567	28. Initial Prosthetic?			
19. Lic. # MM98234789	20. Dentist Phone No. (818) 555-1234	29. Date of Prior Placement:			
		30. Orthodontics?	X		Placement Date:
21. Date of 1st Treatment 07/02/91	22. Place of Treatment Office	23. X-rays enclosed?		X	# 1

I authorize the release of information
Signature on file

I authorize payment of benefits to provider

Identify missing teeth with X

Upper: Right (01) (02) (03) (04) (05) (06) (07) (08) (09) (10) (11) (12) (13) (14) (15) (16) Left
(A) (B) (C) (D) (E) (F) (G) (H) (I) (J)

Lower: Right (32) (31) (30) (29) (28) (27) (26) (25) (24) (23) (22) (21) (20) (19) (18) (17) Left
(T) (S) (R) (Q) (P) (O) (N) (M) (L) (K)

Facial

Tooth #	Surf	Description	Date	PRCDR Code	Fees
		1 Single Film	07/02/91		13.00
		1 Addtl X-Ray	07/02/91		7.00
3		Root Canal Treatment	08/13/91		390.00
		Prophylaxis	07/02/91		50.00

Total Fee	460.00
Patient Paid	
Balance Due	

For official use only

I hereby certify that the services listed above have been performed on the date(s) shown above, and that these are the charges that I actually charged.

Dentist's Signature *Mable Miller, DDS* Date

I hereby certify that the foregoing statements including any accompanying statements are to the best of my knowledge true and correct.
Check: ☐ I do ☒ I do not authorize the administrator to pay directly to the named dentist or any other supplier of services any benefits otherwise payable to me, but not to exceed any of the charges by the dentist or any other supplier of services.
I understand that I am financially responsible for any charges not covered by this authorization.

Employee's Signature *Maria Murdock* Date

Attending Dentist's Statement

Claim 29-3

1. Patient Name	2. Relationship	3. Sex	4. Birthdate	5. FTS
Maedean Murdock	**Daughter**	❑ M ☒ F	**07/21/77**	
5. Employee/Subscriber	7. Social Security No.	9. Name of Group		
Maria Murdock	**111-22-3333**	**XYZ Corporation**		
8. Employee Address		10. Employer Name		
9876 Maraban Lane		**XYZ Corporation**		
City/State/Zip				
Montrose, CA 92318				
11. Group Number	12. Local	13. Are other family members employed? **NO**		
112233		Address:		

15. Is patient covered by another plan?	Name of plan	Union	Number
❑ Y ☒ N			

16. Dentist Name		Is claim related to:	No	Yes	If yes, give date, etc.
Mable Miller, DDS		24. Workers Comp	X		
17. Mailing address		25. Auto Accident?	X		
1895 Myrtle Road		26. Other Accident?	X		
City/State/Zip		27. OIS?	X		
Montrose, CA 92309					
18. Dentist TIN/SS#	**95-1234567**	28. Initial Prosthetic?			
19. Lic. #	20. Dentist Phone No.	29. Date of Prior Placement:			
MM98234789	**(818) 555-1234**	30. Orthodontics?	X		Placement Date:
21. Date of 1st Treatment	22. Place of Treatment	23. X-rays enclosed?	X		#
	Office				

I authorize the release of information	I authorize payment of benefits to provider
Signature on file	**Signature on file**

Identify missing teeth with X

(08) (09)
(07) (10)
(06) (E) (F) (11)
(05) (D) (G) (12)
(04) (C) (H) (13)
(03) (B) (I) (14)
(02) (A) (J) (15)
(01) Upper (16)
Right Left
(32) Lower (17)
(31) (T) (K) (18)
(30) (S) (L) (19)
(29) (R) (M) (20)
(28) (Q) (N) (21)
(27) (P) (O) (22)
(26) (23)
(25) (24)
Facial

Tooth #	Surf	Description	Date	PRCDR Code	Fees
		4 BW X-rays & Exam	**08/28/90**		**25.00**
		3 Addtl X-Rays	**08/28/90**		**10.00**
		Prophy	**08/28/90**		**24.00**
2	**BOL**	**Composite**	**09/11/90**		**74.00**
4	**MOD**	**Composite**	**09/11/90**		**74.00**
5	**DO**	**Composite**	**09/11/90**		**64.00**
14	**BOL**	**Composite**	**09/06/90**		**74.00**
18	**BO**	**Composite**	**09/06/90**		**64.00**
31	**BO**	**Composite**	**09/11/90**		**64.00**

I hereby certify that the services listed above have been performed on the date(s) shown above, and that these are the charges that I actually charged.

Dentist's Signature *Mable Miller, DDS* Date

Total Fee	**473.00**
Patient Paid	**0.00**
Balance Due	**473.00**

For official use only

I hereby certify that the foregoing statements including any accompanying statements are to the best of my knowledge true and correct.
Check: ☒ I do ❑ I do not authorize the administrator to pay directly to the named dentist or any other supplier of services any benefits otherwise payable to me, but not to exceed any of the charges by the dentist or any other supplier of services.
I understand that I am financially responsible for any charges not covered by this authorization.

Employee's Signature *Maria Murdock* Date

Attending Dentist's Statement

Claim 29-4

1. Patient Name	2. Relationship	3. Sex	4. Birthdate	5. FTS
Malcolm Murdock	Son	☒M ☐F	06/20/75	

5. Employee/Subscriber	7. Social Security No.	9. Name of Group
Maria Murdock	111-22-3333	XYZ Corporation

8. Employee Address	10. Employer Name
9876 Maraban Lane	XYZ Corporation
City/State/Zip Montrose, CA 92318	

11. Group Number	12. Local	13. Are other family members employed? NO Address:
112233		

15. Is patient covered by another plan?	Name of plan	Union	Number
☐Y ☒N			

16. Dentist Name: Mable Miller, DDS

17. Mailing address: 1895 Myrtle Road

City/State/Zip: Montrose, CA 92309

18. Dentist TIN/SS#: 95-1234567

19. Lic. #: MM98234789

20. Dentist Phone No.: (818) 555-1234

21. Date of 1st Treatment:

22. Place of Treatment: Office

Is claim related to:	No	Yes	If yes, give date, etc.
24. Workers Comp	X		
25. Auto Accident?	X		
26. Other Accident?	X		
27. OIS?	X		
28. Initial Prosthetic?			
29. Date of Prior Placement:			
30. Orthodontics?	X		Placement Date:
23. X-rays enclosed?		X	# 7

I authorize the release of information: Signature on file

I authorize payment of benefits to provider

Identify missing teeth with X

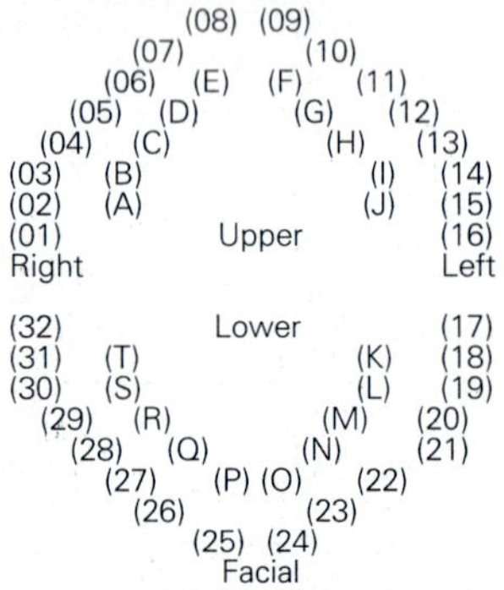

Tooth #	Surf	Description	Date	PRCDR Code	Fees
		Oral Exam	03/28/90		30.00
		Bitewings (2)	03/28/90		25.00
		Add X-rays (5)	03/28/90		25.00
		Prophy	03/28/90		40.00
1	OL	Alloy	05/04/90		50.00
2	OL	Alloy	05/04/90		50.00
12	O	Alloy	05/04/90		45.00
13	O	Alloy	05/04/90		45.00
30		Porcelain Metal Crown	06/19/90		450.00

I hereby certify that the services listed above have been performed on the date(s) shown above, and that these are the charges that I actually charged.

Dentist's Signature *Mable Miller, DDS* Date

Total Fee	760.00
Patient Paid	
Balance Due	

For official use only

I hereby certify that the foregoing statements including any accompanying statements are to the best of my knowledge true and correct.
Check: ☐ I do ☒ I do not authorize the administrator to pay directly to the named dentist or any other supplier of services any benefits otherwise payable to me, but not to exceed any of the charges by the dentist or any other supplier of services.
I understand that I am financially responsible for any charges not covered by this authorization.

Employee's Signature *Maria Murdock* Date

Attending Dentist's Statement

Claim 29-5

1. Patient Name	2. Relationship	3. Sex	4. Birthdate	5. FTS
Maggie Murdock	Child	❑ M ☒ F	09/21/81	

5. Employee/Subscriber	7. Social Security No.	9. Name of Group
Maria Murdock	111-22-3333	XYZ Corporation

8. Employee Address	10. Employer Name
9876 Maraban Lane	XYZ Corporation
City/State/Zip: Montrose, CA 92318	

11. Group Number	12. Local	13. Are other family members employed? NO Address:
112233		

15. Is patient covered by another plan?	Name of plan	Union	Number
❑ Y ☒ N			

16. Dentist Name: Mable Miller, DDS

17. Mailing address: 1895 Myrtle Road

City/State/Zip: Montrose, CA 92309

18. Dentist TIN/SS#: 95-1234567

19. Lic. #: MM98234789

20. Dentist Phone No.: (818) 555-1234

21. Date of 1st Treatment: 05/15/91

22. Place of Treatment: Office

Is claim related to:	No	Yes	If yes, give date, etc.
24. Workers Comp	X		
25. Auto Accident?	X		
26. Other Accident?	X		
27. OIS?	X		
28. Initial Prosthetic?			
29. Date of Prior Placement:			
30. Orthodontics?	X		Placement Date:
23. X-rays enclosed?		X	#

I authorize the release of information: Signature on file

I authorize payment of benefits to provider: Signature on file

Identify missing teeth with X

(08) (09) (07) (10) (06) (E) (F) (11) (05) (D) (G) (12) (04) (C) (H) (13) (03) (B) (I) (14) (02) (A) (J) (15) (01) Upper (16)
Right Left
(32) Lower (17) (31) (T) (K) (18) (30) (S) (L) (19) (29) (R) (M) (20) (28) (Q) (N) (21) (27) (P) (O) (22) (26) (23) (25) (24)
Facial

Tooth #	Surf	Description	Date	PRCDR Code	Fees
		2 Bitewing Films	05/15/91		25.00
		1 Single Film	05/15/91		10.00
		9 Additional Films	05/15/91		45.00
		Oral Exam	05/15/91		45.00
2	O	Amalgam Rest	07/07/91		50.00
3		PFM Crown	07/16/91		450.00
5	DO	Amalgam Rest	07/07/91		60.00
18	O	Amalgam Rest	07/09/91		50.00
19		Root Canal Therapy	07/09/91		425.00
19		Post Buildup	07/14/91		175.00
19		PFM Crown	07/16/91		450.00

I hereby certify that the services listed above have been performed on the date(s) shown above, and that these are the charges that I actually charged.

Dentist's Signature *Mable Miller, DDS* Date

Total Fee	1785.00
Patient Paid	
Balance Due	

For official use only

I hereby certify that the foregoing statements including any accompanying statements are to the best of my knowledge true and correct.
Check: ☒ I do ❑ I do not authorize the administrator to pay directly to the named dentist or any other supplier of services any benefits otherwise payable to me, but not to exceed any of the charges by the dentist or any other supplier of services.
I understand that I am financially responsible for any charges not covered by this authorization.

Employee's Signature *Maria Murdock* Date

Attending Dentist's Statement

Claim 29-6

1. Patient Name	2. Relationship	3. Sex	4. Birthdate	5. FTS
Orville Owen	Self	☒M ❑F	06/03/50	
5. Employee/Subscriber: Orville Owen	7. Social Security No.: 000-55-0000	9. Name of Group: ABC Enterprises		
8. Employee Address: 1000 Oswald Street		10. Employer Name: ABC Enterprises		
City/State/Zip: Ojai, CA 93051				
11. Group Number: 1000001	12. Local: 1001	13. Are other family members employed? NO Address:		
15. Is patient covered by another plan? ❑Y ☒N	Name of plan	Union	Number	

16. Dentist Name: Oliver O'Shea, DDS	Is claim related to:	No	Yes	If yes, give date, etc.
17. Mailing address: 2711 Ornate Blvd.	24. Workers Comp	X		
City/State/Zip: Ojai, CA 93055	25. Auto Accident?	X		
18. Dentist TIN/SS#: 95-0000000	26. Other Accident?	X		
19. Lic. #: 10001	27. OIS?	X		
20. Dentist Phone No.: 000-555-0000	28. Initial Prosthetic?			
21. Date of 1st Treatment	29. Date of Prior Placement:			
22. Place of Treatment: Office	30. Orthodontics?			Placement Date:
	23. X-rays enclosed?			#

I authorize the release of information
Signature on file

I authorize payment of benefits to provider

Identify missing teeth with X

(08) (09) (07) (10) (06) (E) (F) (11) (05) (D) (G) (12) (04) (C) (H) (13) (03) (B) (I) (14) (02) (A) (J) (15) (01) Upper (16)
Right Left
(32) Lower (17) (31) (T) (K) (18) (30) (S) (L) (19) (29) (R) (M) (20) (28) (Q) (N) (21) (27) (P) (O) (22) (26) (23) (25) (24)
Facial

Tooth #	Surf	Description	Date	PRCDR Code	Fees
		Prophylaxis	07/16/90		50.00

I hereby certify that the services listed above have been performed on the date(s) shown above, and that these are the charges that I actually charged.

Total Fee	50.00
Patient Paid	
Balance Due	

Dentist's Signature *Oliver O'Shea DDS* Date

For official use only

I hereby certify that the foregoing statements including any accompanying statements are to the best of my knowledge true and correct.
Check: ❑ I do ☒ I do not authorize the administrator to pay directly to the named dentist or any other supplier of services any benefits otherwise payable to me, but not to exceed any of the charges by the dentist or any other supplier of services.
I understand that I am financially responsible for any charges not covered by this authorization.

Employee's Signature *Orville Owen* Date

Attending Dentist's Statement

Claim 29-7

1. Patient Name	2. Relationship	3. Sex	4. Birthdate	5. FTS
Octavia Owen	Spouse	❑ M ☒ F	12/16/48	

5. Employee/Subscriber	7. Social Security No.	9. Name of Group
Orville Owen	000-55-0000	ABC Enterprises

8. Employee Address	10. Employer Name
1000 Oswald Street	ABC Enterprises
City/State/Zip: Ojai, CA 93051	

11. Group Number	12. Local	13. Are other family members employed? NO
1000001	1001	Address:

15. Is patient covered by another plan?	Name of plan	Union	Number
❑ Y ☒ N			

16. Dentist Name: Oliver O'Shea, DDS

17. Mailing address: 2711 Ornate Blvd.

City/State/Zip: Ojai, CA 93055

18. Dentist TIN/SS#: 95-0000000

19. Lic. #: 10001

20. Dentist Phone No.: 000-555-0000

21. Date of 1st Treatment: 05/12/90

22. Place of Treatment: Office

Is claim related to:	No	Yes	If yes, give date, etc.
24. Workers Comp	X		
25. Auto Accident?	X		
26. Other Accident?	X		
27. OIS?	X		
28. Initial Prosthetic?			
29. Date of Prior Placement:			
30. Orthodontics?	X		Placement Date:
23. X-rays enclosed?		X	# 1

I authorize the release of information: Signature on file

I authorize payment of benefits to provider: Signature on file

Identify missing teeth with X

(08) (09)
(07) (10)
(06) (E) (F) (11)
(05) (D) (G) (12)
(04) (C) (H) (13)
(03) (B) (I) (14)
(02) (A) (J) (15)
(01) Upper (16)
Right Left

Lower
(32) (17)
(31) (T) (K) (18)
(30) (S) (L) (19)
(29) (R) (M) (20)
(28) (Q) (N) (21)
(27) (P) (O) (22)
(26) (23)
(25) (24)
Facial

Tooth #	Surf	Description	Date	PRCDR Code	Fees
		1 Single Film (Root Cnl Fn)	06/13/90		13.00
20		Root Canal Treatment	06/13/90		290.00

I hereby certify that the services listed above have been performed on the date(s) shown above, and that these are the charges that I actually charged.

Dentist's Signature: Oliver O'Shea DDS Date

Total Fee	303.00
Patient Paid	
Balance Due	

For official use only

I hereby certify that the foregoing statements including any accompanying statements are to the best of my knowledge true and correct.
Check: ☑ I do ❑ I do not authorize the administrator to pay directly to the named dentist or any other supplier of services any benefits otherwise payable to me, but not to exceed any of the charges by the dentist or any other supplier of services.
I understand that I am financially responsible for any charges not covered by this authorization.

Employee's Signature: Orville Owen Date

Attending Dentist's Statement

Claim 29-8

1. Patient Name	2. Relationship	3. Sex	4. Birthdate	5. FTS
Odell Owen	Child	☒M ❑F	12/16/81	Ojai Elem.

5. Employee/Subscriber	7. Social Security No.	9. Name of Group
Orville Owen	000-55-0000	ABC Enterprises

8. Employee Address	10. Employer Name
1000 Oswald Street	ABC Enterprises
City/State/Zip Ojai, CA 93051	

11. Group Number	12. Local	13. Are other family members employed? NO Address:
1000001	1001	

15. Is patient covered by another plan?	Name of plan	Union	Number
❑Y ☒N			

Dentist information		Is claim related to:	No	Yes	If yes, give date, etc.
16. Dentist Name Oliver O'Shea, DDS		24. Workers Comp	X		
17. Mailing address 2711 Ornate Blvd.		25. Auto Accident?	X		
City/State/Zip Ojai, CA 93055		26. Other Accident?	X		
		27. OIS?	X		
18. Dentist TIN/SS#	95-0000000	28. Initial Prosthetic?			
19. Lic. # 10001	20. Dentist Phone No. 000-555-0000	29. Date of Prior Placement:			
		30. Orthodontics?			Placement Date:
21. Date of 1st Treatment 05/12/90	22. Place of Treatment Office	23. X-rays enclosed?		X	# 5

I authorize the release of information	I authorize payment of benefits to provider
Signature on file	

Identify missing teeth with X

(08) (09)
(07) (10)
(06) (E) (F) (11)
(05) (D) (G) (12)
(04) (C) (H) (13)
(03) (B) (I) (14)
(02) (A) (J) (15)
(01) Upper (16)
Right Left

(32) Lower (17)
(31) (T) (K) (18)
(30) (S) (L) (19)
(29) (R) (M) (20)
(28) (Q) (N) (21)
(27) (P) (O) (22)
(26) (23)
(25) (24)
Facial

Tooth #	Surf	Description	Date	PRCDR Code	Fees
		1 Single Film	05/12/90		13.00
		4 Additional X-rays	05/12/90		28.00
		1 Gingival Curettage U/R	05/12/90		90.00
		Prophylaxis	06/09/90		50.00
		Complete Oral Exam	05/12/90		30.00

Total Fee	211.00
Patient Paid	
Balance Due	

For official use only

I hereby certify that the services listed above have been performed on the date(s) shown above, and that these are the charges that I actually charged.

Dentist's Signature Date

I hereby certify that the foregoing statements including any accompanying statements are to the best of my knowledge true and correct.
Check: ❑ I do ☑ I do not authorize the administrator to pay directly to the named dentist or any other supplier of services any benefits otherwise payable to me, but not to exceed any of the charges by the dentist or any other supplier of services. I understand that I am financially responsible for any charges not covered by this authorization.

Employee's Signature Date

Attending Dentist's Statement

Claim 29-9

1. Patient Name	2. Relationship	3. Sex	4. Birthdate	5. FTS
Octavia Owen	Spouse	❑ M ☒ F	12/16/48	

5. Employee/Subscriber	7. Social Security No.	9. Name of Group
Orville Owen	000-55-0000	ABC Enterprises

8. Employee Address	10. Employer Name
1000 Oswald Street	ABC Enterprises
City/State/Zip: Ojai, CA 93051	

11. Group Number	12. Local	13. Are other family members employed?
1000001	1001	NO Address:

15. Is patient covered by another plan?	Name of plan	Union	Number
❑ Y ☒ N			

16. Dentist Name: Oliver O'Shea, DDS

17. Mailing address: 2711 Ornate Blvd.

City/State/Zip: Ojai, CA 93055

18. Dentist TIN/SS#: 95-0000000

19. Lic. #: 10001

20. Dentist Phone No.: 000-555-0000

21. Date of 1st Treatment: 03/17/90

22. Place of Treatment: Office

Is claim related to:	No	Yes	If yes, give date, etc.
24. Workers Comp	X		
25. Auto Accident?	X		
26. Other Accident?	X		
27. OIS?	X		
28. Initial Prosthetic?			
29. Date of Prior Placement:			
30. Orthodontics?	X		Placement Date:
23. X-rays enclosed?		X	# 12

I authorize the release of information: Signature on file

I authorize payment of benefits to provider: Signature on file

Identify missing teeth with X

Upper: (01) (02) (03) (04) (05) (06) (07) (08) (09) (10) (11) (12) (13) (14) (15) (16); (A) (B) (C) (D) (E) (F) (G) (H) (I) (J)

Right / Left

Lower: (17) (18) (19) (20) (21) (22) (23) (24) (25) (26) (27) (28) (29) (30) (31) (32); (K) (L) (M) (N) (O) (P) (Q) (R) (S) (T)

Facial

Tooth #	Surf	Description	Date	PRCDR Code	Fees
		Examination	03/17/90		30.00
		Full Mouth X-rays	03/17/90		90.00
		Perio Treatment UL QD	03/17/90		50.00
		Prophylaxis	03/24/90		55.00
8		Ceramco Cr.	04/30/90		400.00
9		Pontic	04/30/90		350.00
10		Ceramco Cr.	04/30/90		400.00
11		Ceramco Cr.	04/30/90		400.00
19	DO	Amal	03/24/90		55.00

I hereby certify that the services listed above have been performed on the date(s) shown above, and that these are the charges that I actually charged.

Dentist's Signature Oliver O'Shea DDS Date

Total Fee	1830.00
Patient Paid	
Balance Due	

For official use only

I hereby certify that the foregoing statements including any accompanying statements are to the best of my knowledge true and correct.

Check: ☒ I do ❑ I do not authorize the administrator to pay directly to the named dentist or any other supplier of services any benefits otherwise payable to me, but not to exceed any of the charges by the dentist or any other supplier of services. I understand that I am financially responsible for any charges not covered by this authorization.

Employee's Signature Orville Owen Date

Attending Dentist's Statement

Claim 29-10

1. Patient Name	2. Relationship	3. Sex	4. Birthdate	5. FTS
Orville Owen	Self	☒M ☐F	06/03/50	

5. Employee/Subscriber	7. Social Security No.	9. Name of Group
Orville Owen	000-55-0000	ABC Enterprises

8. Employee Address	10. Employer Name
1000 Oswald Street	ABC Enterprises
City/State/Zip: Ojai, CA 93051	

11. Group Number	12. Local	13. Are other family members employed? NO
1000001	1001	Address:

15. Is patient covered by another plan?	Name of plan	Union	Number
☐Y ☒N			

16. Dentist Name: Oscar Ortiz, DDS

17. Mailing address: 4444 Olsen Blvd.

City/State/Zip: Orange, CA 92711

18. Dentist TIN/SS#: 95-3333333

19. Lic. #: 13331

20. Dentist Phone No.: 000-555-3333

21. Date of 1st Treatment:

22. Place of Treatment: Office

Is claim related to:	No	Yes	If yes, give date, etc.
24. Workers Comp	X		
25. Auto Accident?	X		
26. Other Accident?	X		
27. OIS?	X		
28. Initial Prosthetic?			
29. Date of Prior Placement:			
30. Orthodontics?			Placement Date:
23. X-rays enclosed?			#

I authorize the release of information: Signature on file

I authorize payment of benefits to provider

Identify missing teeth with X

(08) (09) (07) (10) (06) (E) (F) (11) (05) (D) (G) (12) (04) (C) (H) (13) (03) (B) (I) (14) (02) (A) (J) (15) (01) Upper (16)
Right Left
(32) Lower (17) (31) (T) (K) (18) (30) (S) (L) (19) (29) (R) (M) (20) (28) (Q) (N) (21) (27) (P) (O) (22) (26) (23) (25) (24)
Facial

Tooth #	Surf	Description	Date	PRCDR Code	Fees
		Full Mouth X-rays	04/03/91		45.00
17		Ext. – Part Bone	07/06/91		175.00
18	O	Alloy	07/06/91		40.00
		Perio Root Planing	07/20/91		38.00
		Perio Root Planing	07/20/91		38.00
		Perio Root Planing	07/25/91		38.00
		Perio Root Planing	07/25/91		38.00
		Prophy	08/03/91		45.00

I hereby certify that the services listed above have been performed on the date(s) shown above, and that these are the charges that I actually charged.

Total Fee	457.00
Patient Paid	
Balance Due	

Dentist's Signature Oscar Ortiz, D.D.S. Date

For official use only

I hereby certify that the foregoing statements including any accompanying statements are to the best of my knowledge true and correct.
Check: ☐ I do ☒ I do not authorize the administrator to pay directly to the named dentist or any other supplier of services any benefits otherwise payable to me, but not to exceed any of the charges by the dentist or any other supplier of services.
I understand that I am financially responsible for any charges not covered by this authorization.

Employee's Signature Orville Owen Date

Attending Dentist's Statement

Claim 29-11

1. Patient Name	2. Relationship	3. Sex	4. Birthdate	5. FTS
Sallie Stern	Daughter	❑ M ☒ F	10/28/86	

5. Employee/Subscriber	7. Social Security No.	9. Name of Group
Samuel Stern	999-77-5555	XYZ Corporation

8. Employee Address	10. Employer Name
1708 Simpson Street	XYZ Corporation
City/State/Zip: Sacramento, CA 95266	

11. Group Number	12. Local	13. Are other family members employed?
66677	666	NO Address:

15. Is patient covered by another plan?	Name of plan	Union	Number
❑ Y ☒ N			

16. Dentist Name: Steven Sorby, DDS

17. Mailing address: 676 S. Shapiro Street

City/State/Zip: Sacramento, CA 95258

18. Dentist TIN/SS#: 95-6667777

19. Lic. #	20. Dentist Phone No.
66776	666-7777

21. Date of 1st Treatment	22. Place of Treatment
	Office

Is claim related to:	No	Yes	If yes, give date, etc.
24. Workers Comp	X		
25. Auto Accident?	X		
26. Other Accident?	X		
27. OIS?	X		
28. Initial Prosthetic?			
29. Date of Prior Placement:			
30. Orthodontics?	X		Placement Date:
23. X-rays enclosed?		X	#

I authorize the release of information	I authorize payment of benefits to provider
Signature on file	Signature on file

Identify missing teeth with X

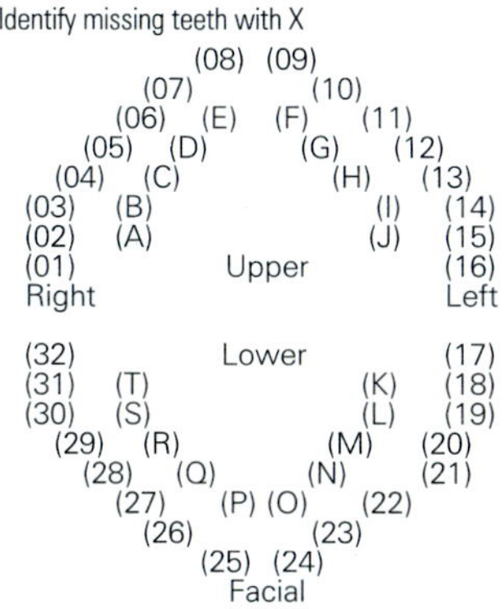

Tooth #	Surf	Description	Date	PRCDR Code	Fees
		Exam	08-08-91		30.00
		BWS	08-08-91		30.00
		ADD PA 2	08-08-91		24.00
		Prophy Fluoride	08-08-91		60.00
A	MOL	AMG	08-10-91		55.00
B	MOD	AMG	08-10-91		55.00
D		EXT	08-10-91		50.00

I hereby certify that the services listed above have been performed on the date(s) shown above, and that these are the charges that I actually charged.

Dentist's Signature *Steven Sorby DDS* Date

Total Fee	304.00
Patient Paid	0.00
Balance Due	304.00

For official use only

I hereby certify that the foregoing statements including any accompanying statements are to the best of my knowledge true and correct.
Check: ☒ I do ❑ I do not authorize the administrator to pay directly to the named dentist or any other supplier of services any benefits otherwise payable to me, but not to exceed any of the charges by the dentist or any other supplier of services.
I understand that I am financially responsible for any charges not covered by this authorization.

Employee's Signature *Samuel Stern* Date

Attending Dentist's Statement

Claim 29-12

1. Patient Name	2. Relationship	3. Sex	4. Birthdate	5. FTS
Susan Stern	Wife	❑ M ☒ F	07/14/50	

5. Employee/Subscriber	7. Social Security No.	9. Name of Group
Samuel Stern	999-77-5555	XYZ Corporation

8. Employee Address	10. Employer Name
1708 Simpson Street	XYZ Corporation
City/State/Zip Sacramento, CA 95266	

11. Group Number	12. Local	13. Are other family members employed? NO Address:
66677	666	

15. Is patient covered by another plan?	Name of plan	Union	Number
❑ Y ☒ N			

16. Dentist Name: Steven Sorby, DDS
17. Mailing address: 676 S. Shapiro Street
City/State/Zip: Sacramento, CA 95258
18. Dentist TIN/SS#: 95-6667777
19. Lic. #: 66776
20. Dentist Phone No.: 666-7777
21. Date of 1st Treatment:
22. Place of Treatment: Office

Is claim related to:	No	Yes	If yes, give date, etc.
24. Workers Comp	X		
25. Auto Accident?	X		
26. Other Accident?	X		
27. OIS?	X		
28. Initial Prosthetic?			
29. Date of Prior Placement:			
30. Orthodontics?	X		Placement Date:
23. X-rays enclosed?	X		#

I authorize the release of information: Signature on file

I authorize payment of benefits to provider

Identify missing teeth with X

(08) (09) (07) (10) (06) (E) (F) (11) (05) (D) (G) (12) (04) (C) (H) (13) (03) (B) (I) (14) (02) (A) (J) (15) (01) Upper (16)
Right Left
(32) Lower (17) (31) (T) (K) (18) (30) (S) (L) (19) (29) (R) (M) (20) (28) (Q) (N) (21) (27) (P) (O) (22) (26) (23) (25) (24)
Facial

Tooth #	Surf	Description	Date	PRCDR Code	Fees
		General Anesthesia Lic#35	06-12-91		155.00
		Biopsy	06-12-91		200.00
		*White Area in Left Cheek			

I hereby certify that the services listed above have been performed on the date(s) shown above, and that these are the charges that I actually charged.

Total Fee	355.00
Patient Paid	0.00
Balance Due	355.00

For official use only

Dentist's Signature Steven Sorby DDS Date

I hereby certify that the foregoing statements including any accompanying statements are to the best of my knowledge true and correct.
Check: ❑ I do ☒ I do not authorize the administrator to pay directly to the named dentist or any other supplier of services any benefits otherwise payable to me, but not to exceed any of the charges by the dentist or any other supplier of services. I understand that I am financially responsible for any charges not covered by this authorization.

Employee's Signature Samuel Stern Date

Attending Dentist's Statement

Claim 29-13

1. Patient Name	2. Relationship	3. Sex	4. Birthdate	5. FTS
Samuel Stern	Self	☒M ❑F	06/18/46	

5. Employee/Subscriber	7. Social Security No.	9. Name of Group
Samuel Stern	999-77-5555	XYZ Corporation

8. Employee Address	10. Employer Name
1708 Simpson Street	XYZ Corporation
City/State/Zip Sacramento, CA 95266	

11. Group Number	12. Local	13. Are other family members employed? NO Address:
66677	666	

15. Is patient covered by another plan?	Name of plan	Union	Number
❑Y ☒N			

16. Dentist Name Steven Sorby, DDS	Is claim related to:	No	Yes	If yes, give date, etc.
17. Mailing address 676 S. Shapiro Street	24. Workers Comp	X		
City/State/Zip Sacramento, CA 95258	25. Auto Accident?	X		
18. Dentist TIN/SS# 95-6667777	26. Other Accident?	X		
19. Lic. # 66776	27. OIS?	X		
20. Dentist Phone No. 666-7777	28. Initial Prosthetic?			
21. Date of 1st Treatment 7-13-91	29. Date of Prior Placement:			
22. Place of Treatment Office	30. Orthodontics?	X		Placement Date:
	23. X-rays enclosed?	X		#

I authorize the release of information
Signature on file

I authorize payment of benefits to provider
Signature on file

Identify missing teeth with X

(08) (09)
(07) (10)
(06) (E) (F) (11)
(05) (D) (G) (12)
(04) (C) (H) (13)
(03) (B) (I) (14)
(02) (A) (J) (15)
(01) Upper (16)
Right Left

(32) Lower (17)
(31) (T) (K) (18)
(30) (S) (L) (19)
(29) (R) (M) (20)
(28) (Q) (N) (21)
(27) (P) (O) (22)
(26) (23)
(25) (24)
Facial

Tooth #	Surf	Description	Date	PRCDR Code	Fees
	UR	Root Plan/Quadrant	07-13-91		95.00

I hereby certify that the services listed above have been performed on the date(s) shown above, and that these are the charges that I actually charged.

Dentist's Signature Steven Sorby DDS Date

Total Fee	95.00
Patient Paid	0.00
Balance Due	95.00

For official use only

I hereby certify that the foregoing statements including any accompanying statements are to the best of my knowledge true and correct.
Check: ☑ I do ❑ I do not authorize the administrator to pay directly to the named dentist or any other supplier of services any benefits otherwise payable to me, but not to exceed any of the charges by the dentist or any other supplier of services.
I understand that I am financially responsible for any charges not covered by this authorization.

Employee's Signature Samuel Stern Date

Attending Dentist's Statement

Claim 29-14

1. Patient Name	2. Relationship	3. Sex	4. Birthdate	5. FTS
Sandra Stern	Child	❑ M ☒ F	06/03/75	
5. Employee/Subscriber: Samuel Stern	7. Social Security No.: 999-77-5555	9. Name of Group: XYZ Corporation		
8. Employee Address: 1708 Simpson Street		10. Employer Name: XYZ Corporation		
City/State/Zip: Sacramento, CA 95266				
11. Group Number: 66677	12. Local: 666	13. Are other family members employed? NO Address:		
15. Is patient covered by another plan? ❑ Y ☒ N		Name of plan	Union	Number

16. Dentist Name	Is claim related to:	No	Yes	If yes, give date, etc.
Steven Sorby, DDS	24. Workers Comp	X		
17. Mailing address: 676 S. Shapiro Street	25. Auto Accident?	X		
City/State/Zip: Sacramento, CA 95258	26. Other Accident?	X		
	27. OIS?	X		
18. Dentist TIN/SS#: 95-6667777	28. Initial Prosthetic?	X		#3 Stnls Stl CR Ill Fit
19. Lic. #: 66776 — 20. Dentist Phone No.: 666-7777	29. Date of Prior Placement:			5 Years Old
21. Date of 1st Treatment — 22. Place of Treatment: Office	30. Orthodontics?			Placement Date:
	23. X-rays enclosed?	X		#

I authorize the release of information: Signature on file

I authorize payment of benefits to provider

Identify missing teeth with X

(08) (09) (07) (10) (06) (E) (F) (11) (05) (D) (G) (12) (04) (C) (H) (13) (03) (B) (I) (14) (02) (A) (J) (15) (01) Upper (16) Right Left

(32) Lower (17) (31) (T) (K) (18) (30) (S) (L) (19) (29) (R) (M) (20) (28) (Q) (N) (21) (27) (P) (O) (22) (26) (23) (25) (24) Facial

Tooth #	Surf	Description	Date	PRCDR Code	Fees
		2 Bitewing Films	05-15-91		25.00
		1 Single Film	05-15-91		10.00
		9 Additional Films	05-15-91		45.00
		Oral Exam	05-15-91		45.00
2	O	Amalgam Rest	07-07-91		50.00
3		PFM Crown	07-16-91		450.00
5	DO	Amalgam Rest	07-07-91		60.00
18	O	Amalgam Rest	07-09-91		50.00
19		Root Canal Therapy	07-09-91		425.00
19		Post Buildup	07-14-91		175.00
19		PFM Crown	07-16-91		450.00
		Prophylaxis	07-16-91		50.00

Total Fee	1835.00
Patient Paid	0.00
Balance Due	1835.00

For official use only

I hereby certify that the services listed above have been performed on the date(s) shown above, and that these are the charges that I actually charged.

Dentist's Signature *Steven Sorby DDS* Date

I hereby certify that the foregoing statements including any accompanying statements are to the best of my knowledge true and correct.
Check: ❑ I do ☒ I do not authorize the administrator to pay directly to the named dentist or any other supplier of services any benefits otherwise payable to me, but not to exceed any of the charges by the dentist or any other supplier of services.
I understand that I am financially responsible for any charges not covered by this authorization.

Employee's Signature *Samuel Stern* Date

Attending Dentist's Statement

Claim 29-15

1. Patient Name	2. Relationship	3. Sex	4. Birthdate	5. FTS
Samuel Stern	Self	☒M ❑F	06/18/46	

5. Employee/Subscriber	7. Social Security No.	9. Name of Group
Samuel Stern	999-77-5555	XYZ Corporation

8. Employee Address	10. Employer Name
1708 Simpson Street	XYZ Corporation
City/State/Zip Sacramento, CA 95266	

11. Group Number	12. Local	13. Are other family members employed? NO Address:
66677	666	

15. Is patient covered by another plan?	Name of plan	Union	Number
❑Y ☒N			

16. Dentist Name: Steven Sorby, DDS

17. Mailing address: 676 S. Shapiro Street

City/State/Zip: Sacramento, CA 95258

18. Dentist TIN/SS#: 95-6667777

19. Lic. #	20. Dentist Phone No.
66776	666-7777

21. Date of 1st Treatment	22. Place of Treatment
06-19-90	Office

Is claim related to:	No	Yes	If yes, give date, etc.
24. Workers Comp	X		
25. Auto Accident?	X		
26. Other Accident?	X		
27. OIS?	X		
28. Initial Prosthetic?			
29. Date of Prior Placement:			
30. Orthodontics?	X		Placement Date:
23. X-rays enclosed?	X		#

I authorize the release of information: Signature on file

I authorize payment of benefits to provider: Signature on file

Identify missing teeth with X

(08) (09)
(07) (10)
(06) (E) (F) (11)
(05) (D) (G) (12)
(04) (C) (H) (13)
(03) (B) (I) (14)
(02) (A) (J) (15)
(01) Upper (16)
Right Left

(32) Lower (17)
(31) (T) (K) (18)
(30) (S) (L) (19)
(29) (R) (M) (20)
(28) (Q) (N) (21)
(27) (P) (O) (22)
(26) (23)
(25) (24)
Facial

Tooth #	Surf	Description	Date	PRCDR Code	Fees
		Initial Oral Exam	6-19-90		30.00
		X-Ray Complete Series	6-19-90		80.00
		Adult FL/Prophy	6-19-90		55.00

Total Fee	165.00
Patient Paid	0.00
Balance Due	165.00

For official use only

I hereby certify that the services listed above have been performed on the date(s) shown above, and that these are the charges that I actually charged.

Dentist's Signature *Steven Sorby DDS* Date

I hereby certify that the foregoing statements including any accompanying statements are to the best of my knowledge true and correct.
Check: ☒ I do ❑ I do not authorize the administrator to pay directly to the named dentist or any other supplier of services any benefits otherwise payable to me, but not to exceed any of the charges by the dentist or any other supplier of services. I understand that I am financially responsible for any charges not covered by this authorization.

Employee's Signature *Samuel Stern* Date

Index

A

AAR; *see* Automatic annual reinstatement
ABC; *see* Alternative birthing center
Abortion, 153
ABP; *see* Alternative benefit plan
Abutment, dental, 325
Accident benefits, 41, 377-378
Accidental death and dismemberment insurance, 3
Accountable Health Partnerships (AHP), 67
Accounting department of insurance companies, 5
Accumulation period, 38
Acid etching, 313
Acquired defects, dental services and coding and, 324
Acrylics, restorative dental services and coding and, 312
Actively-at-work requirement, 38
Acts of third parties (ATP), 48-49, 51, 52, 53, 54
Actuarial department of insurance companies, 5
Acupuncture, 171, 352
ADA; *see* American Dental Association
Additional information letter, 91, 92, 388
Adjustments, 251-254
Administrative Services Only (ASO), 4
Admissions, inpatient, precertification of, 64
Adult normal values, x-ray and laboratory services and, 129-137
Aggravated physical weakness, accident benefits and, 41
Aggregate deductible, 39
Aggressor acts while intoxicated, accident benefits and, 41
Aggressor claims, accident benefits and, 41
AHP; *see* Accountable Health Partnerships
Air ambulance, 226-227
Akin bunionectomy, 217-218
Allergy profiles, x-ray and laboratory services and, 139-140
Allergy testing, x-ray and laboratory services and, 140
Allowable expense, 186
Allowance, basic, 104
Alopecia areata, 158
Alternative benefit plan (ABP), 371
Alternative birthing center (ABC), 180
Alveolar process, oral cavity and, 292
Alveoloplasty, oral surgery and, 327
Amalgam, restorative dental services and coding and, 312
Amastia, 159
Amazia, 159
Ambulance expenses, 225-228
Ambulatory surgical centers, 180
Amendments to Employee Retirement Income Security Act, 25
American Dental Association (ADA) claim form, 355-364
American Dental Association (ADA) Dental Code List, 333-347, 385
Amniocentesis, 153
Ancillary expenses, inpatient hospital claims and, 177-178
Androgenic alopecia, 158
Anemia profiles, x-ray and laboratory services and, 140-141
Anesthesia, 43, 169-174, 329-330, 379-380
Anesthesiologist, 171
Ankyloglossia, 293
Annual maximums, dental, 374
Apexification, 318
Apical curettage, 318
Apicoectomy, 318
Approved charges, Medicare and, 199
Arthritic profiles, x-ray and laboratory services and, 141
Arthrodesis, 219, 220
Arthroplasty, 219, 220
Artificial insemination, 153
ASO; *see* Administrative Services Only
Assistant surgeon, 162-163, 167, 222
Assistant surgery, benefits and, 43
Asterisk procedures, surgery and, 150
Athletic mouth guard fabrication, dental, 319
ATP; *see* Acts of third parties
Attempted suicide, benefits and, 42
Attending dentist's statement, dental claims and, 397-411
Augmentation mammoplasty, 156, 159
Auricular prosthesis, dental services and coding and, 323
Austin bunionectomy, 217
Automated laboratory charge, x-ray and laboratory services and, 126-127
Automatic annual reinstatement (AAR), 38

B

Balance billing, Medicare and, 200-201
Banding fee, dental services and coding and, 329
Base call charge, ambulance expenses and, 226
Basic allowance, 76, 104
Basic benefits, 40, 41-43
Basic dental plans, 366
Basic major medical benefits, 43-44
Bat wing deformity, 158-159
Batch files, claim administration and, 86-87
Behavior modification, TMJ dysfunction and, 352
Benefit credit, 187
Benefit payment, claim administration and, 100-101
Benefits, 37-46
    accident, 41, 377-378
    assignment of, Medicare and, 199-201
    coordination of, 185-194, 384
    definitions of, 38-40, 186-187
    dental, 365-382
    extension of, 24, 39, 368
    maintenance of, Medicare and, 203-204
    Part A of Medicare and, 197-198
    Part B of Medicare and, 199
Bicuspids, 293
Bilateral surgical procedures, 150-152
Biofeedback, 120, 352
Black's Classification System of dental cavities, 299
Blepharochalasis, 155
Blepharoplasty, 154, 155-156
Blepharoptosis, 155
Block procedures, surgery and, 152
Blood, fees for, Medicare supplement and, 205
Blue Book, claim administration and, 106-107
Bone spurs, 220-221
Bone tissue, excision of, oral surgery and, 327-328
BR procedures; *see* By Report procedures
Breast asymmetry, 156, 157
Breast augmentation, 156, 159
Breast prosthesis, 156
Breast reconstruction, 156
Breast reduction, 156, 158, 159
Bridge, dental, 325, 326

Bruxism, 298
Bunions, 217-219
By Report (BR) procedures, 74, 150, 323, 380

C

Calluses, plantar, 220
Canines, 293
Cantilevered bridge, dental, 325
CAPD; *see* Continuous ambulatory peritoneal dialysis
Capitation, Medicare and, 200
Capsulotomy, 219
Cardiovascular care, 121
Caries, dental, 298-299
Carryover deductible, 102
Cavities, 298-299
CCU; *see* Coronary Care Unit
Cephalometric film, dental, 310
CFC; *see* Conversion factor code
Chalazion, 156
CHAMPUS; *see* Civilian Health and Medical Programs of the Uniformed Services
Cheilitis, 292
Cheiloplasty, 156-157
Cheiloschisis, 292
Chemfile combinations, x-ray and laboratory services and, 138
Chemical abrasion, 156
Chemical peel, 156
Chiropractor, 121-122
Chromosomal analysis, 153
Circumvallate papillae, 291
Civilian Health and Medical Programs of the Uniformed Services (CHAMPUS), 190
Claim determination period, 186
Claim files, 86-89, 114
Claim form, dental, 3, 355-364, 383-394, 395-412
Claim inflation indicators of fraud, 112
Claim investigation, 89, 95-96
Claim payment worksheet, dental, 385-388
Claim processing, 95-96, 112
Claim referrals, 89, 90
Claims, prescription, 105-106
Claims administration, 85-108, 386-387
Claims department of insurance companies, 5
Claims examiner's responsibilities, 93-95
Cleft lip and palate, 157-158, 292
Clinical psychologist, 120
C/O; *see* Three-month carryover provision
COBRA; *see* Consolidated Omnibus Budget Reconciliation Act of 1985
Coinsurance, 38, 374
Collagen injections, 158
Common accident provision, 38
Compensation, workers', 3
Competition, managed, cost containment and, 67
Component charges, x-ray and laboratory services and, 127
Composite, restorative dental services and coding and, 312
Composite facial prosthesis, dental services and coding and, 324
Comprehensive major medical benefits, 44
Concurrent review, 64-65
Congenital anomaly, 158
Congenital defects, dental services and coding and, 324
Consideration, contracts and, 11
Consolidated Omnibus Budget Reconciliation Act of 1985 (COBRA), 25-29
Consultation, professional, 119, 330
Contact lenses, prescription of, 121
Continuation of coverage, 24-29
Continuous ambulatory peritoneal dialysis (CAPD), 120-121
Contracts, 9-18
    dental, 367-368
Contributory plan, 22-23
Convalescent hospitals, 180-181
Conventional insurance, 3-4
Conversion factor code (CFC), 74, 75-76, 385, 394
Conversion policies, continuation of coverage and, 24-25
Coordination
    of benefits (COB), 185-194, 384
    with Medicare, 204-205
CoPay, 38-39
Coronary Care Unit (CCU), 177
Coronary profiles, x-ray and laboratory services and, 141-142
Cosmetic services, dental benefit structures and, 380
Cosmetic surgery, 148, 154-161
Cost-containment programs, 63-72, 373-376
Co-surgeons, 162
Coverage
    continuation of, 24-29
    dependent effective date of, eligibility and, 23
    dual, 185-194, 384
    employee effective date of, eligibility and, 22-23
    termination of, 23-24, 29
Covered expense, 39, 368
CPT code; *see* Current Procedural Terminology code
Cranial manipulation, TMJ dysfunction and, 352
Credit reserve, 187
Credit savings, 187
Crown, 296, 297, 314, 315-316, 325
Cumulative benefit, 42
Cupid's bow, cheiloplasty and, 156-157
Current Procedural Terminology (CPT) code, 74, 76, 99
Cuspids, 293
Custodial care, physician's services and, 118
Cysts, removal of, oral surgery and, 327

D

Day care centers, 179
DDS; *see* Doctorate in Dental Surgery
Deciduous teeth, 295
Deductible, 39, 102, 368
Deficit Reduction Act of 1984 (DEFRA), Medicare and, 196
Definitive Observation Unit (DOU), 177
DEFRA; *see* Deficit Reduction Act of 1984
Delivery
    of durable medical equipment, 231
    maternity procedures and, 152-153, 154
Demerol; *see* Meperidine
Dental accidents, 377-378
Dental benefit structures, 365-382
Dental caries, 298-299
Dental claim form, 355-364
Dental claims, 3, 355-364, 383-394, 395-412
Dental Code List, 333-347; *see also* Dental services and coding
Dental contracts, 367-368
Dental form letters, 388
Dental plans, 366-367
Dental plaque, 298
Dental prevailing conversion factors, 394
Dental professionals, 308
Dental prophylaxis, 311

Dental services and coding, 307-348
  ADA Dental Code List, 333-347, 385
  diagnostic, 308, 309-311
  endodontic, 308, 316-318
  oral surgery and, 308, 326-328
  orthodontic services and, 308, 328-329
  periodontic, 308, 318-320
  preventive, 308, 311-312
  prosthodontic, 308, 309, 320-326
  restorative, 308, 312-316
Dental surgery; *see* Oral surgery
Dental terminology, 255-288
Dentalgia, 298
Dentist, 308, 397-411
Dentures, 321, 322-323
Department of insurance, 4, 5-6
Dependent effective date of coverage, eligibility and, 21-22, 23
Dermabrasion, 158
Deviated nasal septum, 158
Diagnosis-related group (DRG) billing, Medicare and, 206
Diagnostic dental services and coding, 308, 309-311
Diagnostic procedures, 148, 149
Diagnostic x-ray and laboratory (DXL) services, 42, 126, 309-310, 352
Dialysis, 120-121
Diazepam (Valium), 171
Disability, per period of, 40
Disability insurance, 3
Distoclusion, 328
DMD; *see* Doctor of Medical Dentistry
DME; *see* Durable medical equipment
Docking device, 324
Doctor
  of Medical Dentistry (DMD), 308
  of Podiatric Medicine (DPM), 216
Doctorate in Dental Surgery (DDS), 308
DOU; *see* Definitive Observation Unit
Dowel pin, 326
DPM; *see* Doctor of Podiatric Medicine
DRG billing; *see* Diagnosis-related group billing
Drifting, space management therapy and, 312
Drug Blue Book, 106-107
Drug Red Book, 106-107
Drugs, prescription; *see* Prescription drugs
Dry needling; *see* Acupuncture
Dual coverage, 185-194, 384
Durable medical equipment (DME), 229-250
Dwyer osteotomy surgical procedure, 220
DXL; *see* Diagnostic x-ray and laboratory charges

E

Ears, protruding, 159-160
Ectropion, 155
Edentulous, 298
Effective date of coverage, eligibility and, 22-23
EGS; *see* Electrogalvanic nerve stimulation/stimulators
Elective abortion, 153
Electrogalvanic nerve stimulation/stimulators (EGS), TMJ dysfunction and, 352
Electrolysis epilation, 158
Electrolyte profile, x-ray and laboratory services and, 142
Eligibility, 19-36
  continuation of coverage and, 24-29
  for dental claims, 384
  for Medicare, 196-198
Emergency, medical, 179
Emergency department services, 118-119
Emergency medical technician (EMT), 227
Emergency response charge, ambulance expenses and, 226
Employee benefits, insurance and, 2-3
Employee effective date of coverage, eligibility and, 22-23
Employee eligibility, 20-21
Employee Retirement Income Security Act (ERISA), 25, 101
EMT; *see* Emergency medical technician
Endocrinology profiles, x-ray and laboratory services and, 142-143
Endodontic dental services and coding, 308, 316-318
Endodontic endosseous implant, 324
Endodontic procedures, 318
Endogenous obesity, 162
Endoscopic procedures, 148
Endosseous implant, 324
End-stage renal disease (ESRD), 120-121, 196-197
Enrollment
  late, penalties for, 376
  open, eligibility and, 23
Entropion, 156
EOB, definition of, 187
Epidural anesthesia, 170, 173
Epilation, electrolysis, 158
ERISA; *see* Employee Retirement Income Security Act
ERISA Right of Review statement, 101
ESRD; *see* End-stage renal disease
Evidence of insurability, 22
Excision pericoronal gingiva, 327
Exclusions, 39, 40, 375
Exclusive provider organizations, cost containment and, 67
Exogenous obesity, 161
Exostosis, 327-328
Expense
  ambulance, 225-228
  covered, 39, 368
Extension of benefits, 24, 39, 368
External fraud, 110, 114
External stimulus, reactions to, accident benefits and, 41
External trauma, internal reaction with, accident benefits and, 41
Extractions, oral surgery and, 326-327
Extraoral prostheses, 323-324
Eyelids, senile ptosis of, 161

F

FACD; *see* Fellow of American College of Dentists
Facelift, 161
Facial moulage, 324
FAGD; *see* Fellow of the Academy of General Dentistry
Family altercations, accident benefits and, 41
Family files, 86
Federal Health Insurance Benefit Plan for the Aged and Disabled; *see* Medicare
Fee schedules, usual, customary, and reasonable fees and, 77
Feeding aid, 324
Fellow of American College of Dentists (FACD), 308
Fertilization, in vitro, 153
Filiform papillae, 291
Fillings, restorative dental services and coding and, 312-314
Flagged providers, referrals and, 89
Flat feet, 222
Flexible hammertoe, 219
Fluoride applicator, 324-325
Fluoride treatments, 311

Follow-up days, surgery and, 149-150
Foot, conditions of, and treatment procedures, 215-224
Fraud, 109-116
  dental claims and, 388-389
  referrals and, 89
Frequency limitations, 374
Full credit adjustment, 252-253
Full veneer crown, 315
Fungiform papillae, 291

G

Ganglions, 222
Gastric balloon/garren gastric bubble, 162
Gastric bypass, 162
Gastric stapling, 162
Gatekeeper PPO, cost containment and, 67
General anesthesia, 170, 173
General plan provisions, 47-62
Genioplasty, 159
Geographic Practice Cost Indices (GPCI), 75, 76
Gingiva, 292
Gingival curettage, 318-319
Gingival flap procedure, 319
Gingivectomy, 319
Gingivitis, 292, 319-320
Glasses, prescription of, 121
Global COB, 187
Gold and metal alloys, restorative dental services and coding and, 313
Gold foil, restorative dental services and coding and, 313
GPCI; *see* Geographic Practice Cost Indices
Group contracts, 10-11
Group insurance versus individual insurance, 3
Group plan, 186
Gums, 292
Gustatory papillae, 291
Gynecomastia, 158

H

Hair transplantation, 158
Hammertoes, 216, 219-220, 222
Health care, rising cost of, 2
Health insurance, 3
Health Insurance Association of America Surgical Prevailing Healthcare Charges System (HIAA), 75
Health Insurance Payment Demand (HIPD), Medicaid and, 210, 211, 212
Health Insurance Purchasing Cooperative (HIPC), 67
Health maintenance organization (HMO), 66, 189
Health questionnaire, 22
Health-care benefits, 2-3
Heel spur, 220-221
Hemodialysis, 120-121
Hepatitis profiles, x-ray and laboratory services and, 143
HIAA; *see* Health Insurance Association of America Surgical Prevailing Healthcare Charges System
High-arched feet, 222
HIPC; *see* Health Insurance Purchasing Cooperative
HIPD; *see* Health Insurance Payment Demand
Hirsutism, 158
History, payment, updating, 101-102, 387-388
Holistic therapy, TMJ dysfunction and, 352
Hordeolum, 156
Hospice care, 181
Hospital benefits, 42
Hospital services, 175-184
  alternative birthing centers and, 180
  convalescent hospitals and, 180-181
  day care centers and, 179
  hospice care and, 181
  inpatient hospital claims and, 176-178
  Medicare supplement and, 205
  nursing homes and, 181
  outpatient hospital claims and, 178
  rehabilitation facilities and, 180
  surgicenters and, 180
  UB-92 billing form and, 176
  urgent care centers and, 179
Human resources department of insurance companies, 4
Hyperkeratosis, 156
Hypertrophied breasts, 158
Hypomastia, 159
Hypomazia, 159

I

ICU; *see* Intensive care unit
Immunizations, 119-120
Immunology profiles, x-ray and laboratory services and, 143-144
Impacted tooth, extraction of, 326-327
Implants, dental services and coding and, 324
In utero fetal surgery, 153
In vitro fertilization, 153
Incentive plans, dental benefit cost containment and, 374
Incisors, 293
Individual deductible, 39
Individual insurance versus group insurance, 3
Infant orthopedic appliance, 325
Influenza virus, 119
Ingrown toenails, 221, 222
Injections of muscle relaxants, TMJ dysfunction and, 352
Inlays, restorative dental services and coding and, 314
Inpatient admissions, precertification of, cost containment and, 64
Inpatient hospital claims, 176-178
Inpatient prescription drugs, 105
Insemination, artificial, 153
Insular COB, 187
Insurability, evidence of, 22
Insurance
  abuse of, checkpoint for spotting, 114
  dental; *see* Dental services and coding
  introduction to, 1-8
Insurance speculation indicators of fraud, 112-113
Integrated dental plans, 366-367
Intensive Care Unit (ICU), 177
Internal fraud, 110, 114
Internal reaction with external trauma, accident benefits and, 41
Internal Revenue Code (IRC), Amendments to, 25
Intertrigo, hypertrophied breasts and, 158
Intoxicated, aggressor acts while, accident benefits and, 41
Intraoral prosthesis, 324
Intravenous (IV) sedation, 170-171
Investigation of fraud, 113-114
IRC; *see* Internal Revenue Code
Itemized billings after delivery, maternity procedures and, 152-153

J

Jaw, 292

K

K wires, podiatric surgery and, 216
Keller bunionectomy with Silastic implants, 218
Keloid, 158
Kidney, transplantation of, 120-121
Kinesiographic analysis, TMJ dysfunction and, 352-353

L

Labial veneer, restorative dental services and coding and, 316
Laboratory profile index, x-ray and laboratory services and, 138-146
Laboratory services; *see* X-ray and laboratory services
Late enrollment penalties, dental benefit cost containment and, 376
Lawsuits, referrals and, 89
LCSW; *see* Licensed Clinical Social Worker
Legal actions, referrals and, 89
Legal department of insurance companies, 5
Legislation issues, referrals and, 89
Lesions, lid, 156
Liability
  normal, 187
  third party, 48-49, 51, 52, 53, 54, 388
Licensed Clinical Social Worker (LCSW), 120
Lid lesions, 156
Life insurance, 3
Lingual bar, 322
Lip stripping and resurfacing, 156
Lipectomy, 158-159, 161
Liposuction, 159
Lips, surgery of, 156-157
Liver profiles, x-ray and laboratory services and, 144
Local anesthesia, 170
Lop ears, 159-160
Loss, stop, 44, 102-104
Loss date, 39
Lump sum billings, maternity procedures and, 152

M

Macromastia, 158
Maintenance therapy, physician's services and, 122
Major medical benefits, 43-44, 104, 376-378
Major medical usual, customary, and reasonable fees, 76
Male pattern baldness, 158
Malocclusions, 328-329
Malpractice, 75
Mammoplasty, 159
Managed care, cost containment and, 66-67
Managed competition, cost containment and, 67
Management service organizations, cost containment and, 67
Mandates, 59-60
Mandible, jaw and, 292
Mandibular guide flange, 325
Mandibular repositioners, TMJ dysfunction and, 353
Mandibular resection prosthesis, 324
Mandibular teeth, 293, 295, 296
Marketing department of insurance companies, 4-5
Marriage, Family and Child Counselor (MFCC), 120
Mastectomy, 158, 159
Maternity procedures, 152-154
Maxilla, jaw and, 292
Maxillary sinusotomy, 328
Maxillary teeth, 293, 295, 296
Maxillofacial prosthetics, 323
McBride procedure, 217
MCM; *see* Medical case management
Medicaid, 3, 209-214
Medical case management (MCM), 67-68, 70-72
Medical emergency, 179
Medical equipment, durable, 229-250
Medical evidence, claim administration and, 96
Medical review, dental benefit cost containment and, 375-376
Medical while hospitalized (MWH), 42-43
Medical/surgical supplies, 232
Medicare, 3, 195-208
Meibomian cyst, 156
Mentoplasty, 159
Meperidine (Demerol), 171
Merck Manual, 55-56
Mesioclusion, 328
MFCC; *see* Marriage, Family and Child Counselor
Microtia, 160
Missing and Unreplaceable rule, 370
Mitchell bunionectomy, 217
Mobile intensive care unit, 227
Modifier codes, 74
Molars, 293
Mole removal, 161
Mouth
  anatomy and physiology of, 289-306
  diseases of, 292-293
  quadrants and sextants of, 295-296, 305
  teeth and; *see* Teeth
Mouth guard fabrication, athletic, 319
Mucogingival surgery, 319
Mucus, saliva and, 291
Multiple surgical procedures, 150-152, 172
Muscle relaxants, injections of, TMJ dysfunction and, 352
MWH; *see* Medical while hospitalized

N

NAIC; *see* National Association of Insurance Commissioners
Nasal prosthesis, 324
Nasal septum, deviated, 158
National Association of Insurance Commissioners (NAIC), 186
National Uniform Billing Committee, 176
Neoplasms, removal of, oral surgery and, 327
Nerve block anesthesia, 170
Nervous/mental care and treatment, physician's services and, 120
Neuromas, 221-222
Neutroclusion, 328
New business department of insurance companies, 5
NL; *see* Normal liability
Nonaccidental injuries, benefits and, 41-42
Nonaggregate deductible, 39
Noncontributory plan, 22-23
Noncovered charges, claim administration and, 104
Nondisabling benefit, 42
Nonintegrated dental plans, 367
Nonparticipating physicians, Medicare and, 200
Normal liability (NL), 187
Nursery, inpatient hospital claims and, 177
Nursing charges, 177, 205
Nursing homes, 181

O

OBD Rules; *see* Order of Benefit Determination Rules
Obesity surgery, 161-162

OBRA 90-Public Law 101-608, 75
Obturator, refitting of, 324
Occlusal equilibration, TMJ dysfunction and, 353
Occlusal rehabilitation, TMJ dysfunction and, 353
Ocular implant, 324
Ocular prosthesis, 324
Office visits, benefits and, 43, 373
Onlays, restorative dental services and coding and, 314
OOP; *see* Out-of-pocket expense
OOP Max, 40
Open enrollment, eligibility and, 23
Ophthalmologist, 121
Ophthalmology, 121
Optometrist, 121
Oral cavity, 290-292
Oral examination, clinical, 309
Oral surgery
    dental services and coding and, 308, 326-328
    TMJ dysfunction and, 353
Orbital implant, 324
Orbital prosthesis, 324
Order of Benefit Determination (OBD) Rules, 187-188
Oroantral fistula closure, 327
Orthodontic dental services and coding, 308, 328-329
Orthodontic x-rays, 379
Orthoptics, 121
Orthotic devices, 222
Osseous grafts, 319
Ostectomy, 327-328
Osteotomy, 219
Otoplasty, 159-160
Outliers, diagnosis-related group billing and, 206
Out-of-pocket (OOP) expense, 40
Outpatient hospital claims, 178
Outpatient prescription drugs, 105
Overhead expense component, 75
Overinsurance, coordination of benefits and, 186
Overpayments, collecting, 253
Oxygen, 231

P

Palatal bar, 322
Palatal lift prosthesis, 324
Palates, 157-158, 291, 292
Palatoplasty, 160
Panel tests, x-ray and laboratory services and, 126
Panniculectomy, 160
Panorex film, 310
Papanicolaou (Pap) smear, 127
Papillae, 291-292
Paramedics, ambulance expenses and, 226, 227
Parotid glands, 291
Partial credit adjustment, 252, 253
Partial veneer crown, 315
Participating physicians, Medicare and, 200
PAT; *see* Preadmission testing
Pathologist, x-ray and laboratory services and, 127
Patient files, 86
Patient Information Sheet, dental, 356, 359-362
Patient's home, durable medical equipment in, 230-231
Payees, 101, 387
Payment
    claim administration and, 105
    facility of, coordination of benefits and, 188
    major medical, 104
Payment demand letter, 49
Payment worksheet, 97-100
Peabody bunionectomy, 217
Pedicle soft tissue grafts, 319
Peel, chemical, 156
Pended claims, 89-93
Per period of disability, 40
Per visit benefit, 42
Periapical services, 318
Periodontal membrane, 297
Periodontic dental services and coding, 308, 318-320
Periodontitis, 292, 319-320
Periodontosis, 292
Perioprophylaxis, 320
Periorecall, 320
Personal items, inpatient hospital claims and, 178
Personnel department of insurance companies, 4
Pes cavus, 222
Pes planus, 222
Phenol, chemical peel and, 156
Photographs, preoperative and postoperative, cosmetic surgery and, 154
PHSA; *see* Public Health Service Act
Physical medicine, physician's services and, 121-122
Physical therapy, TMJ dysfunction and, 353
Physician hospital organizations, cost containment and, 67
Physician work component, 75
Physicians, 153, 199-200
Physician's Desk Reference, 105, 106
Physician's office, surgery in, 149
Physician's services, 117-124
    biofeedback and, 120
    cardiovascular care and, 121
    consultations and, 119
    custodial care and, 118
    dialysis and, 120-121
    emergency department services and, 118-119
    immunizations and, 119-120
    maintenance therapy and, 122
    Medicare supplement and, 205
    nervous/mental care and treatment and, 120
    ophthalmology and, 121
    physical medicine and, 121-122
    second surgical opinion consultations and, 119
    speech therapy and, 121
Pin retention, 314
Plan benefits, 4
Plan UCR, 104
Plantar calluses, 220
Plantar warts, 221
Plaque, dental, 298
Plastics, restorative dental services and coding and, 312
Plasty, 160
Pneumococcal immunization, 119-120
Podiatric surgery, 215-224
Policies, conversion, continuation of coverage and, 24-25
Pontic, 325
Porcelain-faced crown, 315, 316
Positional bunions, 217, 218
Postoperative photographs, cosmetic surgery and, 154
Practice expense component, 75
Preadmission testing (PAT), 64
Precertification, 64-65
Predelivery billings, maternity procedures and, 153
Predetermination, dental benefit cost containment and, 373-374
Preexisting conditions, 51-59

Preexisting exclusion, 40
Preferred Provider Organization (PPO), 66, 67, 189
Prefixes, dental, 256-257
Premium payments, COBRA and, 27-29
Premium services department of insurance companies, 5
Premolars, 293
Prenatal profiles, x-ray and laboratory services and, 144-145
Preoperative care, 149
Preoperative photographs, cosmetic surgery and, 154
Prescription drugs
    claim administration and, 105-106
    dental services and coding and, 330
    inpatient hospital claims and, 178
    Medicare supplement and, 205
    TMJ dysfunction and, 352, 353
Preventive dental services and coding, 308, 311-312
Primary plan, 186
Primary teeth, 295
Private room, inpatient hospital claims and, 177
Procedure code, 74
Processing claim, 99-102, 105, 383-394
Professional component, 127
Professional fees, inpatient hospital claims and, 178
Professional liability component, 75
Professional visits, dental services and coding and, 330
Property and casualty insurance, 3
Prostheses
    dental benefit structures and, 370
    dental services and coding and, 323-325
    durable medical equipment and, 232
    maxillofacial, 323
    TMJ dysfunction and, 353
Prosthodontic dental services and coding, 308, 309, 320-326
Protruding ears, 159-160
Provider authority, dental claims and, 384
Providers, flagged, referrals and, 89
Psychiatrist, 120
Psychologist, clinical, 120
Ptosis, 160, 161
Public Health Service Act (PHSA), Amendments to, 25
Public Law 89-97 of Social Security Act, Title XVIII of; *see* Medicare
Pulp capping, 316-317
Pulpectomy, 317
Pulpotomy, 317
Purchased durable medical equipment, 231

Q

Quadrants of mouth, 295-296, 305

R

Rabies, 119
Radiation carrier, 325
Radical mastectomy, 159
Radiographs; *see* X-ray and laboratory services
Radiologist, x-ray and laboratory services and, 127
Reasonable charges, Medicare and, 199
Reconstruction, 148
Recovery, right of, coordination of benefits and, 188
Red Book, 106-107
Reduction mammoplasty, 156, 159
Referrals, 89, 90, 222-223
Region, 74
Regional anesthesia, 170
Rehabilitation facilities, 180
Reinstatement, automatic annual, 38
Relative Value Not Established (RNE) procedures, 150
Relative value study (RVS), 75, 171
Relative value unit (RVU), 75
Relativity Not Established (RNE) procedure, 74, 323, 380
Relaxation therapy, TMJ dysfunction and, 352
Relining dentures, 323
Rental durable medical equipment, 231
Replacement bridge, 326
Replacement provisions, 372-373
Required participation, dental benefit cost containment and, 376
Resection, submucous, 161
Resource-based relative value study, 75
Restorations, temporary, 378
Restorative dental services and coding, 308, 312-316
Retainers, 325
Retrospective review, 64-65
Reverdin and Green bunionectomy, 217
Rhinomanometry, 161
Rhinoplasty, 160-161
Rhytidectomy, 161
Rhytidoplasty, 161
Riding breeches syndrome, 159
Rigid hammertoe, 219
RNE procedure; *see* Relativity Not Established procedure
Room and board, inpatient hospital claims and, 177-178
Root, dental terminology and, 256-257
Root canal, 296, 316, 317-318
Root extraction, 327
Rue bunionectomy, 217
RVS; *see* Relative value study
RVU; *see* Relative value unit

S

Saddle block anesthesia, 170
Saliva, 291
Salivary amylase, 291
Salivary glands, 291
Sargenti root canal therapy, 317-318
Scaling, 319
Scheduled dental plans, 366
Scope in endoscopic procedures, 148
Sealants, 312
Second dental opinion, 375
Second surgical opinion (SSO) consultation, 65, 119
Secondary plan, 186
Sedative fillings, 380
Self-funded plans, 4
Semiprivate room, inpatient hospital claims and, 177
Senile ptosis of eyelids, 161
Septoplasty, 161
Septum, 161
Sequestrectomy, 328
Seven-eighths crown, 315
Sextants of mouth, 295-296, 305
Sialodentitis, 293
Sialography, 310
Silicate, 312-313
Silver procedure, 217
Sinusotomy, maxillary, 328
Social Security Act
    of 1965, Title XIX of; *see* Medicaid
    Title XVIII of Public Law 89-97 of; *see* Medicare
Social Security Administration (SSA), Medicare and, 196
Space management therapy, dental, 312
Special services, usual, customary, and reasonable fees and, 76-77

Specialized units, inpatient hospital claims and, 177
Speech aid, 324
Speech therapy, 121
Spinal anesthesia anesthesia, 170
Splint(ing), 319, 325, 353
Spontaneous abortion, 153
Spurs, bone, 220-221
SSA; *see* Social Security Administration
SSO consultation; *see* Second surgical opinion consultation
Stainless-steel crown, 315, 316
Statistical adjustment, 252
Steel crown, 315, 316
Stomatitis, 292
Stomatoplasty, 327
Stop loss, 44, 102-104
Stress breaker, 326
Structural bunions, 218-219
Sty, 156
Subcutaneous mastectomy, 159
Sublingual glands, 291
Submandibular glands, 291
Submental lipectomy, 161
Submucous resection, 161
Subperiosteal implant, 324
Subrogation, 49-51, 53
Suffixes, dental, 256-257
Suicide, attempted, benefits and, 42
Supplemental adjustment, 252
Surgeon, assistant, 162-163, 167, 222
Surgery, 147-168
  assistant surgeons and, 162-163, 167, 222
  cosmetic, 148, 154-161
  oral; *see* Oral surgery
  periodontic dental services and coding and, 318-319
  podiatric, 215-224
Surgicenters, 180
Synovial joints, jaw and, 292

T

Take-home prescriptions, inpatient hospital claims and, 178
Tarsal cyst, 156
Taste buds, 291-292
Tattoos, removal of, 160
Tax Equity and Fiscal Responsibility Act of 1982 (TEFRA), Medicare and, 196
Taylor's bunionectomy, 219
TCA; *see* Trichloracetic acid
Technical component, x-ray and laboratory services and, 127
Teeth, 293-299, 301, 302, 303, 304
  impacted, 326-327
  implantation of, 327
  reimplantation of, 327
  transplantation of, 327
TEFRA; *see* Tax Equity and Fiscal Responsibility Act of 1982
Telemetry charges, inpatient hospital claims and, 177
Telephone information sheet, 88
Temporary restorations, 378
Temporomandibular joint (TMJ), 161, 292
Temporomandibular joint (TMJ) dysfunction, 328-329, 349-354
Tenotomy, 219
TENS; *see* Transcutaneous electrical nerve stimulation
Termination of coverage, 23-24, 29
Tetanus toxoid, 120
Therapeutic abortion, 153
Therapeutic procedures, 148, 149-150
Third parties, acts of, 48-49, 51, 52, 53, 54
Third party administrator (TPA), 4
Third party liability (TPL), 48-49, 51, 52, 53, 54, 388
Third party liability reimbursement agreement, 54
Three-month carryover provision (C/O), 40
Time units, anesthesia and, 171-172
Title X, COBRA and, 25
Title XIX of Social Security Act of 1965; *see* Medicaid
Title XVIII of Public Law 89-97 of Social Security Act; *see* Medicare
TMJ dysfunction; *see* Temporomandibular joint dysfunction
Toenails, ingrown, 221, 222
Tongue, 291-292
Topical anesthesia, 170
Total payment, 105
Toxicology profiles, x-ray and laboratory services and, 145-146
TPA; *see* Third party administrator
TPL; *see* Third party liability
Transcutaneous electrical nerve stimulation (TENS), TMJ dysfunction and, 352, 353
Trauma, external, internal reaction with, accident benefits and, 41
Trichloracetic acid (TCA), 156
Tricuspids, 293
Trismus appliance, 325
Tubal ligation, delivery with, 154
Tumor markers, x-ray and laboratory services and, 146
Tumors, excision of, oral surgery and, 327
Turbinates, 161
Twilight sleep, 171

U

UB-92 billing form; *see* Uniform Bill-92 billing form
UCR fees; *see* Usual customary and reasonable fees
Unbundling, x-ray and laboratory services and, 126
Underwriting department of insurance companies, 5
Uniform Bill-92 (UB-92) billing form, 176
Union contracts, 20-21
Unit value, 74
Unna's boot, 216
Unspecified procedures, dental benefit structures and, 380
UR; *see* Utilization review
Urgent care centers, 179
Usual, customary, and reasonable (UCR) fees, 73-84, 104
Utilization review (UR), 64-65

V

Validity, contract, 10
Valium; *see* Diazepam
Van transportation unit, 227
Variable coinsurance, 374
Vestibule, 290
Vestibuloplasty, 319

W

Waiting period, dental benefit cost containment and, 374-375
Ward, inpatient hospital claims and, 177
Warts, 161, 221
Wilson bunionectomy, 217
Wisdom teeth, 293
Workers' compensation, 3, 388
Workflow model, claim administration and, 94

X

X-ray and laboratory services, 125-146
- adult normal values in, 129-137
- allergy profiles in, 139-140
- allergy testing in, 140
- anemia profiles in, 140-141
- arthritic profiles in, 141
- automated laboratory charge and, 126-127
- Chemfile combinations in, 138
- common laboratory tests and, 129-137
- component charges and, 127
- coronary profiles in, 141-142
- dental benefit structures and, 378-379
- diagnostic; *see* Diagnostic x-ray and laboratory services
- electrolyte profile in, 142
- endocrinology profiles in, 142-143
- hepatitis profiles in, 143
- immunology profiles in, 143-144
- laboratory profile index and, 138-146
- liver profiles in, 144
- medical management, 126
- orthodontic, 379
- Papanicolaou smear and, 127
- prenatal profiles in, 144-145
- toxicology profiles in, 145-146
- tumor markers in, 146

Z

Zyderm injections, 158